Nationalism in Asia and Africa

By the same author

England and the Middle East
    The Destruction of the Ottoman Empire 1914-21
Nationalism
Afghani and 'Abduh
    An Essay on Religious Unbelief and
    Political Activism in Modern Islam
The Chatham House Version
    and Other Middle-Eastern Studies

NATIONALISM IN ASIA AND AFRICA

Edited with an Introduction
by ELIE KEDOURIE

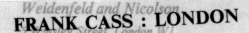

L'invasion des idées a succédé
à l'invasion des barbares.

CHATEAUBRIAND

FRANK CASS : LONDON

FRANK CASS AND COMPANY LIMITED
67 Great Russell Street, London WC1B 3BT

ISBN 0 7146 3046 2 (Case)
ISBN 0 7146 3045 4 (Paper)
SBN 0 297 00358 5 paperback.

Reproduced and Printed in Great Britain by
Redwood Press Limited, Trowbridge & London

for MICHAEL OAKSHOTT

ACKNOWLEDGMENTS

The author is grateful to the following for their kind permission to publish extracts:

Messrs. George Allen and Unwin and Columbia University Press (Z. Gökalp, *Turkish Nationalism and Western Civilization*); Présence Africaine (Cheikh Anta Diop, *Nations nègres et culture*); Mrs. A. Jacques Garvey (*Philosophy and Opinions of Marcus Garvey*); Harvard University Press (R. K. Hall, *Kokutai No Hongi*); Controller, Her Majesty's Stationery Office (*Report of the Commission of Enquiry into Disturbances in the Gold Coast, 1948. Colonial no. 231*, and *Note from the Ministry of the Interior to Sir Eldon Gorst*, Public Record Office, F.O. 371/890); General Administration Department, Government of Maharashtra (*Source Material for a History of the Freedom Movement in India*); Oxford University Press (J. M. Kariuki, *'Mau Mau' Detainee*); Dr. E. Andersson and Uppsala Universsitet Institutionen för allmän och jämförande etnografi (E. Andersson, *Messianic Popular Movements in the Lower Congo*); André Deutsch Ltd. (T. Mboya, *Freedom and After*); MacGibbon and Kee Ltd., (F. Fanon, *The Damned*, trs. C. Farington). M. A. Bennigsen has kindly given permission for an English translation of articles by Sultan Galiev given in a French version in A. Bennigsen and C. Quelquejay, *Les Mouvements nationaux chez les musulmans de Russie*.

CONTENTS

viii   Contents

INTRODUCTION

I

Nationalism in Asia and Africa, it is now generally agreed, is a reaction against European domination. But the nature of this domination, the precise manner in which it has elicited such a reaction, and the character of the reaction itself are issues on which the consensus is perhaps less general. One way of describing the situation current among those who accept Marxism as a gospel, and widely prevalent even among those who do not, is to the effect that nationalism in Asia and Africa is the natural consequence of European exploitation of these areas, an exploitation which goes by the name of imperialism. "It is no ideological assertion, but a simple generalization rooted in empirical observation," we read in a recently published work, "that the prime content of colonial political rule was economic exploitation." And again, the same author, describing European rule overseas, writes as follows: "For the most part, strictly economic exploitation is the predominant element, transforming mere political control into a process which involves nothing short of the revolutionizing of social relations ... the central *raison d'être* of imperialism is the extraction of profit from the labor of the indigenous people by whites by virtue of their control over the political machinery of the state."[1]

This explanation of European activities overseas, now widely accepted all over the world, was invented and propagated by European publicists who have derived from it—and inculcated in their respectful Western audience—powerful and corrosive feelings of guilt. One or two examples of this prevalent attitude are worth giving. We may first look at a passage from a lecture by Professor Arnold Toynbee, delivered under the aegis of the British Broadcasting Corporation, which purports to tell us how matters look "through the eyes of the non-Western majority of mankind": ". . . if any Western inquirer asks them their opinion of the West," declared Professor Toynbee in the first of his 1952 Reith Lectures, "he will hear them all giving him the same answer: Russians, Muslims, Hindus, Chinese, Japanese and all the rest. The West, they will tell him, has been the arch-aggressor of modern times, and each will have their own experience of Western aggression to bring up against him. The Russians will remind him that their country has been invaded by Western armies overland in 1941, 1915, 1812, 1709 and 1610; the peoples of Africa and Asia will remind him that Western missionaries, traders, and soldiers from across the sea have been pushing into their countries from the coasts since the fifteenth century. The Asians will also remind him that, within the same period, the Westerners have occupied the lion's share of the world's last vacant lands in the Americas, Australia, New Zealand, and South and East Africa. The Africans," the relentless indictment continues, "will remind him that they were enslaved and deported across the Atlantic in order to serve the European colonizers of the Americas as living tools to minister to their Western masters' greed for wealth. The descendants of the aboriginal population of North America will remind him that their ancestors were swept aside to make room for the West European intruders and for their African slaves."[2] Let us next listen to Jean-Paul Sartre in merciless invective and self-accusation:

"You well know that we are exploiters. You well know that we have taken the gold, the metals and then the oil of the 'new continents' and have conveyed them to the old metropolitan centers. Not without excellent results: palaces, cathedrals, industrial capitals; and further, when crisis threatened there were the colonial markets to soften its impact or deflect it. Europe, stuffed with wealth, grants humanity *de jure* to all its inhabitants: a man, among us, signifies an accomplice since we have all profited from colonial exploitation." The unbearable situation inspires in Sartre a violent and sanguinary dialectic which elicits the victim's response to the oppressor's oppression and shows nationalism outside Europe erupting out of a dead and confining imperialism in the exhilaration of Sten-gun fire and exploding hand grenades: "When peasants handle rifles, then the old myths pale into insignificance, and one by one prohibitions are overturned: a fighter's weapon is his humanity. Because in the first period of the revolt you must kill: to slaughter a European is to kill two birds with one stone, to do away at the same time with the oppressor and the oppressed: the result is one dead man and one free man; for the first time the survivor feels a *national* earth under his feet. At this moment the Nation is near to him: it is found wherever he goes, wherever he is—never farther, it becomes one with his freedom."[3]

This notion of European or Western imperialism with its characteristic account of economic and political history, now looming so large in political controversy, and generating, as the quotations from Toynbee and Sartre show, so vehement a flow of guilt, indignation, and moral passion, is in fact of very recent origin, and its worldwide popularity is still more recent. Up to the last decade of the nineteenth century or thereabouts the idea of imperialism, which derives originally from the Roman *imperium*, had almost none of the doctrinal accretions and pejorative overtones which have since become attached to it. Webster's International Dictionary in its 1890 edition, for instance, defined imperialism as "the power or character of an emperor; imperial authority; the spirit of empire." Though Webster does not record it, a change had nonetheless occurred in the meaning of the term in the preceding few decades. The origin of this change, as the late Richard Koebner has shown,[4] had to do with the ill-repute which came to attach to Louis Napoleon's resuscitation of his uncle's empire. Since his regime, which many widely suspected of being unconstitutional, antipopular and antiparliamentary, was called an empire, Napoleon III's system was denounced as imperialism: "Imperialism," we find *The Times* writing in a passage of 1869 quoted in The Oxford English Dictionary, "or indeed any worse form of despotism . . . ." After the disappearance of the Second Empire, the term with its new pejorative connotations passed into party-political polemics in Great Britain, and later in the United States. In the former country Disraeli's Liberal and Radical opponents denounced the Conservative minister's methods as imperialism. In using this term, they meant to draw a comparison between Disraeli and Napoleon III in their lack of principle and their appetite for despotism. Disraeli in the eyes of his opponents was a disreputable and dangerous magician who used adventures overseas as an opiate with which to lull the people at home. It is in such a context of party-political warfare that the term "imperialism" came to connote in English the unprincipled and disreputable desire to acquire possessions overseas—a meaning which it has retained to the present day.[5] Similar controversies in the United States during the last decade of the nineteenth century connected with the acquisition of Spanish possessions in the Caribbean served also to fix in popular usage the term's pejorative overtones. We thus find successive editions of Webster from 1909 to the present defining imperialism as "the policy, practice or advocacy of seeking or the acquiescing in the extension of the control or empire of a nation by the acquirement of new territories or dependencies especially when lying outside the nation's natural boundaries, or by the extension of its rule over other races of mankind."

At the beginning of the twentieth century, the term's pejorative implications were made explicit, detailed, and systematic in a new doctrine. This was the invention of an English publicist, John Atkinson Hobson (1858–1940), who offered it to the world in his book *Imperialism*, first published in 1902. Hobson, moderately clever as an economist, supplemented his abilities in the discussion of social and political issues with a vast fund of moral passion imperialism in his eyes was a recent phenomenon, somerning not much more than thirty years old. As he makes clear at the beginning of his work, by imperialism he largely understands the division of Africa between the European Powers in the last twenty years of the nineteenth century, a course of events culminating, so far as he himself was concerned, in the Boer War, the incident which burst the dams of his moral indignation and led him to the study of the subject. Hobson begins by arguing that these new African annexations do not benefit the nation at large. They are of little value to the manufacturer or the trader, since the populations which inhabit them are not great consumers of manufactured goods; again they are largely useless for European settlement. Why then are they acquired? "If, contemplating the enormous expenditure on armaments, the ruinous wars, the diplomatic audacity of knavery by which modern governments seek to extend their territorial power, we put the plain, practical question, *cui bono?*, the first and most obvious answer is," Hobson triumphantly concluded, "the investor." The investor is a man with money to invest; this money has come to him out of the prodigious wealth generated by modern industry. The investor acquires this wealth which is surplus to his needs because the product of industry is, under capitalism, badly and inequitably distributed. If this product were more equally distributed so that the laboring classes, who now live in misery, could increase their consumption, there would be no excess of wealth for which bloated millionaires seek investment opportunities abroad. There would be then no overproduction and no underconsumption in industrial countries, and it is these which are the root cause of economic crises in industrial societies and which drive investors to seek openings for their funds abroad. The economist Maynard Keynes recognized in Hobson a precursor, and indeed Hobson's explanation of economic crises in terms of underconsumption within industrial society has affinities with Keynes's own theory. But Hobson did more than explain the malfunction of capitalist economies; he attempted to explain by this malfunction the annexation of overseas territories by capitalist powers. Since the investor with large surplus funds is, as a significant economic power, a recent phenomenon, it is clear why imperialism must, on Hobson's theory, also be a recent phenomenon.

But to explain imperialism, the investor is not enough. Behind him lurks a more sinister personage: the financier. The financier gains his living by promoting investment schemes, by floating companies, by dealing in shares and stocks, by manipulating the Stock Exchange. Financiers form "the central ganglion of international capitalism." "United by the strongest bonds of organisation, always in closest and quickest touch with one another, situated in the very heart of the business capital of every State, controlled, so far as Europe is concerned, chiefly by men of a single and peculiar race, who have behind them many centuries of financial experience, they are in a unique position to control the policy of nations." "Does anyone seriously suppose," asks Hobson, obviously believing that the question admits of but one answer, "that a great war could be undertaken by any European State, or a great State loan subscribed, if the house of Rothschild and its connections set their face against it?" "There is not a war, a revolution, an anarchist assassination, or any other public shock," Hobson affirms, "which is not gainful to these men; they are harpies who seek their gains from every new forced expenditure and every sudden disturbance of public credit."[6]

This explanation of European annexations overseas is today the most influential one in the field. It has been adopted by a host of publicists and academic writers who have sought to justify it by complicated calculations and subtle reasonings. Of these writers the most influential by far, but not because of his cogency or eloquence, has proved to be Lenin. In 1916, while still an exile in Zurich, he wrote a pamphlet, *Imperialism, the Highest Stage of Capitalism*, which, as he himself acknowledged, leaned heavily on Hobson. Lenin's argument, buttressed by a miscellaneous hotchpotch of industrial and commercial statistics, was neither new nor particularly convincing. But he made large claims for it: "It is proved in the pamphlet," he wrote in the preface to the French and German editions, "that the war of 1914–18 was imperialistic (that is, an annexationist, predatory, plunderous war) on both sides; it was a war for the division of the world, for the partition and repartition of colonies, 'spheres of influence' of finance capital, etc." The world, in the picture he presented, was composed of a handful of "usurer states," as he called them, sucking the substance of all the rest; and the policy of these usurer states is directed and controlled by "finance capital." "Finance capital is such a great, it may be said, such a decisive force in all economic and all international relations, that it is capable of subjecting, and actually does subject, to itself even states enjoying the fullest political independence. . . . Of course," he insisted, "finance capital finds most 'convenient,' and derives the greatest profit from, *such* [control] as involves the loss of the political independence of the subjected countries and peoples."

It is most likely that if Lenin had not seized power in Russia, his pamphlet, the lucubrations of a revolutionary scribbler, having made a modest but useful profit for Parus Publishers who brought it out in Petrograd in April, 1917, would not have been heard of anymore. But Lenin was the head of a revolutionary sect who was enabled by circumstances to seize a powerful and populous country. His opinions, therefore, whatever their intrinsic worth, as official doctrine of the state came to be spread with zeal and conviction by an activist government disposing of all the modern techniques of persuasion and indoctrination. Hobson's theory of imperialism, which asserted a peculiar bond between capitalism and the policies of certain European states, acquired a prodigious currency, and large numbers of people came to believe, for instance, in the words of a manual prepared for the instruction of the Red Army General Staff, that the English king was the "crowned agent of the English banks."[7] The worldwide dissemination and the ensuing popularity of Hobson's doctrine in the decades following the Bolshevik revolution may again be illustrated from the dictionary. Webster, as has been seen, recorded in 1909 the new meaning which had come to attach to the word "imperialism." Another word which has in recent decades begun to be associated with the same range of ideas is the term "colonialism." Such association had not always been the case. In an instance dating from 1889 the two terms are found contrasted rather than associated: "There are three competing influences at work in South Africa," wrote the *Standard* newspaper in a sentence quoted in the Oxford English Dictionary, "Colonialism, Republicanism and Imperialism." A meaning of the term widely current until recently may be gathered from the definition which appears in Webster as late as the 1939 edition. Colonialism, we read there, signifies "the colonial system or policy in industrial legislation or extension of territory." It is clear that such a definition has not yet been touched by Lenin's doctrine. What appears in the 1961 Webster is therefore startling in the sharpness of its contrast; colonialism we now see defined as "the aggregate of various economic, political, and social policies by which an imperial power maintains or extends its control over other areas or peoples." There is no doubt that this is the meaning commonly accepted today, and equally little doubt that this meaning has become so popular only as a result of the dissemination of Lenin's doctrine; and the order in which the dictionary places the policies by which imperial power is maintained may in this respect be significant, for it is of the essence of this doctrine that the economic determines the political. If the dictionary is a true mirror of our condition, we are all Leninists and Hobsonians now.

As has been said, nationalism in Asia and Africa is, according to this influential doctrine, intimately connected with the existence of European imperialism and colonialism. The connection exists because just as imperialism is the expression of finance capitalism, so nationalism is on the one hand the expression of industrial capitalism in Europe and on the other a reaction to European "imperialism" in the colonies and "semicolonies" which finance capitalism has incited European states to establish. This alleged connection between capitalism and nationalism is made clear in a passage which occurs in an essay on *Marxism and the National Question* published in 1913 which the young

Stalin wrote under Lenin's inspiration and at his suggestion. A nation, affirmed the youthful disciple, was "not merely a historical category but a historical category belonging to a definite epoch, the epoch of rising capitalism. The process of elimination of feudalism and development of capitalism is at the same time a process of the constitution of the people into nations." And in this process, it is the bourgeoisie which plays the leading role. Nationalism is thus a phenomenon arising out of early capitalism, when the bourgeoisie in order to make sure of a large market for its capitalist operations works to establish a unified nation-state.

But early capitalism eventually changes into finance capitalism; finance capitalism must seek overseas colonies and exploit their inhabitants; and this exploitation evokes resistance in the masses of Asia and Africa, who embark on "national liberation movements." Some ten years after the publication of his youthful essay, Stalin, now a commissar and a power in the land, delivered some lectures to a university audience on *The Foundations of Leninism* in which he examined the "National Problem." Stalin asserted that it was only in the period of Leninism and only thanks to it that the "scores and hundreds of millions of Asiatic and African peoples who are suffering national oppression in its most savage form" have been acknowledged to exist and to have claims and rights. The situation of these "scores and hundreds of millions" of oppressed peoples Stalin summed up in the following "theses":

a) The world is divided into two camps: the camp of a handful of civilized nations, which possess finance capital and exploit the vast majority of the population of the globe; and the camp of the oppressed and exploited peoples in the colonies and dependent countries, who comprise that majority;

. . . .

c) The revolutionary struggle of the oppressed peoples in the dependent and colonial countries against imperialism is the only road that leads to their emancipation from oppression and exploitation;

d) The most important colonial and dependent countries have already taken the path of the national liberation movement, which cannot but lead to the crisis of world capitalism . . . . [See the text of Stalin's lecture on pp. 552–561.]

How convincing is such an explanation of imperialism and nationalism? We may say, in the first place, that as an account of the motives which have made European governments annex territories overseas, the doctrine of imperialism does not square with the facts. The circumstances in which European governments have annexed such territories have been varied and complicated, and certainly not to be reduced to some simple economic impulse such as the insatiable appetite of financiers for easy and exorbitant profits. In fact, if an economic motive is to be sought for the acquisition and maintenance of colonial possessions, it would more easily be found in a period which preceded by a century or so the appearance of imperialism, as Hobson dates it. As historians know, from the discovery of America until the end of the Napoleonic wars and in some cases well after, European states maintained, with respect to their overseas settlements and establishments, what is known as the mercantilist system—the system of the *Exclusif,* as it is so expressively called in French—which amounted to a monopoly of trade and navigation enforced by the metropolitan country for the benefit of some or all of its merchants.

The intellectual premises of this system were attacked, notably by Adam Smith, who in his *Wealth of Nations* (1776) denounced monopoly in colonial trade along with "the other mean and malignant expedients of the mercantile system." "To found a great empire for the sole purpose of raising up a people of customers," he observed, "may at first sight appear a project fit only for a nation of shopkeepers. It is, however, a project altogether unfit for a nation of shopkeepers; but extremely fit for a nation whose government is influenced by shopkeepers." The reason why mercantilism is unfit for a nation of shopkeepers is essentially simple and transparent: "The interest of a nation in its commercial relations to foreign nations is, like that of a merchant with regard to the different people with whom he deals, to buy as cheap and to sell as dear as possible. But it will be most likely to buy cheap, when by the most perfect freedom of trade it encourages all nations to bring the goods which it has occasion to purchase, and, for the same reason, it will be most likely to sell dear, when its markets are thus filled with the greatest number of buyers."

The sustained intellectual assault on mercantilism, together with changing economic and political conditions, led Britain, which was the leading industrial country in the nineteenth century, to abandon the system and to adopt free international trade, while British preponderance, naval and industrial, persuaded, encouraged, or compelled a great number of countries to follow suit. The new policy may be summed up in the words of Lord Shelburne, who negotiated in 1783 the Treaty of Versailles, which recognized the independence of the United States: "We prefer," he said, "commerce to domination." It may be argued that the British insisted so emphatically on free trade simply because free trade under nineteenth-century conditions suited the British economy, that in fact British industrial preponderance was such that we may speak of the imperialism of free trade. The expression is striking, but what it must chiefly serve to underline here is the fact that British power, in the view of those who directed it, was to be used to create internal and external conditions in Asia and Africa such that free trade would have a chance to function and thus to go on increasing the general welfare. Under such assumptions, there could be no commercial sense in overseas conquest.

But is it anyway the case that the official and ruling classes of Britain or any European Great Power allowed their actions to be much guided by commercial considerations? Is it the case that the governments were, as Adam Smith put it, under the influence of shopkeepers? In an intelligent and stimulating essay on the sociology of imperialism published in 1918–19,[8] the economist Joseph Schumpeter has argued that the appetite of European ruling classes for conquest and overseas territories may be explained by the warlike traditions and antecedents of these ruling classes. And it is true that notwithstanding the industrial revolution, the foreign affairs of European states in the nineteenth century were still in large measure being conducted either by a landed aristocracy unlikely to be much impressed with mercantile views and ambitions or by officials whose instinct and training led them to consider the state not as the representative of a particular class of society and of its interests, but rather as the somewhat remote arbiter, the ultimate judge between claims and pressures by different groups of subjects. So that the considerations likely to weigh with such ruling and official classes were those of political prestige, military preponderance, "law and order," and administrative rectitude. India is very much a case in point. The British connection with India was at the outset purely mercantile. The East India Company came to India in order to buy cheap and sell dear and make the largest possible profit for its shareholders. The decay of the Mughal power and European superiority in military and technical matters gave the Company the opportunity to become a tax-farmer and ruler in Bengal, Madras, and elsewhere, in this respect exactly on the same footing as those Mahratta and Sikh warlords who found their opportunity in the weakness of the Grand Mughal. But a commercial organization justifies itself by making the largest profit possible, not by setting up as policeman, administrator, and judge. When the East India Company took over such functions its commercial character had sooner or later to disappear, had indeed largely disappeared long before its formal extinction at the Mutiny. The thoughts of such men as Elphinstone, who was appointed to the Bengal Civil Service in 1796, Malcolm, who entered the Company's service in 1782, Metcalfe, who began his Indian career in 1801, did not revolve on balance sheets and profit and loss. They were already concerned with the judicial and administrative problems familiar to any member of the later official hierarchy, at the head of which was to stand a viceroy, the heir not of a city merchant but of Akbar and Aurangzeb.

There is then much that is suggestive in Schumpeter's thesis, and if we allow its suggestiveness to work upon us, we may come to see that this modern European expansion overseas has nothing extraordinary about it, nothing at any rate of these peculiar financial or economic factors so much stressed by those who would call this period an imperialist epoch. India again may serve as an illustration.

India, it is quite apparent, was not occupied at the bidding of financiers. Rather, when after some two centuries of operations by the East India Company the country was taken over by the British government, it represented for Great Britain a reservoir of military manpower and a strategic position which, together with the Navy, served to make Great Britain perhaps the most powerful country in the world. The power which India allowed British statesmen to exert in the world was as, if not more, important in their eyes than British investments in India. This power would have remained as precious as it proved to be, even if British investments in India had been negligible. Again, the world was full of places where British investments as, if not more, important than in India had to do without British military protection. It may be argued that these investments were protected indirectly by British preponderance in the world at large, but all that is established by such an argument is that great wealth needs great power to protect it, just as great power makes possible the accumulation of great wealth. In the Victorian age, Great Britain had the good fortune to be both wealthy and powerful, but good fortune, as we know, goes as it comes.

Africa is as instructive a case as India. As recent studies have decisively shown,[9] it was not in order to seek markets or raw materials that Great Britain, France, and Germany annexed most of Africa in the nineteenth century. Strategy, rivalry between Great Powers, prestige, or the sheer force of circumstances inaugurated and continued a process which by the end of the century made almost the whole of Africa a European dependency. In a letter of 1816 to the French ambassador in London, which Professor Brunschwig quotes, the Duc de Richelieu, discussing a dispute with Portugal about Guinea, wrote: "You appreciate that it would be impossible to give in to Portuguese demands, not so much because we have any real interest in retaining a territory which will yield substantial advantages only in a remote future, but rather because the dignity of the

King and of the State would be hurt by a concession which no right whatever on the part of Portugal could justify. This is a most forceful consideration because, in our present situation, any waiving of rights would be taken as a sign of weakness." These are the authentic accents of traditional statecraft, and it is these accents which we hear when we investigate European policies overseas.

At the end the Napoleonic wars, Great Britain occupied the Cape to safeguard the route to India; toward the end of his reign, in 1830, Charles X sent a French expedition to Algiers as a matter of prestige and in order to spread Christianity among the Muslims; Tunisia was occupied by the French Republic not in pursuit of economic advantage but to show, as Gambetta put it in a contemporary letter, that after the debacle of 1870 France was once again a Great Power, and also to protect Algeria's eastern flank and checkmate Italian ambitions in North Africa; Great Britain occupied Egypt in 1882, when a Liberal administratioh, much averse to annexations and foreign wars, was in office, as a result of fortuitous and unwelcome developments. German and Italian policies are no more susceptible of an economic explanation than those of Great Britain and France. The presence on the African continent of these European Great Powers sooner or later led to a play of rivalries which, in the absence of indigenous Powers strong enough to check European annexations, could come to an end only when there were no more territories to annex.

The exception to all this is the extraordinary episode of the Congo Free State which King Leopold II of the Belgians appropriated to himself and treated as a *res nullius* of which he was free to dispose as he pleased. But it is interesting that just as the East India Company could not continue to run a large and populous territory purely as a business enterprise, so again the Congo Free State could not continue for long to be treated as a mere lucrative investment, and its control was transferred in 1908 to the Belgian state, which assumed thereafter the usual responsibilities of a colonial administration.

The connection between overseas possessions and economic

exploitation, it may be objected, cannot be so easily refuted. India was exploited by British manufacturers who poured in their cheap products, thus ruining the traditional Indian textile industry, the products of which had first attracted British merchants to the East India trade. This British dominance in the Indian market, it is further argued, incalculably harmed Indian welfare by inhibiting and retarding the transition from a traditional and agricultural to a modern and industrial economy. But such arguments are not convincing because they try to deal with a fundamental issue in a mystificatory and ideological manner. The modern industrial system undoubtedly brought strain, disruption, and ruin to large numbers of men. But it did so indifferently, in places like India, where it was a foreign importation, and in Europe, where it was a native product. If the modern industrial system ruined traditional crafts and manufactures, it did so equally in Britain and in India; if it atomized stable societies and ground to dust traditional ways of life, its pitiless operation was as evident in the European countryside as in that of India. It is most doubtful whether these effects of the industrial revolution would have stopped short of Asia and Africa if these regions had been able to preserve political independence. We may, if we like to speak in oracular metaphors, say that the very economic inequality between traditional Asia and Africa on the one hand and industrial Europe on the other itself constituted aggression and oppression. This, we must recognize, is to hold industrial Europe guilty of being fortunate. The Bible enjoins us not to honor the person of the mighty, but commands us also in the same verse not to respect the person of the poor either: if good fortune is guilt, then misfortune equally must be.

In this respect also, therefore, the link between European economic power and European rule overseas which Hobsonian doctrine sought to establish fails to hold. It fails not only because the disruptive effects of the industrial system were, in a world in which absolute isolation and autarchy did not obtain, largely independent of political arrangements; it fails also because, in fact, those classes in Europe who benefited most from the industrial revolution were not greatly in favor of overseas annexations; what they wanted was free trade; what they pressed their governments to obtain was the right to trade freely everywhere; and governments did on many occasions use their power and influence in places like China, Japan, and the Ottoman Empire in order to obtain this right for their subjects. This, as has been said above, may be called the imperialism of free trade, but the expression must be recognized as metaphorical and quite innocent of any Hobsonian or Leninist tincture.

Another objection now arises. While industrializing, it may be said, was attended with much disruption in Europe, yet this disruption was made good and compensated by a system which was able eventually and by fits and starts prodigiously to increase wealth and material welfare in Western Europe and America, and thus to provide the indispensable foundation for a new stable society. In Asia and Africa, on the other hand, the impact of industrialism was, it would be pointed out, mainly destructive. The cheap goods it introduced into these traditional societies, the production of "raw materials" which European demand stimulated in Asia and Africa, it would be said, unsettled people, destroyed subsistence agriculture, created new demands and expectations, and in short irrevocably upset a traditional balance between the individual and his society, between the society and its natural environment, which had lasted for thousands of years. For all this damage, it would be claimed, there has been no compensation, and industrialism has not meant in Asia and Africa that enhanced material prosperity which has been its great justification in Europe and America.

This is not wholly true, since it can be shown that contact with the Western economy has meant for Asia and Africa a great enhancement of material welfare.[10] This contact did bring unsettlement and social disruption, but, as has been said, it was not confined to Asia and Africa and was rather the consequence of modern economic activity everywhere. The bearing, therefore, of this argument on the question of European dominance is not obvious. Industrialization, as it happened in Europe and North America, was very much a matter of individual inventiveness, initiative, and ambition. It is of course reasonable to suppose that public administration and state activity in general may actively help or hinder the process. What cannot be established as a general rule is that such action is either necessary or sufficient. Japan never came under foreign rule, and its government took energetic action in the latter half of the nineteenth century to promote industrialization; it may reasonably be supposed that such action did in fact promote Japan's successful industrialization. Turkey under Mustafa Kemal was likewise politically independent, and likewise exerted itself to promote industrialization, but the results were quite mediocre. Among Asian and African countries Japan so far remains the exception and Turkey very much the rule. Governments, whether native or alien, can never tell what contingencies and emergencies they are likely to meet; they are forever groping and whistling in the dark, clinging to the necessary hope that their powerful but crude weapons of coercion and inducement, of taxation and subsidy, will prove adequate; that the obscure mainsprings of individual behavior will work for and not against them; that no unpredictable lurch taken by society at large, a rise in the birthrate, say, or bewitchment by some messianism, will leave them suddenly puzzled and helpless. Assuming—what is normally the case— that rulers in fact rule, that they are not maniacal terrorists like the Nazis, or profit-makers like King Leopold in his Congo Free State, assuming then that they will rule and occasionally exhibit a scruple, it is never very easy to say in advance—or even in retrospect—what they should or should not do. We cannot say that the government of India ought to have done this a hundred years ago, or to have declined to interfere with that fifty years after, and conclude that these acts of omission or commission explain why India is today not industrialized. The British rulers of India a hundred years ago believed in free trade and acted on their belief. Can we say that if they had been Indian they would not have followed some such policy, or that if they had been protectionist India would have been industrialized? The British rulers of India, again, imposed peace over the subcontinent and later, by means of extensive irrigation works, brought into cultivation large areas of the Punjab. Such activities may

have caused the great and continuing increase in the population
of India, an increase which certainly complicates and may eventually defeat the effort to industrialize. Should then the British,
with the eventual welfare of India in mind, have deliberately
encouraged insecurity in the land and kept the Punjab a desert?
If such are the ambiguities in which all government is involved,
can we then say that India was not industrialized because its
government was British? It remains in any case to be seen
whether an Indian government of India will be successful where
its alien predecessor has been retrospectively convicted of
failure.[11]

The notion, then, that it is "imperialism" which conjures up
nationalism in Asia and Africa fails as explanation. It fails when
"imperialism" is understood in the strict Hobsonian sense for
the reasons set out above. But it has an even graver defect, since
nationalism as a distinct political movement antedates "imperialism" as writers like Hobson, Lenin, and Stalin describe it.
It is generally agreed in fact that nationalism first appears in
Europe. In order that one comprehensive explanation should
cover nationalism both in Europe and overseas, Lenin and Stalin
linked its appearance to a particular phase of economic organization. In the case of Europe, so the argument goes (as may be seen
from the passage by Stalin quoted on page 9), nationalism appears when the bourgeois class is powerful enough to challenge
the feudal class and form a unified state to serve as a big market
for its products. The argument, it is obvious, is very lame: a
mechanical application of the "economic" interpretation of history which would have it that the Great Rebellion in seven-
teenth-century England was not about religion and the royal
prerogative, as the protagonists claimed, but "really" an expression of bourgeois aspirations; that the French Revolution likewise was "really" the expression of bourgeois economic power;
that in partitioned Poland—a region where the bourgeoisie in
a Marxist sense hardly existed—Polish nationalism was "really"
a bourgeois movement, etc. The fact is of course that nationalist
ideology has little to do with either capitalism or the industrial
revolution. England, a country where the new industrial system

appeared early and where industrial organization went furthest in the eighteenth and nineteenth centuries, knew nothing of nationalist ideology as it was formulated and proclaimed by numerous writers and political leaders in Germany, Eastern Europe, and the Balkans at a period when these areas had very little industry. Even if by nationalism is meant—albeit loosely and improperly—the formation of centralized territorial sovereignties, a process which took place in Europe in the sixteenth and seventeenth centuries, the role of a capitalist bourgeoisie in this process is not particularly prominent. The truth is that the Leninist and Stalinist glosses merely succeed in making the Hobsonian doctrine even more misleading than it could ever hope to be.

The argument that there is a link between nationalism and economic conditions, particularly in areas like Asia and Africa, sometimes appears in a looser form than that encountered in Hobson and Lenin. In this looser form it may usefully be described as a variant of economism, i.e., of the view that political attitudes and activities are governed by economic conditions.[12] Thus in a recent discussion of social change in the poor and economically backward areas of the world, Professor Ernest Gellner has argued that nationalism is a movement which develops in the poorer parts of an empire in reaction to the wealth of the imperial rulers.[13] But such a statement seems most debatable. Poverty in certain circumstances does breed discontent, just as in other no less important and numerous instances it breeds a passive and fatalistic resignation. Poverty may breed discontent, and this discontent may give rise to a nationalist ideology or facilitate its spread, but the fact is that many well-known nationalist movements arose among populations which were not manifestly poorer than their rulers, while other nationalist movements appeared among populations which were clearly more well-to-do than their rulers, and still other nationalist movements flourished in countries which were not and had never been under alien rule. Thus, to illustrate nationalist movements in the first category, it is quite clear that Polish nationalism or Italian nationalism or Czech nationalism did not result from the manifestly greater poverty of Poles, Italians, and Czechs when compared with their Russian, Prussian, or Austrian masters in the nineteenth century; to illustrate the second category, Greek and Armenian nationalism arose among populations which were generally more prosperous and better able to understand the wealth-generating economies of modern Europe than their Ottoman Muslim overlords; to illustrate, lastly, the third category, Nazism and Japanese nationalism between the wars exercised undisputed sway in countries which were neither "underdeveloped" nor ruled by aliens. If poverty, then, contributes to the appearance or spread of nationalism, it does so only because poverty may give rise, in certain circumstances, to insecurity and social strains making people open to a doctrine which purports to provide for their distempers a sure diagnosis and a certain remedy. But the human condition being generally restless and insecure, poverty is only one of the innumerable justifications which men use when they break out in aggressiveness and destruction: Auschwitz, the *reductio, per terrore, ad absurdum* of nationalism, did not happen because the Germans were poor.

If this is so, then Professor Gellner's further point, namely, that it is the need for economic growth which generates nationalism, seems equally problematic. If people have wants which they are eager to satisfy—and this surely is the mainspring of economic growth—it is only by applying their ingenuity, inventiveness, and capacity for labor to precise and specific tasks that they may hope, with luck, to satisfy these wants. Material wants and their satisfaction have no obvious connection with an ideology like nationalism; a connection may be contrived only through the doubtful expedient of Hobsonian or Leninist doctrine. The idea that the need for economic growth generates nationalism is designed to controvert the contrary assertion, attributed to Professor Walt Whitman Rostow, namely, that it is nationalism which generates economic growth. This proposition seems perhaps even more doubtful than its opposite, since nationalist ideology may require the disruption or distortion of successful economic activity. It is true that nationalist governments in Asia and Africa have used the large amounts of money which the

international situation has enabled them to obtain from the
Great Powers in order to indulge in conspicuous investments,
and this may give Professor Rostow's proposition a semblance
of plausibility; but investment is not necessarily growth, since
not every investment does come to fruition, and international
economic aid, so-called, neither encourages wise investment nor
penalizes wasteful expenditure.

The various theories and doctrines now most frequently invoked to explain the origin and character of Asian and African
nationalism seem then to be in some way or other inadequate
and even misleading. There is one other explanation which is
perhaps even more widespread and acceptable than any of these
doctrines, an explanation which, because of its seeming simplicity, appears to raise no queries, appears indeed to be stating
the obvious. This explanation holds that nationalism is simply
a reaction to conquest and alien rule. The explanation is indeed
simple, but most defective. If it is taken seriously, it must make
nonsense of world history, in which conquest has followed conquest and a ruler's nationality has been almost the last thing men
have worried about. If men had held their nationality and their
language to be the most important fact of politics, there would
have been no Roman Empire, no spread of Islam, no United
States of America, no French or English language, and human
groups would have been still frozen in their most primitive form:
Angles and Saxons and Normans and Huns and Scythians. A
more likely account of the matter is the one given by Daniel
Defoe in "The True-Born Englishman":

> Thus from a mixture of all kinds began
> That heterogeneous thing, an Englishman:
> In eager rapes and furious lust begot
> Between a painted Briton and a Scot;
> Whose gendering offspring quickly learnt to bow
> And yoke their heifers to the Roman plough;
> From whence a mongrel half-bred race there came,
> With neither name nor nation, speech or fame.
> In whose hot veins new mixtures quickly ran,
> Infused between a Saxon and a Dane,

> While their rank daughters, to their parents just,
> Received all nations with promiscuous lust.
> This nauseous brood, directly did contain
> The well extracted blood of Englishmen.

Defoe's "true-born Englishman," in all his variegated hetero-geneity, stands a mirror to all mankind.

Government by aliens has been the rule rather than the exception in world history, and European domination over Asia and Africa in being alien is far from constituting an exception and a novelty which calls for complicated doctrines to account for it; it falls, on the contrary, into a very old and very familiar pattern. If European rule is exceptional, this is because of its remarkable brevity, and we may suspect that the Asian and African nationalism it has undoubtedly conjured up is a reaction to European domination, not because this domination was alien but because it was European.

II

Why then has European domination in Asia and Africa evoked nationalism in these areas? To argue that it was alien is not enough of an explanation; to say that it represented economic exploitation is highly misleading. What then was there in European rule to distinguish it from other alien dominations and to call forth in its subjects such violence and resistance?

According to Professor Peter Worsley, who has already been quoted above, European rule in Asia and Africa has "meant a fundamental transformation of the social life of the ordinary peasant and town-dweller," and European rule overseas, he argues, has been so brief precisely because of the social disturbance it has created.[14] This explanation of the ephemeral character of European rule overseas seems to have little foundation; considering the tremendous technical, administrative, and military superiority which European Powers have even now over their former colonies, it is to be doubted whether any reaction to their rule by their former subjects, however violent, could have dislodged them. The brevity of this rule is better explained by two world wars which were started and conducted by the European Great Powers and which left them in a position of inferiority, not indeed to their colonies, but to the U.S.A. and the U.S.S.R.—two Powers who, albeit for different reasons, have equally adopted the slogan of "anticolonialism." It is surely this inferiority, with all its multifarious and worldwide consequences, which principally accounts for the brevity of European rule overseas.

But whether or not the brevity of European rule is a consequence of the disturbance which it has brought about, there is no gainsaying the fact that Europe has been the origin and center of a deep radical disturbance spreading over the whole world in ever-widening ripples and bringing unsettlement and violence to the traditional societies of Asia and Africa, whether these societies did or did not experience direct European rule. It is this powerful European influence which gives their common features and their family resemblance to nationalist movements, whether in Turkey and Japan, which did not know European rule, or in China, where European annexations were peripheral and European power indirectly exercised, or in Syria and Iraq, where European rule was even more ephemeral than elsewhere, or in those areas, such as India, Algeria, or Indochina, which have been ruled by Europeans for a relatively long time.

What then is the character of this disturbance which Europe has produced in the rest of the world? European military might and European administrative methods, far more powerful and technically superior to anything available to these traditional societies, had over them an effect more pervasive and more drastic than previous conquests. European administrative methods in particular, centralized, impersonal, uniform, undiscriminating in their incidence, had a leveling and pulverizing effect on traditional hierarchies and loyalties, traditional ties of dependence which, however capricious and oppressive in their general effects, did yet have about them a warm and personal quality which made power seem approachable and comprehensible to the humblest and most insignificant man. Anyone who reads of the workings of traditional Islamic society such as they are implied and portrayed in the *Thousand and One Nights* or of traditional Chinese society as it is described in the picaresque novel *Chin P'ing Mei* will know that such societies could not possibly have produced works like Kafka's *The Trial* or *The Castle*, which, whatever their allegorical or philosophical meaning, seem to draw inspiration from, and to achieve some of their effect by, implicit reference to the impersonal, remote, drab, and meticulous bureaucracy assembled and perfected by European enlightened absolutism.

The destructive effect of European administrative methods—whether applied by European officials, as in India and Burma, or by native ones, as in the Ottoman Empire—was greatly magnified by the increasing involvement of these traditional societies with the world economy. These traditional societies had hitherto been largely self-sufficient subsistence economies: they now found themselves, sometimes gradually, sometimes suddenly, linked to a world market which brought them new and vast riches but which was subject to gusts of speculation and to mysterious unpredictable cycles of boom and depression originating in the plans and expectations of city merchants in London or cotton manufacturers in Lancashire, but finally affecting the rice cultivator of Lower Burma or the cotton cultivator of the Egyptian Delta, to whom in their remoteness and helplessness they seemed a new and mysterious scourge.

These forces, so incalculable and haphazard in their incidence, combined to loosen and shake a social fabric which had lasted for centuries, it is true, but which could offer scant resistance to an attack which was powerful in its onset and took forms at once varied and unfamiliar. Whether it was the African chieftain whose authority was undermined by a paramount European power and whose dignity therefore became mere show; or the Indian *ryot* disoriented by the esoteric rigors of a Benthamite penal code; or the peasant of Lower Burma suddenly transformed into the purveyor of rice to the whole world; or the Ottoman conscript learning the strict and outlandish drill of the Franks: all this humanity could not but feel its familiar world suddenly or by degrees become alien, its traditional loyalties drained of significance, and its customary pieties hollow and meaningless.

There is one significant aspect of this disturbance which has to be particularly noticed. This pulverization of traditional societies, this bursting open of self-sufficient economies could not fail to bring about in those who were subject to this process a serious and distressing psychological strain. In a most intelligent and illuminating work, *Psychologie de la Colonisation*,[15] the French colonial administrator and anthropologist O. Mannoni has elucidated the effects of European rule and culture on the traditional society of Madagascar, but the situation which he describes and explains is to be found not only in Madagascar but all over the non-European world. Mannoni makes the point that the ties of traditional Malagasy society are ties of dependence. In this close-knit hierarchical society the individual feels secure and protected because he has a well-defined place in a coherent scheme, the cosmic significance and the reasonableness of which is vouched for by a host of living elders and dead ancestors. European rule pulverizes the traditional society which seemed by its successful working to lend credence to this belief, and European example offers a rival system of beliefs. In this rival system the individual, far from finding fulfillment in the traditional ties of social dependence, will not be content until by his own efforts he achieves intellectual, moral, and economic independence. And it is of course a fact that this aspiration is peculiarly European, having taken root in the European way of life and found its expression in economic and political endeavor as well as in philosophical speculation. Kant and Descartes may be considered to offer a reasoned philosophical justification of this European ideal, Descartes who doubted everything except the scope and power of man's reason, who proclaimed man nature's lord and possessor, and Kant who taught that no action was moral unless it was a freely accepted commitment. This modern European ideal of independent judgment, moral self-determination, and restless individual initiative—which other civilizations, no less sophisticated than those of the modern

West, might consider blindly presumptuous and wilfully self-destructive—became a rival to the traditional outlook, a rival commended to increasing numbers of Asians and Africans by the prestige of Western achievement and prosperity. But an ideal of this kind is a demanding one even in the land of its origin, where social conditions and individual attitudes favored it; how much greater, therefore, the strain and tension which result from the attempt to emulate it in conditions which are wholly unpropitious? Mannoni makes the point that in the conditions of traditional society when the feeling of dependence is undermined, there is generated a feeling of inadequacy and bewilderment: an oppressive sense of inferiority replaces the cozy security of dependence.

Such strain and insecurity in the individual is bound sooner or later to erupt in violent and destructive action which will be the more difficult to contain and control precisely because the social fabric has been weakened beyond repair. Arthur de Gobineau (1816–1882), who was French minister at Tehran in the early eighteen-sixties, tells us in his *Religions and Philosophies of Central Asia* (1864) that he was so curious of the effects of European philosophy on the Oriental mentality that he had Descartes' *Discours de la méthode* translated into Persian so that he might be able to study the reactions of the Persian audience to whom it was read. Gobineau does not tell us the result of this experiment, but his book has a passage worth citing for its acute insight into the corrosive effect of modern European ideals in these ancient societies. "I am inclined to think," he writes of the effects of contact with Europe, "that the dangers for us will not be negligible. Not physical dangers: on this score we may rest easy, for the Asiatics have no swords which can offer resistance to our bayonets. It is to moral dangers that I refer. In this great intellectual swamp some new combustion of principles, of ideas, of pestilential theories will take place, and the poison which it will produce will be transmitted by contact more or less quickly, but surely."[16]

There is, finally, another peculiar characteristic of European influence and rule to notice. It is that unlike past dominations and previous dominant cultures, Europe brought in its wake literacy as an ideal and as a technically feasible goal. Widespread or universal literacy, an indispensable concomitant of industrialism, was in Europe itself quite a recent phenomenon, but the very industrial system which demanded it facilitated its spread far beyond the shores of Europe, since books and newspapers printed cheaply could now be as cheaply scattered by steamship and railway to the four corners of the earth.

The ideas which such publications transmitted came to be known in the first place to those who could read European languages and were more or less acquainted with the kind of experience which lay behind and made sense of what the printed page disclosed. For such people especially, the new things which Europe brought, orderly and scientific administration, the new modes of economic endeavor, the literacy, proved that Europe was technically powerful and intellectually superior, while the traditional societies showed up so lamentably in comparison. Literacy therefore generally meant discontent with existing conditions and a desire to adopt those European "principles" which were thought to be the cause of European superiority. The literate then—literate, that is, in European languages and modes of thought—alienated from their traditional societies became what has been called—not very felicitously—"marginal men," disaffected toward their traditional society, the nucleus and the vanguard of a radical and uncompromising opposition and its battering ram pounding down outmoded and obscurantist institutions. And as the gradual Europeanization of government and economy involved increasing numbers of people in the painful process of rapid and radical change, this nucleus of literate leaders found themselves able to appeal to a disoriented mass which certainly felt the aches and discomforts of its condition but which was unable by itself to diagnose and prescribe for its distemper. When Lenin imposed on the Social Democrats his idea of a party composed of an elite of professional revolutionaries who would lead the inarticulate masses willy-nilly toward the vision by which they themselves had been seized, he was, whether he knew it or not, summing up and codifying the rules of successful political action in all these societies which had been violently wrenched from their age-old moorings by European action or example.

The ideas which came from Europe to the traditional societies were necessarily a haphazard and generally misleading selection from the incoherent medley of European traditions in themselves also incoherent. Such strands from them which happened to be taken up overseas came to be known and adopted either by the accident of transmission and diffusion or because they happened to be emphasized and propagated for some reason in Europe itself. Nationalism is one such idea. Conceived and wholly elaborated in Europe, it knew during the nineteenth century a prodigious popularity in Europe itself and was transmitted and spread to Asia and Africa, where its popularity became as great as in Europe.

"Nationalism is a doctrine invented in Europe at the beginning of the nineteenth century. It pretends to supply a criterion for the determination of the unit of population proper to enjoy a government exclusively its own, for the legitimate exercise of power in the state, and for the right organization of a society of states. Briefly, the doctrine holds that humanity is naturally divided into nations, that nations are known by certain characteristics which can be ascertained, and that the only legitimate type of government is national self-government."[17] Taking this to be a concise but reasonably comprehensive definition of nationalism, we may say that every item of this doctrine can be shown to be either mistaken in its description of reality or misguided and self-defeating in its aims: for humanity is not naturally divided into "nations"; the characteristics of any particular "nation" are neither easily ascertainable nor exclusively inherent in it; while to insist that the only legitimate type of government is national self-government is capriciously to dismiss the great variety of political arrangements to which men have given assent and loyalty and to strive after a state of affairs the attempt to realize which would be, in the nature of things, both ruinous and futile. Nationalism as a doctrinal system can be taken apart and its conclusions accounted for and explained in the light of its various assumptions and arguments,[18] and these will then be seen as a medley derived from various systems of thought, the coherence and plausibility of the doctrine depending on its implicit agreement or affinity with certain strands in the political and intellectual tradition of Europe.

Nationalism as a doctrine argues that humanity must be organized into a world of nation-states. Such a requirement does not seem out of character with European history, seems rather to be a natural extension of a condition which, ever since the disappearance of the Roman Empire in the West, had been customary to Europe, with its feudal divisions, its free cities, its sovereign republics and monarchies in continuous combination, rivalry, and conflict. This lively multiplicity of political authorities, of "states," seems the historical experience which gives body and verisimilitude to the nationalist vision of a world made up of "nation-states." Let it be said in passing that even in Europe "nation-states" are not the natural development of the European state system which they might seem to be at first sight.[19] But Europe is not the world, and the European experience has little parallel in Asia or Africa. The typical Asian polity is the Chinese Empire, or the Empire of the Mughals, or the Ottoman Empire, large, diverse areas administered by a bureaucracy controlled and appointed from one omnipotent center; while Africa before the coming of the Europeans was for the most part given over to a tribal form of government equally removed from Asiatic despotism and from European polycentrism. This form of government—rightly called primitive—is possessed of little articulation or complexity; it is quite unable to withstand a clash with the formidable organization of Europe and is entirely lacking in that reflective self-knowledge which a work such as Aristotle's provides for the polis, or Kautilya's for Oriental despotism, or Hegel's for the European state. Nothing more than this indicates the alien character of nationalism in Asia and Africa, that it is neither something indigenous to these areas nor an irresistible tendency of the human spirit everywhere, but rather an importation from Europe clearly branded with the mark of its origin. Almost any Asian or African nationalism, considered as a scheme of thought or a program of action, suffers from artificiality, from seeming a laborious attempt to introduce outlandish standards and out-of-place categories, and nowhere do they seem more out-of-place than in trying to adopt the European category of the nation-state. Consider, for instance, the arguments by which Choudhary Rahmat Ali justified the creation of Pakistan—a name which he himself invented. (See "The Idea of Pakistan," pp. 245–249.)

As an Indian Muslim, Rahmat Ali was concerned with the Hindu threat to his community, which he thought was best parried by the Muslims of India forming an independent state of their own. This state Rahmat Ali called Pakistan, the Land of the Pure. But his acrostic imagination gave the word a further significance and made it stand "for the names of all our homelands," to wit, *P*anjab, *A*fghania, *K*ashmir, *I*ran, *S*ind, *A*fghanistan, and Balu-chista*n*. And yet this patently fanciful notion, taking its due place in a nationalist system, became all at once the name of a definite territory, the Fatherland of the Pak Nation, and the Pure were seen to inhabit a land with ancient well-defined frontiers and an immemorial history: Pakistan, we discover, "is the land which lies in the northwest of the Continent of Dinia, otherwise known as the Subcontinent of India," that "it constitutes the age-old national stronghold of the people who represent the original core and content of the Millat living in the Orbit of Pakasia," that it is "one of the most ancient and illustrious countries of the Orient," and that "it is the only country in the world which, in the antiquity of its legend and lore as in the character of its history and hopes, compares with Iraq and Egypt—the countries which are known as the cradle of the achievement of Mankind." So we see the problems, fears, and aspirations of the Indian Muslims with all their history as conquerors and rulers of Mughal India, and then as a somewhat backward and fearful minority in British India, transmuted and simplified into a nationalist ideology which requires that Indian Muslims shall be called Paks, that Paks shall be called a nation, that the Pak nation shall be considered a nation-state, and that this nation-state shall be deemed to have lived from of old in a territory known as Pakistan. Such are the triumphs of doctrine.

Nationalist doctrine implicitly takes for granted and assimilates yet another feature of the European tradition. This is the prominent and abiding tendency of European politics to require and enforce uniformity of belief among the members of a body politic. Until very late in its history the Roman Empire was quite indifferent to the beliefs professed by its subjects, provided these beliefs did not threaten the Roman power or endanger the maintenance of law and order. This traditional Roman policy continued almost unchanged until the accession of the Emperor Theodosius in 379 of the Christian era, the opening of whose reign saw an explicit attempt to impose religious uniformity on the Empire: "It is our pleasure," proclaimed the Emperor, "that all the nations which are governed by our clemency and moderation should steadfastly adhere to the religion which was taught by St. Peter to the Romans. . . . According to the discipline of the apostles and the doctrine of the Gospel, let us believe the sole deity of the Father, the Son and the Holy Ghost; under an equal majesty and a pious Trinity. We authorize the followers of this doctrine to assume the title of Catholic Christians; and as we judge that all others are extravagant madmen, we brand them with the infamous name of heretics; and declare that their conventicles shall no longer usurp the respectable appellation of churches. Besides the condemnation of Divine justice, they must expect to suffer the severe penalties which our authority, guided by heavenly wisdom, shall think proper to inflict upon them." A passage in Chapter XXVII of *The Decline and Fall of the Roman Empire* describes the character and intentions of the Theodosian legislation; but the passage may be taken to apply not only to this particular episode but to a remarkably durable strand of the European tradition of which Theodosius' edict is an early and fateful formulation: "The sectaries," observed Gibbon, "were gradually disqualified for the possession of honorable or lucrative employments; and Theodosius was satisfied with his own justice when he decreed, that as the Eunomians distinguished the nature of the Son from that of the Father, they should be incapable of making their wills, or of receiving any advantage from testamentary donations. The guilt of the Manichaean heresy was esteemed of such magnitude that it could be expiated only by the death of the offender; and the same capital punishment was inflicted on the Audians, or *Quartodecimans*, who should dare to perpetrate the atrocious crime of celebrating, on an improper day, the festival of Easter. Every Roman might exercise the right of public accusation; but the office of *Inquisitor* of the Faith, a name so deservedly abhorred, was first instituted under the reign of Theodosius."

It may be that, as Gibbon adds, Theodosius' edicts were seldom enforced, but the hundred and fifty years following saw the gradual extension and the ever more severe enforcement of penalties against Jews and Christian heretics, a progress finally consummated in the legislation of the Emperor Justinian (527–565), who improved on his predecessor Theodosius by depriving pagans, heretics, and Jews of all rights in the body politic, thus effecting a revolutionary and fundamental change in the principles of Roman government. Roman law as codified and proclaimed by the Byzantine emperors was the foundation of European medieval law, and insistence on religious uniformity remained, until the period of enlightened absolutism and the French Revolution, an unquestioned feature of European government—a feature indeed periodically given new life and vigor by the Crusades and the massacre of Jews in Europe which accompanied them, by the Crusade against the Albigensians, by the expulsion of the Jews and Moors from Spain at the Reconquista, by the wars of religion in Central Europe in the sixteenth century and the Peace of Augsburg (1555), which officially and publicly consecrated the rule that the religion of the subject must be the same as that of the ruler. And a century before the outbreak of the Revolution in France, the revocation by Louis XIV of the Edict of Nantes, by which his grandfather had granted toleration to the Huguenots, showed the continuity and abiding vitality of this strand in the European political tradition.

This permanent feature of European politics in medieval and modern times, this emphasis, century after century, on the need for uniformity and homogeneity in the body politic, could not but leave its residue in the assumptions and attitudes of European writers on politics, however secular or even antireligious their outlook. The Savoyard Vicar's Confession of Faith was undoubtedly very different from that "professed by the pontiff Damasus, and by Peter, bishop of Alexandria," which Theodosius was determined to press on his subjects, but there is nothing to choose between the religious uniformity which Theodosius desired to effect by coercion and indoctrination and the political uniformity which Rousseau prescribed in the "civil religion" of his *Contrat Social,* lapses from which this philanthropic and benevolent author proposed to punish with death. What is true of Rousseau is likewise the case with the European inventors of nationalist doctrine. When they invite us to look upon the world as a world of nations, each different from the rest, and each perfectly homogeneous in its history, its speech, its wishes and desires, we may not doubt that we see here erected into a metaphysical principle Theodosius' theory of persecution and the rough justice of the Diet of Augsburg: *cuius regio eius religio.*

It is the opinion of some writers, of whom the best-known today is Professor Arnold Toynbee, that this aggressive pressure for uniformity, this intolerance of heterogeneous beliefs, is a "Judaic" legacy to the Christian politics of Byzantium and Europe, but we observe that another religion, perhaps more closely affiliated to Judaism than Trinitarian Christianity, has, in spite of its warlike beginnings, never demanded religious uniformity and from the start made a place within its polity for those of a different belief, a place which was recognized and sanctioned by law. In this respect Islam, with the protection it vouchsafes to non-Muslims, and the Ottoman Empire, with its highly developed *millet* system, have more affinity than Rome's Byzantine successors to the original character of Roman government. And what is true of Muslim lands is equally true of the lands of Hinduism and Buddhism. In none of these areas before the coming of European influence was a homogeneous population considered a religious or political ideal, nor did the rulers make it a constant maxim of policy to enforce uniformity on their subjects. Here, then, is another aspect of the argument that nationalism is a European doctrine in its unspoken premises and that its spread in Asia and Africa follows the spread of European culture, backed as it was with all the prestige and self-confidence of European power.

The political history of Europe, its variety of independent political authorities, and its traditional emphasis on uniformity of belief are necessary preconditions for nationalist doctrine. Another essential presupposition of this doctrine is provided by a feature of recent European intellectual history, by the fact, namely, that diversity has come to be considered the most important feature of the universe. It was toward the end of the eighteenth century that this idea, which had always been present in European thought, came to be particularly emphasized. What was most significant about things as about men was what made them different from, rather than what made them similar to, other things and men. Men fulfilled themselves when their behavior was in character with the peculiar genius of their group, the outward signs of which were language, social customs, and political traditions. It is this assumption which lies at the back of and justifies the quest of every nationalist doctrine for those singular and unique characteristics which distinguish a particular nation from the rest of mankind. The European writers who did most to develop these ideas, Herder, A.W. Schlegel, Fichte, argued that the characteristics which served to distinguish one human group from another were cultural, and more specifically linguistic, since language was not merely a colorless medium of human communication but a depository of the traditions, attitudes, and habits of the successive generations of a particular group. Hence in nationalist doctrine "nations" are defined by their various languages, and these languages are themselves the outward symbol of a life lived for centuries in common.[20] As F. Schlegel succinctly put it: *"Quot linguae, tot gentes."*

This doctrine transformed language into a political issue the explosive nature of which is sufficiently illustrated by the somber and bloodstained history of Central and Eastern Europe and the

Balkans for the last hundred years. And it may be said that language as a criterion of political organization must bring with it dissension and violence, since, contrary to the assertions of nationalist doctrine, mankind is not naturally divided into distinct "nations," each with its own exclusive territory, and the attempt to make the political map conform to some linguistic criterion is bound to be a brutal and sanguinary affair.

This linguistic and cultural criterion by which nations are defined raises another quite fundamental issue, that of personal identity and of one's attitude toward the past. Nationalist doctrine, in asserting that the only legitimate political association is one which binds together men speaking the same language, sharing the same culture, and cherishing the same heroes and ancestors, expresses in its own ideological way a preoccupation with history which has come to be a dominant theme of the modern European outlook and which has also been taken up wherever European culture has penetrated. History as a distinct mode of thought arose in Europe in the seventeenth century out of the practical preoccupations of religious and political polemic in which men appealed to the past in order to attack or defend an institution or a dogma. Luther, in the sixteenth century, "had not so much as felt," Albert Schweitzer tells us, "that he cared to gain a clear idea of the order of the recorded events. Speaking of the chronology of the cleansing of the Temple, which in John falls at the beginning, in the Synoptists near the close, of Jesus' public life, he remarks: 'The Gospels follow no order in recording the acts and miracles of Jesus, and the matter is not, after all, of much importance. If a difficulty arises in regard to the Holy Scripture and we cannot solve it, we must just let it alone.' "[21] Schweitzer's own work, published in 1906, surveys and illustrates a change in the European consciousness which began to be manifest a century or so after Luther's death and which now seems to be permanent—as permanent, that is, as Western civilization, which has now spread, in varying degrees, throughout the world. The modern attitude toward the past is utterly different from that of Luther's time. To grasp this, we may set side by side with Luther's remark quoted above, a remark which occurs in F. C. Burkitt's preface to the English translation of *The Quest of the Historical Jesus*. "Our first duty with the Gospel as with every other ancient document," wrote this eminent scholar, "is to interpret it with reference to its own time. The true view of the Gospel will be that which explains the course of events in the first century and the second century, rather than that which seems to have spiritual and imaginative value for the twentieth century."[22] For Luther the Gospel is the Word of God, unvarying, eternal, *quod ubique, quod semper, quod ab omnibus creditum est;* for Burkitt it has become a "document" to be interpreted "with reference to its own time."

History thus comes to be seen as that which gives coherence and significance to actions, documents, institutions which had hitherto been accepted as forming an uncomplicated and perhaps timeless tradition. And if the concern with history ceases to be scholarly, as it is in Burkitt's case, and becomes simply practical, then the "past" is used to explain the "present," to give it meaning and legitimacy. The "past" reveals one's identity, and history determines one's role in the drama of human development and progress. Hence these "philosophies of history" which began to be popular in the European enlightenment with Voltaire, Condorcet and Turgot, and which the German romantics, Herder, Fichte, Hegel and many others, helped to swell into a flood.

Nationalist doctrine, insisting that the individual has no identity apart from his nation, and that nations are known by their language, literature, culture, etc., decrees that just as nations exist, so nations by definition must have a past. The spread of nationalist doctrine in Europe has therefore evoked a voluminous literature, historical in its form but apologetic in its substance, which claims to show the rise in remote times, the steady progress and development of this or that nation, and the successive manifestations of its genius in religion, art, science, and literature.[23]

This view of history as providing evidences for a "progress," or a "development," the idea, that is, of a "philosophy of history," had the same far-reaching effects when it spread beyond

Europe and began to subvert and overthrow the views which various Asian and African societies had traditionally held concerning their identity and their place in the world. Thus, to take one example, Muslims, like Luther, held that Divine Revelation vouchsafed to mankind through the Prophet Muhammad was the Truth which could never be subject to variation or emendation. For the believer the past was not a "development" or a "progress" leading up to, explaining, and legitimizing his present; it was rather a store of lessons and warnings illustrating the workings of God's justice: "We tell you," says the Qur'an, "stories of the Apostles which will strengthen your heart, and thus bring you the Truth, an exhortation, and a memorial for believers."[24] "Insight into the history of man," writes again a medieval Muslim chronicler (Hamdani, d. 1127), "is a mirror in which the onlooker finds the verification of good and bad actions and which instructs the men of perfection and natural gifts. Through it God reminds those of His servants whom He finds worthy of such reminder and deserving of His recompense and His reward." But when we come to modern times and contact with European ideas, Islam begins to be regarded by Muslims not so much a Revelation and an immutable truth as a "civilization," a "culture," or even a product of the Arab national genius.[25]

This "transvaluation of values," this appeal to the "past" to provide a new and more satisfying identity, we may illustrate from the career and writings of Adamantios Koraes. A native of Smyrna, Koraes was born a member of the Greek Orthodox community which, with the Ottoman conquest of Constantinople, became repository and heir of the Byzantine tradition. This tradition looked upon Byzantium as the New Israel chosen by God for His own when the Jews forfeited His favor by their rejection of Jesus. While Byzantium flourished, the belief that they were the object of Divine Election was confirmed to the Byzantines by the manifest power and splendor of their Empire; but this belief by no means disappeared when the Empire declined, nor yet when it was finally destroyed. Rather, these misfortunes were considered as a divine chastisement for sin and backsliding which will come to an end at the Second Coming, when God will once again recognize and exalt His own. In this perspective, the Greek Orthodox community of the Ottoman Empire looked upon itself as the guardian of the True Faith against the heresies of the Franks, to whom the Ottomans were infinitely to be preferred. Indeed, as a patriarch of Constantinople argued in a pamphlet published in 1798, Ottoman rule over the Christians was providentially ordained by God in order to safeguard their religious liberty and shield them from the innumerable heresies of the West. Political freedom he denounced as an illusion, "an enticement of the Devil and a murderous poison that will push the people into disorder and destruction." If the Latin West was thus rejected, equally shunned were the ancient Hellenes and their pagan philosophies; indeed, at the end of the eighteenth century it seemed to the leaders of Orthodoxy that the latest Frankish heresies were merely a new version of the old pagan errors. Spinoza, the Freemasons, Voltaire, and Rousseau could be likened not only to earlier Christian heretics but also to Hellenes like Anaximander, Thales, and Orpheus, and a patriarchal encyclical of 1797 asked the faithful "not to cultivate Hellenic letters and the foolish wisdom of the Europeans as being contrary to the Christian life, but only grammar, founded on the exposition of the Church Fathers; as for those Platos and Aristotles, Newtons and Descartes, triangles and logarithms," the encyclical affirmed, "they only cause indifference to things holy."[26]

These statements of the traditional position by the Orthodox hierarchy at the end of the eighteenth century, these warnings to the faithful against new spiritual dangers, were, as is usually the case with such exhortations, altogether late and useless. The sweet and heady poison of Western enlightenment, which in any case had been introduced during the past hundred years or so with the hierarchy's help and encouragement, was past checking by these antidotes. The career and writings of Adamantios Koraes show the radical and far-reaching character of the revolt against tradition.

Koraes (1748–1833) was born and brought up in Smyrna, which before the Greco-Turkish War of 1919–21 was the center of a flourishing Greek settlement and as much a Greek as it was a Muslim city. We are told that in his early youth he became friendly with a Dutch clergyman who officiated in the Dutch Church at Smyrna, and it was contact with this Westerner which first detached the young Koraes from the outlook and traditions of his community. The pastor taught him the elements of Latin, French, and Italian and thus opened up a whole new world, the civilization and learning of the Latin West, which his community and its leaders had usually looked on with hostility, suspicion, or contempt. Indeed, Koraes' own maternal grandfather, whose library he inherited, had published a book written in iambic verses and entitled *Thirty-six Refutations of the Latin Religion.* Pastor Keun contrasted the enlightenment of Europe with the obscurantism and despotism of the Turk and dwelt on the veneration in which European scholarship held the ancient Greeks, their literature and philosophy. Under his influence, Koraes felt attracted to these foreign lands and persuaded his father to allow him to visit them. He went to Holland in 1772 and stayed there until 1778. In Holland he came into more direct and intimate contact with European classical scholarship, which precisely then was maturing and perfecting its knowledge of Greek antiquity, as it had two centuries earlier perfected that of Roman antiquity. If, during the Renaissance, the ideal which the humanists had held up before their disciples was that of civic virtue and Ciceronian philosophy, the students of ancient Greece now conjured up a vision of Hellas in which delectable sensuousness combined with spiritual elevation and philosophical profundity. The lure of Greece has left deep traces in European and particularly German literature of the late eighteenth and early nineteenth centuries, but besides the classical names of Winckelmann, Schiller, Goethe, Hölderlin, Mme. de Staël, and Byron there was a host of popularizers and *vulgarisateurs* who spread among literate Europeans a romantic and sentimental Hellenism which survives to the present day in school manuals and university textbooks. Of this literature a single but significant example may be cited. *The Travels of Anacharsis the Younger in Greece during the Middle of the Fourth Century before the Christian Era* by the Abbé Jean-Jacques Barthélemy is today quite forgotten. But when it was published in Paris in 1788 its five quarto volumes knew an immediate and overwhelming popularity. It went into forty editions and thirteen abridgments and was translated into English, German, Italian, Spanish, Dutch, Danish, Greek, and Armenian. The book recounts the imaginary journey of Anacharsis, a Scythian, who visited Greece from 363 to 338, where he met and talked to Plato, Aristotle, Demosthenes, Xenophon, etc. As Barthélemy described it, Hellas was a society of wise and virtuous men, profound in their thoughts, exquisite in their sensibilities, and elevated in their manners.

Contact with European scholarship and its philhellenism gave Koraes an exalted notion of the greatness of those whom he now learned to consider his ancestors. It is no wonder that on returning to Smyrna he should be filled with disgust at the quality of Greek life as it was actually lived in his community and deep hatred for those who, in his eyes, were chiefly responsible for this degradation: the word "Turk," as he said, became for him synonymous with wild beast. Life in Smyrna he would no longer endure; after four years of discontent he betook himself to Montpellier, never again to see his native land. In Montpellier he was supposed to study medicine; but what seems to have attracted him in medicine was not so much that it could cure disease but that it was yet another example of the transcendent genius of the ancient Greeks: it was to Hippocrates that he devoted his thesis at Montpellier. Medicine had really nothing to attract him, and it was to Greek philology and classical Greek literature that he gave the rest of his life, to this and to the "debarbarization" of the modern Greeks, i.e., their transformation into beings worthy of Pericles and Socrates.

This was an enterprise of some magnitude, involving fundamental change in the language, religion, social relations, and political institutions of the modern Greeks. If the modern Greeks were to become a band of Socrates and Platos, they had to abandon the degraded jargon which they now spoke and revert to the purity of the classical tongue, they had to cleanse

themselves of the superstitions into which a corrupt and scheming clergy had plunged them, and for the present tyranny and
its daughter ignorance they had to substitute the egalitarian
democracy of Solon and Lycurgus. These tasks might seem too
arduous for human capacities, but Koraes was encouraged to
believe that they could be accomplished by the spectacle of the
French Revolution, which he witnessed at close quarters in
Paris, to which he had moved from Montpellier. In fact, for the
modern Greeks to become like their ancestors was to imitate the
enlightened Westerners who were happy and virtuous only because their model and inspiration was fifth-century Athens. His
letters on the eve of, and during, the French Revolution show
us how out of romantic Hellenism and political activism, both
of which loomed so large in his environment, he created the
explosive amalgam of Greek nationalist ideology. In a letter
written from Paris in September, 1788, he describes the splendors of the city which he calls a new Athens, "but," he continues,
"in a Greek who knows that two thousand years ago his ancestors in Athens had reached the same level of civilization (and
perhaps even higher), the wonder is mixed with sadness. When
we also remember that not only have all these beneficent things
flown away but have also been replaced by thousands of evils;
that in the place where the wisest laws of Solon (whose name
I have heard here pronounced by the learned men of Paris with
a kind of religious awe) held sway now reign ignorance, malice,
violence, audacity and impudence; when, I say, an unhappy
Greek sees these things and reflects about the past, then, my
friend, his sadness is changed into indignation and despair."
Exactly a year later, a few months after the outbreak of the
Revolution in France, he writes another letter which is even
more interesting: "I have seen," he informs his friend in Smyrna
in September, 1789, "many horrible things, many curious and
noteworthy things. Is there, for instance, anything more singular
than to see a preacher of the people's party mount the pulpit,
deliver a sermon on liberty taking for his text this passage from
St. Paul's epistle to the Galatians, V, 13: 'For, brethren, ye have
been called unto liberty; only use not liberty for an occasion to

the flesh, but by love serve one another,' and thunder against the aristocrats (that is the bishops and the nobles), saying that those who crucified Jesus Christ were the aristocrats (that is, the monks and the nobles such as the bishops, the scribes, the Pharisees and the leaders of the people)? And this because Jesus defended the Third Estate and taught equality and fraternity." It was not long before Koraes himself began applying these doctrines to his own Greek Orthodox Church. "What good have these monks ever done us?" he asks his friend the precentor of Smyrna Cathedral in a letter of July, 1790. "Have they not always been a cause of trouble, ambitious men and intriguers (if you except from them the truly Christian monks, peaceable, humble and sincere, who lived in the first four or five centuries of our Church)? Are they not the cause of the deplorable slavery in the depth of which the nation finds itself today? Did they not, when the Byzantine Empire was in its agony, concern themselves with 'futile and vain' things, as St. Paul puts it? And not only this, did they not also make of our idiotic emperors theologians instead of soldiers? Try to expel them," he concluded, "it would be agreeable in the sight of God."

The "Report on the Present State of Civilization in Greece" (pp. 153–188), which Koraes delivered before a French audience in Paris in 1803, is a capital document to illustrate the spread of nationalist ideology outside the Western cultural sphere. The lecture has many claims on our interest, the first being that it is a very early statement of those themes which were to recur later again and again in the nationalist doctrines of Asia and Africa. Indeed the lecture shows that the Greek may be considered the first nationalism to appear outside Western Christendom, among a community ruled by non-Christians and itself hitherto violently hostile to all Western notions. We see in the lecture eloquently expressed the customary appeal to a glorious past, earnest of a still more glorious future, and warrant for the subversion of present and existing institutions. We see thus Koraes glorifying the Greeks of his day by reference to Plutarch, Thucydides, and Herodotus. The islanders of Chios founded a school, and this is occasion for Koraes to proclaim that they "have at all times played on the world's stage a part which was as honorable as it was worthy of notice." On the authority of Plutarch, Koraes asserts that for seven hundred years "adultery or any illicit intercourse between free persons" was unheard of among these extraordinary beings; and Thucydides is quoted to the effect that "following the Lacedaemonians they were the only ones to have coupled wisdom with good luck, so that the more their republic flourished, the more they had the good sense to employ all possible means to maintain it in such a state"; and even today in spite of the Turkish yoke they are "the least enslaved, the least poor and the least corrupt." Koraes, again, exalts the Maniots and the Suliots who lived by highway robbery; their turbulence he ascribes to their undying love of liberty, for "they would not have thought of annoying others had they not always been threatened with the loss of that which they prefer to life itself, namely liberty." Their exploits are the very same by which their ancestors opposed Xerxes' aggression and despotism: "Herodotus recounts that the inhabitants of Xanthe, a Cretan colony in Lycia, finding themselves compelled by hard necessity to submit to the yoke of the Persians, who had already subjugated all their neighbors, took a decision which makes humanity tremble, but which at the same time proves that liberty is not an imaginary divinity, since such great sacrifices are made to it." The citizens of Xanthe killed themselves and all their dependents rather than submit to Asiatic despotism; similarly the Suliots "who have certainly not heard of these rare prodigies inspired by despair, have themselves enacted them not long ago"; but as it happened, Fortune "was ashamed not to crown with success the efforts of a people who preferred entirely to disappear from the face of the earth than to live under a despot's yoke." In concluding his lecture, Koraes again emphasized that the modern are the descendants of the ancient Greeks and made the further point that regeneration would come only when the Greeks as a whole became convinced of this: "For the first time," he proclaimed, "the nation surveys the hideous spectacle of its ignorance and trembles in measuring with the eye the distance separating it from its ancestors' glory. This painful discovery, however," he concluded, "does not precipitate the Greeks into despair: *We are the descendants of Greeks*, they implicitly tell themselves, *we must either try to become again worthy of this name, or we must not bear it.*"

Koraes devoted a lifetime to the work of persuading the Greeks that his own version of Greek history was the one which they should, and which they did really, "implicitly" believe. This glorification of classical antiquity, this appeal for its resuscitation was in Koraes' hand a weapon to be turned against existing institutions and particularly the Orthodox Church. The lecture itself is rather circumspect in speaking out against the Church, but its drift is unmistakable: "A good number of Greek ecclesiastics, so far from hindering the nation's education," he says hopefully, "are eager themselves to seek instruction"; they have realized, he says in mild and oblique reproof, "that true piety is enlightened, and that enlightenment so far from being inimical to true religion, gives it, on the contrary, firmer foundations and deeper roots in the hearts of men," etc. In this lecture, no doubt having regard to his enlightened audience, he spoke, as befits an enlightened man, more in sorrow than in anger. But elsewhere, particularly when addressing fellow Greeks, he was more blunt and brutal: the examples quoted above from his private correspondence indicate better than this public utterance the depth and virulence of Koraes' animus against the living traditions and actual arrangements of his community. The love he had for a classical Greece, dead and gone, fed and prospered on this great hatred; for as the poet Yeats says:

> More substance in our enmities
> Than in our love. . . .

Koraes' "Report" is more than a mere specimen of nationalist apologetics—albeit an early and unusually coherent one. Koraes also manages to give us, in his fashion, several important clues about the manner in which nationalist doctrine seeped out and became diffused beyond its area of origin. As has been seen, Koraes affirms that enlightenment is the essential foundation of true religion. Koraes considered himself an enlightened man, and by enlightenment he understood the rationalist criticism of alleged superstitions which Western intellectuals in the eighteenth century claimed to be spread by interested rulers and priests. Koraes echoes the commonplaces of the Enlightenment when he says that "ignorance, daughter of tyranny, is always accompanied by superstition, and superstition insensibly leads to depraved habits" and that "It is useless to seek for virtue in a society which is not ruled by wise and just laws." Koraes also tells us that these ideas, spread by the *Encyclopédie* and like publications, found their way to the eastern Mediterranean, where the Greeks of the Archipelago and of Ionia, following their commercial prosperity, now desired to endow their sons with the latest and most advanced European knowledge. "The light which issued from this literary revolution," says Koraes, referring to the Enlightenment in France, "following the same laws as physical light, had necessarily to shed clarity far from its original source, wherever obstacles did not impede it. ... The Greeks, proud of their origins, far from shutting their eyes to the European enlightenment, never considered the Europeans as other than debtors who were repaying with substantial interest the capital which they had received from their own ancestors." Here then is an early illustration of the general point that an ideological style of politics, of which nationalism is a variant, originated in Europe and owed its popularity to the prestige of the West.[27] And the attraction of European literature and the doctrines it inculcated was reinforced and enhanced by the actual spectacle of European politics at the end of the eighteenth century. This point also comes out toward the end of Koraes' lecture where he says that at the outbreak of the Revolution in France, "Enthusiasm for being ruled only by law became so widespread that people talked of nothing but Frenchmen. Everywhere secret societies of newsgatherers were formed which carefully collected and deliberately spread the good news arriving from France. French victories became their own victories, while French reverses invented or exaggerated by the enemies spread among them pain and consternation."

There is one other point in Koraes' lecture which deserves attention because it illustrates a recurrent feature in the spread of nationalism. Such a spread undoubtedly went hand in hand with the diffusion of European manners and ideas, a diffusion which was haphazard and quite unplanned. But this spread was also assisted at times by the deliberate action of European Great Powers, who have occasionally found it useful to foment nationalist agitations in the territories of rivals or enemies. Koraes notes this with regard to the Greeks and describes how the Russian government, prosecuting a war with the Ottoman Empire in 1769, found it expedient to encourage subversion among the Greek subjects of the Porte: "Russia," he says, "which then had an interest in being considerate to the Greeks, whom she hoped one day to count among her subjects, employed a number of them in this war and attached them to herself by means of honors and rewards. These new auxiliaries espoused the cause of the Court of Petersburg; while the whole nation, from different motives, prayed for the success of Russian arms." Koraes proceeds to set out shrewdly the effects of Russian blandishments on different groups among the Greeks: the great majority, he points out, responded to the Russian call because they looked upon the Russian cause as the cause of religion itself, "and they saw in the Russians merely those who would restore their churches, now either destroyed or turned into mosques." The generality of the people, in other words, at that time still clung to the traditional loyalties, which were those of religion and not of nationality; but there were two small groups whom Koraes mentions and who seem to us now to have been clearly touched by new-fangled notions. They did not see in the Russians those who would "merely" exalt Orthodoxy: those who had taken service with them were "only seeking revenge for their oppressors' injustice," whilst "a small band of sensible people" "looked upon the Russians only as a nation destined to prepare Greece for freedom." The role which Russia attempted to play in Greece in the eighteenth century it played on a larger stage in the Balkans in the nineteenth. And the same dangerous device proved too attractive to the Great Powers for them to leave alone in the desperate contests on which they embarked in the twentieth century. Arabs, Zionists, Indonesians, Somalis, etc., have had dangled before them by some interested Great Power the prospect of some "national liberation" or "national unity."

Koraes saw the modern Greeks through the golden haze of Western Hellenism in the eighteenth century. His writings are a reflection, an echo, of European sentiments and prejudices. Greek nationalist ideology after him continued to follow European fashions. European scholars and writers of the eighteenth century looked upon Periclean Athens as a peak of human achievement and all that followed thereafter in Greek history as lamentable decline and decadence; and Koraes followed suit, as is shown by his violent diatribes against the Orthodox Church of his day and its Byzantine matrix. But European scholarship of the nineteenth century discovered Byzantium and denied that Greek history after Pericles was a tale of unredeemed superstition and obscurantism. Greek nationalist ideology of the nineteenth century followed suit with the glorification of Byzantium as a shining expression of the eternal Greek spirit. The new doctrine is set out in Paparrhegopulos' five-volume *History of the Greek Nation*, published from 1860 to 1877. This "fiery patriot," as a modern scholar calls him, whose work remains "one of the sacred texts" of modern Greece,[28] argued that the whole of Greek history from Pericles in the fifth century before the Christian era to King Otto in his own day formed one consecutive story—a manifestation of that Hellenic spirit which gave it an underlying and essential unity. Pericles might not recognize in Justinian a kindred spirit, Theodosius might consider himself the heir of Augustus rather than of Solon, the people of Constantinople under the Iconoclasts might look upon the term Greek as one of reproach and applicable only to the lower orders of society, and yet, all these men separated by so many centuries, like M. Jourdain who all his life spoke prose without knowing it, were, in the eyes of Paparrhegopulos, in spite of and unbeknown to themselves successive avatars and manifestations of one abiding and eternal Hellenism.

Greek nationalism is a very early instance of the diffusion of this ideology outside the West. It may thus serve to date the beginnings of this diffusion and illustrate its character. But this movement has other claims on our attention. Their neighbors found in the nationalism of the Greeks an inspiration and a model which, because it was near at hand and seemed to have attained its goal, successfully mediated and powerfully reinforced the original European message. Again, not only is Greek nationalist ideology entirely derived from European sources, but, as has been seen, it also followed with admirable docility the changes in intellectual fashions which took place in Europe during the century separating Koraes from Paparrhegopulos. In this too it is a prototype of other nationalisms.

We may illustrate this point by considering the transformations of Turkish nationalist ideology as it appears and spreads among the Greeks' Ottoman overlords. Here too we see the elaboration of a doctrine which substitutes for the traditional view which Ottoman society had of itself a novel account of the past. In this account, the Ottoman Empire no longer was what immemorially it had been taken to be, namely, the work of the House of Osman laboring in the triumphant cause of Islam. The new ideology now considered the Ottoman Empire to be rather an achievement of the Turkish, or more generally the Turanian, genius. The ideologues who propounded these notions in the early decades of the twentieth century called themselves Young Turks and thus, for all their desire to be free of European encroachments, still showed themselves quite enslaved to European fashions in the study of philology and prehistory current during the latter half of the nineteenth century: for "Turk" and "Turanian" are the invention of European philologists and publicists.

The word "Turk" to the Ottomans as late as the nineteenth century meant "peasant, rustic, yokel." But European writers were endowing it then with a noble past and far from rustic splendors. We may see an early example of the eulogies which European publicists began to lavish on the denizens of Tartary —which they considered the original home of the "Turks"—in *A Grammar of the Turkish Language*, which Arthur Lumley

Davids, "Member of the Asiatic Society of Paris, &c., &c." published in 1832, prefacing it with *A Preliminary Discourse on the Language and Literature of the Turkish Nations*. In this lengthy discourse we read of the "ingenious and learned M. Bailly," author of *Lettres sur L'Atlantide de Platon*, who "applied his ingenuity and research to prove that the plains of Tartary had given arts, sciences and civilization to the world, and that its ancient inhabitants were the enlightened preceptors of mankind." Davids feels that these claims are too sweeping, "but although we must reject the system as a whole," he judiciously remarks, "we are yet forced to admit that great and incontestable proofs exist of the advances made by the inhabitants of Tartary in knowledge." These "incontestable" advances include "the invention of the cycle of animals, the use of metals and the works executed to obtain them in the bowels of the earth, the existence of monuments whose ruins still attract the curiosity of the Learned, and the early possession if not the invention of alphabetical characters." Davids was only the harbinger of a numerous host of European writers who labored to create not only the "Language and Literature" but the entire history as well of what Davids called the "Turkish Nations." These labors were not undertaken in vain; they had many repercussions among the "Turkish Nations," of which the most striking perhaps is the name Turkey, by which one of the successor states of the Ottoman Empire has been officially known since 1924. However familiar it became in the European vernaculars, this word was, until fairly recently, quite unknown to the "Turks." It was the Kemalist regime after World War I which, as Professor Bernard Lewis points out, proclaimed that the land of the Turks was Turkey: "So new was this idea," he writes, "that the Turkish language had even lacked a name for it. The Young Ottomans had used the Persian Turkistan; Mehmed Emin [a poet who wrote at the turn of the century] had spoken of *Türkleli*—Turkland, and only during the Young Turk period [1908–1918] had the name *Türkiye* come into common usage."[29] Turkey is, of course, not the only country the name of which has been invented or resuscitated and imposed by a triumphant doctrine.

Iraq, a name with associations going back to the early Islamic conquest of the Sassanid Empire, was chosen by Arab nationalists for another successor state of the Ottoman Empire as an evocation of past and a promise of future Arab glory. *Yugoslavia* and *Romania* in the Balkans are the pure inventions of historical doctrines and philological dogmas, the sweepings and discards of past academic controversies; again, *Ghana, Zambia, Malawi,* etc., are in Africa the factitious and exotic product of shaky historical reconstructions which, for want of anything better, have to satisfy the appetite for historical identity which contact with Europe has aroused in Africans.

Those, then, who had hitherto looked on themselves as Muslims and Ottomans, inspired now by European philology and historiography, began to call themselves "Turks." Mehmed Emin, who has just been mentioned, proclaimed in a poem of 1897:

I am a Turk, my religion and my race are exalted ones.

They were, of course, a very small minority who had access to this European literature. The books they read further told them that they should call themselves not only "Turks" but also "Turanians." "Turan" was originally an Iranian term by which the territory to the northeast of Iran was known. European writers became acquainted with it, and in due course it was transformed into a convenient classificatory term for which ethnologists and philologists found some use. For instance, writers would speak of "Turanian languages," and the expression became, as the scholar Minorsky says, "a regular dumping ground for languages awaiting classification."[30] As nature is said to imitate art, so the philologists' classification from being a ghostly denizen of the learned journals became a thing of flesh and blood, with a history and a destiny of its own. Mongols, Seljuks, Turks, etc., were now discovered to be offshoots of one *Urvolk*, the people of Turan, and their destiny was to reunite what time and chance had severed. This was the Pan-Turanianism or Pan-Turkism in which so many Young Turks believed before World War I, and of which the writer Ziya Gökalp (*c.* 1875–1924) was a prominent advocate.

Mehmed Emin's proclamation in 1897—"I am a Turk"—was improved upon in a poem of 1911 in which Gökalp declaimed:

> The country of the Turks is not Turkey, nor yet Turkestan
> Their country is a broad and everlasting land—Turan.

Gökalp claims that Turan has produced hundreds of great poets, philosophers, and scientists, but "their works are printed some in Arabic, some in Persian, others in Russian or Chinese"; again, it was the Turkish sword which had given the Persians, the Arabs, and the Chinese their history and their deeds of glory. The Turk, the man of Turan, is present everywhere and at all times, he "has not one history, but many." It was presumably to commemorate these mighty and numerous exploits that the Kemalist regime founded banks known as the Bank of the Sumerians or the Bank of the Hittites—Sumerians and Hittites being both manifestations of the protean genius of Turan. The Pan-Turanian movement was, for Gökalp and his associates, a paving of the way for the last and mightiest manifestation of this genius, a re-creation of the glorious times of Attila, Genghis Khan and Tamerlane, when a new Pan-Turanian Attila would appear to unite the Ottomans, the Azerbaijan Turks, the Crimean Turks, the Uzbeks, the Kipchaks, the Kirghiz, and all the other sundered fragments of Turkism into one Turanian nation.

Gökalp wrote most of his works when the Ottoman Empire still existed. The Empire was multiracial, multilinguistic, and multireligious, and a doctrine like Pan-Turanianism was therefore, on the face of it, radically subversive of its constitution. Gökalp did not wish to argue that the Ottoman Empire was well lost for the sake of Turan; rather, he tried to find ways of reconciling the vision with the reality. This led him to practice intellectual acrobatics in search of definitions for words like "nation," "state," and "religion" which might reconcile the irreconcilable. (See pp. 189–206.) We get a glimpse of his problem and of the desperate expedients which he has to employ in a paragraph like the following, published in 1914:

> There is, in fact, a homeland of Islam which is the beloved land of all Muslims. The other one is the national home which, for Turks, is what we call *Turan*. The Ottoman territories are that portion of Islamdom which have remained independent. A portion of these is the home of the Turks, and is at the same time a portion of *Turan*. Another portion of them is the homeland of the Arabs, which is again a part of the great Arab fatherland, etc.

This painful gymnastic establishes to Gökalp's satisfaction that "the Turkish nation today belongs to the Ural-Altaic group of peoples, to the Islamic *ümmet*, and to Western internationality."

But, alas, how perishable the fruits of historical and anthropological endeavor! We have seen how Paparrhegopulos, following the latest European fashions, rehabilitated the Byzantinism which Koraes cursed and execrated. In the same way Gökalp's categorical certainty that the Turks were Turanians of the Ural-Altaic group, buttressed by the authority of Cahun and Vambery, of Bunsen and Max Müller, was shortly afterward shown up as mere superstition by the inexorable advance of anthropological science. For after Gökalp came Tekin Alp who, writing in 1937 (see pp. 207–224), to the nineteenth opposed the twentieth century, and against the authority of Cahun and Vambery pitted that of Legendre and Pittard. "The Turk," affirms Doctor Legendre as quoted by Tekin Alp, "is one of the most beautiful specimens of the white race, big in stature, with an elongated and oval face, a fine nose, either straight or aquiline, sensitive lips, eyes opening widely, quite often grey or blue, and with horizontal palpebral slits." But is this beautiful specimen of the human race, we ask, a Turanian and a member of the Ural-Altaic group? On no account, says Tekin Alp; Turks are wrongly designated as Turanians or as Ural-Altaic; they are pure Aryans: "The word 'ari' means in the Turkish dialect . . . pure, clean, and it is a word much used in the new Turkish language." This "restoration of Turkish history," as its author calls it, was taking place, we observe, when there was much talk in Europe of the superiority of the Aryans, the beauty of their physique, the nobility of their soul, and the preeminence of their achievements.

If the traveler ventures today outside industrialized Europe and North America into one of these areas which, adapting the felicitous phrase of the anthropologist Lévi-Strauss, we might call the *tristes tropiques et sous-tropiques* of the world, he would see most of their past achievements and traditions, whether in manufacture or civility, in religion or architecture, smothered and ruined by Western products and Western manners: wherever he goes, he sees mass-produced ironmongery and plastic ware, newspapers and their cult of the ephemeral (which, as Hegel observed, serve modern man as a substitute for morning prayers), the obsessive and enervating imagery of romantic love, and other similar European inventions. He sees them everywhere, irresistible in their spread, everywhere treasured and sought after. This endless cornucopia of cheap and highly perishable articles seems to smother in a dreary and mechanical sameness cultures which had once been lively and original and not long ago had the power to make whole populations feel at home in the world. This desperate and dreary sameness is nowhere more in evidence than in this craving for "history" which, in spite of numerous local variations, is essentially the same opium, the habit of which Asians and Africans have acquired from its European addicts.

It is the same wherever you go. "Iranians do not forget," exhorts one writer, "we are the sons of the soldiers who, obeying the orders of the King of Kings, and under such commanders as Xerxes, planted the banner of victory over the gates of Athens, the capital of Greece. . . . We are the sons of soldiers who hunted down Kings and Emperors and threw them in the dust at the feet of their King of Kings."[31] They are Parthians and Sasanians, the mighty foes of Rome and Byzantium; this is why the dynasty founded in 1925 by a military usurper of obscure origins needs must adopt the name of *Pahlavi* in commemoration and emulation of Cyrus, Darius, and Xerxes.

If from Persia we pass on to Africa, we see exactly the same process repeated: the attempt to prove by history that Negroes are a people of ancient civilization and of great attainments. There is by now a voluminous literature dedicated to this enterprise. Some of this literature shows great learning and much ingenuity, as for instance the writings of Blyden. Edward W. Blyden (1832–1912), born in the West Indies and mostly self-taught, was a man of great erudition who in his time attained some political eminence as Liberian Secretary of State and subsequently Liberian minister in London and who ended his days as Director of Education in the British colony of Sierra Leone. To prove the ancient civilization of the Negro, Blyden laid under contribution the Bible and Herodotus, together with modern biblical and archaeological scholarship. To his own satisfaction he established that the ancestors of today's Negroes were the same who constructed the Tower of Babel and who originated alphabetic writing, astronomy, history, chronology, architecture, plastic art, sculpture, navigation, agriculture, and textile industry, and he ended his long and eloquent disquisition by exhorting Negroes outside Africa to "betake themselves to their ancestral home, and assist in constructing a Christian AFRICAN EMPIRE." "For we believe," he asserted, "that as descendants of Ham had a share, as the most prominent actors on the scene, in the founding of cities and in the organization of government, so members of the same family, developed under different circumstances, will have an important part in the closing of the great drama." (See pp. 250–274.) Blyden has had many continuators, and the ideas which he tried to buttress with learned proof and complex argument have found modern advocates more extreme and intransigent than the urbane Blyden had it in him to be. One of the latest of these treatises is *Nations nègres et culture* by Cheikh Anta Diop, a very long work stuffed with obscure quotations and ingenious arguments. But for all its length and complication, this work really rests on two simple propositions which are both incapable of proof: the first that the ancient Egyptians were Negroes, and the second that all civilizations originated in Egypt. (See pp. 275–282.)

In the literature of African nationalism we observe the same imitation of passing European fashions that we have had occasion to note in the literature of other nationalisms. Blyden is steeped in biblical and classical scholarship, while Cheikh Anta Diop draws his inspiration from the bulky tomes of French ethnography. Marcus Garvey, who falls midway in time between Blyden and Cheikh Anta Diop, absorbed the language of racialism fashionable in his day. Garvey (1887–1940), born a Jamaican, founded in 1914 in Jamaica the Universal Negro Improvement Association with the motto: "One God! One Aim! One Destiny!" It was however not in Jamaica but among the Negroes of the United States that Garvey found scope for his considerable demagogic abilities in advocating Pan-Africanism and the return of the American Negroes to Africa. He himself never set foot in Africa, but the anthem of his Association began, "Ethiopia, Thou land of Our Fathers," and his writings and speeches developed a theory of the Black Race and of the duty to preserve its purity. Thus in a speech of 1929 he said: "As God divided man into groups, clans and tribes, so he geographically places them in their native habitat. Man because of his powers and because of his weakness has transgressed the laws of God and has invaded others' domains." Again, in another speech of the previous year made to an English audience, he stated: "Just as you are true to your Anglo-Saxon race and type—and you would be unworthy if you were not—so am I true to my African race and African type. Before you became Englishmen you were Anglo-Saxons by race. Before a man is born to a nation he is conceived to a race; so his nationality is only accident whilst his race is positive. I am positively a Negro; there is no mistake about it. Not one drop of anybody else's blood is in my veins— if there were, I would try to get rid of it by draining it out as quickly as possible so that I could be a 100 per cent African as you are 100 per cent Anglo-Saxon. I respect you for your purity of blood, and you ought to respect me for my purity of blood." We see a dogged—and pitifully misplaced—assertion of the Founder's doctrine in a letter from a branch of the Universal Negro Improvement Association to the mayor of New Orleans: "We like," they affirmed, "your 'Jim Crow' laws, in that they defend the purity of races and any person married to any but a Negro cannot become a member of our organization. . . . We are not ashamed," they declared, "of the Race to which we belong and we feel sure that God made black skin and kinky hair because He desired to express Himself in that type."[32]

Of the remarkable Blyden we may say that he knows the meaning of scholarship, of *Nations nègres et culture* that it shows the trappings thereof. What they are both in their different ways bent on proving so laboriously has become the stock-in-trade of publicist and politician. Thus we see the Nigerian Azikiwe declare in 1947: "We have our own traditions and heritage which go back to ancient Egypt," and from a work entitled *Fifty Unknown Facts about the African: With Complete Proof,* we cull the following, no. 8 in the series: "Ethiopia was the first country to appear on earth. Africans from this country were the first to introduce mankind to the worship of Gods and enacted laws. The astronomy we know today came from the Ethiopians. It was the Africans who taught the Greeks geometry."[33] As these ideas percolate from learned journals and academic dissertations they are not merely beaten into slick and simple slogans, they are also souped up for turbulence and incitement. Blyden might endeavor to prove by learned quotations that the Negro was the heir of an ancient civilization but, as he said in a speech of 1907: "I have never written, and will never write, one word derogatory to the special work of the European." It was otherwise with Marcus Garvey. We see him declaim:

> This Christ they killed on Calvary's Cross,
> After His Person around they did toss:
> White men the Savior did crucify,
> For eyes not blue, but blood of Negro tie . . .

Jesus was a Negro, but as we also learn, so were Josephine de Beauharnais and Cleopatra:

> Napoleon fell for a Negro woman;
> So did the Caesars, and the Great Roman.

In sum:

> Africa's millions laughed with the sun
> In the cycle of man a course to run,
> In stepped the white man, bloody and grim,
> The light of these peoples' freedom to dim.[34]

To a sophisticated and fastidious reader, these jingles may sound both childish in their form and crude in their content, but their effect on the kind of audience for which they were intended should not, for all that, be minimized. In considering the writings elicited and brought forth by the spread of universal literacy from the *Communist Manifesto* to *Mein Kampf*, we have to bear this in mind and to remember that the dissemination of cheap literature in recent times has been as politically revolutionary as the invention of the printing press itself.

The exclusively European provenance of all these notions is nowhere better shown than in the case of Gandhi. M.K. Gandhi (1869–1948), the Mahatma or Great Soul as he is universally known, seems at first sight to represent in his utterances authentic and pure Hinduism, rejecting alike European techniques, European institutions, and European notions. Gandhi's ideas are found expressed in a mature form in a series of articles which he wrote in 1908 while he was in South Africa and subsequently collected in a book, *Young India,* the numerous editions of which amply indicate its great popularity. This book is a sustained indictment of Europe and all its works. Of the English Parliament we are told that "It is like a prostitute because it is under the control of ministers who change from time to time. Today it is under Mr. Asquith, tomorrow it may be under Mr. Balfour"; of hospitals, that they are "the worst of all. For the sake of a mistaken care of the human body they kill annually thousands of animals"; also, that they "violate our religious instincts" because their medical preparations "contain either animal fat or spirituous liquors"; again, "the doctors induce us to indulge, and the result is that we have become deprived of self-control and have become effeminate"; "To study European medicine," proclaims the Mahatma, "is to deepen our slavery." Gandhi's indictment of European civilization may finally be summed up thus in his words: "This civilization is such that one has only to be patient and it will be self-destroyed. According to the teaching of Mohammed this would be considered a Satanic civilization. Hinduism calls it the Black Age. I cannot give you an adequate conception of it. It is eating into the vitals of the English nation. It must be shunned."

These are solemn and eloquent words, the words of a prophet who sees clearly the impending doom and warns its victims, but in vain. Here, it seems, we can expect a genuine confrontation between two irreconcilable visions and ways of life. It may well be true, we find ourselves murmuring, that hospitals are engines of destruction and parliaments the emblem of our servitude. It may be that in a flash the seer has penetrated the truth of our condition, that his is a drastic but life-giving surgery. What alternative does Gandhi offer? To the "satanic" civilization of Europe he opposes the "true" civilization of India. "I believe," he tells us, "that the civilization India has evolved is not to be beaten in the world. Nothing can equal the seeds sown by our ancestors. Rome went, Greece shared the same fate, the might of the Pharaohs was broken, Japan has become Westernized, of China nothing can be said, but India is still, somehow or other, sound at the foundation." It is the very backwardness of India which constitutes its virtue: "It was not that we did not know how to invent machinery, but our forefathers knew that, if we set our hearts after such things, we would become slaves and lose our moral fibre. They therefore, after due deliberation, decided that we should only do what we could with our hands and feet.... They further reasoned that large cities were a snare and a useless encumbrance, and that people would not be happy in them.... They were, therefore, satisfied with small villages. They saw that kings and their swords were inferior to the sword of ethics, and they, therefore, held the sovereigns of the earth to be inferior to the Rishis and the Fakirs. A nation with a constitution like this is fitter to teach others than to learn

from others. . . . The common people," the Mahatma says in concluding this idyllic description, "lived independently, and followed their agricultural occupation. They enjoyed true Home
Rule."

It is this idyll which Gandhi offers as the remedy of our ills;
the somber accents of prophecy give way to a charming pastoral
trill; and we who know that the pastoral is an artificial literary
genre, the invention of European literary men, our disappointment is very great. Gandhi, it turns out, no less than Koraes, or
Gökalp, or so many others, has adopted from European authors
a romantic notion of the Indian past and with this fiction confronts present reality. He was, of course, not the first to do so.
Educated Indians of his own and of a previous generation sought
comfort and reassurance in the works of European Orientalists
and from these works derived the notion that their ancestors
were, in the words of a newspaper article written by a Hindu in
1882, "robust, innocent, chaste and simple-minded people," and
that, in the words of another such article, it was now "a well-
established fact that at all events we were among the first civilized nations and that our forefathers were poets and philosophers, logicians and grammarians when those from whom are
descended the present great nations of Europe had hardly risen
above the hunting or nomad state, or had even acquired a distinctive national name." There is, then, nothing particularly
original in Gandhi's contrast between Europe's corruption and
India's innocence. What does seem remarkable in this apostle
of the Indian tradition is not only that his picture of this tradition
is entirely derived from European sources, but that he himself
claims these sources as the warrant of his assertions. When he
published *Young India* in book form, Gandhi added to his articles an appendix of "Testimonies by Eminent Men" who are
called upon to endorse his claim that "ancient Indian civilization
has little to learn from the modern." This galaxy of eminences,
we are interested to see, is made up entirely of Europeans and
includes Victor Cousin, "Founder of Systematic Eclecticism in
Philosophy," Friedrich Max Mueller, LL.D., Colonel Thomas
Munro, "Thirty-two years' service in India," Frederick von

Schlegel, and J. Young, "Secretary, Savon Mechanics' Institutes."

Gandhi's case bears further scrutiny. As is well known, Gandhi was one victim—albeit a prominent one—among a multitude of victims who perished in the partition of India between Hindus and Muslims in 1947–48. He was murdered in the grounds of Birla House in Delhi by a Hindu nationalist who believed that Gandhi was being too sympathetic to Muslims. The partition, and the attendant bloodshed, came about because the two main groups in India were led by politicians who put forward claims couched in a language which made compromise quite impossible. As has been seen above, the Muslim side insisted on transforming the Muslims of India into a hitherto unknown body, namely, the Pak nation, entitled to a territory exclusively its own, i.e., Pakistan. This fiction the Muslim League put forward in order to counter another fiction, put forward by the Congress Party, to the effect that the Indians constituted, and always did constitute, one "nation." Both contentions were patently the outcome of exposure to Western political ideas; they only succeeded in doing violence to the realities of India's past and present and in providing elevated—and hence intransigent—arguments to disguise the appetite and the fear of domination. Now, ever since the end of World War I Gandhi had been the leader and the inspirer of the Congress; and Gandhi, as we discover, held with his peculiar tenacity the view that India was one "nation." We find him stating the tenet in his articles on *Young India:* "The English have taught us that we were not one nation. This," he affirms, "is without foundation. We were one nation before they came to India. One thought inspired us. Our mode of life was the same. It was because we were one nation that they were able to establish one kingdom. Subsequently they divided us." Thirty-six years later, in 1944, in spite of all that had happened in the interval, he utters the same inflexible and empty doctrine. Jinnah, the Muslim leader, writes: "We maintain and hold that Muslims and Hindus are two major nations by any definition or test of a nation. We are a nation of a hundred million, and what is more, we are a nation with our own distinctive culture and civilization, language and literature, art and architecture, names and nomenclature, sense of value and proportion, legal laws and moral codes, customs and calendar, history and traditions, aptitudes and ambitions. In short, we have our own distinctive outlook on life and of life. By all canons of international law we are a nation." To this claim Gandhi opposes a counterclaim utter and absolute: "I am unable to accept the proposition that the Muslims of India are a nation distinct from the rest of the inhabitants of India. Mere assertion is no proof."[35] Mere assertion no proof: a very sound principle, and in equal measure applicable to the briefs of the two advocates, Gandhi and Jinnah. May we not see in these belligerent and frivolous logomachies a prelude to that bloody act consummated four years later on the lawn in New Delhi, a city desolated by wave upon wave of desperate and terrified refugees?

Modern India, we may say, was impaled on the horns of a dilemma which no man could surmount, a dilemma consisting of two propositions, one that India was two nations and the other that India was one nation. This dilemma dominated Indian politics because Indian politicians came to speak a Western political idiom. It was not, to be sure, the only Western idiom of politics; but it happened to be influential and widespread in Europe at a time when Indians were much impressed with all things European, and hence they came to speak it. In this they were like many other Asians and Africans who also picked up the idiom. But in picking it up, did they know what the idiom assumed or entailed? Did they have a clear view of the syntax or some idea of the etymology? It is safe to say that most who spoke this language rather took it for granted, accepted it unquestioningly, in the belief that it was the only possible language in the world, coeval with humanity itself, and unprofitable therefore much to examine and scrutinize. It is only rarely that we find a writer who seems aware of assumptions and implications, who seems to realize that, far from being the natural and obvious language of politics, this idiom is a novelty even in Europe itself, a writer whose attitude, in short, is critical. One such writer is the Bengali Surendranath Banerjea (1848–1926). Very different from Gandhi in the cast of his mind, in his outlook, temperament, and political style, Banerjea was as deeply influenced as Gandhi by European culture and political ideas to which, like Gandhi, he gained entrance through an English education. In his address on "The Study of Indian History" (see pp. 225–244), Banerjea tries to persuade his Indian audience to cultivate "this noble study, the study of the history of our own country." "The study of the history of our own country," Banerjea declares, "furnishes the strongest incentive to the loftiest patriotism. I ask, what Hindu is there, who does not feel himself a nobler being altogether, as he recalls to mind the proud list of his illustrious countrymen, graced by the thrice-immortal names of a Vâlmiki and a Vyâsa, a Pânini and a Patanjali, a Gautama and a Sankaracharya?" "Approach reverentially," he exhorts the 'Hindus, "the sacred records of your sires. Remember that you are studying the sayings and doings of your revered ancestors, of those for whose sake alone you are now remembered, for whose sake alone the intellectual elite of Europe even now feel a deep and an ardent interest in your welfare." So far, Banerjea's argument only articulates and makes explicit the fundamental assumption of nationalist literature, namely that it is the past of a "nation" which gives it an identity, a meaning, and a future. But the address has two other features which greatly add to its interest. Banerjea, in the first place, states that this political role which history has come to have is a very new one: "For, history in the proper sense of the term," he acutely points out, "was not known even in Europe till late in the last century. It was amidst the intellectual ferment and agitation, which preceded the breaking out of that great revolution, the French Revolution, which ushered in the dawn of human liberty and impelled the human mind onwards by giant strides to unknown conquests in unknown regions of thought, that history, in the proper sense of the word, began to be studied." In the second place, Banerjea, in his desire to exalt the Indian past, finds it necessary to establish not only that this past was illustrious and worthy of admiration in the highest degree, but also that the ancient Hindus themselves did write their own history and did thus exhibit that consciousness of their identity as a group which nationalist ideology now requires in a "nation"; and it is one of the main themes of his address that, appearances to the contrary, it is most probable that the ancient Hindus—the Aryans, as educated Hindus learned from European philologists to call their ancestors—wrote history:

We find that in the whole field of Sanskrit literature there is only a single historical work, the Raja-Tarangini or the History of Cashmere, which was commenced by Calhana Pundit about the middle of the twelfth century of the Christian era. Are we then to conclude that our ancestors, the great Aryans of ancient India, were ignorant of the art of historical composition and never wrote histories? . . . Fortunately, however, for the credit of our ancestors, fortunately for the good name of India, we are not wholly driven to that conclusion; and with the arguments I am about to submit for your consideration, it will appear extremely probable that our ancestors were acquainted with the art of historical composition, that they wrote histories, and that if such histories have not come down to us, it is because of the revolutions and convulsions which our country had unhappily too often to pass through, it is because of the carelessness of the Brahmins and the peculiarities of our climate.

For Banerjea, then, the study of Indian history serves to provide an identity for present-day Hindus; the memory of great Hindus of the past serves to minister to the self-esteem of Hindus in the present. He does not present the Buddha as one compassionately seeking to release men from the restless misery which is their lot; rather he hails him as a great representative Hindu, an expression of the Hindu national genius:

But the ancient Hindoos were not only great in literature, great in science, great in war, they were, above all, great in morals. . . . From the frozen waters that skirt the coast of Kamschatka to the extreme south of the island of Ceylon, from the green and verdant isles that fringe the Chinese seas to the arid steppes of Central Asia, Buddhism became the predominating religion. The shivering inhabitant of Siberia, the yellow-complexioned Chinese, the swarthy native of Ceylon, the seminaked barbarian of the steppes, all acknowledged the great Hindoo as their apostle. Gentlemen, Sakya Muni was a Hindoo, and so are we. . . . I ask you, gentlemen, whether standing in his presence, standing in the presence of this noble Hindoo, this illustrious scion of a royal race, who flung away the splendors of a throne in order that he might become the apostle of humanity, you do not feel something of his noble and heroic self-endurance, something of his fervid patriotism, something of his boundless love for mankind? . . . If the noble example of Sakya Muni does not stimulate your patriotism and increase your self-respect, then, I say, you are not his country men. . . .

Buddha as a stimulant to patriotism is certainly a bizarre notion, but one fully consonant with the logic of nationalist doctrine.

In the terms of this doctrine, the past is always by definition the past of the "nation," all achievements "national" achievements, expressions of the "national" genius to be preserved, commemorated, or revived because they establish the "national" identity and foster pride in it. Buddha's function is, in Banerjea's argument, instrumental; so is that of a prophet like Isaiah in Zionist doctrine, of Muhammad in Arab nationalist doctrine, of Confucius in the teaching of Chinese nationalists. Thus for the ideologue of Arab nationalism, Muhammad's message, and the *Islamic* conquests which followed, were a providential prelude for the manifestation of the *Arab* "nation" as he defines it today; so, for instance, Nicholas Ziadeh (see pp. 294–303):

The Arabs occupied these countries and settled them; Islam spread within them. . . . In consequence of the spread of Islam in Iraq, Syria, Egypt and North Africa, the Arabic language, the language of the Glorious Qur'an and the Noble [Prophetic] Tradition, itself spread among the inhabitants of these countries. . . . Arabic therefore penetrated to the soul, the heart and the mind of the people; even those among the natives who remained faithful to their old religion found it necessary to speak, read or write in Arabic.

In brief, without Islam no Arab "nation." A few decades ago, such a notion would have seemed outrageously paradoxical. The term "Arab" was, like the term "Turk," pejorative: its prestige and currency today is another facet of the acceptance of nationalism outside Europe which, in this case, has transformed Muhammad from a prophet and lawgiver into a mere harbinger of Arabism.

What Buddha or Isaiah or Muhammad or Confucius taught
had been for countless generations the light which lighted men
on their way, a rule of life unvarying and stable, that which gave
meaning and coherence to the world, a living, self-confident,
self-contained tradition; they were not symbols and proofs of
national greatness. To a Chinese before the advent of Europe
the teaching of Confucius was worthy of being heeded because
it was wisdom which enabled man to be at peace with himself
and with the world. European ideas cast grave doubts on this
wisdom and the way of life it embodied; to those who practiced
it the tradition gradually became dead and confining, and it
seemed that the only hope of life and vitality lay in repudiating
all that Confucianism stood for. It was only then, after the de-
mise of the living tradition, that Confucianism came to be cherished by Chinese nationalists anxious to assert their equality
with Europe and to show that their "nation" too had great and
original achievements to its credit. In this enterprise Confucianism was to serve as a banner and a symbol behind which the
Chinese could confront the rest of the world. To adopt an apt
and felicitous expression, a civilization was becoming a nation.[36]
"Compared to the other peoples of the world," said Dr. Sun
Yat-sen (1866–1925) in the first of his lectures on *The Three
Principles of the People* of 1924, "we have the greatest population and our civilization is four thousand years old; we should
therefore be advancing in the front rank with the nations of
Europe and America. But the Chinese people have only family
and clan solidarity; they do not have national spirit. Therefore
even though we have four hundred million people gathered
together in one China, in reality they are just a heap of loose
sand." Why has China come to such a pass? It is, says Sun
Yat-sen in his fourth lecture (see pp. 304–317), "because of the
loss of our nationalism." The Chinese had been a powerful entity
with a "divine mission," the equal or the superior of Europe in
science and philosophy. The way for China to regain her past
stature was, said Sun Yat-sen in his sixth lecture, "first [to]
restore our national spirit. . . . Therefore, if we go to the root
of the matter, besides arousing a sense of national solidarity, we

must recover and restore our characteristic, traditional morality. Only thus," he emphasized, "can we hope to attain again the distinctive position of our people." But the labor of the restorers is powerless to revive a tradition dead and gone: what restoration produces is not the living tradition but merely traditionalism to titillate and gratify antiquarian fancy. As the Muslim theologian Ghazali (d.1111) remarked: "There is no hope in returning to a traditional faith after it has once been abandoned, since the essential condition in the holder of a traditional faith is that he should not know he is a traditionalist."

To "arouse" a sense of nationalism, to transform the "heap of loose sand," which is the traditional society battered and pulverized by Europe, into something solid and powerful, into a battering ram, such is the purpose of all these appeals to history, of all these exercises in "restoration." In certain circumstances, and for particular purposes, "restoration" of traditional beliefs and traditional practices is more efficient than the appeal to a new-fangled and unfamiliar history. This is so because the majority in any society respond eagerly to a traditional idiom and its customary associations and do not readily detect that this traditional idiom is not being spoken with their own spontaneous and unquestioning conviction, but used in an operational and, so to speak, Pavlovian mode, to elicit and arouse emotions of solidarity and group loyalty. Such emotions, carefully tended, are a mortar to make the "heap of loose sand" into a solid and compact battering ram. When in 1868 the Tokugawa regime was swept away and the emperor "restored" to his powers, his advisers thought it prudent to revive the Shinto cult in order to promote loyalty to the new political institutions. Shinto has been called a cult of "solar ancestralism,"[37] and of this cult the emperor was the head. An imperial edict of 1868 said: "The worship of the gods and regard for ceremonies of Shinto are the great proprieties of the Empire and the fundamental principles of national polity and education . . ." and in 1870 another edict proclaimed that at the beginning "Religious ceremonies and government were one and the same and the innumerable subjects were united. Government and education were clear to those above, while below them the manners and customs of the people were beautiful." This harmony was afterward broken, but "Now in the cycle of fate all things have become new. Polity and education must be made clear to the nation and the Great Way of obedience to the gods must be promulgated. Therefore do we newly appoint propagandists to proclaim this to the nation." But the Meiji "restoration" coincided with and was precipitated by the forcible opening of Japan to Western ideas and techniques, and with such techniques and ideas a sun cult is not easily compatible. So we find the well-known statesman Prince Ito (1841–1909) writing a few decades after the "restoration": "In our country religion is weak. There is not one that could serve as a principle of state. Buddhism today has fallen into decline. Shinto is based on the precepts of our forefathers and transmits them, yet as a religion it has little power to move men's hearts." But such as it was, this emperor-centered sun cult, nationalists who came to power in the nineteen-thirties chose for indoctrinating the Japanese in order to effect what they called their "spiritual mobilization." In 1937 the Japanese Ministry of Education issued a textbook, *Kokutai No Hongi* (*Cardinal Principles of the National Entity of Japan*; see pp. 318–330), for the guidance of schoolteachers. This manual set out the doctrine of the unity of education, religion, family, and government, a unity held together by the emperor. "The Emperor," we read, "by means of religious ceremonies, becomes one with the divine imperial ancestors, and through participation in the spirit of the imperial ancestors, He is able to educate the subjects of the state ever more and more and promote their prosperity." In this manual we also read that in Japan the relation between emperor and subject is not a public but a private relation, that the whole of Japan is one family, and that the subject owes to the emperor the love and piety he owes to his father and ancestor. Another official manual published in 1941 put the point succinctly: "Our country's being a Family-State does not mean that the state is formed by families but that the state is a family in itself, and individual families exist with the state as their source."

It may perhaps be thought that Shinto, a sun cult and an ancestor cult, is particularly well-suited for use as a national cement; that the Japanese leaders who resuscitated it in the nineteenth century, and who again in the twentieth used all the resources of the state to inculcate it, did not have to do this cult much violence in order to adapt it to new purposes; and that other religions, universal in their appeal and based on a divine revelation, might prove rebellious to such enterprises. But this is not so. Islam, Christianity, and Judaism have proved equally pliable and adaptable to political uses. It is interesting to see that the Arab nationalist Shakib Arslan (1869–1946) quotes precisely the cult of Shinto to his Muslim Arab audience in order to prove that Islam is the necessary foundation for Arab nationalism (see pp. 331–337). "Every nation," he affirms, "clings resolutely to its religion, the constituents of its nationality, and its inherited group characteristics," and one of the examples he puts forward most admiringly is that of Shinto; he refers to an account he had previously published of Japanese coronation rites: "I described how these ceremonies lasted for a whole month, how the Mikado is the Nation's highest priest, how he is a descendant of the gods, *i.e.*, of the sun, how he performed his ablutions in the sacred bath which has been preserved for two thousand years, how he ate in company of the gods the sacred rice planted by the state under priestly supervision," etc. Japan, Shakib Arslan argues, is a modern, powerful state, and yet it clings to its ancient beliefs, and this, he hints, is clearly not accidental. Shakib Arslan, Arab nationalist and Muslim traditionalist as he was, was not a particularly profound or subtle ideologue. That Islam is a buttress of Arabism has been argued by more considerable writers. Michel Aflaq, the well-known leader of the Ba'th Party, has stated that Muhammad was the epitome of all the Arabs and that Islam "represented the ascent of Arabism towards unity, power and progress." Professor Costi Zurayq of the American University of Beirut, who has been called "one of the leaders of modern Arab nationalism," has written that "every Arab, no matter what his sect or community, who takes an interest in his past culture and in its renaissance—and such an interest is at the head of those duties which his nationality imposes on him—should attempt to study Islam and to understand its reality; he should also sanctify the memory of the great Prophet to whom Islam was revealed." Aflaq and Zurayq happen to be Christians, and experience, therefore, no difficulty in looking upon Islam as a mere buttress of Arab nationalism. But the same position is adopted by Abd al-Rahman Bazzaz, who is today perhaps the best Muslim ideologist of Arab nationalism. He argues that Islam is a manifestation of the Arab genius and that "the sending of the Prophet [Muhammad] to the Arabs revived the Arab nation in its entirety and resurrected it."

The same tendency of nationalist doctrine to assimilate a religion to the national folklore is observed in Zionism. Together with the Japanese, Shakib Arslan held up to the Arabs for their emulation the Zionist example; and indeed for Zionism,[38] the Bible becomes a product of the Jewish national genius and useful in fostering and perpetuating this genius. Isaiah is quoted to the effect that "out of Zion shall go forth the law and the word of the Lord from Jerusalem." For Isaiah, of course, the word of the Lord was simply the word of the Lord: that is, a revelation and a command; in the metaphysic of nationalism it is only one of many propositions intended to secure active assent for the doctrine. In the third chapter of Exodus it is related that when Moses wished to investigate the burning bush he heard the command: "Draw not nigh hither: put off thy shoes from off thy feet; for the place whereon thou standest is holy ground." Moses, it is also related, hid his face, "for he was afraid to look upon God." We learn that the burning bush, which shook Moses to the depth of his being, is now symbolized by a sculpture standing at the gate of the Chamber of Deputies in Jerusalem: the noumenal has been degraded into the political.

We may now consider a somewhat different use which nationalists have found for religion. Religion has worth in their eyes because it binds people together, gives them a feeling of solidarity and community which is essential if they are to be made to look upon themselves as a "nation." But this feeling of solidarity, valuable as it is in the eyes of nationalist leaders, is usually inert and passive, no more than an inclination or a disposition. But a disposition can be activated and made to yield its potential in political energy. And nationalism, apart from being a doctrine concerned with the true character of human groups, is also a method of spiritual mobilization, of eliciting, activating, and canalizing dormant political energies. We may therefore say of it not only that it is a doctrine but also that it is an activist doctrine. And this aspect of the doctrine may be illustrated by the manner in which nationalists have made use of religious predispositions in order to arouse their audience and throw them into a formidable, and sometimes successful, assault on power. The methods of the Indian leader Bal Gagandhar Tilak (1856–1920) are worthy of notice. Tilak was a Chitpavan Brahmin, of the caste, that is, which for two centuries enjoyed a monopoly of office in the Mahratta Empire until the Deccan fell under British sway. Himself an able man with a good Western education—a Bachelor of Arts and a Bachelor of Laws—he set out to move and arouse the masses by rehearsing the tale of past Mahratta greatness and by conducting a Hindu revivalist campaign. The worship of the elephant-headed god Ganesh had been a family festival of the Peshwas, the Mahratta ruling house, and had fallen into oblivion. During the last decade of the nineteenth century this worship was revived and popularized by Annasahib, another Brahmin and nationalist leader. Tilak took it up and organized celebrations and processions in honor of Ganesh in the chief centers of the Deccan. His purpose seems to have been to mobilize the Hindus and to provide them with a readily recognizable identity. This organized worship in processions and groups imparted to Hinduism, it has been well said, "a congregational character hitherto unknown to it."[39] This mobilization of the Hindu masses intensified their feeling of communal solidarity, and as the festival was deliberately made to coincide with the traditional Muslim festival of Muharram, when Muslim religious fervor rises to a high pitch, it seems clear that one of its objects was to exacerbate the relations of the Hindus with their Muslim neighbors. Hindu-Muslim riots in the Deccan were the—foreseeable—outcome of Tilak's campaign. In the same cause, and using the same technique, Tilak founded the "Anti-Cow-Killing Society." Since beef is lawful to Muslims and forbidden to Hindus, here was another issue and another battle cry to help on spiritual mobilization. Tilak also inaugurated another cult by resuscitating the memory of Shivaji, the chieftain who had originally established Mahratta fortunes in contest with the Mughals. Tilak organized the celebration of Shivaji's birthday and glorified the memory of his treacherous deed when, inviting the Mughal general Afzul Khan to a peaceful conference, he killed his guest by plunging his steel gauntlet into Afzul's bowels while bending down to greet him. "It is needless," said Tilak in his speech at this celebration, "to make further researches as to the killing of Afzul Khan. Let us even assume that Shivaji deliberately planned and executed the murder. Was the act good or evil? This question cannot be answered from the standpoint of the Penal Code or of the Laws of Manu or according to the principles of morality laid down in the systems of the West or of the East. . . . Great men are above the common principles of morality. . . . The Divine Krishna teaching in the Gita tells us that we may kill even our teachers and our kinsmen, and no blame attaches if we are not actuated by selfish desires. Shivaji did nothing from a desire to fill his own belly. It was in a praiseworthy object that he murdered Afzul Khan for the good of others. . . . Do not circumscribe your vision like frogs in a well. Rise above the Penal Code into the rarefied atmosphere of the sacred Bhaghavad Gita and consider the action of great men." This panegyrist of elevated and altruistic murder also supported, presumably again to further spiritual mobilization, the perpetuation of child marriage in India. He incited the mass against those Hindu reformers who were seeking to make child marriage a little more difficult than heretofore and who, in his scornful words, "because of a few examples of rape committed on small girls . . . ask us to apply to the Government to change the law."

As has been seen, in his apology of political murder Tilak adduced the support of the Bhagavad Gita (The Song of the Lord)—the classic text, now some two thousand years old, of popular Hinduism; also while in prison, he wrote a commentary on the Gita which he considered to be his *magnum opus*. And it is a fact that Indian nationalists found in the Gita a text which could be interpreted in such a way as to convince their audience that there was a religious warrant for violent agitation against British rule. This is because, unlike the earlier and austerer doctrine of the Upanishads, that of the Gita affirmed that not only through abstention but also through action is salvation attainable. "Do your allotted works," Krishna instructs the warrior Arjuna, "for action is superior to nonaction." Krishna also affirms that it is only disinterested action which leads to salvation: "Except for the action done for sacrifice, all men are under the bondage of action. Therefore, O son of Kunti, do you undertake action for that purpose, becoming free from all attachment." This aspect of the teaching of the Gita was used by the nationalist leaders to convince their followers that acts of terrorism in which they imperiled their lives were meritorious. But this they could do only by disregarding other, equally important aspects of the teaching; for Krishna insists that the actions which bring salvation are those which a man performs in pursuit of his caste duties—and the division of society into castes is itself divinely ordained: "The fourfold class system was created by Me in accordance with the varying dispositions and the actions [resulting therefrom]," and again: "Better is one's own dharma [i.e., caste duties] which one may be able to fulfil but imperfectly, than the dharma of others which is more easily accomplished. Better is death in the fulfillment of one's own dharma. To adopt the dharma of others is perilous." In a most perceptive and distinguished study of Hindu nationalist thought, Lord Ronaldshay gives an instance of the perversion of the Gita's teaching by means of this highly selective interpretation. He quotes Tilak, who says of the Gita that its "most practical teaching . . . and one for which it is of abiding interest and value to the men of the world with whom life is a series of struggles, is not to give way to any morbid sentimentality when duty demands sternness and the boldness to face terrible things," and himself comments: "Whatever may have been the intention, the effect of such teaching upon the impressionable youths of Bengal is conclusively demonstrated by the indifference with which members of the revolutionary party committed the most deadly of all sins, the killing of a Brahman. Basanta Kumar Chatterji was a Brahman; but he was also a successful police officer, and he was murdered without the slightest compunction."[40] We remember Tilak proclaiming that "The Divine Krishna teaching in the Gita tells us that we may kill even our teachers and our kinsmen, and no blame attaches if we are not actuated by selfish desires," and we are persuaded that Lord Ronaldshay's observation is the exact and sober truth.

But it is not only the Gita's notion of duty which makes its use for nationalist preaching so illegitimate, rather its whole ethos is far removed from the acrid and turbulent passions which nationalist leaders must either excite or else confess themselves defeated; the ethos of the Gita is a disinterested stoicism; it is restrained and noble, while nationalism is democratic and abandoned in style. To appreciate the contrast we may set side by side with Tilak's oratory the following passage:

He who does not entertain hatred toward any being, who is friendly and ever compassionate, free from all sense of "my-ness," free from egoism, even-tempered in pain and pleasure, forbearing;

He who is ever content, the yogin, possessing self-control, of unshakable resolve; who has dedicated to Me his mind and intellect—he, My devotee, is dear to Me.

He from whom the world shrinks not and who does not shrink from the world; and who is free from elation, impetuosity, fear, and perturbation—he too is dear to Me.

He who has no expectation; who is pure, dexterous, unconcerned, and untroubled; who renounces all acts—he, My devotee, is dear to Me.

He who neither exults nor hates, neither grieves nor yearns; who renounces good and evil; who is full of devotion—he is dear to Me.

He who behaves alike to foe and friend; who, likewise is even-poised in honor or dishonor, who is even-tempered in cold and heat, happiness and sorrow; who is free from attachment;

Who regards praise and censure with equanimity; who is silent, content with anything whatever; who has no fixed abode, who is steadfast in mind, who is full of devotion—that man is dear to Me.

The nationalist interpretation of the Bhagavad-Gita, arbitrary and ill-founded as it was, made it into a subversive book stocked by terrorist societies together with revolvers and sulfuric acid. Tilak was, of course, not the only one to jazz up The Song of the Lord in this manner. A very good and apposite example of this process may be found in the writings of Bipin Chandra Pal (1858–1932). Pal goes so far as to make of the Gita a "messianic" document promising salvation by divine prodigies—a notion entirely alien to Indian thought. The masses, he says, had always believed in Krishna: "What they wanted was a practical application of that faith, not as a mere religious or spiritual force, but as a social, and, perhaps, even as a political, inspiration. Krishna stood too far away from the present. As God, he is no doubt present in spirit always and everywhere. What they craved for was his manifestation in the flesh. . . . A fresh cry now went up from the heart of his chosen people for a fresh advent of the Saviour." We may safely assert that the fresh cry of which Pal speaks did not go up from the masses. Rather—and this is what makes the passage just quoted highly interesting—it was the utterance of the minority of Western-educated Indians who imbibed current European political thought, heavily impregnated as it is with political messianism. Pal shows himself quite aware of the mechanism by which a traditional religion and its venerable sacraments and familiar hymns can be used to mobilize the masses for political ends: "The authors of the French Revolution," he points out, "made grotesque attempts to replace the old sacraments of Catholicism by new ones, representing the new civic order which they were trying to set up in the land. In India, among the Hindus, civic religion is growing through an easy and natural process, out of the old symbolism and ritualism of the people. Hinduism has, indeed, like all ethnic systems, this advantage over credal religions, that its symbols and rituals, its sacraments and mysteries, are all partly religious and partly civic, partly social and partly spiritual. In fact, in Hinduism, the social and the spiritual are strangely blended together. Consequently, the new national spirit has found apt vehicles for expressing itself in the current religious rites and formulas of the people." Pal himself gives a very good instance of this politicization of originally religious notions. The word *Swaraj* is today commonly taken to mean political self-government and is inseparably associated with the struggle of the Congress Party to overthrow British rule. This word was originally a term of Hindu philosophy and meant the state of self-rule or self-control in which a man abstains from action and escapes from the painful and evil cycle of perpetual reincarnation. *Swaraj*, Pal tells us, "was borrowed by politics from the highest philosophical and religious literature of the people. . . . The term is used in the Vedânta to indicate the highest spiritual state, wherein the individual, having realized his identity with the Universal, is not merely freed from all bondage, but is established in perfect harmony with all else in the world." "The concept," he adds, "involves not merely national freedom; but universal federation also"! By the time Gandhi finished with it, *swaraj* was mired in all the impure passions of cupidity and domination and had simply come to mean that not a man called Akbar, or a man called Curzon, but a man called Nehru should rule India.

Pal illustrates also in another way the use of religion for political purposes. In a speech of 1907 he aptly described the British administration as based upon *maya* or illusion, and in the piece reproduced on pp. 338–352 he says that British rule over Indians was not due to their physical or intellectual or moral superiority but to "pure hypnotism." This interesting suggestion is clearly derived from classical Indian thought, for which the world and all phenomena are mere illusion from which the wise man seeks release. This notion that all human actions and feelings are an illusion Pal exploits by suggesting that the proper technique by which to break the spell of the British magic is to weave a more potent counterspell: "The nationalist school exposed the hollowness of all these [British] pretensions. It commenced to make, what are called counterpasses in hypnotism, and at once awoke the people to a sense of their own strength, an appreciation of their own culture, and has created a new conviction that they, too, like the other races of the world, have a distinct mission and destiny." A noble and profound idea is thus drained of its significance and made into a trivial—

albeit powerful—instrument of political warfare.

One of the "counterpasses" which Pal and other Indian nationalists employed was the revival of the cult of Kali, "the grim goddess," as he describes her, "dark and naked, bearing a garland of human heads around her neck—heads from which blood is dripping—and dancing on the prostrate form of Shiva or the Good." It was before Kali, the goddess of destruction, that terrorist societies made their initiates take this vow: "I will not be bound by the tie of affection for father, mother, brother, sister, hearth and home. . . . If I fail to keep this vow, may the curse of Brahmins, of father and mother, and of the great patriots of every country speedily reduce me to ashes." How the cult of Kali and the modalities of this cult were exploited for political ends may again be illustrated by a speech of Pal's at a political rally in which he recommended the worship of Rahbha Kali which is white not black and to which a sacrifice of white, not black, goats was acceptable. If at every new moon 108 white goats were sacrificed, this, Pal said, would be a good thing. The theme was taken up by another speaker whose words made clearer the allusion to the white goats: for this speaker advised his audience to go abroad and learn the manufacturing of bombs and other destructive weapons and then to come back to their country and sacrifice at every new moon 108 whites.

Pal and the other nationalist leaders were educated men, which, in the circumstances, meant that they were touched by European notions and could no longer have an innocent and unselfconscious faith in Kali. How can we explain these fervent appeals to dark goddesses, garlands of human heads, and dripping blood? This was, we suspect, conscious and deliberate manipulation of what must have been, in their eyes, primitive superstition. But Pal and his fellow Indians were not the only nationalist leaders in Asia and Africa to appeal to these superstitions. Jomo Kenyatta, for instance, who studied anthropology with Professor B. Malinowski in London, in his well-known *Facing Mount Kenya*, published in 1938, glorified cliterodectomy as practiced among the Kikuyu. The passage is remarkable and deserves quotation: "When this preparation is finished, a

woman specialist, known as moruithia, who has studied this form
of surgery from childhood, dashes out of the wood, dressed in
a very peculiar way, with her face painted with white and black
ochre. This disguise tends to make her look rather terrifying,
with her rhythmic movements accompanied by the rattles tied
to her legs. She takes out from her pocket . . . the operating
Gikuyu razor . . . and in quick movements, and with the dexterity of a Harley Street surgeon, proceeds to operate upon the girls.
With a stroke she cuts off the tip of the clitoris. . . . As no other
part of the girl's sexual organ is interfered with, this completes
the girl's operation." Kenyatta goes on to attack missionary and
official doctors who denounce cliterodectomy as a barbaric custom and a menace to women in childbirth: they are "irresponsible," "more to be pitied than condemned," and "their objectivity
is blurred in trying to unravel the mystery of the *irua* [i.e.,
circumcision]." This mystagogy Professor Malinowski in his introduction to the book called "a personal statement of the new
outlook of a progressive African," an African "who presents the
facts objectively, and to a large extent without any passion or
feeling." The latter statement may leave us skeptical, but we
cannot help in this case as in that of Bipin Chandra Pal feeling
quite puzzled. How can an educated Hindu promote the worship
of Kali with her necklace of human heads, why does a "progressive African" and a member, to boot, of Professor Malinowski's
discussion class at the London School of Economics celebrate
the mystery of cliterodectomy?

III

The puzzlement arises, the incongruity is felt, because this is not
a consequence generally anticipated from progress and education. It was not what Macaulay anticipated from the spread of
English education in India, it was not what Livingstone anticipated in Africa; it was not what the first Western-educated
Asians and Africans ever imagined Western education would
lead to. True, Gobineau had premonitions, but his influence was
inversely proportional to his insight.

When Europe came into extensive contact with Asia and Africa in the course of the last century, both the Europeans and those whom they came to dominate had a firm and profound belief in the superiority of Western culture and in its power to attract and assimilate alien bodies of people. Other cultures in the past had shown such qualities, had been found attractive by large numbers of conquered aliens, had evoked their devotion and loyalty. This was the case notably with both Hellenic and Roman cultures. The poet Cavafy has a poem which he entitles "Philhellene" and which seems a true imaginative reconstruction of the prestige which in fact attached to Hellenism far beyond its place of origin. In the poem, a Central Asian king gives instructions for the design of a new medal:

> The inscription in Greek, as usual;
> Nothing exaggerated, nothing pompous—
> . . . .

He continues, as if answering the objections of a mocking skeptic:

> Now don't start any of your clever talk,
> Your 'Where are the Greeks?' and 'What Greek can there be
> Here behind Zagros, and beyond Phraata?'
> So many others, more barbarian than we are,
> If they inscribe it, we shall do the same.

Roman civilization also exerted great attractive power over the subjects of Rome. Writing at the beginning of the Christian era the Greek geographer Strabo observed of southern Gaul and Spain: "They have changed their ways and altogether gone over to the Roman fashion. They wear togas and even speak Latin and have changed the pattern of their laws." Tacitus, again, notes the spread of Latin in Britain: "There was no need of compulsion," he remarks, "ambition served instead, and Latin rhetoric became the popular study." Toward the end of the Roman Empire in the West, in 413 of the Christian era, the

Gallic noble Rutilius Claudius Namatianus, on laying down his office of prefect of the city and returning to Gaul, wrote a rather famous poem of farewell which eloquently expresses loyalty and affection to Rome as the center of the world and the source of peace, order, and civilization: "Rome," writes Rutilius, "is the Queen of the world, nurse of men and mother of gods, whose majesty shall not fade from the hearts of men till the sun itself is overwhelmed: her gifts are as widely spread as the sun's rays —the sun which rises and sets on lands ruled by Rome. . . . She had made one fatherland of many nations, and to be brought within her rule was a blessing. What was before the world Rome had turned into one city, offering the conquered partnership in her own law."

A hundred years ago, it would have been reasonable to assume that European civilization would hold the same attraction for its overseas subjects as had Hellenism and the Roman way of life, that it would evoke the same loyalty and affection. To start with, of course, conquest, the putting down of traditional ruling classes, the imposition of new laws, new methods, and new masters, evoked much strenuous but ultimately futile resistance. The Indian Mutiny of 1858 was one notable episode in which the ruling classes and the loyalties of traditional India attempted to make a stand against the British Christian ruler. The famous Abdel Kader of Algeria tried valiantly, but in vain, to resist the French. This alien, relentless, and methodical domination by the European Powers evoked also much bitter lamentation, which finds expression in popular folklore and poetry. This traditional reaction, in its lament for past greatness and present degradation, in its entire innocence of European ideologies and notions, may be illustrated from an anonymous Algerian popular composition of the last century:

The Christian is the master of the two continents [Europe and Africa] and of the sea. He has built fortifications similar to [those of the Romans] the ruins [of which remain] from Suq Akhras to Qantara. Follow the banks of Shatt al-Djarid and, from Bône to Mascara, you will not find a single *douar*. The fires of the Arabs [i.e., the tribes] are dead and cannot roast even a mouse. From Shazwat, on the coast up to Umm

Gherar the companion betrays his companion, neighbour cheats neighbour, and friend slanders friend. The honour of men is demeaned in the [tribal] assemblies. The coming of the *Mahdi* predicted by the Imam Lakhdar is announced by signs which indicate the end of the world. How many men of noble lineage have been degraded into servants! What flies high must now abandon the heights! He who was wealthy has fallen into poverty. The bread of pride gives no sustenance; and the rotten beam will end by cracking! [41]

The poet Rabindranath Tagore also expresses—but in a sophisticated prose, not in the naïve poetry of the popular bard—the native reaction to the destructive impact which European conquest had on traditional society. In an essay entitled *Nationalism*, which he published in 1917, Tagore said of European government that

it is an applied science and therefore more or less similar in its principles wherever it is used. It is like a hydraulic press, whose pressure is impersonal, and on that account completely effective. The amount of its power may vary in different engines. Some may even be driven by hand, thus leaving a margin of comfortable looseness in their tension, but in spirit and in method their differences are small. Our government might have been Dutch, or French, or Portuguese, and its essential features would have remained much the same as they are now.

Traditional domination, it is true, had brought oppression and devastation to India, but the devastation left the essentials of Indian life untouched, and the oppression did not penetrate into the soul: "We had known the hordes of Moghals and Pathans who invaded India, but we had known them as human races, with their own religions and customs, likes and dislikes. . . ." But this new government is remote, lifeless, and inhuman: "In the products of the handloom the magic of man's living fingers finds its expression, and its hum harmonizes with the music of life. But the power-loom is relentlessly lifeless and accurate and monotonous in its production."

But once European rule was established and familiar, it did in fact begin to attract new classes of men who were convinced of the superiority of European civilization over the traditional ways of their own society, who rebelled against this society and wished to remake it in the likeness of Europe. This was the first impulse of the so-called "marginal" men. Such men were aware that they were deliberately breaking with the norms of their own society, but they did so in the belief that the European norms were superior ones.

We read in a poem entitled "To my son going to England," which appeared in an Indian periodical in 1874,

> Go, son belov'd! as pilgrim bold to lands
> Beyond the stormy ocean's wide domain
> Where Commerce, Art and Science freely rain
> On freemen blessings rare with lib'ral hands.
>
> Thou are not tied by false religion's bands,
> Her chains are not round thee, thou'rt nobly free.
> Thou art not one who fears to cross the sea,
> And on the beach by her as spell-bound stands.[42]

The stilted inversions of an outmoded poetical idiom must not prevent a full appreciation of the daring challenge which these lines express. For a Hindu of any standing at all to leave India and venture on the black waters was to risk pollution, to risk becoming an outcaste. Such a journey—and all the European contacts that it implied—was frowned upon in traditional Hindu society, and to undertake it was an act of defiance, a violent sundering of "false religion's bands."

If Asians and Africans were hopeful of acceptance within a European scheme of things, so were their new European masters, provided, of course, that their subjects showed evidence of understanding and accepting this scheme. "I believe," wrote the Indian civilian Sir Bartle Frere (1815–1884), "it is very possible to do much to Anglicize our native servants, not in manner or costume, nor even necessarily in language, but in feeling; to make them feel towards our Government, as being *their* Government, *the* Government to which they belong . . . the best possible Government for India. The feeling may never rise to exactly the same kind of loyalty which is felt for a sovereign of the same race and religion. . . but it might be an identification of interest and feeling. . . ." The same hope and the same outlook were more pithily and strikingly expressed by Cecil Rhodes when he said that his political ideal was to give the vote to every civilized man south of the Zambezi.

When expressing his belief that Indians could be Anglicized and made to identify themselves in feeling and interest with their rulers, Frere admitted that this was "rare now, and is daily, I fear, becoming rarer." In succeeding decades this became increasingly the case. For a variety of complicated reasons those Asians and Africans who had opted for Europe, whose loyalty went to the European ruler and his civilization, found themselves in an equivocal, invidious, and intolerable position. The new ruler introduced new schools and universities, but their graduates found the hopes with which they had embarked on their studies remained bitterly unrealized. Dadabhai Naoroji (1825–1917) voiced the disillusionment of educated Indians in a memorandum which he sent to the secretary of state for India in 1881 (see pp. 353–371): "The thousands that are being sent out by the universities every year," he wrote, "find themselves in a most anomalous position. There is no place for them in their motherland. They may beg in the streets or break stones on the roads, for aught the rulers seem to care for their natural rights, position and duties in their own country." And again: "The educated find themselves simply so many dummies, ornamented with the tinsel of school-education, and then their whole end and aim of life is ended." That there should be such a gap between hope and fulfillment, that the new educated classes should feel themselves "dummies," and that society had no place for them was to some extent inevitable and beyond remedy by a government. But only to some extent, for it was highly imprudent to introduce Western education into India and, as Naoroji put it, to "act as if no such thing had taken place." "Either they have educated or have not. If they deserve the boast, it is a strange self-condemnation, that after half a century or more of such efforts, they have not yet prepared a sufficient number of men fit for the service of their own country." An imperial power may not count on the ties of a common religion or a common language to evoke loyalty to its rule, it cannot buttress its political authority by appealing to the ties of blood or to family and local connection. An imperial government is the public thing, par excellence; it cannot count upon or profit from the complicities of sentiment and private affections. Its prestige and authority must therefore rest on the impartiality and fair-dealing of its servants, on their resolute and unambiguous application of the rule of law—a law publicly known, manifestly equitable, and indifferent to the accident of class or creed or race. When Curzon was viceroy of India he expressed admirably this condition of imperial rule. On one occasion he insisted on collective punishment for a British regiment the soldiers of which had assaulted Indians and remained adamant in his decision even when Edward VII tried to intervene. "If it be known," he wrote to the secretary of state, "that the Viceroy, backed by the Secretary of State, will stand up even against the crack regiment of the British Army, packed though it be with dukes' sons, earls' sons and so on—then a most salutary lesson will be taught to the army." "My first duty," he stated, "lies to my constituents and they are the people of India."[43]

If, therefore, it comes to be generally believed that positions of honor and responsibility are denied on the ground, say, of race, that an Indian graduate, simply because he is an Indian, can never aspire to be a great official in India, much less a great official in London as Rutilius became a great official in Rome, then imperial government is deprived of one of its main justifications, and metropolitan culture will cease to be as attractive and assimilative as *romanitas* had been. Now it does seem to be the case that principles such as those of Rhodes and Curzon, which are the true imperial principles, were not always or perhaps even often the dominant principles of European rule overseas, that the operation of impersonal and impartial criteria of rule was vitiated by racial arrogance. In the circumstances of British India, it was no doubt right to argue as did the Indian civilian Sir George Campbell (1824–1892) that an Indian could be admitted to the civil service only if he had "become so completely Europeanized as to be really and practically on the footing and imbued with the character of an English highly educated gentleman." But it did not prove to be the case that an Indian who had become "imbued" with such a character would be easily or automatically treated like an English gentleman. The loud protests by Englishmen in India at the Ilbert Bill of 1883 were one manifestation of this racial arrogance, and they elicited from educated Indians reactions which were both deep and lasting. The Ilbert Bill proposed to allow Indian-born magistrates to have the same power as their British-born colleagues to try European British subjects. Hitherto Indians were denied this power on the ground of race. Now these Indian magistrates had to have exactly the same qualifications as their British colleagues, and to maintain such a distinction clearly went against those canons of fair and impartial government which were the pride of the British rulers of India. In his memoirs, B.C. Pal has some remarks on this issue which deserve quotation both for their justice and for their penetration. These magistrates, he said, "had not only passed a very rigid test on the same terms as the British members of the service, but had spent the very best years of the formative period of their youth in England. Upon their return to their homeland, they practically lived in the same style as their brother civilians, and almost religiously followed the social conventions and the ethical standards of the latter. In those days, the India-born civilian practically cut himself off from his parent society, and lived and moved and had his being in the atmosphere so beloved of his British colleagues. In mind and manners he was as much an Englishman as any Englishman. It was no small sacrifice for him, because in this way he completely estranged himself from the society of his own people and became socially and morally a pariah among them." "He was," continued Pal, in a striking sentence, "as much a stranger in his own native land as the European residents in the country."[44] It is against these men that the Europeans of Calcutta set up a vociferous agitation which was powerful enough to emasculate the bill and to preserve—albeit in an attenuated form—invidious and dishonoring distinctions between magistrates equal in their professional standing but different in the color of their skin.

The alienation from the foreign ruler and the disaffection toward him which this kind of treatment produced may be illustrated by the case of Surendranath Banerjea, who has been mentioned above. He was a Brahmin and the son of a doctor, one of the first Indians to be admitted to the Indian civil service —only to be dismissed at the start of his career for failing to correct a false report which a subordinate had prepared in his name. Banerjea considered this punishment far in excess of what would be meted out to an English colleague for the same offense and went to London to appeal in person against his dismissal. The appeal was rejected, and Banerjea returned to India persuaded that "the personal wrong done to me was an illustration of the impotency of our people."[45] In the long history of Oriental despotism, wrongful dismissal of an official is not absolutely unknown, but only under modern European rule would a dismissed official consider his grievance to be "an illustration of the impotency of our people" and proceed to organize lecture tours on Mazzini and the struggle of Young Italy against Austrian oppression. In his memoirs B.C. Pal describes the "profound impression" which Banerjea created among the educated classes of Bengal by his recital of the misdeeds of the Austrians who, in particular, "treated even the Italian intellectuals of the middle class as members of an inferior race, indeed literally as helots and slaves."[46] These educated Indians expected educated Englishmen to treat them as their peers; rebuffed and rejected, they took offense; their wholehearted admiration of British achievements was the measure of their fierce and burning resentment. Naoroji in his fervent and admonitory language expresses well this feeling of betrayal: "A misdirected force," he points out, "will hit anywhere and destroy anything. The power that the rulers are, so far to their credit, raising, will, as a nemesis, recoil against themselves. . . ."

These resentments and rebellions and the curious ideological disguises which they sometimes take may be further illustrated

by the cases of George Antonius (1891–1942) and Edward
Atiyah (1903–1964). Both Antonius and Atiyah were Christians
of Lebanese origin, the first Greek Orthodox and the second
Protestant. They both grew up in the shadow of British power
in Egypt and were educated at Victoria College in Alexandria,
an English establishment run on public school lines, and afterward in England: Antonius at King's College, Cambridge, and
Atiyah at Brasenose College, Oxford. After coming down from
Cambridge in 1913 Antonius took employment with the Egyptian government. After the outbreak of war in 1914 he resigned
from his Egyptian post and became deputy chief press censor
with the Egyptian Expeditionary Force which, led by Allenby,
was in 1917–18 to inflict a crushing defeat on the Ottoman Army
and to occupy Palestine and the Levant. When Palestine became
a mandate administered by Great Britain, Antonius was appointed in 1921 senior inspector of education in Jerusalem. All
those who knew Antonius or have read his writings agree that
he had exceptional ability, great industry, and a subtle mind.
Indeed, his British superiors must have recognized his great
talents, for in the nineteen-twenties they employed him in delicate and important diplomatic negotiations with Ibn Saud. And
yet this man, who was formed and molded by English education
at its best, who stood out of the usual run of colonial bureaucrats,
whose career showed how much he identified himself with the
British Empire and its interests, found himself, for some reason
or another, debarred from attaining the highest posts to which
his ability and seniority alike entitled him. The rank of senior
inspector was the utmost he achieved in the Department of
Education; when the post of director was temporarily vacant he
was considered good enough to serve for short periods as acting
director, but director he would never be appointed. After six
years in the department, we find him remarking that no sooner
was there a hint of the director resigning the following year than
everybody's first preoccupation was to find and appoint a successor. "It does not seem to enter their heads," he writes to an
English friend with bitterness, "to give me, if not his succession,
at any rate a trial." Again, when it was desired to reward his

services in the Anglo-Saudi negotiations, the Foreign Office proposed him for the C.M.G.—the usual decoration in these cases, but the Colonial Office, on whose establishment Antonius figured, objected that such a decoration, unusual for a man of his rank in the Palestine administration, would create difficulties, and all that they would allow him was the C.B.E.—the proper decoration for a locally recruited senior inspector. Antonius resigned from the Palestine administration and began to identify himself with the Arab cause in Palestine; his work, *The Arab Awakening*, published in 1938, showed him a most skilled and persuasive advocate of the claims of Arab nationalism. It is not fanciful to think that Antonius espoused this cause—a curious one for somebody of his antecedents and upbringing to take up —because he felt rejected by those whom he expected to treat him as an equal.

The parallel case of Atiyah is equally interesting, the more so in that he has himself left a public record of how he became an Arab nationalist. In his book, *An Arab Tells His Story*, published in 1946, he describes the great prestige which Europe had among the Syrian Christians: "Hero-worship!" he writes. "It is as such that the general attitude of the Syrian Christians to the European nations before the war, and more particularly towards the close of the 19th century, can best be described. The military and naval prowess of Europe, her reputation for culture and scientific advancement; the manifestations of her mechanical greatness— all these factors, with the halo of remoteness and novelty glowing about them, wrought their potent influence on the impressionable Syrian mind." Atiyah then goes on to describe how, growing up in the Anglo-Egyptian Sudan, it became "my lot to adopt England—not the soil of England, for I did not see that till I was nineteen years old—but everything else, the spirit and prestige of England: her kings and heroes, armies, fleets and victories; her history and literature, and all the things that were lacking in my own national background." At the end of his three years at Oxford, he saw himself "as a product of the British liberal tradition, imbued with the humanist spirit. . . . I believed that the British way of life, based on liberal democracy and private enterprise, was the consummation of social and political development and the pattern of progress for the rest of the world. . . . Liberal democracy would become more complete and the rest of the world would approximate to the British model. The East would do so under direct British guidance, until in the fulness of time it was able to rule itself." He went out to Khartoum to teach at Gordon College and found himself segregated from the British staff; after Victoria College and Oxford "I was flung back at one bound into a world of group barriers . . . in which I, despite my long and passionate struggle to assimilate England and be assimilated by her, was consigned to that side of the fence on which I was born." The British in Khartoum did not regard him as one of themselves, and this mortified him: "Mortification was not slow in turning into resentment. The domain from which I was excluded began to arouse my hostility. . . . The manifestations of British privilege and British prestige began to gall me, and for the first time I began to experience towards the British Empire the hostile feelings of a subject who resents its rule and its might, because he has no share in them. What I had taken a personal pride in till then was becoming now the enemy of my pride, and I began to rebel against the glory I could not be associated with." The shock for Atiyah was so tremendous that, as he puts it, his whole life went into reverse gear: "I became myself an Arab nationalist." "I wanted," he also says, "to assert my identity as a Syrian."[47] And for Atiyah, Antonius, the Anglicized Brahmins, and the North African products of French *lycées*, it was indeed a matter of one's identity, of finding an answer to a question the very asking of which betokens unease and anguish, the question: "What am I?" Having been rejected or slighted by the rulers with whom they were culturally one, they now had literally to "assert" a new identity. Assertions are strident: the very title of Atiyah's book is a manifesto. It is an Arab, he affirms, who is telling his story; by calling himself an Arab he is doing much more than to affix an indifferent label on himself: he wishes to be considered a member of a nation, "the Arabs," which to his ancestors and their ancestors before them would have been meaningless and unreal, but the very novelty of which promises release from shock, mortification, and burning resentments.

The revulsion which educated Asians and Africans felt at a racial discrimination so opposed to the character of imperial rule, and so much at variance with what their European rulers had led them to expect, was gradually turned into disaffection; and this disaffection was clothed in an ideology which at once explained their predicament and restored their self-esteem. European rule in Africa sometimes also involved another kind of discrimination equally impossible to reconcile with imperial rule. This also worked to make the metropolitan civilization less assimilative and less attractive. This discrimination arose when Europeans in large numbers settled in the midst of the native population and demanded—sometimes with success—special privileges which nothing justified except racial origin. This happened in the case of the French settlers in North Africa and in the case of British settlers in East and South Africa. Cecil Rhodes, as we have said above, held that the aim in Southern Africa ought to be that every civilized man should have the vote. "Civilization" in this context we may understand presumably to mean familiarity with and ability to work the constitutional and representative government which Europeans carried overseas with them. Such a requirement, onerous as it was, could yet be justified by the fact that the Europeans were the conquerors and the masters. But onerous as it was, it was a requirement which the non-Europeans could hope eventually to meet. It was seldom, however, that they were allowed to meet it. South Africa —with which Cecil Rhodes's name and achievements are linked —is itself a case in point. The Union of South Africa was set up in 1910 in the aftermath of the Boer War. It was composed of the two British colonies of the Cape and Natal and of the two former Boer republics, the Orange Free State and the Transvaal. In respect of the two colonies the British government did not, to start with, allow discrimination based on color in the political rights of British subjects; but in Natal, which had been settled predominantly by men of British stock, the franchise was, by a law of 1896, so defined as to debar in effect Indian immigrants

—who shared the same status of British subjects with the immigrants from Great Britain—from the vote. This law laid it down that no persons could vote who were "Natives or descendants in the male line of Natives of countries which have not hitherto possessed elective representative constitutions founded on Parliamentary Franchise." This law could have been disallowed by the Imperial government; it was suffered to remain on the statute book. In the other British colony, that of the Cape, the franchise was until the South Africa Act of 1910 free from racial distinctions; but in the debates preceding the union the representatives of the Cape were persuaded to abolish the right of non-Europeans to sit in the legislature and thus to fall into line with the practice of the two former Boer republics. The South Africa Act was an act of the Imperial Parliament, and in consenting to such a distinction on the grounds of race, the Parliament clearly derogated from the ideal of a British Empire held together by the rule of law. The British government was aware that such discrimination was an undesirable departure from the principles of colonial legislation but nonetheless acquiesced in it: "I say frankly," stated the secretary of state for the colonies in a debate in the House of Lords, "that there does seem to me to be a strong case against the insertion of such a provision in this act or in any act. There are men not of European descent who are of high standing, of high character, and of high ability. They regard this provision as a slight, and we regret that any loyal subjects of the King should regard themselves slighted"; he went on to say that without such discrimination, no union between the territories of British South Africa would be possible, and that neither the government nor he personally were prepared to oppose such discrimination and then take responsibility for the possible wrecking of the union. To govern is to choose, and no choice is without its attendant evils, proximate or remote. Lord Crewe and his Liberal colleagues chose—no doubt for good and sufficient reasons—to give in to the pressure of Boer and Briton in South Africa. Their decision contributed to make the worldwide British Empire less attractive and less assimilative for a large category of its subjects.

But the revulsion against Europe, the refusal to assimilate its civilization, the appeal to dark gods and their bloody rites, was not only the outcome of rebuffs and mortification suffered by those educated Asians and Africans who had asked for nothing better than to accept and be accepted by Europe. For not all Asians and Africans came under direct European rule, and not all those who came under this rule suffered these insults. There was the spectacle of Europe itself and the example and lessons which European Powers provided for their overseas subjects. This spectacle, from 1914 onward, was one of a savage internecine war in which Europeans humiliated, defeated, and exterminated their European neighbors in large numbers. This spectacle dealt a deadly blow to the prestige of European rulers in Asia and Africa. The German, the Frenchman, the Englishman were in turn found to be not invincible but liable to sudden defeat and humiliating panic, and in prosecuting their wars they could be low, mean, treacherous, and savagely cruel; in fact there was no reconciling this behavior with civilized government and the rule of law which non-Europeans had been taught by their rulers to uphold. Bernard Berenson remarks[48] that the Soviet revolution owed much "to the talk during the first world war of the millions of mobilized but unemployed peasants, who for lack of armaments, were never called to the front, and had nothing to do in their barracks but discuss events and to hear all about the corruption, confusion and incompetence of the government they were serving." The remark is acute and applies *pari passu* to all those Indians, Indochinese, Indonesians, or Africans who either served in the European mass armies and saw for themselves that the European proletariat was not manifestly their superior in manners or sensibility or intelligence or else observed their European rulers defeated, humiliated, and evicted in such places as Malaya, Burma, or the Netherlands East Indies. The reaction of Yen Fu (1854–1921), an educated Chinese who had spent a lifetime familiarizing his fellow countrymen with European thought and literature, to World War I is worthy of notice: "Western culture, after this European War, has been corrupted utterly. . . . It seems to me that in three centuries of progress the peoples of the West have achieved four principles: to be selfish, to kill others, to have little integrity, and to feel little shame."[49] The Indonesian nationalist leader Soetan Sjahrir has a most interesting passage in his memoirs which throws a vivid light on the process by which the moral foundations of Dutch rule and all the standards and attitudes associated with it—and particularly deference to the foreign ruler—were damaged beyond repair by the events of World War II: "As I look back at the Japanese period," he writes, "it is clear to what extent everything in the Indonesian community, spiritually as well as materially, was shaken loose from its old moorings. The fall of the colonial regime was in itself a cause, but what the Japanese showed our people afterward dealt the decisive blow to the old standards and norms. The Japanese gave the people a surprise that was widespread and general. People had expected them to be quite different, stronger and more clever than the Netherlanders they had defeated. What people saw were barbarians who were often more stupid than they themselves. . . . The old experienced Indonesian administrators of the colonial service felt only contempt for the political ignoramuses who were placed over them. As a consequence, all layers of society came to see the past in another light. If these barbarians had been able to replace the old colonial authority, why had that authority been necessary at all?"[50]

IV

Of the dark gods and their rites, we said that they represented a revulsion against Europe. But is this a satisfactory way of describing the matter? As has been seen, the invocation of Kali and the praise of cliterodectomy was the work of men deeply touched by European ideas, men who, in words Malinowski used in introducing the work of his pupil Kenyatta, "have suffered the injury of higher education." The appeal to the past, the idea that every nation is defined by its past and therefore must have a past to be defined by, underlies the doctrine of nationalism, and this strand of the European intellectual tradition was, as we have

shown, taken up by Asians and Africans. Here we may speak
of an adaptation or even imitation of European ideas and not
of revulsion against Europe. And on second thoughts it may
seem to us that the bloodthirsty appeal to Kali and the deliberate
obscurantism apparent in a defense of cliterodectomy are likewise an imitation and adoption of another feature of the European intellectual tradition, a feature which has always existed,
albeit generally hidden and latent, but which has become more
manifest and influential in the last few centuries. It is perfectly
true that the stresses and strains brought about by contact with
and subordination to Europe predisposed Asians and Africans
to the acceptance of this strand in the European tradition,
but the fact remains that this particular strand was dominant in Europe itself at the time of its greatest expansion overseas.

Nationalism, we have said, rests on the assumption that a
nation must have a past. It also rests on another assumption, no
less fundamental, namely, that a nation must have a future. This
assumption is a variant of the idea of progress which has been
the dominant strand in modern European culture. Faith in progress has assumed many forms and variants, but essentially it
is a belief that history will not let us down, that no catastrophe
is final, no disaster irremediable. This is the prevailing note in
modern culture.

The poet T. S. Eliot, in his vision of *The Waste Land*, asks:

> Who are those hooded hordes swarming
> Over endless plains, stumbling in cracked earth
> Ringed by the flat horizon only
> What is the city over the mountains
> Cracks and reforms and bursts in the violet air
> Falling towers
> Jerusalem Athens Alexandria
> Vienna London

The Waste Land was published in 1922, but in spite of all that
has happened in the interval, it would be true to say that this

vision of the doom of each proud Babylon in turn the appointed victim of a catastrophic end remains today as when it was first published a private and eccentric vision, dismissed as mere literature produced by a reactionary poet. What is rather taken for granted, what represents a worldwide consensus today is the view expressed by G.E. Lessing (1729–1781) in his *Education of the Human Race* (1780). In this work, Lessing proclaims in short, emotion-laden paragraphs this religion of progress, with its beatific vision of earthly perfection at the end of time: "... it will come, it will certainly come," affirms Lessing, "this epoch of perfection. . . ."; the course of history he sees as "a large wheel which, in a slow movement, leads the human race to the point of its perfection," or as a "road on which humanity progresses towards perfection." Meliorism, perfectibility, the belief that everything and everybody has a future are considered today natural and harmless; they have been incorporated into the very fabric of our attitudes and ways of thought. We are therefore startled by the fervor of Lessing's language. His enthusiasm should make us suspect that what now seems a commonplace worth hardly a scrutiny was in his day a novelty which could generate violent excitement. On further examination we come to see that the excitement was warranted, that a work like *The Education of the Human Race* was bringing into the open, secularizing, and making respectable an old idea which had led a long and tenacious underground existence among the religious heresies of Christian Europe. Lessing's tract constitutes in fact a landmark on the road which led, to use the title of Professor E.L. Tuveson's work, from millennium to utopia.[51] Lessing himself was quite aware of the origins of the gospel of human and earthly perfection which he was preaching: "It will certainly come," he writes in paragraph 86 of his treatise, "the era of a new, everlasting gospel which is the New Covenant"; and he adds in the following paragraph: "It may be that certain visionaries of the thirteenth and fourteenth centuries were illuminated by some rays of this new eternal gospel, and that their only error lay in believing that its time was nigh." The term "everlasting gospel" to which Lessing refers occurs in the Revelation of St.

John the Divine, chapter 14, verse 6. It figured in the title of the
work *Introductorium in Evangelium Aeternum* which Gerard of
Borgo San Donnino, a young teacher of theology at the University of Paris, published in 1254 and for which he was condemned
to life imprisonment. This work was in turn inspired by the
writings of Joachim of Flora (*c.* 1130–1202). No doubt it was
writers like Joachim and Gerard whom Lessing had in mind
when he spoke of thirteenth- and fourteenth-century visionaries
who had foretold the coming perfection of man.

The visions of these visionaries had to do with the advent of
the millennium as it is spoken of in the Book of Revelation, as
for instance in chapter 20, verse 6: "Blessed and holy is he that
hath part in the first resurrection: on such the second death hath
no power, but they shall be priests of God and of Christ, and
shall reign with him a thousand years," or in chapter 21, verse
1: "And I saw a new heaven and a new earth." Joachim, inspired
by such prophecies, divided human history into three epochs:
the period of law, the period of grace, and the period of love.
The first period is governed by the attributes of the Father, the
second by those of the Son, and the third by those of the Spirit.
The first period is a manifestation of power and dread; the second of humility, truth, and wisdom; the third of love, liberty, and
joy. The first age is a starry night, the second a gray dawn, and
only the third—which is yet to come—is the full day. Joachim's
speculations which may be described as millennial—by reference to the millennium foretold in the Book of Revelation—may
seem quite harmless. Why then should Gerard of Borgo San
Donnino have been put in prison for publicizing them, and why,
in general, should these millennial speculations have attracted
widespread hostility in Judaism, Christianity, and Islam?

For of this hostility there can be no doubt. In all three religions, the orthodox consensus has repeatedly condemned these
speculations. The curse pronounced by the rabbis upon those
who calculate the end[52] has been widely echoed by successive
Muslim and Christian divines. From the early days Christianity
encountered these outbursts of apocalyptic enthusiasm in which
some local religious leader would preach to his followers the

speedy coming of a new heaven and of a new earth. As early as the beginning of the fifth century belief in the millennium was condemned at the Council of Ephesus, in 431; and Catholic interpretation of the Book of Revelation inspired by Augustine and endorsed by Aquinas tried to show that the visions of St. John the Divine do not tell us what the future has in store but are simply allegories of the soul's journey toward salvation and of the trials and pitfalls it encounters on the way.[53] The Lutheran Augsburg Confession of 1530 in its turn condemned the opinion that "before the resurrection of the dead the godly shall occupy the kingdom of the world."

From what Article XVII of the Confession goes on to say we may form an idea of the reasons for which millennial speculation aroused such vehement and continuous hostility, for according to the article the belief that the godly shall occupy the kingdom of the world entailed the further belief that the wicked would be everywhere suppressed, that "the saints alone, the pious shall have a worldly kingdom, and shall exterminate all the godless." Millennial speculation, then, if at all widespread, was seen again and again to carry a threat to law and order. If some distress or discontent rendered a mass of men susceptible to the lure of an imminent, miraculous, collective, and terrestrial redemption, then destructive passions could be unleashed, and the customary checks on which life in society depended would be utterly destroyed.

Joachimism and other forms of millennialism were never completely eradicated from European life but led the usual obscure and disreputable existence of heresies, with occasional violent eruptions whenever chance threw up a prophet to lead a multitude whom the distresses of war, famine, or rapid economic change uprooted or made restless. In modern times, by a process still in large parts obscure but which Professor Tuveson has done much to illuminate, millennialism shed its disreputable origins in medieval heresy and emerged as the respectable and rational doctrine of progress and human perfectibility. The distance traveled from Joachim's everlasting gospel to the enlightened meliorism of the eighteenth century may be illustrated by a quotation from an English theological work published in 1773 which Professor Tuveson cites:

"We have grounds from Scripture," wrote William Worthington in *The Scripture Theory of the Earth . . . from the Creation to the final Renovation of all Things,* "to believe, that natural and moral evil will, in a great measure, yet not totally, be removed and overcome, before the consummation of all things; and that the latter ages of the world, next preceding the final dissolution by fire, will, in general, be the best and happiest; and will approach to the innocence and perfection of the paradisiacal state." The orthodox Worthington, engaged in a polemic against Deism,[54] is making the same point which Lessing, theologically in bad odor, would make so lyrically and fervently only a few years later.

Did this secular apocalypse entirely shed its violent and disreputable origins, or may belief in progress and perfectibility also be associated with those outbreaks which rendered medieval millennialism so terrifying? Let us consider more closely the political style of millennialism. The millennial hope is of the inauguration and institution of a totally new order where love reigns and all men are brothers, where all distinctions and divisions, all selfishness and self-regard are abolished. But a society in which the distinction between public and private is annihilated, in which ranks, orders, classes, associations, and families are all dissolved into one big family, a society in which all articulations and complexities have disappeared—such a society becomes helpless in the hands of those who prophesy the good tidings of the coming salvation. The city of Münster in 1534 received a Dutch baker, Jan Matthys, who prophesied the millennium and called on the people to repent of their sins. He collected a large following and soon became the dominant power in Münster, determined to transform it into a "New Jerusalem purified of all uncleanness." To this end, the prophet proposed the killing of all Lutherans and Roman Catholics, but he was prevailed upon merely to expel them. They were all mercilessly driven out, regardless of age or health, into the bleak winter countryside with no possessions or food of any kind. Münster was henceforth populated by the Children of God, who lived in a community of love, addressing one another as brother and sister. A blacksmith who presumed to murmur against Matthys was publicly stabbed and shot by the prophet in person. Matthys decreed that true Christians should possess everything in common, and by a process of terror and exhortation the believers were induced to hand over to the prophet their money and their gold and silver ornaments. It was next decreed that all commodities would be owned in common; communal kitchens were established, and private stores of food were requisitioned; likewise the exclusive possession of a private dwelling was denounced as sinful. By a natural progress, the prophet next denounced all books save the Bible as of the devil, and they had all to be burned in public. The prophet, now absolute dictator of Münster, was inspired at Easter to go out and do battle against the forces of the bishop of Münster, now besieging the rebellious city. Here he met his death, and he was succeeded in the leadership of the holy community by a disciple, Jan Bockelson, better known as John of Leyden.

Bockelson was the bastard of a Dutch village mayor and a Westphalian serf, and by profession a tailor. He was a man of some education, and when he succeeded his master showed no mean ability in leading and holding together the community which Matthys established. His first important political act was to run naked through the town and then to fall into a silent ecstasy for three days. From this he emerged to declare that God ordered the old constitution of the city to be abolished. In the place of mayor and council Bockelson instituted himself and twelve Elders as the final authority in the city, with power of life and death over all the community. Bockelson next instituted compulsory polygamy and enforced it by decreeing that refusal to comply made a woman liable to the death sentence. Finally, in September, 1534, Bockelson was proclaimed king of the whole world, who was to inaugurate a Third Age, that of the Saints who were now to reign in triumph and prepare a new heaven and a new earth. As a sign of the coming of the new age, Sundays and feast days were abolished, and the days of the week given new names; newborn children were also given new names chosen by the king himself. The new age lasted until June, 1535, when the city was finally taken. Bockelson, captured by the bishop, was publicly tortured to death in Münster with two of his prominent followers: "After the execution the three bodies were suspended from a church tower in the middle of the town, in cages which," according to Professor N. Cohn, "are still to be seen there today."[55]

Bockelson's short-lived universal kingdom in Münster displays almost to perfection the techniques of political activism which seem inseparable from millennial prophecy—techniques designed to upset and destroy traditional and customary social arrangements and to render men, in their shock, bewilderment, and distress, plastic and malleable material, out of which the seer will create tomorrow's world of perfect love and selfless brotherhood. Bockelson's career also illustrates a particularly important distinction on which Professor Cohn insists: the distinction on the one hand between the mundane and ordinary discontents which move the bulk of human beings and which are amenable to ordinary alleviations and remedies, and on the other the obsessive, apocalyptic fantasies of the revolutionaries who harness to their vision the social conflicts of the moment and promise their followers a new world "totally transformed and redeemed."[56]

We may further illuminate the style of millennial politics by considering the aims and policies of the Taiping movement which broke out in China in the first half of the nineteenth century. The founder of this movement, Hung Hsin-ch'üan (1813–1864), came from poor peasant stock in a village near Canton. He was a man of intelligence and ability who acquired enough education to be able to present himself for the civil service examinations at Canton. In spite of repeated attempts, however, he failed to satisfy the examiners, and he seemed destined to a lifetime of disappointment as a village schoolmaster. On one of his visits to Canton, however, Hung heard a Christian missionary speak, and he took back with him to his village some Christian missionary tracts. He fell ill, perhaps as a result of his disappointment, and began to see visions in which God, the Heavenly Father, and Jesus, the Elder Brother, exhorted Hung, the Younger Brother, to stamp out the worship of demons. These visions continued for years to haunt his imagination, but it was only some seven years after he had acquired the religious tracts that Hung actually began to study them. He then began to make converts in his own family circle, to break idols, and to attack the traditional beliefs of his fellow villagers. These activities made him unpopular, and he finally found refuge among the Hakka tribe—his remote kinsmen—in an inaccessible mountainous district of the southwest. He remained there for some years teaching and making converts, and in 1847 he again visited Canton and sat for two months at the feet of a Southern Baptist missionary, the Reverend Issachar J. Roberts, from whom he imbibed tenets of a fundamentalist Christianity which became the foundation of his own peculiar and fantastical theology.

By the late eighteen-forties Hung was at the head of a band of God Worshippers at odds with the government. Southern China in the eighteen-thirties and -forties was in a disturbed state. There had been a steady growth in population in the latter part of the eighteenth and in the early nineteenth century, but this increase was not matched by an increase in resources or production; the use of imported opium meant an ever-larger outflow of silver; the prices of necessaries increased steadily, and the antiquated system of taxation became more oppressive in its incidence and gave greater openings to the greed of corrupt officials. In short, "the position of the peasant had become depressed, insecure, and degraded to what almost amounted to serfdom."[57] In southern China particularly, the prestige and authority of the Manchu rulers were shaken by defeat at the hands of the British in the Opium War (1839–1842); so that, when the Imperial government attempted to put down the God Worshippers, its troops were no match for the band of saints, who fought with discipline and conviction. In December, 1850, Hung proclaimed the inauguration of the Heavenly Kingdom of Great Peace. The Great Peace, or Taiping, was to be an era of peace and harmony, a Kingdom of Heaven, members of which worshiped the one True God. The God Worshippers swiftly cut through Hunan and the Yangtze Valley and in March, 1853, took the city of Nanking, which remained the capital of the Heavenly King, who, until his downfall eleven years later, controlled a rich and extensive part of China with a population of some thirty million.

The literature of the Taipings abounds in many descriptions of the Heavenly Kingdom and of the way to achieve it. In a proclamation of 1851 issued when the first considerable city fell to the God Worshippers, Hung proclaimed: "We sincerely announce to you that, since we have all had the happiness to become sons and daughters of our Heavenly Father, and brothers and sisters of our Celestial Elder Brother, we shall enjoy incomparable dignity in this present world, and interminable felicity in the next." The way to achieve this dignity and felicity is set out in the official Taiping documents. *The Land System of the Heavenly Kingdom* envisages a meticulous control of the whole population in all their activities in peace and war. Private property was abolished, the cultivation of land and the harvesting was to be carried out under official supervision: "During the harvest season, the Group Officer [in charge of a 25-family unit] should direct [the grain collection] by sergeants. Deducting the amount needed to feed the twenty-five families until next harvest season, he should collect the rest of the produce for storage in state granaries. The same method of collection is applicable to other kinds of products . . . for all people under Heaven are of one family belonging to the Heavenly Father, the Supreme Ruler, the Lord God-on-High. Nobody should keep private property. All things should be presented to the Supreme Ruler, so that He will be enabled to make use of them and distribute them equally to all members of his great work-family. Thus all will be sufficiently fed and clothed. . . . For each festival occasion, such as a wedding or the birth of a child, a family is to be allowed 1,000 copper cash and 100 catties of grain, so that there will be a uniform rule throughout the country."

Taiping rule did not last long enough for this program to be realized, but the regimentation of the inhabitants of Nanking by the God Worshippers is a foreshadowing of what they might have accomplished: they segregated bachelors and spinsters and established camps for unmarried women; they regulated sexual intercourse by the most draconian measures, laying down carefully the conditions under which husbands and wives should meet and punishing transgressors by burning them alive, a process known to them as lighting the lamp of heaven; they supervised the systematic and intensive inculcation of their doctrine in public and in private; and in order to keep the population under continual inspection ordered them to keep the doors of their houses perpetually open.

The famous statesman Tseng Kuo-fan (1811–1872), who finally defeated the Taipings, issued in the course of his campaign a proclamation which describes accurately the aims and methods of a movement such as that of the God Worshippers. "From the ancient days of Yao and Shuin [the two model emperors traditionally invoked in Chinese writings]," said the proclamation, "each generation has upheld the far-reaching doctrines which magnify the relation of emperor and statesman, of honorable and humble, of old and young, fixed and irreversible as the positions of the members in the body. But these southern rebels, borrowing the ways of barbarian tribes, and the religion of the 'Lord of Heaven,' depose sovereigns and degrade officials, their 'officials' calling every man 'brother' and every woman 'sister.' " What is said here of the Taipings is *mutatis mutandis* equally true of Münster under the reign of Bockelson and of other millennial outbreaks. All of them announce the gospel of love and brotherhood, and they must therefore destroy all social and political institutions; they must, as Tseng Kuo-fan put it, "depose sovereigns and degrade officials." They have to do this because the stability and the hierarchy which go with any political and social arrangements derogate from the perfection of love and brotherhood: for these are of the spirit and admit of no institutional limitations. The philosopher Hegel showed a profound insight into the workings of millennial politics when he said that the quest for absolute liberty goes hand in hand with terror. Absolute liberty, like love or brotherhood, can never be satisfactorily translated into political and social institutions; the attempt to realize it must involve a permament revolution, and a permament revolution requires terrorism as the method and principle of government. This was clearly seen and asserted by Robespierre when he said in one of his speeches that "the mainspring of popular government in time of revolution is both *virtue and terror:* virtue, without which terror is evil; terror, without which virtue is helpless. Terror," he asserted, "is nothing but justice, prompt, severe and inflexible; it is therefore"—and his terrorist logic is impeccable—"an emanation of virtue."

Mention of Robespierre here serves to make the point that the political style of millennialism, as we have seen it among the Anabaptists and the Taipings, is not linked always and necessarily to the preaching of a strictly religious millennium; that, in fact, it may also accompany the attempt to realize a completely secular vision of man's future. The idea of progress, as we have argued, is a secularized and respectable version of the medieval millennium. The disreputable political style of medieval millennialism erupted, before the French Revolution, only in rare, albeit notable, episodes; it was generally suppressed into the obscure underground of heretical sects. But from the French Revolution onward this style has become increasingly respectable, has indeed shared its respectability with the secular idea of progress, and what we may call *sans-culottisme* has become a striking element in the European political tradition. Among the fragments for an unwritten second volume of *L'Ancien régime et la révolution* which Alexis de Tocqueville left at his death, there is a remark on the political style which the French Revolution bequeathed to posterity: "The Convention," he observes, "which did such harm to contemporaries by its frenzies, did eternal harm by its example. It created the politics of *the impossible*, the theory of madness, the worship of blind audacity." The politics of the impossible in its secular form has had an illustrious career in Europe since the days of 1793 when the new era in its year one began with a new Republican calendar and a decaderian worship of the Supreme Being. The new era of the

French Revolution is duplicated by Mussolini's new era, which was reckoned to have begun with the Fascist march on Rome, and by the Nazi claim to inaugurate a new thousand-year Reich. The French Revolution appeared, as Wordsworth said in his famous poem, a "pleasant exercise of hope and joy"

> the whole earth
> The beauty wore of promise

and all, it seemed,

> Were called upon to exercise their skill,
> Not in Utopia, subterranean fields,
> Or some secreted island, Heaven knows where!
> But in the very world, which is the world
> Of all of us,—the place where in the end
> We find our happiness, or not at all![58]

Exactly the same feeling that universal happiness was at hand was felt in October, 1917, and the enthusiasts of the Russian Revolution at its commencement—and decades afterward—also felt that this was a new dawn in which it was bliss to be alive.

Concluding a notable examination of what he has called "the Democratic Revolution," Professor R.R. Palmer argues that the French Revolution might not have happened if the old privileged orders "had made sagacious concessions"; perhaps they were not sagacious, or perhaps their sagacity would not have saved them; in any event the Revolution happened, and as Professor Palmer correctly points out, all revolutions in Europe, Latin America, Asia, and Africa "have learned from the eighteenth-century Revolution of Western Civilization." It may be true in strict logic that one revolution does not lead to another, that no revolution is inevitable, and that revolution need not be "glorified as a social process."[59] But, in fact, since the French Revolution more and more people have believed revolutions to be inevitable and beneficial and to be glorified "as a social process." This frenzied meliorism, which in its religious form was long suppressed and disreputable, in its secular form became the dominant strand of the political tradition first of Europe and then of the whole world. Nationalism as it appears and spreads in Europe is one of the many forms of this vision of a purified society in which all things are made new. It has of course its own rhetoric, its own structure of metaphysical and anthropological propositions, but what gives the doctrine dynamism, what makes it a mainspring of human action is surely this millennial hope that men can somehow put an end to all oppression and injustice.

Therefore, hand in hand with this meliorism, and called forth by it, went this terrorism which for Robespierre was inseparable from virtue and for Hegel the inevitable result of the quest after absolute liberty. We are fortunate in possessing a startling document which constitutes a paradigm for this particular chapter in the annals of European political thought and attitudes. This document is the *Revolutionary Catechism* which the anarchist Michael Bakunin (1814–1876) wrote in 1869 under the influence of and in collaboration with the famous terrorist Sergei Gennadevich Nechaev (1847–1882), whom he described as one of "these young fanatics, believers without God, heroes without rhetoric." "The revolutionary," says the *Catechism* in its first paragraph, "is a lost man; he has no interest of his own, no cause of his own, no feelings, no habits, no belongings; he does not even have a name. Everything in him is absorbed by a single, exclusive interest, a single thought, a single passion—the revolution." The sixth paragraph declares that the revolutionary must be hard on others as he is on himself: "All the tender feelings of family life, of friendship, love, gratitude and even honor must be stifled in him by a single cold passion for the revolutionary cause." The revolutionary's aim is merciless destruction: "With this aim in view, tirelessly and in cold blood, he must always be prepared to die and to kill with his own hands anyone who stands in the way of achieving it." The only revolution that will achieve anything worthwhile, we read in the twenty-third paragraph, "is one that destroys every established object root and branch, that annihilates all State traditions, orders and classes." To achieve this destruction, the revolutionary, the twenty-fifth paragraph lays down, must draw close to the people. The people are those who have always stood out against the State and organized society: "We must ally ourselves with the doughty world of brigands, who in Russia are the only real revolutionaries." And the following paragraph is categorical and clear: "All our organization, all our conspiracy, all our purpose consists in this: to regroup this world of brigands into an invincible and omni-destructive force."[60]

If, then, we should ask whether the worship of Kali or similar phenomena represent a revulsion against Europe, our answer would have to be negative. These disconcerting reactions by educated and sophisticated men—and it is only the sophisticated who harbor and propagate such notions—represent not so much a revulsion against the European tradition as the adoption and adaptation of certain of its features—features which became prominent in Europe itself at the very moment when it was coming in close and dominating contact with Asia and Africa. Bakunin's aim, "to regroup this world of brigands into an invincible and omni-destructive force," is in a line of succession from Robespierre's conjunction of virtue and terror and has for its counterpart B.C. Pal's glorification of Kali, the goddess of destruction with the garland of human heads round her neck. We may say in short that the mainspring of nationalism in Asia and Africa is the same secular millennialism which had its rise and development in Europe and in which society is subjected to the will of a handful of visionaries who, to achieve their vision, must destroy all barriers between private and public.

In medieval millennialism, as Professor Cohn has pointed out, there is a distinction to be made between the earthly and ordinary discontents which may seize a population at large and the energy of a few who channel their discontents to build the New Jerusalem of their dreams. The distinction, we find, is equally useful in considering nationalist movements in Asia and Africa. As early as 1881 Dadabhai Naoroji pointed out the existence of this class of visionary malcontents which European education had produced in India and prophetically described their role in undermining and destroying the foundation of British rule. "Englishmen," he said, "sometimes indulge the notion that England is secure in the division and disunion among the various races and nationalities of India. But even in this, new forces are working their way. Those Englishmen who sleep such foolish sleep of security, know precious little of what is going on. The kind of education that is being received by thousands of all classes and creeds, is throwing them all in a similar mold; a sympathy of sentiment, ideas, and aspirations is growing among them; and more particularly a political union and sympathy is the first fruit of the new awakening, as all feel alike their deprivation, and the degradation and destruction of their country." (See pp. 353–371.) These thousands finally succeeded in convincing the millions of India's population that "their deprivation, and the degradation and destruction of their country" was the fault of their foreign rulers and that all these things would change if they themselves ruled instead. Nationalism in Africa is still more striking in this respect. As is well known, nationalism on this continent appears only after World War II, and we see it led by men hitherto quite unknown who had spent a lifetime in obscure student agitations or the equally obscure politics of Pan-Africanism, a movement which between the wars led a shadowy existence within Negro communities in Europe and America. The prehistory of the African nationalist movement has been set down for us by the American Negro scholar W.E.B. Du Bois (1868–1963; see pp. 372–387), who was himself one of its leading spirits. There is nothing in the record of this movement, from the first Pan-African Congress at Paris in 1919 to the fifth Congress held in Manchester Town Hall in 1945, to show that it had any contact with or in any way mirrored or represented the society of Black Africa or any of its principal tribal or urban interests. And yet barely a decade afterward, two of the prominent members of the Manchester Congress, Kenyatta and Nkrumah, were leading formidable movements in Kenya and the Gold Coast respectively, and two decades afterward were the absolute rulers of their countries. In 1945, Kenyatta, though he had in the nineteen-twenties taken part in radical Kikuyu politics in Nairobi, had been sixteen years absent from Kenya, while Nkrumah was an utterly obscure graduate of an American Negro university who had no standing whatever in the Gold Coast. How did they come in so short a time to acquire such great, such absolute power?

When Nkrumah was in London in the years 1945–47, a penniless graduate student haunting the decayed purlieus of Kentish Town and the Gray's Inn Road, he set up a society called "The Circle," composed of fellow students from West Africa. As Nkrumah explains in his *Autobiography*, he was chairman of this society, and membership cost seven guineas; its members were "to train themselves in order to be able to commence revolutionary work in any part of the African continent." In 1948, following political riots which he led in Accra, Nkrumah was arrested,[61] and among his papers which the police impounded was a document setting out the duties and obligations of members of "The Circle" (see pp. 388–391). "The Circle," this document stated, was to be confined "to persons who are trained and engaged in political revolution as a profession"; members bound themselves to "accept the Leadership of Kwame Nkrumah," to fast on the twenty-first day of each month, and to meditate daily on "the cause THE CIRCLE stands for"; they were also to take an oath on their "life honour and fortunes . . . [to] live up to the aims and aspirations" of the society, "and that if I dare to divulge any secrets, plans and movements of THE CIRCLE, or betray a member brother or the cause, or use the influence of THE CIRCLE for my own personal interests or advertisement, I do so at my own risk and peril." If we had come upon this document at the time of its composition, we would have taken it to be a childish daydream of absolute power, the very fancifulness of its terms indicating a failure to understand and therefore to control the actual world of politics. But as the sequel showed not long afterward, such a judgment was itself badly mistaken. Mistaken not in thinking of such a scheme as a dream, but in assuming that the dikes of reality are always efficacious against dreams of this kind.

The poet Rimbaud, describing the nature and method of poetic inspiration, declares that the poet "makes himself a *seer* through a long, immense and systematic *derangement* of the senses." This characteristically romantic description of the poetic quest illuminates also the quest for political power as we observe it in cases like Nkrumah's. His power to transform himself, so to speak in the twinkling of an eye, from an anonymous denizen of London into the absolute master of a whole country, and to subvert and overthrow what seemed the solid and tangible reality of British rule, seems to partake of magic, to be indeed the outcome of a self-induced hallucination with which the political seer then proceeds to infect his victims. The systematic derangement of the senses of which Rimbaud speaks is sometimes clearly seen in the personal lives of political leaders, sometimes in the style of their political activity and sometimes in the behavior which they induce in their followers. In his *Young India*, which we have had occasion to mention above, Gandhi describes the method of passive resistance for which he later gained worldwide fame. One of the requisites in a passive resister, says Gandhi, is chastity: "A man who is unchaste loses stamina, becomes emasculated and cowardly. He whose mind is given over to animal passion is not capable of any great effort. This," he asserts, "can be proved by innumerable instances." What, then, are married persons to do? "When a husband and wife gratify the passions," answers Gandhi, "it is no less an animal indulgence on that account. Such an indulgence, except for perpetuating the race, is strictly prohibited. But a passive resister has to avoid even that very limited indulgence, because he can have no desire for progeny. A married man, therefore," he concluded, "can observe perfect chastity." The Mahatma, who had been married at a young age, applied his doctrine to his own life and in 1906, at the age of thirty-seven, vowed to abstain from all sexual relations. He went further; in order to test his resolution he conducted "experiments": "I was informed," writes Nirmal Kumar Bose, one of his close followers, "that he sometimes asked women to share his bed and even the cover which he used, and then tried to ascertain if even the least trace of sensual feeling had been evoked in himself or his companion."

Bose was disturbed by these "experiments" because of their deleterious effects on Gandhi's women disciples, some of whom "regarded Gandhiji as their private possession" and became emotionally unbalanced. But when he questioned Gandhi on the subject of these "experiments," the Mahatma stated: "I have believed in woman's perfect equality with man. My wife was 'inferior' when she was the instrument of my lust. She ceased to be that when she lay naked with me as my sister. If she and I were not lustfully agitated in our minds and bodies, the contact raised both of us.

"Should there be a difference if it is not my wife, as she once was, but some other sister? I do hope you will acquit me of having any lustful designs upon women or girls who have been naked with me. A's or B's hysteria had nothing to do with my experiment, I hope."[62]

It is only the armed prophet, Machiavelli tells us, who can hope to found a new polity: the Mahatma, prophet of a new India, was armed with passive resistance, which, for all its passivity, was just as powerful as more usual and mundane armories. And it was in order to perfect this weapon, we must remember, that the Mahatma conducted these "experiments" in chastity, which like Rimbaud's vastly different experiments may also with equal justice be called an immense and systematic derangement of the senses.

But Gandhi is clearly exceptional. He went further and was more systematic in exploring the hidden unpolitical sources of political power. Others are mostly content with a more superficial understanding, which in practice, however, can prove equally efficient. "I tell you frankly," exclaimed the Indonesian nationalist Sukarno in a speech of 1960, "that I belong to that group of people who are bound in spiritual longing by the romanticism of revolution. I am inspired by it. I am fascinated by it. I am crazed, I am obsessed by the romanticism of revolution. . . . Come, then, keep fanning the flames of the leaping fire of revolution! Brothers and sisters, let us become logs to feed the flames of revolution." This obsession with the romanticism of revolution is what we most frequently encounter among nationalists, an obsession which seizes them, which is cultivated by them, and which is communicated to their followers. Tekin Alp, whose doctrine we discussed above, came from Salonika and was therefore well acquainted with nationalist ardor as it manifested itself in the Macedonian cockpit in all its variety and intensity. In a pamphlet on *The Turkish and Pan-Turkish Ideal* which he published during World War I, he has a chapter on the "The Idealists" whose example he recommends to the Turks:

First let us take the case of a young Bulgarian. He came of a wealthy family and was therefore pampered and indulged in every possible way by his parents. Up to the age of 30 he studies at the University. Does he then move to a luxuriously appointed lawyer's office in Salonica, surrounded by all the most modern comforts? No! His office is in the mountains, his desk is a rock, his pen a gun and dagger, and his clients Turkish gendarmes and Greek robber bands upon whom he passes sentence of death without much ceremony.

Another illustration. The young man has studied medicine in a European University, and returns home with his doctor's degree. Will he now declare war on the microbes and the thousands of diseases which assail human life? No, indeed! He wanders, armed to the teeth, from village to village, from mountain to mountain, dispensing out his only medicine, those death-dealing blue pills, to all the opponents of his ideal, and even to those of his own countrymen who do not share his ideas.

A third picture is afforded by a professor of the highest philosophical attainments. Does he establish a centre of training in Athens, Bucharest, Sofia or Belgrade? No again! In secluded villages such as Grebena and Dikvesh, etc., he instils the Irredenta principles into the minds of the village children, and prepares them to sacrifice life and fortune for this ideal.

During the last few years the prisons of Salonica and Monastir have been filled with a curious class of men. The dark dungeon cells do not hide thieves or ordinary criminals, but chiefly doctors, lawyers, professors, and similar idealists.[63]

And it is doctors, lawyers, professors, and similar idealists who can most appreciate and savor the sophisticated emotions which are the concomitant of political murder. In 1910 a Muslim apothecary in Cairo, Wardany, killed the Coptic Prime Minister of Egypt because he suspected him of subservience to the British.

He was caught, tried, and condemned to death, and the official report of his last days in prison is an illuminating document. (See pp. 392–397.) We learn that he was allowed to retain a few books in his possession which included Bagehot's *English Constitution*, Rousseau's *Contrat Social*, and the Qur'an. "During the early part of his imprisonment, before his condemnation, he was found to have engraved some writings in French and Arabic on the binding of one of these books with a tag of his boot-lace. One of these writings consisted of a series of headings for chapters, such as, Book 1, Chapter I, 'Aperçu du premier Gouvernement'; II 'Démocratie'; III 'Communauté'; IV 'Eléments Sociaux et Politiques.' Book 2, Chapter I, 'Chambre des Députés'; II 'Sénat'; III 'Prince'; IV 'Ministre'; V 'Administration'; etc. When questioned on the subject, the prisoner admitted that these were chapters of a work he intended to compose and which was to be called 'La Constitution d'un Gouvernement Musulman.' "

Wardany and Tekin Alp's "Idealists" are usually called intellectuals. Ideas attract and captivate them, and ideas lead to this derangement of the senses whereby the murder of a minister and the study of Bagehot not only belong to the same universe but somehow also entail one another. But these terrible ideas do not remain confined to the circle of the intellectuals. With the spread of literacy, they reach strata of the population which are generally innocent of intellectual pursuits, and the results they produce are disconcerting and terrifying. An example of this diffusion and of its consequences we may see in the case of Damodar Hari Chapekar. A Chitpavan Brahmin, like Tilak, Damodar Hari Chapekar was the son of a poor itinerant reader of sacred hymns. His education seems to have been largely traditional, but as his autobiography shows he was clearly touched by Tilak's glorification of the Mahratta Empire and of the Peshwas, the Brahmin mayors of the palace who became its effective rulers for many decades until the British extended their rule over the Deccan. His mind is clearly filled with fancies of past greatness, and of resentment against the British for depriving him of his rightful inheritance, and for thwarting his attempts to escape from his present lowly condition. It is only when his application to join the Indian Army, where he hoped to gain glory, is turned down that his hostility to the British is confirmed: "This was," he tells us, "the first and most potent cause of the enmity between the English and ourselves." Damodar Hari Chapekar seems also to have imbibed from Tilak's campaign a hatred of Western habits, ideas, and education. "We are of the opinion," he also tells us, "that the loss of our physical strength is partly to be laid at the door of this Mlenchha* learning. The entire society has devoted itself to education and become much too thoughtful, and thereby has lost manliness"; and again: "The educated are invariably addicted to vice. This may probably be the effect of a liberal education." Statements such as these, which abound in his autobiography, show this terrorist to have been not naïvely traditional but rather deeply touched by the rhetoric of traditionalism as it was purveyed in the vernacular press by Western-educated politicians. For a terrorist Damodar Hari Chapekar finally became. In 1897 the plague broke out in Poona; in order to enforce a minimum of sanitation and limit the ravages of the disease, the authorities organized searches throughout the city to discover and remove the dead and dying. These sanitary activities were denounced in the nationalist press as an act of oppression, and the authorities were accused of using the epidemic as a pretext for looting and violating the privacy of Hindu homes. Damodar Hari Chapekar therefore decided to exact revenge for these insults and oppressions. Together with his brother, he ambushed Mr. Rand, the official who had directed the measures against the plague, and murdered him just as he was leaving an official celebration in honor of Queen Victoria's Golden Jubilee. He was subsequently apprehended and while awaiting trial dictated an autobiography—surely a classic in the literature—copious extracts from which are given on pp. 398–461.

Dedan Kimathi's history is as arresting as Damodar Hari Chapekar's. This tough and ruthless leader of a Mau Mau gang had been born a bastard and, perhaps in consequence, seems to have entertained from his adolescence onward a belief in his own

* I.e., foreign (with highly pejorative connotations).

special destiny. He believed that Ngai—the Kikuyu god—had chosen him to be the head of his tribe: "He dreamed of lands where all the cows were brown; of places in the sky where rows of people sat on wooden benches; of death being like a gate which opened and shut; of rivers running uphill; of people standing before him in white clothes with arms outstretched, and of Ngai speaking to him in his sleep."[64] With the Mau Mau outbreak he became an oath administrator and subsequently escaped into the forest, where he organized and directed a gang of terrorists, for whom he wrote a kind of *Mein Kampf* and whom he dominated with his "magnetic, compelling, irresistible" oratory. He dreamed that he was the "popular Prime Minister of the Southern Hemisphere," at a jungle ceremony dubbed himself K.C.A.E., i.e., Knight Commander of the African Empire, and took the title of "Prime Minister Sir Dedan Kimathi." As government forces began increasingly to harass him and his gang, he grew morbidly and murderously suspicious of his own followers and of terrorists who did not belong to his gang. He appointed himself "Dictator of Justice"; executions became his amusement and killing his sole interest. Just before his capture he dreamed a dream in which he was invested with utter and absolute godlike power: "As I was sleeping," he later told his interrogators, "I felt someone hold my hand. I woke up and heard God say to me, 'My son, come with me.' I stood up, and Ngai took me by my right hand and we walked through a most beautiful forest where there were many red and yellow flowers and big birds with green wings. There were also many big rocks out of which clear springs were flowing. And Ngai took me to a mugumo (wild fig) tree which was bigger and higher than all the other wild fig trees in the forest, a tree that was like the father of all trees. And I rested my hand upon it. When I did that, Ngai spoke to me again and said, 'This is my house in this forest, and here I will guard you.' Then the tree came up out of the ground and went up into the clouds and I did not see it again."

Dedan Kimathi's world seems a world *à rebours*, an evil and nightmarish simulation of the "real" world, with its flesh and blood knight commanders and its tangible prime ministers. But we can easily imagine his fantasies enacted in "reality"; not only in the twilight world of the forest, which for his followers, sweating in terror of his murderous will, was indeed the only reality; but also in the broad daylight world of us all, which not so long ago suffered, with little resistance, the enactment of Hitler's similar fantasies. Dedan Kimathi had something of the essential evil in him; at the age of fifteen he was befriended by an old man who later caught him stealing and chased him away: this old man years later became, at eighty, one of the first victims of the Mau Mau outbreak. It was this outbreak which triggered off, activated, and gave scope to Dedan Kimathi's propensity for evil. Without Mau Mau he might have lived and died a small-time Nairobi thug.

It was as an administrator of Mau Mau oaths that, as we recall, he began his career of political terrorism. The administration of oaths was an essential part of Mau Mau and the mechanism by which members were enrolled and compelled to obey the leaders of the movement.[65] Oaths form an essential part of Kikuyu religion and social behavior. In their legitimate form they are used in initiation ceremonies by which the young are inducted into adult society, in economic transactions, and in judicial ordeals. These oaths are charged for the Kikuyu with a noumenal quality; they were "so terribly feared morally and religiously," wrote Kenyatta in *Facing Mount Kenya*, "that no one dared to take them unless he was perfectly sure and beyond any doubt that he was innocent or that his claim was genuine." It is clear that the binding force of these oaths lies in the fact that they are taken under the aegis of the ancestral spirits of the tribe, who oversee their performance and punish their nonperformance. These legitimate oathing ceremonies, as we also learn from Kenyatta, have an illegitimate, a black counterpart, the ceremonies, namely, of Destructive Magic. These ceremonies are conducted by wizards in "great secrecy and terror." Those taking part meet at "dead hours of the night" and are not allowed to wear any clothing. In these conclaves the wizards, or *arogi*, manufacture *orogi*, or magic poison, which among other ingredients requires the genital organs of both male and female humans, their breasts, tongues, ears, hands and feet, blood, eyes, and noses. The Mau Mau oathings were a nicely—we may perhaps say, scientifically—graded series in which black magic became gradually predominant, but which began by being adaptations, or perhaps perversions, of legitimate public oathings. The first Mau Mau oath as it is described to us by a Kikuyu participant, J.M. Kariuki (see pp. 462–471), was clearly designed to reproduce the strong religious emotions which initiation and circumcision ceremonies seem to evoke in Kikuyu youth. Thus Kariuki tells us that the participants in the first Mau Mau oath began by passing under an arch made of banana stems. This is exactly the kind of arch under which young Kikuyus walked to symbolize their entry into the full membership of the tribe. Indeed, the feelings which this Mau Mau ceremony aroused Kariuki describes in religious terms: "My emotions during the ceremony had been a mixture of fear and elation. Afterwards in the maize I felt exalted with a new spirit of power and strength. All my previous life seemed empty and meaningless. Even my education, of which I was so proud, appeared trivial beside this splendid and terrible force that had been given me. I had been born again. . . . The other three in the maize were all silent and were clearly undergoing the same spiritual rebirth as myself." As Corfield observes, this first oath of initiation into Mau Mau differed from the usual initiation oath only in that it was administered at night, that it could be forcibly administered, and also administered to women.[66] Both the similarity and the differences—which were clearly deliberate—were as clearly meant at the same time to bind members by a strong religious tie and to separate them from the rest of the community by the very secrecy and anomalousness of the rite.

The first Mau Mau oath bound the participants to go forward to fight for the land taken by the Europeans. But Kariuki also tells us of a second, or *Batuni,* oath, which he also took subsequently and which bound him to kill the enemy, whether this enemy were a European or "my father and mother, my brother or sister." The ceremonies held at the *Batuni* oathing have curious similarities with the Destructive Magic as described in Kenyatta's treatise. Kariuki was instructed to squat naked in front of the oath administrator. "He told me to take the thorax of the goat which had been skinned, to put my penis through a hole that had been made in it, and to hold the rest of it in my left hand in front of me. Before me on the ground there were two small wooden stakes between which the thorax (*ngata*) of the goat was suspended and fastened. By my right hand on the floor of the hut were seven small sticks each about four inches long. Biniathi told me to take the sticks one at a time, to put them into the *ngata*, and slowly rub them in it while repeating after him . . . seven vows, one for each stick. (After each promise I was to bite the meat and throw the stick on to the ground on my left side.)" After every promise the oath-taker vowed that if he broke his undertaking, then

> May this oath kill me
> May this he-goat kill me
> May this seven kill me,
> May this meat kill me.

It would seem that there was a whole gradation of these *Batuni* oaths, each more bestial and horrible than the other, requiring ingredients like human flesh, sperm, and menstrual blood and involving public sexual intercourse with animals. These ceremonies were a parody of religious rites and, like the European Black Mass, derived their power over the participants from the fact that they enjoined practices which, for the legitimate religion, were sacrilege and desecration. The purpose of these practices was to bind together the participants in a secret brotherhood of desperadoes, to cut them off from ordinary society, with its restraints and decencies, and thus make them into a frightful and formidable political weapon.

Mau Mau, it is clear, builds on and exploits the traditional institutions and religion of the Kikuyus. But in Mau Mau the tradition, used for political mobilization, is no longer itself;

rather it becomes a mere weapon used to realize a peculiarly European vision. This vision may be summed up exactly in Nkrumah's parody of the Sermon on the Mount: "Seek ye first the political kingdom and all things shall be added unto you."[67] It is for the sake of the millennial political kingdom that the Mau Mau oathings and rites were devised and administered. The same assumptions, invented and spread by Europe, underlie Kenyatta's lyrical defense of cliterodectomy. This defense is not put up by a traditional elder, for whom cliterodectomy is so much a part of the natural order that its defense would be superfluous; it is, we must not forget, the invention of a student of anthropology, for whom contact with Europe has opened up new possibilities of action, influence, and power. European influence is apparent in the—deliberate—transformation of a purely indigenous religion such as that of the Kikuyu; it is perhaps even more apparent when the traditional native religion is superseded and replaced by one introduced and propagated by Europeans —namely, Christianity. While Christian missionary effort has had little effect in the Muslim world or in India or the Far East, the case is otherwise in Africa south of the Sahara. Here Christianity was generally introduced to the African tribesman simultaneously with European domination and the modern cash economy. The new religion, therefore, has provided a hope and a consolation amidst the painful strains and stresses of rapid and drastic change. But it has also sometimes reinforced and complicated the disturbance created by Europe. Christianity in the African's mind was necessarily associated with the European, and sooner or later the Christian message was bound to be contrasted with the behavior of those who propagated the message; Christianity, again, by its appeal to women and to the young, worked a disruption of the traditional tribal hierarchy in a way in which its rival, Islam, so clearly a man's religion, did not. Also in contrast to Islam, Christianity, in forbidding polygamy, set itself up in radical opposition to tribal institutions.[68] The disturbance created by the preaching of Christianity by Europeans at a time when European economic and political activity was subjecting traditional social structures to intolerable strains may be illustrated by a passage from a pamphlet written in 1911 by a Negro Seventh Day Adventist: "There is too much failure among all Europeans in Nyasaland. The three combined bodies, Missionaries, Government and Companies, or gainers of money," affirmed the writer, Charles Domingo, "do form the same rule to look upon the native with mockery eyes. It sometimes startles us to see that the three combined bodies are from Europe, and along with them there is a title 'CHRISTENDOM.' And to compare or make a comparison between the MASTER of the title and his servants it pushes an African away from believing the Master of the title. If we had power enough to communicate ourselves to Europe we would advise them not to call themselves 'Christendom' but 'Europeandom.' Therefore the life of the three combined bodies is altogether too cheaty, too thefty, too mockery. Instead of 'give' they say 'Take away from.' From 6 a.m. to 5 or 6 p.m. there is too much breakage of God's pure law as seen in James Epistle, v. 4."⁶⁹

That Christianity, a hope and a promise, should be preached by Europeans who were also the agents of so much disruption and destruction seemed to the Negro a scandal and a paradox. One way of resolving the paradox was by forming churches in which the white man would have no share. This is the so-called Ethiopianism prevalent among the Bantus and other Negro groups. The appellation "Ethiopian" derives from Psalm 68:31, in which it is said that "Ethiopia shall soon stretch out her hands unto God." By the European missionaries this was taken to be a promise of the coming evangelization of Africa; while those whom they sought to convert took it to signify the institution of purely Negro churches and the election of the Negro in preference to the white for the enjoyment of divine favor either in this world or hereafter. In Ethiopian doctrine the Black Christ stands at the gate of Heaven to admit the Blacks and turn away the whites. Whites have corrupted the Cross and made it a sign of the white race; in the words of a Negro preacher in South Africa: "God is a good God. But he is not a European. Anyone who says that is a fool. Jesus has never set foot on the soil of Europe or America or Australia. But—Jesus has been in

Africa."[70] As part of his ideology, Garvey advocated the adoption of a religion which would show God "made in our own image—black." The chaplain-general of his United Negro Improvement Association became the head of an African Orthodox Church and urged Garveyites to "forget the White Gods." "Erase the white gods from your hearts," he told his congregation, "we must go back to the native church, to our own true God."

The "Ethiopian" reaction to Christian missionary effort sometimes is transformed into an utter rejection of the symbols of Christianity and an assertion that the Negroes have their own prophets and their own Messiah to take the place of Jesus and scriptural revelation. Bishop Sundkler quotes an adaptation by a Zulu Messiah of the well-known Negro spiritual "Were you there/When they crucified my Lord?" which runs as follows:

> Is it that you are Jews
> Are you not Zulus?
> Were you there when they crucified their Lord?

He also quotes the words of an African social worker on the Rand which may be taken to provide a rationale for this significant and fundamental change in the words of the hymn and in its significance: "There is no nation without a God. Each nation," affirmed Bishop Sundkler's informant, "maybe has to have its own God. The only one who could bring about a change in our situation would be a great Bantu prophet who would be prepared to suffer like Christ did."[71] Such a comment brings out and emphasizes the political implications of these African prophets and messiahs. But it is not so much among the South African Bantus whom Bishop Sundkler studied that these implications are best illustrated. Rather, we may find Messianic movements in the Congo for our purpose more apt and more illuminating. This area, which until very recently was administered by the Belgians and the French, saw the appearance of messiahs around whom a religio-political movement grew and flourished in the last few decades. In the Belgian Congo, Simon

Kimbangu (?1889–1950) in 1921 claimed to be divinely inspired and to have healing powers. He gathered a large and devoted following, and the Belgian authorities, alarmed by the possibility of anti-European disorders, immediately arrested and tried him. He was condemned to death, but the sentence was commuted to life imprisonment, and he in fact died in prison. In the nineteen-twenties and -thirties, Simon Kimbangu became the center of a cult with many followers in the Congo, the adepts of which believed that the Prophet (*ngunza*) will soon return to lead his fellow Africans to salvation. In 1939 another native of the Belgian Congo, Simon-Pierre Mpadi, after a period of membership in the Salvation Army, founded his own independent religious movement, the adherents of which—possibly in imitation of the Salvation Army—wore a khaki uniform. Mpadi's movement was thus known as Dibundu dia Khaki, the khaki congregation. The Khaki movement is devoted to the veneration of Kimbangu, the Messiah who will come to give the blacks power and dominion. The fourth article of a creed used in a Khaki congregation in Pointe-Noire (in what was French Equatorial Africa) declares that Kimbangu "is the sacred scepter of dominion, which the Lord God has given to the black race that it may have dominion through it. He is the ruler's rod of the blacks"; while the thirteenth article emphasizes the sacral quality of this earthly dominion, for it declares that Kimbangu "is the open door that the Lord God has opened among the black race that they may enter by it. It is the city of the new Jerusalem, the Jerusalem of the blacks and God's very holiest city. He is the door through which they enter the heaven of their God." (See pp. 472–476.)

A similar cult and legend grew round André Matswa (1899–1942), who originated from the French Congo. After service in the French Army, where he attained noncommissioned rank, Matswa went to Paris, where he frequented extreme left-wing circles and founded a mutual aid association for his fellow Congolese, the "Amicale Balali." Through emissaries and intermediaries he began collecting funds for his association, but these activities aroused the suspicions of the authorities, who arrested and tried him, together with three of his followers. They were sentenced to three years' imprisonment and ten years' exile. The trial—at Brazzaville in 1930—was followed by a popular uprising in which the cry "Kill the Whites" was heard. Like Kimbangu, Matswa has become the center of a cult with its dogmas, rites, and ceremonies; with priests, bishops, and a pope. A photograph of Matswa is placed in front of a chest, which is used as an altar-screen and surrounded by flowers and lighted candles. Wednesday is their weekly day of rest, and the most important celebration of public worship—an imitation of the Mass—takes place on Friday night. To his followers, Matswa was the Messiah: "The whites may perhaps have killed him," his adherents believe, "but he has risen again, and one day he shall return in power and majesty to drive away the whites and their Black troops." Again, in the words of a follower: "Matswa André will come. He will come to save the people from their misery . . . especially from their slavery, for now we are slaves. Today we are slaves, but on the day when Matswa André comes we shall have part in his power and dominion. Yes, then he will in truth rule here, and then the whites must return to their country. And there they may rule themselves, but over us blacks Matswa André shall rule." In due course the cult of Kimbangu and the cult of Matswa were joined in some areas of the Congo in a syncretism in which both Messiahs were invoked and worshiped as in this prayer:

God of Abraham, God of Isaac and God of Jacob, God of Simon Kimbangu and God of Matswa André, when shall we receive the blessing and be free? Thou shalt no more hear the prayers of the whites, for thou hast heard them for a long time and they have received blessing enough. Hear now us. Amen.[72]

Prophetism in South Africa and the Congo is a direct Negro reaction to the preaching of Christian love by Europeans whose ways were clearly not the ways of love and whose presence spelled disturbance, violence, and disruption. But as has been seen, European—and of course American—Christianity was, in some of its many variants, itself emphatically millennial, and it is of some interest to observe the effects of this millennial type of Christianity on native society and behavior. Millennial Christianity came to Africa principally through the agency of the Watch Tower Bible and Tract Society, the forerunner of today's Jehovah's Witnesses.[73] The tenets of the Watch Tower Society were elaborated in the United States by Charles Taze Russell (1852–1916) in a series of books the titles of which are indicative of their tendency and content: *The Divine Plan of the Ages, The Time is at Hand, Thy Kingdom Come, The Battle of Armageddon,* etc. In the Watch Tower scheme of salvation, the Second Coming of Christ is imminent, the present is the time of tribulation which must precede the Coming, and most human governments and churches are in the hands of wicked men, Satan's following and emissaries. "The Devil's organization," said a Watch Tower publication current in the nineteen-thirties, "is made up principally of those that rule and that are called the official part of the nation. This government is represented under the symbol of 'beast.' " "Under the righteous rule of Christ," the same publication affirmed, "there will be no officials who will collect money by taxation and then loan that money to the farmer with a view to making the farmer a serf. There will no more be the harsh and oppressive government agents to browbeat and put in fear the people and harshly judge and misuse them." "The 'Beast,' " another publication of the same period asserted, "is Satan's organization on earth, particularly in the 7th head thereof, to wit, the 7th World Power, which is Great Britain." The millennial hope, it is clear from these quotations, went hand in hand with an outspoken and radical attack on established institutions, religious and political. Watch Tower literature, distributed in Africa, whether in English or in African dialects, stressed the oppressive character of European rule and the violence and corruption of European *mores.* A commission set up by the British Government to investigate disturbances which broke out in the Rhodesian Copperbelt in 1935 took pains to describe some of this literature and the form in which it was disseminated among Africans. The cover of one pamphlet, *Escape to the Kingdom,* represented "four elderly Europeans lying on the ground in a dying condition. Blood is streaming from one or two of them, and it is obvious that they had been cut down by a flaming sword which drips with blood. The sword appears from the upper part of the cover and is held by a purple hand. There is a young European with outstretched arms, who appears to be escaping from the general destruction of the scene. The rest of the picture is of flames, explosions and smoke. . . ." The cover of another pamphlet, entitled *Universal War Near*, shows "four people quarreling over a prone body. One of them is a fat, gross-looking European in a dress suit and top hat with a hunting crop in his hand. The second is a gross-looking European in a frock coat and top hat with a bag of money. The third is an European apache with a drawn dagger in his hand. The fourth is a fat, gross-looking bishop with a miter. Over them is a sword dripping with blood, and on it is written 'For Jehovah and Gideon.' The devil in the form of a black angel is apparently cheering on the disputants. . . ." Yet another Watch Tower tract, *Vindication*, showed on its cover "a group of soldiers marching past a platform, being blessed by a clergyman. Upon the platform are two very stout men who are intended to repel by their grossness. This picture is described at the foot as 'Religious Fornication.'" The commission went on to illustrate the African reaction to Watch Tower teaching by quoting the testimony of a district officer, one of many to the same effect. This district officer while on tour in an area inhabited by a primitive tribe found that as a consequence of Watch Tower teaching in the district the authority of the tribal chief was "completely nullified" and that his own messengers met with opposition "and very rude things had been said to them as Government Messengers. I believe they were called servants of Satan, and things of that nature, and were told that they had no right to come to the villages." The district officer found that it was the women who had imbibed this teaching most. They were "impossible. One could get no reason from them in any way—one could not get them to talk sense. What they had been told they had been told, and that was the limit of their thinking." They had been told "that Armageddon was coming, that God would provide, and all that sort of thing, and they were not taking any care of their

crops and they were not planting." Facing continued recalci-
trance, the district officer sent a native detective to find out what
was happening, but he was eventually recognized and told: "You
can go back and tell that Satan who sent you that the walls of
his gaol will fall." It was the commission's considered judgment
that "the teachings and literature of the Watch Tower bring civil
and spiritual authority, especially native authority, into contempt; that it is a dangerously subversive movement; and that
it is an important predisposing cause of the recent disturbances."[74] The effect of Watch Tower teaching and prophecy was
seen not only in these Copperbelt disturbances of 1935 but in
another more significant and instructive episode, the Chilembwe
rebellion of 1915 in Nyasaland. John Chilembwe (?1871–1915),
a Yao from Nyasaland, was in 1892 taken into the service of
Joseph Booth (1851–1932), who had a long and varied religious
and missionary career in Africa. Booth was the author of a book,
Africa for the Africans (1897), a radical protest against the oppression and maltreatment of the Negroes by whites—planters,
governments, and missionaries. It was Booth also who, after
1907, introduced Watch Tower doctrine and literature into Central Africa. By then he had ceased to have any contact with
Chilembwe. Booth had taken him on a visit to the United States
in 1897, and Chilembwe had attended a Negro Baptist Seminary
in Virginia, whence in 1900 he returned to Nyasaland and
founded the Providence Industrial Mission. In 1915, with a few
helpers and followers he rose in a pitifully ineffective rebellion
which achieved nothing but the murder of a few Europeans.
What led Chilembwe to this sudden, seemingly uncharacteristic
outbreak remains quite obscure, but it is not fanciful to suppose
that Booth's ideas and Pastor Russell's prophecies, which were
known in Nyasaland, worked on him and on his followers and
led them to believe that rebellion was not only righteous but also
timely. For it is a fact that Pastor Russell taught that Jesus had
returned invisibly to earth in 1874, but he prophesied that "the
full end of 'Gentile Times'" would not be seen before October,
1914, and that "The time of trouble or 'day of wrath' which
began October 1874 . . . will cease about 1915."[75] The European

war breaking out in the summer of 1914 must have seemed the fulfillment of Pastor Russell's prophecy. Following the rebellion, a commission of inquiry was set up, and many witnesses testified before it to the fact that millennial expectations and Watch Tower prophecies worked powerfully on Chilembwe's mind and convinced his followers that the appointed hour for the triumph of the righteous over the unrighteous was now come. A native minister of the Church of Scotland Mission, Rev. Stephen Kundecha, described how a little while before the rebellion Chilembwe quoted to him John 8:32: "And ye shall know the truth and the truth shall make you free," and how Chilembwe refused to say what he meant by it remarking: "I shall not be able to explain all to you, because you do not make friendship." Another witness, Rev. Harry Kambwiri of the same mission, told how Chilembwe had asked him "if I know about the first and second resurrection, I could not tell him about it, and then he brought in a blue book, and read from it, and said the first resurrection is freedom from bondage and slavery. And then he said the second resurrection is the future resurrection, and then he said all the Europeans have risen from the first resurrection, and that the natives have not risen from it. I asked him 'How,' and he said 'Because we are ruled by Europeans.' Then he said 'When we shall be free from their rule then we have risen.' " Elliot Kamwana, through whom Joseph Booth first introduced Watch Tower teachings into Nyasaland, also appeared before ᵗhe commission and was examined about a correspondence he had with Chilembwe after August, 1914. In this correspondence he likened the British authorities to Babylon—in obvious reference to the Book of Revelation—and told Chilembwe that between 1914 and 1915 the powers that be would be swept away. He also quoted to him Daniel 2:44: "And in the days of these Kings shall the God of Heaven set up a kingdom which shall never be destroyed: and the kingdom shall not be left to other people, but it shall break in pieces and consume all these kingdoms and it shall stand for ever." Yet another witness, Rev. A.M. Anderson, testified that shortly after the outbreak of war he heard that great excitement prevailed among the followers of Simon Kadewere, one of the leaders of the subsequent rebellion: "In view of the end of the world," he reported, "Simon was exhorting them to eat up their fowls and goats and get baptized at once or they would be lost. Simon and his teachers were carrying spears presumably as symbols of their aggressiveness but at the same time they said they would be required for use against Satan's people—(a term used vaguely). The coming of the end was proved by the fact that wars had come which were according to the Gospel to be one sign of the end."[76]

Mau Mau, Ethiopianism, the cult of Black Messiahs, and the popularity of millenarian varieties of Christianity alike testify to the disturbance and disorientation which contact with Europe brought and which practices and beliefs of this kind promised to assuage and relieve. All of these cults have either been consciously utilized for political ends—as with Mau Mau—or have led their adepts—as in the case of the Watch Tower—to accept the dangers of rebellion. But this religious fervor, this thirst for fulfillment, can also be satisfied directly by a political cause, and the political leader who can capture and channel to his advantage these strong and turbulent emotions disposes of a formidable, a deadly weapon. Many leaders have not only recognized this by attempting to become the focus of the intense yearnings and the blind devotion of their mass following, but have actually in their own writings explained and elucidated the origin and character of their power. For a description which is a model of its kind we are indebted to the Kenyan leader Tom Mboya (see pp. 477–487). "A nationalist movement," he tells us, "should mean the mobilization of all available groups of people in the country for the single struggle. This mobilization is based on a simplification of the struggle into certain slogans and into one distinct idea which everyone can understand without arguing about the details of policy or of governmental program after Independence." This mobilization requires a symbol, and "in many cases," he goes on, "the symbol is the national leader himself, and it is necessary to have this kind of symbol of an heroic father-figure if you are to have unquestioning discipline among the different groups and personalities who should rally their followers behind him. The national leader needs an organization whose pattern allows him to lead and also to impose discipline and demand action whenever it is necessary. This must therefore be a mass movement taking in everybody and anybody." The nationalist movement in Kenya in fact illustrates very well the religious aura which is made to surround the leader from whom the masses await salvation. The hymnbooks of the Kenya African Union in the days of the anti-British struggle presented Jomo Kenyatta as one enjoying special divine favor and inspiration. In passages deliberately echoing the Bible the hymnbooks described how God "told Kenyatta in a vision 'You shall multiply as the stars of heaven, nations will be blessed because of you.' And Kenyatta believed him and God swore to it by his mighty power"; "Kenyatta will find happiness before God," the hymn goes on, "for he is the foundation stone of the kingdom. He has patiently suffered pain in his heart, he is moreover the Judge of the Kikuyu and will dispense justice over the House of Mumbi." Again, one of the hymns, set to the tune of "Jesus Will Come," speaks of "Jomo Kenyatta, son of man"; yet another political hymn parodies "What are you waiting for? Come to Jesus now," and still another is a skit on the hymn "I Trust in the Blood of Jesus."[77] This exploitation of familiar religious images and associations seems—not surprisingly—to have continued after Kenyatta's victory over the British. In a dispatch printed in *The Times* of London on October 18, 1965, its Nairobi correspondent stated that a Roman Catholic priest told a congregation of 5,000 that President Kenyatta had been given special powers by God "to lead Kenya from political darkness to unextinguishable light." This priest also said that Mr. Kenyatta's government was like the Church of Christ—it derived its ministerial powers to administer justice from God. This statement was in celebration of Kenyatta Day, commemorating the President's release from nine years' detention imposed by the same authorities who subsequently made over their power to him. A highlight of this celebration was to be "a last supper" to symbolize "Mr. Kenyatta's last meal before being arrested by the British, but because of an outcry from the Christian Council of Churches and other religious bodies it is now likely," the correspondent informs us, "to be renamed simply 'a supper.' "

In the Gold Coast, again, the Convention People's Party parodied the traditional phraseology of Christianity in order to invest Nkrumah with a religious aura and to harness religious emotions to his cause. Consider this imitation of the Apostles' Creed printed in a party newspaper under the title, "A Verandah Boy's Creed":

> I believe in the Convention People's Party
> The opportune Saviour of Ghana,
> And in Kwame Nkrumah its founder and leader,
> Who is endowed with the Ghana Spirit,
> Born a true Ghanaian for Ghana;
> Suffering under victimizations;
> Was vilified, threatened with deportation;
> He disentangled himself from the clutches of the U.G.C.C.*
> And the same day he rose victorious with the 'verandah boys,'
> Ascended the Political Heights,
> And sitteth at the Supreme head of the C.P.P.**
> From whence he shall demand Full Self-government for Ghana.

Or this version of the Beatitudes printed in the same newspaper:

> Blessed are they who are imprisoned for Self-government's sake: for theirs is the freedom of this land.
> Blessed are ye, when men shall vilify you, and persecute you, and say all things of evil against you, for Convention's People's Party's sake.[78]

Nkrumah's own autobiography provides striking and graphic instances of the effects of this technique. He describes, for instance, the fervor of the women members of his party and the high pitch to which it rose when he was in prison; at one party rally, one woman "who adopted the name of Ama Nkrumah ('Ama' being the female equivalent of 'Kwame') got up on the platform and ended a fiery speech by getting hold of a blade and

* United Gold Coast Convention.
** Convention People's Party.

slashing her face. Then, smearing the blood over her body, she challenged the men present to do likewise in order to show that no sacrifice was too great in their united struggle for freedom and independence."[79]

Another passage in Nkrumah's autobiography is also significant in this respect, for it describes and illustrates the emotional tie between leader and led in the kind of politics of which nationalism is a variant. Nkrumah tells us that at the public meeting where he broke with his original political associates and launched his own movement, "one of the women supporters jumped up on the platform and led the singing of the hymn 'Lead Kindly Light,'[80] a hymn which from that time has been sung at most C.P.P. rallies." "What with the strain of it all and the excitement," Nkrumah goes on, "the singing of this hymn was as much as I felt I could take. I covered my eyes with my handkerchief, a gesture that was followed by many others present."[81] These moments of shared emotion, in which a leader seems to play upon and to control the mass he is leading in exactly the same way in which a musician performs upon and has perfect mastery over his instrument, must give the leader the feeling of absolute power which an artist has over his material, an actor perhaps over his audience, or a seducer over his excited and infatuated victim. It is in such terms that we have to describe an experience which Nkrumah is not the only mass leader to describe. Thus, giving an account of the effect of Bourguiba's oratory on the Tunisian masses, a follower of his speaks of "a union in which the soul of the leader is mixed with the soul of the masses"; they experience the same emotions as he does, they are angry with his anger and even use their minds when he compels them to think.[82] Nehru's *Autobiography* also affords us a candid glimpse into the heady and violent pleasures of mass leadership: " 'Go to the villages' was the slogan, and we trudged many a mile across fields and addressed peasant meetings. I experienced the thrill of mass-feeling, the power of influencing the mass." He was once asked whether he did not feel proud of this hero-worship of the crowd; he answers: "I disliked it, and I wanted to run away from it, and yet I had got used to it, and when it was wholly absent, I rather missed it. Neither way brought satisfaction, but, on the whole, the crowd had filled some inner need of mine. The notion that I could influence them and move them to action gave me a sense of authority over their minds and hearts; and this satisfied, to some extent, my will to power."[83] This emotional link between leader and led, in which the leader satisfies to satiety his will to power and the led, in turn, feel at one with their master, fosters the pathetic fallacy, so profitable to rulers, that there is no difference between them and those whom they rule, that their interests, their preoccupations, their aims are exactly identical. In a word, that the political tie is not a public relation involving power and authority and law, but rather a private, amorous relation, in which the body politic is united by love, and ruler and ruled experience those

> Amorous languishments, luminous trances,
> Delicious deaths, soft exhalations
> Of soul; dear and divine annihilations

which the poet Crashaw associated with mystical experience. Aflaq, the ideologue of the Arab Ba'th Party, indeed envisages nationalism precisely as love. "The nationalism for which we call is love before everything else. It is the very same feeling that binds the individual to his family, because the fatherland is only a large household, and the nation a large family." Just as nationalism is love for Aflaq, so politics has its seat in those affective and obscure regions where originate our most powerful and least controllable impulses: "Any action," he writes in reference to politics, "that does not call forth in us living emotions and does not make us feel the spasm of love, the revulsion of hate, that does not make our blood race in our veins and our pulse beat faster is a sterile action."[84] Frantz Fanon, the ideologue of Algerian nationalism, is more explicit in his metaphors and actually likens the political tie to the intimacy of sexual congress; speaking of the intellectual's relation to the nation, he writes: "when, reaching the height of excitement at rut with his people. . . ."[85]

The pathetic fallacy fostered by the notion that politics is love is also nourished by a well-known feature of nationalism—the idea, namely, that a nation is known by its language, that the members of a nation must speak the same language. This emphasis on language derives from the belief that a language encapsulates the peculiar past of a nation which defines its present existence.[86] The idea that all members of a nation—and hence rulers and ruled also—must speak the same language was originally a corollary of the basic nationalist doctrine that humanity is naturally divided into nations which ought to be self-governing and that language is the supremely differentiating badge of a nation. But this idea—which is untenable—seems now to find less favor than other, more fashionable arguments. Thus, in a work mentioned above,[87] Professor Gellner has argued that modern society, in contrast to primitive and traditional societies, lacks structure, that communication within it is vitally important, and that in this structurally inchoate society where there is little connection between a man's function and his standing in society, it is a common culture which provides the means of communication, which defines a man's identity, and which becomes his passport to citizenship. Culture replaces structure, and a common culture requires linguistic homogeneity. The argument is ingenious, but it has many weak links. Even in modern society, structurally weak as it is, people are not only capable of communicating across cultural barriers, but also manage to coexist in a common political community despite differences in cultures; again, a common culture does not necessarily entail linguistic homogeneity. Another argument of Professor Gellner's is that modern societies have to be industrial and therefore have to be literate. In other words, the proletariat on the factory floor has to be given its marching orders. Since this proletariat is unable to be multilingual, therefore linguistic homogeneity is again necessary. But this argument seems to have little foundation. Large industrial enterprises have taken root and flourished in multilingual societies: in Bohemia and the United States in the nineteenth centuries; in Hong Kong, Israel, French Algeria, India, Ceylon, and Malaya in the twentieth.

A variant of this latter argument asserts that "Wherever the language of the government and the law differs from that of the mass of the people, plans for economic, agricultural and industrial development are more difficult to make . . . and more difficult to put into effect. Linguistic diversity therefore acts as a brake on economic progress."[88] What is asserted here is not that economic development is hindered by linguistic variety but only that "plans" for such development are made more difficult to formulate and to carry out. "Plans" in such a context imply governmental control and direction of the economy, and it is no doubt much easier for governments to direct and control homogeneous and uniform, rather than heterogeneous and diverse, societies. The argument for linguistic homogeneity has here become operational: governments must aim at it because heterogeneity makes social and official control more difficult. This is the view which UNESCO has officially sponsored. In a UNESCO monograph on *The Use of Vernacular Languages in Education* we find asserted that "It is axiomatic that the best medium for teaching a child is his mother tongue. Psychologically, it is the system of meaningful signs that in his mind works automatically for expression and understanding. Sociologically it is a means of identification among the members of the community to which he belongs. Educationally, he learns more quickly through it than through an unfamiliar linguistic medium." These are highly dubious assertions. If they were at all true, we would be quite at a loss to explain the spread of Greek in the Hellenistic world, of Latin in the Roman world, of English and of Russian in large tracts of Asia, Africa, and America in modern times, and of their widespread use by populations of varying origins and diverse histories as a medium of science and scholarship and of civilized discourse. Professor Le Page quotes these UNESCO opinions to disagree with them, yet himself believes that "There can be no doubt that to educate a child in a language which is not that of either of his parents tends to alienate him from his parents; to educate him in a language which is not one of the indigenous languages of the country tends to alienate him from the culture of his country." Professor Le Page also manages to cast aspersions on the very morality of education in a foreign language by saying that "Education through the medium of a foreign language may encourage a kind of opportunism which is not prepared to give any unselfish service back to the community."[89] These assertions conjure up the rhetoric of love and selflessness and assume that this rhetoric is appropriate to political discourse. Since this rhetoric is, in fact, inappropriate and inadequate for the discussion of politics, all that it can effect is to encourage the illusion that relations among citizens and between citizens and government are love relations; and that, therefore, it is the business of government to indoctrinate citizens and to make them "emotionally integrated."[90] In Chapter XVIII of the *Considerations on Representative Government* (1861), which discussed "The Government of Dependencies by Free States," John Stuart Mill stated that "It is always under great difficulties, and very imperfectly, that a country can be governed by foreigners; even where there is no extreme disparity, in habits and ideas, between the rulers and the ruled. Foreigners do not feel with the people. They cannot judge, by the light in which a thing appears to their own minds, or the manner in which it affects their feelings, how it will affect the feelings or appear to the minds of the subject population." This to Mill was a disadvantage; but reflection may lead us to conclude that there may be solid advantages in such a state of affairs; for we will remember that government, whether by foreigner or by native, is exercise of power; and power, it is commonly and rightly said, sets up barriers, isolates, puts him who exercises it in a different world from him who is subject to it. Those who have power and those who do not have power are different species of men. It is therefore safer and more prudent for distances to be kept and for the governed to approach their governors with cautious and mistrustful circumspection. An ancient Chinese sage declared it a mistake to compare the ruler to a father; for, he said, the ruler does not (or at any rate should not) feel affection toward his people. Again, the story is told of another wise Chinese, a ruler who, recovering from an illness, heard that his subjects had sacrificed an ox for his recovery. He thereupon punished those responsible, because love between ruler and subject spoils government and has to be nipped in the bud. Government by foreigners has, then, this advantage at least, that rulers cannot—as they would if they were native—pretend to "feel with the people"; cannot use the complicities of affection and the comforting illusion of affinity to establish and maintain despotism. No foreigner, we reflect, could have founded and maintained the despotisms which Europe has seen in the last few decades and those which have now taken over from European rule in Asia and Africa. These despotisms depend on exploiting the pathetic fallacy, namely, that a government is the same as its subjects and is flesh of their flesh; and the philanthropic fallacy, namely that the aims and interests of government are the very same as those for which the governed work and struggle. It would have been ridiculous of the British rulers of India and Egypt or of the Dutch rulers of the East Indies to claim that they "felt" with their subjects; while their successors confidently, constantly, and most profitably use the rhetoric of the heart, a rhetoric which, with the diffusion of Western mass culture, has spread the world over.

Nationalism, then, to repeat Michel Aflaq's affirmation, "is love before everything else," and nationalist leaders inculcate in their followers the belief, and themselves perhaps believe, that political action will institute a reign of love in society and state. But the love which they speak of, though tender, is also merciless. Only through a tender mercilessness and a loving chastisement will men be brought to know and realize their own deepest urge, which is to love and be at one with the fellow members of their nation. The stern logic of this love is again expounded by Aflaq: "our mercilessness," he writes, "has for its object to bring them back to their true selves which they ignore, to their hidden will which they have not yet clearly discerned and which is with us, even though our swords are raised against them."[91] It is therefore no surprise that the nationalists' avenging sword often claims more victims among their own brethren than among the alien foe. Of this many examples can be quoted, but one may now suffice: the Mau Mau killed two thousand fellow Africans as against thirty-two European civilians.[92] The dialectic of this fraternal and loving violence is displayed for us to see in the most moving record perhaps to come out of the Algerian rebellion of 1954–1962. This is the posthumously published diary which the gifted Kabyle writer and schoolmaster Mouloud Feraoun (1913–1962) kept from 1955 until his murder in Algiers at the hand of European terrorists.[93] Mouloud Feraoun was a native of the Kabyle Mountains who never lost contact with his people. At the beginning of the rebellion he was serving as a teacher in Fort-National in the heart of the Kabyle country, and he had occasion to observe the impact of insurgency on the French and on his own people. Because his Kabyle origin and upbringing and his French education and culture pulled in different, contradictory directions, Mouloud Feraoun could not be fully at home in the society in which he found himself. The events of the rebellion sharpened his awareness of what was equivocal in his position, and this greatly increases the value of his diary as a record left by a humane and subtle mind. In an entry for February 1, 1956, Mouloud Feraoun defines precisely the equivocal character of his position when he writes: "When I say that I am French, I give myself a label which all Frenchmen deny me; I express myself in French, I have been formed by French education. I know as much as an average Frenchman. But, good God, what am I?" His diary throughout in fact shows a man clearly aware of the misunderstandings, of the mutual fear and dislike which divide the French settlers, so long the masters in Algeria, from the native Algerians, even though they might be, as he himself was, indistinguishable from Frenchmen in point of speech and culture. His first reaction to the rebels is one of sympathy, not so much for their violence—for, as his diary shows, he did not profess the cult of violence so popular among modern European writers—as for that warm brotherliness which spoke loud in their anti-French activities, that brotherliness precisely which he missed in relations between Frenchmen and Algerians. "The outlaws are of us," we read in an entry written toward the end of December, 1955. "They behave like Kabyles and are careful not to hurt our feelings. . . . Anybody would feel at ease in the *maquis*. At ease because he knows that he would be among brothers, that he could discuss, defend his own point of view and confront them with other points of view." Another entry, of February 2, 1956, contrasts the cold impersonality of French administration with the warm response which the outlaws elicit in villages which they control: "In short nothing is changed; as in the past, the villages live at the margin of official administrative organization. With this difference only, that there has disappeared this obsession with the *hakem* or the *doula*,* French justice which always and in everybody's mind has been nothing but the cold and cutting sword held by a superior who at once despises and protects you. Now we know we are not protected but we have regained our dignity. This is why people from our parts submit willingly to the *mystique* of the *maquisards;* why they start to rediscover, in all good faith, exceptional virtues in the sacred book of Islam, and great authority in those who invoke it to justify their action." There is then this release from the terrible impersonal sword of French justice, this release into the warm and loving brotherliness of believers. But fraternal love imposes its obligations, perhaps more onerous than the demands of the foreign tax-gatherer and justiciar; an entry in the diary which followed a few days later gives us an inkling of these new burdens: the diarist records a conversation with his French colleagues in which they tell him that they run more risks from the rebels than the Kabyles: "I replied to the Frenchmen: 'You may be right. But only in theory. But up to now your only casualty has been the mayor [of Fort-National]. As for us, we have many killed every day [by the rebels]. And I speak only of what goes on here. Ten Kabyles, one Frenchman. This is the account.' " From day to day, from week to week, from month to month, with a terrible monotony the diary records the fate of the ordinary peaceable Algerians caught between the impersonality of a state threatened in its sovereignty and the equally

---

*Arabic: ruler, state. In the political vocabulary of Islam these terms do in fact suggest the contemptuous and majestic remoteness of government from the governed, and it is curious and significant that Mouloud Feraoun should choose them in order to describe the aspect of French administration which the Kabyles found most striking.

merciless violence of rebels striving for a new reign of fraternity, one calling forth the other and being called forth by it in gruesome and sanguinary conjunction. In an entry of March 9, 1956, he wonders whether the rebels had not in fact decided that the present generation of Algerians should be exterminated and a truly free Algeria created, composed of new men who had not known the French occupant: "The point of view may be logically defended. Too logically, alas! And gradually, from being suspected to being compromised, from being compromised to being accused of treason, we shall all end up by being declared guilty and executed on the spot." "And have I not been told," the same entry continues, "that at home they now behave like masters? Like masters whose arrogance has never been equalled by that of the caids* of painful memory or by that of youthful and impulsive district officers. For the caid was insulting and the *hakem* used the whip. They, they strangle and hang from trees. O Villon! they cut throats, they machine-gun, they mutilate. They, they have no more shame in consorting with easy women who receive them to spite the villagers, who give them shelter and information, who complain to them and get to be feared. In our humiliated villages, it is the whores who lay down the law." An entry of April 3, 1958, sums up his experience of three years of rebellion: "Everybody understands that 'the brethren' are not infallible, are not courageous, are not heroes. But it is also known that they are cruel and hypocritical. They have nothing to give but death, but they, they have to be given everything. [*Ils ne peuvent donner que la mort mais, eux, il faut tout leur donner.*] They go on imposing ransoms, requisitioning, destroying. They go on talking religion, forbidding what they have become accustomed to forbid, and whatever it may take their fancy newly to forbid. They must be called 'brothers' and be venerated like gods." Finally, we may quote an entry of December 9, 1958, which contrasts with some precision the external, impersonal, so to speak routine violence of a state acting in self-defense and the violence of the rebels, which in their eyes serves to establish the kingdom of love, liberty, and brotherhood,

---

* Native chiefs appointed and supported by the French.

and the exercise of which itself proves that brotherhood, liberty, and love are already here: "In brief," writes Mouloud Feraoun, "the French do wrong through ignorance or in order to preserve their interests. An inevitable evil which people are ready to bear because it emanates from the adversary, the enemy from whom one flees, to whom one turns one's back. The soldiers of the liberation do wrong because this freedom which they have assumed from the start must in their eyes primarily be exercised over the people. And they begin by making the people feel that if they are free, it [the people] on the other hand is enslaved. Alas! It is not only enslaved; it is also terrorized."

The Algerian rebellion produced in Mouloud Feraoun a bitterly lucid observer of the dialectic of nationalist revolution, an exact chronicler of those cruelly equivocal emotions which seize ordinary unpolitical men when they experience violence in its most ruthless and least mediated form, practiced in a cause which they feel in some sense to be their own by men who claim with some reason to be saviors and brothers. The Algeria: rebellion has also produced the most eloquent panegyrist of this violence, a writer who celebrates it with savage lyricism. This is Frantz Fanon, who, born in the French West Indies, studied medicine in Paris, specializing in psychiatry. Practicing his specialty in an Algerian hospital during the rebellion, he became convinced that the mental disorders which came under his notice, affecting European and native alike, were the direct consequence of colonialism and of the strains which it created in society and the human personality. Colonialism was responsible for a diabolical and inhuman society, and only its utter eradication could lead men to sanity and happiness. His duty, as he saw it, was to help in this work; he resigned his post and joined the rebellion, for which he became a fluent spokesman, cutting, extreme, acrid, and venomous in the best tradition of European *sans-culottisme*. He died in 1961 at the age of thirty-seven. His piece "Concerning Violence" (see pp. 488–539) preaches that decolonization is always and necessarily a violent phenomenon. Violence for the individual, he says, is a "cleansing force"; "the colonized man finds his freedom in and through violence." For society as a whole, violence is a cement, "a cement which has been mixed with blood and anger." "The practice of violence," he affirms, "binds them together as a whole, since each individual forms a violent link in the great chain, a part of the great organism of violence." In confirmation of his thesis Fanon quotes the rule of the Mau Mau which required that each member of the group should strike a blow at the victim: "Each one was thus personally responsible for the death of the settler. This assumed responsibility for violence allows both strayed and outlawed members of the group to come back again and to find their place once more, to become integrated. Violence is thus seen as comparable to a royal pardon." Decolonization, which requires "absolute violence," is "a program of complete disorder." Its aim is that "the last shall be first and the first last" and "the veritable creation of new men." These "new men" form a homogeneous society from which the alien, the heterogeneous has been cut off. The individual and a society composed of individuals—both of which are colonialist inventions—completely disappear, and in their place arises a new, warm, homogeneous society in which the only appellations to be heard are those of brother, sister, and friend!

With Fanon's celebration of violence went a theory. Quite unoriginal in its main lines, the theory was the very same which asserted the connection between capitalist "exploitation" and imperial rule, the shortcomings and limitations of which we have examined. But his talent is such that he manages to formulate a hackneyed theory in a striking, an arresting manner. Consider for instance his brilliant description—which admittedly owes something to the peculiar condition of Algeria in the last two or three decades—of the colonial world as a "Manichaean world" in which there is absolute and utter contrast and isolation between the world of the colonizers and that of the colonized. "Obedient to the rules of pure Aristotelian logic," he says of these two worlds, "they both follow the principle of reciprocal exclusivity. No conciliation is possible, for of the two terms, one is superfluous. The settler's town is a strongly built town, all made of stone and steel. It is a brightly lit town; the streets are covered with asphalt, and the garbage cans swallow all the leavings, unseen, unknown and hardly thought about. The settler's feet are never visible, except perhaps in the sea; but there you're never close enough to see them. His feet are protected by strong shoes although the streets of his town are clean and even, with no holes or stones. The settler's town is a well-fed town, an easygoing town; its belly always full of good things. The settler's town," he asserts, "is a town of white people, of foreigners." By contrast the native town is dirty, smelly, insanitary, overcrowded: "It is a world without spaciousness; men live there on top of each other, and their huts are built one on top of the other. The native town is a hungry town, starved of bread, of meat, of shoes, of coal, of light. The native town is a crouching village, a town on its knees, a town wallowing in the mire. It is a town," he concludes, "of niggers and dirty arabs." And Fanon sums up the colonial situation by affirming that in the colonies "you are rich because you are white, you are white because you are rich."

For all its brilliance, however, this is no more than specious and bitter invective. The contrast which Fanon describes is of course real enough, but it is not one which obtains only where "white people" and "niggers and dirty arabs" live side by side; it may be equally observed in racially and culturally homogeneous societies whose placid, self-contained agricultural economy was brutally disrupted by industrialization and urbanization. Fanon's words could in fact have applied to London or Manchester in the mid-nineteenth century, and to Bombay or Cairo or Baghdad today. In none of these instances does it make sense to contrast the splendid fortunes of "white people" with the misery of "niggers and dirty arabs." But specious and sophistical as it is, this doctrine has clearly gained a tenacious hold on Fanon's mind; and the warmth and brilliance of his exposition is clearly the outcome of deep conviction. He recognizes the doctrine for what it is, namely, a variant of Marxism-Leninism. Fanon believes, in fact, that the usual Marxism, influenced as it was by European conditions, is not exactly applicable to the colonial situation; Marxist analysis, he states, should be "slightly stretched" every time we have to do with the colonial problem.

He stretches it in two directions. In the first place, the revolutionary class in the colonies is not, as in orthodox Marxism, the industrial proletariat; it is rather the peasantry, he argues, in a manner reminiscent of Mao Tse-tung's: "it is clear that in the colonial countries the peasants alone are revolutionary, for they have nothing to lose and everything to gain. The starving peasant, outside the class system, is the first among the exploited to discover that violence pays. For him there is no compromise, no possible coming to terms; colonization and decolonization are simply a question of relative strength." In the second place, Fanon modifies the Leninist analysis of imperialism by arguing that the struggle between colonizers and colonized is not simply a struggle between capitalism and its victims in which race and color are immaterial, but specifically one between "white people" and "niggers and dirty arabs"; in other words that the anticapitalist struggle is also a nationalist struggle: "And when Mr. Khrouchev casts out his shoe over the United Nations, or thumps the table with it, there's not a single ex-native, nor any representative of an underdeveloped country, who laughs. For what Mr. Khrouchev shows the colonized countries which are looking on is that he, the moujik, who moreover is the possessor of space-rockets, treats these miserable capitalists in the way that they deserve. In the same way, Castro sitting in military uniform in the United Nations Organization does not scandalize the underdeveloped countries. What Castro demonstrates is the consciousness he has of the continuing existence of the rule of violence. The astonishing thing is that he did not come into U.N.O. with a machine gun; but if he had, would anyone have minded? All the *jacqueries* and desperate deeds, all those bands armed with cutlasses or axes find their nationality in the implacable struggle which opposes socialism and capitalism."

The statement that Asians and Africans find their nationality in the struggle between socialism and capitalism is, from a Bolshevik standpoint, dubious and somewhat heretical, since it seems to subordinate the socialist to the nationalist struggle and to make socialism a means or an instrument for the attainment of nationality. The official Bolshevik emphasis is somewhat different. If, as the Second Congress of the Communist International declared in 1920 (see pp. 540–551), Bolsheviks had to "carry out a policy of realizing the closest union between all national and colonial liberation movements and Soviet Russia," this was only because, as another thesis approved by the same congress declared, "One of the main sources from which European capitalism draws its chief strength is to be found in the colonial possessions and dependencies." In his 1924 lectures, Stalin put the matter with extreme clarity. There were "scores and hundreds of millions of Asiatic and African peoples who are suffering national oppression in its most savage and cruel form." These multitudes were the victims of imperialism, which was the highest stage of capitalism, and the destruction of capitalism would be accomplished through an alliance between them and the Soviet Union: "Leninism has proved, and the imperialist war and the revolution in Russia have confirmed, that the national problem can be solved only in connection with and on the basis of the proletarian revolution, and that the road to victory of the revolution in the West lies through the revolutionary alliance with the liberation movement of the colonies and dependent countries against imperialism." (See pp. 552–561.)

The Bolshevik thesis seems from the first to have given rise to objections by non-Europeans. What these were we may gather from a passage in a speech which Zinoviev delivered at the Baku Congress of Oppressed Peoples in September, 1920. "Comrades," he said, "when the East really starts moving, Russia and with it all Europe will be but a small corner in this large picture. True revolution will break out only on the day when we shall have at our side the 850 million of Asia and of the African continent. We hide nothing from you. We define frankly and straightforwardly what divides us from the representatives of the national movement today and what binds us to them. The goal of this movement is to help the East to be rid of English imperialism. But we have another, no smaller, task which is to help the workers of the East to struggle against the wealthy, to help them, as from now, to build up Communist organizations, to explain to them what communism is, to make them ready for a true workers' revolution, for a true equality, for the emancipation of man from every yoke and every oppression." What is interesting to observe is that disagreement with orthodox Bolshevik doctrine came not only from the non-Communists whom Zinoviev was trying to convince but also from within the Soviet Communist Party. This opposition is associated with Sultan Galiev (c.1880–1937), a Volga Tatar from Kazan who before the Bolshevik revolution was active in nationalist and reformist movements among the Muslims of Russia. In November, 1917, he joined the Communist Party and shortly thereafter became, and remained for some three years, Stalin's colleague in the People's Commissariat for Nationalities. It was in the years between 1918 and 1923—when he was accused of having plotted against the revolution, expelled from the Communist Party, and banished from public life—that he developed and propagated his original ideas about world revolution which, in fact, brought about his downfall and perhaps ultimately his execution at Stalin's orders. Sultan Galiev was a Marxist and therefore believed that the proletariat was the "universal class" that exhibited the inhuman condition of class society and the liberation of which spelled the final liberation of all humanity. But for him the proletariat were not the industrial workers of Europe and America. The true proletariat, rather, were the masses of the East, the Muslims, the Hindus, the Chinese, and only their liberation could bring class contradictions to an end. When, therefore, he claimed that "the socialist revolution will never be able to triumph without the participation of the East," he did not mean this in Stalin's or Zinoviev's operational sense, namely that an attack on capitalism in the colonies would bring nearer the true revolution, the only revolution that counted, that of the European and American proletariat. For Galiev, rather, the European and American proletariat were just as much the oppressors of the Eastern masses as the capitalists were; this proletariat were the capitalists' accomplices in "looting" the East, India, and the Americas:

"The greater part of the material and spiritual wealth of the whites derives from Eastern booty, gathered together by the blood and sweat of hundreds of millions of native workers 'of all colors and of all races'"; "Tens of millions of American aborigines and of blacks from Africa had to die, the rich culture of the Incas had completely to disappear in order that present-day 'peace-loving' America should be established with its 'cosmopolitan' culture of progress and technique"; "Christopher Columbus! This name is dear to the heart of European imperialists. It is he who 'opened' to European pirates the way to America. England, France, Spain, Italy and Germany—all have taken equal part in the looting"; "All the history of the Crusades and the long series of wars conducted by the imperialist bourgeoisie in the East are part of a deeply calculated policy destined to subject economically the East to the feudalists of Western Europe and their descendants." (See pp. 562–569.) When he wrote these passages Sultan Galiev was a Soviet official; else there is little doubt that among the oppressors he denounced he would have included the Russians, who had conquered and were still ruling his own people.

In Sultan Galiev's hands the Marxian class struggle became a struggle between the white and the colored races, and it is hardly an exaggeration to say that for him no white could be a true socialist. Sultan Galiev and his followers were speedily suppressed in the Soviet Union, but they were not the only non-European Communists to equate the triumph of socialism with the humiliation and downfall of the Europeans. One of the founders of the Chinese Communist Party, Li Ta-chao (1888–1927), argued in an essay of 1920 that "China really stands in the position of the world proletariat"; the class struggle as he defined it was "between the lower-class colored races and the upper-class white race." In 1924 he gave a lecture on "The Racial Question" to a student society at the University of Peking, and it is curious how similar, not to say identical, the Chinese's and the Tatar's views prove to be. "Given that white men are the pioneers of culture," Li declared, "they look upon colored men as the inferior classes, and themselves occupy the high positions. The result is that, taking the world as a whole, the race problem becomes a class problem. In other words antagonistic classes have come into being. In the future, racial struggles will inevitably break out; this can be predicted with certainty; these struggles will take the form of wars between whites and colored men, and will merge into the 'class struggle'! The proof of this may be found in the Russian Revolution. Whites did take part in the Russian Revolution, but colored men of the oppressed classes also participated in it. Their common aim was to oppose the whites of the oppressing classes; we may already see here roughly sketched the 'class struggle' of colored men and of the lower classes against the upper-class whites; and this struggle is only just beginning."[94] In this remarkable analysis what is so striking is not so much Li's peculiar interpretation of the Bolshevik revolution as his attempt to transform the class struggle into a struggle between the races. This interpretation of the class struggle has also found favor with non-Communists. In the very year in which Sultan Galiev was advocating his new revolutionary strategy, the well-known Japanese ideologue Ikki Kita—whose teachings inspired the turbulent young Japanese nationalist officers in the nineteen-thirties—was arguing that the world was divided into capitalist and proletarian nations; England and Russia were in the first category and Japan in the second: "Why doesn't Japan, which is an area made up of scattered island chains and which is in the position of a proletariat among nations," he asked in 1919 in his programmatic *Outline for the Reconstruction of the Japanese State*, "have the right to start a war in the name of justice, in order to seize [possessions] from these monopolies [i.e., England and Russia]? There are self-contradictions in the fundamental thoughts of those European and American socialists who approve of proletarian class-struggle within a country but who consider international proletarian war as chauvinism and militarism."[95]

Resentment and impatience, the depravity of the rich and the virtue of the poor, the guilt of Europe and the innocence of Asia and Africa, salvation through violence, the coming reign of universal love: these are the elements of the thought of Sultan Galiev and Li Ta-chao, of Ikki Kita, Michel Aflaq, and Frantz Fanon. This theory is now the most popular and influential one in Asia and Africa. It is Europe's latest gift to the world. As Karl Marx remarked, theory itself becomes a material force when it has seized the masses; and with the printing press, the transistor, and television—those other gifts of Europe—it is easy now for theory, any theory, to seize the masses. Theory has become the opium of the masses. Marx, however, was wrong in thinking opium a mere soporific. As the Old Man of the Mountain—whose "theory" was so potent that legend has transmuted it into *hashish*—could have told him, the drug may also excite its addicts to a frenzy of destruction.

NOTES

1. Peter Worsley, *The Third World*, London, 1964, pp. 45, 49.

2. *The World and the West*, London, 1953, pp. 2–3.

3. J.-P. Sartre in Preface to F. Fanon, *Les damnés de la terre*, Paris, 1961, pp. 22–3 and 20.

4. R. Koebner and H.D. Schmidt, *Imperialism*, Cambridge, 1964.

5. A passage occurring in a Liberal newspaper illustrates in its polemical way both the meaning which came to attach to the word and the circumstances in which this occurred: ". . . that odious system of bluster and swagger . . ." wrote the *Daily News* in 1898, ". . . on which Lord Beaconsfield and his colleagues bestowed the tawdry nickname of Imperialism."

6. J.A. Hobson, *Imperialism*, London, 1902, pp. 62, 64–5.

7. Michel Pavlovitch, pseud., *The Foundations of Imperialist Policy*, London, 1922, p. 152.

8. English trs. in *Imperialism and Social Class*, 1951.

9. Henri Brunschwig, *Mythes et réalités de l'imperialisme colonial français, 1871–1914*, Paris, 1960, and Ronald Robinson and John Gallagher with Alice Denny, *Africa and the Victorians: The Official Mind of Imperialism*, London, 1961. See also the excellent pamphlet on *European Rule in Africa* by A.J. Hanna, published by the Historical Association, London, 1961.

10. See, for instance, Peter T. Bauer, "Marxism and the Underdeveloped Countries" in M.M. Drachkovitch, ed., *Marxist Ideology in the Contemporary World—Its Appeals and Paradoxes*, 1966, and the same author's "African Political Economy" in F.S. Meyer, ed., *The African Nettle*, 1965. See also Morris D.

Morris, "Towards a Reinterpretation of Nineteenth-Century Indian Economic History," *The Journal of Economic History*, vol. XXIII (1963), pp. 607–618. In this most original article the author argues that Indian handicrafts did not decline as a result of imports from Lancashire and shows that in this period in which the Indian economy is supposed to have been ravaged and ruined there was in fact a remarkable expansion in commercial activity both domestic and foreign and appreciable population and urban growth.

11. There is no reason to dissent from a judgment like the following: ". . . there can be little doubt that by 1963 the people of India as a whole were not better fed or clad, or housed, and were worse, and more corruptly, governed, and subject to a worse situation of law and order, with higher taxes, ever rising prices, ever acute foreign exchange difficulties, and more unemployment, than in 1946, the year [Nehru] became Head of Government." See Walter Crocker, *Nehru: A Contemporary's Estimate*, 1966, p. 166. The author, formerly Australian High Commissioner in New Delhi, is an admirer of Nehru, and his book is a sympathetic portrait.

12. The term economism has hitherto been confined to Bolshevik controversies, where it is used to describe a heresy into which some of Lenin's doctrinal opponents are supposed to have fallen. But the term is more generally useful and should not remain annexed to a narrow sectarian usage.

13. *Thought and Change*, London, 1964, pp. 167–8.

14. Worsley, *op. cit.*, p. 17.

15. Paris, 1950; English trs. *Prospero and Caliban: The Psychology of Colonization*, New York, 1956.

16. *Les Religions et les philosophies dans l'Asie centrale*, 2nd ed., Paris, 1866, p. 135.

17. E. Kedourie, *Nationalism*, 3rd ed., 1966, p. 9.

18. See *ibid.*

19. See *ibid.*, p. 79.

20. See *ibid.*, chs. IV and V.

21. *The Quest of the Historical Jesus*, Eng. trs., 2nd. ed., 1911, p. 13.

22. *Ibid.*, p. vii.

23. On this literature see Kedourie, *op. cit.*, pp. 75–9.

24. Qur'an, XI, 120.

25. See particularly Professor Wilfred Cantwell Smith's paper, "The Historical Development in Islam of the Concept of Islam as an Historical Development," in B. Lewis and P.M. Holt, eds., *Historians of the Middle East*, London, 1962.

26. Encyclical quoted in Cyril Mango, "Byzantinism and Romantic Hellenism," *Journal of the Warburg and Courtauld Institutes*, Vol. XXVIII (1965), p. 35. The patriarch of Constantinople's pamphlet of 1798, *Paternal Instructions*, is discussed in S.G. Chaconas, *Adamantios Koraes . . .* , New York 1942, pp. 86–7, who attributes it to the patriarch of Jerusalem. See further T. Papadopoullos, *Studies and Documents Relating to the History of the Greek Church and*

People under Turkish Domination, Brussels, 1952, pp. 142–6.

27. Koraes' point that the increasing prosperity of some Greeks made them eager for Western ideas also supports the point made in Part I of the Introduction, that nationalist ideology in some cases spreads because of enhanced material welfare rather than poverty. The well-known Greek economic historian, A. Andreades, in a notable paper has made the point that the Greek Revolution of 1821 could in no way be attributed to financial exploitation by the Ottomans; see his article, "L'Administration financière de la Grèce sous la domination turque," *Revue des études grecques*, 1910.

28. George Ostrogorsky, *History of the Byzantine State*, 1956, and Mango, *loc. cit.*

29. Bernard Lewis, *The Emergence of Modern Turkey*, 1961 p. 347.

30. Article "Turan" in *Encyclopaedia of Islam*.

31. Quoted in F. Kazemzadeh, "Iranian Historiography," B. Lewis and P.M. Holt, eds., *Historians of the Middle East*, pp. 432–3.

32. See E.D. Cronon, *Black Moses*, Madison, Wisc., 1955, p. 195; and no. 8 in the anthology below.

33. Gabriel K. Osei, *Fifty Unknown Facts . . .*, 2nd ed., London, 1964, p. 5.

34. M. Garvey, *The Tragedy of White Injustice*, New York, 1927, pp. 4, 17, and 2.

35. Jinnah to Gandhi September 17 and Gandhi to Jinnah September 22, 1944, in Jamil ud-Din Ahmad, ed., *Some Recent Speeches and Writings of Mr. Jinnah*, vol. II, Lahore 1947, pp. 180 and 191.

36. T'ang Leang-li, *China in Revolt: How a Civilization Became a Nation*, London, 1927. The book does not fullfil the promise of its title.

37. See D.C. Holtom, *Modern Japan and Shinto Nationalism*, revised ed., Chicago 1947, p. 59.

38. Zionism is hardly discussed in these pages, and this for two reasons: in the first place, it is as completely modeled on European ideas as other nationalist ideologies outside Europe and thus presents no special or striking feature; but in the second place, it arose in the European-Christian cultural area, while all the other ideologies I am discussing here appear outside this area—and that they appear outside it is one chief reason for examining them.

39. See Stanley A. Wolpert, *Tilak and Gokhale*, Berkeley, 1962, pp. 67ff.

40. Earl of Ronaldshay, *The Heart of Arya-varta: A Study of the Psychology of Indian Unrest*, London, 1925, pp. 126–7.

41. Elegy recorded by J. Desparmet in "Les réactions nationalitaires en Algérie," *Bulletin de la Société de Géographie d'Alger*, vol. XXXIV, no. 133, 1933, p. 52.

42. Quoted in B.T. McCully, *English Education and the Origins of Indian Nationalism*, New York, 1940, p. 216.

43. See S. Gopal, "Lord Curzon and Indian Nationalism, 1898–1905," *St. Antony's Papers no. 18*, 1966, p. 69.

44. B.C. Pal, *Memories of My Life and Time*, Calcutta, 1932, pp. 408–10.

45. See Banerjea's autobiography, *A Nation in the Making, Being the Reminiscences of Fifty Years in Banerjea's Public Life*, Calcutta, 1925, p. 33.

46. Pal, *op. cit.*, p. 245.

47. *An Arab Tells His Story*, pp. 3, 27, 118, 137, 140, and 148–9.

48. *Sketch for a Self-Portrait*, London, 1949, p. 33.

49. Quoted in H.G. Creel, *Chinese Thought*, 1954, p. 248.

50. *Out of Exile*, New York, 1949.

51. Ernest Lee Tuveson, *Millennium and Utopia: A Study in the Background of the Idea of Progress*, Berkeley, 1949.

52. Babylonian Talmud, Sanhedrin 97b.

53. In Ch. 7, bk. XX of *The City of God*, St. Augustine speaks of the "ridiculous interpretations" of the Book of Revelation "by some of our divines," and adds that such interpretations are "fit for none but carnal men to believe. But they that are truly spiritual do call those of this opinion Chiliasts"—i.e., believers in the millennium.

54. The polemic and Worthington's place in it has been elucidated by R. S. Crane, "Anglican Apologetics and the Idea of Progress 1699–1745," first published in *Modern Philology*, vol. XXXI (1934) and reprinted in Vol. I of his collected papers, *The Idea of the Humanities*, Chicago, 1967.

55. Norman Cohn, *The Pursuit of the Millennium*, 1957, p. 306. The summary of the Anabaptist rebellion in Münster follows closely Professor Cohn's excellent account.

56. N. Cohn, "Medieval Millenarism: Its Bearings on the Comparative Study of Millenarian Movements," in Sylvia L. Thrupp, ed., *Millennial Dreams in Action*, The Hague, 1962, p. 35

57. G.E. Taylor, "The Taiping Rebellion: Its Economic Background and Social Theory," in *Chinese Social and Political Science Review*, Peking, vol. XVI (1933), pp. 545–614.

58. See Wordsworth's poem, "French Revolution As it Appeared to Enthusiasts at its Commencement," composed in 1804.

59. R.R. Palmer, *The Age of the Democratic Revolution*, 2 vols., Princeton, 1959–1964. The passage discussed above is at p. 574 of vol. II.

60. See the chapter on Nechaev in F. Venturi, *Roots of Revolution*, 1960, and particularly pp. 364–7.

61. See *Ghana: The Autobiography of Kwame Nkrumah*, 1957, pp. 60–61.

62. N.K. Bose, *My Days with Gandhi*, Calcutta, 1953, quoted in Ronald Segal, *The Crisis of India*, 1965, pp. 165–6.

63. Tekin Alp, *The Turkish and Pan-Turkish Ideal*, English trs., 1917, pp. 42–3.

64. Ian Henderson with Philip Goodhart, *The Hunt for Kimathi*, 1958, p. 23. The brief account is based on this excellent work.

65. It is not known for certain what the words "Mau Mau" mean. The *Corfield Report* quotes a District Commissioner who wrote in February, 1951: "It is said that *Mau Mau* really means *Uma Uma* (Out, Out), and is a code word based

on the old pre-circumcision secret language game of the Kikuyu young men, in which letters are transposed." See *Historical Survey of the Origins and Growth of Mau Mau*, Cmd. 1030, 1960, p. 104.

66. *Corfield Report*, p. 168.

67. *Ghana: The Autobiography of Kwame Nkrumah*, p. 164. See Matthew 6:33, "But seek ye first the kingdom of God, and his righteousness and all these things shall be added unto you."

68. See G. Balandier, "Messianismes et nationalismes en Afrique noire," *Cahiers internationaux de sociologie*, vol. XIV (1953).

69. James 5: 4 reads: "Behold the hire of the labourers who have reaped down your fields, which is of you kept back by fraud, and the cries of them which have reaped are entered into the ears of the Lord of Sabaoth." Domingo's pamphlet quoted in George Shepperson and Thomas Price, *Independent African*, Edinburgh, 1950, pp. 163–4.

70. See B.G.M. Sundkler, *Bantu Prophets in South Africa*, 2nd edition, 1961, p. 335.

71. *Ibid.*, p. 337.

72. Efraim Andersson, *Messianic Popular Movements in the Lower Congo*, Uppsala, 1958, pp. 124–5 and 193.

73. The name Watch Tower derives, it seems, from Habakkuk 2:1, "I will stand upon my watch, and set me upon the tower, and will watch to see what he will say unto me, and what I shall answer when I am reproved."

74. *Report of the Commission appointed to enquire into the Disturbances in the Copperbelt, Northern Rhodesia, October 1935*. Cmd. 5009 (1935), paras. 100, 104, and 114.

75. Shepperson and Price, *op. cit.*, p. 151, quoting C.T. Russell's *The Battle of Armageddon*. The brief account of Chilembwe's rebellion follows the excellent detailed account by Shepperson and Price and relies also on the evidence given before the Commission of Enquiry into the rebellion which is found in the Public Record Office, London, C.O. 525/66.

76. Passages quoted from the minutes of evidence before the Commission of inquiry annexed to dispatch no. 39, Zomba, 7 February 1916, C.O. 525/66.

77. L.S.B. Leakey, *Defeating Mau Mau*, 1954, pp. 57ff.

78. The Creed and the Beatitudes are quoted in B. Timothy, *Kwame Nkrumah, His Rise to Power*, 1955, pp. 81 and 101–2.

79. *Ghana: The Autobiography of Kwame Nkrumah*, p. 109.

80. Lead, kindly light, amid the encircling gloom,
        Lead thou me on.
The night is dark and I am far from home,
        Lead thou me on.
Keep thou my feet, I do not ask to see
        The distant path, one step's enough for me.

Cardinal Newman's celebrated hymn seems also to have been popular among Pakistani nationalists. One of them used it in dedicating a book to Jinnah; see W. Cantwell Smith, *Modern Islam in India*, 2nd ed., 1946, p. 259.

81. Nkrumah, *op. cit.*, p. 101.

82. Ali Al-Balhawan, *Tunisia in Revolt* (Arabic text), Cairo, 1954, p. 73.

83. Jawaharlal Nehru, *An Autobiography*, pp. 77 and 206.

84. Aflaq quoted in Haim, *Arab Nationalism*, pp. 242 and 70–1.

85. Fanon, *Les damnés de la terre*, p. 165: *"lorsque, parvenu à l'apogée du rut avec son peuple . . ."*

86. See Kedourie, *Nationalism*, ch. 5.

87. *Thought and Change.*

88. R.B. Le Page, *The National Language Question* (Issued under the auspices of the Institute of Race Relations), London, 1964, p. 18.

89. *Ibid.*, pp. 22 and 24–5.

90. The Indian Government set up in fact a Committee on Emotional Integration which actually published a Report (Delhi, 1962).

91. Haim, *op. cit.*, p. 71.

92. See also Kedourie, *Nationalism*, pp. 106–7.

93. *Journal 1955–1962*, Paris, 1962.

94. Passage quoted in Stuart Schram and Hélène Carrère d'Encausse, *Le marxisme et l'Asie 1853–1964*, Paris, 1965, p. 306. See also Maurice Meisner, *Li Ta-chao and the Origins of Chinese Marxism*, Cambridge, Mass., 1967, pp. 144 and 190.

95. Cited in Delmer M. Brown, *Nationalism in Japan*, Berkeley, 1955, p. 182.

1. REPORT ON THE PRESENT STATE OF CIVILIZATION IN GREECE*

ⅬⅬⅬⅬⅬⅬⅬⅬⅬⅬⅬⅬⅬⅬⅬⅬⅬⅬⅬⅬⅬ

Adamantios Koraes

If the state of a nation is to be fruitfully observed, it is mainly in the period when this nation degenerates from the virtues of its ancestors, as well as in the period when it is in the process of regeneration. The observer in both cases is placed at a vantage point which, by placing before him the succession of causes which lead to civilization being fostered or destroyed, affords him lessons useful for humanity.

Such causes may be more or less numerous, more or less efficacious, according as the people among whom such a revolution takes place is more or less removed from other civilized nations, more or less favored by climate, more or less advanced in that civilization which it is on the point of losing, or plunged in the barbaric state from which it is striving to emerge. To these considerations, which the observer must take as a guide, one can and one has to add the kind of barbarism in which the people under observation is stagnating. The same causes do not operate with equal force on a people which is advancing for the first time toward civilization, and on one which is striving to find once

*From *Lettres inédites de Coray à Chardon de la Rochette*, Paris, 1877, pp. 451–490.

again the path from which it had long wandered. The steps of the former are more timid; it progresses but hesitantly; whilst the latter advances more rapidly, provided that monuments of its ancient civilization are still in existence and that external causes do not obstruct its progress.

If I limit myself to man's barbaric or civilized state, if I do not consider him in the savage state, this is because only rarely has the European philosopher been able to reach those remote regions where human reason is still in its cradle, in order to survey the moral infancy of his species; it is also and mainly because in this Report I propose to put before the *Société des observateurs de l'homme*, not the history of man in general but observations which I have actually made on the present state of my own nation. How happy I would be if I could interest my respected colleagues in the fate of a people which is striving to escape from that barbarism in which various causes have plunged it, and to make them feel that delightful emotion which a philosopher's soul must experience at the breathtaking sight of man trying to perfect himself.

May I be allowed to tell the Society that it should not feel mistrust toward me because I am Greek. I may have been mistaken in my observations, or rather in the conclusions which I desired to draw from them. But the reason of my mistake must be sought not in my national prejudices but in the weakness of my reasoning powers. Nothing undoubtedly is more natural than to love the nation to which one belongs more than any other. This preference is as far removed from that partiality for cosmopolitanism so much praised by men who are attached to nothing, as true love is from coquetry; but the man who observes only in order to be instructed, and who does not publish his observations except with the purpose of being useful, must above everything else love the truth.

To want to instruct the Society in what Greece was formerly, in what she successively became through the various revolutions to which she was subjected, would be to rehearse facts which are familiar to it, which are familiar to any man with a good upbringing. The last of these revolutions, dating four centuries back, has plunged her in a state of lethargy similar to that in which Europe was plunged before the Literary Renaissance. Very rarely did she give some faint sign of life: from time to time some men of learning would appear among the nation paying her a tribute of excessive admiration; but, heedless of their voice as of their example, the nation would let them pass on, without reaping from them any advantage; just as during the terror of a dark night one is dazzled rather than illuminated by the meteors which from time to time travel across the vault of the sky.

I will not be asked what, during that unhappy interval, were the moral and religious ideas of the Greeks. Ignorance, daughter of tyranny, is always accompanied by superstition, and superstition insensibly leads to depraved habits. It is useless to seek for virtue in a society which is not ruled by wise and just laws. If a virtuous man happens to be born in such a society, he must be considered, as Socrates said,[1] to be a gift of heaven rather than the handiwork of education.

It is, however, true to say that among European travelers there are some who, not having seen Greece, apparently convinced that in order to know a nation it is unnecessary to move from one's own study, and wishing to give a picture of the degeneration of the modern Greeks, have merely painted a caricature. They did not want to see among the Greeks but what has always been seen among all enslaved peoples; what in fact is seen today among many nations who are not nearly as arbitrarily governed as the Greeks of the present time. These observers, by means of a reckoning which does honor neither to their judgment nor to their heart, have charged the present generation of Greeks with the accumulated vices and errors of all the preceding generations from the day when Greece lost its freedom. These observers have not seen, or have not wanted to see, that the Greeks of today have been the victims of crimes of which they were not the authors. Peoples who have reached such a stage are like unhappy individuals born from parents whom debauchery had exhausted: all that they may be justly reproached with, is not following a contrary mode of life, the only one which can save them from their family's vices; and we shall see by and by that the modern Greeks try to avoid such a reproach. They are infinitely more culpable, those Greeks who first allowed themselves to be corrupted by Macedonian gold, and who, forgetting the brilliant example of virtue and patriotism set by their ancestors, whose tombs were still visible to them and whose voices they could still so to speak hear, sold the freedom which they had inherited; those who afterwards hindered the success of the Achaean League; those who after that by means of their dissensions brought upon themselves Roman arms and the Roman yoke; those, lastly, who, still retaining a shadow of political liberty, allowed themselves to be invaded by a Scythian nation: all these Greeks, I say, are infinitely more guilty than their unhappy descendants to whom all has been left to repair, and not a single error to perpetrate. Deprived of liberty, without pecuniary resources, or those resources which enlightenment procures, abandoned by the whole world, inspiring in some but a feeble interest, in others a sterile pity, in most an indifference which could not but make them despair, what could the modern Greeks do?

What then was to be seen in that unhappy Greece, birthplace of the sciences and of the arts? What in fact may be seen among almost all enslaved peoples: a superstitious and ignorant clergy, leading as they liked an even more ignorant people; so-called notables of the Nation, whose alleged nobility, fed by the sweat of the people whom they tried vexatiously to exploit, was all the more ridiculous because, placed as they were between government and people, they were compelled to abase themselves more and more before the idol of despotism, and were more exposed than the rest of the nation to the blows of arbitrary malice on the part of the rulers; heads of families too exhausted by vexatious demands, or too blinded by superstition to provide a good education for their children; young people deprived therefore of any kind of knowledge and who added to such ignorance the weakness of Sybarites or the strength of savages. If occasionally one saw some young man expatriate himself in order to seek in Europe the enlightenment which he could not find in his own fatherland, such enlightenment was limited to the study of medicine; and Italy, where the subject was studied, represented usually for the modern Greeks what for the ancients the Columns of Hercules were for a time. But, since they went there without any preparation, and rather in order to learn a craft than to acquire a science, and that at a time when in Europe itself medicine was no more than a craft, all that they brought back to their unhappy fatherland, as the fruit of their studies, was the means to do harm accompanied by that presumption which prevents the forestalling or the preventing of it. Sometimes the study of theology was associated to that of medicine; and these theologians, some of them embracing the cause of the Greek Church, others that of the Church of Rome, have been seen to write polemical works which served to nourish, against the spirit of Christianity, the mutual hatreds of the two communions.

These studies usually constituted the limits of enlightenment among educated men. The others hardly knew how to read or write; and yet this part of the nation which, no doubt, was the most ignorant, was yet neither the most superstitious nor the most depraved. It seems to owe this advantage to its very ignorance which prevented it from reading bad books. All that Venice, which was practically the only place in Europe where books for the use of modern Greeks were printed, sent us—if exception is made of works indispensable to religious worship and other elementary works for the use of schoolboys learning ancient Greek—was confined to a few tasteless productions designed more to increase the ignorance of the nation, rather than to enlighten it. It was a happy accident which indebted us to the Venetian printing-press for the translation of *Télémaque* by the immortal archbishop of Cambrai and of Rollin's Ancient History; two books which, as will be seen in the sequel, proved to be of some use to the Greeks.

The nation continued in this deplorable state until after the middle of the last century. Yet it was not difficult for the attentive observer to discern through the heavy darkness which covered unhappy Greece that this state of affairs could not last. On the one hand, the very small number of schools where ancient Greek was taught, in spite of the discouraging imperfection of the teaching methods, in spite of the teachers' ignorance and obstinacy and the small benefit which consequently was derived from them, preserved in the nation the knowledge of its ancestral tongue like a sacred fire which would one day bring it back to life. On the other hand a national vanity, ridiculous in its motives but salutary in its effects, rendered the Greeks as proud of their origin as would be somebody who was the descendant, in direct line, of Miltiades or Themistocles. This vanity, together with the difference in religion and habits and the treatment, equally unworthy and impolitic, which the Greeks received from the hands of their conquerors, resulted in the fact that a large part of the nation always looked upon itself as prisoners of war and never as slaves. It was therefore easy to predict, as I have just observed, that it required only the help of some favorable circumstances for such a state of affairs to change.

It is quite remarkable that one such circumstance was precisely that ever memorable period when the mind of the enlightened part of Europe, tired of systems, and of that scholastic method used in the teaching of the sciences which was then not yet wholly abandoned, felt the need to make a new path for itself, and to take for guide no other but the faithful and exact observation of facts. This happy discovery soon led the Europeans to another—no less important—namely, to look on our sciences not as parts isolated from one another, but rather as the various branches of a great tree, or as the different compartments in a vast edifice, not a single one of which could be studied unless considered in its relation to the rest. It was France which had the glory of being the meeting-place in the middle of the last century of philosophers who were the first to lay the foundations of that vast edifice known as the *Encyclopédie.* The clarity which issued from this literary revolution, following the same laws as physical light, had necessarily to shed light wherever obstacles did not impede it, far from its original source. We have already seen how great these obstacles were on the part of the Greek nation; but, as may also be observed, they were counterbalanced by the feelings which a large part of the nation entertained. The Greeks, proud of their origins, far from shutting their eyes to

European enlightenment, never considered the Europeans as other than debtors who were repaying with substantial interest the capital which they had received from their own ancestors.

In the year 1766 (that is, some fifteen years after the publication of the *Encyclopédie*) appeared among the Greeks for the first time a treatise on Experimental Physics, with plates included, as well as a treatise on Logic. These two works, written in Ancient Greek and published in Leipzig by two respectable Greek ecclesiastics, were as learned as the authors' circumstances then allowed. A little while afterwards, the author of the Logic published a translation of Segnert's Mathematics, and a translation, in Modern Greek, with the original text facing it, of a small work attributed to Voltaire and entitled, *Historical Essay on the Dissensions of the Polish Churches.* This same ecclesiastic has given us, in 1786 and 1791 respectively, a translation in Greek verse of Vergil's Georgics and his Aeneid. This last work, which shows through its accompanying notes the translator's zeal, efforts, and learning and which would have even had some success as a literary work, had it been possible to translate the felicities of one dead language into another dead language, must be remembered all the more by an impartial observer in that it constitutes one of the most characteristic symptoms of present-day intellectual ferment in Greece and indicates that the happy revolution which is working in this country has taken a direction such that nothing can stop it anymore. And yet it was in 1788, two years, that is, after the publication of the Georgics, that Pauw in his *Philosophical Researches Concerning the Greeks,* could prophesy before the whole of Europe, with the tone and confidence of someone inspired, that *among the Greeks ignorance and superstition have put down roots so deep and so tenacious that no force, no human power could extirpate them.* If he had known what was going on among the Greeks, and if he had wanted to reason like a philosopher, as is proclaimed in the ostentatious title of his book, he would have seen and concluded from such an extraordinary phenomenon as the translation of Vergil among a people hardly emerging from barbarism, that among this people an intellectual ferment was going on. Thus the branches of a vigorous tree, bent under the load of an alien force, once rid of this load, grow past the point where they would be at rest; and it is only after much oscillation that they regain their natural position.

I return, however, to the period when for the first time Greece saw treatises on physics and logic written in the manner of the enlightened peoples of Europe. And here we see such a succession of cause and effect, such a concourse of varying circumstances, yet all tending to the same result, that it is quite impossible for me to assign to each its proper place in the sequence of events, or to evaluate with any precision its influence over the moral revolution which is now at work among the Greeks. Such an enterprise may even be unphilosophical, since no revolution, whether moral or political, among any people in the world, has ever been effected through isolated causes. In order to change an individual's condition, one cause may often be sufficient; but men united in society do not move or change their situation except as a result of several causes working jointly and in succession. I must therefore limit myself to presenting in their natural order the most noteworthy events which might be considered to have contributed to the present state of Greece. I myself have been an eyewitness of most of them, and the rest I have collected from the testimony of other eyewitnesses.

The works of which I have spoken were received in the Greek schools (long attached, with the same superstition which has denatured the simplest of religions, to Aristotle's philosophy or rather to his commentators' fancies) by the greater number of the teachers as an innovation which was at the very least useless, and by almost all the students as a curious thing about which one had at least to show oneself to be informed. This curiosity on the part of the youth, however adequately fed by the teaching of the new logic, a teaching which took place for an unfortunately brief period in a school on Mount Athos,[2] this curiosity, I say, would no doubt have remained barren if the Greeks had continued to be as poor as they had been so far, and to vegetate in that discouragement, the deplorable fruit of oppression, which reduces the rational being to a brutish state. Above everything

else man tries to secure his subsistence; and since under a tyrannical government the difficulties of earning it increase by reason
of the oppression, he must continually busy himself with the
means of overcoming these difficulties. It is only when he has
satisfied this primary natural need, and somewhat rendered his
life less precarious, that man looks around him and seeks to
broaden the circle of his understanding. Such has been, always
and everywhere, the course of the human spirit among the
Greeks as I have observed it. At the period of which I speak,
the Greeks were neither free, nor nearly as rich as the inhabitants of a region so marked for the variety and abundance of its
products ought to have been. And even today they can hardly
be considered wealthy; but two noteworthy events have contributed to make them less poor and to inspire in their stricken
souls, not the courage which comes from ease and freedom, but
at least hope, which made them discern at once both the cause
of their unhappy state and the possibility of arresting its nefarious effects.

Because of a new direction which various circumstances gave
to the channels of commerce, many Greek commercial houses
found themselves in a short time in possession of extraordinary
riches; and the word *millionaire* was for the first time heard
among a people who had been accustomed to consider the small
number of those who owned a capital of one hundred purses as
men overwhelmed with the favors of fortune. These newly en-
riched men, who unfortunately had as yet nothing but their
wealth, did not take long to understand that if fortune distributed
her gifts blindly, yet eyes and far-seeing eyes were required to
retain these gifts and render them fruitful. Accustomed hitherto
to use European agents in the management of their businesses,
they now thought they could dispense with these and in fact
replace them, in great part, by the native youth who thanks to
the attraction of large salaries now found themselves tempted
to study.

The study of the languages of those countries with which they
had commercial relations gave them a tincture of learning and
of culture; and by the study of arithmetic and the fine art of

bookkeeping which enable the mind to discover truth by following error to its source, they were, unwittingly, taking a course
in logic. The study of foreign languages made clear the advantage of those who had started by studying their own tongue, or
who were going to study these languages in the countries and
among the peoples where they were spoken. The desire to study
and the desire to go abroad took hold of the young men, therefore, and was seconded by the desire which great riches inspire
in those who possess them, to extend their trade, on the one
hand by opening branches in foreign countries, and on the other
to increase the means of instruction in their own midst if only
for the benefit of their own children. Soon enough, merchants
had established new commercial houses in the ports of Italy, in
Holland, in various parts of Germany, and particularly in
Trieste, which today has a Greek colony composed of hundreds
of families. Thus commerce, by spreading in the nation, saved
from idleness a multitude of young Greeks, and scattered them
into various regions of Europe, and at the same time provided
through the increase of schools more means for the remaining
youth of the nation to educate themselves. The desire to excel
which necessarily arose out of such conditions made a section
of this youth, once their training in the native schools was completed, decide to come to Europe in order to complete their
studies; and here many of them, destined for commerce, have
been seen to desert the countinghouse and take refuge in some
university. Such have been the results of the increase in the
pecuniary means of the Greeks; but at that period nothing contributed more to excite the spirit of emulation, to increase the
intellectual ferment, and to inspire the Greeks with courage than
the event of which I will now speak.

It was in 1769 that Russia declared war on Turkey. This latter
power, however much it had declined from that state of ferocious energy which made her as redoubtable to the European
powers as fearsome to her own subjects, still preserved an appearance of greatness which inspired respect. An illusion difficult to reconcile with the progress of knowledge, and particularly
with the improvement of the art of war, led Europeans to see

in the army of this power the same heroes who had conquered the Eastern Empire, who had expelled the Venetians from Candia and the Peloponnesus, and who, penetrating into the heart of Germany, had dared to lay siege to and almost capture the capital of the Empire. Russia has forever dissipated this illusion, by proving to the whole of Europe that the girth which had been taken to indicate a vigorous constitution was nothing but a dropsy which, sooner or later, would lead the Ottoman Empire to its fate. The effects of this glorious war did not merely serve to enlighten the Europeans. Russia, which then had an interest in being considerate to the Greeks, whom she hoped one day to count among her subjects, employed a number of them in this war and attached them to herself by means of honors and rewards. These new auxiliaries espoused the cause of the Court of Petersburg; while the whole nation, from different motives, prayed for the success of Russian arms.

The latter were only seeking revenge for their oppressors' injustice, whilst for the former Russia's cause was the cause of religion itself and they saw in the Russians merely those who would restore their churches, now either destroyed or turned into mosques; some, however (and they constituted that small band of sensible people who are met with in all countries and ages), looked upon the Russians only as a nation destined to prepare Greece for freedom. In the meantime, those Greeks who had been in the Russian service saw all their hopes frustrated by the peace which the belligerent powers concluded, and had to resume their yoke, but were now moved by sentiments quite different from those they had before throwing it off. Convinced now that their oppressors were men who could be defeated, that in fact they had defeated them by the side of the Russians, and that it would not prove impossible for them to defeat the Ottomans on their own provided they had able men to lead them, they felt in themselves for the first time a spark of pride which only a show of moderation on the part of the Turks has prevented from being rekindled. While the Greeks felt their courage return, the Turks were feeling discouraged and humiliated to an extent such that they felt compelled to show some consideration to those whom they had hitherto treated as mere beasts of burden. Other circumstances came to add to this discouragement. The Russian consuls, gaining in authority from the most glorious peace which their sovereign had just concluded with the Turks, were exercising a kind of dictatorship all through the Levant. They more than once saved Greeks from government persecution on the pretext that they had become Russian subjects or had been in Russian service. The bachas and governors of provinces, on the other hand, who had hitherto been accustomed to receive the orders of the Porte as though they were the decrees of Heaven, came to realize now, as a result of this war in which they had been active eyewitnesses, that the idol which they worshiped rested on nothing but feet of clay. They now received the orders of their emperor with arrogance, more as partners in empire than as slaves. Many of these bachas even raised the standard of rebellion; and there are still some over whom the Turkish government has no more than a precarious authority. This disobedience, an effect of the same cause which had inspired in the Greeks feelings of courage and pride, has itself contributed to strengthen these feelings.

Before this period, the islanders of the Archipelago traded only in moderately small vessels. They carried on *cabotage* from island to island and their longest journeys did not extend beyond Egypt or the Black Sea. But at this period, the new direction in commerce of which I have spoken, the new wealth spreading throughout the nation, and possibly the decrease in the authority of government gave some islanders the idea of building merchant vessels in imitation of and in the manner of the Europeans. The first vessels so constructed were found striking by everybody except the government. Whether it was ignorance, or disdain, or the need and the convenience of finding among the Greeks sailors for the Turkish fleet who were to be sought in vain among the Turks themselves, the Porte, although suspicious by nature, paid no attention to the birth of this merchant fleet. Moreover, it is even said that, by an inconsequence quite common in the annals of despotism, the government even favored it somewhat at the beginning. What at least is certain is that the present

Sultan having at his accession (which took place shortly before the French Revolution) expressed himself in favor of a merchant fleet (a Turkish one naturally), his courtiers hastened to build a few merchant vessels. But being compelled to have them manned by Greek sailors, they put a Turkish captain in command of each vessel in order to save appearances. The fact remains, in any case, that at the present moment the merchant fleet belongs to the Greek islanders alone and that the ships are manned, from the captain down to the apprentice sailor, exclusively by Greeks. Of course, if the government had suspected at the outset that the Greeks would one day own a merchant fleet composed of hundreds of ships, most of them privateers, it would have stifled the enterprise in the cradle. What today prevents it from putting a stop to its further progress is the very help which it derives for its own fleet, for the ignorance of this nation in maritime affairs is as profound as if the seat of its government had been situated in the middle of Asia, hundreds of leagues away from the coast.

It is impossible to predict all the consequences which may flow from the creation of this fleet, or the influence it may come to have over the fate of the oppressed nation, as over its oppressors. It is easier to observe what changes it has worked so far. On the one hand, by helping the trade of the Greeks and increasing their material prosperity, this fleet has powerfully helped in multiplying educational facilities. The islanders, who had been the most ignorant part of the nation, now begin to feel the need and value of enlightenment and rival one another in the foundation of local schools and colleges. On the other hand, owing to the happy influence which this fleet has had over the minds of the rulers whose despotism it has somewhat mitigated, the islanders have acquired and communicated to the rest of the nation a spiritual energy such as had remained unknown ever since the nation lost its freedom. Controlling a large number of sailing ships, solidly and elegantly built by their own hands and manned by crews who are most often linked by blood or marriage, these islanders can, at the least suspicion of intensified oppression, put their families aboard and go to offer themselves to the first nation which would have the sense to accept so substantial a gift. I have myself not long ago heard said to captains from Hydra what Themistocles, who commanded a naval fleet surely much inferior to these islanders' navy, said to the Corinthian admiral who reproached him with the fact that the Athenians had allowed their city to be destroyed by the Persians: "So long as we are in possession of two hundred armed vessels we have a native land and a fatherland."[3]

Among these shipowning islanders, the inhabitants of the small township of Hydra whom I have just mentioned deserve special notice, not only because they are in the first rank, but also because they provide the observer with details about the organization of their fleet, their manner of living and of governing themselves which are all the more curious in that these islanders are still in a state of profound ignorance, in spite of the efforts which they have been making for some time now to emerge from it. Situated in the southeast of the Peloponnesus at some three leagues from the mainland, this island produces almost nothing, and its inhabitants are the less eager to make it more productive in that they are in a position to obtain by means of navigation all the necessary staples, often cheaper than they could be procured in their country of origin.

As I have said, until the Russo-Turkish War, the Hydriots, like the other Greeks, confined themselves to the trade of the Archipelago, of the Black Sea, and sometimes to that of Egypt. When the Turks regained possession of the Archipelago, which the Russians had abandoned, a large portion of the inhabitants of this unhappy region precipitately abandoned their homes in order to escape Turkish vengeance and sought their refuge wherever circumstances and their geographical position afforded them an asylum. Those who transported them were for the most part Hydriots, and Hydra itself became an asylum where a great number of Peloponnesians took refuge together with their families, and with whatever possessions they had not been compelled to abandon to the Turks. These new colonists, transported from a region which produced everything, to a heather-covered rock, so to speak, found themselves reduced to the one expedient of trade and gave themselves up to it all the more willingly since they found themselves living among sailors highly expert in coastal trade and, from a well-acquired and well-merited reputation for good faith, worthy of all their confidence. Even today, the Hydriots do not know in the coastal trade of the Archipelago what in commerce are called *bills of lading*. Large sums of money, packed in bags showing their proprietor's mark and accompanied by a simple letter of advice, are given into their keeping. On arrival to their destination, they deliver both bags and letter; and far from citing examples of fraud, we can record that it has often happened that bags of money remaining unclaimed in the captain's chest for two or three years were finally returned to the owners in the same state in which they had been consigned. Fortunately for the enlightened nations, such instances are by no means easy to find among peoples lacking in education; because, after all, what would be the use of enlightenment if virtue could be attained without its help, if it did not have the advantage over ignorance of forming, even in the midst of nations which dishonor it, a public opinion which resists like a dike the flood of corruption?

Made wealthy by the disastrous events of the Peloponnesus and by the commerce of the new colonists, the Hydriots started to think of nothing else but of making their ships bigger and of undertaking, in rivalry with one another, the most distant journeys. These new Argonauts have been seen in all the ports of Italy and of France, which they supplied with wheat on the occasion of the famine, of the Baltic, and even of America. These journeys presuppose in these sailors a knowledge in proportion to the perils of distant navigation; such knowledge, properly speaking, they do not have; it is in the meantime replaced by the experience of European pilots in those ports only which they approach for the first time, and for the rest by their courage and daring, which are the fruit of their naval regulations and of a singular kind of education, seemingly similar to that of the ancient Greek navigators. Such daring would deserve the name of temerity had not success almost constantly crowned it. Often compelled to fight hand to hand with the Algerines, against whom the Turkish government cannot and frequently does not want to protect them, the Hydriots have made their ships into privateers. Every ship carries from eight to thirty guns and is manned by 35 to 70 men, usually all under 40 years of age, not counting five or six boys of whom the eldest is no more than ten years; sometimes even boys under six years of age are met with. Half the profits of a journey, which in recent years have been considerable, after the payment of interest on the capital used to buy a cargo, belong to the owner; the other half is divided in equal sums among the crew, the children included. The aim of such a division is to make all the members of the crew interested in the success of the expedition; and as for the children, it is to enable them to maintain their families if they should come to lose their fathers, and to help them to marry young. In fact the result of this provident policy has been that the population of Hydra has increased in an extraordinary manner during the last twenty-five years. Boys marry at the age of 18 or 20 and girls at the age of 12. These boys on board ship who one day will become captains and heads of families have to be taught the art, or rather the routine, of navigation. This is how it is done: every time that a ship comes in sight of a coast, a headland, or an island, these boys are brought to the steering wheel and taught the different bearings. At the first opportunity they are summoned again, and their memory tested; and woe to him who does not remember what he had been taught. The lesson is repeated and his attention fixed on it with the help of a whip. The Hydriots are accustomed to lead an extremely frugal life. Thus the provisions they take with them when setting out on a journey amount to very little, except wine, of which they always take care to have an ample supply. But such a precaution is soon found useless, since it happens often that a month's provision of wine is consumed in three days at the start of the journey; and because the young have neither the right nor the power to punish adults, the latter are never weaned from this vice. If anything might excuse such an indulgence, it is that this excess of wine does not render them drunk, or at least not so drunk as to make them careless of anything essential to the success of the expedition, and that in any case they abstain from wine for the rest of the journey as cheerfully as they had indulged in it. This ability to put up with extremes, which is also found in the French character, is common to all the islanders of the Archipelago. It is when they are in port or at home that the Hydriots lead a leisurely life. It is in this arid island that each one then tries to imitate (according to his own taste) the way of life of those nations he has visited. Luxurious habits are introduced; and so long as, without exhausting it, they draw sustenance from the wealth created by trade, these habits must increase civilization and knowledge among them. We may already see in the island houses built with all possible conveniences, with properly appointed dinner tables, the homes of men who lead an almost hermitlike life aboard their ships and who easily take in their stride the most dreadful vicissitudes which weather and different seasons may bring about.

If they have begun to introduce amongst themselves the comforts which Europeans enjoy, they have not failed to realize that these are the fruit of knowledge. They have thus established in the island a college for the study of ancient Greek and a number of schools where reading and writing is taught; they also already have a professor of Italian, the language which today they need most. They have built near the port an edifice which they use as an office and an exchange and in which are transacted all affairs pertaining to their trade and navigation. All this is no doubt too insignificant to attract the attention of the European and particularly of the Frenchman, surrounded as he is by all kinds of universities, colleges, *lycées*, literary societies, and all manner of public institutions. But these things may serve to satisfy the observer who knows that hitherto the Hydriots used to be the most ignorant portion of the Greeks, who will compare what they are today with what they were less than twenty-five years ago, who may consider that such a comparison provides the best augury and will thus entertain for the future hopes which are as flattering as they are well founded.

The revolution which continues to take place in Greece has necessarily had differing effects varying with greater or lesser barbarity, more or less intense passions, more or less abundant resources, varying, in a word, with the circumstances in which it has found the different towns and communities of this region. In those towns which were less poor, which had some well-to-do inhabitants and a few schools, and therefore a few individuals who could at least read and understand the ancient writers, the revolution began earlier and could make more rapid and more comforting progress. In some of these towns, schools are already being enlarged, and the study of foreign languages and even of those sciences which are taught in Europe is being introduced into them. The wealthy sponsor the printing of books translated from Italian, French, German, and English; they send to Europe at their expense young men eager to learn; they give their children a better education, not excepting girls, who had hitherto been deprived of any kind of instruction, as they had been excluded from even the most innocent commerce with men.

A most remarkable thing, which in a way confirms Hippocrates' doctrine concerning the influence of climate, is that in ancient Greece the sciences were born in Ionia and spread from it, and that their rebirth in modern Greece seems to follow the same course. It is common knowledge that Ionia possessed writers of all kinds long before there could be any question of learning in Greece proper. Homer, Hesiod, Thales, Anaximander, Pythagoras preceded, by a greater or smaller number of centuries, Sophocles, Euripides, Aristophanes, Plato, Aristotle, Demosthenes, and all the great writers who adorned Greece's golden century. The Ionian dialect was cultivated and perfected long before that of Athens; and even this latter, which succeeded it, was at the outset identical with the Ionian. The Ionian dialect must have been considered, in the time of Herodotus and Hippocrates—so near to Plato's own period—as the most perfect since both the father of history and the father of medicine chose it for writing their immortal works, even though both of them were of Dorian origin. Plato himself, the most polished and most eloquent of the Attic writers, is influenced by the study of Homer to such an extent that a knowledge of the latter's poems is absolutely essential for a proper understanding of his works.

I have said that the rebirth of letters in Greece seems to take the same course as their birth had taken, originating in Ionia and gradually spreading in the rest of Greece. This is because, although the revolution which forms the subject of my remarks is common to all the Greeks, it is in Homer's own birthplace, in the island of Chios, that modern Greece has had the satisfaction of seeing a few years ago the foundation of some sort of university or polytechnic. This foundation constitutes an epoch in the modern history of this region; and though the institution is still somewhat imperfect, it is nevertheless all the more promising in that it has attracted, at its very inception, eager students coming from all parts of Greece. Their numbers have grown to an extent such that the managers have found it necessary to issue an appeal to the whole nation, inviting the well-to-do to help maintain and enlarge the school by means of their voluntary contributions. Circular letters have been sent everywhere, and everywhere men have been found ready to listen to the voice of the fatherland calling to them. I will allow myself to quote one of these letters addressed to Greek merchants established in different cities of enlightened Europe. This letter describes the revolution I have been speaking of in a manner too striking for me to ignore. "It is from you (say the managers of the school addressing these merchants) particularly from you, dear brethren, that we ought to solicit help. Established in the midst of enlightened cities and nations, you witness with your own eyes the advantages which arts and sciences bring; able to frequent European theaters, where you may see representations of Greek plays and Greek actions, who is better able than you to appreciate our ancestors' values, virtues and learning? Gaining honor from the Greek name, it is in turn your duty to bring it honor, by calling forth once again in the midst of degraded Greece, its ancient exaltation and splendor. In founding this establishment, we have done nothing but obey the voice of the fatherland, nothing but realize the wishes of all the Greeks, and especially yours, because you in your position are best able to judge how far enlightenment might help to gain once more for our nation the esteem of the foreigners which it ought never to have lost."

It is in this manner that the inhabitants of Chios act and speak today.

Even before the beginning of this revolution, it was not difficult to predict that Chios would be among those cities where its effects would be most marked. The inhabitants of this island have at all times played on the world's stage a part which was as honorable as it was worthy of notice. In the time of their prosperity, when they were a free people, they were distinguished by the wisdom of their laws and by a powerful opulence which was the natural consequence of their laws and customs. As Plutarch reports, for the space of seven hundred years, adultery or any illicit intercourse between free persons was unheard of in Chios. In the Ionian-Persian war, the inhabitants of Chios were those who, among the Ionian allies, supplied the greatest number of vessels and men. They fought with a courage such that, if they had been at all supported by their allies, they would have inflicted upon Darius' fleet the same defeat which a few years later his son Xerxes' fleet suffered at the hands of all the Greeks. It is Herodotus who describes these islanders' power and courage which I have just recounted. Thucydides observes that they were thought to be the richest of all the Greeks, and that following the Lacedaemonians they were the only ones to have coupled wisdom with good luck, so that the more their republic flourished, the more they had the good sense to employ all possible means to maintain it in such a state. But what does most honor to these islanders is that having passed from a democratic regime to the subjection of the Macedonians, and then of the Romans, of the Genoese, and finally of the Turks, they have always been, in spite of these vicissitudes, the least enslaved, the least poor and the least corrupt. Unable to answer with force the blows of despotism, they have had recourse to prudence and they have been able to solve this problem: *how to lead a life most devoid of oppression under an arbitrary government.* It must not be thought that they have gained the privilege of being less subject to vexations than the rest of Greece at the price of their own degradation. This is the manner, both simple and ingenious, in which they solved this problem. United among themselves in a rare concord, they take care to put their island under the special protection of some magnate of the Empire; they always have some of their fellow-citizens residing in Constantinople, who see to it that overseers, judges, and other officials for the island's administration are not appointed except by this protector, or at least not appointed against his wishes, and that instructions they receive are such that they are almost unable to do anything without the advice and consent of the Greek municipality on the island. This municipality, elected by the people who confer on it for a year an almost limitless power, never abuses its power; and their fraternal unity is such that they have never requested the dismissal of a Turkish official who had the misfortune of displeasing them, without such a request being satisfied. This unity has meant that even when the times were most calamitous for the Greek nation, they were the least to be pitied; and that a man of feeling, traveling in Greece and seeking rest for his eye tired by the uniform mournfulness of the land, would seek repose on this isle which offered him a more consolatory spectacle. He could see there schools and passably learned teachers, an industrious population, silk factories and various other lucrative trades, a land cultivated or rather created anew, and consequently less misery and more good habits among the people. Thanks to its industry Chios, far from deserving the epithet *stony*, which Homer gives it, is today called *the garden of the Archipelago*. This political phenomenon deserves the legislative and moral philosopher's attention; the more so that these islanders' wisdom does not conflict with an amiable and cheerful disposition, playful to the point of levity, which distinguishes them from the other Greeks. It is presumably this disposition which has led to their being given the title of *Gascons of the Levant*. I myself could prefer to call them the *Frenchmen of the Levant;* a title which they deserve by reason of their past conduct, by the example which they set in founding an educational establishment on the European model and by what, henceforth guided by the torch of learning, they will not fail to do in order to ameliorate their own condition and that of Greece; for we observe that the number of students from the different parts of

Greece who are now in Chios surpasses that of the native Chiot students.

This salutary example which one portion of the Greeks has given will not be lost on the rest of the nation. The return of a large number of young men, now studying in France, Italy, Germany, and England, is being awaited so that schools may be established wherever the locality and other circumstances allow it. The love of learning has spread with all the symptoms of an epidemic, if I may express myself in this fashion; and what is of good augury for the future is that the epidemic has spread among the Greek clergy. Philosophy has walked over the altar's threshold, or rather has descended on it, emerging accompanied by an enlightened religion to instruct the nation. A good number of Greek ecclesiastics, so far from hindering the nation's education, are eager themselves to seek instruction. During the French Revolution priests have been seen coming one after the other from their native countries to seek knowledge in Paris in order to impart it on their return to their compatriots. At this moment Germany harbors an even greater number of them who are busy translating good books into Greek. In a treatise on *Conical Sections* translated by one of my ecclesiastical friends, I note that among the 113 subscribers, 47 are members of the clergy, and of these nine are bishops. These respectable ecclesiastics have realized that true piety is enlightened piety, and that enlightenment so far from being inimical to true religion, gives it, on the contrary, firmer foundations and deeper roots in the hearts of men. They have realized that gratitude by the nation for the services which they render is not to be compared with the foolish incense which superstition lavished on them. I am pleased to give to the Greek clergy their due, who will soon rescue from their dead hand both the altar which they [unenlightened ecclesiastics] did not know how to honor and the nation from whom they can no longer hope to receive a stupid homage.

Until the time when revolution broke out in France, the Greek nation, following an instinct easy to explain, had a kind of partiality for the English and the Russians. These latter have always been the natural enemies of the Turks; while the English were then almost the only nation in Europe to uphold their dignity against the arrogance of a barbaric court. The revolution had barely begun when the very same instinct made and still makes the Greeks take the side of the French. To speak of a confused foreboding of the likely effects and consequences of this revolution may seem romantic. But admiration for the prodigies accomplished by the armies of the Republic spread gradually and served to bring to memory the similar prodigies of the Greek armies in the past. From that moment, national vanity gave way to the countenance of a people preparing to become a nation. Enthusiasm for being ruled only by law became so widespread that people no longer talked of anything but Frenchmen. Everywhere secret societies of newsgatherers were formed which carefully collected and deliberately spread the good news arriving from France. French victories became their own victories, while French reverses invented or exaggerated by the enemies spread among them pain and consternation. This enthusiasm led to actions so extraordinary that I would not dare to recount them had they not been reported to me by eyewitnesses whose truthfulness it is impossible for me to doubt. In some townships of the Peloponnesus administered by Greek municipal bodies who often abused the power given to them by the Turks and oppressed the inhabitants, the people revolted against the municipal authorities, and in order to conform in all points to the French example, the summoning of primary assemblies was suggested. It is in that same period that Greek vessels were seen for the first time to bear the names of illustrious men of antiquity. Up to that period the practice was to give ships names of saints only. Today I know of ships which bear the name of Themistocles and Xenophon. Love of equality penetrated even into the convents, or rather, came back after having been banished for a long time. Exhausted by duties which religion had never imposed but which the haughtiness of their superiors rendered even more painful, the monks yet felt in themselves enough courage to gather in assemblies and summon their superiors to observe once again the ancient rule. Fortunately none of these movements reached the ear of the government, because the oppressors, owing to their relations with the oppressed, themselves had an interest in consigning them to oblivion. This was not the case in those small Greek cantons which, ever since the destruction of the Eastern Empire, have always been successful in maintaining a kind of rebellion against the conquerors of that Empire. Most of these cantons were accustomed to send a slight annual tribute to the Porte without allowing the Turks to come and collect it locally. The Turkish government tolerates these rebel communities, as it calls them, because they are protected for the most part by an almost inaccessible location; but it has neither lost the hope, nor neglected any means to make them submit, although every time that it has attacked them it has been repulsed with a courage akin to that of the ancient Spartans. The French Revolution has augmented this courage to a prodigious degree. I will not speak of the Maniots, whom everybody must know if only because of the highway robberies with which they are usually reproached. Far from justifying these [abuses], I pity those who commit them, for sometimes having recourse to a method which stains the glory of their valor; but also I give them their due and think that they would not have thought of annoying others had they not always been threatened with the loss of that which they prefer to life itself, namely liberty.

I will consider for a moment a small community of brave men which has already excited an English traveler's interest.[4] I will content myself with some incidents taking place after the publication of this traveler's work. It is difficult to believe that a community exists, divided into four villages, the population of which can provide no more than 1,500 arms-bearing men; that these brave men are democratically governed by some dozen chiefs; that they live with all the simplicity of heroic times; that they equal in valor the ancient Spartans; that for some years past they have been defending their freedom against the powerful Bacha of European Turkey, an enemy who is all the more dangerous in that he allies cunning to force; that in emergencies this handful of men call upon the help of three or four hundred of their wives, and that these latter-day Amazons fight by the side of their husbands, their sons, and their fathers, with a courage in no way inferior to that of the men; it is difficult, I say, to believe that such men exist; and yet they do exist. These villages, of which the main one is called Suli, are situated on a plateau in the canton known in ancient times as Cassiope, some fifteen leagues from the ancient oracle of Dodona, three leagues to the southeast from the river Acheron, and some seven or eight leagues distant from the Ionian Sea. Frenchmen must have heard of this ferocious Ali Bacha of Janina in connection with the unheard-of atrocities which he has committed against the Republic's defenders. It is this same monster who, incited by the brave Suliots' resistance, employs all means to exterminate them and who will never vanquish them so long as they are filled with that rare contempt of death of which I shall proceed to give one or two examples.

In an engagement between the Bacha's troops and the Suliots which took place not long ago, an officer of the latter, distinguished by his extreme youth and by a valor immune from all challenge, is struck by a bullet, falls down, and expires in the midst of his comrades. Pain and consternation fill the souls of those present and paralyze all effort: nobody is any longer concerned to repulse the enemy. A woman draws near and asks the reason of the turmoil; she is shown the inanimate remains of the army's Achilles; it was her son. She approaches him and without uttering a word takes her apron and covers his face; she then removes his weapons, puts them on herself, and rallies everybody by the eloquence of her countenance; she rushes on the Turks compelling them to retreat after a frightful massacre; she comes back toward her son and, removing the cover from his face, only then breaks her silence in order to proclaim with a loud voice that she had just revenged his blood.

Herodotus recounts that the inhabitants of Xanthe, a Cretan colony in Lycia, finding themselves compelled by hard necessity to submit to the yoke of the Persians, who had already subjugated all their neighbors, took a decision which makes humanity tremble, but which at the same time proves that liberty is not an imaginary divinity, since such great sacrifices are made to it. They assembled all their goods, their wives, children, and old men in the citadel, to which they set fire; when all was devoured by the flames, all who survived this horrible death, bound by the most sacred oaths, sallied forth against the Persians firmly resolved to die, and in fact died arms in hand. Pausanias records a similar instance of courage which took place, albeit with happier results, in a war waged by the Thessalonians against the inhabitants of Phocis. These latter were prevented from putting their horrible scheme to execution by a victory over their enemies as brilliant as it was unexpected. The brave Suliots, who have certainly not heard of these rare prodigies inspired by despair, have themselves enacted them not long ago. Seeing the enemy on the point of capturing the pass leading to their fastness, they made all individuals whom age or weakness rendered unfit for the carriage of arms stand by the side of a dreadful precipice down which they were resolved to throw them if the enemy should succeed in penetrating to their homes. Fortune, however, was ashamed not to crown with success the efforts of a people who preferred entirely to disappear from the face of the earth than to live under a despot's yoke. They repulsed the Bacha's troops and even captured some. An incident took place on this occasion which is not without interest to an observer of national character, and particularly the character of those people whom civilization has not covered with its varnish. During a truce, an innocent animal, one of those which man, in spite of the services they render to him, is usually pleased to treat harshly and with contempt, broke its lead and wandered off toward the enemy's camp. One of the Suliot captains, addressing himself to the Turks with a stentorian voice, requested them to send back an animal which to them was a necessity. The Turks were for once honest enough to accede to the Suliots' request, and the latter, treating the matter as an exchange of prisoners, sent a Turk in place of the animal. I do not believe that this was only a witty gesture on the part of these braves: even if it were no more than a sign of contempt for their enemies, it would still be characteristic of that heroic simplicity which ordinarily precedes civilized behavior; a rude state no doubt, but unfortunately very often replaced by that falsity on which the name of politeness is bestowed. Homer's heroes do not scruple to insult in a cowardly manner their enemies' inanimate remains. Achilles, however, in spite of so many incitements on Agamemnon's part, contents himself with insulting him and threatening him with the sword; he does not challenge him to single combat; this extravagance has been reserved for more polished and more enlightened ages. What most does honor to the Suliots and proves that they know not only how to defend their birthplace but also how to preserve it by means of good laws, is that in order to put a stop, not to dueling, which they have never known, but to the barbaric custom of mutual killing for frivolous reasons, they have for a short time ago made a law which authorizes them to punish a murderer with a large fine, to raze his home from the soil of the motherland, and to deprive him forever of the right to rebuild it. This law, which would have done honor to a Solon or a Lycurgus, resembles somewhat the expiation which murderers had to make in heroic times. There is another similarity between the Suliots and the ancient Greeks. It is known that these latter never went to war except when accompanied by a diviner. The Suliots' Calchas is called *Father Samuel.* He is no different from the ancient diviners except in that they sought their predictions in the entrails of slaughtered animals, while he finds his oracles in Holy Scripture. To his compatriots he expounds Isaiah, Ezekiel, Daniel, Jeremiah: to Father Samuel the most obscure passages from the prophets are the simplest things in the world; he applies them all to the events of which we have been witness for the last few years, and everywhere in them he finds references to Frenchmen. As he is much venerated in the country, and since his prophecies spread from this new Dodona into the whole of Greece, the French have become the Messiah for most of the Greeks. I have discussed the brave Suliots at such length only because the energy with which, for some years now, they have defended their freedom, enhanced by the events which took place in France, has had a very marked influence over the rest of Greece.

If among the causes of the moral revolution which is now taking place among the Greeks I have listed the French Revolution last, this is precisely because it is last in point of time, although it is the cause which has most contributed to consolidate in the minds of the Greeks the salutary belief in the necessity of enlightenment which they had already conceived. Less than thirty years ago it was still rare to find in the four or five great cities of the Levant two or three Greeks able to speak and understand French tolerably well; it is now almost as common as Italian and becomes daily more so and it gains for the Greeks a more intimate knowledge of the French people and of their books. Another cause, equally derived from the French Revolution, came to increase this knowledge. The deplorable state to which French commerce was then reduced, the scarcity experienced by the valiant Italian Expeditionary Army, and even zeal to serve the French, all these brought a large number of Greek merchants and sailors to France. Here they sold their cargoes with large profits; but the most important profit which they brought back home with them was the greater or smaller amount of education which they acquired in the process. No doubt age, profession, and circumstances did not allow all to acquire instruction; but all, being witness of the nation's greatness and convinced that this greatness was the effect of enlightenment, returned home less ignorant than when they had left it; all came back with the regret of not having been earlier acquainted with France and with the desire to educate their children and to contribute with all their means to the moral revolution already initiated in their country.

The events taking place in France have given to the moral revolution of Greece a more regular rhythm and, if I may so express myself, a greater vitality which are so pronounced that the Greeks can no longer abandon the road which they have opened up for themselves. I will say more: at this moment there exist in Greece European books in translation and educated men in numbers such that as they have made letters flourish in their midst, they would also be able to make them flourish once again in Europe, should Europe perchance once again fall into the barbarism of the thirteenth and fourteenth centuries. It is enough for the impartial observer only to glance at the list of translations into modern Greek made during the last few years in order to be convinced that learned Greeks are today more numerous and much more educated than those Greeks of the fifteenth century who, fleeing a motherland made ready for a foreign yoke by the despotism of the national rulers, came to offer to Europe, as the price of the asylum which she provided, the little learning which yet remained to them.

In the list of translations which I have just mentioned and which would be too long to be given here, a great number of works on mathematics are seen, Locke's *Essay Concerning the Human Understanding*, Condillac's *Logic*, Martin's *Grammar of Philosophical Sciences*, treatises on chemistry, notably Fourcroy's *Chemical Philosophy*, Montesquieu's work concerning *The Causes of the Romans' Greatness and Decadence*. I do not mention a large number of works devoted to amusement and instruction— such as plays, novels, treatises on education— which have been translated and are everyday being translated from the various European languages. The translation of the *Voyage d'Anacharsis*,[5] which was begun and then suspended for reasons on which the honor of the century in which we live requires me to keep silence, will once again be taken up. Works translated and accompanied by notes, and pamphlets originally written in Greek which thirty years ago would have inspired murmurings, are today read with pleasure, or at least do not provoke censure from those who were most interested in censure. Geographical maps in modern Greek became known a few years ago already; and books on geography have appeared where a few Greek cantons are exactly described. A goodly number of Byzantine authors inform the people among whom their works are spread of the true causes of their misfortunes. A Greek dictionary as extensive as Henri Estienne's Thesaurus is projected, and attention extends even to modern Greek. This idiom, deriving from the language of the famous Greek authors of antiquity in the same way as Italian, French, and some other European languages derive from Latin, has over the latter the advantage of being closer to its source. It is, all the same, a new language which is now at the same stage as French was in Montaigne's time. The educated members of the nation who had hitherto neglected and even looked down upon it, compelled as they now are to use it in translating foreign works, have been led to ponder on its native resources and on ways of enriching it. And there is already a feeling that this new language itself constitutes a kind of revolution. Owing to the diversity of literary talents using its medium, it is as yet difficult to foresee exactly its ultimate development or the particular characteristics which will distinguish it from other languages. To judge by its infancy, the language promises to bring together a number of good qualities difficult to find elsewhere. Since among those books which have been translated, a considerable number deal with exact sciences, it is to be presumed that clarity will be one of its qualities; and as it still retains many turns of phrase and a few inversions derived from ancient Greek, it may be hoped that modern writers, far from dismissing these as an obstacle to clarity, will study to reconcile them with the former quality, so that from such a union a language will come forth displaying the flowers of a brilliant imagination together with the ripe fruit of reason. Already at the beginning of the French Revolution, a Greek-French-Italian dictionary had appeared which, however, bears only too visibly the traces of the haste with which it had been compiled; but it at least shows the ferment taking place in Greek minds.

This increase in the number of books is due only to increasing enlightenment. Spread as they are among the nation, they will serve further to increase enlightenment and to purify its customs. The observer may already perceive the influence and effects of this enlightenment with a secret satisfaction. There are already to be seen among the Greeks men with no other education than that afforded by reading, who think and act in a way which gives rise to the most consolatory hopes. There are wealthy men, as I have already said and once more like to repeat, who know how to make a more honorable use of their wealth, and one more worthy of a thinking man. They are seen endowing colleges, encouraging talents, helping with their purse, and honoring with their friendship, I had almost said with their respect, a young generation whose money-making abilities do not equal the passion to learn with which it is devoured. At the present moment there are in Europe many young Greeks who are studying at the expense of their respective communities, and a still greater number who owe their learning to the generosity of private persons.

I feel that in spite of the length of my observations on the present state of Greece, I have succeeded in giving nothing but a sketch. But it is time to end; and I can do so in no better way than by summarizing what I have just been saying.

In the middle of the last century, the Greeks constituted a miserable nation who suffered the most horrible oppression and experienced the nefarious effects of a long period of slavery. There yet remained in the nation's midst a very small number of schools in which a very small number of Greeks acquired only the most superficial knowledge of the Greek language. The rest of the nation was condemned to the crassest ignorance and to the reading of books, acquaintance with which is worse than nonacquaintance. About that period, learning in a large part of Europe takes a new orientation, to which the French philosophes more than others contributed. The *Encyclopédie* was the effect of this new orientation, becoming afterwards the reason for its continuance. Some rays of this enlightenment escape and penetrate into Greece. Greece does not shut her eyes to these rays; but she is still too weak and too poor fully to welcome and withstand their brilliance. Extraordinary circumstances on the one hand open new channels for trade in the Levant, and on the other bring about a war which ends by dissipating all the prestige which surrounded Ottoman power. Following these two developments the Greeks, hitherto stricken, raise their heads in proportion as their oppressors' arrogance abates and their despotism becomes somewhat mitigated. This is the veritable period of Greek awakening. Minds, emerging from their lethargy, are amazed to observe this deplorable state; and that same national vanity which had hitherto prevented them from seeing it, now increases their amazement and irritation. For the first time the nation surveys the hideous spectacle of its ignorance and trembles in measuring with the eye the distance separating it from its ancestors' glory. This painful discovery, however, does not precipitate the Greeks into despair: *We are the descendants of Greeks*, they implicitly told themselves, *we must either try to become again worthy of this name, or we must not bear it*. From that moment the ancient schools began to be reconstituted and new ones came to swell their numbers; young men expatriate themselves in order to learn the languages and acquire the learning of the enlightened nations of Europe; they are hardly back home when they are placed in charge of national education; through their oral tuition, and their translation of various foreign books, the nation becomes educated and increasingly feels the need for more education. All this takes place slowly, but uninterruptedly. The French Revolution comes at last and, as might be expected, does not fail to give a new impulse to the moral revolution which had already begun among the Greeks, an impulse all the stronger in being accompanied by a hope for the improvement of Greek fortunes. Spirits become restless from this new shock and attain such exaltation as to produce prodigies of valor in a few places and vast plans over the greater extent of Greece. The Greeks, seeing in the astonishing successes of the French armies nothing but the effects of enlightenment, seek, proportionately to their admiration for these successes, to multiply educational openings. The translation of foreign books, begun in the first period of the nation's awakening, has never been carried on with greater vigor than during and after the French Revolution. It may be said without exaggeration that during the ten years of this Revolution, which were also the last ten years of the last century, more books containing instruction in various subjects appeared in Greece than had appeared during all the time which elapsed from the destruction of the Eastern Empire. The French Revolution is at an end, and some time before this Revolution the Russians had agreed to make peace with the Turks; but the effects which these two events produced over Greek minds subsist; and it is all the less probable that they would disappear now that the Greeks have more financial resources and are more educated. The small number of books,

ignorance of printing techniques, and bad communications formerly prevented the people from being enlightened and from
recovering the knowledge they had lost. Now it is easier to
transmit knowledge from one country to another than to transport their respective products and staples. And in fact for some
years now the Greeks have added the commerce of science to
their ordinary trade. From all over Europe, and particularly from
France, they export books and knowledge just as they export
cloth, metalwork, and other products of European industry. The
only thing which prevents them from making this commerce as
extensive as it can be is a certain apprehension of the government; a consideration dictated by prudence and by the way in
which this government treats enlightenment.

Such is the present state of Greece; such are the sentiments
of the present generation of modern Greeks. When I took up my
pen in order to describe this state, a struggle began within me
which ended only when I put it down. Truth, with a strict voice,
charged me with the duty of presenting the facts as they were;
the motherland, bent under the yoke, lifted tear-filled eyes and,
showing me her lacerated breast, conjured me, in return for
having given me birth and education, not to reveal to the strangers' eye the truth even of her past state. I render myself justice
if I state that I emerge victorious from this struggle having be-
trayed neither truth nor the motherland. O truth! Do not be
afraid that I would soil my pen with lies; O my motherland! If
I were tempted to speak ill of you, my pen would drop a thousand times from my hands before writing a single word. Your
past faults are no longer yours, and I have recalled them only
in order to emphasize the more the merits of your present conduct. If never to fall is handsome, a virtue more appropriate to
man's nature is that he should attempt to rise up from a fall. Now
that you are making efforts to rise up, what does it matter that
a variety of circumstances did precipitate you into a pit of misfortunes? The deeper this pit, the more your efforts to emerge
from it will be appreciated, and the more glorious will be the
success which must crown them. Your fall is one which many
other peoples have also experienced; but if you continue to

behave as you have been doing for the last few years, you will supply to History's brush the first picture of a people's regeneration. The fall for which you have been so much reproached has not laid you so low as not to have left you some memory of your past greatness.

I have taken up my pen, O my motherland, only in order to be the first to announce that your regeneration has begun, to all Europe and particularly to that hospitable and philanthropic nation in the bosom of which I have found a new motherland since I had the misfortune of being separated from you. It is a debt which I am repaying you, and also a precaution I have thought wise to take for the sake of your future glory. If perchance some magnanimous nation wanted to extend a helping hand to you and to second your efforts, let that nation know that she will be fully entitled to your gratitude and to that of the whole human race, but let her also know in advance that she would not be the first to have dissipated the darkness which enveloped modern Greece. It is on your own, O my motherland, and without foreign help that, as soon as circumstances allowed it, you have opened your eyes to the light, have sought it everywhere, and introduced it in your midst. You have thus proved to the world that if unhappy circumstances may ruin the most fertile soil, yet they cannot deprive it of its natural fertility; a light rain and a little cultivation will suffice for all the riches which used to cover it to germinate anew. No doubt, those happy times when you will be the rival of ancient Greece and even of the most enlightened European nations have not yet arrived for you; but the manner in which you have begun, the ardor and perseverance shown by your young students, the zeal of your wealthy men, all proclaim that you will not always be what you had been for the last few centuries. In the new career which you have opened up for yourself, you have already taken too many steps for you to be able to retreat. As for myself, if I am still clinging to a life which is poisoned by the bitterness of the ills which afflict you, it is only in the hope of seeing you take up once again your proper rank among the nations. In exhibiting your present conduct to the eyes of the Observers of Man, I render justice to the truth, to you, and to the philanthropy of my respected colleagues, who will not fail to interest themselves in your fate.

Postscript On the point of finishing my paper, I receive two printed circulars. The first emanates from the Patriarch and Synod of Constantinople, the second from the four lay administrators named by the Synod for reestablishing on Mount Athos the school mentioned in my paper where logic was taught for the first time, or rather more precisely for establishing a university. In the latter circular, addressed to the whole nation, the four administrators in turn appoint two agents in every city of the Levant which is of any importance and in every European city where Greeks are found for the collection of voluntary contributions in aid of this national establishment. The circular by the Patriarch and Synod begins, after the usual blessings, with these remarkable words: "Every being is endowed with attributes peculiar to itself: man's attribute is reason; but this reason needs to be cultivated, etc." Here then are those superstitious Greeks who, according to a modern thinker, have been only waiting for a propitious moment in order to engage in mutual slaughter in the name of religion;[6] here they are, I say, far from setting up a tribunal of inquisition, peaceably engaged in creating means for the cultivation of their reason; and in such a reform it is the clergy who are taking the initiative.

NOTES

1. Plato, *Republic*, Bk. VI, p. 492.
2. Its own author taught the subject. This respectable prelate is today the dean of all cultured persons in the nation. He was one of the first to have usefully contributed to the moral revolution now at work among the Greeks. I render today my own part of the tribute which is owed to him by the nation all the more willingly that I will always remember with pleasure the desire to excel which the publication of his Logic, to which I owe what little enlightenment I have, excited in me.

3. Herodotus, I, VIII, Chap. LXI.

4. Koraes here refers to the observations on the Suliots contained in W. Eton's work, *A Survey of the Turkish Empire*, London, 1798. E.K.

5. I.e., J.J. Barthélemy, *Voyage du jeune Anarcharsis en Grèce vers le milieu du IVème siècle avant l'ère vulgaire*, 5 vols., Paris, 1788, a work of erudition cast in fictional form quite famous at the time. E.K.

6. Koraes here refers to de Pauw's *Philosophical Researches*. E.K.

2. THE IDEAL OF NATIONALISM: three currents of thought*[1]

⊔⎍⊔⎍⊔⎍⊔⎍⊔⎍⊔⎍⊔⎍⊔⎍⊔⎍⊔⎍⊔⎍⊔

Ziya Gökalp

In our country there are three currents of thought. When we study their history, we see that in the beginning our thinkers realized the need for modernization. The current of thought in that direction, which originated during the reign of Selim III [1789–1807], was followed later by another—the movement toward Islamization. The third, the movement of Turkism, has come forth only recently.

Because the idea of modernization has always been a main theme, it has no particular exponent. Every journal or paper has been an exponent of it in one way or another. Of the doctrine of Islamization, the chief organ is Sirat-i Müstakim ([later] *Sebil-ür Reşat*; and of the school of Turkism, *Türk Yurdu*. We can easily see that all of these trends have been the expression of certain real needs.

Gabriel Tarde tells us that the idea of nationalism has been the product of the newspaper, and gives the following explanation: the newspaper has given a common consciousness to those

*From *Turkish Nationalism and Western Civilization*, translated and edited by N. Berkes, London: George Allen & Unwin, New York: Columbia University Press, 1959, pp. 71–85.

who speak the same language by uniting them into a "public." In addition to this influence, which has been made rather unconsciously and unwillingly, the newspaper, which has spurred the feelings of honor and sacrifice in the masses merely to increase its circulation, has consequently aroused a consciousness of national traditions and of cherished ideals. The sentiment of nationality once it arises amongst the masses spreads easily over neighboring peoples. Once awakened, it leads to revivals in moral life, in language, in literature, and in economic and political life by reinforcing the feelings of solidarity, sacrifice, and struggle among its supporters. Naturally the idea of nationality spreads quickly when emulated by neighboring peoples, especially if they also have the press appealing to the masses in the vernacular.

The idea of nationalism appeared [in the Ottoman Empire] first among the non-Muslims, then among the Albanians and Arabs, and finally among the Turks. The fact that it appeared last among the Turks was not accidental: the Ottoman state was formed by the Turks themselves. The state is a nation already established (*nation de fait*), whereas the ideal of nationalism meant the nucleus of a nationality based on will (*nation de volonté*). With intuitive cautiousness, the Turks were reluctant, in the beginning, to endanger a reality for the sake of an idea. Thus, Turkish thinkers believed not in Turkism but in Ottomanism.

When the movement of modernization started, the supporters of the *Tanzimat* [2] reforms believed that it would be possible to create a nation based on will out of an existing "nation" composed of several nationalities and religions; and they thus attempted to give a new meaning, devoid of any color of nationality, to the older term "Ottoman," which had a certain historical meaning. Painful experiences proved that this new meaning of "Ottoman" had been welcomed by no one save the originators of the term. Inventing this new conception was not only useless but also detrimental, for it gave rise to harmful consequences for the state and the nationalities—and especially for the Turks themselves.

Today the West as well as the East shows unmistakably that our age is the Age of Nations. The most powerful force over the mind of this age is the ideal of nationalism. States, which have to govern on the basis of national consciousness, are doomed to failure if they ignore the existence of this important social factor. If our statesmen and party leaders do not hold this ideal, they cannot establish a spiritual leadership over the communities and the peoples constituting the Ottoman state. The experiences of the last four years have shown that the Turks who, in order to maintain understanding between the nationalities [under the Ottoman rule], denied Turkism and proclaimed Ottomanism, have at last realized bitterly what kind of a conciliation the nationalities would accept. A people moved by the sentiment of nationality can be ruled only by men who have the idea of nationalism in themselves.

The Turks' avoidance of the idea of nationalism was not only harmful for the state and irritating to the diverse nationalities, but it was fatal for the Turks themselves. When the Turks identified the nation and the state with the already existing nation and state, they failed to see that their social and economic existence was deteriorating. When economic and social ascendancy passed into the hands of the [non-Muslim] communities, the Turks did not realize that they were losing everything. They believed that they were the only class constituting the Ottoman nation and did not pay attention to the fact that they were excluded from certain classes, especially from those that constituted the most important strata of their age. They were not bothered by seeing the existence of economic and occupational classes of which they were not a part, from which they were excluded. As a consequence, they ceased to constitute the masses of people even in Anatolia. They were merely government officials and farmers. Farmers and animal breeders live only on the creative powers of nature and are not themselves creative powers. Government officials also are not actively productive. The growth and development of the mental faculties, of will and character, are the products of active occupations, as in industry and manufacturing, and of practical arts like trade and the liberal professions. It is because of this that it is almost impossible to create a national organization out of a people composed solely of farmers and civil servants. Our incompetence in administration, our difficulties in strategy and logistics, which led to the Balkan disaster, are all due to this state of affairs. The nonexistence of efficient government in our country is mainly due to the nonexistence of economic [commercial and industrial] classes among the Turks. Wherever the government is based on economic classes, there an efficient government exists. Business men, artisans, and traders want an efficient government for their own interests. Wherever the government is based on the class of state functionaries, it is always inefficient because those who are dismissed from government service always have their eye on government jobs, and those who are in the administration always have an eye on higher posts, and both are forever discontent with the existing government.

As the nonexistence of the ideal of nationalism among the Turks resulted in the lack of any national economy, so the same factor has been an obstacle to the development of a national language and to the appearance of national patterns in fine arts. And, again, because the ideal of nationalism was not present Turkish morality remained only a personal and familial morality. The notions of solidarity, patriotism, and heroism did not transcend the confines of the family, the village, and the town. As the ideal of *ümmet* [religion] was too large and the ideal of the family too narrow, the Turkish soul remained a stranger to the sort of life and to the intensive moral feelings that should be the bases of sacrifice and altruism. The disintegration seen in our economic, religious, and political institutions is the consequence of this state of affairs.

Turkish nationalism is not contrary to the interests of the Ottoman state; in fact, it is its most important support. As in all young movements, there are some extremists among those who uphold Turkish nationalism, mainly among a portion of the youth, who have caused certain misunderstandings to arise. In fact, Turkism is the real support of Islam and of the Ottoman state, and is against cosmopolitanism.

Tarde had also shown that the idea of internationalism is a product of the book. Since the newspaper appeals to the sentiments of the masses, it uses the vernacular, the living language. Books, on the other hand, appeal to the abstract thinking of the scholar and the scientist, and are dependent upon neologisms rather than the living word. Scientific and philosophical terms, as a rule, do not grow out of the vernacular of the people, which is natural and living, but are artificial constructs, lifeless words. The natural words of the vernacular carry vital and emotional meanings, and as such are not suited to abstract and conceptual usage. For this reason, every nation has borrowed its neologisms from its religious language. European nations have derived their scientific terminology from the Greek in which the Gospels were written and, as Latin became auxiliary to Greek in the Church, the Germanic and Slavonic languages also inherited much from the Latin. Islamic peoples derived their neologisms mainly from Arabic and, secondarily, from Persian. Even today, when we translate contemporary scientific works of the West into our language, we coin Arabic and Persian words for the Greek and Latin terms therein. The earliest books were the Scriptures. As ethics, law, literature, science, and philosophy were developed out of religion as separate branches, books began to be written about them as well.

It follows, then, that as the newspaper helped the rise of the ideal of nationalism by expressing the social and local sentiments of the masses in a colorful way, so the book has been instrumental in the creation of the idea of internationalism, or those aspects of life commonly shared by various nations, by formulating, in an abstract and exact style, the principles, rules, and formulas of civilization whose foundation of knowledge and science originated in religion.

It is not true that the sentiment of internationalism prevailed among men during the earlier stages of history. It is true, however, that there was a sentiment of internationalism during the European Middle Ages. But if we analyze this sentiment, we see that the international love and solidarity of that period was confined only to Christian peoples, and international law likewise pertained only to the rights of the Christian states. The Balkan wars demonstrated to us that even today the European conscience is nothing but a Christian conscience. If we analyze the conscience of the Turk, we shall see that he agrees, for instance, to wed his daughter to an Arab, to an Albanian, to a Kurd, or to a Circassian, but not to a Finn or to a Hungarian. He will not wed her to a Buddhist Mongolian or a Shamanist Tunguz unless he embraces Islam. During the Tripolitanian and Balkan wars, those who shared the griefs of the Turks and gave freely of their moral support were not Hungarians, Mongols, or Manchurians, but Muslims of China, of India, of Java, and of the Sudan, whose names we do not even know. It is because of this that the Turks regard themselves as one of the Muslim nations, although they belong to the Ural-Altai group from the linguistic point of view.

Anthropologically, human beings of the same anatomical types constitute a race, but sociologically the nations that belong to the same civilization constitute an "internationality." When the Turks, as an ethnic people, joined Islamic civilization, the Turkish language assumed an Islamic character with the intro-duction of the Arab script and terms.

Thus, the factor that creates the spirit of internationality, and hence civilization, is the book. Consequently, there is no incompatibility between Turkish nationalism and Islam, since one is nationality and the other internationality. When Turkish thinkers entertained the idea of Ottoman nationality composed of different religious communities, they did not feel the necessity of Islamization, but as soon as the ideal of Turkism arose, the need for Islamization made itself felt.

However, as nationality is the creation of the newspaper and internationality the creation of the book, modernity is the prod-uct of technology. Those peoples are "contemporary" who make and use all those machines made and used by the peoples most advanced in the techniques of the age. For us today moderniza-tion [being contemporary with modern civilization] means to make and use the battleships, cars, and aeroplanes that the Euro-peans are making and using. But this does not mean being like them only in form and in living. When we see ourselves no longer in need of importing manufactured goods and buying knowledge from Europe, then we can speak of being contemporary with it.

As there is no contradiction between the ideals of Turkism and Islamism, there is none between these and the ideal of modernism. The idea of modernity necessitates only the acceptance of the theoretical and practical sciences and techniques from Europe. There are certain moral needs which will be sought in religion and nationality, as there were in Europe, but these cannot be imported from the West as if they were machines and techniques.

It seems, therefore, that we should accept the three ideals at the same time by determining the respective fields of operation of each. To put it in a better way, we have to create "an up-to-date Muslim Turkism," realizing that each of the three ideals is an aspect of the same need taken from a different angle.

Contemporary civilization, which has been coming into existence for some time through the development of modern machines and techniques, is in the process of creating a new internationality. A true internationality based on science is taking the place of the internationality based on religion. The participation of Japan, on the one hand, and of Turkey, on the other, in Western civilization is giving a secular character to European internationality, as we shall show later; and thus the area of the *ümmet* is differentiating itself from the area of internationality increasingly.

In short, the Turkish nation today belongs to the Ural-Altai group of peoples, to the Islamic *ümmet*, and to Western internationality.

Nation and Fatherland [3]

... Currently discussed in the press are three concepts dealing with social questions that need definition: Turkism, Islamism, and Ottomanism. These concepts cannot convey any meaning unless they become symbols of certain social facts and unless

they derive their value from social reality. Without this understanding, they will not yield any fruitful result, even if people
continue to quarrel over them for years to come.

When we look at social realities, we cannot fail to see that an
Islamic *ümmet*, an Ottoman state (*devlet*), a Turkish or an Arab
nation (*millet*) do exist. However, if this statement corresponds
to any reality, the term *"ümmet"* must denote the totality of
those people who profess the same religion, the "state" all those
who are administered under the same government, and the "nation" all those who speak the same language. The statement will
be valid and will correspond to reality only if the above definitions are accepted. It seems, then, that those who do not accept
this statement deny it, not because its meaning does not correspond to reality, but because they do not believe that these words
are suitable for denoting the respective meanings.

The Islamists say that the word "nation" [*millet;* Arabic
milla] denotes what we cover by the word *"ümmet."* The term
"milla," they say, means "sect" in Arabic. The perfection of a
language means the existence of a meaning for every word and
a word for every meaning, and also the existence of words expressing several meanings. Even if we ourselves do not do this,
the language itself will. It is for this reason that the current
[Turkish] language uses the word *"ümmet"* for those who belong to the same religion, and the word *"millet"* for those who
speak the same language. As the majority of the people uses
them with these specific meanings, we too must accept them.
There is no use creating difficulties on questions of terminology.

The Ottomanists, on the other hand, believe that the "state"
and the "nation" are synonymous. To them, the sum total of
the citizens of a state constitutes a nation. This might be true,
if we disregarded reality and took only the logical relation
between the concepts into account. As a matter of fact, to
have a state composed of peoples who speak the same language, or to make only those peoples who speak the same language an independent state, seems more natural and most desirable. But are existing states formed that way? If not, then
how is it justifiable to disregard that which *is* existing and to

believe that what *ought to* exist is really existing?

The Turkists, on the other hand, criticizing the theses of these groups, come to the following conclusions: (a) the *ümmet* and the nation are different things; (b) the nation and the state are also not the same. One may object to these conclusions, but only in so far as they do not correspond to sociological realities, and not by insisting that these realities should not be so. We must fit our concepts to the realities and not the realities to our own concepts!

However, the external realities of the concepts of *ümmet*, nation, and state are not altogether independent of each other. The relation between the *ümmet* and the nation is a relation between the general and the particular. The *ümmet* is a whole which comprises several nations belonging to the same religion. Individuals actually constituting a nation are not the only members of a nation. All those who may speak that language in the future will also be members of that nation. Thus, for example, the Pomaks [Bulgarian Muslims] now speaking Bulgarian and the Cretan Muslims now speaking Greek may learn Turkish in the future and cease to be Bulgarian- or Greek-speaking peoples. This means that nationality is not determined by language alone but also by religion.

There is a more or less similar relation between the terms "nation" and "state." For example, the Ottoman state is a Muslim state—that is, it is formed of Muslim nations. Two great nations, the Turks and the Arabs, by their numbers as well as by their culture and learning, served as the bases of the Ottoman state in such a way that the Ottoman state might even be called a Turkish-Arab state. It should also be remembered that the Turkish and Arab nations are not confined only to those who live within the Ottoman territories. Those who speak the same languages but live under foreign rule also belong to these nations.

About the concept of "fatherland." It means a sacred piece of land for whose sake people shed their blood. Why is it that all other lands are not sacred, but only that which is called fatherland? And how does it happen that those who believe this way do not hesitate to sacrifice their lives, their families, their most beloved ones? Evidently not because of any utilitarian value. The sacredness is certainly derived from something sacred. But what can that sacred thing be?

Is it the state? We have already seen that the state is not a power existing by itself. The state derives its power from the nation and from the *ümmet: sharaf al-makān bil-makin* ["the glory of the residence is with the resident"]! Thus, there are only two things which are sacred: the nation and the *ümmet*. As the objects of reverence are two, their symbols or the homelands which are the seats of these two sacred objects should also be two: the homeland of the *ümmet* and the homeland of the nation.

There is, in fact, a homeland of Islam which is the beloved land of all Muslims. The other one is the national home which, for Turks, is what we call *Turan*.[4] The Ottoman territories are that portion of Islamdom which have remained independent. A portion of these is the home of the Turks, and is at the same time a portion of *Turan*. Another portion of them is the homeland of the Arabs, which is again a part of the great Arab fatherland.

The fact that the Turks have a special love for the home of the Turks, *Turan*, does not necessitate that they forget the Ottoman land which is a small Muslim homeland, or the great land of all Muslims. For national, political, and international[5] ideals are different things and all are sacred ideals.

The Ideal of Nationalism [6]

Youth is asking: "If we believe that ideals are the product of historical disturbance and social crises, will it not then be necessary to assume that another ideal, one which may be born from the impulse of different circumstances, will succeed the ideal of nationalism? Will not, for example, the idea of socialism supersede the sentiment of nationality in the near or distant future?"

My answer to this question is as follows. Essentially an ideal is the actualization of the existence of a social group by its members. The rays of the sun do not have the power to burn unless they are intensified through a lens. Similarly, the group is unable by itself to manifest its "sacredness" unless it reaches a state of social combustion. This sacredness, even before it has reached consciousness, exists in an unconscious state in the psychological unity of the social group. So far it has remained a hidden treasure (*al-kanz al-makhi*), with all its halo of sanctity. The function of the crowd situation is to make this reality manifest to the members of the group by transforming the latter amorphous existence into a clear-cut form. Social agitation becomes a source of ideals by its capacity to transform the group, which until now has been in a loose state, into a compact body. The emergence of an ideal means its rise from the subconscious to the conscious level.

Before the rise of the ideals of Ottomanism, Islamism, and Turkism, the Ottoman state, the Islamic *ümmet*, and the Turkish nationality all existed. The working class existed in a scattered state before the ideal of socialism was born, the latter emerging as a consequence of the concentration of workers, which itself was a result of the development of large-scale industry in Europe.

Therefore, a social group must have an existence, an organized form and institutions, in order to assert its existence in the consciousness of its members in a crowd situation. Its institutions, political, religious, or linguistic, must certainly have an existence. No crowd situation or condition of social agitation can create a group from nothing. Not only do ideals not emerge from a crowd situation that has no organizational basis, but such a crowd is itself inconceivable. Only something which exists in a state of laxity may be transormed into a state of solidity.

It follows from what has been said that any major social emergence taking place in the future must have its basis in already existing conditions. In order for an ideal to arise in the future, it must spring from the intensification of one of the existing groups. Therefore, a great ideal should be born out of the intensification of only that group which, in addition to being the richest and most powerfully organized, is in a position to bring together and assimilate all other groups in its own organization.

Which, then, is this inclusive group? Among the existing ones it is the language group—that is, the nationality group—which is most capable of fulfilling such a function.

First, those who speak the same language are usually descendants of the same stock, and thus a nation also means an ethnic unity. . . . Secondly, language is the carrier of ideas and sentiments, the transmitter of customs and tradition; hence, those who speak the same language share the same aspirations, the same consciousness, and the same mentality. Individuals thus sharing common and homogeneous sentiments are also naturally prone to profess the same faith. It is because of this that language groups in many cases are of the same religion. Even if in the beginning certain conditions interfered somewhat with this religious homogeneity, historical events show that peoples of the same language groups do tend to embrace the same faith. Thus, the Latins have been inclined to Roman Catholicism, the Germanic peoples to Protestantism, and the Slavonic peoples to Eastern Orthodoxy. Of the Ural-Altai group, the Mongols adopted Buddhism, the Manchurians Confucianism, and the Finno-Ugrians Christianity. Various sections of the Turks, in the beginning, had accepted Buddhism, Manichaeism, Judaism, and Christianity; but with the conversion of the majority of Islam, all became Muslims with the exception of the Shamanist Yakuts, who constitute only some two hundred thousand people. The main reason why the latter remained outside Islam is that their home lies far out of the Turkish lands. They will either embrace Islam and remain Turks or become Russified by accepting Christianity.

As language plays a part in deciding religious affiliation, so religion plays a part in determining membership in a nationality. The Protestant French became Germanized when they were expelled from France and settled in Germany. The Turkish aristocracy of the old Bulgars became Slavicized following their conversion to Christianity. And today, the non-Turkish Muslims migrating to Turkey in a scattered way are becoming Turkified because of their religious affiliation. We may conclude, therefore, that there is a close relationship between linguistic and religious association.

Thirdly, when universal military service and sovereignty of the people were introduced, national defense ceased to be the monopoly of a trained and privileged *sipahi* order, and administration of the government was no longer the privilege of a ruling class directly responsible only to the ruler. The peasants who previously had no arms except their plows, and the townsfolk who were used to staying at home, now became soldiers; the people, who had no notion of administration, came to the point where they could control the government. It became necessary to instill in them a sense of patriotism and to teach them how to assume the responsibilities of voting. When the needs of adult and universal education became apparent, conflicts arose among the different ethnic groups in the state over the question of which language should be spoken in the schools. The government began to insist on the dissemination of an official language, but each ethnic group demanded that its own language become the main channel of education and instruction. Thus, in the last century it came to be realized that confining the state and the country to a single language was no longer possible, and, as in the case of Austria-Hungary, the state adopted two main languages. Today in Europe only those states which are based on a single-language group are believed to have a future. Every national group is demonstrating the kind of future to which it aspires by voicing its wishes for a national home, with or without an historical basis.

Today all of us realize that the idea of a state or homeland supposedly common to diverse nationalities, is nothing but a mere concept, devoid of any zeal, enthusiasm, and devotion. Just as it is inconceivable for more than one person to win the love of one individual, so there can be no real common home and fatherland for diverse peoples. A state that is not based on a united spirit can be only a common source of subsistence and nothing more. A land that is not the home of a nation is like a public kitchen where everyone merely feeds himself.

The institutions of state and fatherland achieve permanent life only when based on a national ideal, but they are destined to fall if they are based only on individual interests. Men without ideals are egoistic, self-seeking, pessimistic, faithless, and cowardly; they are lost souls. A state must be founded on national ideals, a country has to be the home of a nationality if it is to have permanent existence.

We see, therefore, that the concept of the language group encompasses the concept of state as well as that of national home. Smaller units, such as family, class, corporation, village, tribe, and religious community, exist within the confines of the national unit. The family is composed of individuals of the same faith. They speak the language of a single nation. Other groups share a common religion and language. They are all, therefore, but smaller, constituent organs of the nation.

In short, all ideals connected with the ethnic unit (*kavm*), religion, state, national home, family, class, corporation, etc., are auxiliary to the national ideals. As long as social evolution substitutes intellectual and sentimental for material factors, the value and effectiveness of the national language as a means of expressing these ideals will increase, and in this way the sentiment of nationality will become a permanent ideal.

It is true that, as large-scale industry grows in Turkey, the ideal of socialism will arise here too. But this ideal is destined to remain auxiliary to the national ideal, as have all other secondary ideals. Although socialism in Europe is constantly gaining strength, we see clearly that it gives way to the national ideal in times of war. Not only during political wars, but even in economic competition, class ideals are subordinated to national ideals.

Furthermore, we can easily detect that the substance of all aspects of social life—such as religion, morality, law, politics, economics, science, and fine arts—is language. Any increase in the importance of these spheres of social life means an increase in the importance of language. Language is the basis of social life, the texture of morality, the substratum of culture and civilization. All future social movements—with respect to any group or activity—will always solidify language groups directly or indirectly, and out of every crisis the ideal of nationalism will effervesce, each time more powerful and with increasing vitality.

National Language [7]

Just as physical bodies have length, width, and depth, so the social consciousness also has three dimensions—nationality, religion, and modernity. I propose to test the validity of this observation first with regard to language, which is the best mirror of social consciousness.

The Turkish language has been in a process of growth for the last fifty or sixty years. As the lights of modern civilization penetrate our country, every day our eyes see new products, our minds think in new concepts. Since the new objects and ideas cannot remain unnamed, our language becomes richer by the addition of several new words every day. We also make translations from the papers and books of the leading nations of our century. In this way, several new concepts which formerly did not exist in our store of knowledge require the creation of new words in our speech.

Thus, the more our language meets the advanced languages, the more it tends to imitate them word by word. It sometimes imitates in form newly coined [Western] words, as we see in the case of words such as *hurdebīn* (microscope) or *dûrbīn* (telescope), or *sehkâr* (masterpiece), or *mefkûre* (ideal). Sometimes it coins new words by imitating meanings, as we see in the case of words such as *tayyare* (aeroplane), *tekâmûl* (evolution), *mesrûtiyet* (constitutionalism), and *bediiyat* (aesthetics).

This tendency suggests the following points for consideration: a day will come when the Turkish language will have all the words corresponding to those that exist in French, English, or German. As speech is an expression of subjective thinking, there grows a language expressing the concepts of our century, to which every national tongue must adapt itself. Until the Turkish language fulfills this requirement, it will not be a modern language—a language fully evolved from the point of view of the needs of our time.

The new words entering our language are of three kinds: (1) foreign words; (2) words derived from Arabic and Persian, or those which were coined from these languages; (3) and those derived or coined from the original Turkish.

The words of the first category enter the language through smuggling. The taste of the language tends to reject these words, and replace them either by Arabic (in the case of scientific terminology) or by Persian words (in the case of general vocabulary). This feature of rejecting foreign words by putting Arabic or Persian roots in their places is peculiar not to Turkish only. All Muslim languages show the same tendency. These languages, which have something in common insofar as the religious terms or the scientific terms derived from religion are concerned, have to maintain this unity in connection with the derivation of new expressions. If, for example, the Turks living in Russia derive their terms from Russian, those in China from Chinese, and if we do it from the French, the Turkish of these peoples will vary from one to the other. But if we take these terms from Arabic or Persian, or from Turkish, they will be more uniform. The terminologies used in the languages spoken in Christendom (*ümmet*) were basically derived from Greek and Latin. The Muslim languages are threatened by the loss of unity in their religious-community (*ümmet*) background by borrowing these terminologies.

However, Muslim languages will not fulfill their duties with respect to this question of religious-community (*ümmet*) background merely by deriving their terminologies from Arabic or Persian. If each one derives its terms from different roots, the desired unity is still not going to be obtained and the religious-community basis of the language will not be maintained. It is for this reason that we [Turks] have to build our terms by adopting those which have already been accepted by other Muslim peoples, or those likely to be accepted by them. To realize this aim, it is necessary to organize societies for introducing new terms into the languages of the Muslim peoples. These organizations must sponsor meetings from time to time to discuss the problems of terminology. When the terms to be used in Muslim languages are decided upon systematically through such meetings, it will be possible to say that our language has completed its growth from a religious point of view, that is, that it has become thoroughly Islamized.

Once our language acquires a dictionary of terminology common to the *ümmet* of Islam, it should avoid any further borrowing from Arabic and Persian. Arabic and Persian words introduced into Turkish have not been confined only to terminology. Several unnecessary words of the vernacular have also been taken from these two languages. Furthermore, the influence of these tongues has not been confined to the mere transmission of words. Certain Arabic and Persian rules of grammar have also entered into Turkish in such a way that Turkish grammar has become a compound of the grammar and syntax of the three languages.

As it is imperative to modernize our language from the point of view of enriching it with new concepts, and to Islamize it from the point of view of unity in matters of terminology, it is equally necessary to Turkify it from the point of view of grammar, syntax, and spelling. Every word in our language, with the exception of scientific terms, must be in Turkish if possible, and, if not possible, at least Turkified. Arabic and Persian rules of grammar should be expelled entirely. We should say, for example, not *suarâ-yi cedîde* but *yeni şairler;* not *edebiyât-i Türkiyye* but *Türk edebiyati;* not *tabîyyet* but *tabîlik;* not *serbestî* but *serbestlik;* not *mûciz bir muharrir* but *îcazli bir muharrir;* not *mûciz bir ifade* but *îcazli bir ifade.* However, it is not enough to restrict Turkification only to vocabulary (*lûgat*). If possible, it would be even better to create all terms from Turkish roots; but if this is not possible, it is preferable to derive them from the Arabic and Persian roots rather than from French or Russian. In any case, it is necessary to make the terms as well as the vocabulary common, if not among all Muslims, at least among the Turks; in other words, all Turks should have a common literary and scientific language. We must not forget, therefore, that when we Turkify our language, we have to develop toward a common Turkish which will be understood by all brothers-in-race.

To summarize, the new concepts are the expression of the modern age, the terms used are the expression of religious-community and the vernacular form, the expression of the nation. Unless Turkish becomes a sensitive reflection of the three aspects of our social consciousness, we cannot speak of a well-established and fully developed language.

NOTES

1. "Üç Cereyan," published in *Türk Yurdu* (III, no. 35, Istanbul, 1913), reprinted in *Türkleşmek, Islâmlaşmak, Muasirlaşmak* (Istanbul, 1918).

2. The policy of reforms initiated by the promulgation of the Reform Charter of 1839.

3. "Millet ve Vatan," published in *Türk Yurdu* (VI, no. 66, Istanbul, 1914), reprinted in *Türkleşmek, Islâmlaşmak, Muasirlaşmak.*

4. *Turan* or Transoxania, the name of the territories beyond the River Oxus, the ancient home of the Turks.

5. Gökalp had used the word *beynelmileliyet* (internationality) when this essay was published in *Türk Yurdu,* but changed this term to *ümmet* when it was reprinted in the book *Türkleşmek, Islâmlaşmak, Muasirlaşmak.*

6. "Milliyet Mefkûresi," *Türkleşmek, Islâmlaşmak, Muasirlaşmak.*

7. "Lisan," published in *Türk Yurdu* (III, no. 36, Istanbul, 1913), reprinted in *Türkleşmek, Islâmlaşmak, Muasirlaşmak.*

3. THE RESTORATION OF TURKISH HISTORY[*]

Tekin Alp

We have reached the year 1929. It is only a few years now that the struggle for the moral independence of the Turkish people has begun to develop. During this brief period, this people has shown a vitality and a dynamism more miraculous than the effort which was exerted during the five years' struggle for material independence. During this brief period, the chains which fettered the moral force of the Turkish people and which it had borne for many centuries were broken. The Chinese wall, which for many centuries was preventing it from following in the wake of Western progress, has been demolished. The peoples of Europe see a new type of man taking his place in their ranks, and marching abreast with them on the road of progress. But what is this new type of man, where does he come from? What is his origin? What is his past? What blood flows in his veins? Will he remain a travel companion until the end of the road, or will he give up in mid-journey? This is why it is interesting to know his antecedents, and his origins.

It must be confessed that many European circles have consid-

[*]From *Le Kémalisme*, by Tekin Alp, Presses Universitaires de France, Paris, 1937, Chapter XV, pp. 109–129.

ered this newcomer an intruder, an intruder—it was said—who is dazzled by the superficial varnish of civilization and who will hasten to return to his former affections at the first sign of fatigue. His past—as it has so far been imagined—was not such as to belie these fears. Does not the Turk belong to a people which gives the impression of being a *parvenu?* Descended from the tribe of Osman, favored for a while by the god of war, the Turk was successful in invading foreign countries and founding an empire which has never belonged to him, in which he has merely camped and acted the policeman, to the benefit of the native populations, whose cultural superiority went on increasing from day to day. Turkish history as it has been conceived so far was not in a position to refute this account characteristic of certain Western circles. Even the history taught in Turkish schools started with the tribe of Osman. And so far as culture and civilization were concerned, the starting point—in this account—was the rising of the sun of Islam over the Turkish people. According to such a history, the Turkish people escaped from ignorance thanks to the light of Islam, and joined the concert of the powers thanks to the success in war of the tribe of Osman, which has even given its name to this people. According to this account, again, the Turkish people did not even exist in history, which recognized only Osmanlis who were members of the great family of Islam.

This is why Turkish and foreign historians have always confused Turkish history with the history of Islam.

The crusade which Christendom has conducted against Islam all through history, has created hatred and prejudice among European historians against the Turks, who have been the advance guard of the Muslim world. Blinded by a fanaticism which is sometimes conscious and sometimes unconscious, historians see in Turkish history nothing but fire and blood. As for Turkish or Muslim historians, they have always obeyed their Islamic conscience and have therefore considered it a duty imposed by the Muslim religion to consign to oblivion the phase in which the Turkish people had not yet had the good fortune of being illumined by the light of Islam.

Following on this came the chimera of Ottomanism, attempting to melt down the various elements of the empire in the Ottoman crucible and to create out of these heterogeneous elements a single unified nation. It was not negligence or forgetfulness that Turkism was not then being spoken of; rather, the very name wherever it might have by accident figured was being obliterated, with a zeal worthy of a better cause. Turkism, the Turkish *élite* sincerely thought, is a reminder of the Tamerlanes, the Genghises, the Attilas, and all those conquerors so much denigrated by Western historians. The Turkish name then necessarily evoked tents, tribes, horses, armies, wars, and massacres. Such was largely the impression gained from a perusal of those historical works found in the hands of Turkish schoolboys who were made to understand that they were nothing but Muslims, Muhammad's noble and grave adepts. Even the most passionate Young Turks have never had the courage to make their history go back beyond Osman's small tribe. The nationalist Young Turks liked to repeat the words of the great patriotic poet, Namik Kemal: "Cihangâranc bir devlet cikardik bir aşirettan," *i.e.*, "We have transformed a tribe into a world-wide empire." On this showing, the Turkish people's history began with this Asiatic tribe numbering four hundred tents. Not only did the Osmanli Turks not wish to make their history go back beyond Osman's tribe, but also they did not wish to be confused with other peoples of the same race. "The word *Türklük,*" writes Vambery, "was taken to be the synonym of boorishness and savagery. When I drew attention to the importance of the Turkish race, which extends from Adrianople to the Pacific Ocean, I was told: *Surely you do not wish to put us in the same category with the Kirghiz and the rude nomads of Tartary.*" Vambery concludes, "With few exceptions, I found nobody in Istanbul who was seriously interested in the question of the Turkish nationality or language."

From the time when he was a schoolboy, Kemal Atatürk has always had a pronounced passion for history in general and for

Turkish history in particular; he has never neglected, even in the midst of his numerous occupations as head of the state, to cultivate passionately this branch of human knowledge. He could not tolerate therefore this false conception of Turkish history which was current even among some of the Turkish intellectuals. He thought it was high time to make the whole world, and to begin with the Turks themselves, understand that Turkish history does not begin with Osman's tribe, but in fact twelve thousand years before Jesus Christ. It is not the history of a tribe of four hundred tents, but that of a great nation, composed of hundreds of millions of souls. The exploits of the Osmanli Turks constitute merely one episode in the history of the Turkish nation which has founded several other empires with their own particular period of brilliant splendor and greatness. It is time that it should be known, thought Atatürk, that the Turk, moving once more on the road of progress and civilization, is only following the example of his prehistoric ancestors, who were the first cultured peoples of the world. The world, including the Turks themselves, has to understand that for thousands of years, when other peoples simply followed their conscience and their instincts, the Turks were agents of culture and progress, and that they have never ceased to be such except when subjugated by foreign cultures and moral forces.

The civilized nations must not take into account this short period of decadence, when the Turkish people were acting out of character; they must understand that this newcomer within their ranks is in reality entitled to the precedence which is due to age.

These words are not inspired by that national vanity which is more or less usual among all nations of the world. International mores admit that what is not allowed to the individual is allowed to nations. Vanity and boastfulness, which are vices in the individual, are considered qualities in nations. Thus the French are allowed to call Paris the *ville-lumière*, the Swiss to proclaim Geneva as the capital of the nations, and the Persians to think that their Shah is the center of the world.

Thus it is thought natural that where courage, generosity,

honesty, and influence in the world are concerned, every nation should arrogate the primacy to itself. But in the present case, it is not a question of vanity which has become a usual part of national habits; it is rather a question of a revolution in the understanding of history, the bringing to light of historical truths which have been unappreciated, the collection of the material necessary to the reconstruction of Turkish history with a view to the rehabilitation of the people's name and its glory, with a view to enhancing the prestige of the Turkish Regeneration by means, so to speak, of a retroactive renascence.

It must be confessed that this new task to which Kemal Atatürk devoted himself was a most difficult one. It was a revolution without precedent in world history. At the outset even Atatürk's most intimate friends received this revolution with some skepticism. The first difficulty to be surmounted was the racial prejudice which has been anchored for some centuries in world opinion as well as in Turkish opinion itself. Eastern and Western historians, and even Turkish historians, have always placed their own nation within the yellow race. Until now nobody has been brave enough to protest against such a prejudice. The Turkists, led by Zia Gök Alp, have timidly replaced the term "Mongol" by "Turanism" or by "Uralo-Altaic." But by so doing they could merely save the appearances. An ethnic term was merely replaced by a geographical one, and this did not prove that the Turks belonged to the great Indo-European family.

Kemal Atatürk, having carefully studied the matter with the help of scientific methods, realized perfectly well that here was a historical prejudice which, in spite of the fact that it has lasted for several centuries, was nonetheless the result of a misconception. He has therefore taken it into his head to eliminate it by means of a new revolutionary outburst which would subject it to the same fate as the other misconceptions from which the Turkish people have suffered for centuries.

A new general mobilization is ordered. The whole Turkish people, as always directed by its leader and with the same impetuosity which it has hitherto so often shown, advances to the conquest of the past, toward the conquest of its own history. As in the other revolutions of the last four years, the vanguard owes its dynamic impetus to that practical school, Tchan-Kaya.* Those who frequent this school have, since the beginning of this campaign, talked of nothing and heard nothing being talked of day and night except Turkish history. All efforts are directed toward one object, namely, to pierce the darkness of the past. Thousands of teachers, and all those intellectuals who could in one way or another contribute toward this objective have been mobilized. The commander-in-chief of the battles of Sakarya and Inonu** has become the commander-in-chief of archaeological excavations and historical research. His directives send his troops not forward by a few kilometers, but many thousands of years back.

After a period of preparation during which minds were thoroughly impressed with Kemal Atatürk's ends and objectives, an institute of historical research is founded. Those notable people who are most knowledgeable in the matter become members of it, and Kemal Atatürk himself effectively presides over it, and endows it with his indefatigable inspiration. The ministry of culture puts at the disposal of this institute all its moral and material resources. By means of periodical publications and *communiqués* published everywhere in the press, the institute enables the whole nation to follow its activities. Periodic congresses called together in Ankara, at which hundreds of delegates from all parts of the country are present, provide an occasion for all citizens to make their contribution to the enterprise of a retroactive renascence.

Today, only a few years after the initiation of the new historical campaign, the age-old prejudice concerning the Mongoloid origins of the Turkish peoples has itself become past history. No one in Turkey believes in it anymore, and many Western specialists and men of learning who have had the opportunity to follow closely the research made on this subject and published in Turkey have become convinced that the Turks occupy a prominent position among the Indo-European peoples.

* The Presidential residence at Ankara. E.K.
** Decisive battles in Atatürk's struggle against the Greeks. E.K.

Following the directive of the commander-in-chief, hundreds of scientific pioneers have advanced on the libraries of the East and of the West, methodically consulting all kinds of old and new works; manuscripts in all languages have been reviewed in search of proofs to buttress the historical truth which Atatürk has proclaimed. The campaign is not yet at an end, but the results obtained so far are sufficient for one to be convinced of this truth.[1]

We see in the first place the most ancient Chinese authors giving a description of the Turkish princes and "Hakans." All these Hakans are big in stature. They have blue eyes, pink faces, and possess remarkable beauty.

Again, Persian works written seven to eight centuries ago give us a picture of the Turkish Seljukid heroes, of the Alp Arslans, of the Melikshahs and their period. Almost all of them have gigantic stature. They have long and wavy hair, beautiful elongated faces, and broad chests. Arab authors of some ten centuries ago describe in their turn the "Atabeys" who ruled for a long time over Syria and Mesopotamia. All the princes of this dynasty are described by the Arab authors as being of a white complexion, of large stature, and as having broad foreheads and large and beautiful eyes. The Arab authors of the time ascribe the same characteristics to the Seljukids of Anatolia.

The pioneers of the Kemalist revolution give long quotations from the celebrated Persian poet Firdevsi, as well as from other Persian poems and epics which describe legendary Turkish heroes whose morphological characteristics have absolutely nothing in common with those of the Mongols. It is particularly the beauty of Turkish women, with their long waistline, their pink complexion, their red lips, their small mouth, their arched eyebrows, their long and abundant hair, which Firdevsi and other famous Persian poets particularly celebrate.

The numerous writings which deal with the Crusaders' exploits and their encounters with the Turks constitute a precious historical source for the pioneers of the Turkish revolution. The Ecclesiastical History written in Latin by the French priest Orderic Vital (1075–1142), in particular, records a great number of happenings in which are involved certain Turkish personalities of the time whose characteristics are described as completely Indo-European.

The most known and the most ancient Turkish historical documents such as the Oguznameh, Dede Korkud, etc., support the Chinese, Persian, Arab, and Latin authors in their description of the morphological characteristics of Turkish racial types. These documents show us the Turkish physical type with his pink and blond complexion, his blue, gray, or azure eyes, his long and slim waistline, and his remarkable beauty.

The different works of Western Sinologists such as Vivien de Saint-Martin, and of historians like Ed. Chavanne and others who deal with the Huns, the Oguz, the Uygurs are copiously drawn upon for proofs which corroborate the Kemalist thesis.

But while the Turkish pioneers indefatigably continue their researches, we see a French man of science, Dr. Legendre, give his categorical verdict: "The Turk is one of the most beautiful specimens of the white race, big in stature, with an elongated and oval face, a fine nose, either straight or aquiline, sensitive lips, eyes opening widely, quite often grey or blue, and with horizontal palpebral slits."[2]

Dr. Legendre most judiciously points out that at the time of the Turkish invasions, the contemporary historians had their attention drawn by the swarms of strange and outlandish Mongol troops who were fighting under the orders of the Turkish conquerors. These, being white and of the same type as the conquered people themselves, did not attract attention and no need was felt to give a description of them.

Pittard, the Swiss anthropologist, also classifies the Turks among the Indo-Europeans and provides the following morphological characteristics: their stature is bigger than the average, they are hyperbrachycephalous, their face is oval, their hair is somewhat thick, their cheekbones are large, their lips are thick, and their nose high and flat.[3] In another passage of the same work Pittard affirms that the Turkish race represents, without any doubt, one of the most beautiful types at the point of junction between Europe and Asia. Relying on his own personal observations, he adds that among the Turks of today, very rarely are types met with who might show the slightest parentage with the Mongols.

Some of the most important proofs collected by the conquerors of Turkish history, the most important, are those supplied by archaeology. The digs undertaken by English, French, German, Russian and Japanese archaeological missions in Eastern Turkestan at the beginning of the twentieth century have given the most brilliant results. A large number of frescoes and statues, as well as pottery and other works of art which go back many centuries before the Christian era, fill the exhibition halls and the ethnographical museums of Leningrad, Paris, and particularly Berlin. These works of art show clearly the morphological characteristics of the Indo-European type in the ancient Turks.

Certain archaeologists such as von le Coq, Grünewald, etc., who do not want to admit the Indo-European origin of the Turks, think that there may have been foreign invasions in the centers of Turkish civilization such as Turfan, Kashgir, etc., and that these frescoes would represent the type of the foreign conquerors. These are obviously gratuitous suppositions which no historical facts support. It must, however, be admitted that the Turkish and Mongol populations who have been neighbors in Central Asia since prehistoric times have undergone, through the ages, substantial crossbreeding. The Mongol populations conquered by the Turks have, in time, ended by adopting the language and culture of their masters and conquerors, and it is perhaps these Turcophone Mongol populations, who are met with even today in certain parts of Asia, who have perhaps given verisimilitude to the historical prejudice which asserts the Mongol origin of the Turkish race.

The institute, for its part, has already compiled a *Turkish and World History* in four volumes, where may be found the new estimate of the role of the Turkish nation in the cultural development of humanity from prehistoric times until our own days. It is this history which, since 1930, is being taught to Turkish and foreign schoolchildren in Turkey. The following are some of the points made in this work:

The motherland of the Turkish people is Central Asia, the region between the Kenyan Mountains and the Baikal Basin and extending through the Altai Mountains to the basin of the Itel, the Caspian Sea, the Hindu Kush, the Karakorum and its neighborhood. Whilst the rest of humanity was living in caves, leading a most primitive life, the Turk had already in his motherland become civilized enough to know the use of wood and metal. The domestication of animals, which is the state of civilization in which men begin for the first time to be distinguished from the beasts, began in the motherland of the Turks. Agriculture too, which constitutes the first stage in the subordination of nature to man, owes its origin to our motherland. It is the motherland of cereals such as wheat, barley, rye, as well as of domestic animals such as the sheep, the goat, the horse, the camel, etc. Meteorological and geological factors, about which foreign specialists are not yet in agreement, led at a certain moment to a complete climatic change in these regions of Central Asia. The Turks, who, for many thousands of years, had benefited from highly favorable climatic conditions and had attained a very high cultural level, began to emigrate in compact masses to China, India, Hither Asia, North Africa, and Europe, to which they brought the cultural gains acquired in their motherland. The introduction of agriculture, the domestication of animals, the use of wood and metal in the whole world is the work of these human waves which swept for thousands of years over these countries. One wave of these Turkish masses swept over China 7,000 years before the Christian era and created there a civilization which, until lately, was the most important one in the world. Another wave invaded India and brought civilization to this region which, as the historians say, was inhabited "by men with black skins who looked like packs of monkeys." Other roads which the emigrants took were those through the Ural Mountains and the Caspian Sea via the northern side of the Black Sea. Historians call this road the gate of the nations. The southern road goes through the mountains of the Caucasus and rejoins the northern road. The caravans which traveled through the southern road settled in Mesopotamia and in Anatolia and from there spread into the islands. Some turned into Syria and Palestine, and from there went on to Egypt. Some of the caravans which took the northern road colonized the Black Sea basin, the banks of the Danube and Thrace, and from this area certain caravans went on to Macedonia, Thessaly and finally to Ionia. It is these groups of emigrants which crossed the Dardanelles and Istanbul and passing westwards settled in Thrace and in the neighborhood of the Danube.

In Lower Mesopotamia, these Turkish immigrants regulated irrigation by draining marshes and digging canals. They made the area healthy and fertile and thus gave on their arrival striking proof of their high cultural level. The civilization which these Turkish tribes founded on the banks of the Euphrates and the Tigris on one side, and on Kirka and Kanuse on the other, gave brilliant results. This is the civilization which history knows under the name of Sumer-Alam.

New archaeological discoveries have proved that the Turks founded in Anatolia the Hittite civilization 4,000 years before the Christian era. The civilization of Anatolia, which the Turks consider as the Holy Land, is thus not less ancient than that of Egypt and Mesopotamia, since Anatolia was colonized in the same period by masses of immigrants arriving from the same motherland.

One portion of the Turkish mass which travelled westwards created the Aegean civilization, the beginnings of which date from 4,000 years before the Christian era, and which with time developed and gave birth to cultural centers known to history as Troy, Crete, Lydia, Ionia, etc. It is thought today that the Etruscans who created Greco-Latin civilization originate from Anatolia, having gone to Italy from there. The history textbook mentioned above tells at length the history of the Turco-Hun Empire in Central Asia of which the best-known chief is Mete, of the Scythian Empire, of that of the Avars, of the Akhuns to the west of Turkestan and the north of Afghanistan, of Tukyu,* of the Seljuks, of Babin in India, of Tamerlane, of Harzem

---

* This is the name given to the Turks by the Chinese, who cannot pronounce the letter R.

throughout the whole of Persia, etc., and particularly emphasizes the importance of the Hittite and Sumerian civilizations of which we shall speak below.[4]

Historians, archaeologists, anthropologists may engage in polemics as much as they like concerning the ethnic origin of this or that people in antiquity which Turkish history includes in the historical genealogy of the Turkish nation. Kemalist Turkey nevertheless firmly safeguards its retrospective conquests. Controversies between men of science on such matters can continue. The new generations of Turkey illuminated by faith will nevertheless know that they have behind them, since prehistoric times, civilizations as varied as that of Sumer, of the Hittites, etc., which fill glorious pages in the history of the nations. In any case, the Ankara Institute of Historical Research continues zealously to search for new proofs to buttress the theses advanced in its history textbook.

Besides the books published under the auspices of the Institute of History, a special chair for Turkish History and Civilization has been created in universities. From the year 1930, therefore, every Turkish child passing through school learns that the true Turks are not those who have been enslaved by the foreigner, by their own tyrannical rulers, by religious obscurantism, and by foreign social and cultural institutions; but that the Turks are rather those who first laid the foundations of civilization in Central Asia thousands of years before the Christian era and spread it thereafter in different parts of the world.

The proceedings of the first Historical Congress, which met at Ankara in July, 1932, attended by hundreds of delegates who had hastened there from all corners of Turkey, and which the whole country followed with great interest, have provided remarkable revelations.

Ihsan Cherif, one of the delegates, arrestingly brought out the importance of these revelations and the rehabilitation of Turkish history through the Kemalist movement of regeneration in the following terms.

"It is now forty-five years that I teach history," he said. "Every year, I went through a period of embarrassment and moral suffering, which was when I had to teach the Turkish portion of history. My words took on a morose and melancholy tone, because I knew very little about what had happened in the heights of Central Asia, which, for thousands of years, has been our ancestors' motherland. Neither did my colleagues know more than myself. The history which we taught in this manner was not made to inspire in our pupils love for the nation and to rekindle the sacred fire of nationalism. But the same magical voice which had cried out in a most pathetic historical moment 'Soldiers, your first objective is the Mediterranean,' now proclaimed that those who had spread throughout the world the seed of civilization were our ancestors. Our immortal Saviour has clarified in a striking manner the history of the Grand Turk, the past of the Great Turkish Race, in the same way that he had the present and the future of our Nation."

Miss Affet, a professor of history who is one of the most zealous frequentors of the Tchan-Kaya School and one of the most eminent members of the Historical Institute, has given two lectures in order to prove, with the help of archaeological and anthropological documents taken in great part from European authors, that the first rays of culture and civilization which lighted the world of antiquity emanated from the heights of Central Asia, the natives of which were the Turks, being wrongly designated as Turanian or as Uralo-Altaic when in fact they were Turkish tribes united by the links of language and culture. That one chief rather than another held sway over these tribes diminishes in no way the cultural and linguistic unity of these tribes.

Having refuted the thesis which confounds the Turks with the Mongols, Miss Affet tries to prove that the Turks are pure Aryans, and that the word Aryan is itself of Turkish origin. The word "ari" in fact means in the Turkish dialect ("Tchagatai"), pure, clean, and it is a word much used in the new Turkish language. Miss Affet ends her lecture with the following passages: "At a time when the Turks had reached a high level of culture in their own motherland, the peoples of Europe were still in a savage state and lived in complete ignorance. The Turkish civilizers who have mixed with the masses in the midst of whom they immigrated, after the passage of many thousands of years and under the influence of many political and religious events, have forgotten their individuality and their motherland. But one memory remained with them, namely their origin, the motherland of the 'Ers,' that is of the 'brave men.' The Europeans later on made of this motherland of the 'Ers' a region which they called 'Ari' and which they situated to the north of the Hindu Kush. They were loth to admit that this region had been inhabited by Turks. In any case these regions were again submerged with new successive invasions by Turks of the Alam, Hun, Avar, Hazar, Oguz, Kuman branches and by other Turkish populations to be distinguished particularly through their cavalry. The Europeans have not understood that these invaders were the racial brothers of the earlier Turks who had brought with them the seeds of culture belonging to the same race of the 'Ers.'

"To summarise, let us repeat therefore," concluded Miss Affet, "that the natives of Central Asia are Turks. It is nonsensical to try to create there an Indo-European race distinct from that of the Turks. What is reasonable and human is to recognize the race which nature has created in the heights of Central Asia and to respect it as such. The Turkish children who today are determined to illuminate their mind and conscience with the last rays of progress, know and will make the whole world know that they are not the descendants of a tribe of four hundred tents, but of the pure race of the Ers or Ari, as the Europeans say, a race which is superior and cultured, and many thousands of years old,"

Professor Keuprulu Fouat, Dean of the Faculty of Letters, who followed her at the rostrum, having supported by means of scientific reasoning the principal points of Bayan* Affet's thesis concluded with these words:

"A nation which looks at its history with the eyes of the foreigner cannot consider itself liberated. The movement towards the reconstruction of our history which our great leader initiated a few years ago proves that the struggle for moral independence has succeeded the struggle for material indepen-

* Miss or Mrs. in the new Turkish.

dence. It is the duty of every Turk who is more or less enlight-ened, as it is that of every schoolmaster, to take part as much as possible in this struggle and to participate in it however mo-destly."

The late Dr. Rechit Galip, former Minister of Education, has also argued, in a public lecture on Turkish race and civilization, that the Turkish race belongs to the brachycephalous and Alpine group and that it is the Turkish tribes who have spread the seed of culture throughout the world. In a passionate peroration he said: "We are the worthy descendants of a prodigious race which carries in its veins treasures of strength and ability and we must do our utmost to make this truth triumph in the eyes of all humanity, and to disperse the dark clouds which, during long centuries, have been heaped by fanaticism over Turkish history . . ."

The Deputy Chemseddin, professor at the university and member of the institute, expounded his thesis on "The Role of the Turks in Muslim Civilization." It is not long ago, he said, that Léon Cahun wrote that without the help of the Turks, Muslim civilization would have never been able to develop to such an extent or to spread into such vast regions. But now that we have deepened our researches in following historical truth, we can correct his conclusions in this fashion:

If the Turks had not entered Muslim society, the civilization which we call Islamic would not have existed. Historical resear-ches, in fact, prove that so long as the Turkish element did not figure in Islamic society, i.e., until the downfall of Ommeyad civilization, there was, in the cultural and intellectual domains of the Muslim world, no movement which could be considered scientific. It is not without reason that the intellectual stagnation which obtained in Muslim society toward the end of Ommeyad rule was transformed into a movement with an intense life as soon as the Turks began to mix in Islamic society and to occupy a predominant position within it. It is because the Turks who created this movement were superior to the other Muslim peo-ples from the point of view of culture and civilization.

The series of lectures and discussions intended to restore

Turkish history and to realize the retrospective renascence of the Turkish people was completed by a discussion by Youssouf Hikmet, successively Minister of Education and Private Secretary of the Presidency of the Republic, who took upon himself the very delicate task of explaining scientifically the causes of Turkish decadence, of that of the oriental peoples, and of the Islamic world in general. According to Bay* Hikmet, these causes must not be sought in ethnic or racial factors, or in geographical or economic ones, but rather in the realm of culture. Whilst the movement of reform and renascence was taking hold of the Western peoples and pushing them irresistibly in the path of progress and recovery, the Turkish people, like so many other Muslim peoples, remained subjugated by theocratic principles and religious obscurantism. According to the ruling notions of that period, the Koran contained everything relating to public and private life. Social, political, administrative, economic, scientific, family, and other relations between men were supposed to continue to be conducted until the end of the world according to the principles of the Koran which Muhammad received by divine inspiration. What was not in the Koran, or rather that which insufficient study is unable to discover therein —since everything is contained in the Koran—must be decided by analogy, according to the jurisprudence of the first four Imams, or from religious tradition. Decision on these subjects belonged exclusively to the Ulemas, the religious scholars. But these Ulemas know nothing about what has gone on in the world after the first two centuries from the Hegira, either from the cultural or the scientific point of view. The Caliph, who exercises both religious and secular power, has an absolute and discretionary power over his subjects. In a word, the Caliph and his executive agencies take no account of any change resulting from the evolution of things in social life and in the realm of science. The principles fixed by the Koran must, in no case, be departed from.

The proof that the causes of decadence are to be found entirely in the theocratic conception of life, and that these causes have

* Mr. in the new Turkish.

nothing to do with racial structure, may be found in the fact that the Hungarians, who belong to the same race as the Turks, have been able to follow the progress of the Western peoples and realize all modern advances.

Turkish decadence begins in the period of Beyazid II. What do we see in that period? An eminent mathematician, Tokatli Lutfi, is condemned to death by a verdict rendered by the Ulema, for having cultivated mathematical sciences which do not derive from the Koran or other religious writings. Masterpieces from the hands of the best European artists of the time which Mehmed the Conqueror had introduced into the palace were destroyed by his son Beyazid. Every work produced by non-believers, by kafirs, had to be destroyed and annihilated. The use of the printing press was considered impious, and according to Diderot's *Encyclopédie*, the use of the printing press was prohibited in Turkey under pain of death. The religious ruling which allowed the use of the printing press was not issued until three centuries after wide use all over Europe of this modern cultural acquisition.

It is during Beyazid's period too that the custom began of reserving the highest offices to Muslims who were not of Turkish nationality. This is the reason why we were not able to participate in the Reform and Renaissance movements which began in Europe during the reign of Salim and Suleyman the Magnificent.

The Institute of Historical Research works with a feverish activity ever since 1930. It has commissioned eminent European scholars to carry out the appropriate archaeological diggings and researches in libraries in order to establish the contribution of the Turkish people to the cultural progress of antiquity. These researches are directed, followed, and encouraged by Kemal Atatürk himself. The Institute neglects no effort to spread the results of these researches as widely as possible. Among those new historical revelations which it desired most to popularize, two deserve special mention: Sumerian civilization and Hittite civilization. The first flourished in all its splendor in Mesopotamia 7,000 years before the Christian era. For many centuries the Sumerians were the carriers and conductors of culture ("Kulturträgers" as the Germans say) throughout the whole world.[5]

NOTES

1. In this connexion, Ismail Hami Danichmend must be specially mentioned for his recently published book, *The Common Origin of the Turks and the Indo-European Peoples* (1935).

2. *L'Illustration*, June 27, 1925.

3. *Les Races et l'histoire*, 1924.

4. In the following chapters. E.K.

5. In the following chapter of his work, the author asserts that archaeological evidence has proved that both the Hittites and the Sumerians were Turks, so much so that the largest national bank the mission of which is to industrialize the country has adopted the name of the latter and is called "Sumer Bank," whilst its Director General himself has adopted the name Sumer as a family name. E.K.

4. THE STUDY OF INDIAN HISTORY*

⊔⊓⊔⊓⊔⊓⊔⊓⊔⊓⊔⊓⊔⊓⊔⊓⊔⊓⊔⊓⊔⊓⊔⊓⊔⊓

Surendranath Banerjea

Those who have their eyes open, and are capable of observing what is going on around us, cannot fail to be painfully impressed with a fact, which we would all do well seriously to ponder over. We have amongst us writers in almost all the varied branches of human knowledge We have poets, novelists, critics, transla-tors, writers on law, mathematics, philosophy, and even on some of the abstruse branches of physical science. But there is one great department of human knowledge which remains almost wholly unexplored by us, yet it is a department which would yield treasures of priceless value to the ardent inquirer, where we would roam amongst the relics of our former greatness, where we would hold communion with the master minds of ancient India, with Vâlmiki and Vyâsa, Pânini and Patanjali, Gautama and Sankaracharya. I purpose this evening, gentlemen, to draw your attention to this noble study, the study of the history of our own country. I purpose to point out its multifari-ous advantages. I purpose to show that the study of the history of our own country, while, perhaps, it cannot be said to possess

Speeches of Babu Surendra Nath Banerjea, 1876–80, edited by Ram Chandra Palit, Calcutta, 1880, pp. 1–18.

that fascinating interest which belongs to those branches of human knowledge which have reference to the amelioration of the miseries, or the promotion of the happiness of our race, nevertheless, presents topics of deep and living interest, and round which the heart of the truly genuine patriot might cling with devout and reverential affection. The study of the history of our own country illustrates in a striking manner the great truth, that miserable and degraded as we are, our degradation has followed upon a chain of sequences, every link of which is explicable, that the iron hand of fate has not been upon us, that we have not been made the hopeless victims of unprecedented calamities, and that whereas circumstances have wholly controlled our destinies, we might, if we chose, have partially controlled those circumstances and thus have changed the face of India, and perhaps of the world at large. Such an assurance is calculated to fill us with hope, to inspire us with enthusiasm and to add stimulus to those noble and patriotic efforts which are being made on all sides around and which I fervently hope, we are now about to enter.

But a difficulty of considerable magnitude meets us on the very threshold of our inquiry. We find that in the whole field of Sanskrit literature there is only a single historical work, the Raja-Tarangini or the History of Cashmere, which was commenced by Calhana Pundit about the middle of the twelfth century of the Christian era. Are we then to conclude, that our ancestors, the great Aryans of ancient India, were ignorant of the art of historical composition and never wrote histories? I would ask you, gentlemen, to approach the consideration of this question with a mind free from prejudice and bias. Let us in this case appeal from the verdict of sentiment to the verdict of sober reason, and if, perchance, that verdict should go against our ancestors, it would then be our duty to submit to it with deference, although it might be with regret. Fortunately, however, for the credit of our ancestors, fortunately for the good name of India, we are not wholly driven to that conclusion; and with the arguments I am about to submit for your consideration, it will appear extremely probable that our ancestors were acquainted with the art of historical composition, that they wrote histories, and that if such histories have not come down to us, it is because of the revolutions and convulsions which our country had unhappily too often to pass through, it is because of the carelessness of the Brahmins and the peculiarities of our climate.

Gentlemen, India emerges upon the pages of authentic history, as forming a satrapy of the great Empire of Darius, and ever since that time, her condition has not improved for the better. The Empire of the Kshatriyas was succeeded by the Empire of the Mussalmans, the Empire of the Mussalmans by the Empire of the Mahrattas, and the Empire of Britain has succeeded and overshadowed them all. Bands of fanatical warriors, enticed by the reports of her extraordinary wealth, again and again poured down upon the fertile plains of Hindustan, spreading death, destruction, desolation, on all sides around. Now, it is my contention that it was amidst these destructive inroads that all traces of our ancient historical literature disappeared; and I am all the more fortified in this conclusion, when I bear in mind that a great many Sanskrit works have not come down to us at all, while there are others which have come down to us only in a fragmentary state. What had been left unfinished by these destructive inroads, was completed by the carelessness of the Brahmins (who were the custodians of all Sanskrit works) and the peculiarities of our climate.

I now pass on, gentlemen, to the consideration of those arguments which, in my humble opinion, make it appear extremely probable that our ancestors were familiar with the art of historical composition and that they wrote histories.

My first argument will be of a presumptive character. Is it at all consistent to reason, that our ancestors who made such great progress in the different branches of human knowledge, in literature, in science, in philosophy, were ignorant of the simple art of recording the sayings and doings of their kings and queens, for that is properly history in its inception? The different branches of human knowledge are interwoven with one another, and is it possible to make any great progress in any one branch without making some progress in—throwing some light on—the other branches of human knowledge? How, again, are we to reconcile this absolute dearth of all historical literature, with the wonderful achievements of the Hindus in some of the most difficult and abstruse departments of human learning—in law, in philosophy, and in astronomy?

But, gentlemen, let us pass on from this presumptive argument and tread on firmer ground. You have all heard of Abul Fazl, the renowned minister of Akber. Well, he wrote an outline of the ancient history of India. Monsieur Abel Remusat very pertinently asks the question, whence did Abul Fazl obtain the materials for his history of India? If he did not draw them from his imagination, he must have obtained them from earlier Hindoo authorities.

But there is yet another argument, still more clenching. About the beginning of the seventh century of the Christian era, a great Chinese traveler visited India. His name was Hiouen Thsang. He was a Buddhist priest, and came here on a pilgrimage to Magadha, the Holy Land of his faith. He was a man of remarkable intelligence, of great powers of observation and of profound genius. He stayed in India for a period of nearly 15 years, and while here, he chiefly employed himself in studying Sanskrit literature, in transcribing Buddhist scriptures, and in acquainting himself with the manners, customs and institutions of that great and interesting people in whose midst he found himself. Hiouen Thsang's travels have now been translated into French by Monsieur Stanislas Julien. Let us see what light the great Chinese traveler throws upon this important point. He says, there were special functionaries charged with the duty of writing the narrative of events; and these narratives were known as the Nilapita or the Blue Collection. But what are narratives of events if not histories? Here, then, we have the testimony of a writer of unquestioned veracity, of remarkable intelligence, and who had unexceptionable opportunities of observation, in support of the conclusion I am endeavoring to establish, viz., that our ancestors were probably familiar with the art of historical composition and that they wrote histories.

But, gentlemen, there remains yet another argument. You have all probably heard of Chand and his bardic poems. Well,

Chand is the bard who relates the exploits of Prithi Raj, that noble Hindu, the last of his race, who died bleeding on the altar of his country's independence. Chand refers to other bardic poems which were extant in his day, but which have not come down to our times. Thus, then, it appears that, not long ago, in the history of our country, these bardic poems occupied a considerable space in our literature. But what are bardic poems but undeveloped history? What dire stroke of fate was it, I ask, that cut short the growth of the Hindu mind in this direction, while in other departments of human knowledge, it marched forward with almost giant strides?

Thus, then, gentlemen, from this series of arguments, from the presumptive argument to which I have already referred, from the inference drawn from Abul Fazl's outlines of ancient India, from the testimony of Hiouen Thsang with regard to the Nilapita, and finally from the existence of the bardic poems of Chand and other bards, it appears to me very probable that our ancestors were familiar with the art of historical composition and that they wrote histories.

But the question might be asked, and indeed it would be a most pertinent question to ask—how are we to explain this singular fact, that while we have Sanskrit works in almost all the branches of human knowledge, which have survived the destructive inroads to which I have already referred, not a single historical work has been preserved, not a single historical work bearing upon it the impress of ancient India has come down to us? I have an explanation to offer, but whether that explanation is to be regarded as satisfactory or not is a point which it is for you to decide. The functionaries, charged with the duty of writing the narrative of events, were government servants. They were entertained by the state. The Nilapita were government records, and would be deposited with other government records, in the palace or the castle. But India, in those days, was the scene of constant revolutions, of constant bloodshed, and of constant changes of dynasty. The castle and the palace would be the central points of attack. They would again and again be assailed, their treasures ransacked and their records destroyed. The Nilapita would thus come to be destroyed, together with other government records. All traces of our early annals would thus disappear.

But, gentlemen, even if it should appear that our ancestors were ignorant of the art of historical composition, it is, after all, a matter of not so very great discredit to them. For, history in the proper sense of the term was not known even in Europe till late in the last century. It was amidst the intellectual ferment and agitation, which preceded the breaking out of that great revolution, the French Revolution, which ushered in the dawn of human liberty and impelled the human mind onwards by giant strides to unknown conquests in unknown regions of thought, that history, in the proper sense of the word, began to be studied.

But, gentlemen, whether our ancestors were familiar with the art of historical composition or not, it becomes a matter of the utmost importance that we should seriously set ourselves to the task of studying the history of our own country. I hope, every one of you here is a patriot, every one of you has a heart that beats in sympathetic response to the miseries of an unhappy fatherland. If you seriously wish to regenerate your country, wish to see her great and prosperous, then you must have a thorough knowledge of the evils that beset her, the miseries that afflict her. First, learn the disease, before you minister to the patient. But the miseries that afflict India, the disease she is suffering from, are not the work of a day. Their roots stretch back into the remote past. The past must be studied, before the work of Indian regeneration could be accomplished. Thus, then, the patriot who really wishes to serve his country, must study its past history. But the study of Indian history is important, considered from another point of view. The policy of the English government in India is profoundly influencing the fortunes of this country, and is not without its effects upon the national character. If, therefore, we desire to understand the policy of the British government in India, it becomes necessary that we should study the history of our own country.

Gentlemen, while upon this subject, I cannot refrain from alluding, for a few moments, to the manner in which sometimes Indian histories are written by English authors. Gentlemen, in the remarks I am about to address you, I do not mean to cast any reflection upon those great and good Englishmen, who have done so much toward elucidating the history of our country. Nobody could be more sensible than myself of the obligations we are all under to these eminent writers. Nobody could be more sensible than myself to the difficulties of their task, difficulties which in their case were enhanced by the circumstance that they were foreigners, writing the history of a country of which they could know but little. But although our obligations to English writers may be very great, we own still higher obligations to truth; and in the interests of truth, it becomes our duty to point out what we conceive to be their errors and their shortcomings.

Gentlemen, it seems to be taken for granted, by most[1] English writers that Suraja Dowlah was the author of the Black Hole tragedy. It is no part of my intention to whitewash the ensanguined fame of a Suraja. I do not wish to paint him in brighter colors than he deserves. I am only anxious that justice should be done to him. The benignant goddess of justice never appears to so much advantage, as when she spreads her wings of protection over those who least deserve such protection. I say then, let justice be done, though a Suraja Dowlah were concerned in the matter. Now, I hold, gentlemen, that Suraja was not concerned in the Black Hole tragedy, or if he was at all concerned, it was as an accessory after the fact.

In order that I may establish this position, I beg of you to dwell with me for a few moments, on the events of the ever-memorable 20th June 1756. On that day, Fort William fell. After the capture of the fort, Mr. Holwell and about 146 other English prisoners were brought before the presence of Suraja Dowlah, bound and fettered. Suraja ordered their chains to be removed and assured Mr. Holwell that no harm would be done to him or to his comrades. At night, when the Nabab had retired to rest, a difficulty arose as to finding a commodious place, where all the prisoners might be safely lodged. The garrison prison was at last fixed upon. It was a small room, about 18 feet square. Into this miserable little place, the hundred and forty-six English prisoners were thrust, on one of the most sultry nights of June. We are all familiar with the terrible events of that awful night, and however much we may desire to exculpate Suraja, we cannot help expressing the deepest sympathy for the fate of those unhappy Englishmen, who were subjected to a punishment so cruel and, in many respects, so undeserved. The morning dawned and revealed the ghastly tale. Of the 146 prisoners, only 23 survived to tell the story of their unutterable sufferings. Now, I ask, gentlemen, what is there to show that the Nabab was in any way concerned in this foul transaction? It is not even pretended that he gave the order. It is admitted that he was asleep, while the prisoners were undergoing the terrible agonies of their incarceration. Indeed, there is nothing to show that he knew anything at all about the tragedy, till it was past and irremediable. Was the feeling of kindliness, I ask, which prompted him to order the removal of the fetters from the English prisoners, consistent with the horrible cruelty which he is alleged to have committed almost immediately after? If he really wanted to massacre the 146 prisoners, would he have allowed twenty-three of them to escape to spread the tale of his monstrous crime and of their own unutterable sufferings? But it might be asked how was it that, if he was not in any way implicated in this foul tragedy, he did not hasten to punish its perpetrators. Suraja Dowlah, it must be remembered, was an Eastern prince, and was one of the worst of his class. He never had any fine sensibility of feeling. On the contrary, the training he had received was such as was calculated to crush out and destroy all the noble qualities of the human heart. Brought up in the school of intemperance, of dissipation, of godlessness, he never knew what it was to sympathize with human misery or human suffering. His courtiers had taught him to think that he was the lord of the universe, and that the rest of mankind had been created to minister to his happiness and to his comfort. Such being his training and his mental temperament, he possibly looked upon the whole affair as a good joke, and its authors as those who had contributed toward his enjoyment.[2]

The next blunder which is often committed by English writers of Indian history, and to which I would draw your attention, is in connection with the events which preceded the breaking out of the second Sikh war. Most English writers hold, that the Sikhs were entirely responsible for the second Sikh war and that, therefore, the annexation of their country was but the proper punishment for their ingratitude and their disloyalty. The Sikhs, they say, were living under British protection. They rebelled against the paramount power. They were worsted in the struggle. The annexation of their country followed as a natural consequence. Now, I hold, gentlemen, that the English were almost as much responsible for the second Sikh war as the Sikhs themselves. The Sikhs were, indeed, goaded into rebellion. Three events chiefly stimulated the Sikhs to revolt, yet these events are not mentioned by most English writers, and for them the English government was responsible. They were (1) The exile of the Maharani Jhunda Koer, the widow of the great Runjeet Singh, to whose memory the Sikhs were so devotedly attached. (2) The unwillingness of the British authorities to fix a day for the marriage of the young Maharaja Dhuleep Singh, a circumstance which served to fill the Sikhs with apprehension with regard to the stability of their kingdom. (3) The treatment of Sirdar Chutter Singh, the father of the Raja Sher Singh, one of the most powerful of the Sikh chieftains. These circumstances, gentlemen, filled the Sikhs with apprehension, with regard to the continuance of the independence of their country. They likewise smarted under the indignities which were freely heaped upon one of the most exalted personages in the land. Under the influence of these feelings, created by the proceedings of the English government, the Sikhs rose in arms against the power that had undertaken to protect them. Who will now say that the Sikhs were wholly responsible for the breaking out of the second Sikh war and that the English were not at all to blame in the matter?

The last historical blunder to which I would draw your attention is in connection with the annexation of Oude. English writers, for the most part, agree in the opinion that Oude was grievously misgoverned under the native dynasty and that, therefore, the protecting power felt itself called upon to annex the country. Now, gentlemen, the misgovernment of Oude appears to me to have been a myth, and not borne out by well-established facts. If Oude were misgoverned, it would be only natural to expect that the people of Oude would emigrate in large numbers to British territory which bordered upon Oude. But there was no such emigration. On the contrary, the stream of emigration tended the other way.[3] What then shall we say of the misgovernment in Oude? But this is not all. You are probably aware that in the year 1801 Lord Wellesley helped himself to a large slice out of Oude, annexed nearly half of that country. Well, we find on the eve of the annexation (1853), and I have Colonel Sleeman's authority for the remark, that whereas the landed aristocracy of Oude under the government of the Nabab remained unimpaired, not a single family of the landed aristocracy remained in British Oude. They had been systematically crushed out. Such a fact as this, leads us to form a very unfavorable opinion with regard to the manner in which the British government in this country is carried on, and ought to make us pause before we feel too certain about the misgovernment in Oude. There remains yet another argument of considerable weight, which has been brought forward, I believe, by Mr. Herman Merivale in the second volume of his Life of Sir Henry Lawrence.[4] In the year 1870, a census was taken of Oude, and from that census it was found that Oude was quite as thickly populated as the most thickly populated countries in Europe—the Netherlands. Now between 1856 and 1870, Oude had passed through a terrible convulsion. Oude was one of the centers of the mutiny. Her towns had been destroyed, her inhabitants massacred, her fields laid waste. Therefore, it is only reasonable to conclude that Oude was at least as thickly populated in 1856 as it was in 1870. But how is that reconcilable with the terrible picture of havoc, desolation, and ruin, drawn by a succession of residents?[5] Thus then, with these facts before me I am led to conclude that the misgovernment in Oude was a plea put forward to justify an act of spoliation.

Up to this time, gentlemen, my attention has been confined to what might be called the objective advantages to be derived from the study of the history of our own country. I now pass on to the consideration of some of the subjective advantages, advantages affecting the human mind, to be derived from the study of the history of our own country. The study of the history of our own country, and indeed the study of all history, is calculated to restrain the exuberance of the imagination. Gentlemen, we are an eminently imaginative people; and I think I do not exaggerate facts when I say that the exuberance of our imagination and our want of practical sagacity have greatly interfered with our success as a nation. If we have to talk of human longevity, we cannot be content with less than about 100,000 years, if we have to talk of a Rakshasa, we must represent him with nostrils several thousands miles long, if we have to speculate about the antiquity of the Vedas and the Institutes of Manu, we must make them several millions of years old. Now, I say, gentlemen, that next to physical science I know of no subject which is so well calculated to restrain the exuberance of our imagination as the study of history.

But there remains yet another subjective advantage, to be derived from the study of Indian history, of greater moment and wider import than the one to which I have already referred. The study of the history of our own country furnishes the strongest incentive to the loftiest patriotism. I ask, what Hindu is there who does not feel himself a nobler being altogether, as he recalls to mind the proud list of his illustrious countrymen, graced by the thrice-immortal names of a Vâlmiki and a Vyâsa, a Pânini and a Patanjali, a Gautama and a Sankaracharya? I ask, what Hindu is there whose patriotism is not stimulated, whose self-respect is not increased, as he contemplates the past history of his country? For ours was a most glorious past. We were great in literature, in science, in war, but above all, great in morals. I would detain you for hours and hours together, were I to expatiate upon the points of beauty and excellence connected with the wonderful language and literature of our fathers. But, I think, gentlemen, I should more profitably occupy your time, if I were to pass on to the consideration of some of those scientific truths, which the ancient Aryans of India have bequeathed to us as a priceless legacy.

Well then, our ancestors were the inventors of the decimal notation; and without the decimal notation, the world could not go on for a day. It is of use in the pettiest commercial computations, as well as in the most difficult astronomical calculations. The ancient Hindus made considerable progress in the science of geometry, and in trigonometry enunciated problems which were not known even in Europe till about the sixteenth century. But it is in the science of algebra that the Hindu mind displayed to the best advantage its marvelous power and resources. The Hindus were the inventors of the science of algebra. The first Arab writer on algebra was Mohamed Musa Kharizmi. Now, there could be no doubt that he obtained his algebra from the Hindus. He abridged an astronomical work founded upon the Indian system, and he was the first to communicate to his countrymen the Indian method of computation. A writer who knew so much of Indian mathematics, who was familiar with our astronomy and our method of computation, might reasonably be presumed to have been familiar with our algebra as well. Indeed the Arabs do not lay any claims to originality in this respect. And it also appears that the Greeks were indebted to the Hindus for their algebra. The first Greek writer on algebra was Diophantus. And we have strong reasons for believing that Diophantus is under very great obligations to the Hindus for his algebra. In 1579, Bombelli published a treatise on algebra. Bombelli says, in this work, that he had translated a part of Diophantus and found that Diophantus cites Indian authorities. Thus, then, Diophantus was familiar with the Indian writers on algebra, and as he often cites them as his authorities, it must be presumed that he was greatly indebted to them.

Passing now from the domain of mathematics, let us dwell for a few moments on the achievements of the Hindus in some of the other departments of science. The Hindus had made considerable progress in chemistry. They knew how to prepare sulfuric acid, nitric acid, muriatic acid, and a great many other chemical substances. We have also good reasons for believing that the Arabs got their chemistry from the Hindus; and it was the Arabs who first introduced chemistry into Europe. We are thus then driven to the conclusion, that that great science whose wonderful results fill the world with so much admiration, and which have contributed in no small degree to promote human happiness and ameliorate human suffering, was of Indian origin. Nor were the Hindus behindhand as regards the science of medicine. The Arabs openly acknowledge their obligations to our ancestors in this respect. Indeed, so great was their respect for the Hindu physicians that two of their number, Saleh and Manka, were retained at the court of Harun-al-Rashed.

But the Hindus were not only great in literature, in science, they were likewise great in war. The Hindu books treat of the subject of tactics. The division of the army into center, flank, wings and reserve, was recognized. Rules are laid down for the order of march and the choice of position. The subject of encampment also received attention.

But the point which possesses the deepest interest in connection with Hindu military science, is the question as to whether our ancestors had any knowledge of firearms. Sir Henry Elliot and perhaps also Professor Wilson incline to the view that the ancient Hindus were acquainted with the use of firearms. Sir Henry Elliot conjectures that they were of an explosive character. The opinions of Wilson and Elliot derive considerable support from the testimony of Greek authors—from the testimony of Philostratus, of Themistius, of Ctesias and Œlian. But, gentlemen, in spite of the weight which must always belong to the opinions of such eminent oriental scholars as Wilson and Elliot, I am led to believe from arguments,[6] which, I am afraid, time will not permit me to enter into, that our ancestors had probably no knowledge of firearms.

But the ancient Hindus were not only great in literature, great in science, great in war, they were, above all, great in morals. If our country had produced no other great man than Sakya Muni, I conceive, we should have been entitled to the gratitude of posterity. The two greatest characters that have adorned the annals of humanity are undoubtedly Jesus Christ and Sakya Muni. It will not be for me to institute any comparison between these two illustrious worthies of our race. Mine will not be the hand that will tear down the veil of sanctity with which the veneration of ages has enshrouded these gifted mortals. I am more concerned here tonight to point out the moral grandeur of ancient India, as typified and exemplified in the life of the great founder of Buddhism. Have the pages of history a nobler instance of self-sacrifice to record than that of Sakya Muni? Born the heir to a magnificent principality, with troops of servants to obey his behests, with a loving wife and affectionate parents, he resolved to forswear the temptations of his lofty position, to rise high above them, and to consecrate his life and his energies to the great task of preaching to the benighted nations of the earth the saving lessons of truth and religion. High mountains, broad rivers, impervious forests, the horrors of the stake, the sword of the executioner, the knife of the assassin, presented no obstacles to the slow, the silent, the steady progress of the religion of Gautama Buddha. From the frozen waters that skirt the coast of Kamaschatka to the extreme south of the island of Ceylon, from the green and verdant isles that fringe the Chinese seas to the arid steppes of Central Asia, Buddhism became the predominating religion. The shivering inhabitant of Siberia, the yellow-complexioned Chinese, the swarthy native of Ceylon, the semi-naked barbarian of the steppes, all acknowledged the great Hindu as their apostle. Gentlemen, Sakya Muni was a Hindu, and so are we; but I ask, where is his heroic and noble self-endurance, where his soul of fire, his heart of love, embracing within its bounds not only man but the whole range of animated beings, aught that could breathe, aught that could feel from the meanest protoplasm to man, the lord of creation? I ask you, gentlemen, whether standing in his presence, standing in the presence of this noble Hindu, this illustrious scion of a royal race, who flung away the splendors of a throne, in order that he might become the apostle of humanity, you do not feel something of his noble and heroic self-endurance, something of his fervid patriotism, something of his boundless love for mankind? If you do not, then I say, call not yourselves the countrymen of Sakya Muni, pride not yourselves on the splendor of his immortal achievements. There is a higher consanguinity than that of blood, a nobler relationship than that of fathers, mothers, brothers, sisters, wives, the consanguinity—the relationship which arises from the unity and the harmony of sentiments, views, and aspirations. If the noble example of Sakya Muni does not stimulate your patriotism and increase your self-respect, then, I say, you are not his countrymen, though the same blood runs through your veins, the same sun warms you, the same moon emparadises your nights, and the same vaulted canopy of heaven, bespangled with its myriads of stars, spreads like a pall over your head.

But, gentlemen, besides Sakya Muni, there were other lights, though not so bright or so gorgeous, which shone on the Indian firmament. It is not necessary that I should allude to them. Contemporary testimony is indeed unequivocal with regard to the moral excellence of the ancient Indians. I dare say, you have all heard of Arrian. He is the historian of Alexander's Indian expedition. Well, Arrian says in his Indica—and I quote this remark with a degree of pride and satisfaction, more to be conceived than described—Arrian says that "No Indian was ever known to tell an untruth." This statement has been regarded as an exaggeration, and that even by so accomplished a scholar as Mr. Cowell. But it finds corroboration from a new and almost unexpected quarter. I have already had occasion to remark that, about the beginning of the seventh century of the Christian era, the great Chinese traveler, Hiouen Thsang visited India. Hiouen Thsang, we have already seen, had unexceptionable opportunities of forming a correct judgment with regard to Indian affairs. Well then, the following is Hiouen Thsang's estimate of the Indian character. He says, "The Indians might be fickle, they might be frivolous, they might be volatile, but they knew not what fraud was." Thus, then, gentlemen, we have the testimony of two writers, separated by age, separated by country, separated by religion, separated by traditions, associations, habits, and institutions, separated, in short, by every thing that constitutes the difference between man and man, uniting to speak in support of the character for truthfulness which our Aryan forefathers bore. And is it possible, in the face of the concurrent testimony of two such witnesses, witnesses whose reputation for veracity is so high, and one of whom, at least, had ample opportunities of forming a correct judgment about the Indian character, to regard the statement of Arrian as an exaggeration? No, gentlemen, our ancestors were a most truthful people. They were likewise one of the bravest nations on the face of the earth. Arrian says they were the bravest soldiers that Alexander encountered on the plains of Asia. In short, as regards everything that constitutes real manliness of character, as regards everything that constitutes true nobility of disposition, the Indians of those days outstripped all Asiatic races and have become the model for our guidance and our imitation.

Our great epic poems—the Ramayana and the Mahabharata —are a monument of the moral worth of our ancestors. Where shall we find sublimer precepts of morality, than those taught in the Ramayana and the Mahabharata? The solemnity of pledges, the great duty of filial obedience, the absolute necessity of self-sacrifice in the discharge of solemn obligations, the supreme virtue of chastity, the sacredness of truth, the heinousness of perjury, are all enforced with a degree of eloquence, of pathos, of sincerity, of depth of conviction, as cannot fail to leave an impression on the mind of even the most careless reader of the Ramayana. The Puranas say, "The world cannot bear a liar." The Ramayana quotes the remark with approbation. When Rama visits Agastya Muni in his hermitage, the great sage tells him that the perjurer feeds on his own flesh in the next world. But no, gentlemen, "Megasthenes," a correspondent of the *Pioneer*, in a letter that he writes to that journal would have us believe that the morality of the Waverly novels and of Shakespeare's writings will do more to regenerate India than the morality of the Ramayana and Mahabharata. Aye forsooth, the morality of Shakespeare's Edmund and of Scott's Wildrake will do more to regenerate India than the noble lessons taught in the lives of Rama and Yudisthira! We do not want such instructors as "Megasthenes," who would rob us of that last consolation left to a fallen and degraded people, the consolation to be derived from the contemplation of our past glories.

Gentlemen, let us sit at the feet of our ancestors and hold communion with the masterminds of ancient India. Such communion is pleasing in these days of gubernatorial repression, in these days of political lifelessness and political stagnation, and when the future outlook is indeed so truly gloomy. I am aware, gentlemen, that in studying the past history of your country, you will find much that is antiquated, much that is obsolete, much, perhaps, that will excite ridicule and laughter. But let not any such feeling overcome you. Approach reverentially the sacred records of your sires. Remember that you are studying the sayings and doings of your revered ancestors, of those for whose sake alone you are now remembered, for whose sake alone the intellectual *elite* of Europe even now feel a deep and an ardent interest in your welfare. If you cannot attain the intellectual eminence of your ancestors, why not strive to emulate their moral grandeur? The road to moral greatness is not so steep, or so slippery. And permit me to remind you that upon the moral regeneration of your country depends its intellectual, its social, and its political regeneration. But the home is the fountainhead of morality. From one's home is derived the impetus to glorious deeds and noble achievements. Let not, then, the clear and pellucid stream of morality be polluted at its very source. I am afraid, gentlemen, there are fathers who seem to think that all they have got to do in reference to their children is to send them to school, and that after that they may lead as dissolute, as abandoned, and as unprincipled a life as they please. I wish to remind such parents that their examples are certain to produce a profound and a most pernicious impression on the minds of their children. I am anxious to remind them that if they wish well to their children, if they wish to see them prosper in life and acquit themselves as the worthy citizens of a great country, then it is for them to set in their own lives an example of high character and honorable dealing. Then, indeed, would they have paved the way for the moral regeneration of this country. Then, indeed, would they have established on a solid basis, their claims to the lasting gratitude of their children.

Gentlemen, I invite you to this noble task, the moral regeneration of your country, a task in every way worthy of your highest ambition; and I am greatly mistaken in the character of my friends, in the character of my countrymen, and in the character of those who are gathered together here this evening, if I cannot assure myself of a cordial and hearty response. If you indeed accomplish this noble task, your names will be emblazoned in characters of gold in the ineffaceable pages of history and will be handed down to remote posterity to receive the countless blessings of unborn generations. Gentlemen, you have your choice between a life of active and patriotic duty and a life of indifference, of carelessness, of disregard of sacred obligations. Countrymen of Vâlmiki and Vyâsa, make your choice, and whether you choose the one line of conduct or the other, remember the hopes of posterity are centered in you and that your great fathers from their high places in heaven are looking down upon you. Oh, Shades of departed sires! Spirits of the mighty dead of ancient India! Where are ye? Oh, cheer us, comfort us, enlighten us, illumine the darkness of our path, so that we might know what course of patriotic duty to adopt and thus hasten the dawn of a bright, of a glorious, and of a noble day upon our country. Gentlemen, with your eyes reverentially fixed upon the past, with your hopes centered in the future, pursue your course of patriotic duty and you will be entitled to the gratitude of your children and your children's children even unto remote generations.

NOTES

1. I should rather say "some" as, for instance, Murray and Sewell.
2. But even if Suraja Dowlah were the real author of the Black Hole tragedy, we should not, perhaps, be too severe in condemning him. Nearly fifty years before his time, a tragedy of a blacker character and of a deeper dye had been perpetrated by a much more enlightened sovereign, and amongst a much more enlightened people. But the Massacre of Glencoe (in which fraud and treachery were combined with murder) can scarcely be said to dim the lustre of William the Third's reign, while the Black Hole tragedy is regarded as the climax of a

life of crime, of folly, and of iniquity. But if historians find enough in the character and achievements of William to atone for the massacre of Glencoe, then surely the youth of Suraja Dowlah, the difficulties of his situation, and the circumstances under which he was brought up, ought to go far to induce us to take a lenient view of his follies and his crimes.

3. "It may naturally be supposed," says General Outram (Oude Blue Book, p. 44), "that the people of Oude, if so greatly oppressed, as has been represented, would emigrate to the neighbouring British districts, which it does not appear, from the replies I have yet received from the magistrates, whom I questioned on the subject, that they do to any great extent."

4. I subjoin the following passage from Herman Merivale's Life of Sir Henry Lawrence, to show that I had not, perhaps, stated the case strongly enough:—

"Such is the description of Oude [a description in which Oude is represented as being covered with thickets of prickly pear, and jungles of bamboo and thorn] before 1853, as drawn by a champion of annexation. Let us tone it down by the application of statistics. Oude contains about 25,000 square miles English; in other words it nearly equals in area the kingdoms of the Netherlands and Belgium together. Sir Henry Lawrence estimated its population (1845) at three millions, a considerable relative number, but (as it turns out) very greatly below the mark. Three or four years ago, it was ascertained to contain eight millions, showing a density equal to that of the two countries aforesaid, the best peopled in Europe; and the annual Blue Book, entitled *Moral and Material Progress of India* for 1869–1870, fixes it at the almost incredible number of eleven millions and a half, or nearly five hundred to the square mile. And yet, to the causes of desolation so rhetorically enumerated in the passage I have quoted, there was afterwards added the Mutiny with its ravages and disastrous results. And British Government, whatever magic we may attribute to it, cannot have had time, in the few years which have since elapsed, to effect any miraculous change.

"Common justice will, therefore, compel us, who have no special political cause to defend with the energy with which sides are usually taken in Indian politics, to own that Oude when we annexed it, was a wealthy, populous commercial region, which might fairly hold a comparison in these respects with many portions of our adjacent empire. Mis-governed it had been, and disgracefully, but not to that extent which really comes home to the mass of the population, and paralyzes industry." (Merivale's Life of Sir Henry Lawrence Vol. II. p. 288.)

5. The cry of the mis-government in Oude, was very popular with a certain class of officials throughout the greater part of this century. Bishop Heber who visited Oude in 1824–25, thus notices the subject:—"We had heard much of the mis-governed and desolate state of the kingdom of Oude;" . . . "I was pleased, however, and surprised after all which I had heard of Oude, to find the country so completely under the plough."

Mr. Shore thus refers to the subject. "This opinion [the misgovernment in Oude] is deduced first from the reports and statement of the different Residents at Lucknow, derived from their sycophant dependents. I believe many of them have officially given opinions quite at variance with their private sentiments, satisfying their consciences by representing them as having been derived from conversations with the people, without discriminating what class of natives were the informants. . . . I have travelled over several parts of Oude and can testify, as far as my own observation went, that it is fully cultivated, according to the population. Between Khanpur (Cawnpur) and Lucknow, numbers must daily pass, who can confirm or deny this statement. Let them declare whether any portion of land there, lies waste which is fit for cultivation. I have known many officers who have been stationed at Scetapore and have made excursions into the neighbouring parts: without an exception, they described the country as a garden. In the number of cattle, horses, and goods which they possess, and in the appearance of their houses and clothes, the people are in no points worse, in many, better off than our own subjects. The wealth of Lucknow not merely of those in authority but the property of the bankers and the shop-keepers, is far superior to that of any city (Calcutta perhaps excepted) in the British domin-ions; so at least the native bankers and merchants who are pretty good judges of such matters universally assert. How can all this be the case, if the government is really so notorious for tyranny and oppression" (Shore on Indian affairs, Vol. I, pp. 152 and 156. Read the whole Chapter.)

6. These arguments are as follows:—If the ancient Hindoos were familiar with the use of fire-arms of any kind, how came they to lose all such knowledge? Is it at all likely, considering the advantages which such a knowledge would confer, that they should ever have forgotten the use of fire-arms, and forgotten it so completely that it is now a matter of warm discussion, as to whether they ever possessed any such knowledge? The necessity there would be, in a rude and turbulent age, of constantly taking the field, whether for purposes of offence or defence, would keep up and improve the knowledge of fire-arms, and it is easy to see how upon such knowledge the national existence would often depend. Unless, therefore, a satisfactory explanation is given, as to how the Hindoos came to lose all knowledge of fire-arms, we are afraid, we must conclude that fire-arms were not known amongst them. Then again, we know that it was the bow which the ancient Hindoos chiefly relied upon in the field of battle. Now, if they possessed any kind of fire-arms, it seems scarcely likely that they should have given the preference to a weapon, infinitely inferior in point of usefulness to fire-arms. Finally, we know that from the earliest times elephants formed an important part in the Indian army. Now this could hardly have been the case, if fire-arms were in use. The great objection to employing elephants in modern warfare, is that they are apt to take fright at the report of guns. Unless, therefore, we suppose that the nature of elephants has, in these modern times, undergone a complete change, they could not have been employed so much in the field as the ancient Aryans appear to have done.

The above points seem to require explanation, before we should feel ourselves at liberty to accept the views of Elliot and Wilson.

5. THE IDEA OF PAKISTAN*

⊓⊔⊓⊔⊓⊔⊓⊔⊓⊔⊓⊔⊓⊔⊓⊔⊓⊔⊓⊔⊓⊔

Choudhary Rahmat Ali

Introductory Sketch:—Pakistan is the Fatherland of the Pak Nation. In other words, it is the land which lies in the northwest of the Continent of Dinia, otherwise known as the Subcontinent of India; and which constitutes the age-old national stronghold of the people who represent the original core and content of the Millat living in the Orbit of Pakasia.

It will therefore be seen that Pakistan is one of the most ancient and illustrious countries of the Orient. Not only that. It is the only country in the world which, in the antiquity of its legend and lore as in the character of its history and hopes, compares with Iraq and Egypt—the countries which are known as the cradle of the achievement of Mankind.

This comparison will serve to remind the reader of certain primordial facts about Pakistan—facts which form the foundation of its own story and provide the pattern of that of Mankind.

What are these facts?

The first is that Pakistan was the birthplace of human culture and civilization. The second is that it was the earliest center of

* From *Pakistan, The Fatherland of the Pak Nation,* by Choudhary Rahmat Ali, Cambridge, 1947, Part I, Ch. 1, pp. 21–25.

the communal aggregation of human society. And the third—the most dynamic of all—is that, ever since the dawn of recorded history, it is the first and the strongest citadel of Islam in the Continent of Dinia and its Dependencies.

It is therefore clear that, seen across the vistas of the ages gone by, these three facts constitute the original credentials of Pakistan in the human family. And, what is more, viewed in the light of its record under the Crescent and Stars, these credentials it has fully sustained in the modern world.

To say that is not to forget its present position in the comity of nations. It is simply to state that, even so, its record is second to that of none in the world. For there are not many countries that can claim to have maintained their national sovereignty for an unbroken period of 1,145 years as can Pakistan from 712 to 1857. Again, there is hardly a country that has to its credit an enlightened and enlightening supremacy over immensely vast and varied territories for 840 years, as has Pakistan over the lands of the Continent of Dinia from 1017 to 1857. And, finally, there are few countries that, in a millennium of history, have suffered subjection for only 89 years, as has Pakistan since its fall in 1857.

Nor is that all. If we turn from the political field to the spiritual and social sphere, we shall find that therein, too, the comparison with that of any other Muslim nation in the world holds good. And no wonder; for, as one of the main pillars of the Fraternity, throughout the eleven centuries of its own freedom and power, it brilliantly served the sacred cause as the standard-bearer of the saving message of Islam, as the herald of its liberating might, as the architect of its greatness in the Continent of Dinia and its Dependencies, and, last but by no means least, as the molder of the fates or fortunes of many a country of the neighboring Continent of Asia.

Even this record, great and glorious as it is, is not the end of the story of Pakistan. On the contrary, it is merely the end of a chapter. It only brings us down to the sad day of the country's eclipse in the last century—an eclipse which some wishful-thinkers mistook for, and misrepresented as, its death. That this was no more than a painful interlude in its life is evident from the fact that, despite desertion and betrayal from within and suppression and exploitation from without, it has, in the course of the past 89 years, accomplished at least three things of supreme importance to its future.

What are those things?

They are first that it has survived and recovered from the paralyzing shock of its fall; secondly, that it has saved its Islamic soul from the dangerous confusion of "Indianism" created by the British-Bania Alliance; and, finally, that since 1933 it has started a new and nobler chapter in its history. That is, a chapter of national regeneration and fraternal reconstruction, the opening lines of which are being written by its people in their heroic fight for its national life and liberty and for its Milli Mission in the Continent of Dinia.

That, in spirit and substance, is Pakistan—of today.

Now, it is this Pakistan, which, within its *present* confines, comprises today, *geographically*, the ancient Mihran Valley, which is also known as the Indus Valley; *territorially*, the provinces of the Punjab, Afghania, Kashmir, Sind, Baluchistan, Kachch, and Kathiawar, and some small tracts; *politically*, the 89-year-old Islamia *irridenta* in the northwest of the Continent of Dinia; and, *historically*, the oldest of the ten nations of the Millat living, on the one side, between the Pamir Plateau and the Dondra Head and, on the other, between the coast of Baluchistan and the borders of Burma.

Again, it is this Pakistan which in its eternal conviction stands today, *spiritually*, as the Frontier-guard of Muslim Asia against the mortal menace of "Indianism"; *nationally*, as the leader of the Muslims' fight against their "minorization," "communalization," and "Indianization"; *internationally*, as the sponsor of the national integration and independence, each in its own fatherland, of all the peoples in the Continent, including the nations of the Millat in Bangistan, Osmanistan, Siddiqistan, Faruqistan, Haidaristan, Muinistan, Maplistan, Safiistan, and Nsaristan; and *ideologically*, as the crusader for the conversion of the "Country of India" into "the Continent of Dinia," for the organization of the Continent of Dinia and its Dependencies into the Cultural Orbit of Pakasia; and, above all, for the rededication of one hundred million Muslims to the achievement of the sovereign freedom of the Millat and the supreme fulfillment of her divine mission throughout the Orbit of Pakasia.

Name:—It must be remembered that, in different periods of its life, Pakistan has had different names—names whose very variety epitomizes its past history, just as its present name symbolizes its present position, its future prospects, and its ultimate destiny in the world.

To explain: In the long eras preceding the advent of the Holy Rasool, the first sovereign-saint of Pakistan, Hazrat Al-Sindh, eponymized its nucleus as Al-Sindh; next, in the age of heathen mythology, its Hindu hegemonists cunningly Sanskritized this eponym as the Sindhu Valley; then, in the epoch of Alexander, its Macedonian invaders hellenically called it the Indus Valley; and after that, in the era of Islam's rise to power, its Muslim liberators historically distinguished it as Al-Sindh. Now, in the present period of British domination, of Indian conglomeration, and of Muslim reintegration, whereas its British captors imperially describe it as northwest India and its Caste Hindu covetors satellitically design it as the hinterland of Hindustan, its own proud, patriotic people nationally designate and fraternally dedicate it as Pakistan.

So, for the purposes of this study the reader should remember that this national designation, which for the sake of consistency and convenience I have used throughout the book, has in fact been borne by the country only since 1933. For, although I actually named it such much earlier, it was not until 28th January, 1933, that, in my first Declaration—*Now or Never*—calling for its separation from "India," I formally used the name, which, by the dispensation of Allah and the blessing of His Rasool, was ordained to ensure the elementary right of its people to a national solidarity under a national appellation. This means:

a right, which springs from the unity of their religion and race, of their language and literature, of their laws of life and liberty, and of their history and hopes;

a solidarity, which symbolizes the cause of their spiritual destiny, the community of their national identity, and the consolidation of their territorial patrimony; and

an appellation, which signalizes the breaking of their foul Indian fetters, the start of their fateful struggle for sovereignty, the reintegration of their national entity with their brethren in Iran, Afghanistan, and Tukharistan, and the strengthening of their fraternal bonds with the other nations of the Crescent in Dinia, in Asia, and in the rest of the world.

6. THE NEGRO IN ANCIENT HISTORY*

ⵗⵗⵗⵗⵗⵗⵗⵗⵗⵗⵗⵗⵗ

Edward W. Blyden

Presuming that no believer in the Bible will admit that the Negro had his origin at the headwaters of the Nile, on the banks of the Gambia, or in the neighborhood of the Zaire, we should like to inquire by what chasm is he separated from other descendants of Noah, who originated the great works of antiquity, so that with any truth it can be said that "if all that Negroes of all generations have ever done were to be obliterated from recollection forever, the world would lose no great truth, no profitable art, no exemplary form of life. The loss of all that is African would offer no memorable deduction from anything but the earth's black catalogue of crimes."[1] In singular contrast with the disparaging statements of the naval officer, Volney the great French Oriental traveler and distinguished linguist, after visiting the wonders of Egypt and Ethiopia, exclaims, as if in mournful indignation, "How are we astonished when we reflect that to the race of Negroes, at present our slaves, and the objects of our extreme contempt, we owe our arts and sciences, and even the

*From *The People of Africa*, by Edward W. Blyden, New York, 1871, pp. 1–34.

very use of speech!" And we do not see how, with the records of the past accessible to us, it is possible to escape from the conclusions of Volney. If it cannot be shown that the Negro race was separated by a wide and unapproachable interval from the founders of Babylon and Nineveh, the builders of Babel and the pyramids, then we claim for them a participation in those ancient works of science and art, and that not merely on the indefinite ground of a common humanity, but on the ground of close and direct relationship.

Let us turn to the tenth chapter of Genesis, and consider the ethnographic allusions therein contained, receiving them in their own grand and catholic spirit. And we the more readily make our appeal to this remarkable portion of Holy Writ because it has "extorted the admiration of modern ethnologists, who continually find in it anticipations of their greatest discoveries." Sir Henry Rawlinson says of this chapter: "The Toldoth Beni Noah (the Hebrew title of the chapter) is undoubtedly *the most authentic* record we possess for the affiliation of those branches of the human race which sprang from the triple stock of the Noachidae." And again: "We must be cautious in drawing direct ethnological inferences from the linguistic indications of a very early age. It would be far *safer*, at any rate, in these early times, to follow the general scheme of ethnic affiliation which is given in the tenth chapter of Genesis."[2]

From the second to the fifth verse of this chapter we have the account of the descendants of Japheth and their places of residence, but we are told nothing of their *doings* or their *productions*. From the twenty-first verse to the end of the chapter we have the account of the descendants of Shem and of their "dwelling." Nothing is said of their *works*. But how different the account of the descendants of Cush, the eldest son of Ham, contained from the seventh to the twelfth verse. We read: "And Cush begat Nimrod: he began to be a mighty one in the earth. He was a mighty hunter before the Lord . . . And the beginning of his kingdom was Babel, and Erech, and Accad, and Calneh, in the land of Shinar. Out of that land he went forth into Asshur (marginal reading), and builded Nineveh, and the city Rehoboth, and Calah, and Resen between Nineveh and Calah: the same is a great city."

We have adopted the marginal reading in our English Bible, which represents Nimrod as having founded Nineveh, in addition to the other great works which he executed. This reading is supported by authorities, both Jewish and Christian, which cannot be set aside. The author of "Foundations of History," without, perhaps, a due consideration of the original, affirms that Asshur was "one of the sons of Shem!" thus despoiling the descendants of Ham of the glory of having "builded" Nineveh. And to confirm this view he tells us that "Micah speaks of the land of Asshur and the land of Nimrod as distinct countries." We have searched in vain for the passage in which the Prophet makes such a representation. The verse to which this author directs us (Micah v. 6) is unfortunate for this theory. It is plain from the closing of the verse that the conjunction "*and,*" in the first clause, is not the simple copulative *and* or *also*, but is employed, according to a well-known Hebrew usage, in the sense of *even* or *namely*, to introduce the words "land of Nimrod" as an explanatory or qualifying addition in apposition to the preceding "land of Assyria."[3]

We must take Asshur in Gen. x. 11, not as the subject of the verb "went," but as the name of the place whither—the *terminus ad quem*. So Drs. Smith and Van Dyck, eminent Oriental scholars, understand the passage, and so they have rendered it in their admirable Arabic translation of the Bible, recently adopted by the British and Foreign Bible Society, namely, "Out of that land he (Nimrod) went forth unto Asshur—Assyria—and builded Nineveh." De Sola, Lindenthal, and Raphall, learned Jews, so translate the passage in their "New Translation of the Book of Genesis."[4] Dr. Kalisch, another Hebrew of the Hebrews, so renders the verse in his "Historical and Critical Commentary on Genesis."[5] All these authorities, and others we might mention, agree that to make the passage descriptive of the Shemite Asshur is to do violence to the passage itself and its context. Asshur, moreover, is mentioned in his proper place in verse 22, and without the least indication of an intention of describing him as the founder of a rival empire to Nimrod.[6] Says Nachmanides (quoted by De Sola, etc.): "It would be strange if Asshur, a son of Shem, were mentioned among the descendants of Ham of whom Nimrod was one. It would be equally strange if the deeds of Asshur were spoken of before his birth and descent had been mentioned."

The grammatical objection of our view is satisfactorily disposed of by Kalisch.[7] On the absence of the (*he*) locale he remarks: "The (*he*) locale, after verbs of motion, though frequently, is by no means uniformly, applied. (1 Kings xi. 17; 2 Kings xv. 14; etc.) Gesenius, whose authority no one will dispute, also admits the probability of the view we have taken, without raising any objection of grammatical structure."

But enough on this point. We may reasonably suppose that the building of the *tower of Babel* was also the work, principally, of Cushites. For we read in the tenth verse that Nimrod's kingdom was in the land of Shinar; and in the second verse of the eleventh chapter we are told that the people who undertook the building of the tower, "found a plain in the land of *Shinar*" which they considered suitable for the ambitious structure. And, no doubt, in the "scattering" which resulted, these sons of Ham found their way into Egypt,[8] where their descendants—inheriting the skill of their fathers, and guided by tradition—erected the pyramids in imitation of the celebrated tower. Herodotus says that the tower was six hundred and sixty feet high, or one hundred and seventy feet higher than the great pyramid of Cheops. It consisted of eight square towers one above another. The winding path is said to have been four miles in length. Strabo calls it a pyramid.

But it may be said, The enterprising people who founded Babylon and Nineveh, settled in Egypt and built the pyramids, though descendants of Ham, were not *black*—were not Negroes; for, granted that the Negro race have descended from Ham, yet, when these great civilizing works were going on the descendants of Ham had not yet reached that portion of Africa, had not come in contact with those conditions of climate and atmosphere which have produced that peculiar development of humanity known as the Negro.

Well, let us see. It is not to be doubted that from the earliest ages the black complexion of some of the descendants of Noah was known. Ham, it would seem, was of a complexion darker than that of his brothers. The root of the name Ham, in Hebrew, *Hamam*, conveys the idea of *hot* or *swarthy*. So the Greeks called the descendants of Ham, from their black complexion, *Ethiopians*, a word signifying *burnt* or *black* face. The Hebrews called them Cushites, a word probably of kindred meaning. Moses is said to have married a Cushite or Ethiopian woman, that is, a *black* woman descended from Cush. The query, "Can the Ethiopian change his skin?" seems to be decisive as to a difference of complexion between the Ethiopian and the Shemite, and the etymology of the word itself determines that the complexion of the former was black. The idea has been thrown out that the three principal colors now in the world—white, brown, and black—were represented in the ark in Japheth, Shem, and Ham.

But were these enterprising descendants of Ham *woolly-haired?*—a peculiarity that, in these days, seems to be considered a characteristic mark of degradation and servility.[9] On this point let us consult Herodotus, called "the father of history." He lived nearly three thousand years ago. Having traveled extensively in Egypt and the neighboring countries, he wrote from personal observation. His testimony is that of an eyewitness. He tells us that there were two divisions of Ethiopians, who did not differ at all from each other in appearance, except in their language and hair; "for the eastern Ethiopians," he says, "are straight-haired, but those of Libya (or Africa) have hair more curly than that of any other people."[10] He records also the following passage, which fixes the physical characteristics of the Egyptians and some of their mighty neighbors:[11]

The Colchians were evidently Egyptians, and I say this, *having myself observed it* before I heard it from others; and as it was a matter of interest to me; I *inquired* of both people, and the Colchians had more recollection of the Egyptians than the Egyptians had of the Colchians;

yet the Egyptians said that they thought the Colchians had descended from the army of Sesotris; and I formed my conjecture, *not only because they are black in complexion and woolly-haired,* for this amounts to nothing, because *others are so likewise,* etc., etc.[12]

Rawlinson has clearly shown[13] that these statements of Herodotus have been too strongly confirmed by all recent researches (among the cuneiform inscriptions) in comparative philology to be set aside by the tottering criticism of such superficial inquirers as the Notts and Gliddons, *et id omne genus,* who base their assertions on ingenious conjectures. Pindar and Æschylus corroborate the assertions of Herodotus.

Homer, who lived still earlier than Herodotus, and who had also traveled in Egypt, makes frequent mention of the Ethiopians. He bears the same testimony as Herodotus as to their division into two sections:

Αἰθίοπας, τοι διχθὰ δεδαίαται, ἔσχατοι ἀνδρῶν,
Ὁι μὲν δυσομένου Ὑπεριονος, οἱ δ᾽ ἀνιόντος—[14]

which Pope freely renders:

"A race divided, whom with sloping rays
The rising and descending sun surveys."

And Homer seems to have entertained the very highest opinion of these Ethiopians. It would appear that he was so struck with the wonderful works of these people, which he saw in Egypt and the surrounding country, that he raises their authors above mortals, and makes them associates of the gods. Jupiter, and sometimes the whole Olympian family with him, is often made to betake himself to Ethiopia to hold converse with and partake of the hospitality of the Ethiopians.[15]

But it may be asked, Are we to suppose that the Guinea Negro, with all his peculiarities, is descended from these people? We answer, Yes. The descendants of Ham, in those early ages, like the European nations of the present day, made extensive migrations and conquests. They occupied a portion of two continents. While the Shemites had but little connection with Africa, the descendants of Ham, on the contrary, beginning their operations in Asia, spread westward and southward, so that as early as the time of Homer they had not only occupied the northern portions of Africa, but had crossed the great desert, penetrated into Sudan, and made their way to the west coast. "As far as we know," says that distinguished Homeric scholar, Mr. Gladstone, "Homer recognized the African coast by placing the Lotophagi upon it, and the *Ethiopians inland from the East all the way to the* extreme West."[16]

Some time ago Professor Owen, of the New York Free Academy, well known for his remarkable accuracy in editing the ancient classics, solicited the opinion of Professor Lewis of the New York University, another eminent scholar, as to the localities to which Homer's Ethiopians ought to be assigned. Professor Lewis gave a reply which so pleased Professor Owen that he gives it entire in his notes on the Odyssey, as "the most rational and veritable comment of any he had met with." It is as follows:

I have always, in commenting on the passage to which you refer, explained it to my classes as denoting the black race, (or Ethiopians, as they were called in Homer's time) living on the eastern and western coast of Africa—the one class inhabiting the country now called Abyssinia, and the other that part of Africa called Guinea or the Slave Coast. The common explanation that it refers to two divisions of Upper Egypt separated by the Nile, besides, as I believe, being geographically incorrect, (the Nile really making no such division), does not seem to be of sufficient importance to warrant the strong expressions of the text. (Odyssey, i. 22–24.) If it be said the view I have taken supposes too great a knowledge of geography in Homer, we need only bear in mind that he had undoubtedly visited Tyre, where the existence of the black race on the West of Africa had been known from the earliest times. The Tyrians, in their long voyages, having discovered a race on the West, in almost every respect similar to those better known in the East, would, from their remote distance from each other, and not knowing of any intervening nations in Africa, naturally style them the two extremities of the earth. (Homer's εσχατνι ανδρων.) Homer elsewhere speaks of the Pigmies, who are described by Herodotus and Diodorus Siculus as residing in the interior of Africa (on a river which I think corresponds to what is now called the Niger). It seems to me too extravagant language, even for poetry, to represent two nations, separated only by a river, as living, one at the rising, the other at the setting sun, although these terms may sometimes be used for East and West. Besides, if I am not mistaken, no such division is recognised in subsequent geography.[17]

Professor Lewis says nothing of the *Asiatic* division of the Ethiopians. But since his letter was penned—more than twenty years ago—floods of light have been thrown upon the subject of Oriental antiquities by the labors of M. Botta, Layard, Rawlinson, Hinks, and others. Even Bunsen, not very long ago, declared that "the idea of an *'Asiatic Cush'* was an imagination of interpreters, the child of despair." But in 1858, Sir Henry Rawlinson, having obtained a number of Babylonian documents more ancient than any previously discovered, was able to declare authoritatively that the early inhabitants of South Babylonia *were of a cognate race with the primitive colonists both of Arabia and of the African Ethiopia.*[18] He found their *vocabulary to be undoubtedly Cushite or Ethiopian,* belonging to that stock of tongues which in the sequel were everywhere more or less mixed up with the Semitic languages, but of which we have the purest modern specimens in the "Mahra of Southern Arabia" and the "Galla of Abyssinia." He also produced evidence of the widely spread settlements of the children of Ham in *Asia as well as Africa,* and (what is more especially valuable in our present inquiry) of the truth of the tenth chapter of Genesis as an ethnographical document of the highest importance.[19]

Now, we should like to ask, If the Negroes found at this moment along the West and East coast, and throughout Central Africa, are not descended from the ancient Ethiopians, from whom are they descended? And if they are the children of the Ethiopians, what is the force of the assertions continually repeated, by even professed friends of the Negro, that the enterprising and good-looking tribes of the continent, such as Lalofs, Mandingoes, and Fulas, are mixed with the blood of Caucasians?[20] With the records of ancient history before us, where is the necessity for supposing such an admixture? May not the intelligence, the activity, the elegant features and limbs of these tribes have been directly transmitted from their ancestors?

The Foulahs have a tradition that they are the descendants of Phut, the son of Ham. Whether this tradition be true or not, it is a singular fact that they have prefixed this name to almost every district of any extent which they have ever occupied. They have Futa-Torro, near Senegal; Futa-Bondu and Futa-Iallon to the north-east of Sierra Leone.[21]

Lenormant was of the opinion that Phut peopled Libya.

We gather from the ancient writers already quoted that the Ethiopians were celebrated for their beauty. Herodotus speaks of them as "men of large stature, *very handsome* and long-lived." And he uses these epithets in connection with the Ethiopians of *West Africa*, as the context shows. The whole passage is as follows:

Where the meridian declines toward the setting sun (that is, south-west from Greece) the Ethiopian territory reaches, being the extreme part of the habitable world. It produces much gold, huge elephants, wild trees of all kinds, *ebony*, and men of large stature, *very handsome*, and long-lived.[22]

Homer frequently tells us of the "handsome Ethiopians," although he and Herodotus do not employ the same Greek word. In Herodotus the word that describes the Ethiopians is καλος — a word denoting both beauty of outward form and moral beauty, or virtue.[23] The epithet (αμνμων) employed by Homer to describe the same people, is by some commentators rendered "blameless," but by the generality "handsome." Anthon says: "It is an epithet given to all men and women distinguished by rank, exploits, or beauty."[24] Mr. Hayman, one of the latest and most industrious editors of Homer, has in one of his notes the following explanation: "Αμνμωγ was at first an epithet of distinctive excellence, but had become a purely conventional style, as applied to a class, like our 'honorable and gallant gentleman.' "[25] Most scholars, however, agree with Mr. Paley, another recent Homeric commentator, that the original signification of the word was "handsome" and that it nearly represented the καλος καγα Ͽος of the Greeks;[26] so that the words which Homer puts into the mouth of Thetis when addressing her disconsolate son (Iliad, i. 423) would be, "Yesterday Jupiter went to Oceanus, to the *handsome* Ethiopians, to a banquet, and with him went all the gods." It is remarkable that the Chaldee, according to Bush, has the following translation of Numbers xii.1: "And Miriam and Aaron spake against Moses because of the beautiful woman whom he had married; for he had married a beautiful woman."[27] Compare with this Solomon's declaration, "I am *black* but *comely,*" or, more exactly, "I am black *and* comely." We see the wise man in his spiritual epithalamium selecting a black woman as a proper representative of the Church and of the highest purity. The Hebrew word, translated in our version *black*, is a correct rendering. So Luther, *schwarz.* It cannot mean *brown*, as rendered by Ostervald (*brune*) and Diodati (*bruna*). In Lev. xiii. 31, 37, it is applied to hair. The verb from which the adjective comes is used (Job xxx. 30) of the countenance blackened by disease. In Solomon's Song, v. 11, it is applied to the plumage of a raven.[28] In the days of Solomon, therefore, black, as a physical attribute, was *comely.*

But when, in the course of ages, the Ethiopians had wandered into the central and southern regions of Africa, encountering a change of climate and altered character of food and modes of living, they fell into intellectual and physical degradation. This degradation did not consist, however, in a change of color, as some suppose, for they were black, as we have seen, before they left their original seat. Nor did it consist in the stiffening and shortening of the hair; for Herodotus tells us that the Ethiopians in Asia were *straight-haired*, while their relatives in Africa, from the same stock and in no lower stage of progress, were *woolly-haired.* The hair, then, is not a fundamental characteristic, nor a mark of degradation. Some suppose that the hair of the Negro is affected by some peculiarity in the African climate and atmosphere—perhaps the influence of the Sahara entering as an important element. We do not profess to know the *fons et origo*, nor have we seen any satisfactory cause for it assigned. We have no consciousness of any inconvenience from it, except that in foreign countries, as a jovial fellow-passenger on an English steamer once reminded us, "it is *unpopular.*"

> "Vuolsi così colà, dove si puote
> Ciò che si vuole: e più non dimandare"[29]

Nor should it be thought strange that the Ethiopians who penetrated into the heart of the African continent should have degenerated, when we consider their distance and isolation from the quickening influence of the arts and sciences in the East; their belief, brought with them, in the most abominable idolatry, "changing the glory of the incorruptible God into an image made like unto corruptible man, and to *birds*, and *four-footed beasts*, and *creeping things*," Rom. i. 23; the ease with which, in the prolific regions to which they had come, they could secure the means of subsistence; and the constant and enervating heat of the climate, indisposing to continuous exertion. Students in natural history tell us that animals of the same species and family, if dispersed and domesticated, show striking modifications of the original type, in their color, hair, integument, structure of limbs, and even in their instincts, habits, and powers. Similar changes are witnessed among mankind. An intelligent writer in No. 48 of the "Dublin University Magazine," says:

There are certain districts in Leitrim, Sligo, and Mayo, chiefly inhabited by the descendants of the native Irish, driven by the British from Armagh and the South of Down about two centuries ago. These people, whose ancestors were well-grown, able-bodied, and comely, are now reduced to an average stature of five feet two inches, are pot-bellied, bow-legged, and abortively featured: and they are especially remarkable for open projecting mouths, and prominent teeth, and exposed gums, their advancing cheek-bones and depressed noses bearing barbarism in their very front. In other words, within so short a period, they seem to have acquired a prognathous type of skull, like the Australian savages.

But these retrogressive changes are taking place in other countries besides Ireland. Acute observers tell us that in England, the abode of the highest civilization of modern times, "a process of de-civilization, a relapse toward barbarism, is seen in the debased and degraded classes, with a coincident deterioration of physical type." Mr. Henry Mayhew, in his "London Labor and London Poor," has remarked that

Among them, according as they partake more or less of the pure vagabond nature, doing nothing whatever for their living, but moving from place to place, preying on the earnings of the more industrious portion of the community, so will the attributes of the nomadic races be found more or less marked in them; and they are more or less distinguished by their high cheek-bones and protruding jaws; thus showing that kind of mixture of the pyramidal with the prognathous type which is to be seen among the most degraded of the Malayo-Polynesian races.

In contrast with this retrogressive process, it may be observed that in proportion as the degraded races are intellectually and morally elevated, their physical appearance improves. Mr. C.S. Roundell, Secretary to the late Royal Commission in Jamaica, tells us that

The Maroons who fell under my (his) own observation in Jamaica, exhibited a marked superiority in respect of comportment, mental capacity, and physical type—a superiority to be referred to the saving effects of long-enjoyed freedom. The Maroons are descendants of runaway Spanish slaves, who at the time of the British conquest established themselves in the mountain fastnesses.[30]

In visiting the native towns interior to Liberia, we have seen striking illustrations of these principles. Among the inhabitants of those towns we could invariably distinguish the free man from the slave. There was about the former a dignity of appearance, an openness of countenance, an independence of air, a firmness of step, which indicated the absence of oppression; while in the latter there was a depression of countenance, a general deformity of appearance, an awkwardness of gait, which seemed to say, "That man is a slave."

Now, with these well-known principles before us, why should it be considered strange that, with their fall into barbarism, the "handsome" Ethiopians of Homer and Herodotus should have deteriorated in physical type—and that this degradation of type should continue reproducing itself in the wilds of Africa and in the Western Hemisphere, where they have been subjected to slavery and various other forms of debasing proscription?

Ημισυ γάρ τ' ἀρετῆς ἀποαινυται εὐρύοπα Ζεὺς
'Ανέρος, εὖτ' ἄν μιν κατὰ δούλιον ἦμαρ ἔλησιν.[31]

The Negro is often taunted by superficial investigators with proofs, as is alleged, taken from the monuments of Egypt, of the servitude of Negroes in very remote ages. But is there anything singular in the fact that in very early times Negroes were held in bondage? Was it not the practice among all the early nations to enslave each other? Why should it be pointed to as an exceptional thing that Ethiopians were represented as slaves? It was very natural that the more powerful Ethiopians should seize upon the weaker, as is done to this day in certain portions of Africa, and reduce them to slavery. And were it not for the abounding light of Christianity now enjoyed in Europe, the same thing would be done at this moment in Rome, Paris, and London. For the sites of those cities in ancient times witnessed all the horrors of a cruel and mercenary slave-trade, not in Negroes, but Caucasian selling Caucasian.[32]

But were there no Caucasian slaves in Egypt? If it be true that no such slaves are represented on the monumental remains, are we, therefore, to infer that they did not exist in that country? Are we to disbelieve that the Jews were in the most rigorous bondage in that land for four hundred years?

Nor everything which is not represented on the monuments was therefore necessarily unknown to the Egyptians. The monuments are neither intended to furnish, nor can they furnish, a complete delineation of all the branches of public and private life, of all the products and phenomena of the whole animal, vegetable, and mineral creations of the country. They cannot be viewed as a complete cyclopaedia of Egyptian customs and civilization. Thus we find no representation of fowls and pigeons, although the country abounded in them; of the wild ass and wild boar, although frequently met with in Egypt; none of the process relating to the casting of statues and other objects in bronze, although many similar subjects connected with the arts are represented; none of the marriage ceremony, and of numerous other subjects.[33]

But we are told that the Negroes of Central and West Africa have proved themselves essentially inferior, from the fact, that in the long period of three thousand years they have shown no signs of progress. In their country, it is alleged, are to be found no indications of architectural taste or skill, or of any susceptibility of aesthetic or artistic improvement; that they have no monuments of past exploits; no paintings or sculptures; and that, therefore, the foreign or American slave-trade was an indispensable agency in the civilization of Africa; that nothing could have been done for the Negro while he remained in his own land, bound to the practices of ages; that he needed the sudden and violent severance from home to deliver him from the quiescent degradation and stagnant barbarism of his ancestors; that otherwise the civilization of Europe could never have impressed him.

In reply to all this we remark: First, That it remains to be proved, by a fuller exploration of the interior, that there are no architectural remains, no works of artistic skill; Secondly, If it should be demonstrated that nothing of the kind exists, this would not necessarily prove essential inferiority on the part of the African. What did the Jews produce in all the long period of their history before and after their bondage to the Egyptians, among whom, it might be supposed, they would have made some progress in science and art? Their forefathers dwelt in tents before their Egyptian residence, and they dwelt in tents after their emancipation. And in all their long national history they produced no remarkable architectural monument but the Temple, which was designed and executed by a man miraculously endowed for the purpose. A high antiquarian authority tells us that pure Shemites had no art.[34] The lack of architectural and artistic skill is no mark of the absence of the higher elements of character.[35] Thirdly, With regard to the necessity of the slave-trade, we remark, without attempting to enter into the secret counsels of the Most High, that without the foreign slave-trade Africa would have been a great deal more accessible to civilization, and would now, had peaceful and legitimate intercourse been kept up with her from the middle of the fifteenth century, be taking her stand next to Europe in civilization, science, and religion. When, four hundred years ago, the Portuguese discovered this coast, they found the natives living in considerable peace and quietness, and with a certain degree of prosperity. Internal feuds, of course, the tribes sometimes had, but by no means so serious as they afterward became under the stimulating influence of the slave-trade. From all we can gather, the tribes in this part of Africa lived in a condition not very different from that of the greater portion of Europe in the Middle Ages. There was the same oppression of the weak by the strong; the same resistance by the weak, often taking the form of general rebellion; the same private and hereditary wars; the same strongholds in every prominent position; the same dependence of the people upon the chief who happened to be in power; the same contentedness of the masses with the tyrannical rule. But there was industry and activity, and in every town there were manufactures, and they sent across the continent to Egypt and the Barbary states other articles besides slaves.

The permanence for centuries of the social and political states of the Africans at home must be attributed, first, to the isolation of the people from the progressive portion of mankind; and, secondly, to the blighting influence of the traffic introduced among them by Europeans. Had not the demand arisen in America for African laborers, and had European nations inaugurated regular traffic with the coast, the natives would have shown themselves as impressible for change, as susceptible of improvement, as capable of acquiring knowledge and accumulating wealth, as the natives of Europe. Combination of capital and cooperation of energies would have done for this land what they have done for others. Private enterprise (which has been entirely destroyed by the nefarious traffic), encouraged by humane intercourse with foreign lands, would have developed agriculture, manufactures, and commerce; would have cleared, drained, and fertilized the country, and built towns; would have improved the looms, brought in plows, steam engines, printing presses, machines, and the thousand processes and appliances by which the comfort, progress, and usefulness of mankind are secured. But, alas! *Dis aliter visum.*

> "Freighted with curses was the bark that bore
> The spoilers of the West to Guinea's shore;
> Heavy with groans of anguish blew the gales
> That swelled that fatal bark's returning sails:
> Loud and perpetual o'er the Atlantic's waves,
> For guilty ages, rolled the tide of slaves;
> A tide that knew no fall, no turn, no rest—
> Constant as day and night from East to West,
> Still widening, deepening, swelling in its course
> With boundless ruin and resistless force."—MONTGOMERY.

But although, amid the violent shocks of those changes and disasters to which the natives of this outraged land have been subject, their knowledge of the elegant arts, brought from the East, declined, they never entirely lost the *necessary* arts of life. They still understand the workmanship of iron, and, in some sections of the country, of gold. The loom and the forge are in constant use among them. In remote regions, where they have no intercourse with Europeans, they raise large herds of cattle and innumerable sheep and goats, capture and train horses, build well-laid-out towns, cultivate extensive fields, and manufacture earthenware and woolen and cotton cloths. Commander Foote says: "The Negro arts are respectable, and would have been more so had not disturbance and waste come with the slave-trade."[36]

And in our own times, on the West Coast of Africa, a native development of literature has been brought to light of genuine home growth. The Vey people, residing halfway between Sierra Leone and Cape Mesurado, have within the last thirty years invented a syllabic alphabet, with which they are now writing their own language and by which they are maintaining among themselves an extensive epistolary correspondence. In 1849 the Church Missionary Society in London, having heard of this invention, authorized their missionary, Rev. S.W. Koelle, to investigate the subject. Mr. Koelle traveled into the interior, and brought away three manuscripts, with translations. The symbols are phonetic, and constitute a syllabarium, not an alphabet; they are nearly two hundred in number. They have been learned so generally that Vey boys in Monrovia frequently receive communications from their friends in the Vey country, to which they readily respond. The Church Missionary Society have had a font of type cast in this new character, and several little tracts have been printed and circulated among the tribe. The principal inventor of this alphabet is now dead; but it is supposed that he died in the Christian faith, having acquired some knowledge of the way of salvation through the medium of this character of his own invention.[37] Dr. Wilson says:

This invention is one of the most remarkable achievements of this or any other age, and is itself enough to silence forever the cavils and sneers of those who think so contemptuously of the intellectual endowments of the African race.

Though "the idea of communicating thoughts in writing was probably suggested by the use of Arabic among the Mandingoes," yet the invention was properly original, showing the existence of genius in the native African who has never been in foreign slavery, and proves that he carries in his bosom germs of intellectual development and self-elevation, which would have enabled him to advance regularly in the path of progress, had it not been for the blighting influence of the slave-trade.

Now are we to believe that such a people have been doomed, by the terms of any curse, to be the "servant of servants," as some upholders of Negro slavery have taught? Would it not have been a very singular theory that a people destined to servitude should begin, the very first thing, as we have endeavored to show, to found "great cities," organize kingdoms, and establish rule—putting up structures which have come down to this day

as a witness to their *superiority* over all their contemporaries—
and that, by a Providential decree, the people whom they had
been fated to serve should be held in bondage by them four
hundred years?

The remarkable enterprise of the Cushite hero, Nimrod; his establishment of imperial power, as an advance on patriarchal government; the
strength of the Egypt of Mizraim, and its long domination over the
house of Israel; and the evidence which now and then appears, that even
Phut (who is the obscurest in his fortunes of all the Hamite race)
maintained a relation to the descendants of Shem which was far from
servile or subject; do all clearly tend to limit the application of Noah's
maledictory prophecy to the precise terms in which it was indited:
"Cursed be Canaan; a servant of servants shall he" (not Cush, not
Mizraim, not Phut, but he) "be to his brethren." If we then confine the
imprecation to Canaan, we can without difficulty trace its accomplishment in the subjugation of the tribes which issued from him to the
children of Israel from the time of Joshua to that of David. Here would
be verified Canaan's servile relation to Shem; and when imperial Rome
finally wrested the sceptre from Judah, and, "dwelling in the tents of
Shem," occupied the East and whatever remnants of Canaan were left
in it, would not this accomplish that further prediction that Japheth,
too, should be lord of Canaan, and that (as it would seem to be tacitly
implied) mediately, through his occupancy of the tents of Shem?[38]

A vigorous writer in the "Princeton Review" has the following:

The Ethiopian race, from whom the modern Negro or African stock
are undoubtedly descended, can claim as early a history, with the exception of the Jews,[39] as any living people on the face of the earth. History,
as well as the monumental discoveries, gives them a place in ancient
history as far back as Egypt herself, if not further. But what has become
of the contemporaneous nations of antiquity, as well as others of much
later origin? Where are the Numidians, Mauritanians, and other powerful names, who once held sway over all Northern Africa? They have
been swept away from the earth, or dwindled down to a handful of
modern Copts and Berbers of doubtful descent.

The Ethiopian, or African race, on the other hand, though they have
long since lost all the civilization which once existed on the Upper Nile,
have, nevertheless, continued to increase and multiply, until they are
now, with the exception of the Chinese, the largest single family of men

on the face of the earth. They have extended themselves in every direction over that great continent, from the southern borders of the Great Sahara to the Cape of Good Hope, and from the Atlantic to the Indian Ocean, and are thus constituted masters of at least three-fourths of the habitable portions of this great continent. And this progress has been made, be it remembered, in despite of the prevalence of the foreign slave-trade, which has carried off so many of their people; of the ceaseless internal feuds and wars that have been waged among themselves; and of a conspiracy, as it were, among all surrounding nations, to trample out their national existence. Surely their history is a remarkable one; but not more so, perhaps, than is foreshadowed in the prophecies of the Old Scriptures. God has watched over and preserved these people through all the vicissitudes of their unwritten history, and no doubt for some great purpose of mercy toward them, as well as for the display of the glory of his own grace and providence, and we may expect to have a full revelation of this purpose and glory as soon as the everlasting Gospel is made known to these benighted millions.[40]

One palpable reason may be assigned why the Ethiopian race has continued to exist under the most adverse circumstances, while other races and tribes have perished from the earth; it is this: *they have never been a bloodthirsty or avaricious people.* From the beginning of their history to the present time their work has been constructive, except when they have been stimulated to wasting wars by the covetous foreigner. They have *built up* in Asia, Africa, and America. They have not delighted in despoiling and oppressing others. The nations enumerated by the reviewer just quoted, and others besides them—all warlike and fighting nations—have passed away or dwindled into utter insignificance. They seem to have been consumed by their own fierce internal passions. The Ethiopians, though brave and powerful, were not a fighting people, that is, were not fond of fighting for the sake of humbling and impoverishing other people. Every reader of history will remember the straightforward, brave, and truly Christian answer returned by the King of the Ethiopians to Cambyses, who was contemplating an invasion of Ethiopia, as recorded by Herodotus. For the sake of those who may not have access to that work, we reproduce the narrative here. About five hundred years before Christ, Cambyses, the great Persian warrior, while invading Egypt, planned an expedition against the

Ethiopians; but before proceeding upon the belligerent enterprises he sent

Spies, in the first instance, who were to see the table of the sun, which was said to exist among the Ethiopians, and besides, to explore other things, and, to cover their design, they were to carry presents to the King . . . When the messengers of Cambyses arrived among the Ethiopians they gave the presents to the King, and addressed him as follows: 'Cambyses, King of the Persians, desirous of becoming your friend and ally, has sent us, bidding us confer with you, and he presents you with these gifts, which are such as he himself most delights in!'

But the Ethiopian knowing that they came as spies, spoke thus to them:

Neither has the King of Persia sent you with these presents to me because he valued my alliance, nor do you speak the truth, for you are come as spies of my kingdom. Nor is he a just man; for if he were just he would not desire any other territory than his own; nor would he reduce people into servitude who have done him no injury. However, give him this bow, and say these words to him: 'The King of the Ethiopians advises the King of the Persians, when the Persians can thus easily draw a bow of this size, then to make war on the Macrobian Ethiopians with more numerous forces; but until that time let him thank the gods, who have not inspired the sons of the Ethiopians with the desire of adding another land to their own.' [41]

Are these a people, with such remarkable antecedents, and in the whole of whose history the hand of God is so plainly seen, to be treated with the contempt which they usually suffer in the lands of their bondage? When we notice the scornful indifference with which the Negro is spoken of by certain politicians in America, we fancy that the attitude of Pharaoh and the aristocratic Egyptians must have been precisely similar toward the Jews. We fancy we see one of the magicians in council, after the first visit of Moses demanding the release of the Israelites, rising up with indignation and pouring out a torrent of scornful invective such as any rabid anti-Negro politician might now indulge in.

What privileges are those that these degraded Hebrews are

craving? What are they? Are they not slaves and the descendants
of slaves? What have they or their ancestors ever done? What
can they do? They did not come hither of their own accord. The
first of them was brought to this country a slave, sold to us by
his own brethren. Others followed him, refugees from the famine
of an impoverished country. What do they know about managing
liberty or controlling themselves? They are idle; they are idle.
Divert their attention from their idle dreams by additional labor
and more exacting tasks.

But what have the ancestors of Negroes ever done? Let Professor Rawlinson answer, as a summing up of our discussion. Says
the learned professor:

For the last three thousand years the world has been mainly indebted
for its advancement to the Semitic and Indo-European races; *but it was
otherwise in the first ages.* Egypt and Babylon, Mizraim and Nimrod—
both descendants of Ham—led the way, and acted as the pioneers of
mankind in the various untrodden fields of art, literature, and science.
Alphabetic writing, astronomy, history, chronology, architecture, plastic art, sculpture, navigation, agriculture, textile industry, seem all of
them to have had their origin in one or other of these two countries.
The beginnings may have been often humble enough. We may laugh
at the rude picture-writing, the uncouth brick pyramid, the coarse fabric, the homely and ill-shapen instruments, as they present themselves
to our notice in the remains of these ancient nations; but they are really
worthier of our admiration than of our ridicule. The inventors of any
art are among the greatest benefactors of their race, and mankind at
the present day lies under infinite obligations to the genius of these early
ages.[42]

There are now, probably, few thoughtful and cultivated men
in the United States who are prepared to advocate the application of the curse of Noah to all the descendants of Ham. The
experience of the last eight years must have convinced the most
ardent theorizer on the subject. Facts have not borne out their
theory and predictions concerning the race. The Lord by his
outstretched arm has dashed their syllogisms to atoms, scattered
their dogmas to the winds, detected the partiality and exaggerating tendency of their method, and shown the injustice of that

heartless philosophy and that unrelenting theology which consigned a whole race of men to hopeless and interminable servitude.

It is difficult, nevertheless, to understand how, with the history of the past accessible, the fact of the present before their eyes, and the prospect of a clouded future, or unveiled only to disclose the indefinite numerical increase of Europeans in the land, the blacks of the United States can hope for any distinct, appreciable influence in the country. We cannot perceive on what grounds the most sanguine among their friends can suppose that there will be so decisive a revolution of popular feeling in favor of their *protégés* as to make them at once the political and social equals of their former masters. Legislation cannot secure them this equality in the United States any more than it has secured it for the blacks in the West Indies. During the time of slavery everything in the laws, in the customs, in the education of the people was contrived with the single view of degrading the Negro in his own estimation and that of others. Now is it possible to change in a day the habits and character which centuries of oppression have entailed? We think not. More than one generation, it appears to us, must pass away before the full effect of education, enlightenment, and social improvement will be visible among the blacks. Meanwhile they are being gradually absorbed by the Caucasian; and before their social equality comes to be conceded they will have lost their identity altogether; a result, in our opinion, extremely undesirable, as we believe that, as Negroes, they might accomplish a great work which others cannot perform. But even if they should not pass away in the mighty embrace of their numerous white neighbors; grant that they could continue to live in the land, a distinct people, with the marked peculiarities they possess, having the same color and hair, badges of a former thraldom—is it to be supposed that they can ever overtake a people who so largely outnumber them, and a large proportion of whom are endowed with wealth, leisure, and the habits and means of study and self-improvement? If they improve in culture and training, as in time they no doubt will, and become intelligent and educated, there may rise up individuals among them, here and there, who will be respected and honored by the whites; but it is plain that, as a class, their inferiority will never cease until they cease to be a distinct people, possessing peculiarities which suggest antecedents of servility and degradation.

We pen these lines with the most solemn feelings—grieved that so many strong, intelligent, and energetic black men should be wasting time and labor in a fruitless contest, which, expended in the primitive land of their fathers—a land that so much needs them—would produce in a comparatively short time results of incalculable importance. But what can we do? Occupying this distant standpoint—an area of Negro freedom and a scene for untrammeled growth and development, but a wide and ever-expanding field for benevolent effort; an outlying or surrounding wilderness to be reclaimed; barbarism of ages to be brought over to Christian life—we can only repeat with undiminished earnestness the wish we have frequently expressed elsewhere, that the *eyes of the blacks may be opened to discern their true mission and destiny;* that, making their escape from the house of bondage, they may *betake themselves to their ancestral home, and assist in constructing a Christian* AFRICAN EMPIRE. For we believe that as descendants of Ham had a share, as the most prominent actors on the scene, in the founding of cities and in the organization of government, so members of the same family, developed under different circumstances, will have an important part in the closing of the great drama.

"Time's noblest offspring is the last."

NOTES

1. Commander Foote, "Africa and the American Flag," p. 207.
2. Quoted by G. Rawlinson in Notes to "Bampton Lectures," 1859.
3. See Conant's Gesenius's Hebrew Grammar, (17th edition) section 155 (a); and for additional examples of this usage, see Judges vii.22; 1 Sam. xvii. 40; Jer. xv. 13, where *even* represents the conjunction *vau* (and) in the original.

4. London, 1844.

5. London, 1858. See Dr. Robinson's view in Gesenius's Hebrew Lexicon, under the word Cush.

6. See Kitto's Biblical Cyclopedia, article, *Ham.* London, 1866.

7. Historical and Critical Commentary on Genesis. Heb. and Eng. P.263.

8. It is certain that Mizraim, with his descendants, settled Egypt, giving his name to the country, which it still retains. The Arabic name for Egypt is *Misr.* In Psalm cv. 23, Egypt is called "the land of Ham."

9. While Rev. Elias Schrenk, a German missionary laboring on the Gold Coast, in giving evidence on the condition of West Africa before a committee of the House of Commons in May, 1865, was making a statement of the proficiency of some of the natives in his school in Greek and other branches of literature, he was interrupted by Mr. Cheetham, a member of the committee, with the inquiry: "Were those young men of *pure* African blood?" "Yes," replied Mr. Schrenk, "decidedly; thick lips and black skin," "And woolly hair?" added Mr. Cheetham. "And woolly hair," subjoined Mr. Schrenk. (See "Parliamentary Report on Western Africa for 1865," p. 145.)

10. Herodotus, iii. 94; vii. 70.

11. It is not necessary, however, to consider *all* Egyptians as Negroes, black in complexion and woolly-haired; this is contradicted by their mummies and portraits. Blumenbach discovered three varieties of physiognomy on the Egyptian paintings and sculptures; but he describes the general or national type as exhibiting a certain approximation to the Negro.

12. Herodotus, ii. 104.

13. Five Great Monarchies, vol. i, chap. 3.

14. Odyssey, i. 23, 24.

15. Iliad, i. 423; xxiii. 206.

16. "Homer and the Homeric Age," vol. iii. p. 305.

17. Owen's Homer's Odyssey (Fifth Ed.), p. 306

18. See Article *Ham*, in Kitto's Cyclopedia. Last Edition.

19. Bowen's "Central Africa," chap. xxii.

20. Rawlinson's Herodotus, Vol. i, p. 442.

21. Wilson's Western Africa, p. 79.

22. Herodotus, iii. 114.

23. Liddell and Scott.

24. Anthon's Homer, p. 491.

25. Hayman's Odyssey, i. 29.

26. Paley's Iliad, p. 215. Note.

27. Bush, *in loco.*

28. A correspondent of the New York Tribune, residing in Syria, describing the appearance of a Negro whom he met there in 1866, says: "He was as *black* as a Mount Lebanon raven." (N.Y. Tribune, October 16, 1866.) Had he been writing in Hebrew he would have employed the descriptive word שחור

29. Dante.

30. "England and her Subjects Races, with special reference to Jamaica." By Charles Saville Roundell, M.A.

31. Odyssey, xvii. 322, 323.

32. Cicero, in one of his letters, speaking of the success of an expedition against Britain, says the only plunder to be found consisted "Ex emancipiis; ex quibus nullos puto te literis aut musicis eruditos expectare"; thus proving, in the same sentence, the existence of the slave trade, and intimating that it was impossible that any Briton should be intelligent enough to be worthy to serve the accomplished Atticus. (Ad. Att., lib. iv. 16.) Henry, in his History of England, gives us also the authority of Strabo for the prevalence of the slave trade among the Britons, and tells us that slaves were once an established article of export. "Great numbers," says he, "were exported from Britain, and were to be seen exposed for sale, like cattle, in the Roman market."— *Henry,* vol. ii. p. 225. Also, Sir T. Fowell Buxton's "Slave Trade and Remedy"—*Introduction.*

33. Dr. Kalisch: "Commentary on Exodus," p. 147. London, 1855.

34. Rev. Stuart Poole, of the British Museum, before the British Association, 1864.

35. Rev. Dr. Goulburn, in his reply to Dr. Temple's celebrated Essay on the "Education of the World," has the following suggestive remark: "We commend to Dr. Temple's notice the pregnant fact, that in the earliest extant history of mankind it is stated that arts, both ornamental and useful, (and arts are the great medium of civilization) took their rise in the family of Cain. In the line of Seth we find none of this mental and social development."—*Replies to Essays and Reviews*, p. 34. When the various causes now cooperating shall have produced a higher religious sense among the nations, and a corresponding revolution shall have taken place in the estimation now put upon material objects, the effort may be to show, to his disparagement—if we could imagine such an unamiable undertaking as compatible with the high state of progress then attained—that the Negro was at the foundation of all material development.

36. "Africa and the American Flag," p. 52.

37. Wilson's "Western Africa," p. 95, and "Princeton Review for July, 1858," p. 488.

38. Dr. Peter Holmes, Oxford, England.

39. The Jews not excepted. Where were they when the Pyramids were built?

40. "Princeton Review," July 1858, pp. 418, 449.

41. Herodotus, iii. 17–22.

42. "Five Great Monarchies," vol. i. pp. 75, 76.

7. THE CONTRIBUTION OF ETHIOPIA-NUBIA AND OF EGYPT TO CIVILIZATION *

ⅬⅬⅬⅬⅬⅬⅬⅬⅬⅬⅬⅬⅬⅬⅬⅬ

Cheikh Anta Diop

According to the unanimous witness of all the ancients, it was first the Ethiopians and then the Egyptians who created and developed to an extraordinary degree all the elements of civilization at a time when all other peoples—and the Eurasians in particular—were plunged in barbarism.

The explanation of this must be sought in the environment in which from the beginning of time their geographical position placed them. In order to adapt himself to it man had to invent the sciences, which were later completed by arts and religion.

It is impossible to exaggerate what the whole world—and in particular the Hellenic world—owes to the Egyptian world. The Greeks only took up and developed, sometimes only to a limited extent, the Egyptian inventions, which, owing to their materialist tendencies, they deprived of the "idealist" cover which protected them. The difficult conditions of life in the Eurasian plain seem on the one hand to have developed the materialist instinct of the people inhabiting it, and on the other to have created ethical values contrary to the Egyptian ethical values which were

*From *Nations nègres et culture*, by Cheikh Anta Diop, Paris, 1955, pp. 249–253.

the outcome of a sedentary collective life, relatively easy and peaceful so long as it was regulated by a few social rules. As much as the Egyptians look with horror upon theft, nomadism, and war, as much are these practices considered on the Eurasian plains to embody ethical values of the first order. No one, except the warrior fallen on the field of battle, may enter Valhalla, the Germanic paradise. Among the Egyptians, on the other hand, no dead man may attain felicity except he who can prove in the tribunal of Osiris that he had never committed a sin and had exercised charity toward the poor. This is in complete opposition to the raiding instinct and the spirit of conquest which in general characterizes the peoples of the north who were so to speak expelled from their country which nature had endowed so poorly. By contrast, life is so easy in the valley of the Nile, a life-giving stream flowing between two deserts, that the Egyptian tends to believe that all of nature falls from heaven. He therefore ends by worshiping the latter in the guise of an All-powerful Being, a Creator, making all that exists and dispensing all goods. The Egyptian's primitive materialism—that is to say his vitalism—is thereafter transposed to heaven and becomes, so to speak, a metaphysical materialism.

In contrast, the Greeks cannot go beyond the visible and material man who subjugates hostile nature. On earth everything revolves round him and the supreme end of art is to produce his exact likeness. In "heaven," paradoxically, none but him may be found with all his faults and earthly weaknesses under the guise of gods who are distinguished from ordinary mortals only by their greater physical strength. When, therefore, the Egyptian god, who is a real god in every sense of the word and who has all the moral perfection resulting from sedentary life, is borrowed by the Greek, the latter will not be able to understand and keep him except by bringing him down to the human level. Thus the Pantheon which the Greek has adopted is nothing more than another version of humanity. It is this anthropomorphism, in this particular case nothing but an extreme materialism, which characterizes the Greek spirit. The Greek miracle, properly speaking, does not exist, since the process of acclimatizing Egyptian values in Greece, and it is this which is in question, has, it is obvious, nothing miraculous about it in the "intellectual" sense of the word. It may be said at the utmost that this tendency toward materialism which characterizes the West is propitious to the development of science.

Once they borrowed Egyptian values, the Greeks were able to develop, owing to their secular genius, which was the result of the influence of the Eurasian steppes and their weak religious temperament, a lay and secular science, taught publicly by philosophers equally secular; whereas among the Egyptians science was the privilege of a sacerdotal corps which jealously stood guard over it, without spreading it among the people and allowing it to be lost in the course of social upheavals:

Spiritual power and dignity which everywhere else exercised an invisible empire, side by side with more visible power, was not, among the Greeks, in the hands of priests or officials, but in those of the researcher and thinker. The latter could, as was clearly the case with Thales, Pythagoras and Empedocles, become the centre of a circle which was something between a religious congregation and a school, of an academy and an order, being sometimes more nearly the one and sometimes the other, having scientific, moral and political goals related to each other in order to constitute a philosophical tradition. (Ernst d'Aster, *Histoire de la Philosophie*, translated by M. Belviares, Payot, 1952, p. 48.)

In these schools scientific and philosophical teaching was provided by lay persons whom nothing distinguished from the people, except perhaps their intellectual level and their aristocratic rank. No halo of sanctity surrounded them. In *Isis and Osiris* Plutarch declares that according to all Greek scientists and philosophers who studied under the Egyptians, Thales, Plato, Lycurgus, Eudoxus, Pythagoras, encountered many difficulties before being initiated by the Egyptians. Again, according to Plutarch, it was Pythagoras who was the Egyptians' favorite owing to his mystical temperament, and Plutarch, in turn, was among the Greeks one of those who most venerated the Egyptians. In an earlier passage Plutarch indicates the esoteric significance of the word AMMON: *i.e.*, , that which is hidden, which is invisible . . .

It is therefore curious that, as Amélineau remarks, the Egyptian contribution to civilization should not be emphasized more.

I saw then, and saw clearly, that the most famous systems of Greece, notably those of Plato and Aristotle, had Egypt for a cradle. I also realized that the Greeks' fine genius, particularly that of Plato, had been able to clothe Egyptian ideas with an incomparable dress: but I thought that what we loved when coming from the Greeks, should not be disdained or looked down upon when found among the Egyptians. When, in our own day, two authors collaborate, they share the fame which accrues from their work: I do not see why ancient Greece should keep for herself alone the honour due to ideas which she had borrowed from Egypt. (Amélineau: *Prolégomènes* . . . Introduction, pp. 8 and 9).

Amélineau shows that if certain of Plato's ideas have become obscure, it is because reference is no longer made to their Egyptian origin; this, for example, is the case with Plato's ideas on the creation of the world by the Demiurge. It is also known that Pythagoras, Thales, Solon, Archimedes, Erastothenes, had gone to study in Egypt itself, and this list is by no means exhaustive. Egypt was in truth the classic land where two-thirds of Greek scientists and philosophers had gone to be initiated. In fact, it may be said that in the Hellenistic period Alexandria was the intellectual center of the world where all the Greek scientists who are spoken of nowadays, were found assembled. One cannot stress too much the fact that these scientists were trained outside Greece, in Egypt itself.

Even Greek architecture has its roots in Egypt. As early as the XIIth dynasty protodoric columns are to be found (the Beni-Hassan tombs).

Greco-Roman monuments are nothing but miniatures when compared to the Egyptian monuments, as is well known. Notre-Dame of Paris including its turrets can be easily accommodated within the hypostyle of the Temple at Karnak; and this is the case *a fortiori* with the Greek Parthenon.*

*The frozen face of the Greek statue, in spite of the other anatomical details, is remote from the later Latin realism, and comes near to the serenity of Egyptian art.

The fable, a literary *genre* which consists in making an animal the hero of a story, is typically Negro—or Cushite, as Lenormant writes—and was introduced into Greece by the Egyptian Negro, Aesop, who inspired La Fontaine to write his fables.

Edgar Poe, in his "Short Discussion with a Mummy" (New Extraordinary Stories) gives a symbolic idea of the breadth of scientific and technical knowledge in ancient Egypt.

Herodotus had already received from the mouth of Egyptian priests indications of the essential mathematics of the Great Pyramid, known as Cheops' Pyramid. Many mathematicians and astronomers have devoted to this pyramid a number of works, the sensational revelations of which have aroused a multitude of queries which cannot, however, be reduced to a coherent scientific exposition. Without getting involved in what may be called an excess of pyramidology, the following figures can be cited:

Astronomers have noted in this pyramid an indication of the sidereal year, of the anomalistic year, of the precession of the equinoxes for a period of 6,000 years, whilst modern astronomy can predict them only for a period of 400 years (according to Riffert, *Grand Pyramid*, London, 1932).

Mathematicians have also noted in the calculations of the Great Pyramid the value of *pi* exactly worked out, the exact average distance from the sun to the earth, the earth's polar diameter, etc.

This list could be made longer by quoting even more sensational figures. Can so many concordances be the effect of chance? As Matila C. Ghyka writes, this would be inconceivable.

Each of these properties may be a coincidence; their fortuitous appearance together would constitute a bundle of coincidences almost as improbable as a temporary reversal of the second law of thermodynamics (that water would freeze over fire, etc.) which physicists evoke in imagination, or as the miracle of monkeys adept at shorthand-typing so dear to M. Emile Borel. (*Esthétique des proportions dans la nature et dans les arts*, Gallimard, Paris, 1927, p. 345.)

Further on, the same author adds (pp. 367–8):

Yet, Viollet-le-Duc's hypothesis concerning the transmission of certain Egyptian diagrams to the Arabs, and afterwards to the Cluniacs through the intermediary of the Greco-Nestorian School at Alexandria, completed and made more precise through the researches of Dieulafoy, E. Mâle and Lun, is quite convincing. The Great Pyramid may well be, astronomically speaking, the "gnomon of the Great Year"; it may also be the "metronome" the harmonious concord of which, sometimes not understood, reverberates in Greek art, Gothic architecture, the first Renaissance and in every art which with "divine proportion" captures the rhythm of life.

The author also cites the Abbé Moreux's opinion, according to whom the Great Pyramid indicates not so much "the tentative beginning of Egyptian civilization and science; but rather the crowning glory of a culture which had reached its apogee and which, on the verge of disappearing had wanted in a gesture of supreme arrogance to bequeath to succeeding civilizations a proud testimony of its superiority." (p. 345)

Such astronomical and mathematical knowledge, far from having totally disappeared in Black Africa, has on the contrary left traces which M. Marcel Griaule has had the merit to have discovered among the Dogons, however surprising this may seem today.

We have many times alluded to the fact that the Greeks took their gods from Egypt; here is the proof of this assertion:

Almost all the names of Gods came from Egypt into Greece. It is absolutely certain that they have come to us from the Barbarians: my researches have convinced me of this. I therefore believe that we derive them principally from the Egyptians. (Herodotus, II, 50.)

Barbarism here means stranger and has no pejorative undertone.

The Egyptian origin of civilization and Greece's extensive

debt to it being historically obvious, one may with Amélineau ask why, in spite of these facts, the Greek role should be so much stressed while that of Egypt is increasingly passed over in silence.

The logic of such an attitude can be grasped only by remembering the substance of the case. Egypt being a country of Negroes, and its civilization being due to Negroes, any thesis trying to assert the contrary has no future; and the protagonists of such a thesis are not the least aware of this fact. It becomes therefore wiser and safer purely and simply to take away from Egypt in the most discreet manner all its achievements, to the benefit of a really white race.

This false attribution of the values of an Egypt described as white to an equally white Greece reveals a profound contradiction which is not the least significant proof of the Negro origin of Egyptian civilization.

As has been seen, colored man far from being unable to create technology, as André Siegfried thinks, is the very being who originated it in the person of the Negro at a time when all the white races, plunged in barbarism, were becoming just ready for civilization.

In saying that it is the ancestors of the Negroes who live today mainly in Black Africa who first invented mathematics, astronomy, the sciences in general, arts, religion, agriculture, social organization, medicine, handwriting, technology, architecture, in saying that it is they who were the first to erect edifices of 6,000,000 tons of stone (the Great Pyramid) in their capacity as architects and engineers—and not only as laborers; that it was they who built the vast temple at Karnak, a veritable forest of columns and its celebrated hypostyle where Notre-Dame with its towers could be accommodated; that it is they who have sculptured the first colossal statues (the Colossi of Memnon, etc.); in saying all this, one is saying no more than the strict and modest truth which nobody, at the present time, can refute with any argument worthy of the name.

This being so, the Negro should be able to recapture the continuity of his national historic past and to derive from it the necessary moral profit to enable him to reconquer his position in the modern world without abandoning himself to the excesses of an inverted Nazism; because the civilization of which he claims to be the heir could have been created by any other human race—in so far as it is possible to speak of race—which found itself placed in such a favorable, such a unique cradle.

8. THE RESURRECTION OF THE NEGRO *

⎍⎍⎍⎍⎍⎍⎍⎍⎍⎍⎍⎍⎍⎍⎍

Marcus Garvey

*Speech Delivered at Liberty Hall, N.Y.C., During
Second International Convention of Negroes, August, 1921**

Four years ago, realizing the oppression and the hardships from which we suffered, we organized ourselves into an organization for the purpose of bettering our condition, and founding a government of our own. The four years of organization have brought good results, in that from an obscure, despised race we have grown into a mighty power, a mighty force whose influence is being felt throughout the length and breadth of the world. The Universal Negro Improvement Association existed but in name four years ago, today it is known as the greatest moving force among Negroes. We have accomplished this through unity of effort and unity of purpose, it is a fair demonstration of what we will be able to accomplish in the very near future, when the millions who are outside the pale of the Universal Negro Improvement Association will have linked themselves up with us.

*From *Philosophy and Opinions of Marcus Garvey*, Vol. I, New York, 1923, pp. 93–97.

By our success of the last four years we will be able to estimate the grander success of a free and redeemed Africa. In climbing the heights to where we are today, we have had to surmount difficulties, we have had to climb over obstacles, but the obstacles were stepping stones to the future greatness of this Cause we represent. Day by day we are writing a new history, recording new deeds of valor performed by this race of ours. It is true that the world has not yet valued us at our true worth, but we are climbing up so fast and with such force that every day the world is changing its attitude toward us. Wheresoever you turn your eyes today you will find the moving influence of the Universal Negro Improvement Association among Negroes from all corners of the globe. We hear among Negroes the cry of "Africa for the Africans." This cry has become a positive, determined one. It is a cry that is raised simultaneously the world over because of the universal oppression that affects the Negro. You who are congregated here tonight as delegates representing the hundreds of branches of the Universal Negro Improvement Association in different parts of the world will realize that we in New York are positive in this great desire of a free and redeemed Africa. We have established this Liberty Hall as the center from which we send out the sparks of liberty to the four corners of the globe, and if you have caught the spark in your section, we want you to keep it a-burning for the great Cause we represent.

There is a mad rush among races everywhere toward national independence. Everywhere we hear the cry of liberty, of freedom, and a demand for democracy. In our corner of the world we are raising the cry for liberty, freedom and democracy. Men who have raised the cry for freedom and liberty in ages past have always made up their minds to die for the realization of the dream. We who are assembled in this convention as delegates representing the Negroes of the world give out the same spirit that the fathers of liberty in this country gave out over one hundred years ago. We give out a spirit that knows no compromise, a spirit that refuses to turn back, a spirit that says "Liberty or Death," and in prosecution of this great ideal—the ideal of a free and redeemed Africa, men may scorn, men may spurn us, and may say that we are on the wrong side of life, but let me tell you that way in which you are traveling is just the way all peoples who are free have traveled in the past. If you want liberty you yourselves must strike the blow. If you must be free you must become so through your own effort, through your own initiative. Those who have discouraged you in the past are those who have enslaved you for centuries and it is not expected that they will admit that you have a right to strike out at this late hour for freedom, liberty, and democracy.

At no time in the history of the world, for the last five hundred years, was there ever a serious attempt made to free Negroes. We have been camouflaged into believing that we were made free by Abraham Lincoln. That we were made free by Victoria of England, but up to now we are still slaves, we are industrial slaves, we are social slaves, we are political slaves, and the new Negro desires a freedom that has no boundary, no limit. We desire a freedom that will lift us to the common standard of all men, whether they be white men of Europe or yellow men of Asia, therefore, in our desire to lift ourselves to that standard we shall stop at nothing until there is a free and redeemed Africa.

I understand that just at this time while we are endeavoring to create public opinion and public sentiment in favor of a free Africa, that others of our race are being subsidized to turn the attention of the world toward a different desire on the part of Negroes, but let me tell you that Africa must be free. The enemy may argue with you to show you the impossibility of a free and redeemed Africa, but I want you to take as your argument the thirteen colonies of America, that once owed their sovereignty to Great Britain, that sovereignty has been destroyed to make a United States of America. George Washington was not God Almighty. He was a man like any Negro in this building, and if he and his associates were able to make a free America, we too can make a free Africa. Hampden, Gladstone, Pitt, and Disraeli were not the representatives of God in the person of Jesus Christ. They were but men, but in their time they worked for the expansion of the British Empire, and today they boast of a British Empire upon which "the sun never sets." As Pitt and

Gladstone were able to work for the expansion of the British Empire, so you and I can work for the expansion of a great African Empire. Voltaire and Mirabeau were not Jesus Christs, they were but men like ourselves. They worked and overturned the French monarchy. They worked for the democracy which France now enjoys, and if they were able to do that, we are able to work for a democracy in Africa. Lenin and Trotsky were not Jesus Christs, but they were able to overthrow the despotism of Russia, and today they have given to the world a social republic, the first of its kind. If Lenin and Trotsky were able to do that for Russia, you and I can do that for Africa. Therefore, let no man, let no power on earth, turn you from this sacred cause of liberty. I prefer to die at this moment rather than not to work for the freedom of Africa. If liberty is good for certain sets of humanity it is good for all. Black men, colored men, Negroes have as much right to be free as any other race that God Almighty ever created, and we desire freedom that is unfettered, freedom that is unlimited, freedom that will give us a chance and opportunity to rise to the fullest of our ambition and that we cannot get in countries where other men rule and dominate.

We have reached the time when every minute, every second must count for something done, something achieved in the cause of Africa. We need the freedom of Africa now, therefore, we desire the kind of leadership that will give it to us as quickly as possible. You will realize that not only individuals, but governments are using their influence against us. But what do we care about the unrighteous influence of any government? Our cause is based upon righteousness. And everything that is not righteous we have no respect for, because God Almighty is our leader and Jesus Christ our standard-bearer. We rely on them for that kind of leadership that will make us free, for it is the same God who inspired the Psalmist to write "Princes shall come out of Egypt and Ethiopia shall stretch out her hands unto God." At this moment methinks I see Ethiopia stretching forth her hands unto God and methinks I see the Angel of God taking up the standard of the Red, the Black, and the Green, and saying "Men of the Negro Race, Men of Ethiopia, follow me." Tonight we

are following. We are following 400,000,000 strong. We are
following with a determination that we must be free before the
wreck of matter, before the crash of worlds.

It falls to our lot to tear off the shackles that bind Mother
Africa. Can you do it? You did it in the Revolutionary War. You
did it in the Civil War; you did it at the Battles of the Marne
and Verdun; you did it in Mesopotamia. You can do it marching
up the battle heights of Africa. Let the world know that 400,-
000,000 Negroes are prepared to die or live as free men. Despise
us as much as you care. Ignore us as much as you care. We are
coming 400,000,000 strong. We are coming with our woes behind us, with the memory of suffering behind us—woes and
suffering of three hundred years—they shall be our inspiration.
My bulwark of strength in the conflict for freedom in Africa, will
be the three hundred years of persecution and hardship left
behind in this Western Hemisphere. The more I remember the
suffering of my forefathers, the more I remember the lynchings
and burnings in the Southern states of America, the more I will
fight on even though the battle seems doubtful. Tell me that I
must turn back, and I laugh you to scorn. Go on! Go on! Climb
ye the heights of liberty and cease not in well doing until you
have planted the banner of the Red, the Black, and the Green
on the hilltops of Africa.

*Easter Sunday Sermon Delivered at Liberty Hall, New York
City, N.Y., April 16th, 1922.* *

The Lord is risen! A little over nineteen hundred years ago
a man came to this world called JESUS. He was sent here for
the propagation of a cause—that of saving fallen humanity.
When He came the world refused to hear Him; the world rejected Him; the world persecuted Him; men crucified Him. A
couple of days ago He was nailed to the cross of Calvary; He
died; He was buried. Today He is risen; risen the spiritual leader
of creation; risen as the first fruit of them that slept. Today that

*From *Philosophy and Opinions of Marcus Garvey*, Vol. I, New York, 1923,
pp. 87–92.

crucified Lord, that crucified Christ sees the affairs of man from His own spiritual throne on high.

After hundreds of years have rolled by, the doctrine He taught has become the accepted religion of hundreds of millions of human beings. He in His resurrection triumphed over death and the grave; He by His resurrection convinced humanity that His cause was spiritual. The world felt the truth about Jesus too late to have accepted His doctrine in His lifetime. But what was done to Jesus in His lifetime is just what is done to all reformers and reform movements. He came to change the spiritual attitude of man toward his brother. That was regarded in His day as an irregularity, even as it is regarded today. The one who attempts to bring about changes in the order of human society becomes a dangerous impostor upon society and to those who control the systems of the day.

The Desire to Enslave Others

It has been an historic attitude of man to keep his brother in slavery—in subjection for the purpose of exploitation. When Jesus came the privileged few were taking advantage of the unfortunate masses. Because the teaching of Jesus sought to equalize the spiritual and even the temporal rights of man, those who held authority, sway, and dominion sought His liberty by prosecution, sought His life by death. He was called to yield up that life for the cause He loved—because He was indeed a true reformer.

The Example Set by Christ

The example set by our Lord and Master nineteen hundred years ago is but the example that every reformer must make up his mind to follow if we are indeed to serve those to whom we minister. Service to humanity means sacrifice. That has been demonstrated by our blessed Lord and Redeemer whose resurrection we commemorate this day. As Christ triumphed nearly two thousand years ago over death and the grave, as He was risen from the dead, so do I hope that 400,000,000 Negroes of today will triumph over the slavishness of the past, intellectually, physically, morally and even religiously; that on this anniversary of our risen Lord, we ourselves will be risen from the slumber of the ages; risen in thought to higher ideals, to a loftier purpose, to a truer conception of life.

The Hope of the U.N.I.A.

It is the hope of the Universal Negro Improvement Association that the 400,000,000 Negroes of the world will get to realize that we are about to live a new life—a risen life—a life of knowing ourselves.

How many of us know ourselves? How many of us understand ourselves? The major number of us for ages have failed to recognize in ourselves the absolute masters of our own destiny—the absolute directors and creators of our own fate.

Today as we think of our risen Lord may we not also think of the life He gave to us—the life that made us His instruments, His children—the life that He gave to us to make us possessors of the land that He himself created through His Father? How many of us can reach out to that higher life; that higher purpose; that creative world that says to you you are a man, a sovereign, a lord—lord of the creation? On this beautiful spring day, may we not realize that God made Nature for us; God has given it to us as our province, our dominion? May we not realize that God has created no superior being to us in this world, but Himself? May we not know that we are the true lords and creators of our own fate and of our own physical destiny?

The work of the Universal Negro Improvement Association for the past four and a half years has been that of guiding us to realize that there should be a resurrection in us, and if at no other time I trust that at this Eastertide we will realize that there is a great need for a resurrection—a resurrection from the lethargy of the past—the sleep of the past—from that feeling that made us accept the idea and opinion that God intended that we should occupy an inferior place in the world.

No Superiority or Inferiority

Men and women of Liberty Hall, men and women of my race, do you know that the God we love, the God we adore, the God who sent His Son to this world nearly two thousand years ago never created an inferior man? That God we love, that God we worship and adore has created man in His own image, equal in every respect, wheresoever he may be; let him be white; let him be yellow; let him be red; let him be black; God has created him the equal of his brother. He is such a loving God. He is such a merciful God. He is such a God that He is no respecter of persons, that He would not in His great love create a superior race and an inferior one. The God that you worship is a God that expects you to be the equal of other men. The God that I adore is such a God and He could be no other.

Some of us seem to accept the fatalist position, the fatalist attitude, that God accorded to us a certain position and condition, and therefore there is no need trying to be otherwise. The moment you accept such an attitude, the moment you accept such an opinion, the moment you harbor such an idea, you hurl an insult at the great God who created you, because you question Him for His love, you question Him for His mercy. God has created man and has placed him in this world as the lord of the creation, as the sovereign of everything that you see, let it be land, let it be sea, let it be the lakes, rivers, and everything therein. All that you see in creation, all that you see in the world, was created by God for the use of man, and you four hundred million black souls have as much right to your possession in this world as any other race.

Created in the image of the same God we have the same common rights, and today I trust that there will be a spiritual and material resurrection among Negroes everywhere; that you will lift yourselves from the doubts of the past, that you will lift yourselves from the slumbers of the past, that you will lift yourselves from the lethargy of the past, and strike out in this new life—in this resurrected life—to see things as they are.

See Life as Others See It

The Universal Negro Improvement Association desires that the four hundred million members of our race see life as the other races see it. The great white race sees life in an attitude of sovereignty; the great yellow race sees life in a similar way, that is to say that man, let him be white or yellow, sees that he is master and owner and possessor of everything that God has created in this world, and given to us in Nature; and that is why by knowing himself, by understanding himself, and by understanding his God, man has gone, throughout the length and breadth of this world, conquering the very elements, harnessing Nature and making a servant of everything that God placed within his reach.

As he has done that for thousands of years pleasing God and justifying his existence, so we are appealing to the members of our race to do that now in this risen life, and if you have never made up your minds before I trust on this Easter Sunday you will do so.

Masters of Your Own Destiny

I repeat that God created you masters of your own destiny, masters of your own fate, and you can pay no higher tribute to your Divine Master than function as man, as He created you.

The highest compliment we can pay to our Creator, the highest respect we can pay to our risen Lord and Saviour, is that of feeling that He has created us as His masterpiece; His perfect instruments of His own existence, because in us is reflected the very being of God. When it is said that we are created in His own image, we ourselves reflect His greatness, we ourselves reflect the part of God the Father, God the Son, and God the Holy Ghost, and when we allow ourselves to be subjected and create others as our superior, we hurl an insult at our Creator, who made us in the fullness of ourselves.

I trust that you will so live today as to realize that you are masters of your own destiny, masters of your fate; if there is anything you want in this world it is for you to strike out with confidence and faith in self and reach for it, because God has created it for your happiness wheresoever you may find it in nature. Nature is bountiful; nature is resourceful, and nature is willing to obey the command of man—Man the sovereign lord; man who is supposed to hold dominion and take possession of this great world of ours.

The Difference Between Strong and Weak Races

The difference between the strong and weak races is that the strong races seem to know themselves; seem to discover themselves; seem to realize and know fully that there is but a link between them and the Creator; that above them there is no other but God and anything that bears human form is but their equal in standing and to that form there should be no obeisance; there should be no regard for superiority. Because of that feeling they have been able to hold their own in this world; they have been able to take care of the situation as it confronts them in nature; but because of our lack of faith and confidence in ourselves we have caused others created in a like image to ourselves, to take advantage of us for hundreds of years.

For hundreds of years we have been the footstool of other races and nations of the earth simply because we have failed to realize, to recognize and know ourselves as other men have known themselves and felt that there is nothing in the world that is above them except the influence of God.

The understanding that others have gotten out of life is the same understanding that 400,000,000 Negroes must get out of this existence of ours. I pray that a new inspiration will come to us as a race; that we will think of nature as our servant; that we will think of man as our partner through life, and go through the length and breadth of this world achieving and doing as other men, as other nations and other races.

*What We Believe**

The Universal Negro Improvement Association advocates the uniting and blending of all Negroes into one strong, healthy race. It is against miscegenation and race suicide.

It believes that the Negro race is as good as any other, and therefore should be as proud of itself as others are.

It believes in the purity of the Negro race and the purity of the white race.

It is against rich blacks marrying poor whites.

It is against rich or poor whites taking advantage of Negro women.

It believes in the spiritual Fatherhood of God and the Brotherhood of Man.

It believes in the social and political physical separation of all peoples to the extent that they promote their own ideals and civilization, the privilege of trading and doing business with each other. It believes in the promotion of a strong and powerful Negro nation in Africa.

It believes in the rights of all men.

UNIVERSAL NEGRO IMPROVEMENT ASSOCIATION

MARCUS GARVEY, President-General

January 1, 1924

---

*From *Philosophy and Opinions of Marcus Garvey*, Vol. II, New York, 1926, p. 81.

9. ARABISM*

⊔⊓⊔⊓⊔⊓⊔⊓⊔⊓⊔⊓⊔⊓⊔⊓⊔⊓⊔⊓⊔⊓⊔⊓⊔⊓

Nicholas Ziadeh

The Arabs are a nation which has been fashioned from three elements, namely race, habitat and history.

Originally the Arabs inhabited the Arabian Peninsula in its known, well-defined boundaries. They filled its mountains, valleys, plains and deserts and came under the influence of its character. They mirrored its divisions, estrangements and enmities, and became as generous as it was avaricious toward them. They cultivated it and settled it to the extent of their power, so that they founded cities in the Yemen and the Hejaz, villages in Najd and elsewhere, and oases in still other areas. They had their culture and traditions, their habitations and meeting places, their religion and language.

In very distant times, groups of them began to spread in areas contiguous to the peninsula. Thus from among them came the Lakhmids of Iraq, the Nabataeans and Ghassanids of Syria, the Harranids of Harran, and the Tadmurites between Iraq and Syria. In these cities spread within and outside the peninsula the remains of which are still extant, Arab states were founded, their

*From *Al-'uruba fi mizan al-qawmiyya* (*Arabism in the Balance of Nationalism*), by Nicholas Ziadeh, Beirut, 1950, pp. 68–81.

civilization flourished, their trade, agriculture and crafts prospered. In these cities they gave and took, constituting a link between the original race and the outside world. They clashed many a time with their powerful neighbors the Persians and the Byzantines, and fought many battles against them, sometimes being defeated and sometimes victorious.

This Arab diffusion in these countries was constant and continuous. This is the reason why we find their inhabitants speaking a pure Arabic and quoting the eloquent Arabic poetry which preceded Islam by some centuries.

When Islam appeared among the Arabs, and they were influenced by its message and emerged from the peninsula in order to spread it, the Christian Arabs of Hira joined the Muslim Arabs of the peninsula, and the two groups fought side by side against the Persians. Something of the kind happened in Syria where the Ghassanids took part with their brethren in war against the Byzantines. The Arabs carried out an offensive against their enemies, and scarcely a century after the death of the Prophet their horses had already reached the Indus and Central Asia to the east and the Pyrenees to the west. This military conquest was accompanied by a migration of Arabs toward the conquered areas where they settled in groups and tribes. We must, however, remember two things in this connection: first that the Arab groups were greater in number and more populous in Iraq, Syria and Egypt than in those other countries which were more distant from the peninsula; and the second is that this migration was not confined to the period of the conquests which may be said to have ended in the third century of the Hegira (the ninth century of the Christian era); but that the migration of Arab groups went on in a manner similar to the pre-Islamic era. In this period, however, these migrations were more extensive and far-flung by reason of the Arab domination over larger areas. In addition to this continuous migration, historical sources have preserved for us the traces of even more extensive and more far-flung movements, in particular two migratory waves which deserve special mention: the first in the fifth century of the Hegira (the eleventh of the Christian era) which was directed toward the Maghreb and the traces of which appear in the Bani Hilal epic, and the second in the Ayyubid period which came to rest perhaps in Syria particularly.

These migrations, and the political domination which the Arabs exercised, made it easy for the Arab race to spread, and for the sphere of its influence to widen. We do not say that this race did away with every other one in the area, but the undoubted truth is that it assimilated all other peoples and gave them its own imprint.

But Arab political domination subsequently retreated from the extremities of the Muslim world, both east and west. Iran and other countries eastwards, and Spain threw off this domination and regained political freedom. The eastern end preserved Islam as a legacy of the Arab conquests, while the withdrawal in the west was complete. As for the countries in between, three things remained constant in their influence: the Arab race, which predominated in the inhabitants; Islam, which spread among them; and the Arabic language, which routed all other languages. The final limits of Arab racial and linguistic predominance are the mountains of Persia to the east, the Taurus and the mountains of Armenia to the north, and the Atlas Mountains to the west. It seems to us that the chief reason for Arabic being arrested in its spread eastwards by the mountains of Persia is the very nature of these mountains, for they constitute the western limit of a vast plateau—the Iranian plateau—and the eastern boundary of a low plain—the plain of Iraq. It was therefore not easy for large groups to migrate from the warm and fertile Iraqi plain to the cold and arid Iranian plateau. The Arabs preferred to settle in the fertile land; and we know that the number of Arabs settled in Khorasan and contiguous areas in Umayyad times—when Arab fortunes were at the apogee—was so small that they were unable to withstand the violent Persian attack. As for the Taurus Mountains, these were from the start a firm barrier against the Arabs which they were but little able to surmount. Perhaps the climatic factor, *i.e.*, the severe cold in these mountains, prevented them from persevering as they persevered in other areas, so that their military, racial and linguistic conquest was arrested. And even the religious conquest, *i.e.*, the spread of Islam, did not take place in Anatolia at the hands of the Arabs, but was carried out by the Turks, both Seljuk and Ottoman.

The conclusion to be drawn from this summary exposition is that the present Arab world, from the mountains of Persia to the Atlas, is Arab. Arab in the sense that the original Arab race has been able, by intermingling, intermarriage and propinquity, to assimilate all other peoples in the area and to Arabize them. These populations are therefore Arab either by origin or by derivation—they are either Arab or Arabized.

This predominance and this Arabization, however, were, as we said in our opening paragraph, not only the result of the spread of the Arab race; but two other factors also cooperated, namely habitat and history.

The area which the Arabs inhabit today may be divided into two main parts: the eastern, which begins with the mountains of Persia and ends at the Western Desert, and the western which begins in Cyrenaica and ends in Morocco, the Western Desert contributing a dividing line between the eastern and the western parts.

If we consider the eastern part, we find that there is great similarity between its various areas, and that its natural frontiers are quite obvious. The Iraqi and Syrian plains and the valley of the Nile are the result of similar factors and similar geological eras. We find also that the Syrian Desert and the mountains of Syria have the Arabian Peninsula for their axis in the same way as the Arabs of Syria depend on the peninsula for their national and spiritual life. In the north and east of this part of the Arab world, we find that the natural frontiers are due to the same geological factors, for these frontiers consist of mountains the formation of which is quite recent.

As for the western part, we find that its mountains and valleys are similar in their configuration and in the nature of their soil from Tunisia to Morocco.

We see from this that the Arab world is a geographical unit with well-defined boundaries, *viz.*, the mountains, the Mediterranean, the African Sahara, the Arab Sea and the Persian Gulf, with clear characteristics, similar in its climate which is Mediterranean except in those areas which show extremes of temperature of one kind or another such as the Arabian Desert, Mount Lebanon and the Atlas.

This area has important economic features. It is rich and its wealth is varied. The Atlas has iron and copper, Iraq and the peninsula possess petroleum, the Dead Sea various chemical salts, etc. Its agricultural products include the main cereals, cotton, olives, fruits of different kinds. It has extensive hydraulic resources. Over and above this, it has special importance as a main world communications center—whether by land, sea or air. Railways and roads cross it, particularly in its eastern part, and the Suez Canal—which is in the heart of the region—links the European with the eastern world. It has also numerous airports.

What is lacking in the Arab geographical area is an organized distribution of its wealth whereby the region takes what it needs and leaves the rest to be exported to those countries from which we can import what we need in the way of machinery and other articles. The utility of such organization would then become apparent.

Let us now turn to the influence of history in the creation of Arab nationality.

This region which the Arab people inhabit has an extremely ancient history. It is here that man took his first steps toward civilization, learned the use of metal for his tools and implements; here that he invented the alphabet to set down his views and thoughts; here that he made the first house; erected the first temple and built the first palace; here that he first showed artistry in his carvings and drawings and sculpture; here that he opened the first school, composed the first poem and wrote the first book; here that he fashioned the first government. These states which arose in the Nile Valley, in Mesopotamia, in the plains and mountains of Syria attempted each in turn to dominate its neighbors. In consequence there arose the Egyptian Empire, the armies of which reached to the Euphrates. It was followed by the Empire of the Hittites, the influence of which extended to the middle of Syria. The Assyrian Empire, whose territory extended to the confines of Egypt arose here to be followed by that of the Chaldeans. When ancient Persia entered the lists as a conqueror its domination extended from the Indus Valley in the east to Upper Egypt in the west. In each case the conquest was military and political and the state relied for its continuance on its garrisons, governors and mercenary armies which were a kind of police force without any influence on the social, spiritual and intellectual life of the people.

Two outside powers came thereafter to this area, *i.e.*, the Greek and the Roman. The first came with Alexander when its dominion included—among the countries which concern us now —Egypt, Syria and Iraq. Alexander, his prominent followers and successors, became the bearers of Hellenic civilization to the east, being themselves firm believers in its universality. They saw, Alexander the first among them, that the best way of spreading Hellenic civilization was to build cities where groups of Greeks would live and become a center from which science and learning would radiate to the inhabitants of the country. The town-dwellers among the natives came under the influence of Hellenic civilization and were attracted by it. Hellenic customs and the Greek language therefore spread among them, and this language became that of rulers, merchants, men of letters, poets and learned men, and anyone who wished to have intercourse with them, as was seen in Antioch, Seleucia, Alexandria, Sidon and elsewhere. If, however, you were to go out of the town and beyond its suburbs and gardens, you would hear people speaking their local language with their particular accents. Thus, the villager outside Antioch used to speak Aramaic, the agriculturist and the shepherd outside Sidon used to speak Phoenician, so that these Hellenic cities came to be like islands in the sea of the original civilization of these countries. This is the reason why we do not find any national feeling in Syria or Iraq, or even Egypt in the Hellenic age.

When the Romans came to occupy these countries, they brought with them a new language, namely Latin, which soon became the official language while Greek remained the language and the channel of thought. No nationalist feeling grew up in Egypt or in Syria in the days of the Romans or of their allies the Byzantines, because the means of communication between the inhabitants were not uniform and their views, customs, traditions and expectations remained disparate.

In the year 15 A.H. (636 of the Christian Era) the Arabs defeated the Byzantines at the battle of the Yarmuk and the Sassanid Persians at the battle of Qadisiyya. A few years later their horses reached the Iranian plateau to the east and the Libyan Desert to the west.

The Arab conquests extended over more than a century after the Prophet's death. They had various characteristics and consequences. They constituted a military conquest which extended up to India and China in the east, and the Atlantic in the west. They also constituted a racial conquest in that the Arab race assimilated the other races or overcame them in some countries rather than others; the nearer the country to the peninsula itself the denser the Arab settlement, and the greater the Arab influence was. They further constituted a linguistic conquest: Arabic spread rapidly in all the conquered countries, and here if anybody has a right to our grateful remembrance it is the two Caliphs 'Abd al-Malik ibn Marwan and al-Ma'mun. The first Arabized the administration by making Arabic the official language of the state; the second encouraged the translation of scientific works to Arabic and thus Arabized the intellectual movement. We must also mention a fourth conquest which took place during the last period, namely the religious conquest. Islam spread in all the conquered countries for reasons which there is no scope to discuss here.

It is these factors which have governed the direction taken by the nations and peoples who have submitted to the Arabs. Those who had submitted purely to Arab political domination attempted revolt or secession, and when circumstances became propitious resumed their previous way of life. Some of these peoples became politically independent but retained as a legacy from military conquest the religion of Islam, which had taken root among them. As for those countries which became Arab by blood, language, mentality and thought, they are those which are bounded by the mountains of Persia to the east, by the Taurus to the north, and which extend westwards, to include Egypt and the whole of North Africa. These linguistic frontiers coincide with natural frontiers which it was difficult for the Arabs to get through in great numbers, so that they did not settle beyond them in large groups, their influence being therefore confined here to religion or politics.

We are not attempting in this essay to study Arab national history in detail or even summarily. What we seek to do is to pause for a few moments in order to consider the history of these Arab countries and discern the main lines of their national evolution. The Arabs occupied these countries and settled them; Islam spread within them; people were attracted to it and adopted it and it was for them a religious message and a source of spiritual strength. It called forth their hidden energies, and under its influence they became an active energetic force in focusing the principles of Greek, Persian and Indian civilization with which they were acquainted, and they fashioned thereafter an Arabic Islamic civilization. In consequence of the spread of Islam in Iraq, Syria, Egypt and North Africa, the Arabic language, the language of the Glorious Qur'an and the Noble [Prophetic] Tradition, itself spread among the inhabitants of these countries. Arabic spread generally among the population, including town-dwellers, villagers and countrymen; the merchant, the agriculturist and the shepherd spoke it, the poet celebrated it in his poetry, the story-teller used it, in it the call to prayer was made, the rituals of worship held and the Qur'an chanted. Arabic therefore penetrated to the soul, the heart and the mind of people; even those among the natives who remained faithful to their old religion found it necessary to speak, read and write in Arabic. Although it did not spread all at once in all these countries, yet it did not take long for Arabic to become the language of society in all matters concerning government, administration, justice, education, science and literature.

The history of these countries from the Arab conquest is an extensive one, comprising both good and evil, the beautiful and the ugly, acts of shining virtue and acts of black wickedness, as is the case with every nation similar to the Arabs in the length of their history and the extensiveness of their domain.

Christianity as a religion, a philosophy and an idea may have its own particular history, and similarly Islam as a religion, a philosophy and an idea. But the Muslims and the Christians of these countries cannot have their own distinct history. The events which befell Iraq or Syria or Egypt did not distinguish between Muslims and Christians, whether these events were harmful or beneficial. Misfortunes were not confined to one group, to the exclusion of the other, neither was good fortune. Syria in the middle ages was exposed to two violent assaults, one from the west at the Crusaders' hands and the other from the east at the Tatars'. The western danger engulfed all the country and all its inhabitants, just as the eastern danger affected all the population regardless of their sects and creeds. The towns destroyed in the wars were inhabited by people of various beliefs; the skulls from which the Mongols built up their various pyramids in Baghdad, Tikrit and Aleppo were the skulls of those whom the sword exterminated without discriminating between their religions; the taxes which the conquerors imposed and the extortions which the invaders exacted were paid by the population of the country as a whole without the conqueror or the invader discriminating between the followers of one religion and those of another. The skilled artisans, architects, artists and the learned men whom Tamerlane carried away from Damascus about the year 1400 of the Christian era were all natives of the city without any particular group being singled out. The scarcities and famines which used to afflict these countries—and still do—do not affect only one category of people to leave the rest unharmed.

We see from this that the events which have befallen the population of the Arab world constitute a common history. That it should have contained faults or mistakes was, as we have said, only natural.

It is this common history which has bequeathed to us Arabs national memories, patriotic experiences, a national literature, popular stories and heroic poetry all written in one Arabic language, read as the product of a single nation, centered on this nation's heroes and located in her mountains, valleys, plains, plateaus, deserts, rivers and shores. There is scarcely a spot which does not evoke in the traveler memories of battles which had ended either in victory or in defeat, or of a hero who had sacrificed himself for us, or of a learned man who had spent a lifetime in educating us, or of a writer who had spent his nights and days toiling for our sake, or of a town, village or fortress the inhabitants of which had died so that we may live. There is nothing in these countries which has not been watered by a generous blood and perfumed by the sweet souls of those ancestors full of piety who have bequeathed to us a country, a fatherland and a nationality. It is this common history which has unified our traditions and habits and kept us close to one another. It is to this history that we return in order to draw from it lessons of experience, ideals and criteria by which to judge good and evil, beauty and ugliness, virtue and vice. It is from this history that we have inherited our unity of feelings, our sentiments of solidarity, of mutual help in difficulty, and of fraternity in troubles.

And it is this history which, above everything else, has given us our Arabic language, and thus imparted unity to our thinking, mentality and views. For language in its larger sense is not a mere collection of vocables and expressions which become ordered by being written down. Language is a civilization and a culture; and unity of language is unity of thought and it is this which forms the nation in its intellectual and sentimental life.

Our history, then, has created us, prescribed our life for us, and renewed our message to the world. We have no means of understanding our life aright, and accomplishing well our mission until each one of us becomes acquainted with his national history, and goes back to his heroes and illustrious men in order to draw inspiration from them; until he returns to his country's soil in order to feel in its savor his very soul, spirit and life; and until he returns to his literature in order to be guided by it.

10. THE PRINCIPLE OF NATIONALISM*

ᒣᒧᒣᒧᒣᒧᒣᒧᒣᒧᒣᒧᒣᒧᒣᒧᒣᒧᒣᒧᒣᒧ

Sun Yat-sen

The population of the world today is approximately a billion and a half. One fourth of this number live in China, which means that one out of every four persons in the world is a Chinese. The total population of the white races of Europe also amounts to four hundred millions. The white division of mankind, which is now the most flourishing, includes four races: in central and northern Europe, the Teutons, who have founded many states, the largest of which is Germany, others being Austria, Sweden, Norway, Holland, and Denmark; in eastern Europe, the Slavs, who also have founded a number of states, the largest being Russia, and, after the European war, the new countries of Czechoslovakia and Yugoslavia; in western Europe, the Saxons or Anglo-Saxons, who have founded two large states—England and the United States of America; in southern Europe, the Latins, who have founded several states, the largest being France, Italy, Spain, and Portugal, and who have migrated to South America forming states there just as the Anglo-Saxons migrated to North America and built up Canada and the United States. The white

*From *San Min Chu I* (*The Three Principles of the People*), by Dr. Sun Yat-sen, tr. F.W. Price, Shanghai, 1929, pp. 77–100.

peoples of Europe, now numbering only four hundred million persons, are divided into four great stocks which have established many states. Because the national spirit of the white race was highly developed, when they had filled up the European continent they expanded to North and South America in the Western Hemisphere and to Africa and Australia in the southern and eastern parts of the Eastern Hemisphere.

The Anglo-Saxons at present occupy more space on the globe than any other race. Although this race originated in Europe, the only European soil it holds are the British Isles—England, Scotland and Ireland—which occupy about the same position in the Atlantic that Japan occupies in the Pacific. The Anglo-Saxons have extended their territory westward to North America, eastward to Australia and New Zealand, and southward to Africa until they possess more land and are wealthier and stronger than any other race. Before the European war the Teutons and the Slavs were the strongest races; moreover, by reason of the sagacity and ability of the Teutonic peoples, Germany was able to unite more than twenty small states into a great German confederation. At the beginning an agricultural nation, it developed into an industrial nation and through industrial prosperity its army and navy became exceedingly powerful.

Before the European war all the European nations had been poisoned by imperialism. What is imperialism? It is the policy of aggression upon other countries by means of political force, or, in the Chinese phrase, "long-range aggression." As all the peoples of Europe were imbued with this policy, wars were continually breaking out; almost every decade had at least one small war and each century one big war. The greatest of all was the recent European war, which may be called the World War because it finally involved the whole world and pulled every nation and people into its vortex. The causes of the European war were, first, the rivalry between the Saxon and Teutonic races for control of the sea. Germany in her rise to greatness had developed her navy until she was the second sea power in the world; Great Britain wanted her own navy to rule the seas so she tried to destroy Germany, whose sea power was next to hers.

From this struggle for first place on the sea came the war.

A second cause was each nation's struggle for more territory. In eastern Europe there is a weak state called Turkey. For the past hundred years the people of the world have called it the "sick man of Europe." Because the government was unenlightened and the sultan was despotic, it became extremely helpless and the European nations wanted to partition it. Because the Turkish question had not been solved for a century and every nation of Europe was trying to solve it, war resulted. The first cause of the European war, then, was the struggle between white races for supremacy; the second cause was the effort to solve critical world problems. If Germany had won the war, she would have held the supreme power on the sea after the war and Great Britain would have lost all her territory, breaking into pieces like the old Roman Empire. But the result of the war was defeat for Germany and the failure of her imperialistic designs.

The recent European war was the most dreadful war in the history of the world. Forty to fifty million men were under arms for a period of four years, and near the end of the war they still could not be divided into conquerors and vanquished. One side in the war was called the Entente; the other side, the Allied Powers. The Allied Powers* at first included Germany and Austria; Turkey and Bulgaria later joined them. The Entente Powers** at first were Serbia, France, Russia, England, and Japan; Italy and the United States joined afterwards. The United States' entry into the war was due entirely to racial considerations. During the first two years of the war Germany and Austria were in the ascendancy. Paris and the English Channel were almost captured by the German and Austrian armies. The Teutons thought that Great Britain was certainly done for, and the British themselves were thoroughly alarmed. Seeing that the American people are of the same race as they, the British used the plea of race relationship to stir up the people of the United States. When America realized that England, of her own race, was in danger of being destroyed by Germany, of an alien race,

* Central Powers.
** The Allies.

inevitably "the creature sorrowed for its kind" and America
threw in her lot with England to defend the existence of the
Anglo-Saxons. Moreover, fearing that her own strength would
be insufficient, America tried with all her might to arouse all the
neutral countries of the world to join in the war to defeat Germany.

During the war there was a great phrase, used by President
Wilson and warmly received everywhere—"self-determination
of peoples." Because Germany was striving by military force to
crush the peoples of the European Entente, Wilson proposed
destroying Germany's power and giving autonomy henceforth
to the weaker and smaller peoples. His idea met a world welcome, and although the common people of India still opposed
Great Britain, their destroyer, yet many small peoples, when
they heard Wilson say that the war was for the freedom of the
weak and small peoples, gladly gave aid to Great Britain. Although Annam had been subjugated by France and the common
people hated the French tyranny, yet during the war they still
helped France to fight, also because they had heard of Wilson's
just proposition. And the reason why other small peoples of
Europe, such as Poland, Czechoslovakia and Romania, all enlisted on the side of the Entente against the Allied Powers was
because of the self-determination principle enunciated by President Wilson. China, too, under the inspiration of the United
States, entered the war; although she sent no armies, yet she did
contribute hundreds of thousands of laborers to dig trenches and
to work behind the lines. As a result of the noble theme propounded by the Entente all the oppressed peoples of Europe and
of Asia finally joined together to help them in their struggle
against the Allied Powers. At the same time, Wilson proposed,
to guard the future peace of the world, fourteen points, of which
the most important was that each people should have the right
of self-determination. When victory and defeat still hung in the
balance, England and France heartily endorsed these points, but
when victory was won and the Peace Conference was opened,
England, France, and Italy realized that Wilson's proposal of
freedom for nations conflicted too seriously with the interests

of imperialism; and so, during the conference, they used all kinds of methods to explain away Wilson's principles. The result was a peace treaty with most unjust terms; the weaker, smaller nations not only did not secure self-determination and freedom but found themselves under an oppression more terrible than before. This shows that the strong states and the powerful races have already forced possession of the globe and that the rights and privileges of other states and nations are monopolized by them. Hoping to make themselves forever secure in their exclusive position and to prevent the smaller and weaker peoples from again reviving, they sing praises to cosmopolitanism, saying that nationalism is too narrow; really their espousal of internationalism is but imperialism and aggression in another guise.

But Wilson's proposals, once set forth, could not be recalled; each one of the weaker, smaller nations who had helped the Entente to defeat the Allied Powers and had hoped to attain freedom as a fruit of the victory was doomed to bitter disappointment by the results of the Peace Conference. Then Annam, Burma, Java, India, the Malay Archipelago, Turkey, Persia, Afghanistan, Egypt, and the scores of weak nations in Europe were stirred with a great, new consciousness; they saw how completely they had been deceived by the Great Powers' advocacy of self-determination and began independently and separately to carry out the principle of the "self-determination of peoples."

Many years of fierce warfare had not been able to destroy imperialism because this was a conflict of imperialisms between states, not a struggle between savagery and civilization or between Might and Right. So the effect of the war was merely the overthrow of one imperialism by another imperialism; what survived was still imperialism. But from the war there was unconsciously born in the heart of mankind a great hope—the Russian Revolution. The Russian Revolution had begun much earlier, as far back as 1905, but had not accomplished its purpose. Now during the European war the efforts of the revolutionists were crowned with success. The reason for the outbreak of revolution again at this time was the great awakening of the people as a result of their war experience. Russia sent over ten million soldiers into the field—not a puny force. Without Russia's part in the war, the Entente's line on the western front would long before have been smashed by Germany; because Russia was embarrassing the Germans on the eastern front, the Entente Powers were able to break even with Germany for two or three years and finally turn defeat into victory. Just halfway through the war, Russia began to reflect, and she realized that in helping the Entente to fight Germany she was merely helping several brute forces to fight one brute force and that no good results would come of it in the end. A group of soldiers and citizens awoke, broke away from the Entente, and concluded a separate peace with Germany.

As far as their legitimate national interests were concerned, the German and the Russian people had absolutely no cause for quarrel; but when it came to imperialistic designs, they vied with each other in aggressions until conflict was inevitable. Moreover, Germany went so far beyond bounds that Russia, in self-protection, could not but move in accord with England, France, and the others. Later, when the Russian people awoke and saw that imperialism was wrong, they started a revolution within their own country, first overthrowing their own imperialism; at the same time, to avoid foreign embarrassments, they made peace with Germany. Before long, the Entente also signed a peace with Germany and then all sent soldiers to fight Russia. Why? Because the Russian people had awakened to the fact that their daily sufferings were due to imperialism and that to get rid of their sufferings they must eliminate imperialism and embrace self-determination. Every other nation opposed this policy and so mobilized to fight Russia, yet Russia's proposal and Wilson's were undesignedly similar; both declared that the weaker, smaller nations had the right of self-determination and freedom. When Russia proclaimed this principle, the weaker, smaller peoples of the world gave their eager support to it and all together began to seek self-determination. The calamitous war through which Europe had passed brought, of course, no great imperialistic gain, but, because of the Russian Revolution, a great hope was born in the heart of mankind.

Of the billion and a half people in the world, the most powerful are the four hundred million whites on the European and American continents; from this base the white races have started out to swallow up other races. The American red aborigines are gone, the African blacks will soon be exterminated, the brown race of India is in the process of dissolution, the yellow races of Asia are now being subjected to the white man's oppression and may, before long, be wiped out.

But the one hundred fifty million Russians, when their revolution succeeded, broke with the other white races and condemned the white man's imperialistic behavior; now they are thinking of throwing in their lot with the weaker, smaller peoples of Asia in a struggle against the tyrannical races. So only two hundred fifty million of tyrannical races are left, but they are still trying by inhuman methods and military force to subjugate the other twelve hundred fifty million. So hereafter mankind will be divided into two camps: on one side will be the twelve hundred fifty million; on the other side, the two hundred fifty million. Although the latter group are in the minority, yet they hold the most powerful positions on the globe and their political and economic strength is immense. With these two forces they are out to exploit the weaker and smaller races. If the political arm of navies and armies is not strong enough, they bear down with economic pressure. If their economic arm is at times weak, they intervene with political force of navies and armies. The way their political power cooperates with their economic power is like the way in which the left arm helps the right arm; with their two arms they have crushed most terribly the twelve hundred fifty million. But "Heaven does not always follow man's desires." The Slavic race of one hundred fifty million suddenly rose up and struck a blow at imperialism and capitalism, warring for mankind against inequality. In my last lecture I told of the Russian who said, "The reason why the Powers have so defamed Lenin is because he dared to assert that the twelve hundred fifty million majority in the world were being oppressed by the two hundred fifty million minority." Lenin not only said this, but also advocated self-determination for the oppressed peoples and launched a campaign for them against injustice. The powers attacked Lenin because they wanted to destroy a prophet and a seer of mankind and obtain security for themselves. But the people of the world now have their eyes opened and know that the rumors created by the powers are false; they will not let themselves be deceived again. The political thinking of the peoples of the world has been enlightened to this extent.

Now we want to revive China's lost nationalism and use the strength of our four hundred million to fight for mankind against injustice; this is our divine mission. The powers are afraid that we will have such thoughts and are setting forth a specious doctrine. They are now advocating cosmopolitanism to inflame us, declaring that, as the civilization of the world advances and as mankind's vision enlarges, nationalism becomes too narrow, unsuited to the present age, and hence that we should espouse cosmopolitanism. In recent years some of China's youths, devotees of the new culture, have been opposing nationalism, led astray by this doctrine. But it is not a doctrine which wronged races should talk about. We, the wronged races, must first recover our position of national freedom and equality before we are fit to discuss cosmopolitanism. The illustration I used in my last lecture of the coolie who won first prize in the lottery has already made this very clear. The lottery ticket represents cosmopolitanism; the bamboo pole, nationalism. The coolie, on winning first prize, immediately threw away his pole* just as we, fooled by the promises of cosmopolitanism, have discarded our nationalism. We must understand that cosmopolitanism grows out of nationalism; if we want to extend cosmopolitanism we must first establish strongly our own nationalism. If nationalism cannot become strong, cosmopolitanism certainly cannot prosper. Thus we see that cosmopolitanism is hidden inside the bamboo pole; if we discard nationalism and go and talk cosmopolitanism we are just like the coolie who threw his bamboo pole into the sea. We put the cart before the horse. I said before that our position is not equal to that of the Annamese or

* In which he had hidden, for safety, his lottery ticket—thus losing both his pole and his prize. E.K.

the Koreans; they are subject peoples and slaves while we cannot even be called slaves. Yet we discourse about cosmopolitanism and say that we do not need nationalism. Gentlemen, is this reasonable?

According to history, our four hundred million Chinese have also come down the road of imperialism. Our forefathers constantly employed political force to encroach upon weaker and smaller nations; but economic force in those days was not a serious thing, so we were not guilty of economic oppression of other peoples. Then compare China's culture with Europe's ancient culture. The Golden Age of European culture was in the time of Greece and Rome, yet Rome at the height of its power was contemporaneous with as late a dynasty in China as the Han. At that time China's political thinking was very profound; many orators were earnestly opposing imperialism and much anti-imperialistic literature was produced, the most famous being "Discussions on Abandoning the Pearl Cliffs." Such writings opposed China's efforts to expand her territory and her struggle over land with the southern barbarians, which shows that as early as the Han dynasty China already discouraged war against outsiders and had developed the peace idea to broad proportions.

In the Sung dynasty, China was not only ceasing to encroach upon other peoples, but she was even being herself invaded by foreigners. The Sung dynasty was overthrown by the Mongols and the nation did not again revive until the Ming dynasty. After this restoration, China became much less aggressive. However, many small states in the South China Sea wanted to bring tribute and to adopt Chinese culture, giving voluntary adherence because of their admiration for our culture and not because of military pressure from China. The small countries in the Malay Archipelago and the South China Sea considered it a great honor for China to annex them and receive their tribute; China's refusal would have brought them disgrace.

The strongest powers in the world today have not succeeded in calling forth a praise like this. Take America's treatment of the Philippines: allowing the Filipinos to organize their own

Assembly and to have a share in the government; allowing them to appoint delegates to the Congress in Washington, not only not requiring a money tribute but subsidizing their main items of expenditure, building roads, and providing education for them. Such benevolent and magnanimous treatment can be considered the limit of generosity, yet the Filipinos even now do not consider it an honor to be Americanized and are every day asking for independence. Or take Nepal in India. The people of Nepal are called Gurkhas, a very brave and warlike race; although England has conquered India she still fears the Gurkhas. She treats them very generously, sending them money each year, just as the Sung dynasty in China, fearing the Kin Tatars, sent them funds, with this difference, that what the Sungs gave to the Kin Tatars was called a tribute, while England's gift to the Gurkhas is probably called a gratuity. But up to the first year of our republic, the Gurkhas were still bringing their tribute to China, which proves that the small nations around China have not yet lost their hope for or faith in her.

About ten years ago, on a visit to the Foreign Office in Siam, I had a conversation with the assistant secretary for foreign affairs. We were discussing various Asiatic problems when the secretary said, "If China could have a revolution and become a strong state and people, we Siamese would gladly renew our allegiance to China and become a province of China." The interview was held in a public office of the Siamese government and the speaker was the assistant secretary for foreign affairs, so he could not be said to be expressing his personal opinion only; he was representing the sentiments of all his people. This shows that even then Siam thought highly of China. But in these last ten years, Siam has become an independent state of Asia, has revised her oppressive treaties with other nations, and has raised her own national standing; hereafter she would hardly be willing to return to China.

I can tell you another very interesting incident. When the European war was raging most fiercely, I was in Canton setting up the constitutional government. One day the British consul came to the headquarters of the commander in chief to see me and to discuss with me the possibility of the Southern Government joining the Entente and sending troops to Europe. I asked the British consul, "Why should we send troops?" He replied: "To fight Germany. Since Germany has invaded Chinese territory and has seized Tsingtao from you, you ought to fight her and recover your possessions." I said: "Tsingtao is rather far away from Canton. What about the place nearest to us—Hong-Kong—or a little farther away, Burma, Bhutan, Nepal, and such places which formerly belonged to China? And now you want to come and take Tibet from us. China hasn't sufficient strength at present to recover her lost territory; if she did, perhaps she might first take back what Great Britain has usurped. Tsingtao, which Germany seized, is comparatively small; Burma is larger and Tibet much larger. If we were out to recover our possessions, we would begin with the large ones." When he heard my argument, he could not control his anger and said, "I came here to discuss public affairs!" For a long time we argued face to face and neither would yield the stage.

Finally I said to him: "Our civilization has already advanced two thousand years beyond yours. We are willing to wait for you to progress and catch up with us, but we cannot recede and let you pull us down. Two thousand years ago we discarded imperialism and advocated a policy of peace, and today the thinking of the Chinese people has fully realized this ideal. You also set up peace as your goal, in the present war. At first we heartily approved, but really you are still fighting, not talking peace; you are talking force, not justice. I consider your characteristic appeal to force as extremely barbarous. Go ahead and fight. We will certainly not join you. When you are worn out with fighting and some day are ready to talk real peace, then we may enlist on your side and seek the world's peace with you. Another strong reason why we are opposing China's entry into the war and the sending of troops is that we are not willing for China to become an unjust power like you. If we followed your advice and joined the Entente, you could send officers to China to train up soldiers; with your experienced leadership and splendid military equipment besides, you could certainly within six months' time train three to five hundred thousand good soldiers and transport them to fight in Europe and defeat Germany. Then you would be bad off!"

"Why bad off?" the British consul asked. I replied: "After using several million soldiers and fighting for years you cannot overcome Germany, yet you think that adding a few hundred thousand Chinese soldiers would spell her defeat! A real result would be the awakening of the martial spirit in China; from the nucleus of these few hundred thousand soldiers the Chinese army would grow to millions and that would be greatly to your disadvantage. Japan is now on your side and is already one of the great powers of the world; with her military prowess she domineers over Asia. Her imperialistic policy is just like that of the powers and you are terribly afraid of her. Yet China's population and resources far exceed Japan's. If we should follow the plan you suggest and China should enter the war on your side, before ten years we would become another Japan. When you think of the size of China's population and territory, we could become ten Japans; then all your world power would hardly be enough for one fight with China. Because we have advanced two thousand years beyond you and have gotten rid of the old savage, pugnacious sentiments and have attained only lately to a true ideal of peace, and because we hope that China will forever cherish her moral code of peace, therefore we are not willing to enter this great conflict." After listening to my speech, the British consul, who half an hour before was ready to fight with me, was deeply impressed and said, "If I were a Chinese, I would undoubtedly think as you do."

Gentlemen, you know that revolution is naturally a thing of bloodshed. Thus, in the revolutions of T'ang and Wu, everyone said that the rebels were "obedient to Heaven and well-pleasing to men" but as to the fighting it was said that they experienced "battle staves floating on rivers of blood." In the Revolution of 1911, when we overthrew the Manchus, how much blood was spilled? The reason for the small bloodshed then was the Chinese people's love of peace, an outstanding quality of the Chinese character. The Chinese are really the greatest lovers of peace in the world. I have constantly urged the people of the world to follow China's example; now the Slavic people of Russia are keeping pace with us and espousing the cause of peace after us, and their one hundred million want to cooperate with us.

Our four hundred million are not only a most peaceful but also a most civilized race. The new cultures which have flourished of late in Europe and which are called anarchism and communism are old things in China. For instance, Hwang-Lao's* political philosophy is really anarchism and what is Lieh-tze's** dream of the land of the Hua-hsü people who lived in a natural state without ruler or laws but another theory of anarchism? Modern youths in China, who have not studied carefully into these old Chinese theories, think that their ideas are the newest things in existence, unaware that, though they may be new in Europe, they are thousands of years old here. What Russia has been putting into practice is not pure communism but Marxism; Marxism is not real communism. What Proudhon and Bakunin advocated is the only real communism. Communism in other countries is still in the stage of discussion; it has not been fully tried out anywhere. But it was applied in China in the time of Hung Hsiu-ch'uan; his economic system was the real thing in communism and not mere theory.

European superiority to China is not in political philosophy but altogether in the field of material civilization, all the daily provisions for clothing, food, housing, and communication have become extremely convenient and time-saving, and the weapons of war—poison gas and such—have become extraordinarily perfected and deadly. All these new inventions and weapons have come since the development of science. It was after the seventeenth and eighteenth centuries, when Bacon, Newton, and other great scholars advocated the use of observation, experiment, and investigation of all things, that science came into being. So when we speak of Europe's scientific progress and of the advance of European material civilization, we are talking about something which has only two hundred years' history. A

* Hwangti and Laotze.
** The name of a philosopher in the Chow dynasty.

few hundred years ago, Europe could not compare with China, so now if we want to learn from Europe we should learn what we ourselves lack—science—but not political philosophy. Europeans are still looking to China for the fundamentals of political philosophy. You all know that the best scholarship today is found in Germany. Yet German scholars are studying Chinese philosophy and even Indian Buddhist principles to supplement their partial conceptions of science. Cosmopolitanism has just flowered out in Europe during this generation, but it was talked of two thousand years ago in China. Europeans cannot yet discern our ancient civilization, yet many of our race have thought of a political world civilization; and as for international morality, our four hundred million have been devoted to the principle of world peace. But because of the loss of our nationalism, our ancient morality and civilization have not been able to manifest themselves and are now even declining.

The cosmopolitanism which Europeans are talking about today is really a principle supported by force without justice. The English expression "might is right" means that fighting for acquisition is just. The Chinese mind has never regarded acquisition by war as right; it considers aggressive warfare barbarous. This pacifist morality is the true spirit of cosmopolitanism. Upon what foundation can we defend and build up this spirit? —Upon nationalism. Russia's one hundred fifty million are the foundation of Europe's cosmopolitanism and China's four hundred million are the foundation of Asia's cosmopolitanism. As a foundation is essential to expansion, so we must talk nationalism first if we want to talk cosmopolitanism. "Those desiring to pacify the world must first govern their own state." Let us revive our lost nationalism and make it shine with greater splendor, then we will have some ground for discussing internationalism.

February 17, 1924.

11. THE NATIONAL ENTITY OF JAPAN AND THE JAPANESE SUBJECT*

꟱꟱꟱꟱꟱꟱꟱꟱꟱꟱꟱꟱꟱꟱꟱꟱

We have already witnessed the boundless Imperial virtues. Wherever this Imperial virtue of compassion radiates, the Way for the subjects naturally becomes clear. The Way of the subjects exists where the entire nation serves the Emperor united in mind in the very spirit in which many deities served at the time when the Imperial Grandchild, Ninigi no Mikoto, descended to earth. That is, we by nature serve the Emperor and walk the Way of the Empire, and it is perfectly natural that we subjects should possess this essential quality.

We subjects are intrinsically quite different from the so-called citizens of Occidental countries. The relationship between ruler and subject is not of a kind in which the people are correlated to the sovereign or in which there is first a people for whose prosperity and well-being a ruler is established. But the reason for erring as to the essential qualities of these subjects or for looking upon them as being the same as so-called citizens, or again for failure to show that at least there is a distinct difference

*From *Kokutai No Hongi (Cardinal Principles of the National Entity of Japan)*, translated by J.O. Gauntlett and edited with an introduction by R.K. Hall, Cambridge, Mass., 1949, pp. 79–92.

between the two, [all of] which happens oftentimes, is that a clear-cut view concerning the cardinal principles of our national entity is lacking and confusion arises as a result of an ambiguous understanding of foreign theories about States. When citizens who are conglomerations of separate individuals independent of each other give support to a ruler in correlation to the ruler, there exists no deep foundation between ruler and citizen to unite them. However, the relationship between the Emperor and his subjects arises from the same fountainhead, and has prospered ever since the founding of the nation as one in essence. This is our nation's great Way and consequently forms the source of the Way of our subjects, and there is a radical difference between [ours] and foreign countries in the matter of choice. Needless to say, even in foreign countries their respective histories, as between ruler and citizens, differ, and there are bonds that attend these relationships. Nevertheless, a country such as ours, which, since its founding, has seen a Way "naturally" one in essence with nature and man united as one, and which thereby has prospered all the more, cannot find its counterpart among foreign countries. Herein lies our national entity which is unparalleled in the world, and the Way of our subjects has its reason for being simply on the basis of this national entity, and on this, too, are based loyalty and filial piety.

Loyalty and patriotism

Our country is established with the Emperor, who is a descendant of Amaterasu Ohmikami, as her center, and our ancestors as well as we ourselves constantly behold in the Emperor the fountainhead of her life and activities. For this reason, to serve the Emperor and to receive the Emperor's great august Will as one's own is the rationale of making our historical "life" live in the present; and on this is based the morality of the people.

Loyalty means to reverence the Emperor as [our] pivot and to follow him implicitly. By implicit obedience is meant casting ourselves aside and serving the Emperor intently. To walk this

Way of loyalty is the sole Way in which we subjects may "live," and the fountainhead of all energy. Hence, offering our lives for the sake of the Emperor does not mean so-called self-sacrifice, but the casting aside of our little selves to live under his august grace and the enhancing of the genuine life of the people of a State. The relationship between the Emperor and the subjects is not an artificial relationship [which means] bowing down to authority, nor a relationship such as [exists] between master and servant as is seen in feudal morals. That means to take a stand at the "source" through the "parts," and to manifest the "source" by fulfilling the "parts." The ideology which interprets the relationship between the Emperor and his subjects as being a reciprocal relationship such as merely [involves] obedience to authority or rights and duties, rests on individualistic ideologies, and is a rationalistic way of thinking that looks on everything as being in equal personal relationships. An individual is an existence belonging to a State and her history, which forms the basis of his origin, and is fundamentally one body with it. However, even if one were to think of a nation contrariwise and also to set up a morality by separating the individual alone from this one body, with this separated individual as the basis, one would only end in a so-called abstract argument that has lost its basis.

In our country, the two Augustnesses, Izanagi no Mikoto and Izanami no Mikoto, are ancestral deities of nature and the deities, and the Emperor is the divine offspring of the Imperial Ancestor who was born of the two Augustnesses. The Imperial Ancestor and the Emperor are in the relationship of parent and child, and the relationship between the Emperor and his subjects is, in its righteousness, that of sovereign and subject and, in its sympathies, that of father and child. This relationship is an "essential"* relationship that is far more fundamental than the rational, obligatory relationships, and herein are the grounds that give birth to the Way of loyalty. From the point of individualistic personal relationships, the relationship between sovereign and subject in our country may [perhaps] be looked upon as that

* In the sense of having to do with natural qualities.

between nonpersonalities. However, this is nothing but an error arising from treating the individual as supreme, from the nation that has individual thoughts for its nucleus, and from personal abstract consciousness. Our relationship between sovereign and subject is by no means a shallow, lateral relationship such as [means] the correlation between ruler and citizen, but is a relationship springing from a basis transcending this correlation, and is that of self-effacement and a return to [the] "one," in which this basis is not lost. This is a thing that can never be understood from an individualistic way of thinking. In our country, this great Way has seen a natural development since the founding of the nation, and the most basic thing that has manifested itself as regards the subjects is in short this Way of loyalty. Herein exists the profound meaning and lofty value of loyalty. Of late years, through the influence of the Occidental individualistic ideology, a way of thinking which has for its basis the individual has become lively. Consequently, this and the true aim of our Way of loyalty which is "essentially" different from it are not necessarily [mutually] consistent. That is, those in our country who at the present time expound loyalty and patriotism are apt to lose [sight of] its true significance, being influenced by Occidental individualism and rationalism. We must sweep aside the corruption of the spirit and the clouding of knowledge that arises from setting up one's "self" and from being taken up with one's "self" and return to a pure and clear state of mind that belongs intrinsically to us as subjects, and thereby fathom the great principle of loyalty.

The Emperor always honors* the Imperial Ancestors, and, taking the lead of his subjects, shows by practice the oneness of ancestor and offspring, and sets an example of reverence for the deities and for the ancestors. Again, we subjects, as descendants of subjects who served the Imperial Ancestors, revere their ancestors, inherit their motives of loyalty, make this [spirit] "live" in the present, and pass it on to posterity. Thus, reverence for the deities and for the ancestors and the Way of loyalty are

* Or, worships. The word is connected with Shintoism and can be variously rendered.

basically entirely one, and are Ways essentially inseparable. Such unity is seen in our country alone, and here, too, is the reason why our national entity is sacred.

The perfect unity between reverence for the deities and the Way of loyalty is also accounted for by the fact that these things and patriotism are one. To begin with, our country is one great family nation [comprising] a union* of sovereign and subject, having the Imperial Household as the head family, and looking up to the Emperor as the focal point from of old to the present. Accordingly, to contribute to the prosperity of the nation is to serve for the prosperity of the Emperor; and to be loyal to the Emperor means nothing short of loving the country and striving for the welfare of the nation. Without loyalty there is no patriotism, and without patriotism there is no loyalty. All patriotism is always impregnated with the highest sentiments of loyalty, and all loyalty is always attended with the zeal of patriotism. Of course, in foreign countries, too, there exists a spirit of patriotism. But this patriotism is not of a kind which, like in our country, is from the very roots one with loyalty and in perfect accord with reverence for the deities and the ancestors.

Indeed, loyalty is our fundamental Way as subjects, and is the basis of our national morality. Through loyalty are we become Japanese subjects; in loyalty do we obtain life and herein do we find the source of all morality. According to our history, the spirit of loyalty always runs through the hearts of the people. The decline of the Imperial Court in the Age of Civil Wars** deeply moves one to awe;† but in this age, too, a hero in carrying out some undertaking could not win the hearts of the people so long as a spirit of reverence for the Emperor was not given recognition. The ability of Oda Nobunaga [A.D. 1534–1582]

* Literally, "one body."

** Sengoku Jidai, from 1490 to 1600, during which Japan was completely involved in civil war.

† The predicate is a common Japanese expression used with regard to the Imperial Household which carries with it a sense of deepest awe, and for which there is no adequate translation.

and Toyotomi Hideyoshi [A.D. 1536–1598] to reap the fruits of their enterprises speaks for the state of affairs at the time. That means that under all circumstances the spirit of reverence for the Emperor is the most powerful thing that moves the nation.

We read in a poem by Ohtomo no Yakamochi [died A.D. 785] in the *Mannyōshū:*

> One known as Ohkumenushi,
> A far-off ancestor of Ohtomo,
> That rendered the Emperor service
> Vowed, "If I traversed the sea,
> A watery corpse I'd be;
> If mountains I traversed,
> A grassy corpse I'd lie;
> If I could only die
> Beside my Emperor,
> Let come what will!"

This song has touched our people's heartstrings since of old, and is still handed down to and sung by us.

In a poem by Tachibana no Moroe [A.D. 684–757] which reads:

> Were I to serve my Lord until
> My hair turned white as the falling snow,
> How exalted I should feel!

a loyalty in serving the Emperor until one's hair turned white is vividly manifested. Then again, Kusunoki Masashige's [A.D. 1294–1336] spirit to serve the nation over seven spans of life is even now stirring the people to the depths. Also, in our country, since of old, there have been not a few utterances in the way of poems expressive of the spirit of loyalty composed at white heat or in deep pain. For instance, such are: Minamoto no Sanetomo's,

> Should it be a world
> Where the mountains crashed

> And the deeps ran dry,
> Could I possess for my Lord
> A double heart!

The priest Gesshō's,

> If it be for my Lord,
> Would I count it a loss—
> Though my body sank deep
> In Satsuma's sea?

Hirano Kuniomi's,

> O that I could die
> Beneath the Emperor's banner,
> Though deserveless of a name!

Umeda Umpin's,

> Thoughtless am I of my being,
> In the singleness of heart that thinks
> For the reign of His Majesty!

Loyalty is realized through the people's constant attention to duties and through faithful devotion to their pursuits. As graciously manifested in the Imperial Rescript on Education: not only to offer oneself courageously to the State, should occasion arise; but also to be filial to one's parents, affectionate to one's brothers and sisters, to be harmonious as husbands and wives, to be true as friends, to bear oneself in modesty and moderation, to extend one's benevolence to all, to pursue learning and to cultivate arts, and thereby to develop intellectual faculties and to perfect moral powers; furthermore, to advance public good and to promote common interests, always to respect the Constitution and to observe the laws, etc., are one and all accounted for by our response to the great august Will and our respectful support for His Majesty's diffusion of His enterprises, and all constitute the Way of loyalty. Tachibana no Moribe relates in the *Taimon Zakki:*

The general public are ready to look upon serving at the Imperial Palace alone as service; but beneath this shining Sun and Moon,* is there anyone that does not serve the Emperor? Beginning with the Gracious Personage who headeth the Government officials right down to the lowest—though there may be differences of high and low—since every one of them is a servant of the Sovereign, to write a thing is for His Majesty, to cure an illness is for His Majesty, to cultivate a field is for His Majesty, and to trade is for His Majesty. But since the lowly are very far separated from His Majesty, they cannot serve the Emperor to the extent of exercising their sympathies for the general public by serving close to the Emperor.

Verily, for those engaged in government, those engaged in industries, those that have dedicated themselves to education or scholastic pursuits, for them to devote themselves to their various fields, is the Way of loyalty to sustain the prosperity of the Imperial Throne, and is by no means a personal Way.

This fact is evidenced by what the Emperor Meiji says in [two of] his poems:

> Lieth Our strength
>   In the people's strength
> That strive to the utmost
>   Each in his sphere.

> Might we serve our Land,
>   Each in our allotted sphere,
> Learning the Way our hearts
>   Should take.

It is the duty of a subject and the noble concern of the Japanese to stand in the deep knowledge that to do one's duty means in effect to sustain the Emperor's great august enterprises, with diligence exercised in perfect accord with the Imperial Will expressed in the words:

* *I.e.,* throughout the whole country.

In private affairs, with prudence and frugality, carry on your daily duties, and order your mode of living; in public affairs, do not pay attention solely to individual benefits, but devote yourselves to the common weal, and thereby give heed to the welfare, peace, and prosperity of the State, and to social well-being.*

Filial piety

In our country filial piety is a Way of the highest importance. Filial piety originates with one's family as its basis, and in its larger sense has the nation for its foundation. Filial piety directly has for its object one's parents, but in its relationship toward the Emperor finds a place within loyalty.

The basis of the nation's livelihood is, as in the Occident, neither the individual nor husband and wife. It is the home. The domestic life does not consist in a lateral relationship, such as between husband and wife or elder brother and younger brother; but that which forms its root is a dimensional** relationship between parent and child. The harmonious merging under the head of a family, in line with our national entity, of a united group of relatives that come together and help each other with the relationship between parent and child for its basis is our nation's home. Consequently, a family is not a body of people established for profit, nor is it anything founded on such a thing as individual or correlative love. Founded on a natural relationship of begetting and being begotten, it has reverence and affection as its kernel and is a place where everybody, from the very moment of his birth, is entrusted with his destiny.

The life of a family in our country is not confined to the present life of a household of parents and children, but beginning with the distant ancestors, is carried on eternally by the descendants. The present life of a family is a link between the past and the future, and while it carries over and develops the objectives of the ancestors, it hands them over to its descendants. Herein

* Part of the Imperial Rescript on the Promotion of the National Spirit, November 10, 1923.

** Or, cubic, solid; used in a geometrical sense.

also lies the reason why since of old a family name has been esteemed in our country. A family name is an honor to a household built up by one's ancestors, so that to stain this may be looked upon not only as a personal disgrace but as a disgrace to a family that has come down in one line linking the past, present, and future. Accordingly, the announcing of one's real name by a knight who has gone out to the battlefield was in the nature of an oath to fight bravely by speaking of one's ancestors and their achievements, so as not to cast a slur on the name of an esteemed family.

Again, since olden times, there have existed such things as family codes, family precepts, and family customs, and these things have been handed down to and developed by one's offspring; and heirlooms have been prized and preserved as symbols of a household's successions, while by the nation as a whole ancestral tablets have been solemnly taken over. Such things as these show that the basis of the nation's life is in the family and that the family is the training ground for moral discipline based on natural sympathies. Thus, the life of a household is not a thing confined to the present, but is an unbroken chain that passes through from ancestor to offspring. In our country, consequently, importance is laid on the succession of a family, and legally, too, there is established a system of succession to the heirship. The fact that at present there is only inheritance but no succession to heirship in the Occident illustrates the fact that a household in the Occident and that in our country are fundamentally different.

The relationship between parent and child is a natural one, and therein springs the affection between parent and child. Parent and child are a continuation of one chain of life; and since parents are the source of the children, there spontaneously arises toward the children a tender feeling to foster them. Since children are expansions of parents, there springs a sense of respect, love for, and indebtedness toward, parents. Since ancient times, as regards relations between parents and children, poems, legends, and historical facts, portraying parents' affection for their children and children's respect for their parents, are exceedingly numerous. In the *Mannyōshū* there is a poem that tells of the love of one Yamanoe no Okura for his child:

> If I eat a melon, it reminds me of my child.
> If I eat a chestnut, it reminds me of my child all the more.
> Whence does it come?
> It rests over my eyes, and I cannot slumber in peace.

Hanka

> Oh, there's nought excels my gem of a child—
>   Gold, silver, or gem though it be!

This poem expresses aptly, though briefly, a love that truly thinks of a child. Also, in a poem which Okura composed lamenting the death of his child Furuhi, too, there is seen an expression of an ardent love of a parent for his child:

> He could not know the way,
>   So tender of years is he—
> Messenger of the shades, I pray,
>   Carry him through on your back.

And the fond respect of a child for its parents is well expressed in poems such as those of Sakimori.

Loyalty and filial piety as one

Filial piety in our country has its true characteristics in its perfect conformity with our national entity by heightening still further the relationship between morality and nature. Our country is a great family nation, and the Imperial Household is the head family of the subjects and the nucleus of national life. The subjects revere the Imperial Household, which is the head family, with the tender esteem they have for their ancestors; and the Emperor loves his subjects as his very own.* The words in

---

* Another word for "subjects," *sekishi*, is here used, which carries with it an idea of endearment, frequently translated as "children."

the august Will left by the Emperor Yūryaky [A.D. 457–479], which says: "Though righteousness may in effect be between sovereign and subject, affection is bound up between father and child," bespeak the great august Will of the successive Emperors. That is to say, the relationship between sovereign and subject is public* and bound with righteousness; and what he states is that it does not end solely in mere righteousness but that it is bound with sympathies similar to those between father and child. "Public" [ōyake] as opposed to "private" [watakushi] signifies the court and means "nation," namely, "house."

Since our ancestors rendered assistance to the spreading of Imperial enterprises by the successive Emperors, for us to show loyalty to the Emperor is in effect a manifestation of the manners and customs of our ancestors; and this is why we show filial piety to our forefathers. In our country there is no filial piety apart from loyalty, and filial piety has loyalty for its basis. The logic of the unity of loyalty and filial piety based on national entity herein shines forth beautifully. Yoshida Shōin says in his *Shiki Shichisoku:*

The Sovereign careth for the well-being of his subjects, and so inheriteth the enterprises of the Imperial Ancestors. The subjects manifest loyalty toward the Emperor, and so inherit the will of their fathers. It is only in our country that sovereign and subject are united, and that loyalty and filial piety converge.

And this is a most appropriate statement on the oneness of the Way of loyalty and filial piety.

In China, too, importance is laid on filial duty, and they say that it is the source of a hundred deeds. In India, too, gratitude to parents is taught. But their filial piety is not of a kind related to or based on the nation. Filial piety is a characteristic of Oriental morals, and it is in its convergence with loyalty that we find a parallel in the world. Accordingly, that which has lost the essential points of these fundamentals cannot be our national

---

* *Oh-yake:* public; open; official; formal.

filial piety. Such things as the announcing of one's name by a knight by way of declaring that his house finds its source in the Imperial Household, and the tracing of the relationship of family codes and family teachings to the Imperial Household as their remote source, are to be looked upon as traceable to the very same reasons.

The poem by Sakura Azumao which runs:

> Precious are my parents that gave me birth,
> So that I might serve His Majesty.

shows that when filial piety is elevated to loyalty, then for the first time it becomes filial piety. The offering of their two sons for the nation by General Nogi and his wife, even counting it an honor to the family, is a manifestation of a mind [which looks upon] the family and the country as a unit* and loyalty and filial piety as one. Thus, the hearts of the subjects that render service through the Way of loyalty and filial piety as one, in uniting with the Emperor's great august heart of benevolence, reap the fruits of concord between the Sovereign and his subjects, and is the basic power of our nation's endless development.

Verily, loyalty and filial piety as one is the flower of our national entity, and is the cardinal point of our people's morals. Hence, national entity forms the foundation not only of morality but of all branches of such things as politics, economics, and industry. Accordingly, the great Way of loyalty and filial piety as one must be made manifest in all practical fields of these national activities and the people's lives. We subjects must strive all the more in loyalty and filial piety for the real manifestation of the immense and endless national entity.

*Literally, "one body."

12. ISLAM AND NATIONALISM*

⎍⎍⎍⎍⎍⎍⎍⎍⎍⎍⎍⎍⎍⎍⎍⎍

Shakib Arslan

How European nations preserve their nationality

If we look at Europe—which today is the ideal to look up to in this connection—we will find no nation willing to be submerged in another. The English want to remain English, the French to remain French, the Germans do not want to be anything but German, the Italians anything but Italian, the Russians bend all efforts to remain Russian, and so on.

This European example becomes all the more impressive when the Irish are considered. Their neighbors the English have for more than seven hundred years employed every conceivable means to absorb this small nation, but the Irish have refused to become English and have clung to their Irish tongue, creed, tastes and customs.

In the same way the Bretons in France insist on preserving their identity. In southern France there is a race called Basques

*From *Limadha ta'akhkhara al-muslimun wa limadha taqaddama ghayru-hum* (*Why Muslims have become backward and why others have advanced*), by Amir Shakib Arslan, 3rd ed., Cairo, 1939, pp. 78–95.

who have preserved their nationality against the Goths, the Arabs, the Spaniards, and the French. They are but a million in number, and to this day have clung to their language, dress, customs and all their other arrangements.

The Flemings refuse to adopt the French language and culture as their own and have kept on protesting until they compelled the Belgian State to recognize Flemish as an official language.

Switzerland is divided into three parts: the German part which amounts to two millions eight hundred thousand, the French-speaking part amounting to eight hundred thousand, and the Italian-speaking part of a little over two hundred thousand. Each part preserves its language, laws and preferences, notwithstanding the fact that they are all united in their political interests and that they all live in one state.

There is no doubt that Denmark, Scandinavia, Holland are branches of the German tree, but they do not desire to be absorbed by the Germans, or to give up their nationality. The Czechs remained hundreds of years under German rule and preserved their identity; after the World War they resumed their political independence, having preserved their tongue and their racial independence for five centuries.

The Germans introduced the Magyars to education, culture and progress, and yet were unable to absorb them in Germanism. You find, in fact, that the Hungarians are the most careful of nations in preserving their original Mongolian tongue and their Magyar nationality.

Mighty Russia kept on attempting for two or three hundred years to assimilate Poland in the Russian race and to persuade the Poles not to preserve their nationality on the argument that the Slavic race includes both Poles and Russians. Their efforts were a failure, and the Poles became once more after the Great War a nation independent in everything, because they did not, not even for a single moment, abandon their nationality.

That a nation of thirty million should refuse to be absorbed in another nation is not surprising, but the Estonians, who are only two million, detached themselves from Russia and refused to be amalgamated with it; they revived their original Mongolian tongue and endowed it with an alphabet. Similarly placed are the Finns, who have seceded from Russia. Russia's efforts in amalgamating the Lithuanians, who number four million, have also failed, and the latter seceded from them after the Great War and became politically independent as they had been nationally distinct. Their neighbors, the Letts, who are only two million, also seceded after the War and founded a republic similar to the other Baltic Republics because they have always been steadfast in preserving their language and race.

The Russians have failed like the Germans in including these nations in their extensive national amalgams. The reason for this is that every people, however small, does not acquiesce in the denial of its origins or in the giving up of its racial independence.

The Croats have preserved their racial independence in spite of the fact that they were surrounded by two great nations, the Latins and the Germans.

The Serbs have preserved their racial independence in spite of a centuries-old Turkish domination.

The Albanians have remained Albanian since time immemorial in spite of the fact that they found themselves between two great nations, the Greeks and the Slavs.

The Bulgarians again have remained obstinately Bulgarian in the midst of Greeks, Slavs and Latins. The Turks conquered them and they learned Turkish but remained Bulgarians.

I do not wish to adduce examples from outside Europe, because if I did then those who wish to give up our nationality will say: We do not wish to emulate backward nations like ourselves.

The nations whose example we have taken are all European, all educated and advanced; their countries are all civilized and well organized, all possessing universities, academies, learned societies, armies and navies, etc.

The lesson of Japanese progress for the Arabs and all the Muslims

Outside Europe I take only the Japanese as an example, because Japanese progress is equal to that of Europe. As in Europe,

Japanese advancement took place within the bounds of the Japanese nationality, language, literature, freedom, religion, ceremonies, feelings, and everything else peculiar to themselves.

I transcribe here for Arabic readers a paragraph from a long dispatch by a European correspondent visiting Japan which appeared in the *Journal de Genève* on 20 October, 1931. He says:

The Japanese loves art above everything else. If you find one engaged in money-making, it is only so that he should have the means to indulge his love of beauty. Apart from this, the other feeling which is impressed on his soul is a powerful national sentiment because he takes pride in the fact that Japan in the space of sixty years has changed from a feudal medieval nation into one of the greatest nations. There is no doubt that the Japanese religion plays a large role in the politics of Japan. Let the reader ponder this. Japanese religion is in fact a philosophy built on the recognition of all that the ancestors have left to their descendants. The modern Japanese is at home in all the aspects of modern life, but he has preserved his partiality for his past and great attachment to his own nationality, thus disregarding the call to Westernization. The Japanese wishes to take from the West only what is necessary to maintain himself successfully against all nations. This is no doubt a unique example in the history of Eastern nations.

He goes on:

The Japanese used to hate travel to distant countries, and to prohibit the entry of foreigners to their own country. But this prohibition was lifted after the modern renascence and Japan made good the errors of the past. The results are before us. The past remains sacred and venerable in the eyes of Japanese of all classes, because it is this sacred past which makes them conscious of their present position. You find them using all the methods of modern civilization without which success is impossible nowadays, yet refusing any element of Westernization which they can do without, and always going back with pleasure to their pure national feeling which enables them to believe in their own superiority.

You will see Shinto shrines, Zen temples and Buddhist shrines venerated, honoured, and their ceremonies performed with the utmost religious enthusiasm and the most steadfast faith, as they have been from of old. In fact it is this extreme reverence which the Japanese have for their past and their divinities which has proved an impregnable fortress against foreign principles and harmful communist ideas.

A few years ago a new book on Japan by the Marquis de la

Mazelière appeared in France which was highly praised in the press. The *Journal des Débats* devoted to it an article of eloquent praise. We would recommend it to anybody interested in trying to understand the Japanese renascence—a subject of the utmost importance for the lessons it provides to all oriental countries— since its author cannot be accused of partiality toward Japan, while I have found him generally to conform to accounts given by Japanese historians and which are translated into French. I must quote here a few paragraphs from La Mazelière's work. Discussing the modern civilization of Japan and its emergence from its ancient isolation, he says:

Japan began to borrow from Europe and America a part of their material civilization, their military organization, their general academic researches, and their financial policy. The reformers attempted to borrow what they considered to be the best from each people. This was therefore a work of renovation, of demolition and reconstruction, the results of which became apparent in all aspects of Japanese life.

He then discussed the Sino-Japanese war and ended with this statement which we translate literally:

The victory of Japan over China does not only prove the superiority of the scientific ideas and principles which Japan adopted from the West, but also that an Asiatic people, has by the exercise of its will and resolution, known how to choose from Western Civilization what was most useful to it while—ponder this carefully—preserving its independence, nationality, mentality, literature and culture.

Some time ago I published in the newspapers an account— which was extremely brief—of the ceremonies by which the Japanese celebrated the coronation of their monarch two years ago. I described how these ceremonies lasted for a whole month, how they were all religious, how the Mikado is the Nation's high priest, how he is a descendant of the gods, *i.e.*, of the sun, how he performed his ablutions in the sacred bath which has been preserved for two thousand years, how he ate in company of the gods the sacred rice planted by the state under priestly supervision—so that its sanctity may not be suspect—and how six hundred thousand Japanese present at this assembly shouted, May the Mikado live for ten thousand years, etc.

Why do we not denounce Europe and Japan as reactionary because of their devotion to their religion?

Japan has made this rapid and astonishing progress, and has become a modern nation the advanced level of which is proverbial, and yet it clings to beliefs, customs and preferences more than two thousand years old, and its emperor is its high priest. I wonder why it is not called reactionary, retrograde, backward or regressive? Indeed if Japan were reactionary, how welcome such backwardness would be.

The King of England and Emperor of India is the sovereign of 450 million souls on earth, white, brown, yellow, red and black; he is the Head of the Anglican Church and his Parliament debates in many sittings the question whether the priest can by his blessing transubstantiate bread and wine into the body of Christ and His blood, or whether this is mere symbolism and ceremony. Yet he is not called reactionary, and his mighty state is not called backward and retrograde. If England were retrograde, how welcome such retrogression would be.

Why is the whole of Europe Christian, proud of its Christianity, boasting of it on every occasion, united in this matter in spite of its other enmities and rivalries, while we cannot dismiss all this as reactionary or retrograde? In fact the religion of Europe is 19 centuries old. This is what may be called an old, a very old covenant. Again, consider the Jews, who, whatever virtues we may deny them, cannot be denied ability, intelligence, practical sense, and great enterprise; yet they are still proud of Scriptures which originated thousands of years ago, and pride in which is shared by the Christians.

Why do we see the most progressive and modern Jewish youth try so hard to revive the Hebrew language, which is so old that its origins are lost, and who yet are not called reactionary, backward or retrogressive?

Weizmann, the President of the Zionist Organization, has been interviewed by the *Matin* newspaper and has declared that one most important achievement and cause for pride is that the whole of modern Palestine speaks in the language of the Prophets. By modern Palestine, he means Jewish Palestine, where the Zionists have spread the old Hebrew tongue and compelled their new generation to speak it so that it would become the universal Jewish language. Who has done this? The answer is, the modern Jews who are most adept at the principles of contemporary science and modern civilization. Let the wise think and ponder. How many more examples can I quote in a treatise as short as this?

Every nation clings resolutely to its religion, the constituents of its nationality, and its inherited group characteristics. None but the Muslims disdain these things. If perchance somebody should tell them to hold fast to their Qur'an, their creed, their characteristics, to the Arabic language and its literature, to an Oriental way of life, those who are diseased in their spirit set up a great clamor and shout: Down with reaction; they say: how can you aspire to progress while you still cling to outworn medieval conditions, while we are in the midst of a new age?

All these men have acquired education, they have advanced and progressed and soared into very heaven, and yet the Christian among them remains faithful to his gospel and the traditions of his church, the Jew holds fast to his Scripture and Talmud, the Japanese to his idol and sacred rice. Every sect among them is well content with its creed, and only the poor Muslim can never advance unless he jettisons his Qur'an, his beliefs, his preferences, his aversions, his inclinations, his customs, his mode of dressing, his favorite meat and drink, his literature, his amusements and all the rest, and detaches himself from the whole of his history. Why, unless he does all this, does he stand no chance to progress?

This is the harm wrought by the ingrate [who spreads such views] who wishes Islam and the whole East ill, and who deceives the simpleminded with his plausible speech.

13. HINDUISM AND INDIAN NATIONALISM*

Bipin Chandra Pal

. . . But the authorities have hardly any appreciation of the gravity of the situation. They are engaged in putting down the outer expressions of an unrest, the root-cause of which lies deep in the spiritual intuitions of the people. Lacking true spiritual perceptions themselves, they are interpreting a deep spiritual upheaval as a mere economic unrest or political ferment. They have no appreciation of the character of the forces that are slowly ranging themselves against them.

These forces are essentially religious and spiritual. They are manifest in every department of the present nationalist activities. A fervent religious spirit breathes through every poem and hymn in which the new nationalist sentiments have found expression during the last five or six years. It has been the inspiration of every nationalist orator who has drawn people in their thousands and tens of thousands, to the nationalist platforms. It has created new symbols—a new form of idolatry, as some perhaps would call it—representing the apotheosis of the geographical habitat of the race. And it is this intensely religious

*From *The Spirit of Indian Nationalism*, by Bipin Chandra Pal, London, 1910, pp. 22–48.

note which constitutes the reality and the gravity of the present situation.

It would be a grievous mistake to think that this religious garb has been given to the new activities by mischievous and intriguing political agitators, eager to rouse the masses and draw them to their propaganda. It is quite possible that some politicians, brought up in alien ways of thinking and drawing their political inspirations from European literature and history, may have been seeking to use the religious instincts of the people in this degrading and diplomatic fashion. But if there be any such, they are survivals of the old political schools, and in no way represent the new national spirit. The real leaders of the people today are men who either never lost, or have come back to, the faith of their fathers. Their faith is larger and deeper, because the result of a new synthesis, than even the uncritical faith of the people. Though products of modern European culture, they have found out the utter inadequacy of the prevailing deism or rationalism of Europe to explain the mysteries of the spiritual life. They have discovered new meaning and inspiration in the ancient symbols and sacraments of their people. To them, Hinduism is not dead, but still living; the religion of the Hindu is not idolatry, not even ideolatry; the old gods are no mere myths. Cosmic evolution has brought forth successive planes of beings from the protozoa to the human kingdom. But is man the last point in this evolutionary process? they ask. He is admittedly the highest—on the sensuous plane; but is there no higher? Cannot there be higher planes above the human, beyond the cognizance of the senses? And it is these higher orders of creation, the possibility of which at least cannot reasonably be denied, that are represented by the gods of the traditional faith. These gods do not make Hinduism polytheistic any more than angelology of the Catholic Church justifies the charge of polytheism against Christianity. These gods, owing to their superior powers, can control, to a large extent, the destinies of men, even as men can control, to some extent, the life and movements of the lower animals. These gods are not imagined—no mere cosmic or poetic symbols—but are entities known by the seers in trance or samâdhi. They are not within the ken of ordinary mortals; but no more do ordinary mortals see the protoplasmic cells upon which the biologist builds his theory of organic evolution. These cells, though invisible to the naked eye, are yet seen with the help of powerful microscopes. The gods also are seen under certain conditions, by man's supersensuous faculties, which are developed through long and laborious psychophysical and psychical disciplines. The supersensuous is not the supernatural. Every human being is endowed with supersensuous faculties, awaiting due development through proper exercise and right discipline. So every man can see the gods by fulfilling the necessary conditions.

This, briefly, is the general line of exegesis by means of which the old gods are being rehabilitated, so to say, in the thoughts of the modern Hindu. The methods of this new exegesis, if it can be called new, may not appeal as strictly rational to all people. They are not likely to be acceptable to those who are still under the spell of nineteenth-century rationalism, whether in India or elsewhere. But this kind of rationality is no test of the reality of human beliefs. And statesmanship is not concerned with the rationality, but simply with the reality, of popular faiths. For it is this reality, the earnestness and sincerity with which particular faiths are held, which lends vitality and strength to historic movements. Both Christianity and Islam have changed the face of a large part of the globe, lending strange vitality and peculiar color to the social and political life of a large section of the human race. But the tremendous influence of these faiths upon contemporary history cannot be measured by the degree of truth or reason which they embodied, but only by the strength of faith which they were able to create. And what we see in India today is the birth of a new exegesis, which is rehabilitating the old beliefs and trying to adjust them to the demands of the modern life and thought. This revived faith of the educated classes of the country in national institutions and scriptures has been rapidly bridging over the gulf which the onrush of foreign ideas and ideals had at one time created between them and the general masses of their countrymen. And it is this religious spirit, at once so real and so conservative, which differentiates the new National Movement from the old, purely secular, political movements in British India.

This religious note is revealed by the messianic aspiration with which the new movement has been associated from its very birth. The messianic idea in Hinduism has found, perhaps, its fullest expression in the well-known verses of the Bhagabad-Geetâ—

Yadâ yadâ hi dharmasya glanirbhavati Bhârata,
Abhyutthânamadharmasya, tadâtmânan sreejâmyaham.
Paritrânâya sâdhunâm vinâshâyaca dushkreetâm,
Dharmasamsthâpanârthâya sambhavâmi yugê, yugê.

Whenever, O Bhârata, there is decadence of Dharma and prevalence of Adharma, I always incarnate myself.
For the protection of the good, for the extirpation of evil-doers, and for the establishment of Dharma, I am born from age to age.

Bunkim Chunder Chatterjee, the author of the Bandê-Mâtaram hymn, stands prominently among those who have helped to call the present national spirit into being; and in modern Bengalee literature we owe the revival of the old Hindu messianic idea to him. It was he who first brought it before his educated countrymen as a mighty molding force in social evolution among intensely religious peoples. To him we owe a new interpretation of the life and character of Sree-Krishna as a great nation-builder in ancient India, and as a divine exemplar to the Hindu people for all time to come. Bunkim Chunder's influence was, however, confined to the educated classes only. Indeed, the masses have always believed in Sree-Krishna, and required, therefore, no new exegesis or interpretation to revive their lost or waning faith. What they wanted was a practical application of that faith, not as a mere religious or spiritual force, but as a social, and, perhaps, even as a political, inspiration. Krishna stood too far away from the present. As God, he is no doubt present in spirit always and everywhere. What they craved for was his manifestation in the flesh. He had incarnated himself repeatedly, from age to age, "for the protection of the good, for the extermination of evil-doers, for the reestablishment of decadent Dharma." A fresh cry now went up from the heart of his chosen people for a fresh advent of the Saviour. This cry is a peculiar feature of the present ferment in India, and more particularly in Bengal, which is, in some sense, the native home of the new Nationalist Movement.

The fundamental point of difference between the older political agitations and the new Nationalist Movement is thus—(1) its intensely spiritual and religious character as compared to the absolutely secular spirit of the former; and (2) its strong grip on the actualities of Indian life and thought as against the imitative character of the older and earlier social and political activities. Nationalism is intensely realistic; the older political and social thought was more or less imitative and imaginative. The older generations drew their inspirations of freedom and progress from European, and especially British, history and literature. The old patriotism did not feed upon the actualities of Indian thought and life, but upon the idealities of Europe and America. Freedom, except in the movements of religious and social revolt where it meant personal freedom only, was a vague idea. The conception of freedom has its natural growth in the sense of bondage, and its vitality is determined by the strength of this sense. There was a keen and growing sense of social and sacerdotal restrictions in the English-educated classes, who were inspired with the ideals of liberty, equality, and fraternity, imbibed from the gospel of the French Revolution, through its English presentations; and consequently there was a real desire for social emancipation, a desire for freedom from the restrictions of caste and custom. But there was hardly any deep and real sense of political wrongs. On the contrary, there was a general impression that the British have established peace where there was turmoil, and a settled government where there was anarchy. Nor was there yet any perception of the ruinous economic conflict between Great Britain and India. Consequently, the desire for political freedom was very weak; and it did not go beyond getting higher appointments in the Administration, and some share in the shaping of the laws of the land. The old patriotism, therefore, simply represented an awakening of the educated classes to a consciousness of their inferior position in the modern world, and a revival of the memories of the past glories of their race. It was just the beginning of a reaction, but not yet the birth of a new life.

A brief survey of the old and the new hymnology of Indian patriotism at once reveals the wide and vital difference between the old political agitations and the new national upheaval. One of the most popular hymns of the old patriotism was this:

When, tell me, O Bhârata (India), wilt thou get across the ocean of thy present misery? Or, wilt thou only sink and sink lower in thy degradations, until thou enterest the nether regions for good? Having gladly made over thy riches and jewels to the stranger, thou bearest to-day only an iron-chain on thy breast!

The lights of the stranger shine in all thy cities; but thou art in darkness all the same!

Another patriotic song declared that "day by day India was being weakened and impoverished through her subjection to the foreigner; a flight of locusts from a high Island, having fallen upon the land, were eating up all the grains, leaving the husks alone for the children of the soil!" Others wept over the glories of the past. These were the dominant notes of Indian patriotism thirty years ago; they are scarcely heard today. The new note is intensely realistic and profoundly religious and spiritual. It breathes no longer the old sense of humiliation and despair, but a new pride of race and a deathless hope in the destiny of the people.

When Lord Curzon divided the old Administration in Bengal into two parts, cutting off the eastern from the western districts, contemptuously rejecting the earnest solicitations of a united people, the nation's reply was,

Wilt thou cut asunder the bonds forged by Providence? Art thou so powerful? Our breaking and building are in thy hands: hast thou this conceit?

Thou wouldst drag us perpetually behind thee, thou wouldst perpetually keep us under thee; but thou hast not the strength, the attempt will not bear the strain.

However close thou may'st draw the cords of repression around us, do not forget that even the weak have their strength. However mighty thou may'st be, there is a God.

By killing our strength, even thou shalt not live. When the cargo is over-full, the boat will sink.

This reference to Providence was distinctly a new note in modern political struggles in India. It showed that the mind of the nation had commenced to turn to higher powers for strength and inspiration. It was no longer a prayer for justice or generosity from man, but a cry for strength and illumination from God. No political conjurer can call up such a cry from a nation's heart.

The immense popularity of these hymns is a proof of the depth of the new patriotic sentiment in the country. In India there are no music halls and but few theaters, which again are completely under the censorship of the police; and the Executive Government, in their campaign against sedition, has of late been exercising this right of censorship to prevent the propagation of almost any kind of nationalist ideas through the national stage. The national songs, however, find extensive circulation in spite of the police and the magistracy. Most of the new hymns, half religious and half political, have, thus, found their way to the most distant corners of the land. The naked cowboy, reclining under the familiar banyan tree, sings out the glories of his country, and calls upon Krishna to come and reestablish the decadent Dharma. Little girls, playing with one another, sing in chorus,

> Cry Bandê-Mâtaram,—Forty million brothers,
> Forty million sisters, are we inferior to any?
> Cry Bandê-Mâtaram!

And holy mendicants chant from door to door,
> Lowly Bhârata cries out to thee, Come, O Murâri.
Murâri is a name of Krishna, which preserves the memory of

his fight with the demon Mura, whom he killed to give relief to his people.

It is in this way that the new National Movement has been working itself into the very heart and soul of the people. Old sacraments that had lost their vitality with their original meaning and significance, have been quickened with a new life under the impulse of this new patriotism. The authors of the French Revolution made grotesque attempts to replace the old sacraments of Catholicism by new ones, representing the new civic order which they were trying to set up in the land. In India, among the Hindus, civic religion is growing through an easy and natural process, out of the old symbolism and ritualism of the people. Hinduism has, indeed, like all ethnic systems, this advantage over credal religions, that its symbols and rituals, its sacraments and mysteries, are all partly religious and partly civic, partly social and partly spiritual. In fact, in Hinduism, the social and the spiritual are strangely blended together. Consequently, the new national spirit has found apt vehicles for expressing itself in the current religious rites and formulas of the people. The common Hindu formula for the sacrificial purification of water—

> Gangêca, Jamunêcaiva, Godâvari, Sarasvati,
> Narmmadâ, Sindhu, Kâveri, jalêsmin sannidhim kuru.
> May the Ganges, the Jumna, the Sarasvati, the Nerbudda,
> the Indus, and the Kaveri, enter into this water—

has become the baptismal formula of the new national life, a sacrament and symbol of Hindu unity. Every orthodox Hindu, during his daily ablutions, repeats this verse. So long it was a mere mantra to the vast majority of the people, a statement of the sanctity of these mighty rivers, along the course of which at one time Hindu life and culture had grown. To the devout few, it has had a sacrificial and supernatural value. But to vast multitudes today it is vested with a new meaning. The swarthy bather, standing knee-deep in a dirty pool and bathing himself with its muddy waters, repeats this mantra, and is conscious that it is the same water in which millions and millions of his brothers and sisters are bathing in different parts of India, and the consciousness helps him to remember his kinship with them and realize the unity of his nation.

The so-called idolatry of Hinduism is also passing through a mighty transfiguration. The process started really with Bunkim Chunder, who interpreted the most popular of the Hindu goddesses as symbolic of the different stages of national evolution. Jagaddhâtri—riding a lion which has the prostrate body of an elephant under its paw—represented the Motherland in the early jungle-clearing stage. This is, says Bunkim Chunder, the Mother as she was. Kâli, the grim goddess, dark and naked, bearing a garland of human heads around her neck—heads from which blood is dripping—and dancing on the prostrate form of Shiva or the Good: this, says Bunkim Chunder, is the Mother as she is; dark, because ignorant of her self; the heads with dripping blood are those of her own children, destroyed by famine and pestilence; the jackals licking these drippings are the symbol of desolation and decadence of social life, and the prostrate form of Shiva means that she is trampling her own good under her feet. Durgâ, the ten-handed goddess—armed with sword and spears in some hands, holding wheat sheaves in some, offering courage and peace with others, riding a lion, fighting with demons—with Sarasvati, or the goddess of Knowledge and Arts, supported by Ganapati, the god of Wisdom, on her one side, and Lakshmi, the goddess of Wealth, protected by Kârtikeya, the leader of the Heavenly army, on the other side: this, says Bunkim Chunder, is the Mother as she will be. This interpretation of the old images of gods and goddesses has imparted a new meaning to the current ceremonialism of the country, and multitudes, while worshiping either Jagaddhâtri, or Kâli, or Durgâ, accost them with devotion and enthusiasm, with the inspiring cry of Bandê-Mâtaram. All these are the most popular objects of worship of the Indian Hindus, especially in Bengal. And the transfiguration of these symbols is at once the cause and the evidence of the depth and strength of the present movement. This wonderful transfiguration of the old gods and goddesses is carrying the message of new nationalism to the women and the masses of the country.

Behind this mighty transfiguration of the old religious ideas and symbols of the country stands, however, a new philosophy of life. Strictly speaking, it is not a new philosophy either, but rather a somewhat new application of the dominant philosophical speculations of the race. Behind the new nationalism in India stands the old Vedantism of the Hindus. This ancient Indian philosophy, divided into many schools, has one general idea running through it from end to end. It is the idea of the essential unity of man and God. According to this philosophy, Substance is one though expressed through many forms. The Reality is one though appearances are multitudinous. Matter, in the eye of this philosophy, is not material, but essentially spiritual; the thought of God concretized. Man is the spirit of God incarnated. The meaning of cosmic evolution is to be found, not in itself, but in the thought of the Absolute. It is, to adopt the Hegelian dictum, the movement of the Self away from itself, to return to itself, to be itself. The Absolute, or Brahman, is the beginning, the middle, and the end of this evolutionary process. He is the Regulative Idea in cosmic evolution. He is progressively revealing himself through the world process. In man, the Divine idea, or the Logos, comes slowly to consciousness of itself. The end of human evolution is the fullest realization of man's unity with God. So long, especially in what may be called the middle ages in India, this essential unity between God and man was sought to be realized through metaphysical abstractions, by a negation of the social and the civic life. There was an undue emphasis on the Subjective and the Universal to the neglect of the realities, however relative they might be, of the Objective and the Particular. Protests had, however, been made from time to time against these monkish abstractions, but in spite of these protests the dominant note continued to be that of Abstract Monism. Neo-Vedantism, which forms the very soul and essence of what may be called Neo-Hinduism, has been seeking to realize the old spiritual ideals of the race, not through monkish negations or medieval abstractions, but by the idealization and the spiritualization of the concrete contents and actual relations of life. It demands, consequently, a social, an economic, and a political reconstruction, such as will be helpful to the highest spiritual life of every individual member of the community. The spiritual note of the present Nationalist Movement in India is entirely derived from this revived Vedantic thought.

Under the influence of this Neo-Vedantism, associated to a large extent with the name of the late Swami Vivekananda, there has been at work a slow and silent process of the liberalization of old social ideas. The old bigotry that anathematized the least deviation from the rules of caste, or the authority of custom, is openly giving way to a spirit of new tolerance. The imperious necessities of national struggle and national life are slowly breaking down, except in purely ceremonial affairs, the old restrictions of caste. In the new movement, old and orthodox Brahmins are rendering open obeisance to the heterodox and non-Brahmin teachers. There is an evident anxiety to discover scriptural and traditional authority for even the outrages that some of these have committed against the old social and sacerdotal order. And where no such authority could be found, their personal freedom of thought and action is being condoned on the principle that those who are to be the saviors of their nation stand, like the mendicant and the holy man, above all law. And all this is a proof of the strange hold that the new nationalist propaganda has got on the real mind and soul of the people.

But this movement has not only developed a strong spiritual note, relating itself thereby to the profound religious consciousness of the people, laying the symbols and sacraments of national religion under contribution for the furtherance of its specific end, namely, the upbuilding of a complete and consolidated national life in the country; but it has struck a strong note of reality in Indian politics also, which it never had before. It has subjected the British policy in India to a rigorous analysis, and has thus revealed its true character with almost cruel candor. It has completely demolished the idea that England is, and has always been, in India mainly for the good of the Indian. Above all, the Nationalist Movement has approached the central political problem in India from a new standpoint, namely, that of psychology.

In fact, it has boldly declared that the real political problem in India is not a strictly political, but essentially a psychological problem. The miracle of British rule in India—the government of 300,000,000 of peoples, spread over a whole continent, by a couple of hundred thousand foreigners, civil and military, all told —was due neither to the physical nor to the intellectual, nor to the moral superiority of the rulers over the ruled, but to pure hypnotism. The people were hypnotized to believe in the altruism of the foreign rulers. Untrained in the crooked ways of civilized diplomacy, they had believed what their rulers had said, either of themselves or of their subjects, as gospel truth. They had been told that the people of India were unfitted to manage their own affairs, and they believed it to be true. They had been told that the people were weak and the foreign government was strong, and they believed it to be true. They had been told that India stood on a lower plane of humanity, and England's mission was to civilize the semibarbarous native, and people believed that they were really low in the scale of civilization. This is how the hypnotism worked. The nationalist school exposed the hollowness of all these pretensions. It commenced to make what are called counterpasses in hypnotism, and at once awoke the people to a sense of their own strength, an appreciation of their own culture, and has created a new conviction that they, too, like the other races of the world, have a distinct mission and destiny.

The Nationalist Movement had been preceded by a general religious and social revival in India. This revival came as a reaction against the earlier movements of religious and social revolt, raised admittedly under the influence of European thoughts and ideals. This revolt was the direct result of the application of the canons of the dominant rationalistic thought of Europe of the later eighteenth and the early nineteenth century to the social and religious life of India. It represented what may be called the outer movement of the modern Indian consciousness. It was soon followed by the necessary return movement. The movement of social and religious revival which preceded the present Nationalist Movement, represented really the return of the national consciousness to itself. It was not really a conflict between the progressive and conservative elements of Indian society, as superficial observers have tried to make it out, but a conflict between aggressive European and progressive Indian culture. It was India's mental and moral protest against the intellectual and ethical domination of Europe. In some sense, it was really the reflex action of the growing appreciation of Eastern, and specially Hindu, thoughts and ideals in Europe and America. Just as foreign Christian missions have very materially helped to develop the self-consciousness of the Christian nations, as civilizers of the world and benefactors of humanity, even so the Hindu and Buddhistic missionary activities in Europe and America have revealed India's place in the evolution of modern world-culture. All these worked together to create a new pride of race; and in this pride of race was really born the new National Spirit in the country. By all these various means the old hypnotism was slowly breaking away. What was needed was only the bold declaration of the new political ideal to complete this work. The Nationalist School came into being, as a new political party in India, with such a declaration. National Autonomy, absolutely free of British control, they declared, was their political ideal. It was a bold declaration, no doubt; nothing like it had been heard before in British Indian politics. It almost staggered both the government and the people. But the mere desire for freedom could not be punished as criminal. The Nationalist leaders also took care, while making this declaration, to publicly announce that, though absolute freedom was their ultimate ideal, considering the state of the country, wisdom counseled the pursuit of this legitimate ideal of absolute freedom, through absolutely peaceful and lawful means. The government was powerless to punish peaceful people simply because they avowed their desire to be free. But while it staggered the authorities, it set the minds of the people free from the moral and intellectual bondage of the old political agitations of the country. As in religion and social life, India had commenced to claim her right to determine her own course of evolution herself, in the light of her own past, untrammeled by overbearing foreign thoughts and ideals; so, in politics also, she claimed her legitimate right of self-control and self-determination, to work out her own problems in her own way, freed from the bondage of European economic or political philosophy. Not self-government, whether colonial or otherwise, which expressed the idea of political freedom in the terms of European thought and experience, but SVARÂJ was proclaimed as the new ideal.

And the significance of this declaration lay mainly in the fact that svarâj was not a mere political term. Indeed, it was borrowed by politics from the highest philosophical and religious literature of the people. The concept was, therefore, a good deal more than what is conveyed by self-government. It is larger than that of the English word *freedom*. Freedom is an essentially negative, svarâj is a positive, concept. The term is used in the Vedânta to indicate the highest spiritual state, wherein the individual, having realized his identity with the Universal, is not merely freed from all bondage, but is established in perfect harmony with all else in the world. Svarâj means cessation of all conflicts. Politically, it means not merely the absence of bondage, but also the settlement of all disputes due to conflict of interests, either national or international. The concept involves not merely national freedom, but universal federation also, without which nations can never be established in perfect harmony with one another.

This term—svarâj—fully represents the spirit of Indian Nationalism. The identification of the individual with the universal, the recognition of the freedom of the individual, not in himself as standing apart from the whole of which the individual is a part, but in and through that whole only—this is the very soul and essence of the concept svarâj. This freedom is possible of realization by those only who recognize unity in diversity, who see that there is really One Life, One Mind, One Will, One Spirit, fulfilling itself through diverse instruments and in diverse ways; and, above all, who recognize in this Unity of the Self, as it is called in the Vedânta—the cancellation of all conflicts and the absolute settlement of all disputes. Viewing life and all its relations and activities from this supremely spiritual standpoint, the Indian Nationalist recognizes a spiritual reference as much in religion proper as in his social economy and political laws and institutions. Politics is, with him, part of his larger religion; it is a department of the science or philosophy of salvation. And, it is therefore, that the word which signifies the highest spiritual end represents also the highest political ideal.

This is the real spirit of Indian Nationalism. It is an essentially religious spirit. Its end is the realization of God-life in and through the activities of the social and the political life. That end is absolutely assured, but whether it will be reached by peaceful means or not will be determined by the capacity or incapacity of British statesmanship to work out the problem that faces it in India.

14. THE MORAL POVERTY OF INDIA AND NATIVE THOUGHTS ON THE PRESENT BRITISH-INDIAN POLICY*

Dadabhai Naoroji

In my last paper, I confined myself to meet Mr. Danvers' line of argument, on the question of the material destruction and impoverishment of India by the present British Indian Policy. I endeavored to show that this impoverishment and destruction of India was mainly caused by the unnatural treatment it received at the hands of its British rulers, in the way of subjecting it to a large variety of expenditure upon a crushing foreign agency both in India and England, whereby the children of the country were displaced and deprived of their natural rights and means of subsistence in their own country. By what was being taken and consumed in India itself and by what was being continuously taken away by such agency clean out of the country, an exhaustion of the very life-blood of the country was unceasingly going on. That till this disastrous drain was not duly checked, and till the people of India were not restored to their natural rights in their own country, there was no hope for the material amelioration of India.

In this Memorandum, I desire to submit for the kind and

*From *Condition of India: Correspondence with the Secretary of State for India*, by Dadabhai Naoroji, Bombay, 1881, pp. 55–69.

generous consideration of His Lordship, the Secretary of State for India, that from the same cause of the deplorable drain, besides the material exhaustion of India, the moral loss to her is no less sad and lamentable.

With the material wealth, go also the wisdom and experience of the country. Europeans occupy almost all the higher places in every department of government, directly or indirectly under its control. While *in* India they acquire India's money, experience and wisdom, and when they go, they carry both away with them, leaving India so much poorer in material and moral wealth. Thus India is left without, and cannot have, those elders in wisdom and experience, who in every country are the natural guides of the rising generations in their national and social conduct, and of the destinies of their country—and a sad, sad loss this is!

Every European is isolated from the people around him. He is not their mental, moral or social leader or companion. For any mental or moral influence or guidance or sympathy with the people, he might just as well be living in the moon. The people know not him, and he knows not, nor cares for, the people. Some honorable exceptions do, now and then, make an effort to do some good they can, but in the very nature of things, these efforts are always feeble, exotic, and of little permanent effect. These men are not always in the place, and their works die away when they go.

The Europeans are not the natural leaders of the people. They do not belong to the people. They cannot enter into their thoughts and feelings; they cannot join or sympathize with their joys or griefs. On the contrary, every day the estrangement is increasing. Europeans deliberately and openly widen it more and more. There may be very few social institutions started by Europeans in which, natives, however fit and desirous to join, are not deliberately and insultingly excluded. The Europeans are and make themselves strangers in every way. All they effectively do, is to eat the substance of India, material and moral, while living there, and when they go, they carry away all they have acquired, and their pensions and future usefulness besides.

This most deplorable moral loss to India needs most serious consideration, as much in its political as in its national aspect. Nationally disastrous as it is, it carries politically with it its own nemesis. Without the guidance of elderly wisdom and experience of their own natural leaders, the education which the rising generations are now receiving, is naturally leading them (or misleading them, if you will) into directions which bode no good to the rulers, and which, instead of being the strength of the rulers as it ought to and can be, will turn out to be their great weakness. The fault will be of the rulers themselves for such a result. The power that is now being raised by the spread of education, though yet slow and small, is one that in time must, for weal or woe, exercise great influence. In fact, it has already begun to do so. However strangely the English rulers, forgetting their English manliness and moral courage, may, like the ostrich, shut their eyes, by gagging acts or otherwise, to the good or bad influences they are raising around them, this good or evil is rising nevertheless. The thousands that are being sent out by the universities every year, find themselves in a most anomalous position. There is no place for them in their motherland. They may beg in the streets or break stones on the roads, for aught the rulers seem to care for their natural rights, position and duties in their own country. They may perish or do what they like or can, but scores of Europeans must go from this country [*i.e.*, Great Britain] to take up what belongs to them, and that, in spite of every profession for years and years past and up to the present day, of English statesmen, that they must govern India for India's good, by solemn acts and declarations of Parliament, and above all, by the words of the August Sovereign Herself. For all practical purposes all these high promises have been hitherto, almost wholly, the purest romance, the reality being quite different.

The educated find themselves simply so many dummies, ornamented with the tinsel of school-education, and then their whole end and aim of life is ended. What must be the inevitable consequence? A wild spirited horse, without curb or reins will run away wild, and kill and trample upon everyone that came in his way. A misdirected force will hit anywhere and destroy anything. The power that the rulers are, so far to their credit, raising, will, as a nemesis, recoil against themselves, if with this blessing of education, they do not do their whole duty to the country which trusts to their righteousness, and thus turn this good power to their own side. The nemesis is as clear from the present violence to nature, as disease and death arise from uncleanliness and rottenness. The voice of the power of the rising education is, no doubt, feeble at present. Like the infant, the present dissatisfaction is only crying at the pains it is suffering. Its notions have not taken any form or shape or course yet, but it is growing. Heaven only knows what it will grow to! He who runs may see, that if the present material and moral destruction of India continues, a great convulsion must inevitably arise, by which either India will be more and more crushed under the iron heel of despotism and destruction, or may succeed in shattering the destroying hand and power. Far, far is it from my earnest prayer and hope, that such should be the result of the British rule. In this rule, there is every element to produce immeasurable good, both to India and England, and no thinking native of India would wish to harm it, with all the hopes that are yet built upon the righteousness and conscience of the British statesmen and nation.

The whole duty and responsibility of bringing about this desired consummation lies upon the head and in the hands of the Indian authorities *in England.* It is no use screening themselves behind the fiction and excuse, that the viceroys and authorities in India are difficult to be got to do what they ought, or that they would do all that may be necessary. They neither can nor will do this. They cannot go against acts of Parliament on the one hand, and on the other, the pressure of European interests, and of European selfishness and guidance, is so heavy in India, that the viceroys in their first years are quite helpless and get committed to certain courses; and if in time, any of them, happening to have sufficient strength of character and confidence in their own judgment, are likely to take matters in their own hands, and with any moral courage, to resist interests, hostile or antagonistic to the good of the people, the end of their time begins to come near, their zeal and interest begin to flag, and soon they go away, leaving India to roll up Sisyphus' stone again, with a new viceroy. It is the highest Indian authority here, the Secretary of State for India, upon whom the responsibility wholly rests. He alone has the power, as a member of and with the weight of the British Cabinet, to guide the Parliament to acts worthy of the English character, conscience and nation. The glory or disgrace of the British in India, is in his hands. He has to make Parliament lay down by clear legislation, how India *shall* be governed for *"India's good,"* or it is hopeless for us to look forward for any relief from our present material and moral destruction, and for future elevation.

Englishmen sometimes indulge the notion that England is secure in the division and disunion among the various races and nationalities of India. But even in this, new forces are working their way. Those Englishmen who sleep such foolish sleep of security know precious little of what is going on. The kind of education that is being received by thousands of all classes and creeds, is throwing them all in a similar mold; a sympathy of sentiment, ideas, and aspirations is growing among them; and more particularly a political union and sympathy is the first fruit of the new awakening, as all feel alike their deprivation, and the degradation and destruction of their country. All differences of race and religion, and rivalry are gradually sinking before this common cause. This beginning, no doubt, is at present insignificant, but it is surely and steadily progressing. Hindus, Mahomadans, and Parsees are asking alike, whether the English rule was to be a blessing or a curse. Politics now engross their attention more and more. This is no longer a secret, or a state of things not quite open to those of our rulers who would see. It may be seen that there is scarcely any union among the different nationalities and races in any shape or ways of life, except only in political associations. In these associations, they go hand in hand with all the fervor and sympathy of a common cause. I would here touch upon a few incidents, little as they are, still showing how nature is working in its own quiet way.

Dr. Birdwood has brought to the notice of the English public certain songs now being spread among the people of Western India, against the destruction of Indian industry and arts. We may laugh at this as a futile attempt to shut out English machine-made cheaper goods against hand-made dearer ones. But little do we think what this movement is likely to grow into, and what new phases it may take in time. The songs are at present directed against English wares, but they are also a natural and effective preparation against other English things when the time comes, if the English in their blindness allow such times to come. The songs are full of loyalty, and I have not the remotest doubt in the sincerity of that loyalty. But if the present downward course of India continue, if the mass of the people at last begin to despair for any amelioration, and if educated youths, without the wisdom and experience of the world, become their leaders, it will be but a *very, very* short step from loyalty to disloyalty, to turn the course of indignation from English wares to English rule. The songs will remain the same; one word of curse for the rule will supply the spark.

Here is another little incident with its own significance. The London Indian Society, a political body of many of the native residents of London, had a dinner the other day, and they invited guests. The three guests were, one Hindu, one Mahomadan, and one Parsee. The society itself is a body representing nearly all the principal classes of India. It is small and may be laughed at as uninfluential and can do nothing. But it shows how a sympathy of political common cause is bringing the different classes together, and how, in time, such small seeds may grow into large trees. Every member of this little body is carrying back with him ideas, which as seeds may produce crops, sweet or bitter according to the cultivation they may receive at our rulers' hands.

I turn to one bright incident on the other side. True to their English nature and character, there are some Englishmen who try to turn the current of native thought toward an appreciation of English intentions, and to direct English thought toward a better understanding of England's duty to India. The East India Association is doing this beneficent work, more especially by the fair and English character of its course of bringing about free and full discussion upon every topic and from every point of view, so that by a sifting of the full expression of different views, truth may be elicited. Though yet little appreciated by the English public, the English members of this association are fulfilling the duty of patriotism to their own country and of benefaction toward India. How far their good efforts will succeed is yet to be seen. But they at least do one thing. These Englishmen, as well as public writers like Fawcett, Hyndman, Perry, Caird, Knight, Bell, Wilson, and others, vindicate to India the English character, and show that when Englishmen as a body will *understand* their duty and responsibility, the natives of India may fairly expect a conduct of which theirs is a sample—a desire and deed to act rightly by India. The example and earnestness of these Englishmen, though yet small their number, keep India's hope alive that England will produce a statesman who will have the moral courage and firmness to face the Indian problem, and do what the world should expect from England's conscience, and from England's mission to humanity.

I have thus touched upon a few incidents only, to illustrate the various influences that are at work. Whether the result of all these forces and influences will be good or bad, remains, as I have said, in the hands of the Secretary of State for India.

In my last paper, I said, the thinking natives were as yet staunch in their loyalty to the British rule, as they were yet fully hopeful of the future from the general character and history of the English people. They believe, that when the conscience of the English nation is awakened, it will not be long before India receives full and thorough redress for all she has been suffering. While thus hopeful of the future, it is desirable that our rulers should know and consider what about the past is passing in many a thinking native mind.

They are as grateful as any people can be, for whatever real good of peace and order and education has been done for them. But they also ask what good upon the whole England has done to India. It is sadly poor and increasing in poverty, both material and moral. They consider and bewail the unnatural treatment India has been receiving.

They dwell upon the strange contrast between the words and

deeds of the English rulers. How often deliberate and solemn promises are made and broken. I need not here instance again what I have at some length shown in my papers on the poverty of India[1] under the heading of "Nonfulfillment of Solemn Promises."[2]

I would refer here to one or two characteristic instances only. The conception for an engineering college in London was no sooner formed than it became an accomplished fact; and Mr. Grant Duff, then Undersecretary of State, in his place in Parliament, proclaimed what great boons "we" were conferring on the English people, but quite oblivious, at whose sacrifices. It was an English interest, and the thing was done as quick as it was thought of. On the other hand, a clause for native interests, proposed in 1867, took 3 years to pass, and in such a form as to be simply ineffectual. I asked Sir Stafford Northcote at the time of the proposal to make it in some way imperative, but without effect. Again, after being passed after 3 years, it remained a dead letter for 7 years more, and might have remained so till doomsday for aught any of the Indian authorities cared. But thanks to the persevering exertions of one of England's true sons, Sir Erskine Perry, some steps were at last taken to frame the rules that were required, and it is now, in the midst of a great deal of fine writing, making some, though very slow, progress. For such even as it is we are thankful, but greater efforts are necessary to stem the torrent of the drain. Turning to the uncovenanted service, Sir Stafford Northcote's dispatch of 8th February, 1868, declared that Europeans should not be allowed in this service to override "the inherent rights of the natives of the country." Now in what spirit was this dispatch treated till very lately? Was it not simply, or is it not even now, almost a dead letter?

In the matter of the load of the public debt of India, it is mainly due to the wars of the English conquests in India, and English wars abroad in the name of India. Not a farthing has been spent by England for its British Indian Empire. The burden of all England's wars in Asia has been thrown on India's shoulders.

In the Abyssinian War, India narrowly and lightly escaped, and in the present Afghan War, her escape from whatever portion she may be saved is not less narrow. Such though the character of nearly the whole of the public debt (excluding for public works) being caused by the actions by which England has become the Mistress of a great Empire and thereby the first nation in the world, she would not move her little finger to give India any such help as is within her power without even any material sacrifice to herself, *viz.*, that of guaranteeing this public debt, so that India may derive some little relief from reduced interest.

When English interests are concerned, their accomplishment is often a foregone conclusion. But India's interests always require long and anxious thought—thought that seldom begins, and when it does begin, seldom ends in any thorough good result. It is useless to conceal that the old pure and simple faith in the honor and word of the English rulers is much shaken, and were it not for the faith in the conscience of the statesmen and people in *this* country, any hope of good by an alteration of the present British Indian policy would be given up.

The English rulers boast and justly so, that they have introduced education and Western civilization into India, but on the other hand, they act as if no such thing had taken place, and as if all this boast was pure moonshine. Either they have educated or have not. If they deserve the boast, it is a strange self-condemnation, that after half a century or more of such efforts, they have not yet prepared a sufficient number of men fit for the service of their own country. Take even the educational department itself. We are made B.A.s and M.A.s and M.D.s, etc., with the strange result that we are not yet considered fit to teach our countrymen. We must have yet forced upon us even in this department, as in every other, every European that can be squeezed in. To keep up the sympathy and connection with the current of European thought, an English head may be appropriately and beneficially retained in a few of the most important institutions. But as matters are at present, all boast of education is exhibited as so much sham and delusion.

In the case of former foreign conquests, the invaders either retired with their plunder and booty, or became the rulers of the country. When they only plundered and went back away, they made no doubt great wounds, but India with her industry revived and healed the wounds. When the invaders became the rulers of the country, they settled down *in* it, and whatever was the condition of their rule, according to the character of the sovereign of the day, there was at least no material or moral drain from the country.[3] Whatever the country produced, remained in the country. Whatever wisdom and experience was acquired in her services, remained among her own people. With the English the case is peculiar. There are the great wounds of the first wars in the burden of the public debt, and those wounds are kept perpetually open and widening, by draining away the life blood in a continuous stream. The former rulers were like butchers hacking here and there, but the English with their scientific scalpel cut to the very heart, and yet, lo! there is no wound to be seen, and soon the plaster of the high talk of civilization, progress, and whatnot covers up the wound! The English rulers stand sentinel at the front door of India, challenging the whole world, that they do and shall protect India against all comers, and themselves carry away by a backdoor the very treasures they stand sentinel to protect.

In short, had England deliberately intended to devise the best means of taking away India's wealth, in a quiet continuous drain, without scandalizing the world, she could not have hit upon a more effectual plan than the present lines of policy. A viceroy tells that the people of India enjoy but scanty subsistence, and this is the outcome of the British rule.

No doubt, the exertions of individual Europeans at the time of famines may be worthy of admiration; the efforts of government and the aid of the contributions of the British people to save life, deserve every gratitude. But how strange it is, that the British rulers do not see that, after all, they themselves are the main cause of the destruction that ensues from droughts; that it is the drain of India's wealth by *them* that lays at their own door the dreadful results of misery, starvation, and deaths of millions. England does not know famines, be the harvest however bad or scanty. She has the means of buying her food from the whole world. India is being unceasingly deprived of these means, and when famine comes, the starving have to be taxed so much more to save the dying.

England's conduct in India is in strange contrast with her conduct with almost any other country. Owing to the false groove in which she is moving, she does violence to her own best instincts. She sympathizes with and helps every nationality that struggles for a constitutional representative government. On the one hand, she is the parent of and maintains the highest constitutionalism, and on the other she exercises a clear and, though thoughtlessly, a despoiling despotism in India, under a pseudo-constitutionalism in the shape of the farce of the present Legislative Councils.

Of all countries in the world, if any one has the greatest claim on England's consideration, to receive the boons of a constitutional representative government at her hands, and to have her people governed as England governs her own—that country is India, her most sacred trust and charge. But England, though she does everything she can for other countries, fights shy of, and makes some excuse or other to avoid, giving to the people of India their fair share in the legislation of their country. Now I do not mean to say that India can suddenly have a full-blown parliament and of such wide spread representation as England enjoys. But has England made any honest efforts to gradually introduce a true representation of the people, excepting some solitary exceptions of partial municipal representation? I need not dwell upon the present farce of the nomination system for the Legislative Councils and of the dummies that are sometimes nominated. I submit that a small beginning can be well made now. I would take the Bombay Presidency as an instance. Suppose the present Legislative Council is extended to 21 members, 13 of these to be nominated from officials and nonofficials by the government, and 8 to be elected by the principal towns of the Presidency. This will give government a clear majority of 5, and the representative element, the minority, cannot do any harm, or hamper government. In England the majority determines the government. In India this cannot be the case at present, and so the majority must follow the government. It would be, when something is extremely outrageous, that the minority would, by force of argument and truth, draw toward it the government majority, and even in any such rare instance, all that will happen will be, that government will be prevented from doing any such outrageous things. In short, in such an arrangement, government will remain all powerful, as it must for a long time to come, while there will be also independent persons actually representing the people to speak the sentiments of the people, thereby giving government the most important help and relieving them from much responsibility, anxiety, and mistakes. The representative element in the minority, will be gradually trained in constitutional government. They will have to maintain the reason of their existence, and will therefore be actuated by caution and good sense. They can do no harm but a vast amount of good both to the government and the governed. The people will have the satisfaction that their rulers were doing their duty and endeavoring to raise them to their own civilization.

There are in the Bombay Presidency the following towns of more than 50,000 population. Bombay having by far the largest, and with its importance as the capital of the Presidency, may be properly allowed 3 representatives.

The towns are:—

BOMBAY[4]	POONA	AHMEDABAD	SURAT	KARACHI	SHOLAPUR
644,405	118,886	116,873	107,149	53,526	53,403

Thus Bombay having 3—the Gujarat division of the Presidency will be represented by Ahmadabad and Surat, the Maharashtra portion by Poona and Sholapur, and Sind by Karachi, making altogether 8 members—which will be a fair though a small representation to begin with. Government may with advantage adopt a larger number; all I desire and insist is there must be a fair *representative* element in the councils. As to the qualifications of electors and candidates for election, government is quite competent to fix upon some, as they did in the case of the Bombay Corporation, and such qualifications may from time to time be modified as experience may suggest. With this modification in the present Legislative Council, a great step will have been taken toward one of the greatest boons which India asks and expects at England's hands. Without some such element of the people's voice in all the Legislative Councils, it is impossible for Englishmen, more and more estranged and isolated as they are becoming, to be able to legislate for India in the true spirit and feeling of her wants.

After having a glorious history of heroic struggles for constitutional government, England is now rearing up a body of Englishmen in India, trained up and accustomed to despotism, with all the feelings of impatience, pride, and high-handedness of the despot becoming gradually ingrained in them, and with the additional training of the dissimulation of constitutionalism. Is it possible that such habits and training of despotism, with which Indian officials return from India, should not, in the course of time, influence the English character and institutions? The English in India, instead of raising India, are hitherto themselves descending and degenerating to the lower level of Asiatic despotism. Is this a nemesis that will in fullness of time show to them, what fruit their conduct in India produced? It is extraordinary how nature may revenge itself for the present unnatural course of England in India, if England, not yet much tainted by this demoralization, do not, in good time, check this new leaven that is gradually fermenting among her people.

There is the opium trade. What a spectacle it is to the world. In England, no statesman dares to propose that opium may be allowed to be sold in public houses at the corners of every street, in the same way as beer or spirits. On the contrary, Parliament, as representing the whole nation, distinctly enacts "opium and all preparations of opium or of poppies" as "poison," to be sold by certified chemists only, and "every box, bottle, vessel, wrapper or cover in which such poison is contained, be distinctly labelled with the name of the article and the word Poison, and with the name and address of the seller of the Poison." And yet, at the other end of the world, this Christian, highly civilized, and humane England forces a "heathen" and "barbarous" power to take this "Poison," and tempts a vast human race to use it, and to degenerate and demoralize themselves with this "Poison." And why—because India cannot fill up the remorseless drain, so China must be dragged in to make it up, even though it be by being "Poisoned." It is wonderful, how England reconciles this to her conscience. This opium trade is a sin on England's head, and a curse on India for her share in being the instrument. This may sound strange as coming from any natives of India, as it is generally represented as if India it was that benefited by the opium trade. The fact simply is, as Mr. Duff said, India is nearly ground down to dust, and the opium trade of China fills up England's drain. India derives not a particle of benefit. All India's profits of trade, and several million from her very produce (scanty as it is and becoming more and more so), and with these, all the profit of opium go the same way of the drain to England. Only, India shares the curse of the Chinese race. Had this cursed opium trade not existed, India's miseries would have much sooner come to the surface, and relief and redress would have come to her long ago. But this trade has prolonged the agonies of India.

In association with this trade is the stigma of the salt tax upon the British name. What a humiliating confession to say that, after the length of the British rule, the people are in such a wretched plight that they have nothing that government can tax, and that government must, therefore, tax an absolute necessary of life to an inordinate extent. The slight flash of prosperity during the American War, showed how the people of India would enjoy and spend, when they have anything to enjoy and spend—and now, can anything be a greater condemnation of the results of British lines of policy than that the people have nothing to spend and enjoy, and pay tax on, but that they must be pinched and starved in a necessary of life.

The English are, and justly and gloriously, the greatest champions of liberty of speech. What a falling off must have taken place in their character, when, after granting this boon to India, they should have even thought of withdrawing it. This act, together with that of disarming the people, is a clear confession by the rulers to the world, that they have no hold as yet upon the affection and loyalty of the people, though in the same breath they make every profession of their belief in the loyalty of the people. Now which is the truth? And are gagging and disarming the outcome of a long benign rule?

Why do the English allow themselves to be so perpetually scared by the fears of Russian or any other foreign invasion? If the people of India be satisfied, if their hearts and hands be with England, she may defy a dozen Russias. On the other hand, do British statesmen think that, however sharp and pointed their bayonets, and however long-flying their bullets, they may not find the two hundred million people of India her political Himalaya to be pierced through, when the present political union among the different peoples is more strengthened and consolidated?

There is the stock argument of overpopulation. They talk, and so far truly, of the increase by British peace, but they quite forget the destruction by the British drain. They talk of the pitiless operations of economic laws, but, somehow, they forget that there is no such thing in India as the natural operation of economic laws. It is not the pitiless operations of economic laws, but it is the thoughtless and pitiless action of the British policy, it is the pitiless eating of India's substance in India, and the further pitiless drain to England—in short, it is the pitiless *perversion* of economic laws by the sad bleeding to which India is subjected that is destroying India. Why blame poor Nature, when the fault lies at your own door. Let natural and economic laws have their full and fair play, and India will become another England, with many fold greater benefit to England herself than at present.

As long as the English do not allow the country to produce what it can produce; as long as the people are not allowed to enjoy what they can produce; as long as the English are the very party on their trial—they have no right, and are not competent, to give an opinion, whether the country is overpopulated or not. In fact, it is absurd to talk of overpopulation, *i.e.*, the country's incapability, by its food or other produce, to supply the means of support to its people, if the country is unceasingly and forcibly deprived of its means or capital. Let the country keep what it produces, and then can any right judgment be formed whether it is overpopulated or not. Let England first hold hands off India's wealth, and then there will be disinterestedness in, and respect for, her judgment. The present cant of the excuse of overpopulation is adding a distressful insult to agonizing injury. To talk of overpopulation at present is just as reasonable as to cut off a man's hands and then to taunt him that he was not able to maintain himself or move his hands.

When persons talk of the operation of economic laws, they forget the very first and fundamental principles. Says Mr. Mill, "Industry is limited by capital." "To employ industry on the land, is to apply capital to the land." "Industry cannot be employed to any greater extent than there is capital to invest." "There can be no more industry than is supplied by materials to work up and food to eat. Yet, in regard to a fact so evident, it was long continued to be believed that laws and governments, without creating capital, could create industry." And while Englishmen are sweeping away this very capital, they raise up their hands and wonder why India cannot have industry.

The English are themselves the head and front of the offending, and yet they talk of overpopulation, and every mortal irrelevant thing, but the right cause, *viz.*, their own drain of the material and moral wealth of the country.

The present form of relations between the paramount power and the Princes of India is un-English and iniquitous. Fancy a people, the greatest champions of fair play and justice, having a system of political agency, by which, as the Princes say, they are stabbed in the dark; the political agents making secret reports and the government often acting thereon, without a fair inquiry or explanation from the Princes. The Princes, therefore, are always in a state of alarm, as to what may befall them unawares. If the British authorities deliberately wished to adopt a method

by which the Princes should always remain alarmed and ir-
ritated, they could not have hit upon a more effective one than
what exists. If these Princes can feel assured that their treaty
rights will be always honorably and faithfully observed, that
there will be no constant nibbling at their powers, that it was not
the ulterior policy of the British to pull them down gradually to
the position of the mere nobles of the country, as the Princes
at present suspect and fear, and if a more just and fair mode of
political agency be adopted, I have not the least hesitation in
saying that, as much from self-interest alone as from any other
motive, these Princes will prove the greatest bulwark and help
to perpetuate British supremacy in India. It stands to reason and
common sense that the native Princes clearly understand their
interest, that by a power like the British only, with all the confidence it may command by its fairness as well as strength, can
they be saved from the paramount power, they will the more
readily listen to counsels of reform which they much need. The
English can then exercise their salutary influence in advising and
helping them to root out the old corrupt regimes, and in making
them and their courtiers to understand that power was not self-
aggrandizement, but responsibility for the good of the people.
I say from personal conversation with some of the Princes, that
they thoroughly understood their interest under the protection
of the present paramount power.

It is useless for the British to compare themselves with the past
native rulers. If the British do not show themselves to be vastly
superior, in proportion to their superior enlightenment and civilization, if India does not prosper and progress under them far
more largely, there will be no justification for their existence in
India. The thoughtless past drain we may consider as our misfortune, but a similar future will, in plain English, be deliberate
plunder and destruction.

I do not repeat here several other views which I have already
expressed in my last Memorandum.

I have thus given a general sketch of what is passing in many
natives' minds on several subjects. It is useless and absurd to
remind us constantly, that, once, the British fiat brought order

out of chaos, and to make that an everlasting excuse for subsequent shortcomings and the material and moral impoverishment of the country. The natives of the present day have not seen that chaos, and do not feel it, and though they understand it, and very thankful they are for the order brought, they see the present drain, distress, and destruction, and they feel it and bewail it.

By all means, let Englishmen be proud of the past. We accord them every credit for the order and law they brought about, and are deeply thankful to them, but let them now face the present, let them clearly realize, and manfully acknowledge the many shortcomings of omission and commission by which, with the best of intentions, they have reduced India to material and moral wretchedness: and let them, in a way worthy of their name and history, repair the injury they have inflicted. It is fully in their power, to make their rule a blessing to India, and a benefit and glory to England, by allowing India her own administration under their superior, controlling and guiding hand—or in their own oft-repeated professions and words, "by governing India for India's good."

May the God of all nations lead the English to a right sense of their duty to India, is my humble and earnest prayer!

NOTES

1. East India Association's journal, Vol. IX, pages 375 to 405.
2. The Duke of Argyll, as Secretary of State for India, said in his speech of 11th March, 1869, with regard to the employment of natives in the covenanted service: "I must say that we have not fulfilled our duty or the promises and engagements which we have made."
3. Sir Stafford Northcote, in his speech in Parliament on 24th May 1867, said: "Nothing could be more wonderful than our empire in India, but we ought to consider on what conditions we held it, and how our predecessors held it. The greatness of the Mogul empire depended upon the liberal policy that was pursued by men like Akbar availing themselves of Hindu talent and assistance, and identifying themselves as far as possible with the people of the country. He thought that they ought to take a lesson from such a circumstance, and if they

were to do their duty towards India they could only discharge that duty by obtaining the assistance and counsel of all who were great and good in that country. It would be absurd in them to say that there was not a large fund of statesmanship and ability in the Indian character."—*Times*, of 25th May, 1867.

4. Statistical abstract of British India—1879, page 21.

15. THE PAN-AFRICAN MOVEMENT *

W. E. Burghardt DuBois

The idea of one Africa uniting the thought and ideals of all native peoples of the dark continent belongs to the twentieth century, and stems naturally from the West Indies and the United States. Here various groups of Africans, quite separate in origin, became so united in experience, and so exposed to the impact of a new culture, that they began to think of Africa as one idea and one land. Thus, late in the eighteenth century, when a separate Negro Church was formed in Philadelphia, it called itself "African"; and there were various "African" societies in many parts of the United States.

It was not, however, until 1900 that a black West Indian barrister, H. Sylvester-Williams, of Trinidad, practicing in London, called together a "Pan-African" Conference. This meeting attracted attention, put the word "Pan-African" in the dictionaries for the first time, and had some thirty delegates, mainly from England and the West Indies, with a few colored Americans. The Conference was welcomed by the Lord Bishop of London, and a promise was obtained from Queen Victoria through Joseph

*From *Colonial and Coloured Unity,* George Padmore, ed., Manchester, n.d., pp. 13–26.

Chamberlain not to "overlook the interests and welfare of the native races."

This meeting had no deep roots in Africa itself, and the movement and the idea died for a generation. Then at its close there was determined agitation for the rights of Negroes throughout the world, particularly in Africa. Meetings were held, a petition was sent to President Wilson, and finally, by indirection, I secured passage on the Creel press boat, the *Orizaba*, and landed in France in December, 1918.

I went with the idea of calling a "Pan-African Congress" and trying to impress upon the members of the Peace Congress sitting at Versailles the importance of Africa in the future world. I was without credentials or influence, but the idea took on.

I tried to get a conference with President Wilson, but only got as far as Colonel House, who was sympathetic but noncommittal. The Chicago *Tribune* said, January 19th, 1919, in a dispatch from Paris dated December 30th, 1918:

An Ethiopian Utopia, to be fashioned out of the German Colonies, is the latest dream of leaders of the Negro race who are here at the invitation of the United States Government as part of the extensive entourage of the American peace delegation. Robert R. Moton, successor of the late Booker Washington as head of Tuskegee Institute, and Dr. William E.B. DuBois, Editor of the *Crisis*, are promoting a Pan-African Conference to be held here during the winter while the Peace Conference is on full blast. It is to embrace Negro leaders from America, Abyssinia, Liberia, Haiti, and the French and British colonies and other parts of the black world. Its object is to get out of the Peace Conference an effort to modernize the dark continent, and in the world reconstruction to provide international machinery looking toward the civilization of the African natives.

The Negro leaders are not agreed upon any definite plan, but Dr. DuBois has mapped out a scheme which he has presented in the form of a memorandum to President Wilson. It is quite Utopian, and it has less than a Chinaman's chance of getting anywhere in the Peace Conference, but it is nevertheless interesting. As "self-determination" is one of the words to conjure with in Paris nowadays, the Negro leaders are seeking to have it applied, if possible, in a measure to their race in Africa.

Dr. DuBois' dream is that the Peace Conference could form an internationalized Africa, to have as its basis the former German colonies, with their 1,000,000 square miles and 12,500,000 population.

"To this," his plan reads, "could be added by negotiation the 800,000 square miles and 9,000,000 inhabitants of Portuguese Africa. It is not impossible that Belgium could be persuaded to add to such a State the 900,000 square miles and 9,000,000 natives of the Congo, making an international Africa with over 2,500,000 square miles of land and over 20,000,000 people.

"This Africa for the Africans could be under the guidance of international organization. The governing international commission should represent not simply Governments, but modern culture, science, commerce, social reform, and religious philanthropy. It must represent not simply the white world, but the civilised Negro world.

"With these two principles the practical policies to be followed out in the government of the new States should involve a thorough and complete system of modern education, built upon the present government, religion, and customary law of the churches. Within ten years 20,000,000 black children ought to be in school. Within a generation young Africa should know the essential outlines of modern culture. From the beginning the actual general government should use both coloured and white officials.

"We can, if we will, inaugurate on the dark continent a last great crusade for humanity. With Africa redeemed, Asia would be safe and Europe indeed triumphant."

Members of the American delegation and associated experts assured me that no congress on this matter could be held in Paris because France was still under martial law; but the ace that I had up my sleeve was Blaise Diagne, the black deputy from Senegal and Commissaire-Général in charge of recruiting native African troops. I went to Diagne and sold him the idea of a Pan-African Congress. He consulted Clemenceau, and the matter was held up two wet, discouraging months. But finally we got permission to hold the Congress in Paris. "Don't advertise it," said Clemenceau, "but go ahead." Walter Lippmann wrote me in his crabbed hand, February 20th, 1919: "I am very much interested in your organization of the Pan-African Conference, and glad that Clemenceau has made it possible. Will you send me whatever reports you may have on the work?"

The *Dispatch*, Pittsburgh, Pennsylvania, February 16th, 1919, said: "Officials here are puzzled by the news from Paris that plans are going forward there for a Pan-African Conference to be held February 19th. Acting Secretary Polk said today the State Department had been officially advised by the French Government that no such Conference would be held. It was announced recently that no passports would be issued for American delegates desiring to attend the meeting." But at the very time that Polk was assuring American Negroes that no Congress would be held, the Congress actually assembled in Paris.

First Pan-African Congress

This Congress represented Africa partially. Of the fifty-seven delegates from fifteen countries, nine were African countries with twelve delegates. The other delegates came from the United States, which sent sixteen, and the West Indies, with twenty-one. Most of these delegates did not come to France for this meeting, but happened to be residing there, mainly for reasons connected with the war. America and all the colonial powers refused to issue special visas.

The Congress influenced the Peace Conference. The New York *Evening Globe*, February 22nd, 1919, described it as "the first assembly of the kind in history, and has for its object the drafting of an appeal to the Peace Conference to give the Negro race of Africa a chance to develop unhindered by other races. Seated at long green tables in the council room today were Negroes in the trim uniform of American Army officers, other American colored men in frock coats or business suits, polished French Negroes who hold public office, Senegalese who sit in the French Chamber of Deputies. . . ."

The Congress specifically asked that the German colonies be turned over to an international organization instead of being handled by the various colonial powers. Out of this idea came the Mandates Commission. The resolutions of the Congress said in part:

(a) That the Allied and Associated Powers establish a code of law for the international protection of the natives of Africa, similar to the proposed international code for labor.

(b) That the League of Nations establish a permanent Bureau charged with the special duty of overseeing the application of these laws to the political, social, and economic welfare of the natives.

(c) The Negroes of the world demand that hereafter the natives of Africa and the peoples of African descent be governed according to the following principles:

1. *The land* and its natural resources shall be held in trust for the natives and at all times they shall have effective ownership of as much land as they can profitably develop.

2. *Capital:* The investment of capital and granting of concessions shall be so regulated as to prevent the exploitation of the natives and the exhaustion of the natural wealth of the country. Concessions shall always be limited in time and subject to State control. The growing social needs of the natives must be regarded and the profits taxed for social and material benefit of the natives.

3. *Labor:* Slavery and corporal punishment shall be abolished and forced labor except in punishment for crime; and the general conditions of labor shall be prescribed and regulated by the State.

4. *Education:* It shall be the right of every native child to learn to read and write his own language and the language of the trustee nation, at public expense, and to be given technical instruction in some branch of industry. The State shall also educate as large a number of natives as possible in higher technical instruction in some branch of industry. The State shall also educate as large a number of natives as possible in higher technical and cultural training and maintain a corps of native teachers . . .

5. *The State:* The natives of Africa must have the right to participate in the Government as far as their development permits in conformity with the principle that the Government exists for the natives, and not the natives for the Government. They shall at once be allowed to participate in local and tribal government according to ancient usage, and this participation shall gradually extend, as education and experience proceeds to the higher offices of State, to the end that, in time, Africa be ruled by consent of the Africans. . . . Whenever it is proven that at the hands of any State or that any State deliberately excludes its civilized citizens or subjects of Negro descent from its body politic and cultural, it shall be the duty of the League of Nations to bring the matter to the civilized World.

The New York *Herald*, Paris, February 24th, 1919, said: "There is nothing unreasonable in the programme, drafted at the

Pan-African Congress which was held in Paris last week. It calls upon the Allied and Associated Powers to draw up an international code of law for the protection of the nations of Africa, and to create, as a section of the League of Nations, a permanent bureau to ensure observance of such laws and thus further the racial, political, and economic interests of the natives."

Second Pan-African Congress

The idea of Pan-Africa having been thus established, we attempted to build a real organization. We went to work first to assemble a more authentic Pan-African Congress and movement. We corresponded with Negroes in all parts of Africa and in other parts of the world, and finally arranged for a Congress to meet in London, Brussels and Paris, in August and September, 1921. Of the hundred and thirteen delegates to this Congress, forty-one were from Africa, thirty-five from the United States, twenty-four represented Negroes living in Europe, and seven were from the West Indies. Thus the African element showed growth. They came for the most part, but not in all cases, as individuals, and more seldom as the representatives of organizations or of groups.

The Pan-African movement thus began to represent a growth and development; but it immediately ran into difficulties. First of all, there was the natural reaction of war and the determination on the part of certain elements in England, Belgium, and elsewhere, to recoup their war losses by intensified exploitation of colonies. They were suspicious of native movements of any sort. Then, too, there came simultaneously another movement, stemming from the West Indies, which accounted for our small West Indian representation. This was in its way a people's movement rather than a movement of the intellectuals. It was led by Marcus Garvey, and it represented a poorly conceived but intensely earnest determination to unite the Negroes of the world, more especially in commercial enterprise. It used all the nationalist and racial paraphernalia of popular agitation, and its strength lay in its backing by the masses of West Indians and by increasing numbers of American Negroes. Its weakness lay in its demagogic leadership, its intemperate propaganda, and the natural fear which it threw into the colonial powers.

The London meetings of the Congress were held in Central Hall, opposite Westminster Abbey, August 28th and 29th, 1921. They were preceded by conference with the International Department of the English Labour Party, where the question of the relation of white and colored labor was discussed. Beatrice Webb, Leonard Woolf, Mr. Gillies, Norman Leys, and others were present.

Paul Otlet, once called Father of the League of Nations, wrote me in April, 1921: "I am very happy to learn your decision. We can put at your disposal the Palais Mondial for your Pan-African Conference, August 31st and September 1st and 2nd." Otlet and La Fontaine, the Belgian leaders of internationalism, welcomed the meeting warmly to Belgium, but strong opposition arose. The movement was immediately confounded by the press and others as a part of, if not the real, "Garvey Movement."

The Brussels *Neptune* wrote, June 14th: "Announcement has been made . . . of a Pan-African Congress organized at the instigation of the National Association for the Advancement of Colored People of New York. It is interesting to note that this association is directed by personages who it is said in the United States have received remuneration from Moscow (Bolsheviki). The association has already organized its propaganda in the lower Congo, and we must not be astonished if some day it causes grave difficulties in the Negro village of Kinshasa, composed of all the ne'er-do-wells of the various tribes of the Colony, aside from some hundreds of laborers."

Nevertheless, meetings of interest and enthusiasm were held. The *Crisis* reported: "The Congress itself was held in the marvelous Palais Mondial, the World Palace situated in the Cinquantenaire Park. We could not have asked for a better setting. But there was a difference. In the first place, there were many more white than colored people—there are not many of us in Brussels—and it was not long before we realized that their interest was deeper, more immediately significant, than that of the white people we had found elsewhere. Many of Belgium's economic and material interests center in Africa in the Belgian Congo. Any interference with the natives might result in an interference with the sources from which so many Belgian capitalists drew their prosperity."

Resolutions which were passed without dissent at the meeting in London contained a statement concerning Belgium, criticizing her colonial regime although giving her credit for plans of reform for the future. This aroused bitter opposition in Brussels, and an attempt was made to substitute an innocuous statement concerning good will and investigation which Diagne declared adopted in the face of a clear majority in opposition.

At the Paris meeting the original London resolutions, with some minor corrections, were adopted. They were in part:

To the World: The absolute equality of races, physical, political, and social, is the founding stone of world and human advancement. No one denies great differences of gift, capacity, and attainment among individuals of all races, but the voice of Science, Religion, and practical Politics is one in denying the God-appointed existence of super-races, or of races, naturally and inevitably and eternally inferior.

That in the vast range of time, one group should in its industrial technique, or social organisation, or spiritual vision, lag a few hundred years behind another, or forge fitfully ahead, or come to differ decidedly in thought, deed and ideal, is proof of the essential richness and variety of human nature, rather than proof of the co-existence of demi-gods and apes in human form. The doctrine of racial equality does not interfere with individual liberty: rather it fulfils it. And of all the various criteria by which masses of men have in the past been prejudged and classified, that of the colour of the skin and texture of the hair is surely the most adventitious and idiotic . . .

The beginning of wisdom in interracial contact is the establishment of political institutions among suppressed peoples. The habit of democracy must be made to encircle the earth. Despite the attempts to prove that its practice is the secret and divine gift of the few, no habit is more natural or more widely spread among primitive people, or more easily capable of development among masses. Local self-government with a minimum of help and oversight can be established tomorrow in Asia, in Africa, America, and the isles of the sea. It will in many instances need general control and guidance, but it will fail only when that guidance seeks ignorantly and consciously its own selfish ends and not the people's liberty and good.

Surely in the twentieth century of the Prince of Peace, in the millennium of Muhammad, and in the mightiest Age of Human Reason, there can be found in the civilized world enough of altruism, yearning, and benevolence to develop native institutions whose aim is not profit and power of the few. . . .

What, then, do those demand who see these evils of the color line and racial discrimination, and who believe in the divine right of suppressed and backward people to learn and aspire and be free? The Negro race through their thinking intelligentsia demand:

1. *The recognition* of civilized men as civilized despite their race or color.
2. *Local* self-government for backward groups, deliberately rising as experience and knowledge grow to complete self-government under the limitation of a self-governed world.
3. *Education* in self-knowledge, in scientific truth, and in industrial technique, undivorced from the art of beauty.
4. *Freedom* in their own religion and social customs and with the right to be different and nonconformist.
5. *Cooperation* with the rest of the world in government, industry, and art on the bases of Justice, Freedom, and Peace.
6. *The return* to Negroes of their land and its natural fruits, and defense against the unrestrained greed of invested capital.
7. *The establishment* under the League of Nations of an international institution for study of the Negro problems.
8. *The establishment* of an international section of the Labor Bureau of the League of Nations, charged with the protection of native labor . . . .

In some such words and thoughts as these we seek to express our will and ideal, and the end of our untiring effort. To our aid, we call all men of the earth who love justice and mercy. Out of the depths we have cried unto the deaf and dumb masters of the world. Out of the depths we cry to our own sleeping souls. The answer is written in the stars.

The whole press of Europe took notice of these meetings, and more especially of the ideas behind the meeting. Gradually they began to distinguish between the Pan-African movement and the Garvey agitation. They praised and criticized. Sir Harry Johnston wrote: "This is the weakness of all the otherwise grand efforts of the Coloured People in the United States to pass on their own elevation and education and political significance to the Coloured Peoples of Africa: they know so little about real Africa."

Even *Punch* took a good-natured jibe (September 7th, 1921): " 'A PAN AFRICAN MANIFESTO,' 'NO ETERNALLY INFERIOR RACES' (headlines in *The Times*). No, but in the opinion of our coloured brothers some infernally superior ones!"

The Second Pan-African Congress had sent me with a committee to interview the officials of the League of Nations in Geneva. I talked with Rappard, who headed the Mandates Commission; I saw the first meeting of the Assembly; and especially I had an interesting interview with Albert Thomas, head of the ILO. Working with Monsieur Bellegarde of Haiti, a member of the Assembly, we brought the status of Africa to the attention of the League. The League published our petition as an official document, saying in part:

The Second Pan-African Congress wishes to suggest that the spirit of the world moves toward self-government as the ultimate aim of all men and nations, and that consequently the mandated areas, being peopled as they are so largely by black folk, have a right to ask that a man of Negro descent, properly fitted in character and training, be appointed a member of the Mandates Commission so soon as a vacancy occurs.

The Second Pan-African Congress desires most earnestly and emphatically to ask the good offices and careful attention of the League of Nations to the condition of civilized persons of Negro descent throughout the world. Consciously and subconsciously, there is in the world today a widespread and growing feeling that it is permissible to treat civilized men as uncivilized if they are colored and more especially of Negro descent. The result of this attitude and many consequent laws, customs, and conventions, is that a bitter feeling of resentment, personal insult, and despair is widespread in the world among those very persons whose rise is the hope of the Negro race.

We are fully aware that the League of Nations has little, if any, direct power to adjust these matters, but it has the vast moral power of public world opinion, and as a body conceived to promote Peace and Justice among men. For this reason we ask and urge that the League of Nations take a firm stand on the absolute equality of races, and that it suggest to the colonial powers connected with the League of Nations to form an International Institute for the study of the Negro problem, and for the evolution and protection of the Negro race.

Later Bellegarde revealed to the world the disgrace of the bombing of the African Bondelschwartz, and in retaliation was recalled by the American forces then in power in Haiti.

We sought to have these meetings result in a permanent organization. A secretariat was set up in Paris and functioned for a couple of years, but it was not successful. Just as the Garvey Movement made its thesis industrial cooperation, so the new young secretary of the Pan-African movement, a colored Paris public school teacher, wanted to combine investment and profit with the idea of Pan-Africa. He wanted American Negro capital for this end. We had other ideas.

Third Pan-African Congress

This crucial difference of aim and method between our Paris office and the American Negroes interested in the movement nearly ruined the organization. The Third Pan-African Congress was called for 1923, but the Paris secretary postponed it. We persevered, and finally, without proper notice or preparation, met in London and Lisbon late in the year. The London session was small and was addressed by Harold Laski and Lord Olivier and attended by H.G. Wells. Ramsay McDonald was kept from attending only by the pending election, but wrote: "Anything I can do to advance the cause of your people on your recommendation, I shall always do gladly."

The meeting of the Congress in Lisbon was more successful. Eleven countries were represented there, and especially Portuguese Africa. The Liga Africana was in charge. "The great association of Portuguese Negroes with headquarters at Lisbon which is called the Liga Africana is an actual federation of all the indigenous associations scattered throughout the five provinces of Portuguese Africa and representing several million individuals. . . . This Liga Africana which functions at Lisbon in the very heart of Portugal, so to speak, has a commission from all the other native organizations and knows how to express to the Government in no ambiguous terms but in a highly dignified manner all that should be said to avoid injustice or to bring about the repeal of harsh laws. That is why the Liga Africana of Lisbon is the director of the Portuguese African movement; but not only in the good sense of the word, but without making any appeal to violence and without leaving constitutional limits."

Two former colonial ministers spoke, and the following demands were made for Africans:

1. *A voice* in their own government.
2. *The right* of access to the land and its resources.
3. *Trial by* juries of their peers under established forms of law.
4. *Free elementary* education for all; broad training in modern industrial technique; and higher training of selected talent.
5. *The development* of Africa for the benefit of Africans, and not merely for the profit of Europeans.
6. *The abolition* of the slave trade and of the liquor traffic.
7. *World disarmament* and the abolition of war; but failing this, and as long as white folk bear arms against black folk, the right of blacks to bear arms in their own defense.
8. *The organization* of commerce and industry so as to make the main objects of capital and labor the welfare of the many rather than the enriching of the few. . . .

In fine, we ask in all the world, that black folk be treated as men. We can see no other road to Peace and Progress. What more paradoxical figure today fronts the world than the official head of a great South African state striving blindly to build Peace and Good Will in Europe by standing on the necks and hearts of millions of black Africans?

From that Lisbon meeting I went to Africa for the first time, to see the land whose history and development I had so long been studying. I held from President Coolidge of the United States status as Special Minister Plenipotentiary and Envoy Extraordinary to represent him at the second inaugural of President King of Liberia.

So far, the Pan-African idea was still American rather than African, but it was growing, and it expressed a real demand for examination of the African situation and a plan of treatment from the native African point of view. With the object of moving the center of this agitation nearer other African centers of population, I planned a Fourth Pan-African Congress in the West Indies in 1925. My idea was to charter a ship and sail down the Caribbean, stopping for meetings in Jamaica, Haiti, Cuba, and the French islands. But here I reckoned without my steamship lines. At first the French Line replied that they could "easily manage the trip," but eventually no accommodation could be found on any line except at the prohibitive price of fifty thousand dollars. I suspect that colonial powers spiked this plan.

Fourth Pan-African Congress

Two years later, in 1927, a Fourth Pan-African Congress was held in New York. Thirteen countries were represented, but direct African participation lagged. There were two hundred and eight delegates from twenty-two American states and ten foreign countries. Africa was sparsely represented by representatives from the Gold Coast, Sierra Leone, Liberia, and Nigeria. Chief Amoah III of the Gold Coast spoke; Herskovits then of Columbia, Mensching of Germany, and John Vandercook were on the program. The resolution stressed six points:

Negroes everywhere need:
1. *A voice* in their own government.
2. *Native rights* to the land and its natural resources.
3. *Modern education* for all children.
4. *The development* of Africa for the Africans and not merely for the profit of Europeans.
5. *The reorganization* of commerce and industry so as to make the main

object of capital and labor the welfare of the many rather than the enriching of the few.

6. *The treatment* of civilized men as civilized despite difference of birth, race, or color.

The Pan-African Movement had been losing ground since 1921. In 1929, to remedy this, we made desperate efforts to hold the Fifth Pan-African Congress on the continent of Africa itself, and selected Tunis because of its accessibility. Elaborate preparations were begun. It looked as though at last the movement was going to be geographically African. But two insuperable difficulties intervened: first, the French Government very politely but firmly informed us that the Congress could take place at Marseilles or any French city, but not in Africa; and finally, there came the Great Depression.

Fifth Pan-African Congress

The Pan-African idea died, apparently, until fifteen years afterwards, in the midst of the Second World War, when it leaped to life again in an astonishing manner. At the Trades Union Conference in London in the winter of 1945 there were black labor representatives from Africa and the West Indies. Among these, aided by colored persons resident in England, there came a spontaneous call for the assembling of another Pan-African Congress in 1945, when the International Trades Union had their meeting in Paris.

After consultation and correspondence a Pan-African Federation was organized.

On August eleventh and twelfth there was convened at Manchester, the headquarters of the Pan-African Federation, a Delegate Conference representing all of the organizations which have been invited to participate in the forthcoming Congress. At that ad hoc meeting a review of the preparatory work was made. From the reports it revealed that the position was as follows:

A number of replies had been received from Labour, Trade Union, Co-operative, and other progressive organizations in the West Indies, West Africa, South and East Africa, in acknowledgment of the formal invitation to attend the Conference. Most of these bodies not only approved and endorsed the agenda, making minor modifications and suggestions here and there, but pledged themselves to send delegates. In cases where either the time is too short or the difficulties of transport at the present time too great to be overcome at such short notice, the organizations will give mandates to the natives of the territories concerned who are travelling to Paris to attend the World Trades Union Conference. Where territories will not be sending delegates to the Trades Union Conference, organizations will mandate individuals already in Great Britain to represent them.

In this way we are assured of the widest representation, either through people travelling directly from the colonial areas to Britain, or individuals from those territories who are already in the British Isles. Apart from these overseas delegates, more than fourteen organizations of Africans and peoples of African descent in Great Britain and Ireland will participate in the Conference.

There is no organization in the British colonial empire which has not been invited. The philosophy back of this meeting has been expressed by the West African Students Union of London in a letter to me:

The idea of a Congress of African nations and all peoples of African descent throughout the world is both useful and timely. Perhaps it is even long overdue. But we observe that four of such Pan-African Congresses had been held in the past, all within recent memory, and that the one at present under discussion will be the fifth. It is unfortunate that all these important conferences should have been held outside Africa, but in European capitals. This point is significant, and should deserve our careful attention. . . .

Our Executive Committee are certainly not in favour of this or any future Pan-African Congress being held anywhere in Europe. We do rather suggest the Republic of Liberia as perhaps an ideal choice. All considerations seem to make that country the most favourable place for our Fifth Pan-African Congress. And, especially, at a time like this when Liberia is planning to celebrate the centenary of the founding of the Republic two years hence, the holding of our Congress there seems most desirable. We have good reason to believe that the Government of Liberia would welcome this idea, and would give us the encouragement and diplomatic assistance that might be necessary to ensure success.

The convening committee agrees that: "After reviewing the

situation, we do feel, like you, that our Conference should be merely a preliminary one to a greater, more representative Congress to be held some time next year, especially as a new Government has come into being in Britain since we started planning the forthcoming Conference." But they decided to call a congress this year in Manchester, since "it is now officially announced that the World Trades Union Conference will begin on September twenty-fifth and close on October ninth, we are planning to convene the Pan-African Congress on October fifteenth. It should last a week. This will enable the colonial delegates to get from France to England between the ninth and fifteenth of October. It will also enable us to hold some informal meetings and finish off our plans."

Difficulties of transportation and passport restrictions may make attendance at this Congress limited. At the same time there is real hope here, that out of Africa itself, and especially out of its laboring masses, has come a distinct idea of unity in ideal and cooperation in action which will lead to a real Pan-African movement.

Singularly enough, there is another "Pan-African" movement. I thought of it as I sat recently in San Francisco and heard Jan Smuts plead for an article on "human rights" in the preamble of the Charter of the United Nations. It was an astonishing paradox. The Pan-African movement which he represents is a union of the white rulers of Kenya, Rhodesia, and Union of South Africa, to rule the African continent in the interest of its white investors and exploiters. This plan has been incubating since 1921, but has been discouraged by the British Colonial Office. Smuts is now pushing it again, and the white legislatures in Africa have asked for it. The San Francisco trusteeship left a door open for this sort of thing. Against this upsurges the movement of black union delegates working in cooperation with the labor delegates of Russia, Great Britain, and the United States in order to build a new world which includes black Africa. We may yet live to see Pan-Africa as a real movement.

16. THE 'CIRCLE'*

⊓⊔⊓⊔⊓⊔⊓⊔⊓⊔⊓⊔⊓⊔⊓⊔⊓⊔⊓⊔⊓

NAME   . . . . THE CIRCLE
MOTTO   . . . . The three S's: Service, Sacrifice, Suffering.
AIM   . . . . 1. To maintain ourselves and The Circle as
                   the Revolutionary Vanguard of the struggle
                   for West Africa Unity and National Inde-
                   pendence.
                2. To support the idea and claims of the All
                   West African National Congress in its
                   struggle to create and maintain a Union of
                   African Socialist Republics.

Introduction

Since no movement can endure unless there is a stable organisation of trained, selected and trusted men to maintain continuity and carry out its programme forward to successful
conclusion.

*From *Report of the Commission of Enquiry into Disturbances in the Gold
Coast, 1948*, Colonial no. 231, Appendix II, p. 92.

And since the more widely the masses of the African peoples are drawn into the struggle for freedom and national independence of their country, the more necessary it is to have an organisation such as THE CIRCLE to establish stability and thereby making it impossible and difficult for demagogues, quislings, traitors, cowards and selfseekers to lead astray any section of the masses of the African peoples.

And since, in a country like West Africa with foreign, despotic and imperialist governments the more necessary it is to restrict THE CIRCLE to persons who are trained and engaged in political revolution as a profession, and who have also been trained in the art of combating all manner of political intrigues and persecutions thereby making it difficult for any one to disrupt the national liberation movement.

I, therefore, accept and abide by the laws of THE CIRCLE which are as follows:—

1. I will irrevocably obey and act upon the orders, commands, instructions and directions of the Grand Council of THE CIRCLE.

2. I will always serve, sacrifice and suffer anything for the cause for which THE CIRCLE stands, and will at all times be ready to go on any mission that I may be called upon to perform.

3. I will always and in all circumstances help a member brother of THE CIRCLE in all things and in all difficulties.

4. I will, except as a last resort, avoid the use of violence.

5. I will make it my aim and duty to foster the cause for which THE CIRCLE stands in any organisation that I may become a member.

6. I will on the 21st day of each month fast from sunrise to sunset and will meditate daily on the cause THE CIRCLE stands for.

7. I accept the Leadership of Kwame Nkrumah.

Oath of Allegiance

On my life honour and fortunes, I solemnly pledge and swear that I shall always live up to the aims and aspirations of the THE CIRCLE, and shall never under any circumstances divulge any secrets, plans or movements of THE CIRCLE, nor betray a member brother of THE CIRCLE; and that if I dare to divulge any secrets, plans and movements of THE CIRCLE, or betray a member brother or the cause, or use the influence of THE CIRCLE for my own personal interests or advertisement, I do so at my own risk and peril.

Duties of Circle Members

1. Each circle member should join an organisation and should adopt two methods of approach:
    a) Advocate and work for the demands and needs of that Organisation.
    b) Infuse that Organisation withe the spirit of national unity and the national independence of West Africa, and the creation and maintenance of the Union of African Socialist Republics.

Circle Fund

Members of each branch of THE CIRCLE shall maintain a fund by voluntary contributions, such fund to be used for furthering the cause of THE CIRCLE only.

Circle Meetings

The Grand Council of THE CIRCLE shall meet at least once a year and shall decide general policy and give directives to territorial and local branches of THE CIRCLE. Members of each branch of THE CIRCLE shall meet on the 21st day of each month, and at such other times as members may deem advisable.

Circle Communication

A close liaison shall at all times be maintained between the Grand council and the individual territorial and local branches of THE CIRCLE. As far as possible all communications should be done by personal contact, couriers and messengers. Letters, telegrams, telephones and cables should be used only for making appointments. Discussions of CIRCLE matters in public places is forbidden.

Circle Member Recognition

Ordinary handshake with thumb pressure.

Circle Goal

At such time as may be deemed advisable THE CIRCLE will come out openly as a political party embracing the whole of West Africa, and whose policy then shall be to maintain the Union of African Socialist Republics.

17. IMPRISONMENT AND EXECUTION OF IBRAHIM NASSIF EL WARDANY*

⎍⎍⎍⎍⎍⎍⎍⎍⎍⎍⎍⎍⎍⎍⎍

I. *Imprisonment*

Ibrahim Nassif El Wardany was arrested on February 20th on the scene of his crime. During the preliminary inquiry he was confined in an isolated cell in the Mousky Police Station, under a strong guard.

On March 3rd he was transferred to the prison of the Appeal Court, where he remained until his execution. Special precautions were adopted. The Governor of the prison was a Copt, and every reliance could be placed upon him. Reliable warders were selected to guard Wardany's cell, and several prison officials, of known nationalist sympathies, were temporarily transferred. In his progress to and from the Court he was guarded by another specially chosen Coptic officer and four European constables.

On the 18th of May sentence of death was pronounced. From that date the number of warders was increased. Two extra sentries were posted and, as a further precaution against any possible attempt at rescue, thirty-two noncommissioned officers and men of the Guard Company, with rifles and ball-cartridge, re-

*Note from the Adviser to the Egyptian Ministry of the Interior to Sir Eldon Gorst, in F.O. 371/890, Public Record Office, London.

mained on duty throughout the night, stationed in two posts of one noncommissioned officer and fifteen men each, at the only two points of the prison from which rescue could have been attempted.

On June 12th, the Court of Cassation rejected Wardany's appeal. From that date, until the end, in addition to the previous guards, a British Head Constable of the Cairo Police was continuously on duty outside the prisoner's cell, being relieved every six hours. The key of his cell was placed under a seal, which could only be broken in the presence of the Governor.

Wardany was, from the moment of his arrest, subjected to the ordinary prison discipline. After the sentence of May 18th, he was confined in a cell reserved for persons condemned to death and was kept under constant observation. He was, in accordance with the provisions of the Code, allowed to wear his own clothes until his sentence had become final on June 18th, at which date he donned the prison dress. There were persistent rumors that he was either to take or to be given poison, and every precaution was adopted. His rations and water were specially inspected, and any extra articles of food ordered for him by the doctors were purchased by the Mamur of the prison in person; that officer tasted not only his food but his cough mixtures and other medicines.

The medical report on the prisoner shows that he suffered from slight anemia and was subject to bronchitis. On the night of the rejection of his appeal by the Court of Cassation, he had a violent gastric attack with vomiting, probably due to emotion.

His conduct in prison was irreproachable. He made no requests and complaints and remained on good terms with all the prison officials.

The only privilege granted to the prisoner was to retain a few books and he spent nearly all his time in reading them. The works in his possession were: *The English Constitution*, by Walter Bagehot; a French political history of contemporary Europe; J.-J. Rousseau's *Contrat Social;* a volume of Arabic poetry and the Koran. During the early part of his imprisonment, before his condemnation, he was found to have engraved some writings in French and Arabic on the binding of one of these books with a tag of his boot-lace. One of these writings consisted of a series of headings for chapters, such as, Book 1, Chapter I: "Aperçu du premier Gouvernement"; II "Démocratie"; III "Communauté"; IV "Eléments Sociaux et Politiques." Book 2, Chapter I, "Chambre des Députés"; II "Sénat"; III "Prince"; IV "Ministre"; V "Administration"; etc. When questioned on the subject, the prisoner admitted that these were chapters of a work he intended to compose and which was to be called "La Constitution d'un Gouvernement Musulman." On the same book he had engraved, after his condemnation, the following lines in Arabic:

> Although death is destruction to the body,
> One like myself will never die;
> Being free, I shall become henceforth the martyr
> for my country.

Also a "hadice" (quotation from the Prophet) "You will have the Governors that you deserve."

Wardany came to be on good terms with Coles Pasha, the Inspector General of Prisons, and Colonel Harvey Pasha, Commandant of the Cairo Police, and he frequently conversed with them. He repeatedly inquired as to the effect of his deed in Egypt and as to whether it would result in good to his country. He said that he did not regret his crime, but was prepared to repeat it as Boutres Pasha had intended to sell his country on the Suez Canal question for £400,000. He maintained that he had committed it entirely of his own accord, without any outside instigation whatsoever, and that he had no accomplices. It was impossible to shake his affirmations on this point. He denied the existence of any secret society for the perpetration of political murders and that any other assassinations were in contemplation.

At interviews, the last of which took place on the eve of his execution, with his uncle and mother the latter reproached him for his crime, and he replied that everyone had to die, but that his name would be immortalized.

He displayed the greatest interest in his will. His sole property consisted in his pharmacy, which he had established at a cost of £300. The concern was, as you are aware, hopelessly bankrupt and he left nothing but debts. Nevertheless, he nominated, to manage this pharmacy after his death, a committee comprising several of the best-known nationalist leaders. He directed that the profits were to be divided into five parts, and distributed, to a reserve fund, to his mother, to a kindergarten, to a girls' school, and to a scientific mission.

This will and his language and attitude throughout his imprisonment tend to prove that he was suffering from a form of megalomania.

II. *Execution*

The fortnight's grace from the final judgment, during which period a pardon might be accorded, expired on June 27th. It had been decided that the execution should take place at the earliest possible date, *viz.*, on the morning of the 28th, but not more than five or six officials were aware of this decision. On the afternoon of June 27th, the necessary document from the Procureur Général, to the effect that the period of grace had expired and that the execution might be carried out, was delivered to me at the Ministry of the Interior and I handed it to Harvey Pasha, who had completed all the necessary arrangements.

Wardany was hanged at 6 A.M. on the following morning in the presence of the Sub-Governor of Cairo, Harvey Pasha, the Governor of the Prison, and two doctors. No other persons were admitted. The prisoner was very nervous, but showed no fear. He was evidently much disappointed at the small number and official character of the persons present. On the scaffold, he endeavored to deliver a speech, but was requested to confine himself to a statement of his last wishes. He then said, "I commend my mother and sister to you— There is only one God and Muhammad is his prophet— Liberty and independence come from God." Death was certified to have been instantaneous.

The native press had announced that the execution would be held on June 26th and, early that morning, a crowd of some 300 loafers of the lowest class assembled round the prison. They were kept moving by the police, but loitered in the neighborhood. During the morning, Ashmawi, the executioner, who had been receiving orders from Harvey Pasha, left the prison and entered a tramway. He was recognized by some of the loafers who, thinking that the execution had taken place, assumed a threatening attitude toward him and began to throw stones at the tramway. The police quickly extricated him; he remained for some time in a neighboring police station and was afterwards sent to Alexandria to await instructions there, and he returned only on the eve of the execution.

The press then announced that June 29th was the date fixed for the event.

On the actual morning of the execution there was scarcely a soul in the vicinity of the prison. The few persons waiting there followed an empty sanitary cart which left the prison yard at 7 A.M. About the same time Wardany's body was removed in a similar cart from a private entrance of the Court of Appeal. Everyone entering the prison on the morning in question, including two journalists who protested loudly, was detained inside until these proceedings were over. Wardany's body was taken to the cemetery of Imam el Shafei, where it was handed over to his uncle, Dr. Zeifal Effendi, an official of the Public Health Department, and quietly interred. Some grave diggers discovered what was taking place and a small crowd began to collect, but was easily persuaded to disperse by some plain-clothes police stationed at the spot. Dr. Zeifal helped to discourage manifestations of sympathy and the authorities are greatly indebted to this gentleman for his cooperation throughout the proceedings. The officer sent to inform Wardany's mother of the execution and to take her and her daughter to the cemetery was unable to find her at her home, but discovered her at the house of a magician, to whom she had promised £23 in order that he should liberate her son by magic. The officer arrived before the money had been paid. The mother is reported to have been much affected and to have repeatedly said, "May God induce those who have persuaded you to fall into the same trap."

Under the provisions of the law, no official ceremony is permitted in the case of persons who have suffered capital punishment, and the family of Wardany was warned to this effect; but a large number of sympathizers, at least four or five hundred, comprising prominent nationalists, students, etc., have called at the mother's house, dressed in deep mourning, to express their condolences.

Although Wardany's fate has undoubtedly provoked very general sympathy, there have been no attempts to disturb public order and perfect quiet prevails throughout the country.

The action of the authorities in avoiding publicity and in not following the usual course of inviting journalists to attend at the execution, has been bitterly criticized in the local press. Publicity would have entailed large crowds round the prison and consequent difficulty in removing the body; it was also undesirable that real or imaginary "last words of Wardany" should be circulated among a credulous public. I venture to submit that the arrangements made, with your approval, were justified, and that the result reflects credit upon Harvey Pasha, who was responsible for them.

(signed): RONALD GRAHAM, June 30th, 1910.

18. THE MAKING OF A TERRORIST: FROM THE AUTOBIOGRAPHY OF DAMODAR HARI CHAPEKAR*

⌐⌐⌐⌐⌐⌐⌐⌐⌐⌐⌐⌐⌐⌐⌐⌐⌐⌐⌐⌐

Meanwhile (the time for holding) the National Congress arrived. As it was to be held at Poona that year, we were desirous of seeing personally what sort of a revolutionary movement it was. Before this, a fierce dispute was going on in the city between the orthodox and the reform parties with regard to the Social Conference. We do not approve of the National Congress, much less of the Social Conference. But though there is no possibility of any good resulting from the National Congress, it does not entail any loss either, except in so far as the expenditure of money is concerned. The lakhs of rupees that are spent upon it are lost (to the country), but it has this redeeming feature that it has nothing to do with religious matters. We, therefore, do not care if the Congress were held even twenty-five times a year. But we cannot view with patience the *chandalin* (*i.e.*, Social Conference) that has been thrust into its bosom by these reformers. This is the principal reason why we look upon them as our inveterate enemies. We are aware that as we are not independent, now, everybody adopts whatever course he likes. We must, however,

*From *Source Material for a History of the Freedom Movement in India*, vol. II, 1885–1920, Bombay, 1958, pp. 978–1015.

conduct ourselves as directed in the Shastras. But as the reformers are endeavoring to circumscribe our freedom of action by laws, why should we not avenge ourselves upon them? There is no reason why we should not. At this time a violent discussion was going on between the two parties. Bal Gangadhar Tilak took up the leadership of one party and Mahadev Govind Ranade that of the other, and a war of words commenced. At this time Shridhar Vithal Date sided with the orthodox party. This man is an enthusiastic admirer of (the Hindu) religion. He is possessed of more self-respect than others and is therefore ever willing to undergo any expense in order to prove the correctness of his own opinions. The cooperation of a man of such determination resulted in a great accession of strength to the orthodox party. But such strength is of no avail because efforts not backed by physical force are doomed to failure. The demands of the National Congress have proved futile for this reason. Englishmen know that the National Congress means eating, drinking, recreation and a profusion of tall talk and nothing more. Had the people been as spirited as the Americans, they (*i.e.,* Englishmen) would have been compelled to take our demands into consideration. The Americans having profited by their National Congress we followed their example, but no one gives thought to what those spirited people did when their demands were refused. To make every meeting of the Congress more imposing than the previous one, is the (sole) object these blockheads have in view. From their point of view, the greater the expenditure on pleasure, on eating and drinking, on illuminations, on talking and writing, the more is the good of the country secured. Let that, however, pass. As I will have to touch upon this topic later on, I shall not dwell upon it further in this place. In short, we did not at all like the wordy warfare that went on between the two parties.

We two brothers, therefore, thought that the chastisement of some prominent individual from amongst the reformers would be conducive to the furtherance (of the cause of the orthodox party). From the very first, we entertained a violent grudge against the Sudharak newspaper, but as we were not able to put our thoughts into execution while Agarkar edited that paper, that sinner escaped (chastisement) at our hands. Being, however, inspired with a strong desire to do something on this occasion, we determined to pounce upon either of the two editors of that paper whom we might be able to catch, and with that object in view we watched for an opportunity. This newspaper always speaks ill of the orthodox party and their way. Its articles have a tendency to produce misapprehension in the minds of the people respecting the Dharma Shastras by placing different interpretations on the precepts contained in them. Being backed by Englishmen, it makes use of such violent language as would wound the feelings of all true lovers of religion. It is impossible for me to describe the state of our minds when we read this paper. On some occasions our wrath was so uncontrollable that we burned the issues of that paper. But as that mode of punishment was not calculated to pacify our feelings, we began to think of inflicting corporal chastisement. As the reflection that the editors were our castemen used to generate compassion in our minds, we resolved that instead of capital punishment they should receive some ordinary chastisement. Then a letter of warning was to be sent to them. If they took that warning, well and good. If not, no pity was to be shown to them. We accordingly marked their houses and watched (their movement). One day we were informed that there was to be a Sanskrit performance at the Anandobhava Theater, and we thought that both the editors would be present there on the occasion. But that day things did not take the turn we wished. We next learned that the students of the Bhave School were to give a performance of "Hamlet" at the Aryabhushana Theater and we concluded that as that institution was not acceptable to the said editors, they would be present at the performance through feelings of jealousy. We, therefore, waited outside that theater, but were unable to ascertain from there as to who were inside. I, therefore, somehow procured four annas (to purchase a ticket with) and went inside the theater. There I saw two persons whom I identified, one of them being Patwardhan, the editor of Sudharak, and the other Kulkarni, a teacher in the New Marathi School. I then came out and informed my brother of this, when he went in and saw them. We then waited for the termination of the performance. It soon came to an end. Kulkarni was the first to leave the theater, and I dealt him a blow, which was not heavy, near the entrance to the lane opposite Hamjekjan's gymnasium. It must have struck him lightly on the back and part of the head. Two or three persons were walking with him at the time. Having dealt the blow, I hurried away. Patwardhan, who left (the theater) after (Kulkarni), was closely followed by my brother, whom I joined in the Budhwar (Peth). While we were thus following him, we reached a place just below the dilapidated tower in the Shalukar lane, when my brother, stepping forward, gave a blow to Patwardhan with a piece of iron piping. That blow must have struck him on the head near the ear. About three or four persons must have been walking with him at this time. After execution of this deed, we returned home and heartily thanked God. On the next day we waited to hear what the people would say about the matter. It appeared that all orthodox people were much gratified. We were delighted to know this, and believed that we had done a great service to our religion. We then thought that after what had happened there was no objection to send them a letter of warning. Although we two alone (had punished them) it was necessary to make them understand that we had a following, so that they might be overawed and thus prevented from traducing (the orthodox) faith. With this object in view we penned a letter. We did not keep a copy of it, but in substance it was as follows.

"Like your association for removing the obstacles in the way of widow-remarriage (we also) have formed a society for removing the obstacles in the way of the Aryan religion, that is to say, a league, prepared to lay down their lives as well as to take the lives of others for the sake of that religion. This society does not want the beggarly Congress, much less the Social Conference. We like all the Hindu customs, whatever they may be, including even the evil practices of the Shimga, which are condemned by the reformers. There is no necessity for any innovation whatever either in our religious observances or our customs of the present day. Both the reformers and the nonreformers are, therefore, hereby warned that although the reformers are forgiven for whatever they have done hitherto, they should conduct themselves with great caution hereafter, as, otherwise, it would be our sad and painful duty to put them to the sword. You should, therefore, take note of this warning and conduct yourself with caution. Remember your forefathers and do not incur the hostility of the whole community by interference with religion. If you disregard this, Nemesis (will overtake you)."

This letter was sent to the address of Devdhar (one of) the editors of the Sudharak at the New English School. He gave a substance of it in the issue of the Sudharak dated 25th November 1895. Afterwards, a meeting against the Social Conference was held at Thakurdwar in Bombay. On that occasion, we stepped forward and recited two shloks composed by my brother. We can compose poetry fairly suited to any occasion, though we are not poets. Being, however, actuated by a desire to do everything that was necessary for popularizing our favorite subject, and thinking that as metrical compositions commended themselves to the popular taste it would be better to lay our views before the public in that form, we studiously devoted ourselves to the art of versification. I, in particular, had a great predilection for versification and composed many verses on patriotism. Although my brother had not the same predilection, still he could compose excellent verses whenever he was in a mood to do so. As the habit of indulging in loquacity in public meetings did not meet with our approval, my brother composed two shloks with a view to make known his inmost thoughts to the discerning portion of the public. One of them deals with the Social Conference and the other is about Daji Abaji Khare, High Court Pleader. It was at that time proved that this vilest of Brahmins had eaten beef while dining with Badruddin Tyabji. When we heard of this we could not restrain our feelings, and having composed a shlok about him, we recited it at the meeting. I give below the abovementioned two shloks:

l. Listen! Should the Social Conference be held in the National (Congress) pandal, the Aryans must certainly withhold their help from that lusterless institution. We shall never tolerate any revilement of our religion in the (Social) Conference; we shall first, with a rod in our hand, strike down the army of reformers.

2. That religion-destroyer Khare, having invited Mlenchas and others to dine with him, partook, in defiance of the precepts of his religion, of biscuits, loaves, flesh and spirits in their company. He should forever be looked down upon as a Chandal. How is it that the reformers are not ashamed! Let us strike him with shoes.

As I have already said above that we are not good poets, my readers will kindly overlook the many blemishes that may be found in the above verses if tested by the rule of prosody and only appreciate our meaning. These verses were received with cheers by many in the audience. The reformers, however, appeared to be stung by them and left the meeting. These people, having received a thrashing at our hands, were well kept in check. Every one of them engaged Purbhayas for his personal protection and none dared to go out of his house except in carriage. They saw from the signs that a riot would certainly take place if the Social Conference were held in the National Congress pavilion and so decided to hold its sitting in a different place. The people were much gratified at this, and we ourselves felt particularly joyful for what we had done. Still we persisted in our efforts to burn down the Social Conference mandap. Two or three times did we go to the hill near the Fergusson College at 2 o'clock at night, taking with us materials for setting fire to it, but as the work of construction was going on day and night to the last moment, our plan proved futile. (Like the National Congress) the Social Conference too had issued tickets to its delegates. We sought to gain admittance into that assembly (by that channel). We, therefore, asked some educated youths to start a reform club to enable us to obtain tickets of admission to the Conference. Being thus pressed by us, they got up a Young Men's Reform Club and applied for tickets of admission to the Conference in its name. Thereupon Mahadev Govind Ranade asked that the Secretary (of the club) should be sent to see him with the papers of the club. Our educated friends, however, got frightened at this invitation and none of them would go to him. I, therefore, prepared some bogus papers, and styling myself the Secretary of the club, took them to Mr. Ranade's house at about 8 o'clock in the evening. This oldest leader of the reformers was sitting in a swinging seat at this time, chatting with a stranger. I was given a chair near them. They continued chatting for a pretty long time, but as the conversation was carried on in a jargon, half English and half Marathi, I was not able to understand the whole of it. The assault on Patwardhan was mentioned in the course of their conversation, but they were not aware that the prime mover in that incident was then sitting by their side. When he finished the conversation Mr. Ranade turned to me, and having inquired about myself, asked a man to examine my papers. He examined those bogus papers, and inquired of me as to why I had not brought the originals. I replied that we never took the original papers outside our club. Thereupon Mr. Ranade said that I would be provided with tickets if I produced a recommendatory note from some respectable gentleman. I said in reply, "I am a respectable gentleman myself, and therefore do not stand in need of any introduction from others. If you believe me, give me the tickets: if not, I do not want them." I then left the place. Subsequently, a man came from him to pay me a visit, but I refused to see him. By and by, the day fixed for the Congress approached. The city became thronged with people arriving from outside. The delight of our educated men knew no bounds. All were in a hurry and bustle. This put us in mind of the little girls in our houses. The doings of these self-styled educated men can only be compared with the play of these girls when they celebrate the marriage of their dolls, taking much more delight therein than in real marriage ceremonies, while people of maturer understanding instead of taking any interest in their play, only laugh at their childishness and fondle and caress them because they are children. These educated classes have got up a toy regiment, as it were, and have become absorbed in witnessing its unarmed drill. But as it is uninteresting to see girls playing with lifeless dolls, so the feeble display of a regiment without the soul-stirring equipment of arms excites no enthusiasm. Being aware that it was impossible to gauge the real nature of the Congress without entering (its pavilion), we began to try for a free ticket of admission. In the meanwhile seeing a Madrasi gentleman taking a stroll on a hill behind the Fergusson College, we entered into conversation with him, and being convinced that he was a reformer in his opinions, we snatched away his ticket from him and ran away.

With that ticket we gained admission into the pavilion by turns and saw the fun. We came to know many things on these occasions. These self-styled educated men find fault with Bajirao the Second, and accuse him of having lost his kingdom by his habits of luxury and sensuality; but the conduct of these people is such as will throw his acts into the shade. I ask these wiseacres, who must have perused their historical books over and over again, if they have any instance in history wherein empty talk and indulgence in eating and drinking has accomplished the good of one's country. Has even one of the men famous in history ever tried to unite the world by holding National Congresses or by delivering speeches? The answer must be in the negative. It is a matter for deep regret that our educated men of the present day should not have sense enough to understand that the good of one's country is accomplished only when crores of meritorious men, reckless of their lives for the sake of their country, encounter death at the edge of the sword on a battlefield, and by no other means. Where is the use of simply learning history by rote when at school? There is nothing to be gained by learning by heart the dates of the birth and death of Shivaji. The object of studying his life is to know what he did in his lifetime: whether he started a National Congress, collected money from the poor and squandered it on pleasure in the company of false patriots like himself gathered together once a year under the pretext of promoting the good of his country; or whether he, with a view to the execution of some serious design, suffered privations all his life, along with his similarly inspired friends, in his attempt to achieve the good of his country. If the lessons contained (in the lives of such men) are not followed, where is the use of learning history? A perusal of the proceedings of the Congress which appeared every year in the newspapers had convinced me that it was all a sham. It is necessary that I should give here the conclusions at which I have arrived after a full consideration of the matter.

The first thought struck me was how far the originators of the Congress, *viz.*, Hume, Bradlaugh, and others, being Europeans, could be trusted. It was inexplicable to us how those very Englishmen who in this country send us to lifelong transportation for the mildest unfavorable comments (upon the acts of Government) could permit Messrs. Hume, Bradlaugh and others of their own race to remain alive in England even though they have incited us (to act) in opposition (to Government). For, the fomentation of dissensions in the country is the last thing that (a nation) can tolerate. I, therefore, began to consider how, in the face of the above facts, this was possible. And I came to the conclusion that all this was a sham and nothing more. I was convinced that those people were acting under the instigation of our wily administrators and had come forward to deceive the Hindus and to give a harmless turn to their activities with a view never to allow their thoughts to turn towards deeds of cruelty. Had the case been otherwise, they would long before this have suffered death at the hands of their countrymen. This is one of the modes of deceiving the public. Whenever an Englishman has a craving for popularity among the Hindus, he knows how to espouse the cause of India when an Indian question crops up in Parliament. The moment he does so, our educated people begin to dance with joy and dub him as the defender of the cause of India. If he afterwards visits India, they will draw his carriage and have illuminations and processions in his honor. And they think that by doing so the welfare of the country is gained. I remember having seen two or three such celebrations in honor of Europeans. We two brothers felt exasperated at these sights. Just as Arjun, after enjoying himself at Dwarka under the disguise of a sanyasi, carried away Subhadra in the end, so these Englishmen, having come to India, deceive the people and carry away to their country the prize of great glory. The only difference is that, while the people of Dwarka recognized in the disguised sanyasi the cunning Arjun after Subhadra had been taken away, our educated classes fail to understand the true character (of these men). Otherwise, none of them would have had a blind regard for the English. Let that pass.

The National Congress having been held this year in Poona itself, we had an opportunity of personally witnessing the great efforts of our educated classes in the interests of our country. An influential gentleman from Madras by the name of Manmohan Ghosh, or some such other name which I do not remember, (had come down to Poona) and was working heart and soul in the cause of Congress. He is a great devotee of the Congress. It is his special characteristic that, though a Hindu by religion, he dresses like a European from top to toe, and shaves his moustache like a eunuch. Had he been a fair-looking man this European dress might have looked graceful, but being of dark complexion and having no moustache, he presented a very queer appearance in that attire. He looked just as if he were a pervert. He had a European to drive his carriage, and had to pay him a salary of Rs. 500 a month. In this particular, above all others, is his love of his country seen to the greatest advantage. (The reason) is simple. While engaged in promoting the welfare of the country innumerable obstacles are sure to arise in one's way and consequently charioteering skill of no common order is requisite for surmounting them. As, however, such skillful men are not to be found in India they must needs be imported from England. Here, however, a doubt crosses our mind. How can a country which cannot furnish a skillful charioteer produce a warrior fitted to sit on a chariot? The status of the latter is considerably higher than that of the former. When I first saw this man driving in his carriage, I mistook the driver for Ghose and Ghose himself for the lackey. Let that, however, pass. This incarnation of patriotism had come (to Poona) in advance (of the Congress) to assist the Poonaites in their preparations. All the Brahmins in our city, both young and old, including the schoolboys, were also heartily exerting themselves (in the Congress movement). I must, however, explain here what the expression "exerting oneself "means;

for, in other lands, the expression "exerting oneself for the good of one's country" is understood to have a significance different from what it had in this country. The people of these lands might be led to think that our patriots, reckless of their lives, must have prepared themselves to die for the good of their country. But that would be a wrong impression. The brave patriots from all parts of the country who had congregated in the city of Poona on this occasion were received at the railways station by the volunteers, who, taking up their baggage and (even) their shoes in their hands, guided them with such words as these, "Sir, place your foot here carefully, there is a stone in front," to a small but handsome pavilion erected near the station, and here their first adoration took place. The guests were served with fruits, tea and coffee to their heart's content and garlands of fragrant flowers were put round their necks. Then they were taken in tongas to the small rooms built near the Congress pavilion for their use and asked to sit on the mattresses of small but neatly made bedsteads. These rooms contained all conveniences. I do not know whether women too were provided there, but every article of food and drink was ready at hand. There was plenty of every kind of prohibited food and drink. Warm-water shower-baths were also there, and after our patriots had seated themselves on beautiful square slabs in the bathrooms, warm-water showers poured down on their heads. And so they proceeded to bring about the country's good. At night electric lamps were lit, and in their moonlike refulgence these patriots wandered about and thus advanced the good of the country. Their national darbar was held during the day, and on that occasion the veteran patriots were lustily cheered when they entered the pavilion. Tilak was cheered, Ranade was cheered, and Surendranath Banarji was cheered, for hours together, because, forsooth, he was the Indra, the chief of all the gods, and was therefore escorted by the toy regiment referred to above. After these, the best heroes had assembled, the war of words began. But singularly enough, their opponent, *viz.*, the Englishman, was conspicuous by his absence. He was represented there by some solitary blackcoat. (Even) this sight was sufficient to confound these men, who were bold only in speech. If asked by some Government official or placed before a court of justice, they would protest against (an unfavorable) interpretation being placed upon their speeches, and would engage a pleader at some expense to defend themselves. Alas!

Oh my countrymen, how have you been reduced to such a helpless condition! How is it that your intellect is incapable of thinking aright! When Shivaji, Bajirao, Nana Phadnavis and other ancestors of yours determined to advance the good of their country, were they ever required to take the advice of either Hume or Bradlaugh? When those worthy personages made determined efforts to get their rights from the Yavanas, did they achieve their end by gathering together Banias and traders, and seths and bankers, from all parts of the country in a national pavilion, illuminated with electric lights and erected on the plain of Chatursingi, and by indulging in loquacity by day and lounging upon sofas by night? Have you ever read that such was the case? If you contend that it was the National Congress that has done good to America, I have already traversed that argument on the last page. Though I can neither speak nor read English, the information I have collected on the subject is reliable, and I can write very extensively on this topic. I, however, stated here in short what I have to say: "My friends, be mindful of the old adage, 'Wisdom is powerless before authority.' You should, therefore, adapt yourselves (to the ways of your rulers) and thus accomplish whatever good you can. Even if they imposed taxes upon you, submit to them with the thought that they are foreigners after all. Tall talk and writing articles in newspapers will be of no avail against them. If you are unable to bear the oppression of these foreigners, then give up all hope of your life, wealth, relations, friends and acquaintances, sons and wives, and make a demand for your rights and support it with physical force. I, however, do not think that you are capable of achieving that. Because had you possessed that ability, you would have long before this understood the matter. Do not render yourselves liable to punishment with hard labor by indulging in vain talk and by using your pens against Englishmen. Do not glory in so doing. If you shower flowers on one who has been sentenced for simply indulging in tall talk, what will you do to discharge your obligations to a warrior like Shivaji should he be fortunately born in this century? I ask this question because you have already conferred all kinds of honor on persons of ordinary abilities. Nay, you have honored such insignificant persons as Surendranath Banarji, Dadabhai Naoroji, Hume and others in a manner Shivaji was not honored during his time. Do you think nothing remains to be done for the good of the country beyond this? You are mistaken. A little consideration will teach you the lesson conveyed by the adage 'A thundercloud produces no rain, a talkative man will not act.' I ask you to consider this adage and proceed with my narrative." The sight of this national festival grieved us very much. We had even planned to burn down its pavilion. But considering (that the institution had gained) popular favor, we thought it would not be right to do so. Had the Social Conference been held in that pavilion, we would certainly have made an attempt to set it on fire, but our initial experiment having compelled the Conference to wind up its belongings, we spent our days only in observing carefully the inconsistent proceedings (of the Congress).

After its puerile game was over, all the patriots left for their respective places. Then we began to harass the missionaries. While we were at Bombay, we used to annoy in various ways the European missionaries who were to be seen (preaching) at the Back Bay. We pelted them with stones (and) created an uproar. Once we snatched away a handbag from a European lady who was there. We found in it some English books, some visiting cards bearing her name, a bunch of keys and a beautiful purse. The last was a very convenient article, but we found in it (only) one pice and a postal stamp worth two annas and a half. We went and saw the bungalow of the lady who resides at Grant Road. Once we took away the signboard of the Church Mission Hall on the Palva Road and burned it. After coming down to Poona, we determined to harass the European missionaries at this place. On inquiry we learned that they used to preach in the upper storey of a building occupied by Messrs. Philips and Company.

There, in the first instance, I advised my Aryan brethren not to go upstairs, and several of my friends accordingly desisted from going there. When their time of preaching arrived, there was not a soul present at the place and so the missionaries were in a fix. The men whom I had prevented from going there had not returned to their homes, but were standing together on the road. When the missionaries, who were on the upper story, came to know that a particular individual had prevented all persons from going up there, they came down to me and said that I was doing an unlawful act and that they would prosecute me. After this they had a conversation with the police and it appeared as if they were going to carry out their intentions. I, therefore, slipped away from the place, and considering that such attempts were futile, resolved to make a desperate effort (to gain our object).

With a view to prevent all persons from giving any place to these (missionaries) we began to devise plans to set the said building on fire. The staircase leading to the upper storey opens on the main Budhwar Road. It has got one door at its foot and another at the top. The missionaries, when leaving the place, used to lock the latter door, while they merely chained the former. We, therefore, determined to open the door at the foot of the staircase and to slip away after having set fire to the upper one. Lest what was going on inside might be clearly observed through a latticed window above the lower door by the people outside, we hit upon the following plan by which the flames were to blaze up inside after we had left the place. We took a big uparna and, having saturated it with kerosene oil, firmly attached it to the upper door. To this uparna we tied a long strip of cloth similarly saturated, and having stretched it for a long distance along the ground placed hollow tiles upon it in a line, so as to form a sort of tunnel. The (other end of the) strip peeped a little out of this tunnel. Our object was to set fire to this end and then to slip away. The tiles were to prevent the light of the burning strip from being seen outside and there being a lack of air there, the strip was to burn slowly and set fire to the cloth (attached to the door) after we had gone a considerable distance. To carry out this plan, we first of all sent a friend of ours named Bhuskute upstairs, and we two disguised as Mavlas, sat below eating fried rice, in order to protect him. Thinking that it would be found difficult to extinguish the fire if the lower door were locked while leaving the place we purchased a lock for four pice and gave it to Bhuskute when he went upstairs. But that being the first occasion of its kind, he got confounded and, having bungled the work, came down and told us that he had done all. We, therefore, told him to go home and walked about (in the street) waiting to witness the fun. But we heard no alarm of fire. When an hour elapsed, we were convinced that the bungler had certainly failed to set fire (to the place). I, therefore, went upstairs, while my brother remained below. I returned after having set fire to the strip. Then we went away, having locked the door. We had not proceeded far when we heard a fire bugle. Just as we reached home, we also caught the sound of the bugle of the fire engine located near our house, but after a short while, a telephone message was received announcing that the fire had been extinguished. We were much disheartened at this news, because our attempt had not proved as successful as we had wished. On inquiry we learned that as the padlock which had been attached to the lower door was a worthless one, Dagdu confectioner, a gymnast of our city, forced it open by breaking the lock. How long could a padlock worth only one anna hold out? This weak point in our plans was due to our inability to spend more on the padlock. After this, we sent a warning to the owner of the house to evict the missionaries, as otherwise the attempt (at incendiarism) was sure to be repeated some other day. As we were fired with an ambition to follow a military career we were unceasingly exerting ourselves (to gain our object).

We went to the old market every Sunday and Wednesday and accosted the native soldiers visiting that place, with a view to elicit information from them on this subject of special interest to us. I had given up conversing with the Marathas among them, as Englishmen have fairly imbued their minds with the idea that the Brahmins were the cause of their ruin. My intelligent readers are doubtless aware of the existence at Poona and Bombay of a large anti-Brahmin association founded by one Jotiba Fule.

The sole aim of this association is to stir up hatred against the Brahmins among all other castes. Its members are always moving about the country, delivering lectures to create a feeling of animosity against the Brahmins. Their principal organ is the Din Bandhu, a weekly newspaper, published in Bombay. Its columns are usually filled with the abuse of Brahmins. On the death of Jotiba Fule, one Lokhande took up the lead in the matter. This Lokhande, although a perfect numskull, has been honored with the distinction of a Justice of the Peace by Englishmen for the simple reason that he has undertaken this important task of creating dissensions among his own countrymen. Careful observers will see that most English people assist these men in the above manner. But the Deccan Brahmins alone are so (spitefully) dealt with. It will upon inquiry be found that no people in India are so greatly devoted to politics and are so persistent in applying their intelligence and ardor in that direction as the Deccan Brahmins are. The foreigners, therefore, deeming it to be inadvisable that the public should view with favor these scheming men, have by conferring honors upon such ignorant people made them adopt this attitude (of hostility to Brahmins). There is no doubt about this. This suicidal policy of theirs has been, is, and will be the cause of great detriment to us and will greatly benefit the foreigners.

On this occasion I deem it necessary to controvert their opinions in this place. It is the stock argument of these ignorant men that the Brahmins lost the (Maratha) kingdom and that they are selfish. On the strength of these two charges they abuse the Brahmins to their heart's content. The first charge about losing the (Maratha) kingdom is based on the maladministration of the country by Bajirao the Second. It must be within the memory of students of history that this Bajirao allowed foreigners to swallow up (his kingdom) by feasting Brahmins and by indulging in vicious habits. This Bajirao had never earned, and will never earn hereafter, a good name among Brahmins. There is no difference of opinion as to the fact that his acts were highly reprehensible and ruinous to the interests of the country. But I ask these Brahmin-haters (the following questions): Were the Maratha

Sardars, such as Scindia, Holkar, Gaikwad, Bhosle, Satarkar and Kolhapurkar, dead and gone at the time Bajirao lost his kingdom? Or, being alive, were they, with bangles on their hands and sadis round their bodies, shamefacedly hiding themselves in their harems? Or, had they become eunuchs by divesting themselves of their moustaches? What was the matter with them? The Maratha states cover nearly the whole of India, and yet how was it that they were not ashamed, on that occasion, to throw down their swords, shake hands with Englishmen, and declare themselves to be their friends? If Bajirao was really loose in his morals, why did they not protest (against his conduct), throw him into prison and install a capable ruler on the throne? On the contrary, while the far-seeing Nana Phadnavis was repeatedly advising them not to ruin the country by placing this dastardly Bajirao on the throne, it was the Scindia of Gwalior who espoused his cause and installed him. This explains who it was that lost the kingdom. Although all of them were the Sardars of the Peshwa, they treacherously sided with the English and thus kept their state intact. How will they answer for this ingratitude? All the native states that are at present to be seen in India owe their existence to their disloyalty to their sovereign as well as to their treachery in siding with the English. Otherwise, the English would have swallowed them up long ago. Perhaps some might say that they fell off from Bajirao because he was not a good sovereign. To such people I ask the question as to what they would have said to Moropant Peshwa, had he gone over to the side of Aurangzeb because of Sambhaji's misconduct. If the history of the calamities which befell the country in the reign of Sambhaji and after his death be read, it would convince you that those times were a hundredfold more troublous than the times of Bajirao. It is but proper to eulogize those who with perseverance strenuously exerted themselves as for the welfare of their country during those times.

If Scindia and Holkar, who styled themselves the Sardars of the Peshwa, had exerted themselves as strenuously then, they would not have been reduced to their present plight and exposed themselves to censure. Is there a single descendant of the Peshwas, who were the real sovereigns of the country, now living in ignominy under a foreign yoke? Bajirao handed over the kingdom to the English and, having retired to Brahmavarta, passed his life there in devotion; but his adopted son, Dhondopant Nana, as if with a view to wipe off the stigma cast on his father's name, distinguished himself on the battlefield and departed to the other world along with his friends Bala Saheb, Rao Saheb, Tatya Tope and Lakshmibai of Jhansi. Had Scindia and Holkar not resorted to treachery on that occasion they as well as ourselves (Brahmins) would not have been reduced to this plight. Even a Brahmin lady fought at that time, while men with beards and moustaches, whose ancestors served their masters with true wholeheartedness, fell off from their master's son and went over to the English, the enemy of their sovereign, of their religion, and of their country. Could the meanness of the Marathas go further? Think over this and do not needlessly raise a hue and cry against Brahmins.

I do not mean to say that Brahmins have no black sheep amongst them. Like other castes they too have their black sheep. Are there no Marathas among you of the type of the Brahmin Natus, who, having gone over to the English, are now enjoying a life of pleasure? How many instances do you want? As a rule, all those who are at present eating the crumbs of ease under the cool shadow of the English did at one time turn ungrateful to the Peshwa and were thus guilty of treason. They come from all classes and castes—Brahmins, Marathas and Mussulmans. There is no reason for one of them to laugh at the others. Was not the ruler of Hyderabad independent at that time? Why then did he remain indifferent? Was it because of the Brahmin Bajirao? Is there any Brahmin agency at work in Manipur, Burma and similar other states which are now being swallowed up by the English? You revile the Brahmins without any reason. I for my part find fault with our evil stars. Infatuation precedes all (evil) things. Accordingly, divergent counsels having prevailed among the different native states of India, the English could easily do what they liked.

Who should blame whom in this matter? I, for my part, blame

one and all. They, and they alone, who laid down their lives on the battlefield in measuring their swords with the English are free from any blame. Such worthy men are to be found only among the Brahmins. Even if you look to the present times, you will be convinced of what I say. In 1857, Nana Saheb (showed himself to be a Brahmin of this type), then Wasudev Balwant, and after that we two brothers, Damodar and Balkrishna Hari Chapekar. Excepting these, has any Maratha or Muhammadan become a martyr for his religion and his country? According to the adage, "The master is reduced to distress while thieves roll in plenty," the Peshwas have passed away, while these ingrates are still living and enjoying the jaghirs conferred upon them by the Peshwas. What sort of hell might have been created for (the punishment) of such men? I do not wish to say anything further about these ungrateful wretches; for, my blood boils whenever I think of their treacherous deeds, and I much regret that we could not wreak our vengeance upon them. We were burning with rage at Dinkarrao Rajwade, the late Diwan of Scindia. But we were disappointed when a few days ago we heard that he was dead. Now of course the execution of all our designs must be deferred to our next existence. May Heaven fulfill our desires in our future lives! The second charge remains yet to be refuted, but I do not wish to enlarge upon that insignificant point here. In connection with this matter, I recommend my readers to peruse the criticism of the late Vishnu Shastri Chiplunkar on the "Lokahitavadi." Therein he has ably dealt with the subject. In short, this anti-Brahmin spirit has spread amongst people of all castes. From my personal experience I know that this feeling is very strong among the Deccan Marathas employed in the regiments.

I was well acquainted with Kashinath Baneh, the Subhedar Major of the 4th (Infantry) Regiment. At my first visit to him he asked me what I had come for. I said to him, "I am very fond of a military career. Can I be enrolled (in your regiment)." Thereupon that man knit his brows and, giving an emphatic nasal twang to his voice, said to me in the Konkani dialect, "Bhatji Bova, what you say is true, but how will you be able to observe the customs of your caste in the regiment? A regiment is not a place for eating sweetmeat balls. Look at my feet, and see how very bronzed they have become. This is the way we are required to move about (from place to place); we alone can do that." He philosophized much in this fashion, but as I had no desire to argue with him I quietly heard what he said. I tickled him with the following words: "Subhedar Saheb, what a brave man you are! Certainly you are the men to fight battles. Your bronzed feet strike me with wonder. What toil you must have undergone!" I tickled him in this manner, but at the same time taunted him as follows: "Did the Peshwas observe the customs of their caste when they crossed the Attock? Was it by tasting sweetmeat balls that they confounded the Persians?" At this the Subhedar softened his tone and said, "I do not mean that; I only wanted to say that it is not possible to observe the caste customs in a regiment." I thus made various attempts to get myself enlisted in the army. But as the Deccan Maratha sepoys used to deride and jeer at us, I refused to see them anymore.

We sought information about regimental matters by making friends with native soldiers (of other castes). None of them, however, encouraged us in our desire to enlist in the army. They used to tell us that it was through their ill-luck that they got themselves enlisted in the army. We did not, however, appreciate what they said and so vigorously prosecuted our efforts, which, however, proved futile. We were thus helpless in the matter. We then directed our efforts toward Hindustan (*sic*). We had interviews with many influential persons at Baroda, Gwalior, Indore, Hyderabad, Sangli, etc., and expressed to them our desire to serve in a cavalry regiment. But each one of them declined to do anything for us. Then we applied to the Portuguese Government at Goa, but were not favored with a reply. Afterwards someone explained to us the futility of applying to subordinate European officers, and advised us to address the Commander-in-Chief at Simla, where our request would be favorably considered. Four times did I address the Commander-in-Chief in the matter and received replies to my petitions, but they were all to no purpose. In other words, all the replies were of a negative character. I have handed over copies of them to my friends, Brewin and Kennedy. I have also got (a copy of) the application which I sent to the Chief of Sangli. I desire that all these should be printed hereafter.

On receiving such a sour reply from Simla, we thought that it would be far better to settle in a foreign country than to remain in one where liberty did not exist even in so small a measure. Therefore knowing Nepal to be an independent country, my brother (determined to) set out for it. We were under the impression that our parents would not allow us to go to such a distant country, as hitherto we had never left them to follow our own inclinations. But now we thought we would be wasting away the very prime of our lives if we were to remain inactive. We also thought it undesirable to delay our plans as it was necessary that the art of war which we aspired to learn should be studied while one possessed a strong physique. But another difficulty as to how to arrange for our parents in our absence presented itself. Being conscious that it was our duty not to forsake them, we decided that I should remain at home and my brother should proceed to Nepal for the achievement of our purpose. There he was to arrange everything for both of us and then inform me of his having done so. We then fixed an auspicious day for (his) departure. All the members of our family were quite happy at this time. Readers! my father's profession of kirtan enabled him to earn plenty of money. He was liberal in his expenditure, and so every holiday was well enjoyed. As my father was very hospitable to his guests, there was scarcely a day on which we did not partake of sweetmeats with our guests and friends. Our family having increased by the grace of God, our happiness also increased in the same proportion. It is a fact to be particularly remembered that our family possessed in a full measure that affection (for one another) which is the source of all domestic happiness. I have seen a good many families, but have never come across a single one which is free from domestic quarrels. Fire seize their other comforts! There are many who possess wealth, and are also blessed with large families, but no two members of the family live in harmony. Such, however, was not the case with our family. All those who were younger than myself were obedient to me, and they never showed any disrespect to me. I do not know how I can requite them for all this. May Heaven bless them! My family thus consisted of my loving brothers and sisters, my father and mother, and my wife and son; but the actions of our former existence having given a peculiar turn to our predilections, our minds deviated from all domestic concerns and took a different direction.

An auspicious day having been fixed for my brother's departure to Nepal, he took with him Rs. 40 for his traveling expenses. This amount had been accumulated by us laying aside small sums of money for this long journey. He also took with him other necessary things. As we had settled that my brother should start by the morning train, both of us left our beds early in the morning and adored the Deity, and prayed to Him that, as we were leaving (the city) with a good object in view, He should vouchsafe success to us. Then considering my seniority in age, I gave him some advice, after which I was for a moment plunged in sadness at the thought of (our impending) separation. As the members of our family had never before separated from each other, this (separation) was found by us to be extremely unbearable. Besides, the affection mutually felt by us was not like that felt by other brothers for each other. My brother saluted me, made a mental (*sic*) obeisance to our parents, uttered the name of Gajanan and stepped out of the house. Having gone as far as Budhwar (Peth) to see him off, I returned. My mind, however, was filled with sadness, and it having occurred to me that contrary to the rules laid down in the Shastras he had set out on a journey without taking any companion with him, I prayed that God might keep him happy. I then came home. At 10 o'clock in the morning, as my brother was not present at dinnertime, my father suspected that he must have gone to some (distant) place. My father being very astute could at once divine (the motive of) our conduct. Our mother was indeed of an unsuspecting nature, but our father gave her to understand that Balkrishna had left home for some (unknown) place. Thereupon she persisted in saying that I knew his whereabouts and refused to eat anything unless I brought him back by writing to him. I told her that he had not apprised me of his departure. But would she believe it? How could our parents, who knew our daily mode of life, believe what I told them? Then I thought that I had not acted properly in remaining behind. I could not bear to hear my mother's lamentations. But what could I do? Wishing to get out of the difficulty anyhow, I assured her that he had gone to Baroda, and made her take her meal. My mother importuned me daily (to give information about my brother), but every day I basely deluded her with some fresh explanation. Our parents led a moral life and I was heartily grieved to have abandoned them and caused them trouble. Everyone in the town would ask me where my brother had gone, and I would reply that he had gone to Baroda, in search of employment. In this manner about fifteen days elapsed, but I received no letter giving any account of his health, etc. This circumstance caused me great anxiety. One day, however, I unexpectedly received a telegram, requesting me to remit Rs. 25 to him by a telegraphic money order. The perusal thereof removed my anxiety, as I learned from it that my brother was in good health. I then began to guess why he wanted money. That, however, was no proper time for (idle) conjectures, and so I began to consider how I might procure the requisite amount. Though a perusal of our lives would lead the reader to suppose that we were expert thieves, we never unjustly took a single chhadam from anyone. On the contrary, in money matters we obliged others, but never incurred any debt ourselves. Not being addicted to any vice we never wanted money. If we at all wanted money, it was for the good of the country. As we thus lived a life of probity, we had considerable credit with the people. I was sure that my request for money would not be refused by any one (of our friends). Accordingly, when I asked for the said amount of one of our friends he at once paid it. I heartily thanked him for this and at once remitted the amount by a telegraphic money order to my brother's address at the Allahabad Post Office according to his instructions. From my brother's (continued) absence my father concluded that I, his eldest son, would also follow him, and even sent letters to that effect to his friends and acquaintances. Not having received any letters from my brother for fifteen days after I had remitted the said amount to him, I became anxious, when one day, as I awoke at dawn, I heard my dear brother's voice, to my great delight. First of all I devoutly thanked God on seeing my brother in sound health. I was especially delighted at the thought that my mother would rejoice (at my brother's return). Accordingly, when she saw Balkrishna that morning her face plainly indicated the joy felt by her. Then on the second or third day after my brother's return, I asked him to give an account of what had occurred at the place to which he had gone. This he did in detail. I think that the high hopes which we had entertained about Nepal were wholly destroyed. I wish that my brother should himself write an account of the perilous position in which he had found himself. I, therefore, omit it from this narrative. After this, we determined to accomplish our object by remaining in our country, regardless of consequences. We also determined never to abandon our parents. Having pondered over what we should do next, I said to my brother that we might make one more application (to Government), stating. "Since you decline to appoint to suitable posts men like ourselves, who are fond of the art of war, how should we gratify our desire? Should we rebel?" Considering that the making of such an application would be tantamount to open hostility, we decided that since the English were our implacable enemies and the cause of our subjection, we should commit as many hostile acts against them as we could. This was the first and the most potent cause of the enmity between the English and ourselves.

Just at this time, the first occasion on which the anniversary of Shivaji's birth was to be celebrated with festivities approached. My brother and myself do not at all like this festival. Such undertakings as involved a great deal of talk highly exasperated us. Besides, some features of the festival held in honor of Shivaji are so extravagant that he himself would not have liked them. In the first place, he would not at all have approved of the custom of celebrating the anniversary of his birth as it was tantamount to placing him on an equal footing with God. For though he was a most ambitious man, and this was natural, since he who would expose his life to such dangers would do so only for glory, he would not have insisted on being worshiped like God. Even his preceptor, Shri Samarth Ramdas, was not considered worthy of being ranked with God. How could then Shivaji, his disciple, at once attain such rank? No jayanti is celebrated in honor of Ramdas. Only his punyatith is celebrated. A jayanti is celebrated only in commemoration of the incarnation assumed by God at various times. It cannot be celebrated in connection with any other event. If the custom of celebrating jayantis of men be once introduced, anyone will be able to celebrate a jayanti in honor of anyone he likes. It will be possible to celebrate a jayanti in honor of even Tilak and Agarkar. We, therefore, do not at all like that these wiseacres should, by holding a festival in honor of Shivaji, raise him to the rank of God. The first of such festivals was celebrated in Natus' Garden in Sadashiv Peth. We attended the festivities, but were much grieved to see the childishness of our people. We could not endure that all people, old and young, should behave in a puerile manner instead of taking such a lesson from Shivaji's life as they ought to have. My brother, therefore, composed two shloks, which are excellent. We learned them by heart at the opportune moment and recited them at a meeting at which a vehement discussion took place between Jinsiwale and the reformer Bhau. These shloks also referred to loquacious men like Jinsiwale and Bhau. The shloks recited at the gathering held in honor of Shivaji are as follows:

No one has ever heard of the lofty trees of lipbravery bearing good fruit; kissing a woman's lips in a dream never produced offspring; you may speak, but do not thunder like clouds which give no showers; a woman's counsel, being unaccompanied by prowess, is ridiculed by the world; merely reciting Shivaji's story like a bard does not secure independence; it is necessary to be prompt in engaging in desperate enterprises like Shivaji and Baji; knowing this you good people take up swords and shields at all events now. Rap your upper arms (like wrestlers) and we shall cut off countless heads of enemies.

On reading the above shloks someone may ask. "You find

fault with others, but what have you yourselves done?" Many persons privately asked us the above question. Considering that if we were asked it in a full assembly it would be incumbent upon us to make our vow known to the public, my brother composed the following shlok anent our vow:

Listen. We shall risk our lives on the battlefield in a national war. Do not look upon our utterances in the presence of many people as a mere farce. We shall assuredly shed upon the earth the life-blood of the enemies who destroy (our) religion. We shall die after killing only. While you yourselves will hear the story like women?

The recitation of the above shloks during the Shivaji festival was followed by loud cheers. After this I also composed some shloks intended to be recited during the Ganpati festival at Bombay. I have already stated that after our hopes of getting enlisted in some regiment were completely destroyed, we became implacable enemies of the English. The drift of all our shloks will be found to be simply this: "Do not talk that idly, (but) do something." In the Ganpati festival we two brothers put on masculine attire and accompanied our recitations with such gestures as were calculated to properly impress the drift of our shloks upon the minds of the assembled people. The shloks referred to are as follows:

Fools, what is the use of your being men? Of what use are your big moustaches? Alas. You are not ashamed to remain in servitude; try, therefore, to commit suicide. Alas. Like butchers the wicked in their monstrous atrocity kill calves and kine. Free her (the cow) from her trouble, die (but) kill the English. Do not remain idle and (thereby) burden the earth. This is called Hindustan (land of the Hindus). How is it that the English rule here? It is a great shame. Do not forget (your) name. Dearly cherish patriotism in your minds. Rise, rap your upper arms, encounter (the enemies). May you succeed in slaughtering the wicked. How valiant were our forefathers on the battlefield. They died after winning glory in the defense of their country. We who have sprung from them are like Saturn whom the Sun has produced. We are not ashamed though our kingdom has been wrested (from us).

Whenever we recited the above shloks we were cheered. Some

people warned us that though what we recited was true, we should be cautious as there were detective policemen among the assembled people. Though we recited the above shloks only at four or five places in Bombay, that was sufficient to make us the subject of popular talk for a long time. We then returned to Poona. One day I went alone to the Anandobhava Theater to hear a lecture annually delivered there. Tilak graced the presidential chair. Seeing Daji Abaji Khare rise to deliver a speech about Shivaji, the cow protector, I flew into a rage. I consider it a disgrace that a vile cow-eater, who ate beef in company with Muhammadans, should deliver a speech about Shivaji the cow-protector, and that the audience should quietly listen to him. Accordingly I said to some mischief-makers, who were sure to reduce a new speaker to a miserable plight: "Friends, mischief-making is reprehensible. But if you indulge in it on an exceptional occasion like the present one, it would reflect credit on the Hindu community to which you belong." Though I made the above request in various ways, none of the blockheads would accede to it. Thereupon I resolved to insult Khare, whom I considered to be a disgrace to our religion, by reciting a shlok which I had composed about him. Accordingly, I approached the speaker's platform, where sat the leading reformers and non-reformers. Someone having told me that if I intended to speak I should first obtain the manager's permission to do so, I requested the manager, by name Mande, to grant it. He, however, refused it. Caring little for his refusal, I advanced with the intention of reciting the shlok. A serious altercation then took place between the manager and myself, and at last some Brahmin wrestler was sent to drive me out. Readers, I had till then neither put up with the slightest insult nor gone to any place where I did not expect to be treated with consideration. I, therefore, leave it to you to imagine how intolerable must have been this insult offered in full assembly to me, who am so jealous of my honor. I was so greatly incensed that I longed to make the educated brutes at once feel what dishonor is and at the same time to let them know how men of honor act. These professors

of law have a notion that every case is to be disposed of by a
court of justice. They do not know for whom laws are made. I
wished to make these modern scholars know that he who can
secure all his rights by the strength of his arm has no occasion
to resort to a court of justice. I wished to deal the wrestler, who
had come to seize me by the arm and drive me out, a blow on
the head with the stick in my hand so as to let him understand
that his artful twists would not prove serviceable to him on every
occasion, and then to punish Tilak, the president of the meeting,
who had sent him (to drive me out). Many of my readers will,
on reading this, feel indignant and say that I am not a patriot
but an enemy of my country. Poor fellows. Let them say it. I
know that many people have a good opinion of Tilak, but they
must be devoid of reason. In my opinion, according to the saying, "Alas (he is) neither a Hindu nor a Yavan." Tilak is neither
a thorough reformer nor is he thoroughly orthodox. For if we
were to credit him with devotion to his own religion, (we must
remember that) he is a member of the association for the removal
of obstacles in the way of widow-remarriage. This sanctimonious
individual is the dear friend of the beef-eater Daji Abaji Khare
(donkey), to whose house he goes occasionally and with whom
he takes meals without any hesitation. This worthy individual
was ashamed to undergo expiation for eating biscuits, but was
not ashamed to take tea. Had he consented to have his moustache shaved off in deference to popular opinion, would forty
generations (of his ancestors) have been consigned to hell? He
tried to place himself on a footing of equality with the authors
of the Smritis by introducing certain innovations in the marriage
ritual. I do not think that anyone had ever seen him performing
such pious acts as hearing a kirtan or puran or visiting a temple.
He did many other similar acts which would be disgraceful to
any man calling himself religious. I have mentioned (only) some
of them. Owing to these acts we have no good opinion of him.
We, however, consider him to be a far better man than a reformer. Latterly, he had adapted his manners to the opinions of
his community, and this had considerably checked his irregular

conduct. We hoped that after some time he would be much improved.

In short, we Chapekars are the slaves of those who are sincerely devoted to their religion, but the implacable enemies of those who are not so. Besides, it was natural that an insult offered in a full assembly to a haughty man like myself, without any consideration of my worth, should incense me. When the above thought occurred to me, I closed my eyes for a little while and questioned God who resides in my heart, "Oh God, how should I act in my present condition?" He inspired me as follows: "You, who are desirous of cleaving your enemies' hearts, have become ready to strike men of your own caste. (But) take heed. You will not succeed in this. It was through ignorance that they insulted you. They do not know you." On learning the will of God to the above effect, I at once left the meeting before the wrestler could seize my hand. I was much dejected for the next two or four days. After my brother and myself had held a consultation, we vowed never to go from that day to any meeting held in connection with any question of public interest. This vow proved of great use to us. As we were not seen taking part in any wild scheme affecting the public we ceased to be reckoned among the well-wishers of the country—a result which was very beneficial to us.

Afterwards, according to our practice every year, we went to Bombay for spending the four monsoon months there. As we were often badly in want of money, it occurred to me, after some consideration of the matter, that I might offer for sale a book designed for the use of the Ganpati melas of that year. Accordingly, I composed one such book and took it to the Suvarna Printing Press for being printed. As might have been expected from our temperament, the tone of the book was rather severe. Before it was printed the proprietor of the press altered it in some places. As it attracted the notice of the Bombay police, they attached all the copies of the book found in the Suvarna Printing Press and ordered me to be present in the Police (Commissioner's) Office the next day. Some copies of the (said) book had (already) been sold. In the evening a detective policeman came to my residence in Vithalvadi under the pretext of buying (some) books, (but really) to ascertain whether I had got any more copies of it. But in accordance with the saying "Set a thief to catch a thief" we recognized him and prevented him from obtaining any material information. Next day I had to appear before Vincent in the Police Office. As the police are discourteous, I, in order to avoid being insulted by them, most humbly prayed to God to preserve my honor, and then went with the proprietor of the said press (to the Police Commissioner's Office). The police directly took us before Vincent. Inspector Roshan Ali and Jamadar Lakshman, of the Detective Police, were present there. The proprietor of the said press was first examined and Mr. Vincent made many cutting remarks about him. Hearing this, I became apprehensive that he might abuse me in the same manner and that a serious altercation might take place between us. But I am very glad to state that owing to the miraculous power of God, he questioned me very calmly and with a smiling face. As I answered his questions with much adroitness he was pleased with me, and told me that my books had been temporarily attached and that I might take them back after the Ganpati festival was over. This gave me much relief. This case taught us the lesson that we should never do anything likely to attract the notice of the Police. I had sent another poem (to the press) for being printed, but in view of the fate of my first book I revoked the order for printing it.

We then became anxious as to what we should do in order to acquire greater boldness, when we heard that only recently an educated Hindu, who had risen to a professorship, had, as it was to be expected from his antecedents, become an apostate and embraced Christianity. Considering him to be a proper person on whom we might inflict punishment, we began to make inquiries about him. We first inquired at the Wilson College where his bungalow was and afterwards saw it in person. On considering how we might accomplish our object, we two brothers came to the conclusion that at first one of us should see the professor and express his desire of being initiated into the Christian religion, and by visiting him for one or two days more obtain information about his mode of life, his family, (the time of) his going out and returning, and other more or less useful particulars, and that further arrangements should be made afterwards. After careful consideration we decided that our dear friend, Bhuskute, who knew English well enough for practical purposes, should see the professor and express a desire as stated above. Accordingly, we gave him elaborate instructions as to how he was to act and sent him there. After his entrance into the bungalow we used to wait somewhere on the outside. After learning on his return what had occurred at the interview, we used to tutor him for the next day's visit. He had assumed the name of Kirtane. He discovered from the expression of Velankar's face that the latter was greatly delighted to hear of Bhuskute's intention of embracing Christianity. Bhuskute must have seen Velankar only three or four times. It was then decided (by us) that Bhuskute should tell Velankar that as one of his friends had expressed a desire to embrace Christianity he would introduce him to Velankar, that my brother should accompany Bhuskute and that he should strike Velankar on the same day. Bhuskute acted in accordance with the above plan, and my brother, Balwantrao, went with him. We two always used to carry our offensive weapons concealed about our persons. They two went into Velankar's bungalow and I stood on the outside. As my brother found no favorable opportunity he abandoned his design of striking (Velankar) on that day. A long discussion about the Christian religion took place between them and Velankar on that day. My brother told (Velankar) that his surname was Sathe. We now feel deep regret for the serious mistake committed by my brother in assuming the above name. Had he assumed any other name instead of the above one, the present calamity would perhaps have not befallen us. When my brother went to see Velankar, the latter had left the bungalow which he had rented and was living in one which he himself had built. In this manner even my brother paid two or three fruitless visits to Velankar. He treated them with much more respect than they deserved and manifested great affection for them. The cause of all this was that the rascally missionary, believing that Bhuskute and my brother intended to embrace

Christianity, tried all means of pleasing them. He always used
to tell them "my friend Dr. Mackichan was greatly delighted to
hear of your intention of embracing Christianity and he is very
eager to see you. We shall, therefore, at once go to see him."
My brother, however, wishing to execute his design without
letting his own face be seen by Velankar's friends, used to put
off his compliance with the said proposal by promising to go (to
Dr. Mackichan) on some future day. As the matter was thus
progressing we fixed a day, *viz.*, Gokul Ashtami, for executing
our design without failure. On that day we were to make Velankar undergo a slight expiation for his act (of becoming a convert). He had given us two books for reading, *viz.*, copies of "An
Indian Youth" and the New Testament. It was decided that the
third man (*i.e.*, myself) should also go to Velankar's house on
the Gokul Ashtami day. It was settled that I should pretend to
be Sathe's brother-in-law and to have come (to Bombay) to make
inquiries about him in consequence of a rumor of his intended
conversion. He (Bhuskute) had already told Velankar that Sathe
used to live at Bandra. Two days before the date fixed Bhuskute
told Velankar that Sathe's brother-in-law, by name Bhide (*i.e.*,
myself), had come to take him away, that Sathe would bring him
with himself two days after by the 10 P.M. train and that the three
persons would come to his (Velankar's) house at about 11 o'-
clock on that night; and he, therefore, requested him not to retire
till that time. When that auspicious day came we devoutly
prayed to God as follows: "Oh God, this day thou didst become
incarnate as Krishna in order to destroy the wicked, and didst
slay Kamsa and Chanur. As thou hatest the wicked very much,
do thou give success to us who too have girded up our loins to
destroy the wicked." Having offered this prayer, we started from
our residence at about half past 8 and went to the Grant Road
Station, where we anxiously waited for the desired opportunity.
When it was just close upon half past 10 we uttered God's name
and went to Velankar's house. He was talking with someone on
the upper story. Being informed of our arrival, he after some time
came downstairs with a candlelight and entered a shed outside
his bungalow. There we three entered into conversation with

him. Being introduced to him, I said, "My friend Sathe having left his family has been living here for many days. I hear that he has now some improper idea in his head. As he has full confidence in you, you should, by giving him proper advice, induce him to go back to and live with his family." Hearing this Velankar said, "Mr. Bhide, what you say is true. But every man is independent in the matter of religion and it is a great sin to throw obstacles in his way. In my case also, when my intended conversion became known to all, all my relatives, friends and acquaintances advised me in many ways (to give up my intention). I, however, without caring for their advice carried out my intention. You should not, therefore, make me act sinfully in this matter." At this I pretended to be silenced. We then talked upon other subjects, and at last upon the story of Krishna. When Velankar, who had disgraced his family, began to find fault with the eternal Krishna, we could not put up with it, and Sathe struck a very severe blow with his steel-bound stick on Velankar's head and a moderately severe one on the back. We then returned home and expressed our gratitude to God.

On the next day news of the above occurrence spread in all parts of Bombay, and all Hindus and Muhammadans appeared to be greatly rejoiced at it. The Police also began to make very searching inquiries. At 2 P.M. on the next day, a European constable with one or two (Police) peons came to Kamat Company's chawl in which we lived, to enquire about Kirtane and Sathe. They asked the inmates of every room whether two men by name Sathe and Kirtane respectively were living there. On our telling them that neither of them lived there, they went away. Apprehending that the two books in our possession (which we had received from Velankar) might serve as evidence (against us), we burned them. The *Times* (of India), the *Bombay Gazette* and the other English and Marathi newspapers then began to write about this Velankar affair with vehemence. In these articles the police were blamed for their inability to detect such a (serious) offense. Thereupon the police feeling rather ashamed began to arrest persons indiscriminately, take them to Velankar for identification, and release them on his failing to identify them. Apprehensive of falling into the clutches of the police, we determined to play a very clever trick on them in order to mislead them. We had already told him (Velankar) that all of us were inhabitants of Kolhapur. We now wrote in the Balbodh character a letter to the following effect in the style of an illiterate man:

You abandoned your own religion and became a convert to another and thereby disgraced the Maratha Community to which we belong. We, therefore, inflicted a light punishment upon you and left for Kolhapur.

In order to convince him (of the truth of the above statements) allusions were made in that letter to the books (given to us by him) and to certain incidents in our conversation with him. We caused Bhuskute to post it at Poona. We addressed it from Kothrud in order to make Velankar believe that we had started for Kolhapur on foot. When it reached him he showed it to the police and said, "Do not make any more fruitless inquiries or bring any more men to me for identification. I am certain that they have gone to Kolhapur." As soon as the police heard this, they relaxed their efforts to our satisfaction. The English papers, however, continued to discuss the matter now and then. Hearing that Dr. Mackichan was more exasperated than any other person, we also found out and marked his bungalow. A few days afterwards, the bubonic plague now prevailing in the country broke out in Bombay.

In the meanwhile we again tried to get ourselves enlisted in a regiment, but failed. This was the last disappointment suffered by us and we strongly reviled the English as follows: "A system of administration so cruel as that of the English cannot, if search be made, be found in any region of this globe. Far better were the tyrannical Yavan kings, who, with sword in hand, actually cut the throats of men as if they were so many goats. But the English are perfidious and I positively declare that no other people can be found on this earth who are as villainous as they and who like them ruin others by a show of kindness. As God has given men different features, so He has endowed them with different temperaments. Men's desires necessarily vary according to their temperaments. The three principles of sattva (goodness or excellence), raja (passion or foulness) and tama (darkness or ignorance) exist in a greater or less proportion in all men and are the cause of the difference between their respective bent of mind as manifested in their conduct. If a sovereign were to act in opposition to human disposition or inclinations implanted by God, would not that be tantamount to ordering an innocent man, on the strength of authority, to do a particular act against his will or, in other words, to sentencing him to rigorous imprisonment? If he be found to entertain any immoral desire it would be right to check him. But our request, though legal, was refused. Who will call him king who exercises such arbitrary powers? Hitherto there have been many cruel Yavan kings in India, but they made no rules for excluding Hindus from particular appointments or for limiting the number of those open to them. It is a fact well known in history that our people have even discharged the duties of a premier requiring tact and trustworthiness. It is also possible even now to point out the descendants of persons who served in the army and obtained jaghirs by performing deeds of valor." These thoughts created in our minds a violent prejudice against the English and we resolved to persecute them in future. We knew only one or two on our side, while those against whom we were only to commence hostilities were far more powerful than ourselves. The difference between them and ourselves was as great as that between the sky and the regions under the earth. Many people will ask why we formed such an absurd design as the above in the face of the rule, "In marriage, enmity and love the parties must be each other's equals." But, friends, I interpret the above (rule of the) Shastra in a manner very different from yours. The meaning of the rule "We should form (an alliance by) marriage with one who is our equal" is as follows: We should form it with good qualities, irrespectively of his outward riches. Accordingly, I have seen several great men give their daughters in marriage to poor but (otherwise) eligible persons and also make over their riches to them. So also, love and enmity depend on greatness of mind. What does it matter if a man be not fortunate enough to have riches? He whose mind is great (under any circumstances), though he may have no riches, that does not in the least detract from his greatness of mind. The wise must not forget this. Though we are destitute of wealth, we feel proud to say that our family is noble. Our parents are highborn, possessed of greatness of mind, generous and virtuous, and we owe our origin to them. Friends, there being at present a lack of discerning men capable of properly appreciating the merits of our parents and ourselves, and my end having approached, I am compelled to indulge in self-glorification, for which I beg my Aryan brethren to excuse me. (In forming an estimate of our merits) my friends must not confine their attention only to the fact that our father used to perform kirtans and we used to beat tall behind him. If they make careful inquiries about the innate disposition and outward conduct of our parents and ourselves, they will come to know the truth. In short, though we have neither an army, nor territory, nor money, we still possess greatness of mind and are therefore competent to pit ourselves against any being except God. Success or failure depends upon chance and has no connection whatever with greatness.

Taking this view, we girded up our loins to enter upon a struggle with the English. We began to consider to what undertaking we should first put our hand. It must be a very grave one and of such a nature that our success in accomplishing it might be the talk of all, rejoice our Aryan brethren, fill the English with sorrow, and put upon us the indelible brand of treason. While pondering over this, we were inspired with the following idea: There is a statue of the Queen of England situated at a certain crossing off our roads in the Fort in Bombay. This place is an important one. This woman, after the Mutiny of 1857, acquired the universal sovereignty of India by making fair but deceitful promises. She alone is the real enemy of our people. Other white men are our enemies only insofar as they are her subjects. We should, therefore, begin at this place. Other acts (should be done) afterwards. Had she been in India we would have tried to wreak vengeance upon herself even at the risk of losing our lives. We would not have cared for other less eminent people. It is, however, to be deeply regretted that owing to our misfortune she is not here and it is not likely that she will ever come to this country. We, therefore, resolved to make an auspicious beginning by first dealing with her stone image, and proceeded to make the necessary arrangements.

We at first carefully examined the spot and thought over all the conveniences and inconveniences, and considered in what way we should deal with the statue. Our first thought was to break its head into small pieces by means of a large hammer with a long handle. But on mature consideration, we thought it difficult to do this in a short time and therefore resolved only to disfigure it. Considering that "He who does not act up to his professions gets his face blackened," we resolved to inflict the same punishment on her. Proceeding to make arrangements for the execution of our design, we decided to put round the neck of the statue a string of precious gems in the form of shoes as a token of our devotion. But whence were the gems to be brought? We wanted small ones and began to look for them. Moreover, it was necessary that the shoes should be old. The older they were, the better would they suit our purpose. How were these conditions to be fulfilled? As these could not be purchased with money in the market, we searched many rubbish heaps, but could not obtain any such gems there. But as our devotion is genuine, God helped us. While in Bombay, I used to go to a large house in Kandewadi belonging to a gentleman by name Wagle, for the purpose of bathing, performing sandhya and making prostrations (to the sun). While searching there for these gems I found them in a basket lying in disorder under a staircase among other things. I stole them with great dexterity and formed them into a necklace, in the middle of which we attached tassels of a very filthy substance. I cannot mention that substance here. The shoes forming the necklace were of three or four sorts. Having finished the necklace, we intended to execute our design on the (auspicious) day of Dasara because on that day our ancestors used to set out for the purpose of overpowering their enemies. In accordance with this our ancient custom we decided to make a beginning (on the said day). On consulting astrological works we found two very auspicious periods, one occurring at dawn on the Dasara day and the other at 2 P.M. on the second day after Dasara. As our object was to carry out our design in the manner enjoined by the Shastras, we resolved to execute it on the day fixed (as above). We bought six annas worth of dammar. It was very liquid. In order to make it into a very hard plaster we mixed with it some gram-flour and the filthy substance above referred to. Having thus prepared the mixture we kept it in a long tube of zinc and awaited the arrival of the appointed auspicious hour. On the approach of the Dasara day we devoutly prayed to God to give us success in our undertaking and resolved to get up at the earliest dawn. But as we awoke from sleep at a late hour on that day, our whole plan failed. We, therefore, resolved not to fail (to execute our design) at the second auspicious hour. That night we kept awake praying to God all the time. Soon after 8 o'clock at night, we took the tube containing dammar and the necklace of shoes to a certain spot marked by us. Just before 2 o'clock we remembered Gajanan and started from our residence. At that time there was bright moonlight. The police were standing motionless at various places on the road. I carried in my hand a stick long enough to reach my ears and was walking at a distance (from my brother). My brother carried an iron pipe in his hand. We were walking at a distance from each other. Instead of going by the metaled road, we passed through the open space adjoining the Marine Battalion (Lines), and after reaching the back part of the police station near the Queen's statue went a little farther. We stopped for a while at a certain spot, and my brother went near the statue and came back. We then decided that one of us should worship the statue and the other should defend him (if necessary). Though any obstacle were to arise the worshiper was to finish his task quietly, while the guard was to silently remove the obstacle by the use of the last expedient, *viz.*, violence. Accordingly, I undertook to act as a guard, while my brother undertook the worship and both of us started. My brother crossed the railing on the right of the statue and entered the compound, while, fully equipped, I stood on the (left) side of the statue toward the police station. At that time the light in the lantern at the police station was dimly burning. One or two peons were indistinctly observed in the dark to be smoking cigarettes. From the spot where I stood I could distinctly see the statue as well as perceive any movement on the part of the men in the police station. A little while before my brother climbed the statue a man went by the road which passes the police station. In our opinion this man was a police Havaldar or Jamadar. I thought that the man might happen to see what we were doing and that I might have to discharge my duty. But nothing of the sort took place and the man went on without stopping. In the meantime my brother had finished the worship (of the statue). When the necklace was thrown round the neck (of the statue) it struck its chest and made a sound which, however, failed to draw the attention of the (police) sepoy. My brother got out of the compound by leaping over the railing and then I too joined him on the road. By way of precaution we had previously seen some other roads by which we might return home in case of necessity. But no such necessity having arisen, we returned home by the high road. On our return home, we, as usual, praised God by reciting hymns and then retired. When next morning we went to see the statue, we saw many Hindus, Parsis, Muhammadans and Europeans assembled there. All except the Europeans appeared to be delighted. The police also had gathered there. They removed the necklace from the statue and kept it at the police station and tried to remove the dammar by a powerful jet of water. Just then a prohibitory order was received from the police authorities for stopping the use of all remedies for the present. Seeing this we returned home. At about 12 o'clock the news spread over the town, while at night it became the subject of general talk. All began to admire the daring of the author of the deed. Many columns of newspapers edited by Europeans were devoted to this topic. The (editors of) Marathi papers were inwardly delighted, but outwardly they said that the bad character (who had perpetrated the deed) ought to be arrested and punished. Specu-

lation was rife. Some said that the deed was done not by any
Hindu or Muhammadan, but by a European. Others said that
a Muhammadan had done it. Everyone said that such a daring
deed could not have been done by a Hindu. We were highly
offended to hear such disagreeable words uttered by anyone.
With a view to make it generally known that a Hindu had done
the deed, we had already written a letter and placed it on the
statue. We were hitherto in doubt as to whether the police had
got it or not. I now learn that they did not get it. It, therefore,
seems that it was blown away by the wind. The Times (of India)
gave a full description of the occurrence, with the exception of
the tassels attached to the necklace and the letter. We, therefore,
thought of writing a letter to that paper. As, however, we do not
know English, we had recourse to the following artifice: As the
tenor of our letter made it desirable that it should be posted at
Thana, we addressed the following anonymous letter written in
Marathi to the editor of the Suryodaya, a newspaper published
in that town:—

We have formed an association called Dandapani. Our fixed determination is to die and kill (others) for the sake of our religion. The association was formed on the recent auspicious day of Dasara. Its first
achievement was the blackening of the face of (the statue of) the Queen
of England who made a distinction between natives and Europeans.
Having done this the association informs the public as follows: This
Dandapani Association will not be overawed by anyone. Anyone who
encourages immorality, whether the Queen or someone superior to her,
is the enemy of this association. This detailed statement will certainly
enable all to comprehend its object. We, therefore, request you to take
the trouble of forwarding an English version of this letter to the Times
(of India). You will thereby earn credit for having assisted the said
association.

The purport of the letter was only that. That letter is with my
friend Mr. Brewin, and I am of the opinion that it should be
published. We sent the above letter to the editor of the Suryodaya. But as it was not published in the Times (of India) we
concluded that the editor (of the Suryodaya) had not forwarded
it to the Times (of India). I, however, now learn that he had
forwarded it. In this manner our first undertaking, *viz.*, this affair

of the Queen's statue, was successfully accomplished. The people, however, continued to talk about the matter more or less till recently. In the course of that talk, they gave utterance to some very amusing things, not even a hundredth part of which I can mention here for fear of prolixity.

At that time the bubonic plague was on the increase. All began to complain loudly of the increasing oppression on the part of the Government. People began to leave Bombay for the districts through fear (of the plague), while those in the mofussil ceased to go to Bombay owing to the same cause.

In the meantime the date of the Matriculation Examination was drawing near. As usual a fine mandap was put up near Colaba for the said examination. As the plague was increasing every moment, people from all parts (of the Presidency) petitioned the authorities concerned for a postponement of the examination. The people of Poona made strenuous efforts in the matter. As, however, the authorities were inexorable, we resolved to take up the matter into our hands, being satisfied that we might settle it in a manner that would procure us popular applause. Besides, we are dead against (higher) education, which has a bad effect on the boys. We are of opinion that the loss of our physical strength is partly to be laid at the door of this Mlenchha learning. The entire society has devoted itself to education and become much too thoughtful, and thereby has lost manliness. At present (such is our condition that) if anyone were to kick and cuff us soundly, we shall only weary ourselves by holding meetings, making petitions and discussing the matter. Though we have already lost so much by education, our educated men complain that Government does not give us higher education. A vicious but poor man, in order to gratify his evil inclination, at first spends his own money to seduce some rich man's son into an evil habit, but when the latter has become a slave to the habit, withholds his own money and leads a life of pleasure and ease (at his expense and) in his company so long as he has any money with him. In like manner when the English assumed the administration of India, they thought it necessary to extinguish the spirit of the Hindus by making them addicted to the vice of education. They, therefore, spent their own money at first. Seeing that the people have become pretty well addicted to it, they are now withholding their own money. The more they do so, the more our people think that they are unwilling to give us education, because it is the only means of securing our good. They, therefore, devote themselves to education, with still greater enthusiasm. But my brethren, you commit a mistake in thinking so. They will not lose but gain by giving you education. They wish to close the schools and colleges, not for stopping education but for reducing expenditure. They know that if they were to sever all connection with education, the people being enthusiastically attached to it will pay constant visits to them at their bungalows and invite them to pan-supari in order to obtain permission to open schools and colleges at their own expenses. This is actually the case at present. If they are (really) unwilling to educate people, why are they so anxious to educate women? They always endeavor to educate the lower orders because they wish to make those castes addicted to it which are now free from it and then to enjoy the fun. The Marathas, etc., have lately begun to complain as follows:"We do not receive education. Only the Brahmins become educated. Even in former times they, with like selfishness, educated themselves, but kept us in ignorance. We, therefore, pray that the paternal Government will be graciously pleased to give us education." They repeatedly make such petitions (to Government). But they fail to understand that it was by receiving education that the Brahmins destroyed their religious observances, caste, families, morality and immorality, manliness and impotence. If in spite of the above results of that baleful education the Marathas, etc., wish to acquire it let them do so by all means and become effeminate. Many people, on reading these our opinions which are quite opposed to education, will call us fools. Poor things, let them do so. In a village inhabited by naked persons, a person wearing a dhoti is sure to be called a downright fool. But he alone will be called wise by discerning persons. I can write much on this topic, but refrain from doing so with a view to avoid prolixity. To be brief, as the University was acting in opposition to (the wishes of) the people and was not also liked by us, we thought of inflicting some damage on that body and accordingly began to make inquiries about the mandap referred to above. We saw the mandap which was being put up near Colaba. Our intention was to set fire to it only one day before the date of the examination, because in that case no new mandap could be put up before the time of the examination, which, therefore, would be necessarily postponed. But afterwards it occurred to us that if we did not find any opportunity on the previous day, the examination would begin on the next day. We, therefore, thought that there was no objection to setting fire to it one or two days before (the examination day). On examining the mandap, we considered on what side it would be convenient to set it on fire, and proceeded to make the necessary arrangements. Knowing that it would be difficult to go a long way in the latter part of the night we resolved to do the business before 9 o'clock. The mandap was to be set on fire on the side toward the railway compound. The materials and the method employed were similar to those employed in setting fire to the upper story of the building belonging to Messrs. Philips & Co., Bhudwar Peth, Poona, which had been occupied by a certain missionary. After setting fire to the mandap we got out of the compound by leaping (over the fence), walked along the seashore as far as the Churney Road Station and thence got home. After we had walked over a considerable distance, we could see the glare of the fire. By the time we got home, the fire (had attained such dimensions that it) could easily be seen from our chawl. But the people (in our chawl) did not know that the mandap was on fire. All of them had assembled in the upper gallery to see the fire and wondered where it had occurred. We also stood among them. They were in doubt (as to the origin of the fire). Though we had no doubt whatever (on that point), we did not disclose the true facts to them, but looked on with them in (feigned) astonishment. The next day the people knew for certain that the mandap had been burned down. The educated people in particular were much delighted to hear this. The police shifted their own responsibility by giving out that the fire had been caused by a spark from the engine of a railway train. There was, however, a very general rumor among the people that the fire had been caused by some Poonaite. A similar suspicion of the Poonaites had been expressed in papers edited by Englishmen, in connection with the blackening of the face of the Queen's statue, though it cannot be known on what grounds they thought so. As, however, we are very proud of Poona, once the capital of the Peshwas, we were delighted to hear the above reports. The mandap being thus consumed by fire like an offering, the authorities were compelled to postpone the examination, in consequence of which the people highly praised the authors of the said deed. We were greatly delighted to hear ourselves thus praised. A few days after this we returned to Poona with our family. On our return we began to look out for some serious enterprise, but could not soon find any. As, however, we had made it our vocation to persecute the irreligious and glorify the religious, we could not feel easy at heart unless we did something toward the accomplishment of our object. We were always absorbed in thinking what we should do and how we should do it. The good or evil acts of the irreligious did not remain hidden from our keen observation. Our wrath was specially directed against the Sudharak and Dnyan Chakshu newspapers. We had obtained full information about the editors and proprietors of both these newspapers. My readers must be aware of the fact that one of the editors of the Sudharak was some time ago first lightly punished and then even a letter of warning was sent to him; but I am very sorry to observe that he heeded our warning only in the first issue of the paper published after it was given, but thereafter he reverted to his old practices and thus treated us with contempt. As we could not put up with this, we resolved to cut off the head of this Devdhar (the said editor) and thus show to the world what severe punishment is deserved by persons for the great sin (committed by them) of vilifying their own religion. But on mature consideration it was resolved to kill an offending European in the first place and then, after warning these brutes in human form to the effect that those on whom they rely so much were dealt with by us in this manner, to ask them once more to beware. Having resolved that, if even after such warning these men should fail to mend their ways, they were mercilessly killed without delay. After this we ceased to give any further thought to these educated blockheads.

In the meantime, our dear friend, Bhuskute, reported (to us) that Mr. Thorat, a teacher in Bhave School, was a very bad man, being addicted to the vice of sodomy. This educated teacher was in the habit of showing favor and giving higher rank to those boys only who were handsome and young. We had already known Mr. Thorat to be a man of such character. We used to keep a register of all ill-behaved men. There are in our register (the names of) many men who are very vile and whose conduct is disgusting. All of them were to suffer at our hands one after another, but the Almighty does not seem inclined to get this service done by us. God's will prevails. The educated are invariably addicted to vice. This may probably be the effect of a liberal education. Let us proceed. We had many a time sent anonymous letters to Mr. Bhave of the Bhave School representing that the conduct of Thorat was such that it was not advisable to retain him in the school as the boys might contract evil habits, and that it would be to his (Bhave's) interest to dismiss him from the school; but no satisfactory arrangements were made. Later on, when we came to know of many of his other vices, *viz.*, eating flesh, drinking wine, vilifying the gods and the (Hindu) religion, etc., Bhuskute was strongly of opinion that he should receive chastisement at our hands. It was resolved to get this done by Bhuskute in order to inspire him with courage, and we made careful inspection of the place where he resided. He used to live on the first floor of Mantri's Wada in a room overlooking the street. When my brother and Bhuskute entered the room through a small window overlooking the road, they perceived that he was awake. He was sleeping in a cloth-partitioned room. When, on hearing footsteps, he repeatedly asked in a low voice, "Who is there? Who is there?" my brother told (Bhuskute) to strike him and he struck him one blow; but the blow was feeble as Bhuskute was in a state of nervous excitement and he (Thorat) raised an alarm. Thereupon, my brother gave him a heavier blow and both then swiftly jumped out of the window and escaped. The two pieces of iron piping (carried by them) in their hands remained on the floor while jumping down, and were taken charge of by the police. The next day this circumstance was much talked of in the town, but our object was not accomplished. The people said that some thieves had come, but not being able to steal anything went away. As he was, however, not a well-known man, no one said anything about his vices. We did not derive any great satisfaction from this affair as our pride for (our) religion did not come to light. After this, with the intention of doing something, we one night took off the signboard at the office of the Sudharak and placed it on Khasgiwale's privy which faced the high road, and, having filled an earthen jar with the ordure in that privy, suspended it from the door chain of the office of the Sudharak, and wrote on that jar the words "Remove our excrements." Having done this during the night, we went in the morning to the spot (Sudharak's office) to see the fun; but as this state of things did not last for a long time, the people could not enjoy the fun to their hearts' content. The matter, however, was to some extent talked about in the city.

Some days after this incident a European brought down some kind of show to the new Market. Its big apparatus had already arrived there two days before. On seeing the apparatus we could not make out what wonderful show it was. But all our doubts were removed when he (the European) set up the show by arranging its several parts. It is necessary to place before the reader a description of this show. Friends, this show was not so very wonderful. It is, however, the ignorance of our people which is unparalleled. In this India of ours, I have seen this show set up by the poor people at their fairs and gatherings. A big pillar is set up on the ground and on the top of it a canopy, to which (wooden) horses and camels are attached, is made to turn round. On payment of one pice, a ride on these (wooden animals) is allowed. Generally, boys and country-people take a ride on these wooden horses, but gentlemen never do so. In short, a show similar to that which we consider to be so very vulgar was brought into the Market, the only difference being that it was of an improved type. It consisted of two divisions; the upper division was in a manner decorated and couches were placed therein at intervals. The canopy was overdecorated with tinsel. Some sort of music was played while the canopy turned round. At night it glittered with lamps. The proprietor of the show had fixed two rates of admission, namely, two annas for (a seat on) the lower division and four annas for (a seat on) the upper one. While whirling round, this show afforded the same pleasure as is derived from our country merry-go-rounds. But as it was brought there by a European, our wiseacres flocked to see it like ghosts. The show for which our poor people charge only one pice a head, and thus earn their livelihood, is not patronized by our people professing themselves to be refined. But as soon as they see that a European (has brought one), they, forgetful of their position, over and over again visit it like boys, paying four annas a head each time. I, therefore, am at a loss to know how to characterize these wiseacres. Many reformers had stigmatized us by being born amongst us. These fools have no idea of patriotism. We two brothers shall never admire, or derive any pleasure from, any invention of the English, though it might show the highest inventive skill. Though many admirable amusements like the phonograph have hitherto been introduced into India, our patriotism has never permitted us to see them even though people persuaded us to do so and were prepared to pay for us. If we have at all seen any, we have never in consequence of our patriotic feeling been inspired with admiration for them. We have not starved for not having seen the extraordinary novelties introduced by foreigners, nor do the unpatriotic reformers seem to have grown fat for having seen them. It is the foreigners who fill their own coffers by plundering us and then bid good-bye to the country. We used to feel greatly exasperated at these things, but what could we do? How were we to expostulate with these idiots (though they call themselves learned, I reckon them among perfect idiots)? Thinking that the best course would be to get rid of that apparently seductive show, we resolved to set fire to it. We accordingly procured phosphorus, and having made it into tablets, stuck pins into them to be handy for use. We then arranged that Bhuskute and my brother, Bapurao, should go into the upper division (of the show) and make use of (some of) them (to set fire to it), while I should use others in (setting fire to) the private tent (of the proprietor) that was pitched on the ground, so that both the (merry-go-round and the) tent should be ablaze simultaneously. Accordingly, my brother went into the upper division of the show, and when he was about to come down, I, on my part, set fire below and immediately the tent on the ground was ablaze. Thereupon, all the spectators came down to extinguish the fire. We were waiting to see the show also in a similar condition, but through some inexplicable cause it did not catch fire. The fire engine having come to the spot put down the fire. The proprietor of the show suffered a good deal of loss. The next day the police came there to keep order, but we having showered stones upon them they could not do anything. On the third day, a larger number of police came to the assistance (of the showman). In spite of them, however, we again attacked the show and some of the lamps and (wooden) horses and camels having been broken on the occasion, the showman was subjected to considerable loss. At last that European got disgusted and removed his show to a place near the (railway) station. We then let him alone. We did not derive any great pleasure from this performance, but only felt that we had not wasted our hours of leisure.

In the meanwhile rumors about the increase of the bubonic plague in the city began to spread, and people began to say that Government intended to make effective arrangements regarding it. They also said that the arrangements (here) would be similar to those in Bombay. But as we were not in the least satisfied with the preventive measures adopted in Bombay, we determined to make an attempt to oppose the measures if the oppression practiced in Bombay were repeated here.

While we were thus considering the matter, that very system was gradually put into operation, and after a few days we heard that one Mr. Rand was appointed to give effect to it. On inquiry we learned that he was the same Mr. Rand who had sentenced (some) respectable gentlemen of Wai to imprisonment. We, therefore, resolved not to trouble the other officers of the (Plague) Committee, lest they might get alarmed, but to punish the principal officer alone. We then made careful inquiries (to find out) whether Mr. Rand was a good or a bad man. It was rumored in the city that he was a wicked man. His notorious injustice at Wai was the index of his perversity. We had, however, a great desire to witness personally his iniquitous practices in our own city. As soon as we heard of Mr. Rand's appointment, we three, *viz.*, we two brothers and Bhuskute, began to look for him. But he could not be seen anywhere. Some said he had not yet arrived, while others said he had. Such were the conflicting rumors that flew about in the city. Every day we went into the Cantonment, but his bungalow could not be found. Many a time did we go to (office of the Plague) Committee. There we saw Beveridge of Hong Kong, Colonel Philips, Dr. Jones and other Europeans. We had mistaken Colonel Philips for Mr. Rand, but one day that illusion was dispelled unmistakably. How to learn his identity was then our sole anxiety. We could not openly question anybody on the point for fear of exciting suspicion. Thus we spent several days in simply trying to have a look at Mr. Rand. But he had not arrived till then. The rumors that he had come and taken over charge of his duties were groundless. We think that he took charge of his duties long after (this time). We had a full view of this individual on the day the inspection commenced; but still we took care to ascertain his identity from many persons. We then saw his carriage, and, on inquiry of the coachman through Bhuskute as to where Mr. Rand had put up, we learned that he was staying at the Club. We then paid frequent visits to the Club premises, but could get no inkling of his whereabouts. We all three then ceased to visit the Cantonment and took to visiting the Municipal (office) where we could see him in the mornings as well as in the evenings. Ever since the commencement of the house-to-house visitation, he used to come to Bhudhwar (Peth) every morning and thence proceed to the places where the inspection was to take place. Many people used to collect together in Budhwar (Peth) in order to see him when he came there. On the first day, the work of inspection began in Budhwar and the sight was an unprecedented one. The people, being unused to such inspections, were off their guard.

Had they known that this inspection meant only spoliation; that the white men carrying on that work were marauders with Colonel Philips, Lewis and other white men as their ringleaders; that Mr. Rand was the chief in command over them; that it was merely for the sake of carrying on this premeditated and extensive loot that one Dr. Jones was appointed beforehand; that as a preliminary step these English marauders had caused him to make large openings in the houses of the rich as well as of the poor with the only object of rendering visible, while on their raid in broad daylight, the treasury boxes and other articles placed in the dark; that like the Ramoshi dacoits of our own country, who first make careful inquiries (about the belongings of their victims) to enable them to commit dacoities during night, Dr. Jones had, at the outset, by means of a general inquiry prepared a list of the rich as well as the poor people of the city and had handed it over to those marauders at the commencement of the operations; and that those marauders, taking advantage of the mildness of the Hindus, were about to commence their pillage under the guise of law; (in short) if the rayats had known beforehand that their paternal Government was about to cut the throats of their own subjects in the above manner, they would have, to save themselves, migrated to some other place with all their belongings. But as they failed to perceive this state of things beforehand they remained in their homes (confident of their) security. Meanwhile a band of these marauders paid their first visit to Budhwar (Peth). Immediately on their arrival, they stationed guards at the corner of the street and began to break open shops by picking the locks. Oh! what a spectacle it was. Indeed, neither history nor tradition can show such treatment accorded to a subject people by their rulers. One can understand an army raised to meet an enemy being used in repelling an invading foe; but here we see our valiant Englishmen (utilizing) their brave and well-equipped forces in swooping down upon moribund victims (of the plague) and packing them off to hospitals. How very brave of them. Would (any other) ruler on the face of the globe use his forces in such a fashion? Our English (rulers), however, appear to think that valor consists not in striking down a man in full possession of his powers, which anyone can do, but in capturing those who are stricken with illness and are unable to move an inch. It is for this reason that they employed their well-drilled soldiers on such operations. In this way did these plunderers commence their depredations. We always followed (the parties which carried on) this plunder, with the object of seeing with our own eyes their high-handed proceedings. I prefer to call these operations a loot rather than inspection. While this loot was going on, high officers of Government with Mr. Rand at their head paraded in the streets and supervised the breaking of locks, the making away with furniture and (other) lawless proceedings and also saw that all these operations were duly carried on. They were at this time (so much) blinded (with authority) that they cared not for any Hindu gentleman (however high his position might be). Nothing but burning, demolition, wreckage and arrests were to be seen in those parts which this band of raiders visited. I do not think that those who have seen such sights would characterize these vilest men otherwise than as marauders. Rules were framed for regulating the manner in which this pillage was to be carried on. The rules which were reduced to writing were in themselves mild in a large measure, but the manner in which they were carried out appeared to be quite the reverse. It was expressly laid down in the rules that no one should so act as to wound the religious susceptibilities of anyone. But these white men purposely acted in such a way as to exasperate us, and Mr. Rand witnessed this spectacle with great satisfaction.

I am unable to describe how exasperated we felt on such occasions. We resolved to take his (Mr. Rand's) life at all risks. Having formed this resolve we set to work. We possessed swords only. We had two pistols but had no gunpowder and hence they were useless. A pistol was, of course, the most convenient weapon for a swift action, but what was to be done? Whence was the ammunition to be procured? We, therefore, resolved to perpetrate the deed with swords alone. We selected two of the best we possessed and attached to them straps of tape to sling them from our shoulders. The sheaths which were of black (leather) were wrapped in pieces of white turban and thus made to appear white. Having made these preparations, we began to look out for a suitable spot (to execute our design), but did not succeed in fixing upon any. We, therefore, determined to perpetrate the deed near the (Municipal) Committee's office, the only restriction being that it was to be executed not earlier than 8 o'clock in the evening. The idlers in the city had, however, put Mr. Rand on his guard by sending intimidatory anonymous letters to him. This put us to a great deal of trouble. He would not remain in the city after nightfall, and began to take with him an escort of sowars on his way (to the Municipal office) and back. We, however, did not allow ourselves to be discouraged in the least. We resolved to kill both (Mr. Rand and the sowars). But we could not move out with swords except at night time, while he (Mr. Rand) would not allow nightfall to overtake him (in the city). Several days elapsed in this manner. Oppression as well as the plague increased in the city (and) it was wholly abandoned by its inhabitants. Our father received invitations from distant places to go there as the plague was raging (in Poona) and he made preparations to go to a distant place, and, therefore, we began to put impediments in the way of his going. When, however, we saw that he very much wished to leave Poona, we decided that it would be more convenient (for us) to go to our house at Chinchwad than to any distant place. Chinchwad being (only) ten miles distant from Poona, we thought that, in case we went to that place, we could come here any day and execute our design. Accordingly, we proposed to go to Chinchwad, and our father, having approved of the proposal, wrote about it to our uncle at the place; but the latter raised many objections (to our proposal) and wrote back to say that it was not advisable for us to remove there. Thus did he manifest his brotherly feeling. As we could not secure any other place in the vicinity of Poona, we made a request to our vyahi, Mr. Paranjpe, in the matter and obtained his permission to remove to his garden at Kirkee. We found this place more convenient than Chinchwad and shifted there on an auspicious (day).

We took great care not to allow anyone even to suspect that we three were bent upon the perpetration of a terrible deed. While at Kirkee, we formed the acquaintance of one R. Jones, a missionary, living in the Kirkee bazaar. We asked for and obtained 25 to 30 percussion caps from him, but gunpowder could not be obtained anywhere. Being, however, informed by Bhuskute that we would be able to procure gunpowder at the house of Kachare, a mali in a garden at Kothrud, we three proceeded thither one night as if for pleasure and made away with some gunpowder and small shot. (In the meanwhile) Mr. Rand had carried his oppression to the highest pitch. The people talked about (the advisability of) taking his life and lamented that there was no religious enthusiast amongst them who could do that work. The people of other places scoffed at the Poonaites, and the newspapers wrote in derision about the city, calling it garrulous and nothing more. Every day saw new modes of oppression. Temples were desecrated in one part of the city, in another women were outraged and idols broken. The poor and the helpless were the greatest sufferers at the hands of these marauders. While this state of things was going on, we every day came to Poona from Kirkee and returned home in the evening. Our father did not like to see us go to and return from Poona in the noon-day sun. He pointed out to us in various ways that the course we were following would be deleterious to our health, but as we were bent upon the execution of our object we persisted in paying stealthy visits to Poona. When our father came to know of this, he got angry with us and moved back to Poona, and we too with all the members of our family followed suit. The bubonic plague was raging in the city at this time, but we had the consolation that it would now be easy for us to make an attempt to carry out our plan.

In the meanwhile, our dear friend, Dattatraya Bhuskute, was seized with this deadly fever. On the day he fell ill, he came and told us about it. He, however, said that as the fever was of an ordinary type we need not entertain any fears on that score.

After this he went home and we never saw him again. As no member of his family knew that we were his friends, we could not call at his house to inquire after his health. I, however, sent my youngest brother on this mission, but everybody being apprehensive of these marauders, none would admit that Bhuskute was ill. Great God, where (art) thou. To what depths of dependence have we Hindus sunk. As we could not hear any news about Bhuskute's health, we resolved that he should, while yet on his sick-bed, hear that the wretch (Mr. Rand) had been punished. With this object in view we strained every nerve for the execution of our design, but instead of a favorable opportunity offering itself for the perpetration of the deed the evil news that Bhuskute had departed this life fell on our ears. Our grief knew no bounds when we received this news. It is easy to imagine how difficult it is to find a bosom friend who will cooperate with one in such work as we had undertaken. Unfortunately for us, our friend was not spared to us. We went outside the city, and stretching out our hands toward heaven, uttered the following words with up-turned faces:"Friend, you have strenuously exerted yourself along with us in the interest of our religion. May God grant you eternal happiness. That wretch will shortly be dispatched to the world of Pluto. You need not entertain any anxiety on that score. That is the only way by which we can fulfill your desires." Having addressed these words to (the spirit of) Bhuskute, we retraced our way to town, meditating on the transitoriness of our material existence. The fate of our friend filled us with utter despondence as regards this world, and thinking that God might one day snatch us away in a similar manner we made up our mind that, come what might, we must execute our design even in broad daylight if we could not find a suitable opportunity at night. So the death of our friend, instead of disheartening us, spurred us on to set about our undertaking with greater vigor. As far as possible we were resolved not to run any personal risk in our attempt, but if that was not found possible, we were determined to carry out our plan even at the sacrifice of our lives. Whenever a gang of the marauders visited our Peth, they found us fully prepared (to meet them). We were determined to make

the European (soldiers) pay with their lives in case they misconducted themselves in our house. At the same time we thought
the killing of those worthless soldiers too trivial an affair, and
therefore with a view not to allow Mr. Rand to escape unscathed,
one of us kept an eye on the spot where he took his stand. Our
object was that the moment the soldiers misconducted themselves in our house I was to strike them down, while my brother
was to deal similarly with Mr. Rand. We were prepared every
day to act in this manner. Fortunately, however, the soldiers did
not act against our wishes in our house. Once it so happened that
my brother was rather indisposed at the time these marauders
visited our house, but even on that occasion we took care to be
ready with our arms to impress upon the minds of the marauders
that we at all events were men of self-respect in the town. In our
house we used to take these marauders only into my brother's
room and to the storey of our house occupied by our father, but
did not allow the brutes to trespass into the god-house, nor into
the kitchen, nor into the women's apartments. Our she-buffalo,
which was tethered in the back yard of our house, used to fiercely
rush at the European (soldiers) whenever it saw them. They,
therefore, being terrified at its fierce look, did not venture into
that part of the house. We are very proud of the fact that even
our she-buffalo was such a fierce animal. As we used to be in
such a state of preparedness, God took care of us. The Europeans acted in accordance with our wishes in our house. One
day, however, a European insisted upon entering our house,
but when we both of us told him in an indignant tone that it
was impossible for him to do so, he being inspired by God in
some unknown manner quietly went away. Though I personally witnessed outrages committed at other places, nothing
calculated to provoke us occurred in our own house and consequently we were calmly maturing our plans concerning Mr.
Rand. Many a trivial quarrel took place between the soldiers
and ourselves on the road, but all this originated in our own
tricks.

The epidemic of fever and tyranny, having increased in the

above manner, now began to abate by the will of God. After some days house-to-house visitation was discontinued, but the police stations established at the cemeteries were retained. Each of these stations had two armed sentries and we became fired with a desire to make away with their guns. With that object in view we examined all the stations and found the one located on Lakdipul to be the most convenient one (for our purposes). I then went there four or five times disguised as a pujari, and on one occasion having made my prostrations to Balbhima, snatched away with his permission two Henri-Martinis and one sword and took them to our house. This was a source of extreme delight to us both. I cannot describe how joyful we felt. We now felt confident enough to face even an army. Our ill-luck, however, did not show us that day, nor is there any prospect of our ever seeing it hereafter. We had procured the guns but where were cartridges to be found? It was our intention to attempt to procure them later on. On the following day the news of the theft of the guns spread in the city, and in very flattering terms did the people speak of the discipline and bravery of the soldiers concerned. The people (however) were wonder-struck at the (boldness of the) person who had stolen the guns. This circumstance delighted us the most. But as there was no possibility of the guns being of any use to us in our undertaking in the absence of cartridges, we stowed them away with great care. Since the house-to-house visitation system was discontinued, Mr. Rand was not very punctual in coming to and going from the city. He came and went at any time he liked. Consequently, our intention of accomplishing our design in the city fell through. Then we began visiting the Club in the Cantonment in order to find out his room. Having found it out, we went to the Cantonment every evening and watched the movements of Mr. Rand. Every Wednesday and Sunday he was in the habit of going to St. Mary's Church for evening service. Five or seven times did we lie in wait for him at this place, but could not succeed in our object. While there, we once happened to enter into conversation with a European constable. We also went to the Club three or four times, and in the course of our visits to that place we came into collision with a European constable. It would be wearisome if I entered into full details about the various attempts made by us as stated above. I would, therefore, content myself by giving here only a resume of what we did and then conclude. The adage "God helps those who help themselves" is not untrue. We were unremitting in our efforts, but the time of our departure for Bombay having approached, we were filled with anxiety as to how God would enable us to commit the deed. We prayed to God repeatedly to make us His instruments in committing the deed, and thus enable us to do some service to our religion. Whenever we heard the utterances of the people about the oppression which they were suffering, we imagined that they were laying their grievances before us just as people seek redress from a king. We thought that we owed these people a debt which would remain undischarged if the deed were not perpetrated, and then we would be ashamed to show our face to the public. We, therefore, often prayed to Shri Gajanan to save us from such disgrace. As time passed on, the Jubilee day approached. The newspapers began to be filled with descriptions of the manner in which this grand festival was to be celebrated, and we believed that Europeans of all ranks would go to the Government House at Ganesh Khind on that occasion. Thinking, therefore, that would be a fitting time for us, both of us started to reconnoiter that part of the country and inspected all the large and small roads in the vicinity thereof. After examining all the places, we resolved to cross the Lakdi Bridge and the canal flowing past the yellow bungalow situated on this side of the spot where the pandal of the National Congress was erected and then to debouch on the high road leading to Ganesh Khind at a point where it passes the yellow bungalow and there execute our commendable deed and then return. We had (also) fixed upon certain unoccupied bungalows in the neighborhood for the purpose of taking shelter therein in case it should rain at the time. While crossing the canal in the course of our inspection of the places, we needlessly remonstrated with certain European girls who were paddling in the water near the yellow bungalow and then proceeded to do our homage to the goddess Chatursingi, the mother of the universe. There we prayed to her by reciting the following song:—

Pad. Oh mother of the universe, we are about to perform a commendable deed; vouchsafe success to us.

Confer on us, Oh mother Bhavani, the blessing of subduing the enemy; Oh mother, etc.

We have no other supporter in (this) world except thyself. Rand has completely destroyed the (Hindu) religion in the holy city (Poona).

(That) wretch has ruined all.

Oh mother give us firmness and daring in killing that inconsiderate man with our own hands; Oh mother of the universe.

Having invoked her in this way we came back. On our return home we began our devotions to the Almighty. The Lord of the universe alone knows how devoutly we prayed to Gajanan, offering him our bodies, our minds and our belongings. We believe that Gajanan answered our prayer. Our first consideration was what weapons we should take with us, (and) we resolved that each of us should arm himself with a sword and a pistol. My brother Bapurao determined to take with him a hatchet in addition. He intended to use these arms according to the exigencies of the occasion. My readers will remember that we had already kept the sword ready (for use). The pistol which I had chosen to take with me was out of order. Only one of its chambers could be used. That of Bapurao had a single barrel, but it was of large bore. Having determined to arm ourselves with these weapons, we waited for the occasion. We spent the whole day in offering prayers to the Almighty. As we were quite uncertain as to the success or failure of this undertaking, we were altogether unmindful of our domestic concerns. But one thing remains to be described. Government wished that the Jubilee festival should be celebrated by the rayats. Accordingly, in the city (Poona), nay, in the whole of India, that festival was most loyally observed even by Princes and Chiefs. Viewed in a proper light this was not a time for rejoicing.

There was plague in the Bombay Presidency, earthquakes on the Calcutta side and a terrible famine all over India. How ungenerous it was (for the Queen of England) to cause the rayats, already beset with three such formidable calamities, to celebrate the sixtieth year of her reign at such a critical juncture instead of relieving them from those calamities. This behoves only the Queen of England. According to our Shastras, a king and his subjects are in the same relationship as a father and a son. On this principle, the Queen is the mother of her subjects. But judging from her actions there is no reason why, instead of being styled a subject-protecting mother, she should not be called a female fiend who devours her own progeny. Had the Queen a generous heart, she would have on the said joyful occasion earned the blessings of her subjects by feeding them. But as we saw nothing of that sort, we did not like the festival at all and thought that it was the duty of every true Aryan to show his indifference rather than to take part in rejoicings. We do not at all like to make a false display of loyalty by means of hypocritical newspaper articles or speeches. India is, at this moment, full of such imbeciles. Though these good-for-nothing people do not at all like the policy of the British Government, they make a great show of their loyalty in their newspapers and speeches. Some shower upon the Queen covert ridicule in a variety of ways, but when charged under section 124 defend their writings by asserting that they did not mean what is alleged of them. Thinking that it was a thousand times better to openly spurn the English people, their authority and their Queen, and to bring them into disgrace, we exerted ourselves in that direction. Our people being conscious of the truth of the adage "Wisdom prevails not against authority" were celebrating the Jubilee festival in a half-hearted manner, though they were unwilling to take part in the rejoicings. We, however, do not consider ourselves to be her loyal subjects, and therefore, with a view to mar the rejoicings, instead of joining in them we resolved to set up an image of the

Queen of England at some conspicuous and central spot in the Budhwar Street on the morning of the Jubilee day. We laboriously searched many rubbish heaps and procured with great difficulty some extremely old and tattered shoes. We could get only six of them and no more. We set up these shoes on the main Budhwar road, with a picture of the Queen stuck to the sole of each saying that we did this stealthily and not openly, yes, friends, yes; though we did it stealthily at that time, we knew full well that some day we would have to come forward and that we would do so with great pride. That blessed day has now fortunately dawned upon me, for which I thank Gajanan. Having done this in the morning we prepared ourselves to go to the Ganesh Khind as soon as it was dusk. At the time of our departure we relinquished all hopes of our home, wives, children, parents, friends and relatives. When leaving our house, we devoutly made obeisance to Shri Mangalmurti and, muttering his name, made a mental obeisance to our parents and bid adieu in our minds to all, young and old, nay, we even touched our extremely favorite she-buffalo and took leave of them all. Similarly, with the words "Dear brethren. May the merits of you all help us in the attainment of success," we left the house. We even took with us our sacred scripture, the Gita.

It was about 7 or 7:30 o'clock and the sun had just set. Darkness was increasing every moment. After we had gone out of the city, we recited the above mentioned verses in praise of the Chatursingi Bhavani and, taking the appointed route, soon reached Ganesh Khind. As soon as we arrived there we saw Mr. Rand's carriage pass by, but not being quite sure that it was his, we postponed the execution of the deed till the time of his return (from the Government House). A large concourse of people had gathered there to witness the spectacle, but there were very few Brahmins among them. Owing to the bonfires on the hilltops and the crowd of spectators, it became difficult for us to walk about with our swords. We, therefore, deposited the two swords and one hatchet under the stone culvert situated in the vicinity of the bungalow in such a way as to easily reach them in case of need. This enabled us to move about with the greatest ease. For fear of coming across any acquaintance, we, instead of walking about on the public road, betook ourselves to a field in the dark and there leisurely devoted ourselves to divine contemplation. When (I saw that) no more carriages were coming from the city and those which had already gone there (Government House) had begun to return, I proceeded to the gate and took my stand near it. It was arranged between ourselves that I was to run after the carriage (of Mr. Rand) and my brother was to come to my assistance near the yellow bungalow in the execution of the deed, and that while running after the carriage I was to call out "Gondya" as a signal to him, so that he might understand that the carriage was coming and prepare himself for action. Having made this arrangement, I approached the gate. The carriage in question came up after many others had preceded it, and having fully identified it, I gave it chase, running at a distance of some 10 or 15 paces behind. As the carriage neared the yellow bungalow, I made up the distance (between it and myself) and called out "Gondya." My brother came up to me directly. I undid the button of the flap of the carriage, raised it, and fired from a distance of about a span. Our original plan was to empty both the pistols at Mr. Rand so as to leave no room for doubt about his death. But as my brother lagged behind, the charge from my pistol (alone) hit Mr. Rand and his carriage rolled onwards. My brother, suspecting that the occupants of the carriage behind were, on seeing us, whispering to each other, aimed his pistol at the head of (one of them) from behind the carriage and fired a bullet.

We then went away with speed by the prearranged route. We intended to take away the swords on the following day. On our return home we offered fervent prayers to the Almighty. We could not sleep that night owing to excess of delight. Having bathed early in the morning we went out and passed the Faraskhana and the Municipal Office to see if there was any excitement in the city over the matter. But people appeared to know nothing about the incident. The news began to spread in the city at about 10 or 11 A.M. By evening the incident was everywhere talked about and everyone was overjoyed. All Hindus and Muhammadans, whether rich or poor, young or old, reformers or non-reformers, shared equally this feeling of extreme delight, and every one distributed according to his means either sugar-candy or sweetmeats. I leave it to my readers to imagine what gratification we must have felt when the universal feeling of joy was so great. We were delighted because the people were delighted; otherwise, we had no ill-feeling against Mr. Rand.

Had he been careful not to interfere with our religion, that is to say, had he taken notice of the lawless conduct of the soldiery, we would not have been compelled to perpetrate the deed. We had been following Mr. Rand's movements for nearly three months and a half, and during that period we came to entertain a very good opinion of him. He was a proud man like ourselves and we believe that he was not addicted to any vice. There was no meanness in his character. We had seen him playing lawn-tennis at the Gymkhana. He would never play with ladies, and from this (we inferred) that he disliked associating with the wives of others. We had marked this and many other traits in his character. But of what avail was all this? As he made himself an enemy of our religion, we deemed it necessary to take revenge upon him. We could not help it. This incident threw the police into a great commotion, and innumerable were the rumors that circulated in the city. Some said that they were going to search all the houses for weapons. As we had to remove to Bombay, we thought it undesirable to leave our weapons behind. We, therefore, tied them up in a bundle and threw them in a well appertaining to the house of Londhe. Having learned that the swords which we had left underneath the culvert had been taken away by the police to the Faraskhana, we did not go there. But we went to pay a visit to Jagadamba and, having filled the lap of that deity with a khan and a coconut, returned home. The next day we left for Bombay with all the members of our family by the 1:30 P.M. train. On our way to the railway station some members of the Bombay Police Force passed by us in a carriage, and we at once recognized them. We desired to be in Poona at this time, but it was just as well that our wish was not fulfilled, for had we remained there we might have been tempted to do something. We were thus a prey to alternate feelings of relief and sorrow. In this state we arrived in Bombay. The troubles which the English as well as the natives had to undergo in consequence of this act of ours (if narrated) would fill a big volume. I do not, therefore, think it desirable to narrate them.

As they (the English) suspected that the Brahmins alone were responsible for this affair, we hit upon a device to transfer their suspicion to the Muhammadans by sending a letter (to the newspapers?) purporting to be signed by a Ghazi. We thought it would be a good thing if the letter were written in Hindustani, but as there was no one amongst us who knew the language, we decided to send it in English, and just as we had made the editor of the Suryodaya to publish a letter in connection with a previous incident, *viz.*, the tarring of the Queen's statue, so we wrote to the editor of the Mumbai Vaibhav asking him to send (to the newspaper) a letter in English signed "A Ghazi" who should take upon himself the responsibility for the deed.

A copy of that letter must be in the possession of the police, and I am of opinion that it should be published along with this. We sent that letter, but did not gain anything by doing so. On the contrary, we were placed at a disadvantage. That letter only led Mr. Brewin to hit upon the idea that the man connected with the tarring of the Queen's statue and the assault of Mr. Velankar must be the author of the present deed also. With this clue he began his investigations. We came to know of this, but we could not rectify our mistake. The assault on Mr. Velankar had placed us in a very unfavorable situation as he could have identified us. This was a very good clue for the police, and everyone whom they suspected was taken by them to Mr. Velankar for identification.

We passed three months in Bombay vigilantly, when all of a sudden I one day received a call from the police. It was in connection with Gopalrao Sathe. I obeyed the summons, and they (the police) took me to Poona and placed me before Mr. Brewin. There in the presence of Superintendents Kennedy and Brewin I, in the interest of the public, made, on certain conditions, a confession of murder and proudly detailed the particulars connected therewith, with a view to earn renown. To convince them, I of my own accord gave them many a minute detail. Nay, I adduced evidence in support of my statements. The fact that (I was connected with) the tarring of the Queen's statue and that the shoes made use of in the affair belonged to Wagle was proved by me to their satisfaction. As for Velankar, I got my statement corroborated in his presence. I made a confession in Bombay before Mr. Hamilton and I signed it. I had at first informed the police that I had done this deed single-handed, but I had subsequently to retract that statement owing to a turban and a piece of tape having been found in the bundle of weapons. As the police had come to the conclusion that the (murders) must have been committed by two men, I mentioned the name of my brother and thus made him a participator in the glory. It was I alone who supplied the police with all the evidence in the case. I have entirely forgotten my long-cherished hatred of the English owing to the intercourse I subsequently had with Superintendents Kennedy and Brewin. These gentlemen have, till now, shown themselves to be true to their word in their treatment of me, and I pray to God that they might continue to do so until the end. The next part (of this autobiography) will contain a narration in detail of what has taken place since my removal by the police from Bombay to Poona. I now conclude the account of Rand's assassination.

[Signed] DAMODAR HARI CHAPEKAR

19. THE "MAU MAU" OATH*

⊓⎍⊓⎍⊓⎍⊓⎍⊓⎍⊓⎍⊓⎍⊓⎍⊓⎍⊓⎍⊓⎍⊓⎍⊓⎍

Josiah Mwangi Kariuki

I have myself taken the oath twice. On the evening of 20 December 1953 a friend of mine called Kanyoi Githenji, who had been my school mate at K.I.S.A.** Kabati-ini School, came to see me at Wangui's hut. He invited me to come over to his house and drink a cup of tea with him. While we were drinking he went out several times and once I heard him asking someone outside if they had a *mukuha*. This is an instrument like a pin used for removing jiggers (an insect which bores into the feet) or mending broken calabashes. When it was dark he suggested we go for a walk together. After going about three hundred yards along a narrow path into the fields we suddenly came upon some men and women sitting down in the maize on our left and I saw immediately to the right an arch between six and seven feet high, made of two banana stems joined at the top and plaited with bean stalks and the leaves of the *mugere* bush.

I was very surprised to see banana stems as to the best of my knowledge there were no banana plantations in this part of the Rift Valley Province but Kanyoi told me that they had been cut

*From '*Mau Mau' Detainee*, by Josiah Mwangi Kariuki, 1963, pp. 25–33.
**Kikuyu Independent Schools Association. E.K.

in Kabatini Forest from the *shamba* of a man called Kaburu Chege, who was known to me and who had lived there in the forest for many years. It was clear to me that this was where the oath would be given. Kanyoi had been behaving strangely throughout the evening and in some ways I think I had begun much earlier to guess what was about to happen. I was told to move over to a place where three other people who were all known to me were standing. We were to take the oath together. We were then ordered to remove our shoes and our watches and any other metal things we had with us. Kanyoi pointed at me and told the people that I was a student from school who seemed to have a sincere wish to help the country and had been very active in persuading people to join the Kenya African Union. He believed that I was, therefore, the right sort of person to be given the Oath of Unity, *Ndemwa Ithatu*, as I was likely to be just as active in serving this movement as I had been in K.A.U. The other three who were in my group were hit about a little, but because of Kanyoi's remarks about me the people said "Do not beat the student," and I was left alone. We passed through the arch seven times in single file and then stood silently in a line facing the oath administrator, whose name was Biniathi, waiting for the next part of the ceremony.

Biniathi held the lungs of a goat in his right hand and another piece of goat's meat in his left. We bowed toward the ground as he circled our heads seven times with the meat, counting aloud in Kikuyu. He then gave each of us in turn the lungs and told us to bite them. Next he ordered us to repeat slowly after him the following sentence:

I speak the truth and vow before God
And before this movement,
The movement of Unity,
The Unity which is put to the test
The Unity that is mocked with the name of "Mau Mau,"
That I shall go forward to fight for the land,
The lands of Kirinyaga that we cultivated,
The lands which were taken by the Europeans

And if I fail to do this
May this oath kill me,
May this seven kill me,
May this meat kill me.

I speak the truth that I shall be working together
With the forces of the movement of Unity
And I shall help it with any contribution for which I am asked,
I am going to pay sixty-two shillings and fifty cents and a ram for
the movement
If I do not have them now I shall pay in the future.
And if I fail to do this
May this oath kill me,
May this seven kill me,
May this meat kill me.

I was given a box on the ears for failing to repeat one sentence correctly. It was delivered by the administrator's assistant, who was standing beside him holding a gourd full of the blood of the goat used for the ceremony. Biniathi anointed each of us on the forehead with the blood, saying that he did this to remind us that we were now fighting for our land and to warn us never to think of selling our country.

After this Biniathi came to each of us individually and made three tiny scratches on our left wrists. This was the meaning of *Ndemwa Ithatu* (three cuts) and it also explained Kanyoi's earlier search for a *mukuha*. He then brought the other piece of meat to our wrists so that a few drops of blood went on to it. Next he gave us in turn the meat to bite and while we were doing this he said, "The act of eating this meat with the blood of each one of you on it shows that you are now united one to the other and with us." This was the end of the ceremony and all four of us then went over to sit down with Kanyoi, who wrote out our names and asked us to give him the five shillings special oathing fee, which we all did. We then went to wait among the other people in the maize and our shoes and watches were returned to us.

My emotions during the ceremony had been a mixture of fear

and elation. Afterwards in the maize I felt exalted with a new spirit of power and strength. All my previous life seemed empty and meaningless. Even my education, of which I was so proud, appeared trivial beside this splendid and terrible force that had been given me. I had been born again and I sensed once more the feeling of opportunity and adventure that I had had on the first day my mother started teaching me to read and write. The other three in the maize were all silent and were clearly undergoing the same spiritual rebirth as myself.

Biniathi was aged about forty and was of medium height and build. Four of his front teeth were missing. He wore a black coat and gray trousers, a black, yellow, and gray check shirt and no tie. No one of our people at Bahati knew how to administer the oath and he had recently come from Kiamu District to help. After each ceremony he used to receive such money as the local committee (*athuri a kirira*), of which I was not a member, decided. He was an excellent oath administrator and a humble man who gave very good advice to people on their problems and difficulties.

I asked Kanyoi if it was right for me to continue recruiting for K.A.U. He told me that K.A.U. was a completely different organization from this one but that some of those at the ceremony were also members of it. There was no objection to my carrying on with K.A.U. but I should be careful not to tell any of the K.A.U. people about my membership of this other movement, which must remain secret. Kanyoi, whom I now looked upon as my teacher, also warned us not to sleep with a woman for seven days after the ceremony. If we wanted to know if someone we met had taken the oath we should ask them, "Where were you circumcised?" If the person gives a normal truthful answer to this question we would know that he had not taken the oath. Should the answer, however, be "I was circumcised at Karimania's with Karimania," this would be sufficient sign that the person had taken the oath. I had never heard the word "Karimania" used as a name before. It can be translated "to turn the soil over and over," as in cultivation and it is the word used for this in the oath.

I had slept that night at Kanyoi's house. I did not talk much, as my head was still full of the promises I had made at the ceremony. In the morning, after eating some porridge with Kanyoi, I returned to my aunt's house. Some days later I informed Kanyoi that the time had come for me to return to Nakuru and he asked me to come and visit him on the Sunday before I left. I met Biniathi there and another man called Muthee, who later went to fight in the forest and was killed by an ambush of the King's African Rifles when he was searching for food. We spent the day quietly, discussing politics and our land grievances, especially the barriers to African ownership of land in the White Highlands. We had the sense of frustration about this that the owner of a house would feel if he were turned out by a guest he had innocently welcomed. In the evening we all went to another house where some people had been skinning a goat. We sat down and Biniathi then told us to take all our clothes off except our trousers, and we stood patiently waiting to be called by him. I was called second after Kanyoi and there was no disobeying the summons.

I took off my trousers and squatted facing Biniathi. He told me to take the thorax of the goat which had been skinned, to put my penis through a hole that had been made in it, and to hold the rest of it in my left hand in front of me. Before me on the ground there were two small wooden stakes between which the thorax (*ngata*) of the goat was suspended and fastened. By my right hand on the floor of the hut were seven small sticks each about four inches long. Biniathi told me to take the sticks one at a time, to put them into the *ngata*, and slowly rub them in it while repeating after him these seven vows, one for each stick. (After each promise I was to bite the meat and throw the stick on to the ground on my left side.)

1. I speak the truth and vow before our God
   And by this *Batuni* oath of our movement
   Which is called the movement of fighting
   That if I am called on to kill for our soil
   If I am called on to shed my blood for it

I shall obey and I shall never surrender
And if I fail to go

> May this oath kill me,
> May this he-goat kill me,
> May this seven kill me,
> May this meat kill me.

2. I speak the truth and vow before our God
   And before our people of Africa
   That I shall never betray our country
   That I shall never betray anybody of this movement to the enemy
   Whether the enemy be European or African
   And if I do this
   > May this oath kill me, etc.

3. I speak the truth and vow before our God
   That if I am called during the night or the day
   To go to burn the store of a European who is our enemy
   I shall go forth without fear and I shall never surrender
   And if I fail to do this
   > May this oath kill me, etc.

4. I speak the truth and vow before our God
   That if I am called to go to fight the enemy
   Or to kill the enemy—I shall go
   Even if the enemy be my father and mother, my brother or sister
   And if I refuse
   > May this oath kill me, etc.

5. I speak the truth and vow before our God
   That if the people of the movement come to me by day or night
   And if they ask me to hide them
   I shall do so and I shall help them
   And if
   I fail to do this
   > May this oath kill me, etc.

6. I speak the truth and vow before our God
   That I shall never take away the woman of another man

That I shall never walk with prostitutes
That I shall never steal anything belonging to another person
in the movement
Nor shall I hate any other member for his actions
And if I do any of these things
May this oath kill me, etc.

7. I speak the truth and vow before our God
And by this *Batuni* oath of our movement
That I shall never sell my country for money or any other thing
That I shall abide until my death by all the promises
that I have made this day
That I shall never disclose our secrets to our enemy
Nor shall I disclose them to anybody who does not belong
to the movement
And if I transgress against any of the vows that I have
thus consciously made
I shall agree to any punishment that the movement shall
decide to give me
And if I fail to do these things
May this oath kill me, etc.

When I had said these things I removed the thorax and laid
it on the ground, put on my trousers and went to another part
of the hut where I paid to Kanyoi six shillings and fifty cents,
which was the oathing fee. Thus it was that I took the second
or *Batuni* oath. This word seems to be derived from the English
"platoon" and the oath itself was taken by all those who were
likely to be called on to give active service to the movement.

This second oath was much stronger than the first and left my
mind full of strange and excited feelings. My initiation was now
complete and I had become a true Kikuyu with no doubts where
I stood in the revolt of my tribe. Complete secrecy had again
been enjoined on us as even some of those administering the first
oath had not yet taken the *Batuni*. After the ceremony I returned to my aunt's hut for the night. Three days later I went
to Nakuru to stay with Obadiah Mwaniki, the man who had
come to our house with a bicycle so many years before. He was

still a staunch Christian and President of the Nakuru African Court and because he was a Christian, and because of the promises I made in the oath, I did not tell him what had been happening. Although there was no clause in the oath which forbade me to go to church or to remain a Christian, ever since the time of my first oath my belief in the God of Christ had been fading and I no longer went to church services without an ulterior reason. However, since Obadiah was so militant a Christian, while staying with him I went to church every Sunday lest he should become suspicious or angry.

The *Muma wa Thenge* (the he-goat oath) is a prominent feature of our social life, an integral part of the ceremonies uniting partners in marriages, in the exchange or sale of land (before the Europeans came, when land was plentiful, the sale of land was almost unknown), or in transactions involving cattle or goats. The warriors also took an oath, known as *Muma wa Aanake* (the oath of the warriors) to bind them before going on a raid. The purpose of all these oaths was to give those participating a feeling of mutual respect, unity, and shared love, to strengthen their relationship, to keep away any bad feelings, and to prevent any disputes. Most important of all, groups bound together by this ceremony would never invoke sorcery against each other. The fear of being killed by sorcery was prevalent among our people. The *muma* (oath) removed that fear and created a new and special relationship between the families and clans involved. Envy, hate, and enmity would be unknown between them.

The Oath of Unity (given the mysterious and sinister name of "Mau Mau" by a cunning propaganda machine) had the same background. It was intended to unite not only the Kikuyu, Embu, and Meru but all the other Kenya tribes. These might not give their oaths in the same way, but every tribe in Kenya had an oath for bringing together and solemnizing certain transactions. It is not really surprising that the movement should have started first among the Kikuyu. They more than any other tribe felt the despair brought by pressing economic poverty; they more than any other tribe by their proximity to the forcing house of Nairobi were subject to urban pressures and the great increase in understanding and frustration brought by education; they more than any other tribe daily saw the lands that had been taken from them producing rich fruits for Europeans.

There is no question that at times the oath was forced upon people who did not wish to take it, though these were nothing like so many as the Government spokesmen would have had us believe: it was important for them to conceal from the outside world the real springs and motives of the Movement. It is also true that by 1953 and 1954 severe punishment sometimes including death was meted out by the courts of the Movement to those whom it considered traitors or spies. This was not the first political organization, nor will it be the last, which has been driven to set up its own judicial system parallel to that of the state. We had rejected the authority of the Kenya Government. We had organized in its place another Government, accepted by the large majority of our people, which was compelled to undertake in its infancy a desperate battle for survival, with the odds weighted most heavily against it. It is not surprising that the leaders insisted on military discipline or that failure to join and obey were considered most serious crimes against our Government. Nothing but absolute unity, implicit obedience, and a sublime faith in our cause could bring victory against the guns, the armies, the money, and the brains of the Kenya Government. It was a war for our homes, our land, and our country in which the price of failure was death.

Many false notions have spread round the world about these oaths. It is said that a book has been placed in the library of the House of Commons describing the unnatural and obscene practices supposedly indulged in during the ceremonies. Some people are alleged to have been given as many as fourteen oaths, each one more foul and disgusting than the last. The two oaths which I have described above were the only legitimate ones. Naturally, as there was no central control of the organization, there were minor variations in the different districts and oath administrators did not everywhere use exactly the same technique.

The stories of the widespread use of the menstrual blood of

women, of bestial intercourse with animals, of the eating of the embryos of unborn children ripped from their mothers' wombs, all these are either fabrications or, if anyone can prove any truth in them (and they have not yet done so to my satisfaction), they must have been confined to a minute number of perverted individuals driven crazy by their isolation in the forests. To imply that these sorts of oaths were indulged in wholesale by most of the Kikuyu tribe is like saying that all Englishmen are child-rapers and murderers simply because a few Englishmen do this every year.

In our society the sacredness of the menstrual blood is impressed on our young men and women by their mentors (*Atiri*) at the time of circumcision. Abuse of it was a sin (*thahu*) which led to barrenness and other disasters and could only be purified in a most solemn ceremony. No Kikuyu leader in his senses would make use of such an ominous substance in a movement which could in no way afford to flaunt the spirits of our ancestors.

20. A MESSIANIC CREED FROM THE CONGO*

⎍⎍⎍⎍⎍⎍⎍⎍⎍⎍⎍⎍⎍⎍⎍⎍⎍⎍⎍

The most interesting document concerning the messianic role that according to his followers SIMON KIMBANGU will one day come to play consists in a sort of creed that has been and probably still is in use in the Ngunza-Khaki congregation in Pointe-Noire.[1]

The creed has the form of a number of commandments revealed by God Himself to SIMON KIMBANGU. It makes us in an incomparable way acquainted with some of the essential features of the movement, it shows what the members believe and hope. The text from Pointe-Noire bears the characteristic title "The twelve words (commandments, doctrines) which Mfumu SIMON KIMBANGU received from Yave Wanzambi (the Lord God)."[2] The catechism is drawn up in the form of twelve, or rather, thirteen, questions, in which the true being of SIMON KIMBANGU is represented.

1. Who is Mfumu S.K. in the first person?[3]

ANSWER: Mfumu S.K. is the executor, he who realizes the reve-

*From *Messianic Popular Movements in the Lower Congo*, by E. Andersson, Uppsala, 1958, pp. 134–6.

lation through the words of grace, through the words of power and through the words of miracles, he is the one who realizes the blessing. He is the one in whom lives the Lord God, the gracious father of the blacks.

2. Who is Mfumu S.K. in the second person?

ANSWER: Mfumu S.K. is the priest that the Lord God has exalted to be an eternal priest, like the priesthood of Melchizedek.[4] He is the priest of the black race.

3. Who is Mfumu S.K. in the third person?

ANSWER: Mfumu S.K. is the cup with the oil of blessing or the calabash with the oil of blessing that the Lord God has given to the black race that it may be blessed in Him. He is the cup with the oil of blessing for the black race.

4. Who is Mfumu S.K. in the fourth person?

ANSWER: Mfumu S.K. is the sacred scepter of dominion, which the Lord God has given to the black race that it may have dominion through it. He is the ruler's rod of the blacks.

5. Who is Mfumu S.K. in the fifth person?

ANSWER: Mfumu S.K. is the mighty sword of government that the Lord God has given to the black race. He is the saber with the keen edge or the three-edged bayonet, in him is the message of salvation for the wicked that the Lord God has given to the black race.

6. Who is Mfumu S.K. in the sixth person?

ANSWER: Mfumu S.K. is the banner of dominion that the Lord God has given to the black race that it may rule through it. He is the banner of dominion for the black race.

7. Who is Mfumu S.K. in the seventh person?

ANSWER: Mfumu S.K. is the shining lamp over the way that the Lord God has given to the black race so that the blacks, when they come to the valley of the shadow of death, may be able to take this lamp in their hand, and thus the night shall be no more for their eyes. And they shall see clearly the way to the city above; all stumbling blocks, all pits, the whole North and the wicked lions, all who are enemies of the Saviour. All people, when they journey on the way, shall see many evil things on the way and they shall fight with them. They shall fight and gain the victory and enter in God's heaven. This is why he is called the lamp on the way to heaven.

8. Who is Mfumu S.K. in the eighth person?

ANSWER: Mfumu S.K. is the open and prepared way that the Lord God has opened on the earth in the heart of the black race so that they may journey thereon to God's heaven. He is the prepared way upon which the black race may enter heaven.

9. Who is Mfumu S.K. in the ninth person?

ANSWER: Mfumu S.K. is the shield of battle on the way to heaven that the Lord God has given to the black race so that when they have stood up to travel the road to heaven they may arm themselves and fight the fight against Satan who is our enemy on the way to heaven.

10. Who is Mfumu S.K. in the tenth person?

ANSWER: Mfumu S.K. is the river with the living water that the Lord God has given to the black race. The blacks wish to drink from this river and they shall receive eternal life and enter the gate of heaven. He is the river with the living water for the black race.

11. Who is Mfumu S.K. in the eleventh person?

ANSWER: Mfumu S.K. is the canoe that the Lord God has put in the river of death, so that the blacks shall go on board that boat and cross death's river courageously. He is the ferry of the black race.

12. Who is Mfumu S.K. in the twelfth person?

ANSWER: Mfumu S.K. is the sacrifice of atonement that the Lord
God has allowed to descend among the black race so that
they may enter in at the gate of heaven as a group. He
has become the ladder on which the human race reaches
up to God's heaven. He has become the stair on which
they reach the heaven of their God.

13. Who is Mfumu S.K. in the thirteenth person?[5]

ANSWER: Mfumu S.K. is the open door that the Lord God has
opened among the black race that they may enter by it.
It is the city of the new Jerusalem, the Jerusalem of the
blacks and God's very holiest city. He is the door
through which they enter the heaven of their God.

Amen, Amen.

P.S.P. Nkuluntu azintumwa.[6]

Translated by the Secretary General in M.B.R.M. 4/7/47.

Chief scribe Seule traville sentelesvwrw S.STR[7]

NOTES

1. The original document from which the creed in question is taken has the form
of a battered notebook in which a former member of the congregation has noted
down the main features in the doctrine of the movement. After his return to the
mission he lent this to the African pastor YAYAKA JEAN. The latter and E.
BERG were kind enough to have most of the contents copied out for my
account. As the text is difficult to interpret, the copying and translation especially of certain "technical terms" entailed a lot of work, and NKODIA JEAN
also helped in this work (as YAYAKA, one of the present writer's old pupils).

2. The introduction or subtitle runs as follows: "These are the twelve words
that Mfumu S.K. received from God, in which you learn of your Saviour's birth
and the twelve passwords for the black race to God's heaven."

3. The phrase "Who is Mfumu S.K. in the first person?" is obscure. Probably
it constitutes a free application of the doctrine of the Trinity to SIMON KIM-
BANGU, here multiplied to a doctrine of twelve (or rather thirteen) persons.

4. GENESIS 14:18; PSALMS 110:4; HEBR. 5:6.

5. Despite the title, this creed of the Ngunza-Khaki contains thirteen ques-

tions and answers. The explanation of the contradiction given by the blacks is that the twelve articles of belief are intended to be "kifwani ye minlongi mia Yesu" (an image of Jesus' apostles). The thirteenth paragraph is added on account of SIMON KIMBANGU, who is "the thirteenth that Jesus has chosen." As the thirteenth apostle SIMON KIMBANGU is "nzila yampulusu kwa bandombe," i.e. "the way of salvation for the blacks" (BERG, 15/9 1950).

6. Nkuluntu azintumwa means the supreme (oldest) high priest. According to YAYAKA JEAN, the initials P.S.P. stand for "Papa SIMON PADI." The word papa or perhaps "phaapa" is a Congoized form of the French pape, Pope (LDKF, p. 844). It is used mostly by the Catholics in its French form (see e.g. C. JAFFRÉ, Catéchisme-Lari, pp. 53 f.). Among the natives the word has become papa or Phaapa. The interpretation shows that SIMON MPADI had great pretensions to being superior to all other leaders in the movement. The initials P.S.P. have, however, also been interpreted to mean "Pasteur SIMON PADI." But it is not very likely that the simple title of pasteur should have been given to the foremost of all the "apostles," and the first-mentioned interpretation is doubtless nearer the truth.

7. None of the Africans questioned by E. BERG has been able to say what the initials M.B.R.M. stand for. The words "seule traville" presumably indicate that the secretary general in question was the only person who had worked with the translation. The words "sentelesvwrw S.STR" it has so far not been possible to interpret (BERG, 31/5 1954).

21. THE MASS MOVEMENT*

ⅬⅬⅬⅬⅬⅬⅬⅬⅬⅬⅬⅬⅬⅬⅬⅬⅬ

Tom Mboya

For the effective struggle against colonialism and for the work of economic reconstruction after Independence, it has come to be accepted that you need a nationalist movement. I use these words advisedly, as opposed to a political party. A nationalist movement should mean the mobilization of all available groups of people in the country for the single struggle. This mobilization is based on a simplification of the struggle into certain slogans and into one distinct idea, which everyone can understand without arguing about the details of policy or of governmental program after Independence. Mobilization is planned on the assumption that, for the time being, what is needed is to win independence and gain power to determine one's own destiny.

Everyone is taught to know the one enemy—the colonial power—and the one goal—independence. This is conveyed by the one word round which the movement's slogans are built. In Ghana it was "Free-dom," in East Africa it is "Uhuru" and in Northern Rhodesia and Nyasaland "Kwacha" (the dawn). In this way one word summarizes for everyone the meaning of the struggle, and within this broad meaning everyone has his own

*From *Freedom and After*, by Tom Mboya, 1963, pp. 61–72.

interpretation of what Uhuru will bring for him. The simple peasant may think of Uhuru in terms of farm credits, more food, schools for his children. The office clerk may see it as meaning promotion to an executive job. The apprentice may interpret it as a chance to qualify as a technician, the schoolboy as a chance for a scholarship overseas, the sick person as the provision of better hospital facilities, the aged worker as the hope of pensions and security in old age. The interpretation of the goal is not immediately relevant or important, when compared with the importance of mobilization of the entire population. This kind of approach is not unique to Africa: despite his spiritual approach Gandhi used virtually the same tactics—his slogan was Self-rule.

The people have to be organized so that they are like an army: they must have a general, they must have discipline, they must have a symbol. In many cases the symbol is the national leader himself, and it is necessary to have this kind of symbol of an heroic father-figure if you are to have unquestioning discipline among the different groups and personalities who should rally their followers behind him. The national leader needs an organization, whose pattern allows him to lead and also to impose discipline and demand action whenever it is necessary. This must therefore be a mass movement taking in everybody and anybody, and an important feature of it is the series of mass political rallies held all over the country.

Some foreign visitors have expressed surprise about the political rallies they have seen in Africa. There is the huge crowd, streaming toward a stadium or an open piece of ground, sitting patiently for hours while a dozen politicians make speeches. The speakers do not seem to make many new points—or, at least, for every new idea there is a great deal which everyone has heard often before. The speeches are frequently interrupted by the speaker calling on the crowd to thunder back at him a series of slogans:

"Uhuru!"

"Uhuru!"

"Uhuru na umoja!"

"Uhuru na umoja!"
"Uhuru na KANU!"
"Uhuru na KANU!"
"Uhuru na Kenyatta!"
"Uhuru na Kenyatta!" and so on. The crowd is good-natured, it is true, and seems to look on it as a festival occasion. In fact, in the front is a women's choir with bark-cloth dresses and painted faces and a curious mixture of Western ornaments like dark glasses, and tin cans round their ankles. But what is the point of it all? It may help to boost the people's morale a bit, but don't they get bored after the first once or twice? And why do so many leaders spend so much time at these rallies?

This is how some foreigners feel at first, but it is easy to show them the importance of these rallies. They are intended to have an impact both on the population and on the colonial power. They are intended to show the colonial power the strength and unity ("umoja") of the people and the leadership, and the unanimity of the people in their demand for Uhuru. And, among the people themselves, they are intended to show the strength of the leader and the complete loyalty of his followers, and to persuade the few who may doubt the rightness of the cause that after all everybody else believes in it. The rallies tackle the task, in the early days of a national movement, of creating among Africans a sense of self-confidence, a feeling that it is not only right to fight for his independence but that it is possible to win his independence. Further, that it is not only right he should be free, but that he has a duty to free himself. The rallies are intended to create a revolutionary spirit, to wipe away the acquiescence he has shown before and the obedience which was expected of him.

For a nationalist movement faces the problem of changing attitudes inculcated by the colonial power. Schools have taught Africans to accept the inevitability of gradualism in the development of their countries and the attainment of independence. They have taught the "never-never policy"—independence cannot come in your lifetime, it is too complicated to hope to win, you cannot run a government unless you have reached a certain

high standard of education. They have taught that certain traditional forms of government must be maintained if independence
is to survive, and in many cases they have taught that the African
is inferior to the white man and must depend on him for guidance. In Kenya and other colonies many people—and especially
chiefs—were convinced through the administrative set-up that
the white man's position was indestructible and no amount of
agitation was going to move it. Africans who had worked for
years with missionaries, and the older African teachers and Africans employed by district administrations, were all conditioned
in this manner. They will always give you long sermons about
gradualism, and they dislike every aspect of nationalist agitation
as a threat to good order. In the initial stages of the struggle, their
opposition is one of the big problems. I remember, when I had
decided to become involved in KAU* in 1952, how not only my
father but other elders in my tribe often told me: "We can never
compete with the European. After all, he has aeroplanes, he flies
about while we walk on foot. He has cars and he has guns."

I was virtually told we were beating our heads against a brick
wall. But I did not find it strange, because I knew various District
Commissioners who at Barazas (meetings) had told the people
they could not compete with the white man because they had
not learned how to make a nail. To foster this spirit of inferiority
among Africans, the administration had identified everything
good with the European and everything bad or inferior with the
African. Thus first-grade maize or eggs or potatoes were designated "European-type maize (or eggs or potatoes)," and all inferior maize, eggs or potatoes or even cattle were described as
African-type ("Mahindi ya Kizungu" and "Viazi vya Kiafrika").
To overcome this feeling of inferiority, the nationalist rallies play
a vital part.

A nationalist movement cannot immediately be run on the
same basis as a modern political party in Britain or Europe or
North America, with committees and research workers and discussion groups on this and that problem. Such a system brings
people too much into discussion of details and creates too many

*Kenya African Union. E.K.

opportunities for differences and divisions. The mass movement must be organized on a foundation of strong membership, but the organizing machinery should concern itself with increasing membership and raising funds and not with too much study of aspects of future policy. When we organized the Peoples Convention Party in Nairobi in 1957 and 1958, we had on each housing estate an organizing cell with a committee of six whose task was to run a local membership drive. It was never intended those cells should be intellectual discussion groups on policies, studying the problems of education and agriculture and so on.

The concentration on Uhuru does not date from the beginning of the nationalist struggle, it must be added. In the days of KAU, independence was referred to, but the main emphasis was on the struggle against the color bar and the reservation of land for white farmers. The British Government did not in those days dream of talking about dates for independence. When a United Nations Visiting Committee spoke in 1956 of a target for Tanganyika's Independence in 1972, the British Government went nearly berserk; and for their part African leaders were prepared to accept the UN line, because it stated the principle of independence, although it did not press for an earlier date. The main focus on independence came from 1957 onwards, because Ghana set a precedent in that year for the rest of Africa. Before Ghana there were only Egypt, Liberia, Sudan and Ethiopia as independent states, and their history was so different they did not have a similar impact on postwar nationalist aspirations in the rest of Africa. The first conference of Independent African States was held in Accra in April 1958, and it passed resolutions which highlighted the struggle for independence. Delegates to the first All-African Peoples Conference in that December could read on the plinth of Kwame Nkrumah's statue the declaration that the independence of Ghana was meaningless unless it was linked to the liberation of all Africa. The whole trend changed from emphasizing the struggle against piecemeal acts of injustice, and everyone decided to prepare the nationalist movement to fight for the independence within which all other problems would be solved. Once again Nkrumah's remark should be quoted: "Seek ye first the political king-dom and everything else shall be added unto you."

In this respect the position of our friends in Central and South Africa is no different from our own. We fought against the exclu-sive reservations of land, South Rhodesians fought primarily until 1959 against injustices done to farmers under the Land Husbandry Act, Nyasas and Northern Rhodesians have fought against Federation. In fact, in Northern Rhodesia it remained the prime target: during the elections in October 1962, when Kenneth Kaunda shouted "Kwacha" at a rally the answering call from the crowd was always "Federation must Go!" They are mobilizing on slogans which appeal to emotion on matters close to the ordinary man. But the issues change swiftly: when in Southern Rhodesia the municipalities opened the swimming baths to all races at the end of a tough struggle between reform-ers and reactionaries, Joshua Nkomo told officials: "We don't want to swim in your swimming pools. We want to swim with you in parliament." He had moved on to demand greater repre-sentation than just a few "lower roll" seats in the legislature.

So the slogan "Uhuru" only came into universal use in East Africa in 1958. From then on we were often criticized for being unrealistic when we called for "Uhuru Sasa" (Freedom now). Our critics thought we were merely stating a date for independ-ence. The slogan was coined to convey the people's sense of urgency and their conviction that freedom is a birthright and not a right to be acquired by qualification. It was a revolt against the colonialist argument that "You cannot be free because you are not sufficiently educated; you do not have enough doctors and engineers and lawyers." It was a refutation of those people who laid down criteria for voters, that they should be "responsible and civilized," of the Capricorn Africa Society whose leaders declared "a vote is not a right, but a privilege," and of the Tredgold Commission which confined the vote in Southern Rhodesia in 1957 to those who it thought would exercise it "with reason, judgment and public spirit"—and these turned out to be (in the Commission's judgment) only those earning more than £ 300 a year who had been at school for ten years. So "Uhuru

Sasa" was our declaration in simple words that we had always possessed the right to be free, and freedom had nothing to do with riches or schooling or civilization.

In the process of mass mobilization, leadership is needed to act as a rallying point, and one problem which sometimes has to be faced is a clash of personalities when trying to create the national leader. The clash may come because of tribalist tendencies. It has been said that Nigeria is perhaps an example to quote in this respect, because each region has produced its own leader —Awolowo in the West, Azikiwe in the East and the Sardauna of Sokoto in the North—but I feel this is a simplification of the Nigerian position because the country was too vast and the communications too undeveloped for a mass movement to be created. But Nigeria has been mentioned frequently in discussions of this question of tribalism—and so, in another sense, have events in Kenya—and I would like therefore to discuss at this point the issue of tribalism, and put it in the context of politicians organizing a national movement.

To anyone concerned with African unity, tribalism presents one of the major problems. We discussed at length this problem at the All-African Peoples Conference in 1958: the question of traditional rulers, the problems of language and customs. We concluded that, if governments tried to destroy tribal culture and customs, language and ethnical groupings, they would create such a vacuum that the African might find he had nothing to stand upon and become a most bewildered person in this modern world. We thought it essential to isolate what you might call "negative tribalism" from tribalism in the form of customs and culture.

Let me state the positive contributions of tribalism first. At this stage of economic emancipation, with many more Africans moving into the money economy, they have to decide whether to allow themselves to be completely uprooted from all their past beliefs. I believe it is unwise to destroy this African structure of interdependence within the community, where each man knows he has certain responsibilities and duties and where there are certain sanctions against those who do not fulfill expectations.

There is, for instance, inherent generosity within a tribe or clan. From the moment a child is born, he is virtually the property of the whole clan, and not just of his father and mother. He is expected to serve everybody, and also to receive from everybody. As a young child he herds cattle in a group with other children of the clan. Later he will work with other girls and boys in other people's fields, or build a hut for a member of the clan without distinction of family. When he comes to marry, his own father may be poor, but if he has even only a distant uncle with property he does not hesitate to go ahead and contract a marriage. If that uncle refuses to part with cattle—for a bride-price —he is entitled to take them away with the support of the elders. If, on the other hand, he has not as a youth made his full contribution to the community, then he does not stand a chance with the clan elders when he comes to the age of marriage. When he is in need, his demands will often be disregarded and the elders are bound to tell him he deserves nothing better until he proves himself. This is an aspect of the African tribal system I would hate to see die. It provides the discipline, self-reliance and stability needed in the new nations.

People have done their worst in attacking tribalism, and never differentiating what was positive and worth preserving. Missionaries taught Africans to despise their tribal culture, telling them it was in conflict with the modern world. No effort was made to trace what was good, or to point out to the potential leaders of a community how some customs could be modified to suit the changes in the world. People were simply taught European social behavior and the way European workmen lived their lives, without any reference to African customs. This tended to raise a serious conflict in the minds of unsophisticated Africans, as to whether they should remain entirely tribal, or shift completely to the European way of life. Yet this is not a question which should be posed at all. The question is whether we can develop within Africa a system which reflects the African personality, but is at the same time a growing system in which a man does not have to cling to tribal customs in the raw and primitive sense. For example, some people have told unsophisticated Africans that wearing clothes and washing with soap means moving away from the African tribal life. "Wash with this piece of soap, and you will have reflected the European way of life!" You can imagine how this approach destroys his confidence in what is good in African society.

After the influence of schools comes that of money. When a man earns his own salary and begins to buy a gramophone or a bicycle or a suit of clothes, he ceases to look on certain things as belonging to the community and begins to regard them as personal. This is a main area of conflict with tribalism, where adjustment is most necessary. He asks himself: "Am I going to become individualistic like the Europeans, or can I own something of my own and still belong to the tribe?" To a large extent, even African leaders and heads of African states have not succeeded in transforming themselves completely into individual personalities: they are still to some degree "communal" because of their background and their relatives remaining tribal, and so they themselves cannot afford to change at the risk of offending and losing their family. In a European society I would expect that, when people came to my house, they would first telephone to say they were coming or if they were coming to stay they would advise me in advance. But to expect this from my relations would be asking the impossible. I have learned to expect them when I see them, and I also know they may not telephone me even if they have a telephone in their house. But I do not object to this: I regard it as part of the Africanism which I think can synthesize with what is modern to create something African.

But I would never pretend that there is not a negative form of tribalism, which is most harmful in Africa. The man who tries to live so completely within the confines of his tribe, not so much revering its customs as discriminating against other tribes, represents the kind of tribalism of which Africa must beware. The Luo, who thinks nothing good can come from other tribes or continuously protects a person merely because he is a fellow Luo; the Kikuyu, who thinks it only suitable to meet other Kikuyu and disregards merit and ability in other people because and only because they do not belong to his tribe; this is negative tribalism which cannot allow for unity. That we are born of different tribes we cannot change; but I refuse to believe that, because our tribes have different backgrounds and culture and customs, we cannot create an African community or a nation.

The European colonial powers and even missionaries for a long time tended to build up tribal antagonism. It made it easier to influence the people, if they could find an amenable tribe to use against another tribe which was hostile. This was the straightforward tactic of "divide and rule," and it cannot be excused as part of the British public school attitude of administrators backing "my team" against the "other chaps." We must also beware of people, including the colonial powers in these last stages, trying to re-create old tribal hostilities. In Kenya the Masai used to fight the Kikuyu, either for cattle or women, and Luo had boundary clashes with the Kisii. Some political leaders have revived these old hostilities for their own personal reasons. When a leader feels himself weak on the national platform, he begins to calculate that the only support he may have will come from his own tribe: he starts to create an antagonism of this sort, so that he can at least entrench himself as a leader of his tribe.

Education is one weapon against negative tribalism: not bookish education, but practical civics and general sophistication, for instance in the form of people working together to form a trade union and fighting for their rights as a workers' movement. The trade union movement can be a very useful instrument of education against negative tribalism, even among illiterate people. But perhaps the strongest weapon is the political party machinery, in which everyone is mobilized for the struggle regardless of tribe or language and in which leadership is given to the person who merits it, regardless of his tribe. Again, there is education involved in the social intercourse which takes place in urban communities, where people of all tribes live together and go to the same beer house and dances and football matches. A long time ago in Nairobi the antagonism between Kikuyu and Luo was such that they fought on sight. They did not even quarrel about anything, they just fought. As soon as a Kikuyu saw a Luo, the first thing he did was pick up a stone and hit his head. We have come a long way since those days, and men like Kenyatta have done much to educate the people away from negative tribalism.

Nevertheless, tribalism is one of the basic differences between KANU* and KADU** in Kenya and perhaps is the origin of these differences. Some will say the smaller tribes must be protected from the bigger tribes. Such people refuse to accept the challenge of tribalism, and instead of fighting it have given in and are actually promoting it. The difference between KANU and KADU over tribalism is this: KANU concedes that tribal feelings exist but says they can be eliminated by wise leadership and positive action; KADU is exaggerating these feelings to entrench tribalism. These were the dangers of tribalism to which we referred at the Accra conference.

* Kenya African National Union. E.K.
** Kenya African Democratic Union. E.K.

22. CONCERNING VIOLENCE*

⊓⌐⊔⌐⊔⌐⊔⌐⊔⌐⊔⌐⊔⌐⊔⌐⊔⌐⊔⌐⊔⌐⊔⊓

Frantz Fanon

National liberation, national renaissance, the restoration of nationhood to the people, commonwealth: whatever may be the headings used or the new formulas introduced, decolonization is always a violent phenomenon. At whatever level we study it —relationships between individuals, new names for sports clubs, the human admixture at cocktail parties, in the police, on the directing boards of national or private banks—decolonization is quite simply the replacing of a certain "species" of men by another "species" of men. Without any period of transition, there is a total, complete and absolute substitution. It is true that we could equally well stress the rise of a new nation, the setting up of a new state, its diplomatic relations, and its economic and political trends. But we have precisely chosen to speak of that kind of *tabula rasa* which characterizes at the outset all decolonization. Its unusual importance is that it constitutes, from the very first day, the minimum demands of the colonized. To tell the truth, the proof of success lies in a whole social structure being changed from the bottom up. The extraordinary impor-

*From *The Damned,* by Frantz Fanon, trs. Constance Farrington, Paris, 1963, pp. 29–74.

tance of this change is that it is willed, called for, demanded. The need for this change exists in its crude state, impetuous and compelling, in the consciousness and in the lives of the men and women who are colonized. But the possibility of this change is equally experienced in the form of a terrifying future in the consciousness of another "species" of men and women: the colonizers.

Decolonization, which sets out to change the order of the world, is, obviously, a program of complete disorder. But it cannot come as a result of magical practices, nor of a natural shock, nor of a friendly understanding. Decolonization, as we know, is a historical process: that is to say that it cannot be understood, it cannot become intelligible nor clear to itself except in the exact measure that we can discern the movements which give it historical form and content. Decolonization is the meeting of two forces, opposed to each other by their very nature which results from and is nourished by the situation in the colonies. Their first encounter was marked by violence and their existence together—that is to say the exploitation of the native by the settler—was carried on by dint of a great array of bayonets and cannon. The settler and the native are old acquaintances. In fact, the settler is right when he speaks of knowing "them" well. For it is the settler who has brought the native into existence and who perpetuates his existence. The settler owes the fact of his very existence, that is to say his property, to the colonial system.

Decolonization never takes place unnoticed, for it influences individuals and modifies them fundamentally. It transforms spectators crushed with their inessentiality into privileged actors, with the grandiose glare of history's floodlights upon them. It brings a natural rhythm into existence, introduced by new men, and with it a new language and a new humanity. Decolonization is the veritable creation of new men. But this creation owes nothing of its legitimacy to any supernatural power; the "thing" which has been colonized becomes man during the same process by which it frees itself.

In decolonization, there is therefore the need of a complete calling in question of the colonial situation. If we wish to describe it precisely, we might find it in the well-known words: "The last shall be first and the first last." Decolonization is the putting into practice of this sentence. That is why, if we try to describe it, all decolonization is successful.

The naked truth of decolonization evokes for us the searing bullets and bloodstained knives which emanate from it. For if the last shall be first, this will only come to pass after a murderous and decisive struggle between the two protagonists. That affirmed intention to place the last at the head of things, and to make them climb at a pace (too quickly, some say) the well-known steps which characterize an organized society, can only triumph if we use all means to turn the scale, including, of course, that of violence.

You do not turn any society, however primitive it may be, upside down with such a program if you are not decided from the very beginning, that is to say from the actual formulation of that program, to overcome all the obstacles that you will come across in so doing. The native who decides to put the program into practice, and to become its moving force, is ready for violence at all times. From birth it is clear to him that this narrow world, strewn with prohibitions, can only be called in question by absolute violence.

The colonial world is a world divided into compartments. It is probably unnecessary to recall the existence of native quarters and European quarters, of schools for natives and schools for Europeans; in the same way we need not recall Apartheid in South Africa. Yet, if we examine closely this system of compartments, we will at least be able to reveal the lines of force it implies. This approach to the colonial world, its ordering and its geographical layout, will allow us to mark out the lines on which a decolonized society will be reorganized.

The colonial world is a world cut in two. The dividing line, the frontiers are shown by barracks and police stations. In the colonies it is the policeman and the soldier who are the official, instituted go-betweens, the spokesmen of the settler and his rule of oppression. In capitalist societies the educational system, whether lay or clerical, the structure of moral reflexes handed down from father to son, the exemplary honesty of workers who are given a medal after fifty years of good and loyal service, and the affection which springs from harmonious relations and good behavior—all these aesthetic expressions of respect for the established order serve to create around the exploited person an atmosphere of submission and of inhibition which lightens the task of policing considerably. In the capitalist countries a multitude of moral teachers, counselors and "bewilderers" separate the exploited from those in power. In the colonial countries, on the contrary, the policeman and the soldier, by their immediate presence and their frequent and direct action maintain contact with the native and advise him by means of rifle butts and napalm not to budge. It is obvious here that the agents of government speak the language of pure force. The intermediary does not lighten the oppression, nor seek to hide the domination; he shows them up and puts them into practice with the clear conscience of an upholder of the peace; yet he is the bringer of violence into the home and into the mind of the native.

The zone where the natives live is not complementary to the zone inhabited by the settlers. The two zones are opposed, but not in the service of higher unity. Obedient to the rules of pure Aristotelian logic, they both follow the principle of reciprocal exclusivity. No conciliation is possible, for of the two terms, one is superfluous. The settlers' town is a strongly built town, all made of stone and steel. It is a brightly lit town; the streets are covered with asphalt, and the garbage cans swallow all the leavings, unseen, unknown and hardly thought about. The settler's feet are never visible, except perhaps in the sea; but there you're never close enough to see them. His feet are protected by strong shoes although the streets of his town are clean and even, with no holes or stones. The settler's town is a well-fed town, an easygoing town; its belly is always full of good things. The settler's town is a town of white people, of foreigners.

The town belonging to the colonized people, or at least the native town, the Negro village, the medina, the reservation, is a place of ill fame, peopled by men of evil repute. They are born there, it matters little where or how; they die there, it matters not where, nor how. It is a world without spaciousness; men live there on top of each other, and their huts are built one on top of the other. The native town is a hungry town, starved of bread, of meat, of shoes, of coal, of light. The native town is a crouching village, a town on its knees, a town wallowing in the mire. It is a town of niggers and dirty arabs. The look that the native turns on the settler's town is a look of lust, a look of envy; it expresses his dreams of possession—all manner of possession: to sit at the settler's table, to sleep in the settler's bed, with his wife if possible. The colonized man is an envious man. And this the settler knows very well; when their glances meet he ascertains bitterly, always on the defensive, "They want to take our place." It is true, for there is no native who does not dream at least once a day of setting himself up in the settler's place.

This world divided into compartments, this world cut in two is inhabited by two different species. The originality of the colonial context is that economic reality, inequality and the immense difference of ways of life never come to mask the human realities. When you examine at close quarters the colonial context, it is evident that what parcels out the world is to begin with the fact of belonging to or not belonging to a given race, a given species. In the colonies the economic substructure is also a superstructure. The cause is the consequence; you are rich because you are white, you are white because you are rich. This is why Marxist analysis should always be slightly stretched every time we have to do with the colonial problem.

Everything up to and including the very nature of precapitalist society, so well explained by Marx, must here be thought out again. The serf is in essence different from the knight, but a reference to divine right is necessary to legitimize this statutory difference. In the colonies, the foreigner coming from another country imposed his rule by means of guns and machines. In defiance of his successful transplantation, in spite of his appropriation, the settler still remains a foreigner. It is neither the act of owning factories, nor estates, nor a bank balance which distinguishes the governing classes. The governing race is first and foremost those who come from elsewhere, those who are unlike the original inhabitants, "the others."

The violence which has ruled over the ordering of the colonial world, which has ceaselessly drummed the rhythm for the destruction of native social forms and broken up without reserve the systems of reference of the economy, the customs of dress and external life, that same violence will be claimed and taken over by the native at the moment when, deciding to embody history in his own person, he surges into the forbidden quarters. To wreck the colonial world is henceforward a mental picture of action which is very clear, very easy to understand and which may be assumed by each one of the individuals which constitute the colonized people. To break up the colonial world does not mean that after the frontiers have been abolished lines of communication will be set up between the two zones. The destruction of the colonial world is no more and no less than the abolition of one zone, its burial in the depths of the earth or its expulsion from the country.

The natives' challenge to the colonial world is not a rational confrontation of points of view. It is not a treatise on the universal, but the untidy affirmation of an original idea propounded as an absolute. The colonial world is a Manichaean world. It is not enough for the settler to delimit physically, that is to say with the help of the army and the police force, the place of the native. As if to show the totalitarian character of colonial exploitation the settler paints the native as a sort of quintessence of evil.[1] Native society is not simply described as a society lacking in values. It is not enough for the colonist to affirm that those values have disappeared from, or still better never existed in, the colonial world. The native is declared insensible to ethics; he represents not only the absence of values, but also the negation of values. He is, let us dare to admit, the enemy of values, and in this sense he is the absolute evil. He is the corrosive element, destroying all that comes near him; he is the deforming element, disfiguring all that has to do with beauty or morality; he is the depository of maleficent powers, the unconscious and irretrievable instrument of blind forces. Monsieur Meyer could thus state seriously in the French National Assembly that the Republic must not be prostituted by allowing the Algerian people to become part of it. All values, in fact are irrevocably poisoned and diseased as soon as they are allowed in contact with the colonized race. The customs of the colonized people, their traditions, their myths—above all, their myths—are the very sign of that poverty of spirit and of their constitutional depravity. That is why we must put the DDT which destroys parasites, the bearers of disease, on the same level as the Christian religion which wages war on embryonic heresies and instincts, and on evil as yet unborn. The recession of yellow fever and the advance of evangelization form part of the same balance sheet. But the triumphant *communiqués* from the missions are in fact a source of information concerning the implantation of foreign influences in the core of the colonized people. I speak of the Christian religion, and no one need be astonished. The Church in the colonies is the white people's Church, the foreigner's Church, She does not call the native to God's ways but to the ways of the white man, of the master, of the oppressor. And as we know, in this matter many are called but few chosen.

At times this Manichaeism goes to its logical conclusion and dehumanizes the native, or to speak plainly it turns him into an animal. In fact, the terms the settler uses when he mentions the native are zoological terms. He speaks of the yellow man's reptilian motions, of the stink of the native quarter, of breeding swarms, of foulness, of spawn, of gesticulations. When the settler seeks to describe the native fully in exact terms he constantly refers to the bestiary. The European rarely hits on a picturesque style; but the native, who knows what is in the mind of the settler, guesses at once what he is thinking of. Those hordes of vital statistics, those hysterical masses, those faces bereft of all humanity, those distended bodies which are like nothing on earth, that mob without beginning or end, those children who seem to belong to nobody, that laziness stretched out in the sun, that vegetative rhythm of life—all this forms part of the colonial vocabulary. General de Gaulle speaks of "the yellow multitudes" and François Mauriac of the black, brown and yellow masses which soon will be unleashed. The native knows all this, and laughs to himself every time he spots an allusion to the animal world in the other's words. For he knows that he is not an animal; and it is precisely at the moment he realizes his humanity that he begins to sharpen the weapons with which he will secure its victory.

As soon as the native begins to pull on his moorings, and to cause anxiety to the settler, he is handed over to well-meaning souls who in cultural congresses point out to him the specificity and wealth of Western values. But every time Western values are mentioned they produce in the native a sort of stiffening or muscular lockjaw. During the period of decolonization, the native's reason is appealed to. He is offered definite values, he is told frequently that decolonization need not mean regression, and that he must put his trust in qualities which are well-tried, solid and highly esteemed. But it so happens that when the native hears a speech about Western culture he pulls out his knife —or at least he makes sure it is within reach. The violence with which the supremacy of white values is affirmed and the aggressiveness which has permeated the victory of these values over the ways of life and of thought of the native mean that, in revenge, the native laughs in mockery when Western values are mentioned in front of him. In the colonial context the settler only ends his work of breaking in the native when the latter admits loudly and intelligibly the supremacy of the white man's values. In the period of decolonization, the colonized masses mock at these very values, insult them and vomit them up.

This phenomenon is in the ordinary way masked because, during the period of decolonization, certain colonized intellectuals have begun a dialogue with the bourgeoisie of the colonialist country. During this phase, the indigenous population is discerned only as an indistinct mass. The few native personalities whom the colonialist bourgeois have come to know here and there have not sufficient influence on that immediate discernment to give rise to nuances. On the other hand, during the period of liberation, the colonialist bourgeoisie looks feverishly for contacts with the *élite*, and it is with this *élite* that the familiar dialogue concerning values is carried on. The colonialist bourgeoisie, when it realises that it is impossible for it to maintain its domination over the colonial countries, decides to carry out a rearguard action with regard to culture, values, techniques and so on. Now what we must never forget is that the immense majority of colonized peoples is oblivious of these problems. For a colonized people the most essential value, because the most concrete, is first and foremost the land; the land which will bring them bread and, above all, dignity. But this dignity has nothing to do with the dignity of the human individual: for that human individual has never heard tell of it. All that the native has seen in his country is that they can freely arrest him, beat him, starve him: and no professor of ethics, no priest has ever come to be beaten in his place, or to share their bread with him. As far as the native is concerned, morality is very concrete; it is to silence the settler's defiance, to break his flaunting violence—in a word, to put him out of the picture. The well-known principle that all men are equal will be illustrated in the colonies from the moment that the native claims that he is the equal of the settler. One step more, and he is ready to fight to be more than the settler. In fact, he has already decided to eject him and to take his place; as we see it, it is a whole material and moral universe which is breaking up. The intellectual who for his part has followed the colonialist with regard to the universal abstract will fight in order that the settler and the native may live together in peace in a new world. But the thing he does not see, precisely because he is impermeated by colonialism and all its ways of thinking, is that the settler, from the moment that the colonial context disappears, has no longer any interest in remaining or in coexisting. It is not by chance that, even before any negotiation[2] between the Algerian and French governments has taken place, the European minority which calls itself "liberal" has already made its position clear: it demands nothing more nor less than twofold citizenship. By setting themselves apart in an abstract manner, the liberals try to force the settler into taking a very concrete jump into the unknown. Let us admit it, the settler knows perfectly well that no phraseology can be a substitute for reality.

Thus the native discovers that his life, his breath, his beating heart are the same as those of the settler. He finds out that the settler's skin is not of any more value than a native's skin; and it must be said that this discovery shakes the world in a very necessary manner. All the new, revolutionary assurance of the native stems from it. For if, in fact, my life is worth as much as the settler's, his glance no longer shrivels me up nor freezes me, and his voice no longer turns me into stone. I am no longer on tenterhooks in his presence; in fact, I don't give a damn for him. Not only does his presence no longer trouble me, but I am already preparing such efficient ambushes for him that soon there will be no way out but that of flight.

We have said that the colonial context is characterized by the dichotomy which it imposes upon the whole people. Decolonization unifies that people by the radical decision to remove from it its heterogenity, and by unifying it on a national, sometimes a racial, basis. We know the fierce words of the Senegalese patriots, referring to the maneuvers of their president, Senghor: "We have demanded that the higher posts should be given to Africans; and now Senghor is Africanizing the Europeans." That is to say that the native can see clearly and immediately if decolonization has come to pass or no, for his minimum demands are simply that the last shall be first.

But the native intellectual brings variants to this petition, and, in fact, he seems to have good reasons: higher civil servants, technicians, specialists—all seem to be needed. Now, the ordinary native interprets these unfair promotions as so many acts of sabotage, and he is often heard to declare: "It wasn't worth while, then, our becoming independent. . . ."

In the colonial countries where a real struggle for freedom has taken place, where the blood of the people has flowed and where the length of the period of armed warfare has favored the backward surge of intellectuals toward bases grounded in the people, we can observe a genuine eradication of the superstructure built by these intellectuals from the bourgeois colonialist environment. The colonialist bourgeoisie, in its narcissistic dialogue, expounded by the members of its universities, had in fact deeply implanted in the minds of the colonized intellectual that the essential qualities remain eternal in spite of all the blunders men may make: the essential qualities of the West, of course. The native intellectual accepted the cogency of these ideas, and deep down in his brain you could always find a vigilant sentinel ready to defend the Greco-Latin pedestal. Now it so happens that during the struggle for liberation, at the moment that the native intellectual comes into touch again with his people, this artificial sentinel is turned into dust. All the Mediterranean values—the triumph of the human individual, of clarity and of beauty—become lifeless, colorless knick-knacks. All those speeches seem like collections of dead words; those values which seemed to uplift the soul are revealed as worthless, simply because they have nothing to do with the concrete conflict in which the people is engaged.

Individualism is the first to disappear. The native intellectual had learned from his masters that the individual ought to express himself fully. The colonialist bourgeoisie had hammered into the native's mind the idea of a society of individuals where each person shuts himself up in his own subjectivity, and whose only wealth is individual thought. Now the native who has the opportunity to return to the people during the struggle for freedom will discover the falseness of this theory. The very forms of organization of the struggle will suggest to him a different vocabulary. Brother, sister, friend—these are words outlawed by the colonialist bourgeoisie, because for them my brother is my purse, my friend is part of my scheme for getting on. The native intellectual takes part, in a sort of *auto-da-fé*, in the destruction of all his idols: egoism, recrimination that springs from pride, and the childish stupidity of those who always want to have the last word. Such a colonized intellectual, dusted over by colonial culture, will in the same way discover the substance of village assemblies, the cohesion of people's committees, and the extraordinary fruitfulness of local meetings and groupments. Henceforward, the interests of one will be the interests of all, for in concrete fact *everyone* will be discovered by the troops, *everyone* will be massacred—or everyone will be saved. The motto "look out for yourself," the atheist's method of salvation, is in this context forbidden.

Self-criticism has been much talked about of late, but few people realize that it is an African institution. Whether in the *djemaas** of northern Africa or in the meetings of western Africa, tradition demands that the quarrels which occur in a village should be settled in public. It is communal self-criticism, of course, and with a note of humor, because everybody is relaxed, and because in the last resort we all want the same things. But the more the intellectual imbibes the atmosphere of the people, the more completely he abandons the habits of calculation, of unwonted silence, of mental reservations, and shakes off the spirit of concealment. And it is true that already at that level we can say that the community triumphs, and that it spreads its own light and its own reason.

But it so happens that decolonization occurs in areas which have not been sufficiently shaken by the struggle for liberation, and there may be found those same know-all, smart, wily intellectuals. We find intact in them the manners and forms of thought picked up during their association with the colonialist bourgeoisie. Spoiled children of yesterday's colonialism and of today's national governments, they organize the loot of whatever national resources exist. Without pity, they use today's national distress as a means of getting on through scheming and legal robbery, by import-export combines, limited liability companies, gambling on the stock exchange, or unfair promotion. They are insistent in their demands for the nationalization of commerce, that is to say the reservation of markets and advantageous bargains for nationals only. As far as doctrine is concerned, they proclaim the pressing necessity of nationalizing the robbery of the nation. In this arid phase of national life, the so-called period of austerity, the success of their depredations is swift to call forth the violence and anger of the people. For this same people, poverty-stricken yet independent, comes very quickly to possess a social conscience in the African and international context of today; and

* Village assemblies. (Trans.)

this the petty individualists will quickly learn.

In order to assimilate and to experience the oppressor's culture, the native has had to leave certain of his intellectual possessions in pawn. These pledges include his adoption of the forms of thought of the colonialist bourgeoisie. This is very noticeable in the inaptitude of the native intellectual to carry on a dialogical discussion; for he cannot eliminate himself when confronted with an object or an idea. On the other hand, when once he begins to militate among the people he is struck with wonder and amazement; he is literally disarmed by their good faith and honesty. The danger that will haunt him continually is that of becoming the uncritical mouthpiece of the masses; he becomes a kind of yes-man who nods assent at every word coming from the people, which he interprets as considered judgments. Now, the *fellah*, the unemployed man, the starving native do not lay a claim to the truth; they do not *say* that they represent the truth, for they *are* the truth.

Objectively, the intellectual behaves in this phase like a common opportunist. In fact he has not stopped maneuvering. There is never any question of his being either rejected or welcomed by the people. What they ask is simply that all resources should be pooled. The inclusion of the native intellectual in the upward surge of the masses will in this case be differentiated by a curious cult of detail. That is not to say that the people are hostile to analysis; on the contrary, they like having things explained to them, they are glad to understand a line of argument and they like to see where they are going. But at the beginning of his association with the people the native intellectual overstresses details and thereby comes to forget that the defeat of colonialism is the real object of the struggle. Carried away by the multitudinous aspects of the fight, he tends to concentrate on local tasks, performed with enthusiasm but almost always too solemnly. He fails to see the whole of the movement all the time. He introduces the idea of special disciplines, of specialized functions, of departments within the terrible stone-crusher, the fierce mixing machine which is a popular revolution. He is occupied in action on a particular front, and it so happens that he loses sight of the unity of the movement. Thus, if a local defeat is inflicted, he may well be drawn into doubt, and from thence to despair. The people, on the other hand, take their stand from the start on the broad and inclusive positions of *Bread and the land:* how can we obtain the land, and bread to eat? And this obstinate point of view of the masses, which may seem shrunken and limited, is in the end the most worthwhile and the most efficient mode of procedure.

The problem of truth ought also to be considered. In every age, among the people, truth is the property of the national cause. No absolute verity, no discourse on the purity of the soul can shake this position. The native replies to the living lie of the colonial situation by an equal falsehood. His dealings with his fellow-nationals are open; they are strained and incomprehensible with regard to the settlers. Truth is that which hurries on the breakup of the colonialist regime; it is all that protects the natives, and ruins the foreigners. In this colonialist context there is no truthful behavior: and the good is quite simply that which is evil for *"them."*

Thus we see that the primary Manichaeism which governed colonial society is preserved intact during the period of decolonization; that is to say that the settler never ceases to be the enemy, the opponent, the foe that must be overthrown. The oppressor, in his own sphere, starts the process, a process of domination, of exploitation and of pillage, and in the other sphere the coiled, plundered creature which is the native provides fodder for the process as best he can, the process which moves uninterruptedly from the banks of the colonial territory to the palaces and the docks of the mother-country. In this becalmed zone the sea has a smooth surface, the palm tree stirs gently in the breeze, the waves lap against the pebbles, and raw materials are ceaselessly transported, justifying the presence of the settler: and all the while the native, bent double, more dead than alive, exists interminably in an unchanging dream. The settler makes history; his life is an epoch, an Odyssey. He is the absolute beginning: "This land was created by us"; he is the unceasing cause: "If we leave, all is lost, and the country will go back to the Middle Ages."

Over against him torpid creatures, wasted by fevers, obsessed by ancestral customs, form an almost inorganic background for the innovating dynamism of colonial mercantilism.

The settler makes history and is conscious of making it. And because he constantly refers to the history of his mother-country, he clearly indicates that he himself is the extension of that mother-country. Thus the history which he writes is not the history of the country which he plunders but the history of his own nation in regard to all that she skims off, all that she violates and starves.

The immobility to which the native is condemned can only be called in question if the native decides to put an end to the history of colonization—the history of pillage—and to bring into existence the history of the nation—the history of decolonization.

A world divided into compartments, a motionless, Manichae-istic world, a world of statues: the statue of the general who carried out the conquest, the statue of the engineer who built the bridge; a world which is sure of itself, which crushes with its stones the backs flayed by whips: this is the colonial world. The native is a being hemmed in; Apartheid is simply one form of the division into compartments of the colonial world. The first thing which the native learns is to stay in his place, and not go beyond certain limits. This is why the dreams of the native are always of muscular prowess; his dreams are of action and of aggression. I dream I am jumping, swimming, running, climbing; I dream that I burst out laughing, that I span a river in one stride, or that I am followed by a flood of motorcars which never catch up with me. During the period of colonization, the native never stops achieving his freedom from nine in the evening until six in the morning.

The colonized man will first manifest this aggressiveness which has been deposited in his bones against his own people. This is the period when the niggers beat each other up, and the police and magistrates do not know which way to turn when faced with the astonishing waves of crime in North Africa. We shall see later how this phenomenon should be judged.[3] When the native is confronted with the colonial order of things, he finds he is in a state of permanent tension. The settler's world is a hostile world, which spurns the native, but at the same time it is a world of which he is envious. We have seen that the native never ceases to dream of putting himself in the place of the settler—not of becoming the settler but of substituting himself for the settler. This hostile world, ponderous and aggressive because it fends off the colonized masses with all the harshness it is capable of, represents not merely a hell from which the swiftest flight possible is desirable, but also a paradise close at hand which is guarded by terrible watchdogs.

The native is always on the alert, for since he can only make out with difficulty the many symbols of the colonial world, he is never sure whether or not he has crossed the frontier. Confronted with a world ruled by the settler, the native is always presumed guilty. But the native's guilt is never a guilt which he accepts; it is rather a kind of curse; a sort of sword of Damocles, for, in his innermost spirit, the native admits no accusation. He is not convinced of his inferiority. He is patiently waiting until the settler is off his guard to fly at him. The native's muscles are always tensed. You can't say that he is terrorized, or even apprehensive. He is in fact ready at a moment's notice to exchange the *role* of the quarry for that of the hunter. The native is an oppressed person whose permanent dream is to become the persecutor. The symbols of social order—the police, the bugle-calls in the barracks, military parades and the waving flags—are at one and the same time inhibitory and stimulating: for they do not convey the message "Don't dare to budge"; rather, they cry out "Get ready to attack." And, in fact, if the native had any tendency to fall asleep and to forget, the settler's morgue and the settler's anxiety to test the strength of the colonial system would remind him at every turn that the great showdown cannot be put off indefinitely. That impulse to take the settler's place implies a tonicity of muscles the whole time; and in fact we know that in certain emotional conditions the presence of an obstacle accentuates the tendency toward motion.

The settler-native relationship is a mass relationship. The settler pits brute force against the weight of numbers. He is an exhibitionist. His preoccupation with security makes him remind the native out loud that he alone is master. The settler keeps alive in the native an anger which he deprives of outlet; the native is trapped in the tight links of the chains of colonialism. But we have seen that inwardly the settler can only achieve a pseudo petrification. The native's muscular tension finds outlet regularly in bloodthirsty explosions—in tribal warfare, in feuds between sects, and in quarrels between individuals.

Where individuals are concerned, a positive negation of common sense is evident. While the settler or the policeman has the right the livelong day to strike the native, to insult him and to make him crawl to them, you will see the native reaching for his knife at the slightest hostile or aggressive glance cast on him by another native; for the last resort of the native is to defend his personality *vis-à-vis* his brother. Tribal feuds only serve to perpetuate old grudges deep buried in the memory. By throwing himself with all his force into the *vendetta*, the native tries to persuade himself that colonialism does not exist, that everything is going on as before, that history continues. Here on the level of communal organizations we clearly discern the well-known behavior patterns of avoidance. It is as if plunging into a fraternal blood-bath allowed them to ignore the obstacle, and to put off till later the choice, nevertheless inevitable, which opens up the question of armed resistance to colonialism. Thus collective autodestruction in a very concrete form is one of the ways in which the native's muscular tension is set free. All these patterns of conduct are those of the death reflex when faced with danger, a suicidal behavior which proves to the settler (whose existence and domination is by them all the more justified) that these men are not reasonable human beings. In the same way the native manages to bypass the settler. A belief in fatality removes all blame from the oppressor; the cause of misfortunes and of poverty is attributed to God; He is Fate. In this way the individual accepts the disintegration ordained by God, bows down before the settler and his lot, and by a kind of interior restabilization acquires a stony calm.

Meanwhile, however, life goes on, and the native will strengthen the inhibitions which contain his aggressiveness by drawing on the terrifying myths which are so frequently found in underdeveloped communities. There are maleficent spirits which intervene every time a step is taken in the wrong direction, leopard-men, serpent-men, six-legged dogs, zombies—a whole series of tiny animals or giants which create around the native a world of prohibitions, of barriers and of inhibitions far more terrifying than the world of the settler. This magical superstructure which permeates native society fulfills certain well-defined functions in the dynamism of the libido. One of the characteristics of underdeveloped societies is in fact that the libido is first and foremost the concern of a group, or of the family. The feature of communities whereby a man who dreams that he has sexual relations with a woman other than his own must confess it in public and pay a fine in kind or in working days to the injured husband or family is fully described by ethnologists. We may note in passing that this proves that the so-called prehistoric societies attach great importance to the unconscious.

The atmosphere of myth and magic frightens me and so takes on an undoubted reality. By terrifying me, it integrates me in the traditions and the history of my district or of my tribe, and at the same time it reassures me, it gives me a status, as it were an identification paper. In underdeveloped countries the occult sphere is a sphere belonging to the community which is entirely under magical jurisdiction. By entangling myself in this inextricable network where actions are repeated with crystalline inevitability, I find the everlasting world which belongs to me, and the perenniality which is thereby affirmed of the world belonging to us. Believe me, the zombies are more terrifying than the settlers; and in consequence the problem is no longer that of keeping oneself right with the colonial world and its barbed-wire entanglements, but of considering three times before urinating, spitting or going out into the night.

The supernatural, magical powers reveal themselves as essentially personal; the settler's powers are infinitely shrunken, stamped with their alien origin. We no longer really need to fight against them since what counts is the frightening enemy created by myths. We perceive that all is settled by a permanent confrontation on the phantasmic plane.

It has always happened in the struggle for freedom that such a people, formerly lost in an imaginary maze, a prey to unspeakable terrors yet happy to lose themselves in a dreamlike torment, such a people becomes unhinged, reorganizes itself, and in blood and tears gives birth to very real and immediate action. Feeding the *moudjahidines**, posting sentinels, coming to the help of families which lack the bare necessities, or taking the place of a husband who has been killed or imprisoned: such are the concrete tasks to which the people is called during the struggle for freedom.

In the colonial world, the emotional sensitivity of the native is kept on the surface of his skin like an open sore which flinches from the caustic agent; and the psychism shrinks back, obliterates itself and finds outlet in muscular demonstrations which have caused certain very wise men to say that the native is a hysterical type. This sensitive emotionalism, watched by invisible keepers who are however in unbroken contact with the core of the personality, will find its fulfillment through eroticism in the driving forces behind the crisis' dissolution.

On another level we see the native's emotional sensibility exhausting itself in dances which are more or less ecstatic. This is why any study of the colonial world should take into consideration the phenomena of the dance and of possession. The native's relaxation takes precisely the form of a muscular orgy in which the most acute aggressivity and the most impelling violence are canalized, transformed and conjured away. The circle of the dance is a permissive circle: it protects and permits. At certain times on certain days, men and women come together at a given place, and there, under the solemn eye of the tribe, fling themselves into a seemingly unorganized pantomime, which is in reality extremely systematic, in which by various

* Highly trained soldiers who are completely dedicated to the Muslim cause. (Trans.)

means—shakes of the head, bending of the spinal column, throwing of the whole body backwards—may be deciphered as in an open book the huge effort of a community to exorcise itself, to liberate itself, to explain itself. There are no limits—inside the circle. The hillock up which you have toiled as if to be nearer to the moon; the river bank down which you slip as if to show the connection between the dance and ablutions, cleansing and purification—these are sacred places. There are no limits—for in reality your purpose in coming together is to allow the accumulated libido, the hampered aggressivity to dissolve as in a volcanic eruption. Symbolical killings, fantastic rides, imaginary mass murders—all must be brought out. The evil humors are undammed, and flow away with a din as of molten lava.

One step further and you are completely possessed. In fact, these are actually organized *séances* of possession and exorcism; they include vampirism, possession by djinns, by zombies, and by Legba, the famous god of the Voodoo. This disintegrating of the personality, this splitting and dissolution, all this fulfills a primordial function in the organism of the colonial world. When they set out, the men and women were impatient, stamping their feet in a state of nervous excitement; when they return, peace has been restored to the village; it is once more calm and unmoved.

During the struggle for freedom, a marked alienation from these practices is observed. The native's back is to the wall, the knife is at his throat (or, more precisely, the electrode at his genitals): he will have no more call for his fancies. After centuries of unreality, after having wallowed in the most outlandish phantoms, at long last the native, gun in hand, stands face to face with the only forces which contend for his life—the forces of colonialism. And the youth of a colonized country, growing up in an atmosphere of shot and fire, may well make a mock of, and does not hesitate to pour scorn upon the zombies of his ancestors, the horses with two heads, the dead who rise again, and the djinns who rush into your body while you yawn. The native discovers reality and transforms it into the pattern of his customs, into the practice of violence and into his plan for freedom.

We have seen that this same violence, though kept very much on the surface all through the colonial period, yet turns in the void. We have also seen that it is canalized by the emotional outlets of dance and possession by spirits; we have seen how it is exhausted in fratricidal combats. Now the problem is to lay hold of this violence which is changing direction. When formerly it was appeased by myths and exercised its talents in finding fresh ways of committing mass suicide, now new conditions will make possible a completely new line of action.

Nowadays a theoretical problem of prime importance is being set, on the historical plane as well as on the level of political tactics, by the liberation of the colonies: when can one affirm that the situation is ripe for a movement of national liberation? In what form should it first be manifested? Because the various means whereby decolonization has been carried out have appeared in many different aspects, reason hesitates and refuses to say which is a true decolonization, and which a false. We shall see that for a man who is in the thick of the fight it is an urgent matter to decide on the means and the tactics to employ: that is to say, how to conduct and organize the movement. If this coherence is not present there is only a blind will toward freedom, with the terribly reactionary risks which it entails.

What are the forces which in the colonial period open up new outlets and engender new aims to the violence of colonized peoples? In the first place there are the political parties and the intellectual or commercial *élites*. Now, the characteristic feature of certain political structures is that they proclaim abstract principles but refrain from issuing definite commands. The entire action of these nationalist political parties during the colonial period is action of the electoral type: a string of philosophico-political dissertations on the themes of the rights of peoples to self-determination, the rights of man to freedom from hunger and human dignity, and the unceasing affirmation of the principle: "One man, one vote." The national political parties never lay stress upon the necessity of a trial of armed strength, for the good reason that their objective is not the radical overthrowing of the system. Pacifists and legalists, they are in fact partisans of order, the new order—but to the colonialist bourgeoisie they put bluntly enough the demand which to them is the main one: "Give us more power." On the specific question of violence, the *élite* are ambiguous. They are violent in their words and reformist in their attitudes. When the nationalist political leaders *say* something, they make quite clear that they do not really *think* it.

This characteristic on the part of the nationalist political parties should be interpreted in the light both of the makeup of their leaders and the nature of their followings. The rank-and-file of a nationalist party is urban. The workers, primary schoolteachers, artisans and small shopkeepers who have begun to profit— at a discount, to be sure—from the colonial setup, have special interests at heart. What this sort of following demands is the betterment of their particular lot: increased salaries, for example. The dialogue between these political parties and colonialism is never broken off. Improvements are discussed, such as full electoral representation, the liberty of the press, and liberty of association. Reforms are debated. Thus it need not astonish anyone to notice that a large number of natives are militant members of the branches of political parties which stem from the mother-country. These natives fight under an abstract watchword: "Government by the workers," and they forget that in their country it should be *nationalist* watchwords which are first in the field. The native intellectual has clothed his aggressiveness in his barely veiled desire to assimilate himself to the colonial world. He has used his aggressiveness to serve his own individual interests.

Thus there is very easily brought into being a kind of class of affranchised slaves, or slaves who are individually free. What the intellectual demands is the right to multiply the emancipated, and the opportunity to organize a genuine class of emancipated citizens. On the other hand, the mass of the people have no intention of standing by and watching individuals increase their chances of success. What they demand is not the settler's act of parliament, but the settler's place. The immense majority of natives want the settler's farm. For them, there is no question of entering into competition with the settler. They want to take his place.

The peasantry is systematically disregarded for the most part by the propaganda put out by the nationalist parties. And it is clear that in the colonial countries the peasants alone are revolutionary, for they have nothing to lose and everything to gain. The starving peasant, outside the class system, is the first among the exploited to discover that only violence pays. For him there is no compromise, no possible coming to terms; colonization and decolonization are simply a question of relative strength. The exploited man sees that his liberation implies the use of all means, and that of force first and foremost. When in 1956, after the capitulation of Monsieur Guy Mollet to the settlers in Algeria, the *Front de Libération Nationale*, in a famous leaflet, stated that colonialism only loosens its hold when the knife is at its throat, no Algerian really found these terms too violent. The leaflet only expressed what every Algerian felt at heart: colonialism is not a thinking machine, nor a body endowed with reasoning faculties. It is violence in its natural state, and it will only yield when confronted with greater violence.

At the decisive moment, the colonialist bourgeoisie, which up till then has remained inactive, comes into the field. It introduces that new idea which is in proper parlance a creation of the colonial situation: nonviolence. In its simplest form this nonviolence signifies to the intellectual and economic *élite* of the colonized country that the bourgeoisie has the same interests as them and that it is therefore urgent and indispensable to come to terms for the public good. Nonviolence is an attempt to settle the colonial problem around a green baize table, before any regrettable act has been performed or irreparable gesture made, before any blood has been shed. But if the masses, without waiting for the chairs to be arranged around the baize table, listen to their own voice and begin committing outrages and setting fire to buildings, the *élites* and the nationalist bourgeois parties will be seen rushing to the colonialists to exclaim "This is very serious! We do not know how it will end; we must find a solution—some sort of compromise."

This idea of compromise is very important in the phenomenon of decolonization, for it is very far from being a simple one. Compromise involves the colonial system and the young nationalist bourgeoisie at one and the same time. The partisans of the colonial system discover that the masses may destroy everything. Blown-up bridges, ravaged farms, repressions and fighting harshly disrupt the economy. Compromise is equally attractive to the nationalist bourgeoisie, who, since they are not clearly aware of the possible consequences of the rising storm, are genuinely afraid of being swept away by this huge hurricane and never stop saying to the settlers: "We are still capable of stopping the slaughter; the masses still have confidence in us; act quickly if you do not want to put everything in jeopardy." One step more, and the leader of the nationalist party keeps his distance with regard to that violence. He loudly proclaims that he has nothing to do with these Mau-Mau, these terrorists, these throat-slitters. At best, he shuts himself off in a no-man's-land between the terrorists and the settlers and willingly offers his services as go-between; that is to say, that as the settlers cannot discuss terms with these Mau-Mau, he himself will be quite willing to begin negotiations. Thus it is that the rearguard of the national struggle, that very party of people who have never ceased to be on the other side in the fight, find themselves somersaulted into the van of negotiations and compromise—precisely because that party has taken very good care never to break contact with colonialism.

Before negotiations have been set on foot, the majority of nationalist parties confine themselves for the most part to explaining and excusing this "savagery." They do not assert that the people have to use physical force, and it sometimes even happens that they go so far as to condemn, in private, the spectacular deeds which are declared to be hateful by the press and public opinion in the mother-country. The legitimate excuse for this ultraconservative policy is the desire to see things in an objective light; but this traditional attitude of the native intellectual and of the leaders of the nationalist parties is not, in reality, in the least objective. For in fact they are not at all convinced that this impatient violence of the masses is the most efficient means of defending their own interests. Moreover, there are some individuals who are convinced of the ineffectiveness of violent methods; for them, there is no doubt about it, every attempt to break colonial oppression by force is a hopeless effort, an attempt at suicide, because in the innermost recesses of their brains the settler's tanks and aeroplanes occupy a huge place. When they are told "Action must be taken," they see bombs raining down on them, armored cars coming at them on every path, machine-gunning and police action . . . and they sit quiet. They are beaten from the start. There is no need to demonstrate their incapacity to triumph by violent methods; they take it for granted in their everyday life and in their political maneuvers. They have remained in the same childish position as Engels took up in his famous polemic with that monument of puerility, Monsieur Dühring:

In the same way that Robinson (Crusoe) was able to obtain a sword, we can just as well suppose that (Man) Friday might appear one fine morning with a loaded revolver in his hand, and from then on the whole relationship of violence is reversed: Man Friday gives the orders and Crusoe is obliged to work. . . . Thus, the revolver triumphs over the sword, and even the most childish believer in axioms will doubtless form the conclusion that violence is not a simple act of will, but needs for its realisation certain very concrete preliminary conditions, and in particular the implements of violence; and the more highly-developed of these implements will carry the day against primitive ones. Moreover, the very fact of the ability to produce such weapons signifies that the producer of highly-developed weapons, in everyday speech the arms manufacturer, triumphs over the producer of primitive weapons. To put it briefly, the triumph of violence depends on production in general, and thus . . . on economic strength, on the economy of the State, and in the last resort on the material means which that violence commands.[4]

In fact, the leaders of reform have nothing else to say than: "With what are you going to fight the settlers? With your knives? Your shotguns?"

It is true that weapons are important when violence comes into play, since all finally depends on the distribution of these implements. But it so happens that the liberation of colonial countries throws new light on the subject. For example, we have seen that during the Spanish campaign, which was a very genuine colonial war, that Napoleon, in spite of an army which reached in the offensives of the Spring of 1810 the huge figure of 400,000 men, was forced to retreat. Yet the French army made the whole of Europe tremble by its weapons of war, by the bravery of its soldiers and by the military genius of its leaders. Face to face with the enormous potentials of the Napoleonic troops, the Spaniards, inspired by an unshakable national ardor, rediscovered the famous methods of guerilla warfare which, twenty-five years before, the American militia had tried out on the English forces. But the native's guerilla warfare would be of no value as opposed to other means of violence if it did not form a new element in the world-wide process of competition between trusts and monopolies.

In the early days of colonization, a single column could occupy immense stretches of country: the Congo, Nigeria, the Ivory Coast, and so on. Today, however, the colonized countries' national struggle crops up in a completely new international situation. Capitalism, in its early days, saw in the colonies a source of raw materials which, once turned into manufactured goods, could be distributed on the European market. After a phase of accumulation of capital, capitalism has today come to modify its conception of the profit-earning capacity of a commercial enterprise. The colonies have become a market. The colonial population is a customer who is ready to buy goods. Consequently, if the garrison has to be perpetually reinforced, if buying and selling slackens off, that is to say if manufactured and finished goods can no longer be expected, there is clear proof that the solution of military force must be set aside. A blind domination founded on slavery is not economically speaking worthwhile for the bourgeoisie of the mother-country. The monopolistic group within this bourgeoisie does not support a government whose policy is solely that of the sword. What the factory-owners and finance magnates of the mother-country expect from their government is not that it should decimate the colonial peoples, but that it should safeguard with the help of economic conventions their own "legitimate interests."

Thus there exists a sort of detached complicity between capitalism and the violent forces which blaze up in colonial territory. What is more, the native is not alone against the oppressor, for indeed there is also the political and diplomatic support of progressive countries and peoples. But above all there is competition, that pitiless war which financial groups wage upon each other. A Berlin Conference was able to tear Africa into shreds and divide her up between three or four imperial flags. At the moment, the important thing is not whether such-and-such a region in Africa is under French or Belgian sovereignty, but rather that the economic zones are respected. Today, wars of repression are no longer waged against rebel sultans; everything is more elegant, less bloodthirsty; the liquidation of the Castro régime will be quite peaceful. They do all they can to strangle Guinea and they eliminate Mossadek. Thus the nationalist leader who is frightened of violence is wrong if he imagines that colonialism is going to "massacre all of us." The military will of course go on playing with tin soldiers which date from the time of the conquest, but higher finance will soon bring the truth home to them.

This is why reasonable nationalist political parties are asked to set out their claims as clearly as possible, and to seek with their colonialist opposite numbers, calmly and without passion, for a solution which will take the interests of both parties into consideration. We see that if this nationalist reformist tendency which often takes the form of a kind of caricature of trades unionism decides to take action, it will only do so in a highly peaceful fashion, through stoppages of work in the few industries which have been set up in the towns, mass demonstrations to cheer the leaders, and the boycotting of buses or of imported commodities. All these forms of action serve at one and the same time to bring pressure to bear on the forces of colonialism, and to allow the people to work off their energy. This practice of therapy by hibernation, this sleep-cure used on the people, may sometimes be successful; thus out of the conference around the green baize table comes the political selectiveness which enables Monsieur M'ba, the president of the Republic of Gabon, to state in all seriousness on his arrival in Paris for an official visit: "Gabon is independent, but between Gabon and France nothing has changed; everything goes on as before." In fact, the only change is that Monsieur M'ba is president of the Gabonese Republic and that he is received by the president of the French Republic.

The colonialist bourgeoisie is helped in its work of calming down the natives by the inevitable religion. All those saints who have turned the other cheek, who have forgiven trespasses against them, and who have been spat on and insulted without shrinking are studied and held up as examples. On the other hand, the *élites* of the colonial countries, those slaves set free, when at the head of the movement inevitably end up by producing an ersatz conflict. They use "their brothers' slavery" to shame the slave-drivers or to provide an ideological policy of quaint humanitarianism for their oppressors' financial competitors. The truth is that they never make any real appeal to the aforesaid slaves; they never mobilize them in concrete terms. On the contrary, at the decisive moment (that is to say, from their point of view the moment of indecision) they brandish the danger of a "mass mobilization" as the crucial weapon which would bring about as if by magic the "end of the colonial régime." Obviously there are to be found at the core of the political parties and among their leaders certain revolutionaries who deliberately turn their backs upon the farce of national independence. But very quickly their questionings, their energy and their anger obstruct the party machine; and these elements are gradually isolated, and then quite simply brushed aside. At this moment, as if there existed a dialectic concomitance, the colonialist police will fall upon them. With no security in the towns, avoided by the militants of their former party and rejected by its leaders, these undesirable firebrands will be stranded in country districts. Then it is that they will realize bewilderedly that the peasant masses catch on to what they have to say immediately, and without delay ask them the question to which they have not yet prepared the answer: "When do we start?"

This meeting of revolutionaries coming from the town and country-dwellers will be dealt with later on. For the moment we must go back to the political parties, in order to show the nature of their action, which is all the same progressive. In their speeches the political leaders give a name to the nation. In this way the native's demands are given shape.

There is, however, no definite subject-matter and no political or social program. There is a vague outline or skeleton, which is nevertheless national in form, what we describe as "minimum requirements." The politicians who make speeches and who write in the nationalist newspapers make the people dream dreams. They avoid the actual overthrowing of the state, but in fact they introduce into their readers' or hearers' consciousness the terrible ferment of subversion. The national or tribal language is often used. Here, once again, dreams are encouraged, and the imagination is let loose outside the bounds of the colonial order; and sometimes these politicians speak of "We Negroes, we Arabs," and these terms which are so profoundly ambivalent take on during the colonial epoch a sacramental signification. The nationalist politicians are playing with fire: for, as an African leader recently warned a group of young intellectuals, "Think well before you speak to the masses, for they flare up quickly." This is one of the tricks that destiny plays in the colonies.

When a political leader calls a mass meeting, we may say that there is blood in the air. Yet the same leader very often is above all anxious to "make a show" of force, so that in fact he need not use it. But the agitation which ensues, the coming and going, the listening to speeches, seeing the people assembled in one place, with the police all around, the military demonstrations, arrests, and the deportation of the leaders—all this hubbub makes the people think that the moment has come for them to take action. In these times of instability the political parties multiply their appeals for calm to the left, while on their right they scan the horizon, trying to make out the liberal intentions of colonialism.

In the same way the people make use of certain episodes in the life of the community in order to hold themselves ready and to keep alive their revolutionary zeal. For example, the gangster who holds up the police set on to track him down for days on end, or who dies in single combat after having killed four or five policemen, or who commits suicide in order not to give away his accomplices—these types light the way for the people, form the blueprints for action and become heroes. Obviously, it's a waste of breath to say that such-and-such a hero is a thief, a scoundrel or a reprobate. If the act for which he is prosecuted by the colonial authorities is an act exclusively directed against a colonialist person or colonialist property, the demarcation line is definite and manifest. The process of identification is automatic.

We must also notice in this ripening process the *role* played by the history of the resistance at the time of the conquest. The great figures of the colonized people are always those who led the national resistance to invasion. Behanzin, Soundiata, Samory, Abdel Kader—all spring again to life with peculiar intensity in the period which comes directly before action. This is the proof that the people are getting ready to begin to go forward again, to put an end to the static period begun by colonization, and to make history.

The uprising of the new nation and the breaking down of colonial structures are the result of two causes: either of a violent struggle of the people in their own right, or of action on the part of surrounding colonized peoples which acts as a brake on the colonial régime in question.

A colonized people is not alone. In spite of all that colonialism can do, its frontiers remain open to new ideas and echoes from the world outside. It discovers that violence is in the atmosphere, that it here and there bursts out, and here and there sweeps away the colonial régime—that same violence which fulfills for the native a *role* that is not simply informatory, but also operative. The great victory of the Vietnamese people at Dien Ben Phu is no longer, strictly speaking, a Vietnamese victory. Since July 1954, the question which the colonized peoples have asked themselves has been "What must be done to bring about another Dien Ben Phu? How can we manage it?" Not a single colonized individual could ever again doubt the possibility of a Dien Ben Phu; the only problem was how best to use the forces at their disposal, how to organize them, and when to bring them into action. This encompassing violence does not work upon the colonized people only; it modifies the attitude of the colonialists who become aware of manifold Dien Ben Phus. This is why a veritable panic takes hold of the colonialist governments in turn. Their purpose is to capture the vanguard, to turn the movement of liberation toward the right, and to disarm the people: quick, quick, let's decolonize. Decolonize the Congo before it turns into another Algeria. Vote the constitutional framework for all Africa, create the French *Communauté*, renovate that same *Communauté*, but for God's sake let's decolonize quick. . . . And they decolonize at such a rate that they impose independence on Houphouët-Boigny. To the strategy of Dien Ben Phu, defined by the colonized peoples, the colonialist replies by the strategy of encirclement—based on the respect of the sovereignty of states.

But let us return to that atmosphere of violence, that violence which is just under the skin. We have seen that in its process toward maturity many leads are attached to it, to control it and show it the way out. Yet in spite of the metamorphoses which the colonial régime imposes upon it in the way of tribal or regional quarrels, that violence makes its way forward, and the native identifies his enemy and recognizes all his misfortunes, throwing all the exacerbated might of his hate and anger into this new channel. But how do we pass from the atmosphere of violence to violence in action? What makes the lid blow off? There is first of all the fact that this development does not leave the settler's blissful existence intact. The settler who "understands" the natives is made aware by several straws showing the wind that something is afoot. "Good" natives become scarce; silence falls when the oppressor approaches; sometimes looks are black, and attitudes and remarks openly aggressive. The nationalist parties are astir, they hold a great many meetings, the police are increased and reinforcements of soldiers are brought in. The settlers, above all the farmers isolated on their land, are the first to become alarmed. They call for energetic measures.

The authorities do in fact take some spectacular measures. They arrest one or two leaders, they organize military parades and maneuvers, and air force displays. But the demonstrations and warlike exercises, the smell of gunpowder which now fills the atmosphere, these things do not make the people draw back. Those bayonets and cannonades only serve to reinforce their aggressiveness. The atmosphere becomes dramatic, and everyone wishes to show that they are ready for anything. And it is in these circumstances that the guns go off by themselves, for nerves are jangled, fear reigns and everyone is trigger-happy. A single commonplace incident is enough to start the machine-gunning: Setif in Algeria, the Central Quarries in Morocco, Moramanga in Madagascar.

The repressions, far from calling a halt to the forward rush of national consciousness, urge it on. Mass slaughter in the colonies at a certain stage of the embryonic development of consciousness increases that consciousness, for the hecatombs are an indication that between oppressors and oppressed everything can be solved by force. It must be remarked here that the political parties have not called for armed insurrection, and have made no preparations for such an insurrection. All these repressive measures, all those actions which are a result of fear are not within the leader's intentions; they are overtaken by events. At this moment, then, colonialism may decide to arrest the nationalist leaders. But today the governments of colonized countries know very well that it is extremely dangerous to deprive the masses of their leaders; for then the people, unbridled, fling themselves into *jacqueries*, mutinies, and "brutish murders." The masses give free rein to their "bloodthirsty instincts" and force colonialism to free their leaders, to whom falls the difficult task of bringing them back to order. The colonized people, who have spontaneously brought their violence to the colossal task of destroying the colonial system, will very soon find themselves with the barren, inert slogan "Release X or Y."⁵ Then colonialism will release these men, and hold discussions with them. The time for dancing in the streets has come.

In certain circumstances, the party political machine may remain intact. But as a result of the colonialist repression and of the spontaneous reaction of the people the parties find themselves outdistanced by their militants. The violence of the masses is vigorously pitted against the military forces of the occupying power, and the situation deteriorates and comes to a head. Those leaders who are free remain, therefore, on the touchline. They have suddenly become useless, with their bureaucracy and their reasonable demands; yet we see them, far removed from events, attempting the crowning imposture—that of "speaking in the name of the silenced nation." As a general rule, colonialism welcomes this godsend with open arms, transforms these "blind mouths" into spokesmen, and in two minutes endows them with independence, on condition that they restore order.

So we see that all parties are aware of the power of such violence and that the question is not always to reply to it by a greater violence, but rather to see how to relax the tension.

What is the real nature of this violence? We have seen that it is the intuition of the colonized masses that their liberation must, and can only, be achieved by force. By what spiritual aberration do these men, without technique, starving and enfeebled, confronted with the military and economic might of the occupation, come to believe that violence alone will free them? How can they hope to triumph?

It is because violence (and this is the disgraceful thing) may constitute, in so far as it forms part of its system, the slogan of a political party. The leaders may call on the people to enter upon an armed struggle. This problematical question has to be thought over. When militarist Germany decides to settle its frontier disputes by force, we are not in the least surprised; but when the people of Angola, for example, decide to take up arms, when the Algerian people reject all means which are not violent, these are proofs that something has happened or is happening at this very moment. The colonized races, those slaves of mod-

ern times, are impatient. They know that alone this apparent
folly can put them out of reach of colonial oppression. A new
type of relations is established in the world. The underdeveloped
peoples try to break their chains, and the extraordinary thing is
that they succeed. It could be argued that in these days of sput-
niks it is ridiculous to die of hunger; but for the colonized masses
the argument is more down-to-earth. The truth is that there is
no colonial power today which is capable of adopting the only
form of contest which has a chance of succeeding, namely, the
prolonged establishment of large forces of occupation.

As far as their internal situation is concerned, the colonialist
countries find themselves faced with contradictions in the form
of working-class demands which necessitate the use of their
police forces. As well, in the present international situation,
these countries need their troops to protect their régimes. Finally there is the well-known myth of liberating movements
directed from Moscow. In the régime's panic-stricken reasoning,
this signifies "If that goes on, there is a risk that the communists
will turn the troubles to account and infiltrate into these parts."

In the native's eagerness, the fact that he openly brandishes
the threat of violence proves that he is conscious of the unusual
character of the contemporary situation and that he means to
profit by it. But, still on the level of immediate experience, the
native, who has seen the modern world penetrate into the fur-
thermost corners of the bush, is most acutely aware of all the
things he does not possess. The masses by a sort of (if we may
say so) childlike process of reasoning convince themselves that
they have been robbed of all these things. That is why in certain
underdeveloped countries the masses forge ahead very quickly,
and realize two or three years after independence that they have
been frustrated, that "it wasn't worthwhile" fighting, and that
nothing could really change. In 1789, after the bourgeois revolution, the smallest French peasants benefited substantially from
the upheaval. But it is a commonplace to observe and to say that
in the majority of cases, for 95 percent of the population of
underdeveloped countries, independence brings no immediate
change. The enlightened observer takes note of the existence of

a kind of masked discontent, like the smoking ashes of a burned-down house after the fire has been put out, which still threaten to burst into flames again.

So they say that the natives want to go too quickly. No, let us never forget that only a very short time ago they complained of their slowness, their laziness and their fatalism. Already we see that violence used in specific ways at the moment of the struggle for freedom does not magically disappear after the ceremony of trooping the national colors. It has all the less reason for disappearing since the reconstruction of the nation continues within the framework of cutthroat competition between capitalism and socialism.

This competition gives an almost universal dimension to even the most localized demands. Every meeting held, every act of repression committed, reverberates in the international arena. The murders of Sharpeville shook public opinion for months. In the newspapers, over the wavelengths and in private conversations Sharpeville has become a symbol. It was through Sharpeville that men and women first became acquainted with the problem of Apartheid in South Africa. Moreover, we cannot believe that demagogy alone is the explanation for the sudden interest the big powers show in the petty affairs of under-developed regions. Each *jacquerie*, each act of sedition in the Third World makes up part of a picture framed by the Cold War. Two men are beaten up at Salisbury, and at once the whole of a *bloc* goes into action, talks about those two men, and uses the beating-up incident to bring up the particular problem of Rhodesia, linking it, moreover, with the whole African question and with the whole question of colonized people. The other *bloc*, however, is equally concerned in measuring by the magnitude of the campaign the local weaknesses of its system. Thus the colonized peoples realize that neither clan remains outside local incidents. They no longer limit themselves to regional horizons, for they have caught on to the fact that they live in an atmosphere of international stress.

When every three months or so we hear that the sixth or seventh flotilla is moving toward such-and-such a coast; when

Khrouchev threatens to come to Castro's help with gunshot; when Kennedy decides upon some desperate solution for the Laos question, the colonized person or the newly independent native has the impression that whether he will it or not he is being carried away in a kind of frantic cavalcade. In fact he is marching in it already. Let us take, for example, the case of the governments of recently liberated countries. The men at the head of affairs spend two-thirds of their time in watching the approaches and trying to anticipate the dangers which threaten them, and the remaining one-third of their time in working for their country. At the same time, they search for allies. Obedient to the same dialectic, the national parties of opposition leave the paths of parliamentary behavior. They also look for allies to support them in their ruthless ventures into sedition. The atmosphere of violence, after having colored all the colonial phase, continues to dominate national life, for, as we have already said, the Third World is not cut off from the rest. Quite on the contrary, it is at the middle of the whirlpool. This is why the statesmen of under-developed countries keep up indefinitely the tone of aggressiveness and exasperation in their public speeches which in the normal way ought to have disappeared. Herein, also, may be found the reasons for that lack of politeness so often spoken of in connection with newly established rulers. But what is less visible is the extreme courtesy of these same rulers in their contacts with their brothers or their comrades. Discourtesy is first and foremost a manner to be used in dealings with the others, with the former colonists who come to observe and to investigate. The "ex-native" too often gets the impression that these reports are already written. The photos which illustrate the article are simply a proof that one knows what one is talking about, and that one has visited the country. The report intends to verify the evidence: everything's going badly out there since we left. Frequently reporters complain of being badly received, of being forced to work under bad conditions and of being fenced round by indifference or hostility: all this is quite normal. The nationalist leaders know that international opinion is formed solely by the Western press. Now, when a journalist from the

West asks us questions it is seldom in order to help us. In the Algerian war, for example, even the most liberal of the French reporters never ceased to use ambiguous terms in describing our struggle. When we reproached them for this, they replied in all good faith that they were being objective. For the native, objectivity is always directed against him. We may in the same way come to understand the new tone which swamped international diplomacy at the United Nations General Assembly in September 1960. The representatives of the colonial countries were aggressive and violent, and carried things to extremes, but the colonial peoples did not find that they exaggerated. The radicalism of the African spokesmen brought the abcess to a head and showed up the inadmissible nature of the veto and of the dialogue between the great powers, and above all the tiny *role* reserved for the Third World.

Diplomacy, as inaugurated by the newly independent peoples, is no longer an affair of nuances, of implications, and of hypnotic passes. For the nation's spokesmen are responsible at one and the same time for safeguarding the unity of the nation, the progress of the masses toward a state of well-being and the right of all peoples to bread and liberty. Thus it is a diplomacy which never stops moving, a diplomacy which leaps ahead, in strange contrast to the motionless, petrified world of colonization. And when Mr. Khrouchev casts out his shoe over the United Nations, or thumps the table with it, there's not a single ex-native, nor any representative of an underdeveloped country, who laughs. For what Mr. Khrouchev shows the colonized countries which are looking on is that he, the moujik, who moreover is the possessor of space rockets, treats these miserable capitalists in the way that they deserve. In the same way, Castro sitting in military uniform in the United Nations Organization does not scandalize the underdeveloped countries. What Castro demonstrates is the consciousness he has of the continuing existence of the rule of violence. The astonishing thing is that he did not come into U.N.O. with a machine gun; but if he had, would anyone have minded? All the *jacqueries* and desperate deeds, all those bands armed with cutlasses or axes find their nationality in the implacable struggle which opposes socialism and capitalism.

In 1945, the 45,000 dead at Setif could pass unnoticed; in 1947, the 90,000 dead in Madagascar could be the subject of a simple paragraph in the papers; in 1952, the 200,000 victims of the repression in Kenya could meet with relative indifference. This was because the international contradictions were not sufficiently distinct. Already the Korean and Indochinese wars had begun a new phase. But it is above all Budapest and Suez which constitute the decisive moments of this confrontation.

Strengthened by the unconditional support of the socialist countries, the colonized peoples fling themselves with whatever arms they have against the impregnable citadel of colonialism. If this citadel is invulnerable to knives and naked fists, it is no longer so when we decide to take into account the context of the cold war.

In this fresh juncture, the Americans take their *role* of patron of international capitalism very seriously. Early on, they advise the European countries to decolonize in friendly fashion. Later on, they do not hesitate to proclaim first the respect for and then the support of the principle of "Africa for the Africans." The United States are not afraid today of stating officially that they are the defenders of the right of all peoples to self-determination. Mr. Mennen Williams' last journey is only the illustration of the consciousness which the Americans have that the Third World ought not to be sacrificed. From then on we understand why the violence of the native is only hopeless if we compare it in the abstract to the military machine of the oppressor. On the other hand, if we situate that violence in the dynamics of the international situation, we see at once that it constitutes a terrible menace for the oppressor. Persistent *jacqueries* and Mau-Mau disturbances unbalance the colony's economic life but do not endanger the mother-country. What is more important in the eyes of imperialism is the opportunity for socialist propaganda to infiltrate among the masses and to contaminate them. This is already a serious danger in the cold war; but what would happen to that colony in case of real war, riddled as it is by murderous guerillas?

Thus capitalism realizes that its military strategy has everything to lose by the outbreak of nationalist wars. Again, within
the framework of peaceful coexistence, all colonies are destined
to disappear, and in the long run neutralism is destined to be
respected by capitalism. What must at all costs be avoided is
strategic insecurity: the breakthrough of enemy doctrine into the
masses and the deep-rooted hatred of millions of men. The colonized peoples are very well aware of these imperatives which
rule international political life; for this reason even those who
thunder denunciations of violence take their decisions and act
in terms of this universal violence. Today, peaceful coexistence
between the two *blocs* provokes and feeds violence in the
colonial countries. Tomorrow, perhaps, we shall see the shifting
of that violence after the complete liberation of the colonial
territories. Perhaps we will see the question of minorities crop-
ping up. Already certain minority groups do not hesitate to
preach violent methods for resolving their problems and it is not
by chance (so the story runs) that in consequence Negro extremists in the United States organize a militia and arm themselves.
It is not by chance, either, that in the so-called free world there
exist committees for the defense of Jewish minorities in USSR,
nor an accident if General de Gaulle in one of his orations sheds
tears over the millions of Muslims oppressed by Communist
dictatorship. Both capitalism and imperialism are convinced that
the struggle against racialism and the movements toward national freedom are purely and simply directed by remote control,
fomented from outside. So they decide to use that very efficacious tactic, the Free Europe Broadcasting Station, voice of the
Committee for the aid of overruled minorities. . . . They practice
anti-colonialism, as did the French colonels in Algeria when
they carried on subversive warfare with the S.A.S.* of the psychological services. They "use the people against the people."
We have seen with what results.

This atmosphere of violence and menaces, these rockets bran-
dished by both sides, do not frighten nor deflect the colonized

* Section Administrative Spéciale, an officers' corps whose task was to
strengthen contact with Algerians in nonmilitary matters.

peoples. We have seen that all their recent history has prepared them to understand and grasp the situation. Between the violence of the colonies and that peaceful violence that the world is steeped in, there is a kind of complicit agreement, a sort of homogeneity. The colonized peoples are well adapted to this atmosphere; for once, they are up to date. Sometimes people wonder that the native, rather than give his wife a dress, buys instead a transistor radio. There is no reason to be astonished. The natives are convinced that their fate is in the balance, here and now. They live in the atmosphere of doomsday, and they consider that nothing ought to be let pass unnoticed. That is why they understand very well Phouma and Phoumi, Lumumba and Tschombe, Ahidjo and Moumie, Kenyatta, and the men that are pushed forward regularly to replace him. They understand all these figures very well, for they can unmask the forces working behind them. The native and the underdeveloped man are today political animals in the most universal sense of the word.

It is true to say that independence has brought moral compensation to colonized peoples, and has established their dignity. But they have not yet had time to elaborate a society, or to build up and affirm values. The warming, lightgiving center where man and citizen develop and enrich their experience in wider and still wider fields does not yet exist. Set in a kind of irresolution, such men persuade themselves fairly easily that everything is going to be decided elsewhere, for everybody, at the same time. As for the political leaders, when faced with this situation they first hesitate and then choose neutralism.

There is plenty to be said on the subject of neutralism. Some equate it with a sort of tainted mercantilism which consists of taking what it can get from both sides. In fact, neutralism, a state of affairs created by the cold war, if it allows underdeveloped countries to receive economic help from both sides, does not allow either party to aid underdeveloped areas to the extent that is necessary. Those literally astronomical sums of money which are invested in military research, those engineers who are transformed into technicians of nuclear war, could in the space of

fifteen years raise the standard of living of underdeveloped countries by 60 percent. So we see that the true interests of underdeveloped countries do not lie in the protraction nor in the
accentuation of this cold war. But it so happens that no one asks
their advice. Therefore, when they can, they cut loose from it.
But can they really remain outside it? At the very moment,
France is trying out her atomic bombs in Africa. Apart from the
passing of motions, the holding of meetings and the shattering
of diplomatic relations, we cannot say that the peoples of Africa
have had much influence, in this particular sector, on France's
attitude.

Neutralism produces in the citizen of the Third World a state
of mind which is expressed in everyday life by a fearlessness and
an ancestral pride strangely resembling defiance. The flagrant
refusal to compromise and the tough will that sets itself against
getting tied-up is reminiscent of the behavior of proud, poverty-
stricken adolescents, who are always ready to risk their necks
in order to have the last word. All this leaves Western observers
dumbfounded, for to tell the truth there is a glaring divergence
between what these men set up to be and what they have behind
them. These countries without tramways, without troops and
without money have no justification for the bravado that they
display in broad daylight. Undoubtedly, they are impostors. The
Third World often gives the impression that it rejoices in sensa-
tion and that it must have its weekly dose of crises. These men
at the head of empty countries, who talk too loud, are most
irritating. You'd like to shut them up. But, on the contrary, they
are in great demand. They are given bouquets; they are invited
to dinner. In fact, we quarrel over who shall have them. And this
is neutralism. They are 98 percent illiterate, but they are the
subject of a huge body of literature. They travel a great deal: the
governing classes and students of underdeveloped countries are
goldmines for airline companies. African and Asian officials may
in the same months follow a course on socialist planning in
Moscow and one on the advantages of the liberal economy in
London or at Columbia University. African trades union leaders
leap ahead at a great rate in their own field. Hardly have they

been appointed to posts in managerial organizations when they decide to form themselves into autonomous bodies. They haven't the requisite fifty years' experience of practical trade-unionism in the framework of an industrial country, but they already know that nonpolitical trade-unionism doesn't make sense. They haven't come to grips with the bourgeois machine, nor developed their consciousness in the class struggle; but perhaps this isn't necessary. Perhaps. We shall see that this will to sum everything up, which caricatures itself often in facile internationalism, is one of the most fundamental characteristics of underdeveloped countries.

Let us return to considering the single combat between native and settler. We have seen that it takes the form of an armed and open struggle. There is no lack of historical examples: Indochina, Indonesia, and of course North Africa. But what we must not lose sight of is that this struggle could have broken out anywhere, in Guinea as well as Somaliland, and moreover today it could break out in every place where colonialism means to stay on, in Angola, for example. The existence of an armed struggle shows that the people are decided to trust to violent methods only. He of whom *they* have never stopped saying that the only language he understands is that of force, decides to give utterance by force. In fact, as always, the settler has shown him the way he should take if he is to become free. The argument the native chooses has been furnished by the settler, and by an ironic turning of the tables it is the native who now affirms that the colonialist understands nothing but force. The colonial régime owes its legitimacy to force and at no time tries to hide this aspect of things. Every statue, whether of Faidherbe or of Lyautey, of Bugeaud or of Sergent Blandan—all these *conquistadors* perched on colonial soil do not cease from proclaiming one and the same thing: "We are here by the force of bayonets. . . ."[6] The sentence is easily completed. During the phase of insurrection, each settler reasons on a basis of simple arithmetic. This logic does not surprise the other settlers, but it is important to point out that it does not surprise the natives either. To begin with, the affirmation of the principle "It's them or us" does not constitute a paradox, since colonialism, as we have seen, is in fact the organization of a Manichaean world, a world divided up into compartments. And when in laying down precise methods the settler asks each member of the oppressing minority to shoot down 30 or 100 or 200 natives, he sees that nobody shows any indignation and that the whole problem is to decide whether it can be done all at once or by stages.[7]

This chain of reasoning which presumes very arithmetically the disappearance of the colonized people does not leave the native overcome with moral indignation. He has always known that his duel with the settler would take place in the arena. The native loses no time in lamentations, and he hardly ever seeks for justice in the colonial framework. The fact is that if the settler's logic leaves the native unshaken, it is because the latter has practically stated the problem of his liberation in identical terms: "We must form ourselves into groups of two hundred or five hundred, and each group must deal with a settler." It is in this manner of thinking that each of the protagonists begins the struggle.

For the native, this violence represents the absolute line of action. The militant is also a man who works. The questions that the organization asks the militant bear the mark of this way of looking at things: "Where have you worked? With whom? What have you accomplished?" The group requires that each individual perform an irrevocable action. In Algeria, for example, where almost all the men who called on the people to join in the national struggle were condemned to death or searched for by the French police, confidence was proportional to the hopelessness of each case. You could be sure of a new recruit when he could no longer go back into the colonial system. This mechanism, it seems, had existed in Kenya among the Mau-Mau, who required that each member of the group should strike a blow at the victim. Each one was thus personally responsible for the death of the settler. This assumed responsibility for violence allows both strayed and outlawed members of the group to come back again and to find their place once more, to become integrated. Violence is thus seen as comparable to a royal pardon.

The colonized man finds his freedom in and through violence. This rule of conduct enlightens the agent because it indicates to him the means and the end. The poetry of Césaire takes on in this precise aspect of violence a prophetic significance. We may recall one of the most decisive pages of his tragedy where the Rebel (indeed!) explains his conduct:

THE REBEL (harshly)

My name—an offense; my Christian name—humiliation; my status—a rebel; my age—that of the stones.

THE MOTHER

My race—the human race. My religion—brotherhood.

THE REBEL

My race: that of the fallen. My religion . . . but it's not you that will show it to me with your disarmament. . . . 'tis I myself, with my rebellion and my poor fists clenched and my woolly head. . . .

(Very calm): I remember one November day; it was hardly six months ago. . . . The master came into the cabin in a cloud of smoke like an April moon. He was flexing his short muscular arms—he was a very good master—and he was rubbing his little dimpled face with his fat fingers. His blue eyes were smiling and he couldn't get the honeyed words out of his mouth quick enough. "The kid will be a decent fellow," he said looking at me, and he said other pleasant things too, the master—that you had to start very early, that twenty years was not too much to make a good Christian and a good slave, a steady, devoted boy, a good commander's chain-gang captain, sharp-eyed and strong-armed. And all that man saw of my son's cradle was that it was the cradle of a chain-gang captain.

We crept in knife in hand. . . .

THE MOTHER

Alas, you'll die for it.

THE REBEL

Killed . . . I killed him with my own hands. . . .
Yes, 'twas a fruitful death, a copious death. . . .
It was night. We crept among the sugar canes.
The knives sang to the stars, but we did not heed the stars.
The sugar canes scarred our faces with streams of green blades.

THE MOTHER
And I had dreamed of a son to close his mother's eyes.

THE REBEL
But I chose to open my son's eyes upon another sun.

THE MOTHER
O my son, son of evil and unlucky death—

THE REBEL
Mother of living and splendid death,

THE MOTHER
Because he has hated too much.

THE REBEL
Because he has too much loved.

THE MOTHER
Spare me, I am choking in your bonds. I bleed from your wounds.

THE REBEL
And the world does not spare me. . . . There is not anywhere in the world a poor creature who's been lynched or tortured in whom I am not murdered and humiliated. . . .

THE MOTHER
God of Heaven, deliver him!

THE REBEL
My heart, thou wilt not deliver me from all that I remember. . . .
It was an evening in November. . . .
And suddenly shouts lit up the silence;
We had attacked, we the slaves; we, the dung underfoot, we the animals with patient hooves,
We were running like madmen; shots rang out. . . . We were striking. Blood and sweat cooled and refreshed us. We were striking where the shouts came from, and the shouts became more strident and a great clamor rose from the east: it was the outhouses burning and the flames flickered sweetly on our cheeks.

Then was the assault made on the master's house.
They were firing from the windows.
We broke in the doors.
The master's room was wide open. The master's room was brilliantly
lighted, and the master was there, very calm ... and our people stopped
dead ... it was the master ... I went in. "It's you," he said, very calm.
It was I, even I, and I told him so, the good slave, the faithful slave,
the slave of slaves, and suddenly his eyes were like two cockroaches,
frightened in the rainy season. . . . I struck, and the blood spurted; that
is the only baptism that I remember today.[8]

It is understandable that in this atmosphere, daily life becomes
quite simply impossible. You can no longer be a *fellah*, a pimp
or an alcoholic as before. The violence of the colonial regime
and the counterviolence of the native balance each other and
respond to each other in an extraordinary reciprocal
homogeneity. This reign of violence will be the more terrible in
proportion to the size of the implantation from the mother country. The development of violence among the colonized people
will be proportionate to the violence exercised by the threatened
colonial régime. In the first phase of this insurrectional period,
the home governments are the slaves of the settlers, and these
settlers seek to intimidate the natives and their home governments at one and the same time. They use the same methods
against both of them. The assassination of the Mayor of Evian,
in its method and motivation, is identifiable with the assassination of Ali Boumendjel. For the settlers, the alternative is not
between *Algérie algérienne* and *Algérie française* but between an
independent Algeria and a colonial Algeria, and anything else
is mere talk or attempts at treason. The settler's logic is implacable and one is only staggered by the counterlogic visible in the
behavior of the native insofar as one has not clearly understood
beforehand the mechanisms of the settler's ideas. From the moment that the native has chosen the methods of counterviolence,
police reprisals automatically call forth reprisals on the side of
the nationalists. However, the results are not equivalent, for
machine-gunning from aeroplanes and bombardments from the
fleet go far beyond in horror and magnitude any answer the

natives can make. This recurring terror demystifies once and for all the most estranged member of the colonized race. They find out on the spot that all the piles of speeches on the equality of human beings do not hide the commonplace fact that the seven Frenchmen killed or wounded at the Col de Sakamody kindles the indignation of all civilized consciences, whereas the sack of the douars* of Guergour and of the dechras of Djerah and the massacre of whole populations—which had merely called forth the Sakamody ambush as a reprisal—all this is of not the slightest importance. Terror, counterterror, violence, counterviolence: that is what observers bitterly record when they describe the circle of hate, which is so tenacious and so evident in Algeria.

In all armed struggles, there exists what we might call the point of final departure. Almost always it is marked off by a huge and all-inclusive repression which engulfs all sectors of the colonized people. This point was reached in Algeria in 1955 with the 12,000 victims of Phillippeville, and in 1956 with Lacoste's instituting of urban and rural militias.[9]

Then it became clear to everybody, including even the settlers, that "things couldn't go on as before." Yet the colonized people do not chalk up the reckoning. They record the huge gaps made in their ranks as a sort of necessary evil. Since they have decided to reply by violence, they therefore are ready to take all its consequences. They only insist in return that no reckoning should be kept, either, for the others. To the saying "All natives are the same" the colonized person replies, "All settlers are the same."[10]

When the native is tortured, when his wife is killed or raped, he complains to no one. The oppressor's government can set up commissions of inquiry and of information daily if it wants to; in the eyes of the native, these commissions do not exist. The fact is that soon we shall have had seven years of crimes in Algeria and there has not yet been a single Frenchman indicted before a French court of justice for the murder of an Algerian. In Indochina, in Madagascar or in the colonies the native has always known that he need expect nothing from the other side.

* Temporary village for the use of shepherds. (Trans.)

The settler's work is to make even dreams of liberty impossible for the native. The native's work is to imagine all possible methods for destroying the settler. On the logical plane, the Manichaeism of the settler produces a Manichaeism of the native. To the theory of the "absolute evil of the native" the theory of the "absolute evil of the settler" replies.

The appearance of the settler has meant in the terms of syncretism the death of the aboriginal society, cultural lethargy, and the petrification of individuals. For the native, life can only spring up again out of the rotting corpse of the settler. This, then is the correspondence, term by term, between the two trains of reasoning.

But it so happens that for the colonized people this violence, because it constitutes their only work, invests their characters with positive and creative qualities. The practice of violence binds them together as a whole, since each individual forms a violent link in the great chain, a part of the great organism of violence which has surged upwards in reaction to the settler's violence in the beginning. The groups recognize each other and the future nation is already indivisible. The armed struggle mobilizes the people; that is to say, it throws them in one way and in one direction.

The mobilization of the masses, when it arises out of the war of liberation, introduces into each man's consciousness the ideas of a common cause, of a national destiny and of a collective history. In the same way the second phase, that of the building-up of the nation, is helped on by the existence of this cement which has been mixed with blood and anger. Thus we come to a fuller appreciation of the originality of the words used in these underdeveloped countries. During the colonial period the people are called upon to fight against oppression; after national liberation, they are called upon to fight against poverty, illiteracy and underdevelopment. The struggle, they say, goes on. The people realize that life is an unending contest.

We have said that the native's violence unifies the people. By its very structure, colonialism is separatist and regionalist. Colonialism does not simply state the existence of tribes; it also reinforces it and separates them. The colonial system encourages chieftaincies and keeps alive the old Marabout confraternities. Violence is in action all-inclusive and national. It follows that it is closely involved in the liquidation of regionalism and of tribalism. Thus the national parties show no pity at all toward the caids and the customary chiefs. Their destruction is the preliminary to the unification of the people.

At the level of individuals, violence is a cleansing force. It frees the native from his inferiority complex and from his despair and inaction; it makes him fearless and restores his self-respect. Even if the armed struggle has been symbolic and the nation is demolished through a rapid movement of decolonization, the people have the time to see that the liberation has been the business of each and all and that the leader has no special merit. From thence comes that type of aggressive reticence with regard to the machinery of protocol which young governments quickly show. When the people have taken violent part in the national liberation they will allow no one to set themselves up as "liberators." They show themselves to be jealous of the results of their action and take good care not to place their future, their destiny or the fate of their country in the hands of a living god. Yesterday they were completely irresponsible; today they mean to understand everything and make all decisions. Illuminated by violence, the consciousness of the people rebels against any pacification. From now on the demagogues, the opportunists and the magicians have a difficult task. The action which has thrown them into a hand-to-hand struggle confers upon the masses a voracious taste for the concrete. The attempt at mystification becomes, in the long run, practically impossible.

NOTES

1. We have demonstrated the mechanism of this Manichaean world in *Peau Noire, Masques Blancs* (Editions du Seuil).
2. Fanon is writing in 1961. (Transl.)

3. See chap. V [of *The Damned*]. *Colonial war and mental disorders.*

4. Engels: "Anti-Duhring," Part II, Chapter III, Theory of Violence. Editions Sociales, p. 199.

5. It may happen that the arrested leader is in fact the authentic mouthpiece of the colonized masses. In this case colonialism will make use of his period of detention to try to launch new leaders.

6. Refers to Mirabeau's famous saying: "I am here by the will of the People; I shall leave only by the force of bayonets." (Transl.)

7. It is evident that this vacuum cleaning destroys the very thing that they want to preserve. Sartre points this out when he says:

In short by the very fact of repeating them (concerning racist ideas) it is revealed that the simultaneous union of all against the natives is unrealisable. Such union only recurs from time to time and moreover it can only come into being as an active grouping in order to massacre the natives— an absurd though perpetual temptation to the settlers, which even if it was feasible would only succeed in abolishing colonization at one blow." ("Critique de la Raison Dialectique", p. 346.)

8. Aimé Césaire: *Les Armes Miraculeuses.* (*Et les chiens se taisaient*), pp. 133 to 137. Publ. Gallimard.

9. We must go back to this period in order to judge the importance of this decision on the part of the French government in Algeria. Thus we may read in "Résistance Algérienne," no. 4, dated 28th March 1957, the following:

In reply to the wish expressed by the General Assembly of the United Nations, the French Government has now decided to create urban militias in Algeria. "Enough blood has been spilled" was what the United Nations said: Lacoste replies "Let us form militias." "Cease fire," advised U.N.O.; Lacoste vociferates, "We must arm the civilians." Whereas the two parties face-to-face with each other were on the recommendation of the United Nations invited to contact each other with a view to coming to an agreement and finding a peaceful and democratic solution, Lacoste decrees that henceforward every European will be armed and should open fire on any person who seems to him suspect. It was then agreed (in the Assembly) that savage and iniquitous repression verging on genocide ought at all costs to be opposed by the authorities: but Lacoste replies, "Let us systematise the repression and organize the Algerian manhunt!" And, symbolically, he entrusts the military with civil powers, and gives military powers to civilians. The ring is closed. In the middle, the Algerian, disarmed, famished, tracked down, jostled, struck, lynched, will soon be slaughtered as a suspect. Today, in Algeria, there is not a single Frenchman who is not authorized and even invited to use his weapons. There is not a single Frenchman, in Algeria, one month after the appeal for calm made by U.N.O. who is not permitted, and obliged to search out, investigate and pursue suspects.

One month after the vote on the final motion of the General Assembly of the United Nations, there is not one European in Algeria who is not party to the most frightful work of extermination of modern times. A democratic solution? Right, Lacoste concedes; let's begin by exterminating the Algerians, and to do that, let's arm the civilians and give them *carte blanche*. The Paris press, on the whole, has welcomed the creation of these armed groups with reserve. Fascist militias, they've been called. Yes; but on the individual level, on the plane of human rights, what is fascism if not colonialism when rooted in a traditionally colonialist country? The opinion has been advanced that they are systematically legalized and commended; but does not the body of Algeria bear for the last one hundred and thirty years wounds which gape still wider, more numerous and more deep-seated than ever? "Take care," advises Monsieur Kenne-Vignes, member of parliament for the M.R.P., "do we not by the creation of these militias risk seeing the gap widen between the two communities in Algeria?" Yes; but is not colonial status simply the organized reduction to slavery of a whole people? The Algerian revolution is precisely the affirmed contestation of that slavery and that abyss. The Algerian revolution speaks to the occupying nation and says: "Take your fangs out of the bleeding flesh of Algeria! Let the people of Algeria speak!"

The creation of militias, they say, will lighten the tasks of the Army. It will free certain units whose mission will be to protect the Moroccan and Tunisian borders. In Algeria, the Army is six hundred thousand strong. Almost all the Navy and the Air Force are based there. There is an enormous, speedy police force with a horribly good record since it has absorbed the ex-torturers from Morocco and Tunisia. The territorial units are one hundred thousand strong. The task of the Army, all the same, must be lightened. So let us create urban militias. The fact remains that the hysterical and criminal frenzy of Lacoste imposes them even on clear-sighted French people. The truth is that the creation of militias carries its contradiction even in its justification. The task of the French Army is never-ending. Consequently, when it is given as an objective the gagging of the Algerian people, the door is closed on the future forever. Above all, it is forbidden to analyze, to understand or to measure the depth and the density of the Algerian Revolution: departmental leaders, housing-estate leaders, street leaders, house leaders, leaders who control each landing. . . . Today, to the surface checkerboard is added an underground network.

In 48 hours two thousand volunteers were enrolled. The Europeans of Algeria responded immediately to Lacoste's call to kill. From now on, each European must check up on all surviving Algerians in his sector; and in addition he will be responsible for information, for a "quick response" to acts of terrorism, for the detection of suspects, for the liquidation of runaways and for the reinforcement of police services. Certainly, the tasks of the Army must be lightened. Today, to the surface mopping-up is added a deeper harrowing. Today, to the killing which is all in the day's work is added planified murder. "Stop the bloodshed," was the advice given by

U.N.O." "The best way of doing this," replied Lacoste, "is to make sure there remains no blood to shed." The Algerian people, after having been delivered up to Massu's hordes, is put under the protection of the urban militias. By his decision to create these militias, Lacoste shows quite plainly that he will brook no interference with HIS war. It is a proof that there are no limits once the rot has set in. True, he is at the moment a prisoner of the situation; but what a consolation to drag everyone down in one's fall!

After each of these decisions, the Algerian people tense their muscles still more and fight still harder. After each of these organized, deliberately sought-after assassinations, the Algerian people builds up its awareness of self, and consolidates its resistance. Yes; the tasks of the French Army are infinite: for oh, how infinite is the unity of the people of Algeria!

10. This is why there are no prisoners when the fighting first starts. It is only through educating the local leaders politically that those at the head of the movement can make the masses accept 1) that people coming from the mother-country do not always act of their own free will and are sometimes even disgusted by the war; 2) that it is of immediate advantage to the movement that its supporters should show by their actions that they respect certain international conventions; 3) that an army which takes prisoners is an army, and ceases to be considered as a group of wayside bandits; 4) that whatever the circumstances, the possession of prisoners constitutes a means of exerting pressure which must not be overlooked in order to protect our men who are in enemy hands.

23. THESES OF THE SECOND CONGRESS OF THE COMMUNIST INTERNATIONAL ON THE NATIONAL AND COLONIAL QUESTIONS *

ⅬⅬⅬⅬⅬⅬⅬⅬⅬⅬⅬⅬⅬⅬⅬ

(A.) THESES

1. It is typical of the very nature of bourgeois democracy to take an abstract or formal attitude toward the question of the colonies in general, and to that of national equality in particular. With the formula of the equality of human beings in general, bourgeois democracy proclaims the formal or juridical equality of the proprietor and the proletarian, of the exploiter and the exploited, thereby greatly deceiving the oppressed classes. On the pretext of absolute equality of human beings, the bourgeoisie converts the idea of equality, which is in itself but a reflection of the relations caused by commodity production, into an instrument in the struggle against the abolition of classes. But the real essence of the demand for equality is based on the demand for the abolition of classes.

2. In conformity with its chief task—the struggle against bourgeois democracy and the denunciation of its lies and deceptions,

* From *Report of the Proceedings*, Communist International, 2nd Congress, Moscow, 1920, pp. 571–9.

the Communist Party, as the class-conscious expression of the struggle of the proletariat to cast off the yoke of the bourgeoisie, must not advance any abstract and formal principles on the national question, but must first analyze the historical, and especially the economic conditions; second, it must clearly distinguish the interest of the oppressed classes, of the toilers, of the exploited from the general conception of national interests which in reality means the interests of the ruling class; third, it must equally separate the oppressed and subject nations from the dominating nations, in contradistinction to the bourgeois democratic lies concealing the enslavement of a vast majority of the population of the earth by an insignificant minority of the advanced capitalist nations, which is peculiar to the epoch of financial capital and imperialism.

3. The imperialist war of 1914 has demonstrated very clearly to all nations and to all oppressed classes of the world the deceitfulness of bourgeois democratic phraseology. That war was waged on both sides under the false pretense of the freedom of nations and national self-determination. But the Brest-Litovsk and Bucharest peaces on the one hand, and the Versailles and Saint-Germain peaces on the other, have shown how the bourgeoisie establishes even "national" boundaries in conformity with its own economic interests. "National" boundaries are for the bourgeoisie nothing but market commodities. The so-called "League of Nations" is nothing but an insurance policy in which the victors mutually guarantee each other their prey. The striving for the reconstruction of national unity and of the "reunion of separated territories" on the part of the bourgeoisie, is nothing but an attempt of the vanquished to gather forces for new wars. The reuniting of the nationalities artificially torn asunder corresponds also to the interests of the proletariat, but real national freedom and unity can be achieved by the proletariat only through revolutionary struggle and by the overthrow of the bourgeoisie. The League of Nations and the policy of the imperialist powers after the war demonstrates this even more clearly and definitely, making the revolutionary struggle in the advanced

countries more acute, increasing the ferment of the working masses of the colonies and the subject countries, and dispelling the middle-class nationalist illusion of the possibility of peaceful collaboration and equality of nations under capitalism.

4. It follows from the fundamental principles laid down above that the policy of the Communist International on national and colonial questions must be chiefly to bring about a union of the proletarian and working masses of all nations and countries for a joint revolutionary struggle leading to the overthrow of capitalism, without which national equality and oppression cannot be abolished.

5. The political situation of the world at the present time has placed the question of the dictatorship of the proletariat in the foreground, and all the events of world politics are inevitably concentrating around one point, namely, the struggle of the bourgeois world against the Russian Soviet Republic, which is grouping around itself the Soviet movements of the vanguard of the workers of all countries, and all national liberation movements of the colonial and subject countries, which have been taught by bitter experience that there can be no salvation for them outside of a union with the revolutionary proletariat, and the triumph of the Soviet power over imperialism.

6. Consequently, we must not content ourselves with a mere recognition or declaration concerning the unity of the workers of different nations, but we must carry out a policy of realizing the closest union between all national and colonial liberation movements and Soviet Russia, determining the forms of this union in accordance with the stage of development of the Communist movement among the proletariat of each country, or the revolutionary liberation movement in the subject nations and backward countries.

7. Federation is a transitional form toward the complete union of the workers of all countries. It has already proved its efficiency in practice in the relations of the Socialist Federated Soviet Republic of Russia to the other Soviet Republics (Hungary, Fin-

land, and Latvia, in the past, and Azerbeidjan and the Ukraine in the present), as also within the borders of the Socialist Federal Republic of Russia with regard to the nationalities which had neither their own government nor any self-governing institutions (for example, the autonomous Bashkir Republic and the Tartar Republic, which were formed in 1919–1920 by the R.S.F.S.R.).

8. It is the task of the Communist International in this matter not only to develop further, but also to study and test by experience these federations which have arisen out of the Soviet order and the Soviet movement. Recognizing federation as a transition form toward complete union, we must strive for ever closer federal connections, bearing in mind (1) the impossibility of maintaining the Soviet Republic surrounded by powerful imperialist nations, without a close union with other Soviet Republics, (2) the necessity of a close economic union of the Soviet Republics, without which the restoration of the forces of production destroyed by imperialism and the assuring of the welfare of the workers is impossible, (3) the striving toward the creation of a unified world economy based on one general plan and regulated by the proletariat of all the nations of the world. This tendency has already manifested itself under capitalism, and is undoubtedly going to be further developed and perfected by Socialism.

9. With regard to interstate relations, the international policy of the Communist International cannot limit itself to a mere formal verbal declaration of the recognition of the equality of nations, which does not involve any practical obligations, such as has been made by the bourgeois democrats who styled themselves Socialists. The constant violations of the equality of nations and the infringement of the rights of national minorities practiced in all the capitalist States, in spite of democratic constitutions, must be denounced in all the propaganda and agitational activity of the Communist International, within, as well as outside of Parliament. It is likewise necessary, first, to explain constantly that only the Soviet regime is able to give the nations real equality, by uniting the proletariat and all the masses of the

workers in the struggle against the bourgeoisie; second, to support the revolutionary movement among the subject nations (for example, Ireland, American Negroes, etc.) and in the colonies.

Without this last especially important condition, the struggle against the oppression of dependent nations and colonies, as well as the recognition of their right to an independent existence, is only a misleading signpost, such as has been exhibited by the parties of the Second International.

10. It is the habitual practice not only of the Center Parties of the Second International, but also of those which have left it, to recognize internationalism in words and then to adulterate it in their propaganda, agitation, and practical activities by mixing it up with petty bourgeois nationalism and pacifism. This is to be found even among those parties that at present call themselves Communist. The struggle against this evil, and against the deep-rooted petty bourgeois national prejudices (manifesting themselves in various forms, such as race hatred, national antagonism and anti-Semitism), must be brought to the foreground the more vigorously because of the urgent necessity of transforming the dictatorship of the proletariat and changing it from a national basis (i.e., existing in one country and incapable of exercising an influence over world politics), into an international dictatorship (i.e., a dictatorship of the proletariat of at least several advanced countries capable of exercising a determined influence upon world politics). Petty bourgeois internationalism means the mere recognition of the rights of national equality, and preserves intact national egotism. Proletarian internationalism, on the other hand, demands: (1) the subordination of the interests of the proletarian struggle in one country to the interests of that struggle on an international scale; (2) the capability and the readiness on the part of any one nation which has gained a victory over the bourgeoisie, of making the greatest national sacrifices for the overthrow of international capitalism.

In the countries in which fully developed capitalist states exist, the workers' parties comprising the vanguard of the proletariat must consider it as their primary and most important task to combat the opportunist and petty bourgeois pacifist confusion of the ideas and the policy of internationalism.

11. With regard to those states and nationalities where a backward, mainly feudal, patriarchal, or patriarchal-agrarian regime prevails, the following must be borne in mind: (1) All Communist parties must give active support to the revolutionary movements of liberation, the form of support to be determined by a study of existing conditions. This duty of rendering active support is to be imposed in the first place on the workers of those countries on whom the subject nation is dependent in a colonial or financial way; (2) Naturally a struggle must be carried on against the reactionary medieval influences of the clergy, the Christian missions and similar elements; (3) It is also necessary to combat the pan-Islam and pan-Asiatic and similar movements, which are endeavoring to utilize the liberation struggle against European and American imperialism for the purpose of strengthening the power of Turkish and Japanese imperialists, of the nobility, of the large landowners, of the clergy, etc.; (4) It is of special importance to support the peasant movements in backward countries against the landowners and all feudal survivals; above all, we must strive as far as possible to give the peasant movement a revolutionary character, to organize the peasants and all the exploited classes into the Soviets, and thus bring about the closest possible union between the Communist proletariat of western Europe and the revolutionary peasant movement of the East and of the colonial and subject countries; (5) It is likewise necessary to wage determined war against the attempt of quasi-Communist revolutionists to cloak the liberation movement in the backward countries with a Communist garb. It is the duty of the Communist International to support the revolutionary movement in the colonies and in the backward countries, for the exclusive purpose of uniting the various units of the future proletarian parties—such as are Communist not only in name—in all backward countries and educate them to the consciousness of their specific tasks, i.e., to the tasks of the struggle against the bourgeois democratic tendencies within

their respective nationalities. The Communist International must establish temporary relations and even unions with the revolutionary movements in the colonies and backward countries, without, however, amalgamating with them, but preserving the independent character of the proletarian movement even though it be still in its embryonic state; (6) It is essential to expose continually the deception fostered among the masses of the toilers in all, and especially in the backward countries, by the imperialist powers aided by the privileged classes of the subject countries, in creating under the mask of political independence various government and state institutions which are in reality completely dependent upon them economically, financially and in a military sense. As a striking example of the deception practiced upon the working class of a subject country through the combined efforts of Allied imperialism and the bourgeoisie of the given nation, we may cite the Palestine affair of the Zionists, where under the pretext of creating a Jewish state in Palestine, in which the Jews form only an insignificant part of the population, Zionism has delivered the native Arab working population to the exploitation of England. Only a union of Soviet Republics can bring salvation to the dependent and weak nationalities under present international conditions.

12. The age-long enslavement of the colonial and weak nationalities by the imperialist powers, has given rise to a feeling of rancor among the masses of the enslaved countries, as well as to a feeling of distrust toward the oppressing nations in general and toward the proletariat of those nations. These sentiments have become strengthened by the base treachery of the majority of the official leaders of the proletariat in the years of 1914–1919, when the social patriots came out in defense of their fatherlands and of the "rights" of their bourgeoisie to enslave the colonies and to plunder the financially dependent countries. These sentiments can be completely rooted out only by the abolition of imperialism in the advanced countries and the radical transformation of all the foundations of economic life in the backward countries. Thus, it will take a long time for these

national prejudices to disappear. This imposes upon the class-conscious proletariat of all countries the duty of exercising special caution and care with regard to these national sentiments still surviving in the countries and nationalities which have been subjected to lasting enslavement, and also of making necessary concessions in order more speedily to remove this distrust and prejudice. The victory over capitalism cannot be fully achieved and carried to its ultimate goal unless the proletariat and the toiling masses of all nations of the world rally of their own accord in a heartfelt and close union.

(B.) ADDITIONAL THESES

(1.) To determine more especially the relation of the Communist International to the revolutionary movements in the countries dominated by capitalist imperialism, for instance, in China and India, is one of the most important questions before the Second Congress of the Third International. The history of the world revolution has come to a period when a proper understanding of this relation is indispensable. The great European War and its result has shown clearly that the masses of non-European subjected countries are inseparably connected with the proletarian movement in Europe, as a consequence of the centralization of world capitalism; for instance, the sending of colonial troops and huge armies of workers to the battle front during the war, etc.

(2.) One of the main sources from which European capitalism draws its chief strength is to be found in the colonial possessions and dependencies. Without the control of the extensive markets and vast fields of exploitation in the colonies, the capitalist powers of Europe cannot maintain their existence even for a short time. England, the stronghold of imperialism, has been suffering from overproduction since more than a century ago. But for the extensive colonial possessions acquired for the sale of her surplus products and as a source of raw materials for her ever-growing industries, the capitalist structure of England would have been crushed under its own weight long ago. By enslaving the hundreds of millions of inhabitants of Asia and Africa, English imperialism succeeds so far in keeping the British proletariat under the domination of the bourgeoisie.

(3.) Extra profit gained in the colonies is the mainstay of modern capitalism, and so long as the latter is not deprived of this source of extra profit it will not be easy for the European working class to overthrow the capitalist order. Thanks to the possibility of the extensive and intensive exploitation of human labor and natural resources in the colonies, the capitalist nations of Europe are trying, not without success, to recover from their present bankruptcy. By exploiting the masses in the colonies, European imperialism will be in a position to give concession after concession to the labor aristocracy at home. Whilst on the one hand, European imperialism seeks to lower the standard of living of the home proletariat by bringing into competition the productions of the lower-paid workers in subject countries; on the other hand, it will not hesitate to go to the extent of sacrificing the entire surplus value in the home country so long as it continues to gain huge superprofits in the colonies.

(4.) The breaking up of the colonial empire, together with a proletarian revolution in the home country, will overthrow the capitalist system in Europe. Consequently, the Communist International must widen the sphere of its activities. It must establish relations with those revolutionary forces that are working for the overthrow of imperialism in the countries subjected politically and economically. These two forces must be coordinated if the final success of the world revolution is to be guaranteed.

(5.) The Communist International is the concentrated will of the world revolutionary proletariat. Its mission is to organize the working class of the whole world for the overthrow of the capitalist order and the establishment of Communism. The Third International is a fighting body which must assume the task of combining the revolutionary forces of all the countries of the world. Dominated as it was by a group of politicians, permeated with bourgeois ideas, the Second International failed to appreciate the importance of the colonial question. For them the world did not exist outside of Europe. They could not see the necessity of coordinating the revolutionary movement of Europe with those in the non-European countries. Instead of giving moral and material help to the revolutionary movement in the colonies, the members of the Second International themselves became imperialists.

(6.) Foreign imperialism, imposed on the Eastern peoples, prevented them from developing, socially and economically, side by side with their fellows in Europe and America. Owing to the imperialist policy of preventing industrial development in the colonies, a proletarian class, in the strict sense of the word, could not come into existence there until recently. Skilled craft industries were destroyed to make room for the products of the centralized industries in the imperialist countries; consequently a majority of the population was driven to the land to produce food grains and raw materials for export to foreign lands. On the other hand, there followed a rapid concentration of land in the hands of the big landowners, of financial capitalists and the state, thus creating a huge landless peasantry. The great bulk of the population was kept in a state of illiteracy. As a result of this policy, the spirit of revolt latent in every subject people, found its expression only through the small, educated middle class.

Foreign domination has obstructed the free development of the social forces, therefore its overthrow is the first step toward a revolution in the colonies. So to help overthrow the foreign rule in the colonies is not to endorse the nationalist aspirations of the native bourgeoisie, but to open the way to the smothered proletariat there.

(7.) There are to be found in the dependent countries two distinct movements which every day grow farther apart from each other. One is the bourgeois democratic nationalist movement, with a program of political independence under the bourgeois order, and the other is the mass action of the poor and ignorant peasants and workers for their liberation from all forms of exploitation. The former endeavors to control the latter, and often succeeds to a certain extent, but the Communist International and the parties affected must struggle against such control and help to develop class-consciousness in the working masses of the colonies. For the overthrow of foreign capitalism, which is the first step toward revolution in the colonies, the cooperation of the bourgeois nationalist revolutionary elements is useful.

But the first and most necessary task is the formation of Communist Parties which will organize the peasants and workers and lead them to the revolution and to the establishment of Soviet Republics. Thus the masses in the backward countries may reach Communism, not through capitalist development, but led by the class-conscious proletariat of the advanced capitalist countries.

(8.) The real strength of the liberation movements in the colonies is no longer confined to the narrow circle of bourgeois democratic nationalists. In most of the colonies there already exist organized revolutionary parties which strive to be in close connection with the working masses. (The relation of the Communist International with the revolutionary movement in the colonies should be realized through the mediums of these parties or groups, because they were the vanguard of the working class in their respective countries.) They are not very large today, but they reflect the aspirations of the masses, and the latter will follow them to the revolution. The Communist Parties of the different imperialist countries must work in conjunction with these proletarian parties of the colonies, and through them give all moral and material support to the revolutionary movement in general.

(9.) The revolution in the colonies is not going to be a Communist revolution in its first stages. But if from the outset the leadership is in the hands of a Communist vanguard, the revolutionary masses will not be led astray, but may go ahead through the successive periods of development of revolutionary experience. Indeed, it would be extremely erroneous in many of the

Oriental countries to try to solve the agrarian problem according to pure Communist principles. In its first stages, the revolution in the colonies must be carried on with a program which will include many petty bourgeois reforms, such as division of land, etc. But from this it does not follow at all that the leadership of the revolution will have to be surrendered to the bourgeois democrats. On the contrary, the proletarian parties must carry on vigorous and systematic propaganda of the Soviet idea and organize the peasants and workers Soviets as soon as possible. These Soviets will work in cooperation with the Soviet Republics in the advanced capitalist countries for the ultimate overthrow of the capitalist order throughout the world.

24. NATIONALISM OUTSIDE EUROPE*

⊓⊔⊓⊔⊓⊔⊓⊔⊓⊔⊓⊔⊓⊔⊓⊔⊓⊔⊓⊔⊓⊔⊓⊔

Joseph Stalin

From this theme I take the two main questions: a) the presentation of the problem; b) the liberation movement of the oppressed peoples and the proletarian revolution.

1. *The presentation of the problem.* During the last twenty years the national problem has undergone a number of very important changes. The national problem in the period of the Second International and the national problem in the period of Leninism are far from being the same thing. They differ profoundly from each other, not only in their scope, but also in their intrinsic character.

Formerly, the national problem was usually confined to a narrow circle of questions, concerning, primarily, "cultured" nationalities. The Irish, the Hungarians, the Poles, the Finns, the Serbs, and several other European nationalities—that was the circle of disfranchised peoples in whose destinies the heroes of the Second International were interested. The scores and hundreds of millions of Asiatic and African peoples who are suffering national oppression in its most savage and cruel form usually

*From *Foundations of Leninism*, by Joseph Stalin, 1924, reprinted in *Problems of Leninism*, Moscow, 1945, pp. 59–67.

remained outside of their field of vision. They hesitated to put white and black, "civilized" and "uncivilized" on the same plane. Two or three meaningless, lukewarm resolutions, which carefully evaded the question of liberating the colonies—that was all the leaders of the Second International could boast of. Now we can say that this duplicity and half-heartedness in dealing with the national problem has been brought to an end. Leninism laid bare this crying incongruity, broke down the wall between whites and blacks, between Europeans and Asiatics, between the "civilized" and "uncivilized" slaves of imperialism, and thus linked the national problem with the problem of the colonies. The national problem was thereby transformed from a particular and internal state problem into a general and international problem, into a world problem of emancipating the oppressed peoples in the dependent countries and colonies from the yoke of imperialism.

Formerly, the principle of self-determination of nations was usually misinterpreted, and not infrequently it was narrowed down to the idea of the right of nations to autonomy. Certain leaders of the Second International even went so far as to represent the right to self-determination as meaning the right to cultivate autonomy, *i.e.*, the right of oppressed nations to have their own cultural institutions, leaving all political power in the hands of the ruling nation. As a consequence the idea of self-determination stood in danger of becoming transformed from an instrument for combating annexations into an instrument for justifying them. Now we can say that this confusion has been cleared up. Leninism broadened the conception of self-determination and interpreted it as the right of the oppressed peoples of the dependent countries and colonies to complete secession, as the right of nations to independent existence as states. This precluded the possibility of justifying annexations by interpreting the right to self-determination to mean the right to autonomy. Thus the principle of self-determination itself was transformed from an instrument for deceiving the masses, which it was, into an instrument for exposing all and sundry imperialist aspirations and chauvinist machinations, into an instrument for the political education of the masses in the spirit of internationalism.

Formerly, the question of the oppressed nations was usually regarded as purely a juridical question. Solemn proclamations regarding "national equality," innumerable declarations about the "equality of nations"—that was the fare of the parties of the Second International which glossed over the fact that "equality of nations" under imperialism, where one group of nations (a minority) lives by exploiting another group of nations, is sheer mockery of the oppressed nations. Now we can say that this bourgeois-juridical point of view on the national question has been exposed. Leninism brought the national problem down from the lofty heights of high-sounding declarations to solid ground, and declared that pronouncements about the "equality of nations" which are not backed by the direct support of the proletarian parties for the liberation struggle of the oppressed nations, are meaningless and false. In this way the question of the oppressed nations became a question of supporting, of rendering real and continuous assistance to the oppressed nations in their struggle against imperialism for real equality of nations, for their independent existence as states.

Formerly, the national problem was regarded from a reformist point of view, as an independent problem having no connection with the general problems of the rule of capital, of the overthrow of imperialism, of the proletarian revolution. It was tacitly assumed that the victory of the proletariat in Europe was possible without a direct alliance with the liberation movement in the colonies, that the national-colonial problem could be solved on the quiet, "of its own accord," off the high road of the proletarian revolution, without a revolutionary struggle against imperialism. Now we can say that this antirevolutionary point of view has been exposed. Leninism has proved, and the imperialist war and the revolution in Russia have confirmed, that the national problem can be solved only in connection with and on the basis of the proletarian revolution, and that the road to victory of the revolution in the West lies through the revolutionary alliance with the liberation movement of the colonies and dependent countries against imperialism. The national problem is a part of the general problem of the proletarian revolution, a part of the problem of the dictatorship of the proletariat.

The question presents itself as follows: Are the revolutionary possibilities latent in the revolutionary liberation movement of the oppressed countries *already exhausted* or not; and if not, is there any hope, any ground to expect that these possibilities can be utilized for the proletarian revolution, that the dependent and colonial countries can be transformed from a reserve of the imperialist bourgeoisie into a reserve of the revolutionary proletariat, into an ally of the latter?

Leninism replies to this question in the affirmative, *i.e.*, to the effect that it recognizes the latent revolutionary capabilities of the national liberation movement of the oppressed countries, and to the effect that it is possible to use these for the purpose of overthrowing the common enemy, for the purpose of overthrowing imperialism. The mechanics of the development of imperialism, the imperialist war and the revolution in Russia, wholly confirm the conclusions of Leninism on this score.

Hence the necessity for the proletariat to support—resolutely and actively to support—the national liberation movement of the oppressed and dependent peoples.

This does not mean, of course, that the proletariat must support *every* national movement, everywhere and always, in every single concrete case. It means that support must be given to such national movements as tend to weaken, to overthrow imperialism, and not to strengthen and preserve it. Cases occur when the national movements in certain oppressed countries come into conflict with the interests of the development of the proletarian movement. In such cases support is, of course, entirely out of the question. The question of the rights of nations is not an isolated self-sufficient question; it is a part of the general problem of the proletarian revolution, subordinate to the whole, and must be considered from the point of view of the whole. In the forties of the last century Marx supported the national movement of the Poles and Hungarians and was opposed to the national movement of the Czechs and the South Slavs. Why? Because the Czechs and the South Slavs were then "reactionary nations," "Russian outposts" in Europe, outposts of absolutism; whereas the Poles and the Hungarians were "revolutionary nations," fighting against absolutism. Because support of the national movement of the Czechs and the South Slavs was at that time equivalent to indirect support for tsarism, the most dangerous enemy of the revolutionary movement in Europe.

"The various demands of democracy," writes Lenin, "including self-determination, are not an absolute, but a *small part* of the general democratic (now: general Socialist) *world* movement. In individual concrete cases, the part may contradict the whole; if so, it must be rejected." (Lenin, *Collected Works*, Russian edition, Vol. XIX, pp. 257–58.)

This is the position in regard to the question of certain national movements, of the possible reactionary character of these movements—if, of course, they are appraised not from the formal point of view, not from the point of view of abstract rights, but concretely, from the point of view of the interests of the revolutionary movement.

The same must be said of the revolutionary character of national movements in general. The unquestionably revolutionary character of the overwhelming majority of national movements is as relative and peculiar as is the possible reactionary character of certain particular national movements. The revolutionary character of a national movement under the conditions of imperialist oppression does not necessarily presuppose the existence of proletarian elements in the movement, the existence of a revolutionary or a republican program of the movement, the existence of a democratic basis of the movement. The struggle the Emir of Afghanistan is waging for the independence of Afghanistan is objectively a *revolutionary* struggle, despite the monarchist views of the Emir and his associates, for it weakens, disintegrates and undermines imperialism; whereas the struggle "desperate" Democrats and "Socialists," "revolutionaries" and republicans, such as, for example, Kerensky and Tsereteli, Renaudel and Scheidemann, Chernov and Dan, Henderson and Clynes, waged during the imperialist war was a *reactionary* struggle, for its result was the whitewashing, the strengthening, the victory of imperialism. For the same reasons, the struggle the Egyptian merchants and bourgeois intellectuals are waging for the independence of Egypt is objectively a *revolutionary* struggle, despite the bourgeois origin and bourgeois title of the leaders of the Egyptian national movement, despite the fact that they are opposed to Socialism; whereas the fight the British Labour Government is waging to perpetuate Egypt's dependent position is for the same reasons a *reactionary* struggle, despite the proletarian origin and the proletarian title of the members of that government, despite the fact that they are "for" Socialism. I need not speak of the national movement in other, larger, colonial and dependent countries, such as India and China, every step of which along the road to liberation, even if it runs counter to the demands of formal democracy, is a steam-hammer blow at imperialism, *i.e.*, is undoubtedly a *revolutionary* step.

Lenin was right in saying that the national movement of the oppressed countries should be appraised not from the point of view of formal democracy, but from the point of view of the actual results obtained, as shown by the general balance sheet of the struggle against imperialism, that is to say, "not in isolation, but on . . . a world scale." (Lenin, *Collected Works*, Russian edition, Vol. XIX, p. 257.)

2. *The liberation movement of the oppressed peoples and the proletarian revolution.* In solving the national problem Leninism proceeds from the following theses:

a) The world is divided into two camps: the camp of a handful of civilized nations, which possess finance capital and exploit the vast majority of the population of the globe; and the camp of the oppressed and exploited peoples in the colonies and dependent countries, who comprise that majority;

b) The colonies and the dependent countries, oppressed and exploited by finance capital, constitute a very large reserve and a very important source of strength for imperialism;

c) The revolutionary struggle of the oppressed peoples in the dependent and colonial countries against imperialism is the only road that leads to their emancipation from oppression and exploitation;

d) The most important colonial and dependent countries have already taken the path of the national liberation movement, which cannot but lead to the crisis of world capitalism;

e) The interests of the proletarian movement in the developed countries and of the national liberation movement in the colonies call for the amalgamation of these two forms of the revolutionary movement into a common front against the common enemy, against imperialism.

f) The victory of the working class in the developed countries and the liberation of the oppressed peoples from the yoke of imperialism are impossible without the formation and the consolidation of a common revolutionary front;

g) The formation of a common revolutionary front is impossible unless the proletariat of the oppressor nations renders direct and determined support to the liberation movement of the oppressed peoples against the imperialism of its "own country," for "no nation can be free if it oppresses other nations" (*Marx*);

h) This support implies the advocacy, defense and carrying out of the slogan of the right of nations to secession, to independent existence as states;

i) Unless this slogan is carried out, the union and collaboration of nations within a single world economic system, which is the material basis for the victory of Socialism, cannot be brought about;

j) This union can only be voluntary, and can arise only on the basis of mutual confidence and fraternal relations among nations.

Hence the two sides, the two tendencies in the national problem: the tendency toward political emancipation from the shackles of imperialism and toward the formation of an independent national state—a tendency which arose as a consequence of imperialist oppression and colonial exploitation; and the tend-

ency toward an economic rapprochement among nations, which
arose as a result of the formation of a world market and a world
economic system.

"Developing capitalism," says Lenin, "knows of two historical tendencies in the national problem. First: the awakening of national life
and of national movements, the struggle against all national oppressions, the creation of national states. Second: the development and
growing frequency of all sorts of intercourse among nations; the breaking down of national barriers; the creation of the international unity of
capital, of economic life in general, of politics, of science, and so forth.
Both tendencies are the universal law of capitalism. The first predomi-
nates at the beginning of the development of capitalism; the second
characterizes mature capitalism, heading toward its transformation into
Socialist society." (Lenin, *Collected Works*, Russian edition, Vol. XVII,
pp. 139–40.)

For imperialism these two tendencies represent irreconcilable
contradictions; because imperialism cannot exist without exploiting colonies and forcibly retaining them within the framework of the "integral whole"; because imperialism can bring
nations together only by means of annexations and colonial
conquest, without which it is, generally speaking, inconceivable.

For Communism, on the contrary, these tendencies are but
two sides of a single cause—the cause of the emancipation of
the oppressed peoples from the yoke of imperialism; because
Communism knows that the union of the nations in a single
world economic system is possible only on the basis of mutual
confidence and voluntary agreement, and that the road to the
formation of a voluntary union of nations lies through the separation of the colonies from the "integral" imperialist "whole,"
through the transformation of the colonies into independent
states.

Hence the necessity of a stubborn, continuous and determined
struggle against the imperialist chauvinism of the "Socialists" of
the ruling nations (Great Britain, France, America, Italy, Japan,
etc.), who do not want to fight their imperialist governments,

who do not want to support the struggle of the oppressed peoples in "their" colonies for emancipation from oppression, for secession.

Without such a struggle the education of the working class of the ruling nations in the spirit of true internationalism, in the spirit of rapprochement with the toiling masses of the dependent countries and colonies, in the spirit of real preparation for the proletarian revolution, is inconceivable. The revolution would not have been victorious in Russia, and Kolchak and Denikin would not have been crushed, had not the Russian proletariat enjoyed the sympathy and support of the oppressed peoples of the former Russian empire. But to win the sympathy and support of these peoples it had first of all to break the fetters of Russian imperialism and free these peoples from the yoke of national oppression. Without this it would have been impossible to consolidate the Soviet power, to implant true internationalism and to create that remarkable organization for the collaboration of nations which is called the Union of Soviet Socialist Republics —the living prototype of the future union of nations in a single world economic system.

Hence the necessity of fighting against the national insularity, narrowness and aloofness of the Socialists in the oppressed countries, who do not want to rise above their national steeple and who do not understand the connection between the liberation movement in their various countries and the proletarian movement in the ruling countries.

Without such a struggle it is inconceivable that the proletariat of the oppressed nations can maintain an independent policy and its class solidarity with the proletariat of the ruling countries in the fight for the overthrow of the common enemy, in the fight for the overthrow of imperialism; without such a struggle, internationalism would be impossible.

This is how the toiling masses of the ruling nations and of the oppressed nations should be educated in the spirit of revolutionary internationalism.

Here is what Lenin says about this twofold task of Communism in educating the workers in the spirit of internationalism:

"... Can such education ... be *concretely identical* in great, oppressing nations and in small, oppressed nations, in annexing nations and in annexed nations?

"Obviously not. The way to the one goal—to complete equality, to the closest intimacy and the subsequent *amalgamation of all* nations —obviously proceeds here by different routes in each concrete case; in the same way, let us say, as the route to a point in the middle of a page lies towards the left from one edge and towards the right from the opposite edge. If a Social-Democrat belonging to a great, oppressing, annexing nation, while advocating the amalgamation of nations in general, were to forget even for one moment that 'his' Nicholas II, 'his' Wilhelm, George, Poincaré, etc., *also stand for amalgamation* with small nations (by means of annexations)—Nicholas II being for 'amalgamating' with Galicia, Wilhelm II for 'amalgamating' with Belgium, etc.—such a Social-Democrat would be a ridiculous doctrinaire in theory and an abettor of imperialism in practice.

"The weight of emphasis in the internationalist education of the workers in the oppressing countries must necessarily consist in advocating and urging them to demand freedom of secession for oppressed countries. Without this there can be *no* internationalism. It is our right and duty to treat every Social-Democrat of an opppressing nation who *fails* to conduct such propaganda as an imperialist and a scoundrel. This is an absolute demand, even if the *chance* of secession being possible and 'feasible' before the introduction of Socialism is only one in a thousand . . .

"On the other hand, a Social-Democrat belonging to a small nation must emphasize in his agitation the *second* word of our general formula: 'voluntary *union*' of nations. He may, without violating his duties as an internationalist, be in favor of *either* the political independence of his nation *or* its inclusion in a neighbouring state X, Y, Z, etc. But in all cases he must fight *against* small-nation narrowmindedness, insularity and aloofness, he must fight for the recognition of the whole and the general, for the subordination of the interests of the particular to the interests of the general.

"People who have not gone thoroughly into the question think there is a 'contradiction' in Social-Democrats of oppressing nations insisting on 'freedom of *secession*,' while Social-Democrats of oppressed nations insist on 'freedom of *union*.' However, a little reflection will show that there is not, nor can there be, any *other* road leading from the *given* situation to internationalism and the amalgamation of nations, any other road to this goal." (Lenin, *Collected Works*, Russian edition, Vol. XIX, pp. 261–62.)

25. SOCIAL REVOLUTION AND THE EAST *

⎍⎍⎍⎍⎍⎍⎍⎍⎍⎍⎍⎍⎍⎍⎍⎍⎍⎍⎍

Sultan Galiev

I

The socialist revolution in Russia is only the beginning and only a phase of the international socialist revolution. Sooner or later, it must change into a revolutionary struggle, a desperate hand-to-hand fight between two irreconcilable enemies, two forces opposed to one another—the international proletariat and international imperialism. The civil war which rages today within the confines of the old Russian Empire will have to spread and deepen both its internal content and its external manifestations. With the spread of the revolution, peoples and entire countries will be compelled, whether they like it or not, to take part in this conflict—which will constitute the last world-wide carnage in human history. This is inevitable because the old world is decrepit; it is groaning and tottering; the whole earth looks forward to and demands a renewal and a total transformation. The deci-

*An article in three parts published in *Zizn' Nacional' nortej* (*Life of the Nationalities*), Moscow, official organ of the Peoples' Commissariat for Nationalities, in the issues for 5 and 12 October, and 2 November, 1919.

sive moment has come not only for individuals but also for peoples and for states, to decide their own fate and to choose irrevocably on which side of the barricades they are to stand. Whether you like it or not, you must take part in this war and, consciously or unconsciously, become either "Red" or "White."

Yes, it is so, the October Revolution had hardly broken out when, in Russia, Capital and Labor, the Bourgeoisie and the Proletariat, began to differentiate themselves from one another, to define themselves and to prepare for the decisive battle.

The October Revolution was no more than the moment of encounter for these forces in Russia, when the Russian bourgeoisie, crushed on its native soil, concentrated its remaining forces where it was assured of a "free" existence for a more or less brief period, that is, on the confines of Russia and in the countries of the Entente.

But from this moment the struggle against the Revolution took on an international character. In the struggle against the Russian workers and peasants who had vanquished their bourgeoisie, not only the Russian bourgeoisie were to participate, but also fractions of the international bourgeoisie, their efforts being first scattered and then united. The League of Nations has become their central general staff where, as in a focus, the counterrevolutionary forces of the whole world are concentrated, a "black international" which brings together all that which, in one way or another, might serve as a barrier to the Revolution.

Such are, at the present moment, the premises of the world socialist revolution. It is only by proceeding from them that we can predict the forms which it will take in future.

One of the essential problems which confront us is that of the East. This problem is indissolubly linked to the natural development of world revolution. It is this which constitutes its imminence and its inevitable character.

Even if we had wanted not to admit it and even if we were ready to ignore it, this problem would confront us in all its diversity and its internal and external complexity. We would also be wrong to give it a superficial solution. It is necessary to study it attentively under all its aspects, both from the economic and social point of view, and from that of international politics.

We must examine and define all the concrete forms which the international class war may take in the East and thus define once and for all our attitude to it, with all the consequences which have to follow.

However justified our strategy in regard to the social revolution may seem to us, it is all the same necessary to admit that our policy toward the East requires serious amendment. It must be recognized that up to now all the measures we have taken in order to define the relations between Soviet Russia and the East have been temporary palliatives. We did not have in this area a firm and precise policy. It was, at worst, the reflection and the admission of our pitiful impotence, as was, for example, the removal of Russian troops from Persian territory; and at best the expression of an entirely Platonic sympathy toward national movements, and a promise of support for Eastern revolutionary aspirations, as for example after the Afghan rising against the English.

Our action did not begin to have a more or less defined character until the failure of social revolution in the West became clear, when the very course of events (the crushing of the *Spartakists* in Germany, the end of the General Strike protesting against intervention in Russian affairs, and the collapse of the Hungarian Soviet Republic), compelled us to recognize this truth which is yet very simple: the socialist revolution will never be able to triumph without the participation of the East. But even today our policy does not have that character of precision which the laws of correct development of a socialist revolution require.

The aim of the present article is precisely to give a complete analysis of this problem.

II

The Soviet order and communism are opposed to the bourgeois capitalist state. These two orders can neither coexist nor live at peace side by side. They can tolerate each other only provisionally, until the moment when one or other of the two protagonists shall have acquired a certain superiority which will necessarily lead him to attack the weaker enemy.

In virtue of this law of the development of the social revolution, which is fundamental and beyond discussion, it was incumbent on the Russian Revolution from its earliest days to become a world revolution; otherwise the Russian Soviets would have been no more than a tiny oasis in the stormy sea of imperialism, threatened daily with obliteration by the world imperialist bacchanalia.

The leaders of the October Revolution who had a perfect understanding of this law were endeavoring to change the Russian Revolution into a world revolution. Nothing else was possible, for otherwise the socialist revolution in Russia would have lost all its meaning. From the tactical point of view, however, the revolution has been badly oriented: what might have seemed important if considered on its own (the *Spartakist* movement in Germany, the Hungarian Revolution, etc. . . .) was in the general context no more than secondary. This was due to the fact that the revolutionary leaders' attention was fully absorbed by the West. The transformation of the October Revolution into a world socialist revolution was entirely understood as the transmission of Russian revolutionary energy to the West, that is, to that part of the world where, apparently, the contradictions between the class interests of the proletariat and the bourgeoisie were most acute and where therefore the ground seemed ready for the development of the revolution.

In contrast, the East, with its population of a milliard and a half human beings, oppressed by the West European bourgeoisie, was almost entirely forgotten. The current of the international class war bypassed the East and the problem of revolution in the East existed only in the minds of a few scattered individuals, who were mere drops of water lost in the surging sea of the revolution.

Owing to the ignorance about the East and to the fear which it inspired, there was a refusal to admit that the East could take part in world revolution.

However, the exclusive orientation of the international socialist revolution toward the West was a mistake.

It is true that the states of Western Europe, and their ally America, were the bastions where all the material and "moral" forces of international imperialism were to be found concentrated. But we are not sure that the strength of the West European proletariat would be alone sufficient to crush the bourgeoisie of Western Europe, for the simple reason that this bourgeoisie is international, world-wide, and that the will and revolutionary energy of the whole of the international proletariat, the Eastern proletariat included, are required in order to destroy it.

While throwing the proletariat of Western Europe alone against international imperialism, we leave to the latter full freedom of action and maneuver in the East. So long as international imperialism, incarnated by the Entente, can retain the East as a colony of the natural wealth of which it may dispose as an absolute master, so long will it remain confident of a favorable outcome to an isolated economic conflict with the laboring masses of the metropolis, since it has the possibility of "shutting their mouths" by satisfying their economic demands.

The fact that our expectation of revolutionary aid from the West in the first years of the revolution in Russia has proved vain eloquently confirms our thesis.

Even if the West European worker were successful in overcoming his bourgeoisie, we would inevitably come into collision with the East, since the bourgeoisie of Western Europe will, similarly to the Russian bourgeoisie, concentrate all its forces on the "confines," and primarily in the East. In order to crush the social revolution in Western Europe, she will not hesitate to utilize the secular hatred, both national and social, of the East against the West which has been the center of imperialist oppression, and would throw against Europe an army of Negroes.

Not only do we recognize this possibility, but also we are convinced of it because the experience of two years' struggle by the Russian proletariat against its bourgeoisie has taught us many things on this score.

III

If the East is studied from the economic and social points of view, it is seen that all of it is the object of capitalist exploitation by Western Europe. It supplies the principal materials for its industry and as such constitutes for us very rich and very "inflammable" matter.

If we could calculate the degree of exploitation of the East by West European capital and, starting from this, evaluate its indirect contribution to the establishment and to the power of the noisy bourgeois culture and civilization of Europe and America, we would observe that the greater part of the material and spiritual wealth of the whites derives from Eastern booty, gathered together by the blood and sweat of hundreds of millions of native workers "of all colors and of all races."

Tens of millions of American aborigines and of blacks from Africa had to die, the rich culture of the Incas had completely to disappear in order that present-day "peace-loving" America should be established, with its "cosmopolitan" culture of progress and technique. The proud skyscrapers of Chicago, New York and other cities of "Europeanized" America have been built on the bones of the "redskins" and Negroes assassinated by inhuman plantation owners, and on the smoking ruins of Inca cities.

Christopher Columbus! This name is dear to the heart of European imperialists. It is he who "opened" to European pirates the way to America. England, France, Spain, Italy and Germany—all have taken equal part in the looting, the ruining and the devastation of "native" America, by building at its expense their capitalist cities and their bourgeois imperialist culture. The invasions of Europe by the Tamerlanes, the Genghis Khans and other Mongol princes pale before the cruelty, the power of devastation, and all that the Europeans have done in this America "discovered" by them.

The thesis which I formulated at the beginning of this article is strikingly confirmed by the later history of West European imperialism when, having looted "native" America to satiety, it turned its attention toward the East, and particularly toward India which, from the very first appearance of this imperialism, has not ceased to excite its cupidity.

All the history of the Crusades and the long series of wars conducted by the imperialist bourgeoisie in the East are part of a deeply calculated policy destined to subject economically the East to the feudalists of Western Europe and their descendants. This policy has finally been crowned with an almost complete success.

If we now examine the relations between Western European industry and the East during their last stage, that is at the outset of the imperialist world war, we see that during this period the East, powerfully subjugated, was writhing convulsively, held in the vice of international capitalism.

All Asia and all Africa found themselves divided into "zones of influence"; only a few states such as China, Persia and Turkey still enjoyed a fictional independence.

The great imperialist war was the last manifestation of this policy when international imperialism, feeling its end coming, found itself compelled to go to war with itself.

At the present moment, with the victory of the Entente over Germany, the Eastern Question has received a temporary solution which confirms the domination of the Entente over the East.

But even now, although the situation in the East is not yet absolutely clear, contradictions are beginning to appear between the interests of the principal members of this *"union sacrée,"* and sooner or later a serious conflict will break out between the imperialist great powers in the bosom of the criminal "League of Nations."

We must not lose sight of another factor which exerts over the Eastern situation an "internal" pressure which is no less hoary—the existence of a national bourgeoisie.

We must never forget that the socialist revolution in the East must in no case be limited to the abolition of the power of European imperialism; this revolution must spread and must put to the East the question of the destruction of its own bourgeoisie which calls itself liberal but which is in reality brutally despotic; it is clerical and feudal, and capable in order to satisfy its selfish interests of changing every minute its position toward its quite recent foreign adversaries.

We must understand that the East is the principal source which feeds international imperialism. In the conditions of a world-wide civil war, this factor is highly favorable to us while it is very unfavorable to the international imperialists.

Deprived of the East and cut off from India, Afghanistan, Persia and other Asiatic and African colonies, Western European imperialism will be ruined and will die a natural death.

But the East is also the cradle of despotism and we are not sure that, once Western imperialism is overthrown, an Eastern imperialism will not flourish which finds itself for the time being under the heavy pressure of its European colleague. There is no guarantee that, "liberated" with our help from the foreign yoke, the feudalists of China, India, Persia and Turkey will not ally themselves to imperialist Japan or to some other European imperialism, and will not organize an expedition against their liberators in order to preserve themselves from "Bolshevist" infection.*

*According to A. Bennigsen and C. Quelquejay, *Les mouvements nationaux chez les musulmans de Russie*, Paris, 1960, p. 212, the conclusion of this article, promised at the end of its third section, in fact never appeared. E.K.

INDEX*

* This index covers the introduction.

ABOUT THE EDITOR

Elie Kedourie was educated at the London School of Economics and at St. Antony's College, Oxford, where he was a senior scholar. He has been teaching at the University of London (London School of Economics) since 1953 and is now Professor of Politics. Recently, he was Visiting Professor of History at Harvard College.

Mr. Kedourie is the editor of the journal *Middle Eastern Studies*. His principal publications are *Nationalism; England and the Middle East: The Destruction of the Ottoman Empire 1914–1921;* and *Afghani and Abduh: An Essay on Religious Unbelief and Political Activism in Modern Islam.*